THE **C** *Graphics* **HANDBOOK**

THE C *Graphics* HANDBOOK

ROGER T. STEVENS

ACADEMIC PRESS, INC.
Harcourt Brace Jovanovich, Publishers

Boston   San Diego   New York
London   Sydney   Tokyo   Toronto

ACADEMIC PRESS, INC.
1250 Sixth Avenue, San Diego, CA 92101-4311

United Kingdom edtion published by
ACADEMIC PRESS LIMITED
24-28 Oval Road, London NW1 7DX

Library of Congress Cataloging-in-Publication Data

Stevens, Roger T., 1927–
     The C graphics handbook / Roger T. Stevens.
        p.   cm.
     Includes index.
     ISBN 0-12-668320-4 (alk. paper)
     1. C (Computer program language)   2. Computer graphics.
     I. Title.
QA76.73.C15S7349   1992
006.6'762—dc20   92-11251
                                              CIP

Printed in the United States of America
92 93 94 95   MM   9 8 7 6 5 4 3 2 1

For my daughter Peggy
who gave me the bear shown in Plate 30
and who loves computers–
with much love.

Acknowledgments

All of the Software in this book was written in Borland C++, furnished by Borland International, 4385 Scotts Valley Drive, Scotts Valley, California 95066.

Computer graphics were tested on a Powergraph ERGO-VGA board with 1 megabyte of memory furnished by STB Systems, Inc., 1651 N. Glenville, Suite 210, Richardson, Texas 75081, on a Vega 1024i board furnished by Headland Technology Inc., 46221 Landing Parkway, Fremont, California 94538 and on an ATI VGA Wonder XL board with 1 megabyte of memory furnished by ATI Technologies Inc., 3761 Victoria Park Avenue, Scarborough, Ontario, Canada M1W 3S2.

Color pictures were viewed on a NEC Multisync Plus Color Monitor furnished by NEC Home Electronics (U.S.A.) Inc.

LIMITED WARRANTY AND DISCLAIMER OF LIABILITY

Table of Contents

Contents

Chapter 14. Drawing and Filling Ellipses   **391**

Chapter 15. Drawing and Filling Circular Arcs   **423**

Chapter 16. Drawing and Fast Filling Polygons   **453**

Chapter 17. Drawing and Filling Rounded Rectangles   **489**

Chapter 18. Smooth Curves with Bezier and B-Spline Functions   **501**

Chapter 19. Displaying Text in the Graphics Modes   **531**

Contents

List of Color Plates

Introduction

Only four years ago, there wasn't a single C compiler that included a graphics package. If you wanted to produce graphics in your C programs, you either had to buy an add-on package or start from scratch. What was needed then, was a basic book which told you how to produce your own graphics functions and use them. Today, programmers are much more sophisticated. We know a lot more about graphics than we did then. We have better tools, newer and better compilers with built-in graphics packages, and Super VGA display adapter cards that can do things that we never even dreamed of a few years ago. Does this mean that we can create graphics with a few simple commands so that a book explaining these sophisticated graphics techniques is unnecessary? Unfortunately the answer to this is "No!". The new techniques require a lot more learning on your part. To get the best graphics displays, you'll have to learn how to implement Super VGA high resolution modes, which unfortunately are not standardized from one brand of display adapter card to another. You'll need to know about undocumented display modes. You'll need to be able to save graphics displays to a disk file in a number of different standard formats and to restore the disk file data to a screen display. A little grounding in three-dimensional techniques won't do any harm, either.

Another important aspect of implementing graphics is to obtain flexibility and speed. Every graphics package that is included with a compiler has to make certain compromises, either limiting features to those that the compiler developer feels are important or adding a lot of extra code to make the package work in every possible situation, or both. In designing your own graphics functions, you can tailor the function to do exactly the job that you want it to. For example, say that you want to draw an oval after specifying the coordinates of the center, the x and y axis lengths and the color. No problem; you can design your oval drawing function to work exactly this way. On the other hand if you want to specify the top left and bottom right coordinates of a rectangle and draw your oval inside this box, your function can just as easily be designed to use this mode of operation. You don't need to try to create an omnibus oval drawing function that will use all of the possible modes of specifying the oval parameters, nor do you need to hold committee meetings to try to determine which method of specifying the oval will satisfy the greatest number of users. You can design your function to do what is right for you. Similarly, you don't need to create a huge function that will draw ovals for every graphics display mode ever thought up by the human mind, nor do you need to make it work with every type of display adapter card ever designed. Instead, you can make the function work with only your hardware configuration and the display mode that you want to use. The function will be much simpler and much faster. You can also be more flexible than the commercial graphics packages. For example, Borland C++ allows you to draw lines that are either one pixel wide or three pixels wide. What if you want to draw a line 10 pixels wide? Sorry, you're just out of luck. Now if you are going to want to draw only one or three pixel wide lines, you have no problem with the standard graphics package. However, if you want to draw 10 or 20 or 30 pixel wide lines, you can easily include in your own graphics programs a feature that allows you to make lines of any desired width.

Programming Style

Every programmer has his or her own style. When you're writing a book like this, that style is ideally one that will enable the reader to use the programs and functions with minimal effort. One thing that I have done to encourage this end is to put every curly bracket on a separate line and to match the indentation of the beginning and ending curly brackets for a section of code. This assures that you can look at a listing and tell which curly brackets encompass each section of code. Another thing that I have done, that many programmers disagree with, is to eliminate almost all comments from the code listing itself. I've done this for several reasons. First, I've tried to keep each function and program simple enough so that continual comments are unnecessary to understanding the code. Any additional exposition that is needed is included in the accompanying text. Second, if you didn't buy the disk and are trying to type in some of the code to your computer, you'll be eternally grateful for all those thousands of comment characters that you didn't have to type in and that, if you had typed them, would make no contribution to running the code itself. Finally, if you are actually working with the listings, you will often want to comment out some sections of code. For example, if you decide to make major modifications of the code, you'll probably want to copy the entire section you are working with, using the editor, and then comment it out. Then if your modifications mess up the original section of program beyond recovery, you can always return to that section that you copied and at least be back where you started. But if a section of the program already contains a lot of comments, you can't just put comment symbols at the beginning and end to comment it out; instead you have to go down through and modify each comment that is within the block. In summary, I hope you like the programming style that I have used and find it easy to work with, but if you don't like it, please don't write me to argue about it.

An Overview of the Book

In this book, we want to supply you with a variety of ways of performing basic graphics operations such as plotting points, drawing lines, and drawing and filling polygons and ellipses. We also want you to have a good understanding of display modes and of the use of the ROM BIOS video services. Along with most types of functions will be test programs which permit you to see the functions in action and analyze the advantages and disadvantages of different techniques for performing an operation. We also want you to have a good grounding in how to use extended high resolution modes of the Super VGAs. The number of Super VGAs is increasing every day, and there is presently little or no standardization of high resolution modes, so it is impossible to cover all possibilities in a single book. However, we've done the next best thing and given you information on five typical Super VGA cards. We have personally tested the programs and functions given in this book with each of these five cards and know that they will work as listed. Finally, we've given detailed information on three accepted formats for storing display information on a disk file and retrieving this information. The ultimate goal is to provide you with all of the information that you need to develop your own customized set of graphics routines and to provide test programs which can be used to verify that your graphics functions are working in the way that you intended.

Hardware Considerations

Four years ago, there were such significant differences in motherboards and other computer hardware that a PC compatible was usually not quite compatible. Thus a great deal of effort was needed to assure that software routines would work with a widely varied set of hardware considerations. It was also usually a good idea to list the actual hardware that made up the test computer configuration so that readers would have a baseline reference point if things went wrong. Today, most of the hardware compatibility problems involve the Super VGA cards. I am routinely developing software on two 386 machines, two 386SX machines and a 286 machine, all using different VGA display adapter cards. Each VGA card has a set of registers that are completely compatible with the IBM VGA cards and there is no problem in transferring software between any of the machines. On the other hand, each of the Super VGA cards that I am using has a different set of registers for extended (high resolution) modes and different commands to run these modes. Chapter 2 of this book describes the display adapter cards, showing how the hardware evolved from the monochrome adapter to the CGA, EGA, VGA, and ultimately the Super VGA.

Display Adapter Card Registers

Proper programming of the display adapters requires an intimate knowledge of the workings of the display adapter registers, since these control the display timings and the way that display memory interacts to produce various colors on the screen. This is particularly true if you are interested in using unusual display modes that are off the beaten track of what is handled by the ROM BIOS video services. Chapter 3 describes the contents and functions of the EGA/VGA registers in detail. Chapter 4 provides this same information for the extended registers that are used in five typical Super VGA display adapter cards. Using this information, you'll at least be able to get some idea of the techniques used with Super VGA cards, in case you have a Super VGA that is not covered in the book.

Display Modes

The first consideration in creating computer graphics is determining the display mode that is to be used. Display adapter cards have a number of modes that are supported by the ROM BIOS video services and others that are not documented but can be created through judicious manipulation of the display adapter card registers. In addition are the many new modes supported by the Super VGAs. Chapter 5 describes all these modes, the resolutions and colors involved, memory requirements, and character cell sizes for text. With this information, you can select the mode that is most suited to your graphics purposes within the limitations of your equipment configuration.

Plotting a Pixel on the Screen

Although the ROM BIOS video services provide a means for plotting a pixel on the screen in any of the supported video modes, this service is usually too slow and may also be inadequate for some purposes. Chapter 6 describes several methods of plotting a pixel to the screen through direct access of the VGA registers. Methods are included for both 16 color and 256 color modes.

Lines and Rectangles

Line drawing is one of the more important aspects of graphics. Not only can the line drawing function be used for drawing straight lines, but also complicated curves can be drawn in the form of tiny line segments. Chapter 7 goes into the details of line drawing. In addition to general purpose line drawing functions, a fast horizontal line drawing function is described that can be used for fast filling of various geometric shapes. Methods for drawing wide lines, and dotted, dashed and other stylized lines are given. The chapter also discusses how to join straight line segments appropriately.

Undocumented Display Modes

Several new display modes have recently been discovered which appear to work with every VGA and which offer better resolution and other advantages in the 256 color mode over the standard 320 pixel by 200 pixel by 256 color mode (mode 13H). These modes can be set up by first using the ROM BIOS video service to set mode 13H and then changing the contents of some of the VGA registers. The method of plotting points in these modes is different from anything that has ever been used before. Chapter 8 describes these modes, gives the necessary functions to set them up and plot to them and provides a test program for observing their use in actual displays.

Extended High Resolution Super VGA Modes

Each of the five Super VGA display adapter cards described in this book has a different set of extended modes and uses different methods for activating these modes and plotting points in them. Chapter 9 provides a description of these modes for the five cards, gives *setMode* and *plot* functions for them and provides a test function that can be used to observe a typical high resolution display.

ROM BIOS Video Services

The ROM BIOS video services provide a number of methods of direct access to the display adapter cards. There is a basic set of these services that is common to every VGA and Super VGA card. In addition, a particular card can supply additions which modify existing services or add new ones to make provision for treating extended resolution display modes. Chapter 10 documents all of these services, both for the original display adapter cards (CGA, EGA, and VGA) and for the five typical Super VGA cards described in this book.

System Display Coordinates

Some graphics functions, such as those that draw circles or squares, work properly only when the pixels are square (the amount of the screen covered by a pixel is the same in the horizontal and vertical directions. If this is not the case, circles will appear as ellipses and squares as rectangles. Since not all display modes have a square pixel system, it is often advantageous to set up a set of system coordinates for your graphics work and then convert from them to the actual screen coordinates at appropriate places in the program. Another good reason for setting up a set of system coordinates is that screen coordinate systems usually have their origin at the top left-hand corner of the screen, with increasingly positive values of x going toward the right and increasingly positive values of y going downward, which is totally unlike most mathematical coordinate systems. Chapter 11 describes how to set up coordinate systems, how and where to perform the conversion to screen coordinates, and the relationships that must exist between system and screen coordinates in order to assure that unfortunate interactions do not occur to degrade the display.

Clipping Techniques

It is often possible to design programs in such a way that calls to graphics functions that draw points, lines, circles, etc. on the screen never designate points that are outside the screen boundaries. If this is the case, you don't need to worry about clipping, and your functions will be the fastest that are achievable. There are other times, however, when points may be outside the screen boundaries and, if no precautions are taken, may produce disturbing and unwanted displays. In this case, clipping operations are necessary to prevent any attempts at displaying points outside the screen boundaries. On the most primitive level, this means checking every pixel to be displayed against the boundary parameters. It is often possible, however, to modify line endpoints to assure that all points are within the screen boundaries. This is a much faster way of performing necessary clipping. Chapter 12 describes the clipping problem and shows various solutions that may be used.

Drawing and Filling Circles

Drawing and filling circles using a rectangular coordinate system is a difficult problem, particularly if the circle boundary is a wide line that needs to be completely filled in. Using Bresenham's algorithm, there are a number of ways of solving this problem. Chapter 13 shows some of the best and fastest methods of drawing and filling circles.

Drawing and Filling Ellipses

One good aspect of drawing circles is that the circle has a symmetry such that we need only compute one-eighth of the circle and then draw this repeatedly to complete the figure. Unfortunately, this is not true of ellipses, so that the problem becomes much more complicated. Furthermore, we may not be satisfied with ellipses oriented along the coordinate axes, but may want to tilt them in various ways. Chapter 14 describes the solutions for various ellipse drawing and filling problems.

Drawing and Filling Circular Arcs

Given that we have a good function for drawing circles, and that we know the beginning and ending angles of an arc, we can draw that arc if we figure out how the function can know which points on the circle it calculates are within the arc and therefore should be drawn, and which are not and therefore should be skipped. Filling an arc may seem meaningless to you at first; what we mean is that we draw lines from the center of the circle to the endpoints of the arc and then fill the area enclosed by the arc and these two lines. Chapter 15 describes how we approach these arc problems and provides functions to perform the desired operations.

Drawing and Fast Filling of Polygons

Drawing an irregular polygon is simply a process of drawing a series of line segments and making sure that there is a closing connection from the last set of coordinates specified to the first. There are different ways to handle the passing of the points to the drawing function, however. The best method may depend upon the nature of the polygons and how many pairs of coordinates are used to define it. Filling an irregular polygon is much more complicated, since even if we have collected the coordinate pairs of all the points that make up the polygon boundary, we still have to figure out whether we are inside or outside the polygon if each fill line is to be drawn correctly. Finally, if a polygon, or other closed figure, is bounded by lines whose exact location is not known to us, we need a fill technique that starts somewhere within the closed surface and keeps on filling until everything up to the boundary line is filled, no matter how peculiar the shape of the boundary is. Chapter 16 discusses these problems and lists some fast functions for performing the various operations.

Drawing and Filling Rounded Rectangles

A rectangle with its corners rounded makes a nice background for displaying menus or text panels. It also turns out to be rather easy to create a rounded rectangle outline or a filled rounded rectangle by using a combination of the functions developed for circles and rectangles. Chapter 17 describes how to do this.

Bezier and B-Spline Curves

Chapter 18 addresses the problem of how to draw a nicely shaped curve when several reference points are given to specify the curve shape. We don't want to just connect the specified points together with line segments; instead we want a curve whose shape is both smooth and pleasing to the eye. Two mathematical methods are given for doing this; the Bezier curve and the B-spline curve.

Displaying Text in the Graphics Modes

The ROM BIOS for a VGA card contains several character sets for use in displaying characters on the screen. If you know how to use the character sets properly, you can overcome quite a few limitations that are built in to their normal use. For example, the usual C routines for printing characters to the screen won't work properly when you have moved to a portion of the display outside the normal screen boundaries, but a custom routine will enable you to place characters anywhere you desire. A custom function will also let you place alphanumerics on a screen generated by one of the undocumented display modes, which is impossible with the regular functions. You can also make functions to display large characters or vertical characters. Finally, you can mix 8 x 8 and 8 x 16 characters (to make superscripts, for example). Chapter 19 shows you how to do all of these things.

Rotating Geometric Figures

Our chapter on ellipses introduced the notion of rotating a figure. Chapter 20 takes a more general approach to the problem of coordinate rotation and geometric figure rotation and gives the matrices that may be used to perform these operations.

Three-Dimensional Rotation, Translation and Projection

Chapter 21 extends coordinate rotation and translation to cover three dimensions and also presents the mathematics of projecting a three dimensional figure onto a two-dimensional screen.

Solid Modeling Techniques

Chapter 22 extends the three-dimensional techniques to provide all of the functions needed to define three-dimensional figures, rotate, translate and scale them, determine the lighting of facets and identify which facets are visible, and finally to project the resulting figure as a realistic two-dimensional display.

Improving 3D Graphics with C++

Chapter 23 shows how the functions that were developed for three-dimensional graphics using ordinary C may be improved in speed, simplicity, and clarity by making use of the object definition and operator overriding capabilities of C++.

Saving and Restoring Displays with the *.PCX* Format

Chapter 24 describes the run length compression technique and the file contents for the ZSoft *.PCX* graphics storage files and demonstrates the problems involved in reading and writing such files.

Displaying *.IMG* Files

Chapter 25 describes the run length compression technique and the file contents for the Digital Research *.IMG* graphics storage files and demonstrates the problems involved in reading and writing such files.

Saving and Restoring Displays with the *.GIF* Format

Chapter 26 describes the LZW compression technique and the file contents for CompuServe *.GIF* graphics storage files and demonstrates the problems involved in reading and writing such files.

How Display Adapter Card Hardware Works

You don't have to be a hardware expert to create breathtaking displays with a PC and a VGA card and monitor, but it does help a lot to have some basic knowledge of how the computer, display adapter card, and monitor work together to produce a graphics display. Each particular hardware configuration has a lot of constraints built in, but there are often ways around these constraints, and sometimes there are hidden features that you can exploit if you know how the whole system works. Furthermore, if you are going to upgrade your PC with a new display adapter card and monitor, it is important to know just what you are getting for your money. In this chapter, we're going to look at the basics of display adapter card and monitor hardware. By the time we're through, you should have the answers to any of your questions about how the hardware works.

The Monitor

First, we're going to look at the monitor, which is the fundamental thing that determines the color and resolution of your computer display. Display adapter cards exist simply to supply the monitor with the signals that it needs to produce a useful display. All desktop computers use a monitor whose display device is a cathode ray tube (CRT). The CRT has a florescent screen which, for a color tube, when examined under a microscope is seen to consist of a lot of groups of red, green, and blue dots. Three electron guns at the base of the tube are arranged with a set of optics so that the red gun can only impinge upon red dots, the green gun on green dots, and the blue gun on blue dots. Which clump of dots is illuminated at any time is determined by a deflection yoke, which surrounds the neck of the CRT and provides magnetic fields that independently bend the electron beam in the horizontal and vertical directions.

The usual method of scanning the screen is to deflect the beam from the top left-hand corner of the screen toward the right. When the beam reaches the right-hand edge of the screen, one horizontal scan line is complete, and the beam is blanked and returned as quickly as possible to the left side of the screen to begin another line. (This quick return is called *horizontal retrace*.) Meanwhile, the vertical deflection is changing at a much slower rate, so that by the time the next horizontal scan line starts, the beam is positioned just below the previous line. (You can see that the horizontal scan lines are not quite horizontal; they slant downward just a little bit because of the changing vertical deflection.) When all the horizontal scan lines are completed, a vertical retrace takes place, in which the beam is blanked and returned as quickly as possible to the top of the screen.

Before we leave this topic, one more thing needs to be explained, namely, the concept of interlace. Sometimes, one would like to have better resolution than can be achieved with a given monitor's parameters. One way to do this is to perform the preceding process for only half the scan lines that you would like to see on the screen and then, on the vertical retrace, establish an initial vertical position right between the first two horizontal scan lines that were previously displayed. You can now write another set of scan lines that contains the rest of the display data. This is the technique used on all television sets. It isn't as good a method as scanning the whole display screen in one frame, first, because it requires extra complications in the display adapter card to sort out what part of the display needs to be sent to the CRT for any scan line, and second, because any jitter in the CRT deflection is much more evident when the interlaced technique is used. (The latter doesn't matter too much on a television, because most of the jitter is at the power line frequency and the vertical display frequency is synched to this; it is much more of a problem with computer displays, where the vertical frequency and the power line frequency are different.)

Before going into how a display is created, lets look a little deeper into the constraints of the CRT deflection system. The description just given might lead you to think that you could select almost any horizontal and vertical frequencies that you wanted, and the monitor deflection system would then provide the proper deflection. Actually, however, the horizontal and vertical deflection yokes can be designed to work efficiently only over a very narrow range of frequencies. Consequently, the driver circuits for these deflection circuits are designed as an integral part of the whole deflection system and have similar frequency constraints. Usually, they have frequency ranges at which they operate naturally, and the only control of the exact frequencies is by horizontal and vertical sync signals that are sent from the display adapter card. If the sync signals are close enough in frequency to the natural frequencies of the monitor deflection system, they will lock the deflection system to their exact frequencies, and everything will be fine. If they are too far off, the monitor will go its own merry way, and all that will appear on your screen is a meaningless jumble. Worse yet, it is sometimes possible to send a wrong sync frequency to a monitor that will lock the monitor into a wrong frequency which results in self-destruction.

What about multi-sync monitors? These have to include techniques that make the deflection circuits work efficiently at several different sets of frequencies. This may be done electronically or by relays that switch when a different frequency is recognized. In any case, more sophisticated and more expensive circuits are required, and that is why multi-sync monitors cost more. (You also need to know that the higher frequencies associated with higher resolution display modes are the ones that require the most complicated and expensive hardware.) It would be nice if the specs for a monitor told you how good the method for changing frequencies was and whether the monitor was subject to self-destruction if the wrong sync frequencies are applied. Since this is the kind of information that manufacturers don't want to talk about, they only way to be sure of a new monitor is to watch a demo unit in operation for all of the display modes that you are interested in using. If there are disturbing clunks when shifting from one mode to another, if there are strange flashes and changes in display size, or if you just don't like the appearance of the display, try another model.

We now know how the deflection system works, but just sweeping a beam across the face of a CRT doesn't result in a display. What happens is that, while the beam position is being swept across the face of the CRT, signals applied to the red, green and blue electron guns determine how large a stream of electrons hits the florescent dots on the front of the screen. If you don't want anything displayed on the screen at a particular point, you make sure that all beams are off at that point; if you want a brilliant red at a particular point, you make sure the red gun is on full and the other two are off and so forth. The VGA card takes care of determining what signals are sent to what guns. (The VGA requires an analog monitor, which means that the gun signals can take on any value over some specified range, giving a lot more color combinations than the EGA, which uses a digital monitor that has only a few discrete levels possible for each color gun signal.) To paint two adjacent pixels on the CRT screen in different colors, you have to be able to switch the gun levels in the time required for the deflection system to move the beams from the one pixel location to the other. This time can be determined by the fact that we know how many pixels are in a line, how many lines are in a screen, and how many screens are displayed in a second. The reciprocal of the pixel time determines the video frequency at which all of the monitor circuitry that carries red, green and blue signals from the monitor inputs to the electron guns must work. You don't have to worry about this; it is a problem for the engineers who designed the monitor. However, you should note that the higher the video frequency, the more expensive the video circuits are to build, so that this also causes the price of high resolution monitors to go up. It is possible to design a monitor with a video frequency bandwidth that is too small for the resolutions that are to be supported. This makes the monitor cheaper (this is done all the time with television sets) but you'll notice the difference in the blurring of your high resolution displays.

Finally, no matter how good the frequency response (and consequently the resolution) of your video system, the ultimate limit to how good the resolution on the screen can be is the size of the florescent dots on the front of the screen. Most high resolution multi-sync monitors have dot sizes of 0.28 mm to 0.31 mm. In this case, the smaller the dot size, the better resolution you get. Of course if you are using nothing but the very lowest resolution modes, small dot size is a waste, since it will just give you a display with a lot of black space between dots, but generally, as graphics capabilities improve, you're going to want all of the resolution you can get.

The Video Graphics Array (VGA) Card

The Video Graphics Array (VGA) card accepts digital data from the computer, converts it in various ways, stores it in four memory planes, and converts it to analog signals for transmission to the red, green and blue inputs of the monitor. It also sets up all the proper timing relationships and sends the horizontal and vertical sync signals to the monitor. Figure 2-1 shows a block diagram of the VGA circuitry.

All of the operations of the VGA are controlled by registers on the card that store critical parameters. Chapter 3 will describe these registers and their contents in detail. Here, we're just giving an overview. The CRT Controller Registers, shown at the upper right of the block diagram, determine all of the timing parameters for the card and monitor. For any supported display mode, they send the proper horizontal and vertical sync signals to the monitor. These are derived from a high frequency master clock, which also produces the proper timing signals that are used by the Digital-to-Analog converter to convert the color information for each pixel into analog red, green and blue voltages for output to the monitor. The remainder of the card consists of four memory planes and the control circuits needed to process data to and from memory.

The reason for four memory planes is that the original VGA modes required 256K of memory to store the data for the highest resolution screen, whereas only 64K of computer memory space was available. Consequently, IBM broke the necessary memory up into four planes, all four being addressed by the same 64K memory address space. Through the use of the graphics, sequencer and attribute registers, data from the computer for a particular memory address is routed to those of the four memory planes that must be activated for a particular color. Super VGA boards now use much more than 256K of memory (1 Megabyte boards are common) so that additional paging schemes are needed to fit into the 64K computer memory address space.

In 16 color modes with default color selection, the four memory planes correspond to the red, green, blue and intensity portions of the color signal, but as colors or modes are changed, this is more often an abstraction than a reality. To get back to the reality of colors, there are 256 color registers each of which contains 18 bits, 6 bits for red, 6 bits for green, and 6 bits for blue. Consequently, a color register can

Figure 2-1. Block Diagram of Video Graphics Array (VGA)

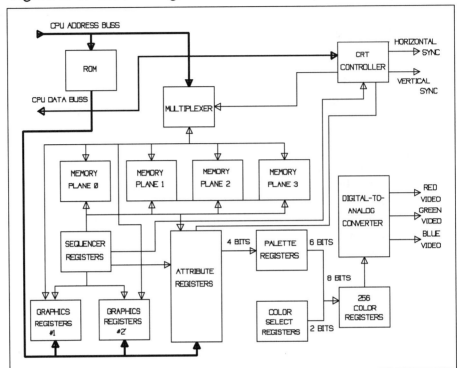

define one of 262,144 shades of color. For 256 color display modes, the information from the memory planes selects one of these 256 registers, and it in turn controls generation of the proper voltages for the monitor color inputs. For the 16 color display modes, the information from the memory planes selects one of 16 palette registers. Each palette register can contain a value from 0 to 63 (6 bits), which is combined with 2 bits of information from the Color Select Registers to create an 8 bit signal that selects one of the 256 color registers to control the color of a designated pixel. Thus, by changing the palette register contents, it is possible to select 16 from 64 possible choices and then, by resetting the color select registers, it is possible to choose any one of four different sets of color registers designated by the same palette register assignments.

This gives you some idea of how all of the registers and hardware tie together. In the next chapter, we give details of the register assignments and usages, which will bring you a lot closer to making use of some of the interesting features that are hidden in the register capabilities.

The Enhanced Graphics Adapter (EGA)

The Enhanced Graphics Adapter (EGA) is just like the VGA if you chop off the digital-to-analog converter, the 256 color registers, and the color select register. The EGA has no 256 color modes. For the 16 color modes, the outputs from the palette registers are used directly to select 16 of 64 possible colors. The six bits from the palette registers correspond to 25% levels of red, green and blue and 75% levels of red, green and blue respectively. Thus four levels of each color are possible, 0, 25%, 75%, and 100%, by the right combinations of these bits. These bits are sent directly to the monitor which has digital inputs for the 6 bits.

VGA/EGA Display Adapter Card Registers

No matter what display adapter card your PC uses, be it the Monochrome Graphics Adapter (MGA), the Color Graphics Adapter (CGA), the Enhanced Graphics Adapter (EGA), or the Video Graphics Array (VGA), or one of the super VGAs, operations of the card are controlled by a series of registers, which store information used to determine the display resolution, color properties and many other parameters that are needed to generate the proper display mode. The original IBM PC display adapters (MGA and CGA) as well as the Hercules Graphics Adapter (HGA) use the Motorola 6845 integrated circuit to control display operations. This integrated circuit has a set of basic registers for display control. All display adapters developed since then have similar sets of registers so that downward compatibility can be maintained (at least at the ROM BIOS level). Improvements in display resolution, etc., have made some of the 6845 registers inadequate, so the EGA and VGA have some changes and some additional registers in the CRT controller register set. These changes and additions have been made in such a way that any software developed for the MGA, CGA or HGA that works through the ROM BIOS will work equally well with one of the more advanced display adapter cards. However, software designed to send commands directly to the registers of the MGA, CGA, or HGA may need modification to work with EGA or VGA to achieve the same type of display that would have been produced on the screen by one of the original 6845 equipped adapters. When you look at the comparison of the EGA/VGA Controller Registers and the 6845, which will be given in Figure 3-2, you'll note some differences that can cause troubles in conversion. This will provide a starting point if difficulties occur with using various software packages.

In addition to duplicating the characteristics of the registers in the 6845, the EGA and VGA have a number of other registers used, for example, in manipulating the memory planes and determining which colors are to be output to the screen. The newer, so-called Super VGA cards have additional registers besides those specified for the EGA and VGA. Unfortunately, there is no standardization of Super VGA characteristics, so that the added registers and their uses differ for each different manufacturer of a Super VGA chip set. Furthermore, manufacturers of these chip sets are continually coming up with improved versions, in which the additional registers and how they operate may have changed from the previous version. All this means that, first, we can't possibly describe in this book the operation of all the chip sets currently on the market and, second, even if we could, the information could very well be obsolete by the time you get it. Therefore, in Chapter 5, we are going to describe the registers and their use for five different chip sets that we have personally used and tested with the programs described in the remainder of this book. This will give you at least the flavor of how different manufacturers perform the Super VGA display operations. If you are lucky enough to have a Super VGA card that includes one of the chip sets described, you can use the programs without modification. If you have a card that includes a new version of one of the described chip sets, the programs for that set may still work. If neither of these situations applies, you'll need to get the manufacturer's technical data on how the chip set works and devise your own programs. Sometimes this is easy; STB, for example, provides detailed technical information that includes everything you need to know to program the Super VGA modes. But other card manufacturers often do not furnish the information you need to branch out on your own. In some cases, it is almost impossible to get; in others you can get it in the form of a technical manual available from the manufacturer at extra cost. If you are in the market for a new Super VGA card, you might well consider the availability of technical information as one of the important considerations in determining which card to buy.

The remainder of this chapter will be devoted to a detailed description of the registers that are used in the standard VGA card. This will include those registers that are a part of the earlier cards and an indication of differences you should be aware of if you are programming for an earlier card or if you want your programs to be able to run on any display adapter that a potential user may have in his system.

General Registers

Table 3-1 lists the general registers included with the EGA/VGA. There are five of these registers, each with its own port address, so that no indexing is necessary. Please note that one port address may be used both to write to one register and to read from a different one when the first register is write only and the second register is read only.

TABLE 3-1. GENERAL REGISTERS

Register	Address	Status
Miscellaneous Output Register.	Write: 3C2H. Read: 3CCH.	Write/Read (through different ports).
Feature Control Register.	Monochrome Adapters: 3BAH. Color Adapters: 3DAH.	Write only.
Input Status Register Zero.	3C2H.	Read Only.
Input Status Register One.	Monochrome adapters: 3BAH. Color Adapters: 3DAH.	Read only.
VGA Enable Register.	3C3H or 46E8H.	Read/Write.

MISCELLANEOUS OUTPUT REGISTER

Write Register Address: 3C2H   Read Register Address: 3CCH

Bit 7	Bit 6	Bit 5	Bit 4	Bit 3	Bit 2	Bit 1	Bit 0
Vertical Sync Polarity. 0 = +. 1 = -.	Horizontal Sync Polarity. 0 = +. 1 = -.	0=Page 0. 1= Page 1. for Modes 0,1,2, 3,7.	Disable Internal Video Drivers.	Clock Select 1.	Clock Select 0.	Enable RAM. 0 = disable. 1 = enable.	I/O Address Select. 0=3BxH. 1=3DxH.

The **Sync Polarity** bits control the polarity of the sync signals that are sent to the monitor. VGA monitors not only use the sync signals to lock in the line and frame frequencies, but also make use of the polarity information to determine how many lines make up a frame. The number of lines per frame is shown in the following table:

Bits 7 and 6	Resolution
00	Reserved.
01	400 lines.
10	350 lines.
11	480 lines.

The **Odd/Even Page** bit selects which page is used for display when in modes 0, 1, 2, 3 and 7.

The **Disable Video** bit enables the video drivers for normal operation or disables them for control of the display through the feature connector.

The **Clock Select** bits determine the clock frequency. They have the following meaning:

Bits 3 and 2	EGA Clock Frequency	VGA Clock Frequency
11	Reserved	Reserved.
10	External clock	Reserved (may be used on super VGAs).
01	16.257 MHz.	28.322 MHz.
00	14.161 MHz.	25.175 MHz.

The **Enable RAM** bit determines whether display memory can be accessed by the processor.

The **I/O Address Select** bit determines whether the display adapter registers are at the monochrome display address block (3BxH) or the color display address block (3DxH).

FEATURE CONTROL REGISTER

Register Write Address: Register Read Address (VGA Only): 3CAH
        Monochrome Adapters: 3BAH
        Color Adapters: 3DAH

Bit 7	Bit 6	Bit 5	Bit 4	Bit 3	Bit 2	Bit 1	Bit 0
				Reserved.		Feature Control Bit 1.	Feature Control Bit 0.

The two **Feature Control** bits, when set to 1, cause the corresponding bits on the feature connector to go high; when set to 0, these bits cause the corresponding bits on the feature connector to go low.

INPUT STATUS REGISTER ZERO

Read Register Address: 3C2H   (Read Only)

Bit 7	Bit 6	Bit 5	Bit 4	Bit 3	Bit 2	Bit 1	Bit 0
CRT Vertical Retrace Pending.	Feature Connector Bit 1.	Feature Connector Bit 0.	Switch Sense.				

The **Vertical Retrace Pending** bit, when 1, indicates that a vertical retrace interrupt is being processed; when set to 0, the vertical retrace interrupt has been cleared.

Feature Connector bit 1 indicates the status of the feature control bit 1 on pin 20 (for EGA) or pin 17 (VGA) of the feature connector; feature connector bit 0 indicates the setting of the feature control bit 0 on pin 21 (EGA) or pin 19 (VGA) of the feature connector.

The **Sense Switch** bit reports the status of a selected sense switch (0 = off; 1 = on). There are four sense switches; the one that is read is determined by the clock select bits (bits 3 and 2) of the Miscellaneous Output Register.

INPUT STATUS REGISTER ONE

Read Register Address: (Read Only)
      Monochrome Adapters: 3BAH
      Color Adapters: 3DAH

Bit 7	Bit 6	Bit 5	Bit 4	Bit 3	Bit 2	Bit 1	Bit 0
		Diagnostic 1.	Diagnostic 0.	Vertical Retrace.			Display Enable.

The **Diagnostic** bits are connected to two of the eight color outputs of the Attribute Controller. The Color Plane Enable (bits 5 and 4 of Attribute Register 12H) determines which color outputs appear at these bits as follows:

Color Plane Register		Input Status Register One	
Bit 5	Bit 4	Bit 5	Bit 4
0	0	P2	P0
0	1	P5	P4
1	0	P3	P1
1	1	P7	P6

When using the EGA, the only method for determining the contents of the color lookup table in the Attribute Controller is through the use of these diagnostic bits. With the VGA, the Attribute Register contents can be read directly.

The **Display Enable** bit, when 0, indicates that the display is in the display mode. When this bit is 1, the display is not in the display mode (either horizontal or vertical retrace is occurring).

CRT Controller Registers

Table 3-2 describes the CRT controller registers, comparing the 6845 version with the EGA/VGA version. If you are trying to convert programs that have direct access to the 6845 to use with the EGA or VGA, you need to note particularly the differences in registers 3, 4, 5, 6, 7 and 8.

TABLE 3-2. CRT CONTROLLER REGISTERS

Index Register Address:
  Monochrome Adapters: 3B4H
  Color Adapters: 3D4H

Data Register Address:
  Monochrome Adapters: 3B5H
  Color Adapters: 3D5H

Register Number	6845 Register Description	EGA/VGA Register Description
00H	Total Horizontal Columns	Total Horizontal Columns
01H	Horizontal Display End	Horizontal Display End
02H	Horizontal Sync Position	Start Horizontal Blank
03H	Horizontal Sync Width	End Horizontal Blank
04H	Total Vertical Lines	Horizontal Sync Start
05H	Vertical Adjust	Horizontal Sync End
06H	Vertical Displayed	Vertical Total
07H	Vert Sync Position	Overflow
08H	Interlace Mode	Initial Row Address
09H	Max Scan Line Address	Max Row Address
0AH	Cursor Start Register	Cursor Start Position
0BH	Cursor End Register	Cursor End Position
0CH	Screen Start Address (MSB)	Start Address (MSB)
0DH	Screen Start Address (LSB)	Start Address (LSB)
0EH	Cursor Address (MSB)	Cursor Location (MSB)

(continued)

TABLE 3-2. CRT CONTROLLER REGISTERS (Cont.)

Index Register Address:
    Monochrome Adapters: 3B4H
    Color Adapters: 3D4H

Data Register Address:
    Monochrome Adapters: 3B5H
    Color Adapters: 3D5H

Register Number	6845 Register Description	EGA/VGA Register Description
0FH	Cursor Address (LSB)	Cursor Location (LSB)
10H	Light Pen Register (MSB)	Vertical Sync Start
11H	Light Pen Register (LSB)	Vertical Sync End
12H		Vertical Display End
13H		Row Offset
14H		Underline Row Address
15H		Start Vertical Blank
16H		End Vertical Blank
17H		CRTC Mode Control
18H		Line Compare

A number of the CRT controller registers are devoted to the timing of the display. The horizontal timing descriptors are shown in Figure 3-1. They include the total length of a horizontal line in characters, the beginning and end of the horizontal blanking and retrace signals, and the length of the displayed portion of the line. They are defined a little differently than one might ordinarily think of doing it, so look at the diagram carefully when you are adjusting the contents of these registers. Figure 3-2 shows the vertical timing descriptors. These differ from the horizontal ones in that they are measured in terms of scan lines, rather than characters.

Figure 3-1. Horizontal Timing Diagram

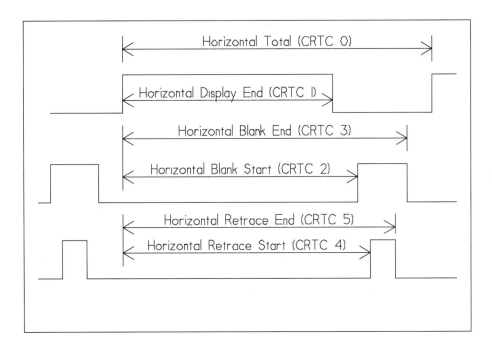

Figure 3-2. Vertical Timing Diagram

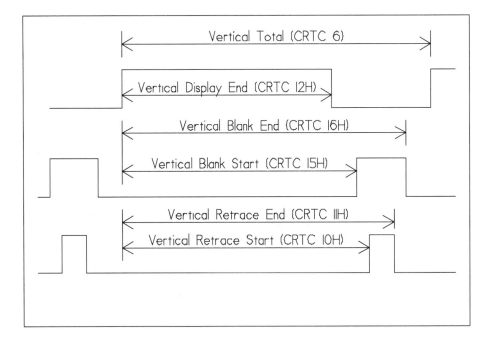

CRT CONTROLLER REGISTER 00H—HORIZONTAL TOTAL

Index Register Address: Index = 0
      Monochrome Adapters: 3B4H
      Color Adapters: 3D4H
Data Register Address:
      Monochrome Adapters: 3B5H
      Color Adapters: 3D5H

Bit 7	Bit 6	Bit 5	Bit 4	Bit 3	Bit 2	Bit 1	Bit 0
Total number of character times per horizontal scan -5 for VGA. Total number of character times per horizontal scan -2 for EGA.							

This register contains the number of characters that make up a total scan line, including border and blanked character positions. For obscure reasons, the actual number in the register is two less than the actual total for the EGA and five less for the VGA.

CRT CONTROLLER REGISTER 01H—HORIZONTAL DISPLAY END

Index Register Address: Index = 1
      Monochrome Adapters: 3B4H
      Color Adapters: 3D4H
Data Register Address:
      Monochrome Adapters: 3B5H
      Color Adapters: 3D5H

Bit 7	Bit 6	Bit 5	Bit 4	Bit 3	Bit 2	Bit 1	Bit 0
Character count at which horizontal display is to end - 1							

This is the total number of characters that are actually displayed minus one. Note that the character is defined as consisting of eight pixels, so that with a one-byte register we can have a resolution of up to 2040 pixels, which is more than adequate for all display systems currently available.

CRT CONTROLLER REGISTER 02H—HORIZONTAL BLANK START

Index Register Address: Index = 2
    Monochrome Adapters: 3B4H
    Color Adapters: 3D4H
Data Register Address:
    Monochrome Adapters: 3B5H
    Color Adapters: 3D5H

Bit 7	Bit 6	Bit 5	Bit 4	Bit 3	Bit 2	Bit 1	Bit 0
Character count at which horizontal blanking is to start.							

The horizontal blanking pulse will begin at the start of the character whose number is given in this register.

CRT CONTROLLER REGISTER 03H—HORIZONTAL BLANK END

Index Register Address: Index = 3
    Monochrome Adapters: 3B4H
    Color Adapters: 3D4H
Data Register Address:
    Monochrome Adapters: 3B5H
    Color Adapters: 3D5H

Bit 7	Bit 6	Bit 5	Bit 4	Bit 3	Bit 2	Bit 1	Bit 0
Test bit. Normally set to 1.	Horizontal display enable skew. 00 = 0 character clocks. 01 = 1 character clock. 10 = 2 character clocks. 11 = 3 character clocks.		Character count for end of horizontal blanking modulo 32 for EGA. Character count for end of horizontal blanking modulo 64 for VGA (the most significant bit is found in bit 7 of CRTC Register 5 — Horizontal Sync End.				

The **Test** bit should always be set to 1 for normal operation.

The **Horizontal Enable Skew** bits determine the number of character times to skew (delay) the horizontal timing to obtain proper synchronization.

The **End Horizontal Blanking** bits determine the character position for the end of the horizontal blanking pulse. Actually only the five least significant bits of this value are given. The display adapter begins checking character position values after the blanking pulse begins, and as soon as the last five bits match, the blanking pulse is terminated. For the VGA there is a sixth (most significant) bit for this quantity, which is found in CRT Controller Register 05H—Horizontal Sync End register.

CRT CONTROLLER REGISTER 04H—HORIZONTAL SYNC START

Index Register Address: Index = 4
    Monochrome Adapters: 3B4H
    Color Adapters: 3D4H
Data Register Address:
    Monochrome Adapters: 3B5H
    Color Adapters: 3D5H

Bit 7	Bit 6	Bit 5	Bit 4	Bit 3	Bit 2	Bit 1	Bit 0
Character count at which horizontal sync (retrace) begins							

This is the character count at which the horizontal sync (retrace) pulse begins. The monitor uses a sawtooth waveform to scan the screen horizontally. The voltage of this waveform starts at zero and increases at a constant rate to sweep the trace across the monitor screen. When the end of the horizontal line is reached, there is a sudden drop to zero, which causes the trace to jump back to the beginning of the line. This pulse provides the signal that it is time for that jump to begin.

CRT CONTROLLER REGISTER 05H—HORIZONTAL SYNC END

Index Register Address:
    Monochrome Adapters: 3B4H
    Color Adapters: 3D4H
Data Register Address:
    Monochrome Adapters: 3B5H
    Color Adapters: 3D5H

Index = 5

Bit 7	Bit 6	Bit 5	Bit 4	Bit 3	Bit 2	Bit 1	Bit 0
Bit 5 of Horizontal Blank End for VGA modes	Horizontal sync skew 00 = 0 character clocks 01 = 1 character clock 10 = 2 character clocks 11 = 3 character clocks		Horizontal sync end Character count for horizontal sync (retrace) end modulo 32				

The **Horizontal Blank End** bit is the most significant bit of the Horizontal Blank End value given in CRT Controller Register 03H—Horizontal Blank End Register for VGAs only.

The **Horizontal Sync Skew** bits determine the number of character times to skew (delay) the horizontal sync to obtain proper synchronization.

The **Horizontal Sync End** bits determine the character position for the end of the horizontal sync pulse. Actually only the 5 least significant bits of this value are given. The display adapter begins checking character position values after the blanking pulse begins, and as soon as the last five bits match, the horizontal sync pulse is terminated.

CRT CONTROLLER REGISTER 06H—VERTICAL TOTAL

Index Register Address: Index = 6
      Monochrome Adapters: 3B4H
      Color Adapters: 3D4H
Data Register Address:
      Monochrome Adapters: 3B5H
      Color Adapters: 3D5H

Bit 7	Bit 6	Bit 5	Bit 4	Bit 3	Bit 2	Bit 1	Bit 0
VGA modes: Horizontal scan lines per vertical frame - 2. (Eight least significant bits. Most significant bits are found in bit 5 and bit 0 of CRT Controller Register 07H—Overflow register.) EGA modes: Horizontal scan lines per vertical frame - 1. (Eight least significant bits. Most significant bits are found in bit 5 and bit 0 of CRT Controller Register 07H—Overflow register.)							

This register contains the eight least significant bits total number of horizontal scan lines that make up a vertical frame (minus 2 for the VGA and minus 1 for the EGA). The most significant bit is bit 5 and the next most significant bit is bit 0 in the CRT Controller Register 07H—Overflow Register.

CRT CONTROLLER REGISTER 07H—OVERFLOW

Index Register Address: Index = 7
      Monochrome Adapters: 3B4H
      Color Adapters: 3D4H
Data Register Address:
      Monochrome Adapters: 3B5H
      Color Adapters: 3D5H

Bit 7	Bit 6	Bit 5	Bit 4	Bit 3	Bit 2	Bit 1	Bit 0
Vertical Sync Start (bit 9).	Vertical Display Enable End (bit 9).	Vertical Total (bit 9).	Line Compare (Split Screen) (bit 8).	Vertical Blank Start (bit 8).	Vertical Sync Start (bit 8).	Vertical Display Enable End (bit 8).	Vertical Total (bit 8).

The Overflow Register provides a place to store additional bits needed to expand quantities contained in other registers that need to be expanded for the EGA/VGA. The designations of the bits are shown in the table; a full description of each quantity is given in connection with the register where its main portion is stored.

CRT CONTROLLER REGISTER 08H— PRESET ROW SCAN/INITIAL ROW ADDRESS

Index Register Address: Index = 8
    Monochrome Adapters: 3B4H
    Color Adapters: 3D4H
Data Register Address:
    Monochrome Adapters: 3B5H
    Color Adapters: 3D5H

Bit 7	Bit 6	Bit 5	Bit 4	Bit 3	Bit 2	Bit 1	Bit 0
Reserved.	Byte Panning Control. Number of bytes to pan for horizontal panning.		Preset row scan. Starting row for first character to be displayed on screen (normally 0).				

The **Reserved** bit should not be used.

The **Byte Panning Control** bits indicate the number of bytes to pan during a horizontal panning operation.

The **Preset Row Scan** bits indicate the starting row of the character box for the first line of characters to be displayed at the top of the screen. Normally, this is 0, to display the full characters. If one desires to provide a smooth scrolling of the display vertically, rather than having the display scroll by jumping a row of characters at a time, then the beginning row of the character box of the first character line must change incrementally. This is done by incrementing the number in this section of this register.

CRT CONTROLLER REGISTER 09H—MAXIMUM ROW ADDRESS

Index Register Address: Index = 9
        Monochrome Adapters: 3B4H
        Color Adapters: 3D4H
Data Register Address:
        Monochrome Adapters: 3B5H
        Color Adapters: 3D5H

Bit 7	Bit 6	Bit 5	Bit 4	Bit 3	Bit 2	Bit 1	Bit 0
Enable Double Scan. 0 = normal 200 line scan. 1 = converts 200 line scan to 400 line scan.	Line compare. (Split Screen) (bit 9).	Vertical Blank Start (bit 9).	Number of scan lines per character row -1.				

The **Enable Double Scan** bit, when set to 1, divides the clock in the row scan counter by two so that each horizontal line is displayed twice, enabling a 200 line resolution display to be displayed in 400 lines. (This gives better apparent resolution than an ordinary 200 line display.) When this bit is set to 0, the normal 200 line display is produced.

The **Line Compare** bit is the most significant bit for the line compare value, which is described under CRT Controller Register 18H—Line Compare Register.

The **Vertical Blank Start** bit is the most significant bit for the vertical blank start value, which is described under CRT Controller Register 15H—Vertical Blank Start.

The **Number of Scan Lines Per Character Row** bits define the height of character row in scan lines.

CRT CONTROLLER REGISTER 0AH—CURSOR START ROW ADDRESS

Index Register Address: Index = 0AH
 Monochrome Adapters: 3B4H
 Color Adapters: 3D4H
Data Register Address:
 Monochrome Adapters: 3B5H
 Color Adapters: 3D5H

Bit 7	Bit 6	Bit 5	Bit 4	Bit 3	Bit 2	Bit 1	Bit 0
Reserved.		Cursor on/off. 0 = cursor on. 1 = cursor off.	Cursor Start Row Address. Address of first character scan line at which cursor is enabled.				

The **Cursor On/Off** bit determines if the cursor will be displayed.

The **Cursor Start Row Address** bits indicate the cursor start line of the character cell.

CRT CONTROLLER REGISTER 0BH—CURSOR END ROW ADDRESS

Index Register Address: Index = 0BH
 Monochrome Adapters: 3B4H
 Color Adapters: 3D4H
Data Register Address:
 Monochrome Adapters: 3B5H
 Color Adapters: 3D5H

Bit 7	Bit 6	Bit 5	Bit 4	Bit 3	Bit 2	Bit 1	Bit 0
Reserved	Cursor skew 00 = 0 character clocks 01 = 1 character clock 10 = 2 character clocks 11 = 3 character clocks		Address of character scan line at which cursor is disabled				

The **Reserved** bit should not be used.

The **Cursor Skew** bit defines the skew of the cursor signal in character clocks.

The **Cursor End Row Address** bits indicate the line of the character cell at which the cursor should stop being enabled.

CRT CONTROLLER REGISTER 0CH—START ADDRESS HIGH

Index Register Address: Index = 0CH
    Monochrome Adapters: 3B4H
    Color Adapters: 3D4H
Data Register Address:
    Monochrome Adapters: 3B5H
    Color Adapters: 3D5H

Bit 7	Bit 6	Bit 5	Bit 4	Bit 3	Bit 2	Bit 1	Bit 0
Display memory address of top lefthand pixel on the screen. This is a 16 bit address. This register contains bits 8–15 of the address. Bits 0–7 are found in CRT Controller Register 0DH—Start Address Low.							

This is the high byte of the 16 bit display memory address of the top lefthand pixel on the screen.

CRT CONTROLLER REGISTER 0DH—START ADDRESS LOW

Index Register Address: Index = 0DH
      Monochrome Adapters: 3B4H
      Color Adapters: 3D4H
Data Register Address:
      Monochrome Adapters: 3B5H
      Color Adapters: 3D5H

Bit 7	Bit 6	Bit 5	Bit 4	Bit 3	Bit 2	Bit 1	Bit 0
Display memory address of top lefthand pixel on the screen. This is a 16 bit address. This register contains bits 0–7 of the address. Bits 8–15 are found in CRT Controller Register 0CH—Start Address High.							

This is the low byte of the 16 bit display memory address of the top left hand pixel on the screen.

CRT CONTROLLER REGISTER 0EH—CURSOR LOCATION HIGH

Index Register Address: Index = 0EH
      Monochrome Adapters: 3B4H
      Color Adapters: 3D4H
Data Register Address:
      Monochrome Adapters: 3B5H
      Color Adapters: 3D5H

Bit 7	Bit 6	Bit 5	Bit 4	Bit 3	Bit 2	Bit 1	Bit 0
Display memory address of cursor location on the screen. This is a 16 bit address. This register contains bits 8–15 of the address. Bits 0–7 are found in CRT Controller Register 0FH—Cursor Location Low.							

This is the high byte of the 16 bit display memory address of the cursor location on the screen.

CRT CONTROLLER REGISTER 0FH—CURSOR LOCATION LOW

Index Register Address: Index = 0FH
      Monochrome Adapters: 3B4H
      Color Adapters: 3D4H
Data Register Address:
      Monochrome Adapters: 3B5H
      Color Adapters: 3D5H

Bit 7	Bit 6	Bit 5	Bit 4	Bit 3	Bit 2	Bit 1	Bit 0
Display memory address of the cursor location on the screen. This is a 16 bit address. This register contains bits 0–7 of the address. Bits 8–15 are found in CRT Controller Register 0EH—Cursor Location High.								

This is the low byte of the 16 bit display memory address of the cursor location on the screen.

CRT CONTROLLER REGISTER 10H—VERTICAL SYNC START

Index Register Address: Index = 10H
      Monochrome Adapters: 3B4H
      Color Adapters: 3D4H
Data Register Address:
      Monochrome Adapters: 3B5H
      Color Adapters: 3D5H

Bit 7	Bit 6	Bit 5	Bit 4	Bit 3	Bit 2	Bit 1	Bit 0
These are the lower 8 bits of a 10 bit number specifying the value of the internal line counter when the vertical sync (retrace) pulse begins. Bit 8 of this number is found in bit 2 and bit 9 is found in bit 7 of CRT Controller Register 07H—Overflow.								

These are the eight least significant bytes of the number of the scan line at which vertical retrace starts. The two most significant bytes are in CRT Controller Register 7.

CRT CONTROLLER REGISTER 11H—VERTICAL SYNC END

Index Register Address: Index = 11H
      Monochrome Adapters: 3B4H
      Color Adapters: 3D4H
Data Register Address:
      Monochrome Adapters: 3B5H
      Color Adapters: 3D5H

Bit 7	Bit 6	Bit 5	Bit 4	Bit 3	Bit 2	Bit 1	Bit 0
Protection bit. 0 = can write to CRTC registers 0–7. 1 = cannot write to CRTC registers 0–7.	Reserved.	Vertical interrupt enable. 0 = vertical interrupt can occur. 1 = vertical interrupt cannot occur.	Vertical interrupt clear. 0 = clear vertical interrupt 1 = no effect.	Scan line at which vertical sync ends modulo 16. Compared with 4 LSB of line counter after vertical sync begins to determine when vertical sync should end.			

It is important to note that if the **Protection** bit is not set to 0, you will not be able to write any data to CRT Controller registers 0 to 7 (described previously). This make it impossible to inadvertently change the contents of these registers and thereby damage your monitor. To write to these registers, you must first set the **Protection** bit to 0. When writing is complete, you should reset the **Protection** bit to 1.

The **Reserved** bit should not be used.

The **Vertical Interrupt Enable** bit, when set to zero, causes the *INTL* line to be asserted when the vertical interrupt signal becomes true.

The **Clear Vertical Interrupt** bit should be set to 0 to clear the vertical interrupt after a vertical interrupt is processed and before interrupts are reenabled.

The **Vertical Sync End** bits determine the value of the internal line counter for the end of the vertical sync (retrace) pulse. Actually only the four least significant bits of this value are given. The display adapter begins checking the line counter values after the vertical sync pulse begins, and as soon as the last four bits match, the vertical sync pulse is terminated.

CRT CONTROLLER REGISTER 12H—VERTICAL DISPLAY END

Index Register Address: Index = 12H
     Monochrome Adapters: 3B4H
     Color Adapters: 3D4H
Data Register Address:
     Monochrome Adapters: 3B5H
     Color Adapters: 3D5H

Bit 7	Bit 6	Bit 5	Bit 4	Bit 3	Bit 2	Bit 1	Bit 0
These are the lower 8 bits of a 10 bit number specifying the number of the last scan line displayed vertically. Bit 8 of this number is found in bit 1 and bit 9 is found in bit 6 of CRT Controller Register 07H—Overflow Register.								

This register contains the eight least significant bits of the number of the last horizontal line that is displayed at the bottom of the screen. The two most significant bits of this number are found as bits 6 and 1, respectively, of CRT Controller Register 07H—Overflow Register.

CRT CONTROLLER REGISTER 13H—ROW OFFSET

Index Register Address: Index = 13H
     Monochrome Adapters: 3B4H
     Color Adapters: 3D4H
Data Register Address:
     Monochrome Adapters: 3B5H
     Color Adapters: 3D5H

Bit 7	Bit 6	Bit 5	Bit 4	Bit 3	Bit 2	Bit 1	Bit 0
Display width (difference in memory addresses of two adjacent vertical pixels) in 16 bit words (if bit 6 of CRTC register 17H—Mode is 1) or in 32 bit double words (if bit 6 of CRTC register 17H—Mode is 0).							

This register specifies the amount that is to be added to the current display memory address to advance from one screen row to the next. This amount is in 16 bit words if bit 6 of CRT Controller Register 17H—Mode Register is set to 1 or in 32 bit double words if bit 6 of CRT Controller Register 17H—Mode Register is set to 0. For example, in a 640 pixel, 16 color mode, each pixel on the screen occupies one bit in the memory addressing space. Thus one line requires 80 bytes, so in mode 1, this register would be programmed to 80/2 or 40 (28H) words. For a 320 pixel, 256 color mode, each pixel on the screen occupies one byte in the memory addressing space. Thus one line requires 320 bytes, so in mode 0, this register would be programmed to 320/4 or 80 (50H) double words.

Actually, this register can define a virtual screen that is wider than the actual displayed screen. The display screen can then be considered a window looking at part of this virtual screen, and the horizontal panning capability of the display adapter card can be used to move the window back and forth to display different portions of this virtual screen.

CRT CONTROLLER REGISTER 14H—UNDERLINE ROW ADDRESS

Index Register Address: Index = 14H
      Monochrome Adapters: 3B4H
      Color Adapters: 3D4H
Data Register Address:
      Monochrome Adapters: 3B5H
      Color Adapters: 3D5H

Bit 7	Bit 6	Bit 5	Bit 4	Bit 3	Bit 2	Bit 1	Bit 0
Reserved = 0.	Double Word Mode. 0 = normal word memory addressing. 1 = double word memory addressing.	Count by 4. 0 = normal clocking of memory address counter. 1 = memory address counter is character clock divided by four.	Row address at which underline will occur.				

The **Reserved** bit should always be zero.

The **Double Word Mode** bit indicates whether the display memory is to be addressed in words or double words.

The **Count by 4** bit clocks the memory address counter with the character clock when set to 0. When set to 1, the memory address counter is clocked by the character clock divided by four (for proper timing when double word addressing is used). If bit 3 of CRT Controller Register 17H—Mode Register is set to 1, the linear counter will increment twice for each character.

CRT CONTROLLER REGISTER 15H—VERTICAL BLANK START

Index Register Address: Index = 15H
     Monochrome Adapters: 3B4H
     Color Adapters: 3D4H
Data Register Address:
     Monochrome Adapters: 3B5H
     Color Adapters: 3D5H

Bit 7	Bit 6	Bit 5	Bit 4	Bit 3	Bit 2	Bit 1	Bit 0
The 8 LSB of a 10 bit number specifying the value of the line counter at which the vertical blanking interval should start minus one. The ninth bit is found as bit 3 of CRTC Register 07H—Overflow Register and the tenth bit is found as bit 5 of CRTC Register 09H—Maximum Row Address Register.							

These are the eight least significant bits of the number of the scan line at which vertical blanking starts. The ninth bit is in CRT Controller Register 07H—Overflow Register and the tenth bit is found in CRT Controller Register 09H—Maximum Row Address Register.

CRT CONTROLLER REGISTER 16H—VERTICAL BLANK END

Index Register Address: Index = 16H
     Monochrome Adapters: 3B4H
     Color Adapters: 3D4H
Data Register Address:
     Monochrome Adapters: 3B5H
     Color Adapters: 3D5H

Bit 7	Bit 6	Bit 5	Bit 4	Bit 3	Bit 2	Bit 1	Bit 0
Scan line at which vertical blanking ends modulo 256. Vertical blanking ends when the eight LSB of the line counter first matches this number after vertical blanking has begun.							

The **Vertical Blanking End** bits determine the value of the internal line counter for the end of the vertical blanking signal. This register contains the eight least significant bits of this value. The display adapter begins checking the line counter values after the vertical blanking signal begins, and as soon as the last eight bits match, the vertical blanking signal is terminated.

CRT CONTROLLER REGISTER 17H—MODE

Index Register Address:
      Monochrome Adapters: 3B4H
      Color Adapters: 3D4H
Data Register Address:
      Monochrome Adapters: 3B5H
      Color Adapters: 3D5H

Index = 17H

Bit 7	Bit 6	Bit 5	Bit 4	Bit 3	Bit 2	Bit 1	Bit 0
Retrace Enable. 0=places all horizontal and vertical control timings in a hold state. 1=enables horizontal and vertical control signals.	Word/ Byte mode. 0=word mode. 1=byte mode.	Address wrap. When in word mode: 0 = address bit 13 sent to LSB bit of display memory (scan lines separated by 8K bytes). 1=address bit 15 sent to LSB of display memory (scan lines separated by 32K bytes).	Memory address output control. 0=enable EGA output drivers. 1=Disable EGA output drivers. Useage varies for different VGA boards.	Linear counter. 0=memory address counter clocked by character clock. 1=memory address counter clocked by every other character clock.	Line counter. 0=clock scan line counter with every horizontal retrace. 1=clock scan line counter with every other horizontal retrace.	Select row scan counter. 0=row scan counter bit 1 is placed on memory address bus bit 14 during active display time. 1=memory addresses are output sequentially. This provides Hercules GA compatibility.	Compatibility mode support. 0=row scan counter bit 0 is placed on memory address bus bit 13 during active display time. 1=memory addresses output sequentially. This provides HGA compatibility.

The **Retrace Enable** bit disables all horizontal and vertical timing signals when set to 0. When set to 1, all timing signals are enabled.

The **Word/Byte Mode** bit, when set to 0, permits CGA emulation by shifting the display memory address one position to the left and then placing either address bit 13 or 15 (depending upon the setting of the Address Wrap bit) in the least significant bit position. When set to 1, addresses are transferred to display memory unaltered. To understand how this works, we need to look at how the CGA is designed. When sending consecutively displayed data to the CGA, all odd numbered bytes are sent to consecutive display memory addresses, beginning with B8000H. Even numbered bytes are sent to consecutive display memory addresses starting at BA000H. If we have data addressed to the CGA like this and want to use it with the EGA or VGA, we set the Word/Byte Mode bit to 1, which shifts the addresses one bit to the left and then moves bit 13 (or 15) to the LSB, causing all of the data now to be addressed consecutively as needed for the EGA/VGA.

The **Address Wrap** bit determines whether address bit 13 or 15 should be output to the display memory least significant address line when in the word mode.

The **Memory Address Output Control** bit, when set to 1, disables the EGA display memory drivers. Usage varies on VGA Boards. Consult the literature from the manufacturer of your VGA board to determine the use of this bit.

The **Linear Counter** bit increments the linear counter at each character clock when set to 0. When set to 1, the linear counter is incremented on every other character clock.

The **Line Counter** bit increments the line counter at each scan line when set to 0. When set to 1, the line counter is incremented on every other scan line, thereby doubling the vertical timings without affecting the horizontal timings.

The **Select Row Scan Counter** bit, when set to 0, permits compatibility with the Hercules Graphics Adapter (HGA), which uses a four bank memory, by using the contents of address bit 14 to drive display address bit 1.

The **Compatibility Mode Support** bit, when set to 0, permits compatibility with the CGA, which uses a two bank memory, by using the contents of address bit 13 to drive display address bit 0.

CRT CONTROLLER REGISTER 18H—LINE COMPARE

Index Register Address: Index = 18H
      Monochrome Adapters: 3B4H
      Color Adapters: 3D4H
Data Register Address:
      Monochrome Adapters: 3B5H
      Color Adapters: 3D5H

Bit 7	Bit 6	Bit 5	Bit 4	Bit 3	Bit 2	Bit 1	Bit 0

Display address of start of second window of split screen display. This is a 10 bit address. The 8 least significant bits (bits 0–7) are in this register. Bit 8 is bit 4 of CRTC Register 07H—Overflow and bit 9 is bit 5 of CRTC Register 09H—Maximum Row Address.

The display is divided into two windows by clearing the display memory address counter when the horizontal line counter reaches this register's value.

Sequencer Registers

Table 3-3 describes the sequencer registers. These registers control timing and access to the planes of the display memory. To access one of the registers, one first outputs the index number of the register to port 3C4H. The indexed register is then available at port 3C5H.

TABLE 3-3. SEQUENCER REGISTERS

Index Register Address: 3C4H   Data Register Address: 3C5H

Register Name	Index	Status
Reset Register	00H	Read/Write
Clock Mode Register	01H	Read/Write
Write Plane Enable Register	02H	Read/Write
Font Select Register	03H	Read/Write
Memory Mode Register	04H	Read/Write

SEQUENCER REGISTER 00H—RESET

Index Register Address: 3C4H   Index = 0
Data Register Address: 3C5H

Bit 7	Bit 6	Bit 5	Bit 4	Bit 3	Bit 2	Bit 1	Bit 0
						Synchronous Reset and Halt Both must be 1 for sequencer to operate	Asynchronous Reset and Halt

Bit 1 commands the timing synchronizer to synchronously clear and halt. Bit 0 commands the timing synchronizer to asynchronously clear and halt. Both bits should be set to one for the display to run. Bit 1 should be set to 0 while selecting a new clock frequency. If the synchronous reset period is too long, data may be lost from display memory.

SEQUENCER REGISTER 01H—CLOCKING MODE

Index Register Address: 3C4H   Index = 1
Data Register Address: 3C5H

Bit 7	Bit 6	Bit 5	Bit 4	Bit 3	Bit 2	Bit 1	Bit 0
		Display off. 0 = screen is turned off. 1 = screen is turned on.	32 bit fetch. 0 = load video shifter input latches at normal clock rate. 1 = load video shifter input latches at quarter of clock rate.	Divide by 2. 0 = normal dot clock. 1 = dot clock is master dot clock /2.	16 bit fetch. 0 = load video shifter input latches at normal clock rate. 1 = load video shifter at half of clock rate. (This bit only active if bit 4 is 0.)	Reserved.	8/9 Dot Clocks. 0 = 9 dot clocks per character. 1 = 8 dot clocks per character.

The **Display Off** bit, when set to 0, turns off the screen and picture generating logic. Since refreshing of the screen is not taking place, memory access by the processor is faster, permitting speedier rewrite of screen data.

The **32 Bit Fetch** bit allows the video serializer to be loaded at quarter rate, which is necessary if dealing with 32 bit double words. This bit is normally not set.

The **Divide by 2** bit when set to 1, causes the dot clock to be divided by two. This causes the EGA/VGA to operate at the 320 pixel per scan line rate. If set to 0, the normal dot clock rate is used, resulting in 640 pixels per scan line.

SEQUENCER REGISTER 02H—MAP MASK

Index Register Address: 3C4H   Index = 2
Data Register Address: 3C5H

Bit 7	Bit 6	Bit 5	Bit 4	Bit 3	Bit 2	Bit 1	Bit 0
				0 = Disable memory plane 3. 1 = Enable memory plane 3.	0 = Disable memory plane 2. 1 = Enable memory plane 2.	0 = Disable memory plane 1. 1 = Enable memory plane 1.	0 = Disable memory plane 0. 1 = Enable memory plane 0.

The **Write Enable** bits enable or disable write access to the respective memory planes on a plane by plane basis. This is useful only when the memory planes are not chained. When the planes are chained (as for the 256 color mode) all these bits should be set to 1.

SEQUENCER REGISTER 03H—CHARACTER MAP SELECT

Index Register Address: 3C4H

Index = 3

Data Register Address: 3C5H

Bit 7	Bit 6	Bit 5	Bit 4	Bit 3	Bit 2	Bit 1	Bit 0
		Character map select A (High bit for VGA)	Character map select B (High bit for VGA)	Character map select A		Character map select B	
		EGA Character Mapping: 00 = First 8K of bank 0 (0–7K). 01 = First 8K of bank 1 (16–23K). 10 = First 8K of bank 2 (32–39K). 11 = First 8K of bank 3 (48–55K). VGA Character Mapping 000 = Address offset of first character 0K. 001 = Address offset of first character 16K. 010 = Address offset of first character 32K. 011 = Address offset of first character 48K. 100 = Address offset of first character 8K. 101 = Address offset of first character 24K. 110 = Address offset of first character 40K. 111 = Address offset of first character 56K.							

In the text modes, the **Character Select A** bits select which character set will be used for a character whose attribute bit 3 is set to 0. The **Character Select B** bits select which character set will be used for a character whose attribute bit 3 is set to 1.

SEQUENCER REGISTER 04H—MEMORY MODE

Index Register Address: 3C4H   Index = 4
Data Register Address: 3C5H

Bit 7	Bit 6	Bit 5	Bit 4	Bit 3	Bit 2	Bit 1	Bit 0
Reserved.				Chain 4. 0 = Display planes not chained. 1 = Display planes chained.	Odd/Even. 0 = Odd/even storage. 1 = sequential storage.	Extended memory. 0 = no memory extension. 1 = memory extension.	Alpha/Graphics Mode. 0 = graphics mode. 1 = Text mode.

The **Reserved** bits should not be used.

The **Chain 4** bit controls the way in which display memory planes are accessed. When set to 0, the planes are not chained together; any combination of the four display memory planes may be accessed by Sequencer Register 02H—Map Mask Register. When this bit is set to 1, the four memory planes are chained together. In this case, the two least significant bits of the memory address are used to select one of the four memory planes. Thus only every fourth byte of each memory plane is used.

The **Odd/Even** bit, when set to 0, causes odd memory addresses to access odd memory planes and even memory addresses to access even memory planes. When set to 1, memory planes are written to according to the Map Mask register.

The **Extended Memory** bit indicates whether display memory is greater or less than 64K bytes.

The **Alpha/Graphics Mode** bit, when set to 0, indicates that a graphics display mode has been selected. When set to 1, this bit indicates that an alphanumerics display mode has been selected.

Graphics Registers

The graphics registers are described in Table 3-4. The graphics controller forms the interface between the processor and the display memory and determines how data is transferred to the four memory planes.

TABLE 3-4. GRAPHICS REGISTERS

Index Register Address: 3CEH   Data Register Address: 3CFH

Register Name	Index	Status
Set/Reset Register	00H	Read/Write
Set/Reset Enable Register	01H	Read/Write
Color Compare Register	02H	Read/Write
Data Rotate/Function Select	03H	Read/Write
Read Plane Select Register	04H	Read/Write
Mode Register	05H	Read/Write
Miscellaneous Register	06H	Read/Write
Color Don't Care Register	07H	Read/Write
Bit Mask Register	08H	Read/Write

GRAPHICS REGISTER 00H - SET/RESET

Index Register Address: 3CEH   Index = 0
Data Register Address: 3CFH

Bit 7	Bit 6	Bit 5	Bit 4	Bit 3	Bit 2	Bit 1	Bit 0
				Fill data for memory plane 3.	Fill data for memory plane 2.	Fill data for memory plane 1.	Fill data for memory plane 0.

If a memory plane is enabled by Graphics Controller Register 01H—Enable Set/Reset and the write mode is 0 (Graphics Controller Register 05H—Mode, then a write to a memory address will cause the entire byte in the selected memory plane to be filled by the value (1 or 0) in that plane's bit in this register.

GRAPHICS REGISTER 01H—ENABLE SET/RESET

Index Register Address: 3CEH   Index = 1
Data Register Address: 3CFH

Bit 7	Bit 6	Bit 5	Bit 4	Bit 3	Bit 2	Bit 1	Bit 0
				0 = Disable memory plane 3 Set/Reset. 1 = Enable memory plane 3 Set/Reset.	0 = Disable memory plane 2 Set/Reset. 1 = Enable memory plane 2 Set/Reset.	0 = Disable memory plane 1 Set/Reset. 1 = Enable memory plane 1 Set/Reset.	0 = Disable memory plane 0 Set/Reset. 1 = Enable memory plane 0 Set/Reset.

This register selects those memory planes for which Graphics Controller Register 0—Set/Reset supplies color data in write mode 0.

GRAPHICS REGISTER 02H—COLOR COMPARE

Index Register Address: 3CEH   Index = 2
Data Register Address: 3CFH

Bit 7	Bit 6	Bit 5	Bit 4	Bit 3	Bit 2	Bit 1	Bit 0
				Color compare value for memory plane 3.	Color compare value for memory plane 2.	Color compare value for memory plane 1.	Color compare value for memory plane 0.

This register establishes a reference color against which data for each pixel from all four memory planes may be compared during a memory read cycle. The return from the memory read is a byte representing eight consecutive pixels beginning at the memory address. Each bit in this byte that is set to 1 indicates that the appropriate pixel matched the color established in this register; each bit that is set to 0 indicates no match. This read mode is set by setting bit 3 of Graphics Controller Register 05H—Mode to 1.

GRAPHICS REGISTER 03H—DATA ROTATE/FUNCTION SELECT

Index Register Address: 3CEH   Index = 3
Data Register Address: 3CFH

Bit 7	Bit 6	Bit 5	Bit 4	Bit 3	Bit 2	Bit 1	Bit 0
			Function Select. 00 = Data overwritten in specified color. 01 = Data ANDED with latched data. 10 = Data ORed with latched data. 11 = Data XORed with latched data.		Rotate Count. Binary representation of the number of bit positions to rotate processor data to the right.		

The **Function Select** bits determine how the data sent to display memory by the processor is combined with the existing data at that memory location before the data is actually transferred to display memory. The processor data may overwrite the existing data or be logically combined with it in some way.

The **Rotate Count** bits determine how many bit positions (from 0 to 7) data is rotated to the right before being written to display memory when in write mode 0.

GRAPHICS REGISTER 04H—READ MAP SELECT

Index Register Address: 3CEH

Index = 4

Data Register Address: 3CFH

Bit 7	Bit 6	Bit 5	Bit 4	Bit 3	Bit 2	Bit 1	Bit 0
						Binary representation of the number of the memory plane to be read by the processor.	

This register determines which color plane is enabled for reading by the processor (when not in the Color Compare mode).

GRAPHICS REGISTER 05H—MODE

Index Register Address: 3CEH

Index = 5

Data Register Address: 3CFH

Bit 7	Bit 6	Bit 5	Bit 4	Bit 3	Bit 2	Bit 1	Bit 0
	Shift register mode. 00=output data in serial fashion (standard EGA format). 01=CGA compatible output (modes 4 and 5). 11 or 10= output data 8 bits at a time from four mem- ory planes (256 color VGA modes).		Odd/Even. 0 = normal EGA/VGA operating mode. 1 = CGA compatible; even addresses access planes 0 and 2, odd addresses access planes 1 and 3.	Read mode. 0 = read from plane selected by graphics data register 4. 1 = do color compare.	Test condition. 0 = Normal operation. 1 = Put all outputs in high impedance state for testing.	Write mode. 00 = Direct write (modified by data rotate and set/reset as applicable). 01 = Write with contents of processor latches. 10 = Memory plane 0–3 filled with 8 bits of of data bit 0–3. 11 = Write with (rotated, if applicable) write data ANDed with Bit Mask (graphics data register 8). Set/reset enabled for all planes.	

The **Shift Register Mode** bits determine how data from the shift registers is transferred to create the serial display output. When bit 6 is set to 1, the serial output is the four most significant bits of plane 0 followed by the four least significant bits from plane 0. This is followed by the four most significant bits of plane 1, and so forth, cycling through the four planes. Each byte selects one of the 256 Digital to Analog registers to output its color selections to the red, green and blue guns of the cathode ray tube. This method is used for display mode 13H, the 320 by 200 pixel by 256 color mode. When bit 6 is set to 0, the shift register mode is determined by bit 5. When it is set to 0, the Digital to Analog register is selected by the value in the Palette Register and the value in the Color Select register. The proper Palette Register (1 of 16) is selected by four bits, one from each bit plane. This is the 16 color EGA/VGA mode. When bit 5 is 1, the contents of memory planes 0 and 1 are output on both the plane 0 and plane 1 serial outputs and the contents of memory planes 2 and 3 are output on both the plane 2 and plane 3 serial outputs. This is the CGA compatible mode of transferring color information.

The **Odd/Even** bit determines which display map data is routed to the processor data bus on a memory read when Sequencer Register 04H— Memory Mode bit 2 is set to 1 (the Odd/Even mode). If bit 4 is set to 0, a normal EGA/VGA memory read occurs. If bit 4 is set to 1, odd memory addresses read data from an even memory map if the address LSB is 0 and from an odd memory map if the address LSB is 1.

The **Read Mode** bit, if set to 0, reads data from the memory plane selected by Graphics Controller Register 04H—Read Map Select. When set to 1, a data read operation performs the color compare (see Graphics Controller Register 02H—Color Compare).

The **Write Mode** bits select the write mode as indicated in the following table:

Bit 1	Bit 0	Write Mode
0	0	0
0	1	1
1	0	2
1	1	3

Write Mode 0. The data addressed to display memory is rotated by the current rotation setting (Graphics Register 03H—Data Rotate/Function Select) and then combined with the latched data for each memory plane in accordance with the current logical function selected (Graphics Register 03H—Data Rotate/Function Select) for each bit for which the bit mask (Graphics Register 08H—Bit Mask) is set to 1. If the bit mask is set to 0, the latched bits are returned to their appropriate memory planes unchanged. If the set/reset function is enabled for any memory plane (Graphics Register 01H—Enable Set/Reset) then the set/reset value for that memory plane that is contained in Graphics Controller Register 02H—Color Compare will be written to every unmasked bit of the addressed byte, ignoring the data written by the processor.

Write Mode 1. The data in the memory latches is written to all memory planes at the addressed byte. The bit map, selected logical function and set/reset function are ignored. This mode permits fast transfer of data within the display memory, since a single read operation at one address will fill the latches with the data from all four memory planes at that address and then a single write to another memory address will transfer this data to the new address.

Write Mode 2. Each of the four least significant bits (bits 0–3) of the processor data is extended to a byte and written to the corresponding memory plane. Thus bit 0 forms the byte written to memory plane 0, bit 1 forms the byte written to memory plane 1, etc. The newly created byte is operated upon by the bit mask, the selected logical function and the set/reset registers, as described for **Write Mode 0**. Graphics Register 03H—Data Rotate/Function Select has no effect.

Write Mode 3. The processor data is operated upon by Graphics Register 03H—Data Rotate/Function Select and the resulting byte is

ANDed with the data from Graphics Register 08H—Bit Mask. The result is used as the bit mask in writing eight bits of the value in Graphics Register 00H—Set/Reset to each memory plane.

GRAPHICS REGISTER 06H—MISCELLANEOUS

Index Register Address: 3CEH   Index = 6
Data Register Address: 3CFH

Bit 7	Bit 6	Bit 5	Bit 4	Bit 3	Bit 2	Bit 1	Bit 0
Reserved.				Memory map 00 = A0000H for 128K bytes 01 = A0000H for 64K bytes 10 = B0000H for 32K bytes 11 = B8000H for 32K bytes		Chain odd maps to even	Display mode. 0 = Text mode 1 = Graphics mode

The **Reserved** bits must all be set to 0.

The **Memory Map** bits determine the size of the display memory window in the processor memory addressing space and the initial address for this window. Note that if you are in a mode that is addressed at A0000H and then shift to a mode that is addressed at B0000H without clearing the memory, then whatever data you had in memory at A0000H will now be at memory address B0000H; you're not getting a new, unused section of memory as you might wish.

The **Chain Odd/Even** bit, when set to 1, enables an odd/even mode in which the least significant bit of the processor memory address is used to select an odd or even memory plane, and this bit is then replaced by a high order bit of the address data before the display memory is actually addressed. This provides CGA compatibility. When this bit is set to 0, normal display memory addressing occurs.

The Display Mode bit, when set to 0, enables the text mode of display. When set to 1, the graphics display mode is enabled.

GRAPHICS REGISTER 07H—COLOR DON'T CARE

Index Register Address: 3CEH   Index = 7
Data Register Address: 3CFH

Bit 7	Bit 6	Bit 5	Bit 4	Bit 3	Bit 2	Bit 1	Bit 0
Reserved.				0 = compare color plane 3. 1 = color plane 3 don't care.	0 = compare color plane 2. 1 = color plane 2 don't care.	0 = compare color plane 1. 1 = color plane 1 don't care.	0 = compare color plane 0. 1 = color plane 0 don't care.

Bits 0 to 3 determine which display memory planes will be used in a read mode 1 color comparison. If a bit is set to 1, the corresponding color plane will be used in the color comparison; it the bit is set to 0, it will not be used.

GRAPHICS REGISTER 08H—BIT MASK

Index Register Address: 3CEH   Index = 8
Data Register Address: 3CFH

Bit 7	Bit 6	Bit 5	Bit 4	Bit 3	Bit 2	Bit 1	Bit 0
For each bit position containing a 0, that bit position is immune to change in each memory plane for a write to the same address as was last read from. For each bit position containing a 1, that bit position in the memory plane can be replaced by the written bit upon a write to the same address as was last read from.							

This register determines which bit positions are immune to change when a display memory write action takes place.

Attribute Registers

Table 3-5 describes the attribute registers. There are 20 registers for the EGA and 21 for the VGA. They are primarily concerned with determining the colors to be displayed on the screen. There is no separate port address for the index register. Instead, a toggle action occurs at the common port address of 3C0H. The first port access sends an index. The next port access writes to the register just indexed. The next port address sends another index, and so forth. If you don't know which toggle state the port is in, you can force it to the state of accepting an index by doing a read of port 3D2H. With the VGA, you can read from the indexed register by reading port 3C1H.

TABLE 3-5. ATTRIBUTE REGISTERS

Address: 3C0H Toggles between index and data registers. Toggle set to index by read of 3D2H.

Register Name	Index	Status
Palette Registers	00H to 0FH	Read/Write
Mode Control Register	10H	Read/Write
Overscan Color Register	11H	Read/Write
Color Plane Enable	12H	Read/Write
Horizontal Pixel Scanning Register	13H	Read/Write
Color Select Register	14H	Read/Write

ATTRIBUTE REGISTERS 00H TO 0FH—PALETTE

Write Index Register Address: 3C0H   Index = 00H to 0FH
Write Data Register Address: 3C0H
Read Index Register Address: 3C1H (VGA only)
Read Data Register Address: 3C1H (VGA only)

16 Registers - one to define each of the 16 EGA colors.

Bit 7	Bit 6	Bit 5	Bit 4	Bit 3	Bit 2	Bit 1	Bit 0
		Red 2/3 satura-tion.	Green 2/3 satura-tion.	Blue 2/3 satura-tion.	Red 1/3 satura-tion.	Green 1/3 satura-tion.	Blue 1/3 satura-tion.
		Note that when the 2/3 saturation and 1/3 saturation bits for a given color are both on, the result is 3/3 or 100% saturation.					

Each of these registers determines 1 of the 16 colors that can be displayed simultaneously in the 16 color modes. for the VGA, the six bit color value in the palette register selects one of 64 colors whose components are shown in the table. For the VGA, the six bit value in the palette register selects one of the first 64 color registers, whose colors are the same as the EGA colors in the default condition.

ATTRIBUTE REGISTER 10H—MODE CONTROL

Write Index Register Address: 3C0H   Index = 10H
Write Data Register Address: 3C0H
Read Index Register Address: 3C1H (VGA only)
Read Data Register Address: 3C1H (VGA only)

Bit 7	Bit 6	Bit 5	Bit 4	Bit 3	Bit 2	Bit 1	Bit 0
Source select. 0=palette register source of color bits 4 & 5. 1 = color select register source of color bits 4 & 5.	Clock select. 0=pixel changes at each dot clock. 1 = pixel changes every other dot clock.	Panning. 0=enables split screen mode pixel panning. 1=disables split screen mode pixel panning.		Blinking. 0=bit 7 of character attribute sets background color. 1=bit 7 of character attribute selects blinking.	Character codes. 0=9th dot same as background. 1=9th dot same as 8th dot.	Display Type. 0 = monochrome. 1 = color.	Display mode. 0 = text. 1 = graphics.

The **Source Select** bit (bit 7) selects the source for outputs to bits 4 and 5 of the digital to analog converters. When set to 0, the 256 color registers of the VGA are segmented as four groups of 64 registers each. The six bits in a palette register are the address of 1 of the 64 registers in the segment selected by bits 6 and 7 of Attribute Register 14H—Color Select. If bit 7 is set to 1, the 256 color registers are segmented into 16 groups of 16 registers each. The first four bits from a palette register select 1 of the 16 registers in a segment selected by bits 4, 5, 6 and 7 of Attribute Register 14H—Color Select.

The **Clock Select** bit controls clocking of the pixel data. When set to 1, it allows eight bits of data to select one of 256 colors, by changing pixel data on every other clock cycle. At this setting, bits 5 and 6 of Graphics Controller Register 05H—Mode must be set to 1 to permit the eight bits of data to be loaded to the shift registers in two successive operations. When set to 0, the normal clock rate is used, transferring four bits to the shift registers for 16 color modes.

The **Panning** bit, when set to 1, enables the operation of CRT Controller Register 18H—Line Compare, which permits one part of a split screen to be scrolled while the other part remains stationary. When set to 0, independent panning is prevented.

The **Blinking** bit, when set to 1, causes a 1 in the most significant bit of a character attribute to make the character blink on the display. When this bit is set to 0, the most significant bit of the character attribute causes the character background to be high intensity when it is 1.

The **Character Codes** bit, when set to 1, sets the ninth horizontal pixel of a character to be the same as the eighth pixel when a nine pixel wide character cell is used with an eight pixel wide character set. Under the same circumstances, setting the bit to 0 will cause the ninth pixel to be the same color as the background.

The **Display Type** bit, when set to 0, causes display attributes to be displayed as color attributes; when set to 1, display attributes are displayed as monochrome attributes (as defined for the IBM Monochrome Display Adapter).

The **Display Mode** bit determines whether the display is to be text (alphanumerics) or graphics.

ATTRIBUTE REGISTER 11H—OVERSCAN COLOR

Write Index Register Address: 3C0H   Index = 11H
Write Data Register Address: 3C0H
Read Index Register Address: 3C1H (VGA only)
Read Data Register Address: 3C1H (VGA only)

Bit 7	Bit 6	Bit 5	Bit 4	Bit 3	Bit 2	Bit 1	Bit 0
		1 = secondary red border.	1 = secondary green border.	1 = secondary blue border.	1 = red border.	1 = green border.	1 = blue border.

This register determines the color for the overscan region, which is the space on the display between the end of blanking and the beginning of the display at the top and left and between the end of the display and the beginning of blanking at the bottom and right. The color selection is the same as described for Attribute Registers 00–0FH (Palette Registers). Unfortunately, for most EGA and VGA implementations, this feature does not work properly if the color is set to anything other than black (00).

ATTRIBUTE REGISTER 12H—COLOR PLANE ENABLE

Write Index Register Address: 3C0H   Index = 12H
Write Data Register Address: 3C0H
Read Index Register Address: 3C1H (VGA only)
Read Data Register Address: 3C1H (VGA only)

Bit 7	Bit 6	Bit 5	Bit 4	Bit 3	Bit 2	Bit 1	Bit 0
		Video status multiplex		Enable color plane 3	Enable color plane 2	Enable color plane 1	Enable color plane 0

The **Video Status Multiplex** bits select which two of eight color outputs are returned by the Diagnostic bits of Input Status Register One, as follows:

Attribute Register 12H		Input Status Register One	
Bit 5	Bit 4	Bit 5	Bit 4
0	0	Primary red	Primary blue
0	1	Secondary green	Secondary blue
1	0	Primary intensity	Primary green
1	1	Secondary intensity	Secondary red

The **Enable Color Plane** bits determine which color planes are enabled in the 16 color configurations.

ATTRIBUTE REGISTER 13H—HORIZONTAL PIXEL PANNING

Write Index Register Address: 3C0H   Index = 13H
Write Data Register Address: 3C0H
Read Index Register Address: 3C1H (VGA only)
Read Data Register Address: 3C1H (VGA only)

Bit 7	Bit 6	Bit 5	Bit 4	Bit 3	Bit 2	Bit 1	Bit 0
				Horizontal pixel panning. Binary representation of number of pixels to shift character to the left.			

The **Horizontal Pixel Panning** bits specify the number of pixels to the left that the video data is to be shifted. The relationship of the number in this field to the number of pixels the character is to be shifted depends upon the specified width of the character, as follows:

Dots / Pixel	Horizontal Panning Value															
	0	1	2	3	4	5	6	7	8	9	A	B	C	D	E	F
6																
8	0	1	2	3	4	5	6	7	-	-	-	-	-	-	-	-
9	8	0	1	2	3	4	5	6	7	-	-	-	-	-	-	-
12	B	A	9	8	0	1	2	3	4	5	6	7	-	-	-	-
16	F	E	D	C	B	A	9	8	0	1	2	3	4	5	6	7

This pixel by pixel shifting permits sliding the display to the left smoothly rather than having to jump character by character.

ATTRIBUTE REGISTER 14H—COLOR SELECT

Write Index Register Address: 3C0H   Index = 14H
Write Data Register Address: 3C0H
Read Index Register Address: 3C1H (VGA only)
Read Data Register Address: 3C1H (VGA only)

Bit 7	Bit 6	Bit 5	Bit 4	Bit 3	Bit 2	Bit 1	Bit 0
				Color bit 7.	Color bit 6.	Color bit 5.	Color bit 4.

Color bits 7 and 6 are used as the high order bits of the eight bit address for selecting which of the 256 color registers are used for colors in the 16 color modes. Therefore by changing these bits, one may select one of four sets of 64 color registers.

Color bits 4 and 5 are are used along with **Color Bits 6 and 7** to select 1 of 16 sets of 16 color registers in the 16 color modes when Attribute Register 10H—Mode Control bit 7 is set to 1.

Video Digital-to-Analog Converter Registers

Table 3-6 presents an overview of the Video Digital-to-Analog converter registers. There are 256 internal color registers which store the 256 VGA colors. Each is 18 bits long, containing 6 bits of red data, 6 bits of green data and 6 bits of blue data. There are five registers used to communicate with these internal color registers. They are the Color Data Register Write Index Register, the Color Data Register Read Index Register (write only), the DAC State Register (read only), the Pixel Data Register, and the Pixel Mask Register. Descriptions of these registers follow.

TABLE 3-6. VIDEO DIGITAL-TO-ANALOG CONVERTER REGISTERS

Register	Address	Status
Color Data Register Write Index Register.	3C8H	Read/Write.
Color Data Register Read Index Register.	3C7H	Write only.
DAC State	3C7H	Read Only.
Pixel Data Register	3C9H	Read/Write.
Pixel Mask Register	3C6H	Read/Write.

COLOR DATA REGISTER WRITE INDEX REGISTER

Write Data Register Address: 3C8H
Read Data Register Address: 3C8H

Bit 7	Bit 6	Bit 5	Bit 4	Bit 3	Bit 2	Bit 1	Bit 0
Address of color register during write mode.							

This register contains the address used to access 1 of the 256 color registers for a write operation. A write operation consists of three inputs to the Pixel Data register, to load red, green and blue values to the register. When these three inputs are complete, the address in this register is incremented so that the programmer does not need to supply a new index value to this register for each successive set of color inputs.

COLOR DATA REGISTER READ INDEX REGISTER

Write Data Register Address: 3C7H

Bit 7	Bit 6	Bit 5	Bit 4	Bit 3	Bit 2	Bit 1	Bit 0
Address of color register during read mode.							

This register contains the address used to access one of the 256 color registers for a read operation, which consists of reading three bytes from the Pixel Data register to obtain red, green and blue values from the register. When these three bytes have been read, the address in this register is incremented to point to the next color register in case successive color register values are to be read.

PIXEL DATA REGISTER

Write Data Register Address: 3C9H
Read Data Register Address: 3C9H

Bit 7	Bit 6	Bit 5	Bit 4	Bit 3	Bit 2	Bit 1	Bit 0
		Color Data.					

This register provides the interface to whichever of the 256 18 bit color registers is addressed by one of the two preceding registers. For write operations, the six color data bits sent to this register on three successive write operations are transferred to the red, green and blue portions of the color data register addressed by the Color Data Register Write Index Register. That register is then incremented to address the next color data register. For a read operation, three successive reads of this register will obtain the red, green and blue color information from the Color Data Register addressed by the Color Data Register Read Index Register, after which that register is incremented to address the next color data register.

DAC STATE REGISTER

Read Data Register Address: 3C7H

Bit 7	Bit 6	Bit 5	Bit 4	Bit 3	Bit 2	Bit 1	Bit 0
						DAC State. 0 = Color Data Register Index Read Register was accessed last. 3 = Color Data Register Index Write Register was accessed last.	

This register indicates whether a read or write operation to the Color Data Registers is in effect.

PIXEL MASK REGISTER

Write Data Register Address: 3C6H
Read Data Register Address: 3C6H

Bit 7	Bit 6	Bit 5	Bit 4	Bit 3	Bit 2	Bit 1	Bit 0
Set to FFH by BIOS mode call.							

This register should not be modified by the programmer.

Chapter 4

Extended Registers for Super VGA Cards

Each Super VGA display adapter card has additional internal registers and/or extensions to existing register sets, which are used for paging of the additional memory required for high resolution modes, for setting up these modes, and for other advanced capabilities of the card. Unfortunately, there is currently no standardization of the way in which Super VGA cards are used. Recently a new industry standards organization has been established to attempt to set up standards that will provide some compatibility of Super VGA boards from different vendors. This organization is known as the Video Electronics Standards Association (VESA). VESA has set up a set of additional ROM BIOS video services that should work with newer Super VGA display adapter cards regardless of their manufacturer. The standard includes the definition of nine high resolution extended video graphics modes. The new ROM BIOS video services permit setting the computer to these modes and interacting with the Super VGA to use them in programs. Unfortunately, the standardization does not extend to register definitions. Since even with these new standards, the problem still exists that writing graphics to the screen through the ROM BIOS video services is usually too slow to be acceptable, we are still faced with many different techniques that are required for writing pixels, and we have to select the correct one for the Super VGA that we are using. So, even with the new standards, you aren't going to be able to escape learning something about the detailed operation of special Super VGA registers, if you are serious about programming in high resolution extended graphics modes. In the sections that follow, we will describe the additional registers used in five typical Super VGA display adapter cards. These are the STB

PowerGraph card (which uses the Tseng Labs, Inc. ET4000 chip set), the Headlands Technology (formerly Video Seven) 1024i Super VGA board (which uses Headlands Technology's own chip set), the Logix Super VGA board (which uses the Trident 8800CS chip set), the Paradise Super VGA board as used in the Dell 310 (which uses the Western Digital/Paradise chip set), and the ATI VGAWONDER Super VGA board (which uses the ATI Technologies chip set). If you have a different Super VGA board that uses one of these chip sets your chances are quite good that you can use the information in this book to run high resolution modes successfully. Registers and techniques for using them remain the same for all boards that use the same chip set, but each board manufacturer writes its own extensions for the ROM BIOS video services, so you will need to use caution when working with these. If you have one of the many Super VGA boards that are not covered by this book, you should be able to observe how the boards that are covered are treated and extend these methods to write your own functions. To do this, you'll need some detailed information on the internal registers and BIOS extensions. If you're planning to buy a Super VGA board, it will be a lot easier if you get one of the ones covered in detail in this book. I highly recommend the STB PowerGraph board, which is easy to program and has given excellent results in testing the software developed for this book. If you insist on buying a board that is not covered, make sure before you buy that you will receive all of the technical information necessary to program the extended graphics modes.

Additional Registers Used in the STB PowerGraph VGA Display Adapter Card (Tseng Labs, Inc. ET4000 Chip Set)

FEATURE CONTROL REGISTER

Read Register Address: 3CAH

Write Register Address:
      Monochrome Adapters: 3BAH
      Color Adapters: 3DAH

Bit 7	Bit 6	Bit 5	Bit 4	Bit 3	Bit 2	Bit 1	Bit 0
Enable NMI Generation. 1 = Enable NMI. 2 = Disable NMI.	Reserved.					Feature Connector Bit 1.	Feature Connector Bit 0.

The **Enable NMI Generation** bit can only be set to 1 when bit 7 of CRT Controller Register 34H is set to 1. This bit can be read only when the *Key* is set. This is done by writing 03H to Hercules Compatibility Register 3BFH and A0H to Mode Control Register 3B8H (monochrome) or 3D8H (color). The *Key* also needs to be set in order to read bits 5 and 6 of Input Status Register Zero.

VIDEO SUBSYSTEM REGISTER

Read/Write Register Address: 3C3H/46E8H

Bit 7	Bit 6	Bit 5	Bit 4	Bit 3	Bit 2	Bit 1	Bit 0
Reserved.				Select video subsystem address (46E8H).	Reserved.		Select video subsystem address (03CFH).

The default configuration of the chip set is for CRT controller register index 34 bit 3 to be set to 0. This sets the port address for this register to 3C3. In this situation, if bit 0 is set to 1, the video subsystem is enabled; otherwise it is disabled. When CRT Controller Register 34H bit 3 is set to 1, the port address for this register is set to 46E8H. In this situation, if bit 3 is set to 1, the video subsystem is enabled; otherwise it is disabled.

DISPLAY MODE CONTROL REGISTER

Read/Write Register Address:
  Monochrome Adapters: 3B8H
  Color Adapters: 3D8H

Register contents for color adapters:

Bit 7	Bit 6	Bit 5	Bit 4	Bit 3	Bit 2	Bit 1	Bit 0
Reserved.	Bit 1 of Hercules Compatibility Register (3BFH).	Enable Blink (Text mode only).	640 x 200 mode.	Enable screen display.	B&W mode	Enable graphics mode	80x25 text mode

Register contents for monochrome adapters:

Bit 7	Bit 6	Bit 5	Bit 4	Bit 3	Bit 2	Bit 1	Bit 0
Page select.	Bit 1 of Hercules Compatibility Register (3BFH).	Enable Blink.	Reserved.	Enable screen display.	Reserved.	Monochrome graphics mode.	80x25 text mode.

COLOR SELECT REGISTER

Write Only Register Address: 3D9H

Bit 7	Bit 6	Bit 5	Bit 4	Bit 3	Bit 2	Bit 1	Bit 0
Reserved.		0 = modes 4 & 5 colors are green, red, brown. 1 = modes 4 & 5 colors are cyan, magenta, white.	0 = mode 4 & 5 foreground colors are not intensified. 1 = modes 4 & 5 foreground colors are intensified.	Border color for modes 0–3 & 7. Background color for modes 4 & 5. Foreground color for mode 6. Intensity.	Red.	Green.	Blue.

Bit 5 selects the palette color set for CGA type modes. The two palettes are numbered 0 and 1.

Color Number	Palette 0 (Bit 5 = 0)	Palette 1 (Bit 5 = 1)
0	Background (defined by bits 0–3)	
1	Green.	Cyan.
2	Red.	Magenta.
3	Brown.	White.

Bit 4 selects intensified colors for the 320 x 200 graphics mode when set to 1.

Bits 0–3 select the background color for the 320 x 200 graphics mode, the foreground color for the 640 x 200 graphics mode, and the border color for the 40 x 24 alphanumeric (text) mode.

AT&T MODE CONTROL REGISTER

Register Address: (Write only) 3DE

Bit 7	Bit 6	Bit 5	Bit 4	Bit 3	Bit 2	Bit 1	Bit 0
Reserved.	Underline color attribute.			Alternate page select.	Alternate font select.	Reserved.	Double scan line mode.

This register permits compatibility with the 640 x 400 pixel AT&T display system. Bit 7 of the CRT Controller Register 34H—6845 Compatibility Control must be set to enable this register. (Bit 6 of CRTC 34 enables bit 6 of this register; bits 6 and 7 of CRTC 34 enables bit 0 of this register.) Miscellaneous Output Register bit 0 must be set to 1 for color mode before this register can be set.

The **Underline color attribute enable** bit sets the foreground color attribute to blue when set to 0 and the underline attribute to white when set to 1.

The **Alternate page select** bit selects the first 16K memory page when set to 0 and the second 16K memory page when set to 1 (if bit 0 = 0).

The **Alternate font select** bit selects the font stored in block 0 when set to 0 and the font stored in block 1 when set to 1.

The **Double scan line** bit causes the display mode to simulate IBM 200-line graphics when set to 0 and to simulate AT&T 400 line graphics when set to 1.

HERCULES COMPATIBILITY REGISTER

Register Address: (Write only) 3BF

Bit 7	Bit 6	Bit 5	Bit 4	Bit 3	Bit 2	Bit 1	Bit 0
Reserved.						Enable second page.	Reserved.

This register permits enabling the second page of memory to provide full 64K display memory compatibility with Hercules graphics.

The **Enable second page** bit, when set to one, enables the second page of memory at address B8000H.

CRT CONTROLLER REGISTER 32H—RAS/CAS CONFIGURATION

Index Register Address: Index = 32H
        Monochrome Adapters: 3B4H
        Color Adapters: 3D4H
Data Register Address:
        Monochrome Adapters: 3B5H
        Color Adapters: 3D5H

Bit 7	Bit 6	Bit 5	Bit 4	Bit 3	Bit 2	Bit 1	Bit 0
Static Memory.	Column set-up time.	RCD RAS to CAS time. 1=3 clock. 0=2 clock.	RAS precharge time.		CAS pre-charge time.	CAS low pulse width.	

The timing signals described for this register are part of the timing for refreshing the display memory on-board the VGA card. The values are normally set by the manufacturer to match the type of memory chips used. They should not be modified by the user or programmer. Therefore we haven't attempted to define these signals. Unless you are a dynamic memory expert, the timings will seem somewhat obscure to you.

The **Static Memory** bit, when set to 0, toggles the CAS during a fast page memory read operation. When set to 1, it causes the CAS outputs to remain active during the entire memory read operation.

The **Column setup time** bit, when set to 1, causes an additional clock period to be added to the RAS low pulse width and an additional clock period to be added to the last CAS low pulse width of every RAS cycle.

The **RCD RAS to CAS time** bit causes the *Trcd* time to be 2 clock periods when set to zero and 3 clock periods when set to one.

The value of the **RAS precharge time** bits plus 2 is the width of the RAS precharge control high pulse width in clock periods.

The value of the **CAS precharge time** bit plus 1 is the width of the CAS precharge control high pulse width in clock periods.

CRT CONTROLLER REGISTER 33H—EXTENDED START ADDRESS

Index Register Address: Index = 33H
        Monochrome Adapters: 3B4H
        Color Adapters: 3D4H
Data Register Address:
        Monochrome Adapters: 3B5H
        Color Adapters: 3D5H

Bit 7	Bit 6	Bit 5	Bit 4	Bit 3	Bit 2	Bit 1	Bit 0
				Cursor address bits 16 and 17.		Linear start address bits 16 and 17.	

These extend the specified quantities to handle the larger memory size required for the extended display modes.

CRT CONTROLLER REGISTER 34H—6845 COMPATIBILITY CONTROL

Index Register Address: Index = 34
      Monochrome Adapters: 3B4H
      Color Adapters: 3D4H
Data Register Address:
      Monochrome Adapters: 3B5H
      Color Adapters: 3D5H

Bit 7	Bit 6	Bit 5	Bit 4	Bit 3	Bit 2	Bit 1	Bit 0
1=enable 6845 compatibility.	Enable double scan/underline in AT&T mode select.	1=enable translation ROM for CRTC and MISCOUT.	1=enable translation ROM for CRTC and MISCOUT read.	Set video sub-system enable address. 0=3C3. 1=46E8.	1=tri-state output.	Clock select 2.	1=enable CS0 translation.

The **Enable 6845 compatibility** bit, when set to 0 makes the CRTC registers EGA/VGA compatible. When set to 1, it makes these registers fully compatible with the 6845 integrated circuit.

Bit 6 enables the double scan and underline color attributes for AT&T mode. (See the AT&T Model Control Register).

Bits 4 and 5, when set to 1 disable the read and write respectively to the CRTC data registers and the MISCOUT register and allow for the substitution of external ROM.

Bit 3 determines the port address of the video subsystem enable register. If set to 0, the address is 3C3; if set to 1, the address is 46E8.

The **Tri-state output** bit, when set to 1, causes all output pins to go to a tri-state condition.

The **Clock select 2** bit is used as the most significant bit of a three bit number whose least significant bits are bits 3 and 2 of the

Miscellaneous output register. **Bit 0** enables the use of this bit. When bit 0 is set to 0, only the two bits from the Miscellaneous Output Register select one of four possible clock rates. When bit 0 is set to 1, bit 1 of this register together with the two bits from the Miscellaneous Output Register select one of eight possible clock rates.

Additional Registers Used in the Headlands Technology 1024i VGA Display Adapter Card

EXTENDED REGISTER 06H—EXTENSION CONTROL

Index Register Address: 3C4H   Index = 6
Data Register Address: 3C5H

Bit 7	Bit 6	Bit 5	Bit 4	Bit 3	Bit 2	Bit 1	Bit 0
Unused.							Extensions access enable.

The **Extensions access enable** bit, when set to 1, permits access to all the extended registers described later. When it is set to 0, these registers are not accessible.

EXTENDED REGISTER 1FH—IDENTIFICATION

Index Register Address: 3C4H   Index = 1FH
Data Read Only Register Address: 3C5H

Bit 7	Bit 6	Bit 5	Bit 4	Bit 3	Bit 2	Bit 1	Bit 0
Most significant byte of display memory address of top left hand pixel on screen XORed with EAH.							

This register returns the most significant byte of the display memory address of the top left-hand pixel of the display screen (the contents of CRTC Register 0CH) exclusive ORed with EAH. It may be used to identify the presence of a Headlands Technology VGA board, in which case E0H is returned.

EXTENDED REGISTER 8EH and 8FH—VGA CHIP REVISION

Index Register Address: 3C4H
Data Read Only Register Address: 3C5H

Index = 8EH or 8FH

Bit 7	Bit 6	Bit 5	Bit 4	Bit 3	Bit 2	Bit 1	Bit 0
00000000–0011FFFF (00H to 6FH) Reserved for future Headlands Technology products. 01110000 (70H) = V7VGA chip revisions 1, 2, or 3. 01110001 (71H) = V7VGA chip revision 4. 01110010–01111111 (72H to 7FH) = Reserved for future versions of V7VGA. 10000000–11111111 (80H to FFH) = VEGA VGA chip.							

EXTENDED REGISTER 94H—POINTER ADDRESS PATTERN ADDRESS

Index Register Address: 3C4H
Data Register Address: 3C5H

Index = 94H

Bit 7	Bit 6	Bit 5	Bit 4	Bit 3	Bit 2	Bit 1	Bit 0
Part of address for memory location of the cursor pattern. The two most significant bits (A15 and A14) are bits 6 and 5 of Extended register FFH.							
A13	A12	A11	A10	A9	A8	A7	A6

The VGA1024i supports a hardware cursor for graphics modes that unfortunately does not work with the 256 color modes. The advantage of the hardware cursor is that, when it is displayed and moved, the underlying display information is not disturbed. Therefore there is no need to save the display data under the cursor and restore it when the cursor is moved. The graphics cursor is a 32 pixel by 32 pixel pattern that is stored in a 256 byte block of off-screen video memory whose offset from the base display memory address is given by the address that is partially in this register. (The six least significant bits of this offset address are always zero.) The cursor pattern consists of a 128 byte AND mask followed by a 128 byte XOR mask.

EXTENDED REGISTER 9CH—CURSOR HORIZONTAL POSITION HIGH

Index Register Address: 3C4H   Index = 9CH
Data Register Address: 3C5H

Bit 7	Bit 6	Bit 5	Bit 4	Bit 3	Bit 2	Bit 1	Bit 0

Most significant byte of the horizontal position (column) of the hardware cursor on the display screen.

EXTENDED REGISTER 9DH—CURSOR HORIZONTAL POSITION LOW

Index Register Address: 3C4H   Index = 9DH
Data Register Address: 3C5H

Bit 7	Bit 6	Bit 5	Bit 4	Bit 3	Bit 2	Bit 1	Bit 0

Least significant byte of the horizontal position (column) of the hardware cursor on the display screen.

EXTENDED REGISTER 9EH—CURSOR VERTICAL POSITION HIGH

Index Register Address: 3C4H   Index = 9EH
Data Register Address: 3C5H

Bit 7	Bit 6	Bit 5	Bit 4	Bit 3	Bit 2	Bit 1	Bit 0

Most significant byte of the vertical position (row) of the hardware cursor on the display screen.

EXTENDED REGISTER 9FH—CURSOR VERTICAL POSITION LOW

Index Register Address: 3C4H   Index = 9FH
Data Register Address: 3C5H

Bit 7	Bit 6	Bit 5	Bit 4	Bit 3	Bit 2	Bit 1	Bit 0
Least significant byte of vertical position (row) of hardware cursor on the display screen.							

EXTENDED REGISTER A0H—PLANE 0 DATA LATCH

Index Register Address: 3C4H   Index = A0H
Data Register Address: 3C5H

Bit 7	Bit 6	Bit 5	Bit 4	Bit 3	Bit 2	Bit 1	Bit 0
Data latch for display memory plane 0.							

The data in the four display memory planes is accessible only through an indirect process wherein input data manipulates four memory latch registers, whose contents is then transferred to the memory planes by a display memory write. Sending data to this register sends it directly to the plane 0 memory latch register.

EXTENDED REGISTER A1H—PLANE 1 DATA LATCH

Index Register Address: 3C4H   Index = A1H
Data Register Address: 3C5H

Bit 7	Bit 6	Bit 5	Bit 4	Bit 3	Bit 2	Bit 1	Bit 0
Data latch for display memory plane 1.							

The data in the four display memory planes is accessible only through an indirect process wherein input data manipulates four memory latch registers, whose contents is then transferred to the memory planes by a display memory write. Sending data to this register sends it directly to the plane 1 memory latch register.

EXTENDED REGISTER A2H—PLANE 2 DATA LATCH

Index Register Address: 3C4H   Index = A2H
Data Register Address: 3C5H

Bit 7	Bit 6	Bit 5	Bit 4	Bit 3	Bit 2	Bit 1	Bit 0
Data latch for display memory plane 2.							

The data in the four display memory planes is accessible only through an indirect process wherein input data manipulates four memory latch registers, whose contents is then transferred to the memory planes by a display memory write. Sending data to this register sends it directly to the plane 2 memory latch register.

EXTENDED REGISTER A3H—PLANE 3 DATA LATCH

Index Register Address: 3C4H   Index = A3H
Data Register Address: 3C5H

Bit 7	Bit 6	Bit 5	Bit 4	Bit 3	Bit 2	Bit 1	Bit 0
Data latch for display memory plane 3.							

The data in the four display memory planes is accessible only through an indirect process wherein input data manipulates four memory latch registers, whose contents is then transferred to the memory planes by a display memory write. Sending data to this register sends it directly to the plane 3 memory latch register.

EXTENDED REGISTER A4H—CLOCK SELECT

Index Register Address: 3C4H   Index = A4H
Data Register Address: 3C5H

Bit 7	Bit 6	Bit 5	Bit 4	Bit 3	Bit 2	Bit 1	Bit 0
			Clock select bit 2.				

The **Clock select bit 2** is the most significant bit of a three bit clock select number formed with bits 3 and 2 of the Miscellaneous Output Register. This selects one of eight clock signals as follows:

Bit 4	Misc Output Register bit 3	Misc Output Register bit 2	Clock Source	Comments
0	0	0	25.175 MHz.	VGA standard.
0	0	1	16.257 MHz.	VGA standard.
0	1	0	Feature connector.	VGA standard.
0	1	1	00.000 MHz.	VGA standard.
1	0	0	50.350 MHz.	V7 VGA extension.
1	0	1	65.000 MHz.	V7 VGA extension.
1	1	0	Feature connector.	V7 VGA extension.
1	1	1	40.000 MHz.	V7 VGA extension.

EXTENDED REGISTER A5H—CURSOR ATTRIBUTES

Index Register Address: 3C4H
Data Register Address: 3C5H

Index = A5H

Bit 7	Bit 6	Bit 5	Bit 4	Bit 3	Bit 2	Bit 1	Bit 0
1=Hardware graphics cursor enable.	Not used.			Text cursor mode. 0=replace. 1=XOR.			Cursor blink disable. 1=disable. 0=enable.

The **Hardware graphics cursor enable** bit, when set to 1, enables the use of the hardware graphics cursor.

The **Text cursor mode** bit, when set to 1, causes the hardware cursor to overwrite the existing display data. When set to 0, this bit causes the hardware cursor to be XORed with the display data.

EXTENDED REGISTER EAH—SWITCH DATA STROBE

Index Register Address: 3C4H
Data Write Only Register Address: 3C5H

Index = EAH

Bit 7	Bit 6	Bit 5	Bit 4	Bit 3	Bit 2	Bit 1	Bit 0
Switch data strobe.							

When a write is performed to this register, the actual write data is ignored, but is used to strobe the state of on-board switches into Extended register F7H—Switch Readback. The switch information may then be obtained by reading that register.

EXTENDED REGISTER EBH—EMULATION CONTROL

Index Register Address: 3C4H   Index = EBH
Data Register Address: 3C5H

Bit 7	Bit 6	Bit 5	Bit 4	Bit 3	Bit 2	Bit 1	Bit 0
Emulation enable.	Hercules bit map enable.	Write protect range 2.	Write protect range 1.	Write protect range 0.	NMI enable range 2.	NMI enable range 1.	NMI enable range 0

The **Emulation Enable** bit, when set to 1, permits the 1024i VGA to emulate the Video Seven IUO chip.

The **Hercules bit map enable** bit, when set to 1, forces the V7 VGA to decode a memory mapping at B0000H for 64K (for Hercules graphics modes) regardless of the settings of bits 3 and 2 of Graphics Register 06H—Miscellaneous register.

The **Write Protect Range 2** bit, when set to 1, write protects CRT Controller Registers 00H to 08H.

The **Write Protect Range 1** bit, when set to 1, write protects CRT Controller Registers 09H to 0BH.

The **Write Protect Range 0** bit, when set to 1, write protects CRT Controller Register 0CH.

The **NMI Enable Range 2** bit, when set to 1, generates a strobe for the IOU's external event pin upon any write to CRT Controller Registers 00H to 08H.

The **NMI Enable Range 1** bit, when set to 1, generates a strobe for the IOU's external event pin upon any write to CRT Controller Registers 09H to 0BH.

The **NMI Enable Range 0** bit, when set to 1, generates a strobe for the IOU's external event pin upon any write to CRT Controller Register 0CH.

EXTENDED REGISTER ECH—FOREGROUND PLANE 0 LATCH

Index Register Address: 3C4H   Index = ECH
Data Register Address: 3C5H

Bit 7	Bit 6	Bit 5	Bit 4	Bit 3	Bit 2	Bit 1	Bit 0
Input byte for memory plane 0 when bits 3 and 2 of Extended Register FEH are 10.							

This provides a dithered foreground pattern for display memory plane 0 when Extended Register FEH—Foreground/Background Control has bits 3 and 2 set to the dithered foreground mode (10).

EXTENDED REGISTER EDH—FOREGROUND PLANE 1 LATCH

Index Register Address: 3C4H   Index = EDH
Data Register Address: 3C5H

Bit 7	Bit 6	Bit 5	Bit 4	Bit 3	Bit 2	Bit 1	Bit 0
Input byte for memory plane 1 when bits 3 and 2 of Extended Register FEH are 10.							

This provides a dithered foreground pattern for display memory plane 1 when Extended Register FEH—Foreground/Background Control has bits 3 and 2 set to the dithered foreground mode (10).

EXTENDED REGISTER EEH—FOREGROUND PLANE 2 LATCH

Index Register Address: 3C4H   Index = EEH
Data Register Address: 3C5H

Bit 7	Bit 6	Bit 5	Bit 4	Bit 3	Bit 2	Bit 1	Bit 0
Input byte for memory plane 2 when bits 3 and 2 of Extended Register FEH are 10.							

This provides a dithered foreground pattern for display memory plane 2 when Extended Register FEH—Foreground/Background Control has bits 3 and 2 set to the dithered foreground mode (10).

EXTENDED REGISTER EFH—FOREGROUND PLANE 3 LATCH

Index Register Address: 3C4H   Index = EFH
Data Register Address: 3C5H

Bit 7	Bit 6	Bit 5	Bit 4	Bit 3	Bit 2	Bit 1	Bit 0
Input byte for memory plane 3 when bits 3 and 2 of Extended Register FEH are 10.							

This provides a dithered foreground pattern for display memory plane 3 when Extended Register FEH—Foreground/Background Control has bits 3 and 2 set to the dithered foreground mode (10).

EXTENDED REGISTER F0H—FAST FOREGROUND LATCH

Index Register Address: 3C4H   Index = F0H
Data Register Address: 3C5H

Bit 7	Bit 6	Bit 5	Bit 4	Bit 3	Bit 2	Bit 1	Bit 0
Input bytes for registers ECH through EFH when bits 3 and 2 of Extended Register FEH are 10.							

This is not an actual physical register. It permits sequential loading of all four foreground pattern registers (ECH through EFH) by four sequential writes to this address. Reading from this register will reset it so that the next write will be to the first register (ECH).

EXTENDED REGISTER F1H—FAST LATCH LOAD STATE

Index Register Address: 3C4H   Index = F1H
Data Register Address: 3C5H

Bit 7	Bit 6	Bit 5	Bit 4	Bit 3	Bit 2	Bit 1	Bit 0
Not used.		Foreground latch load state.		Not used.		Background latch load state.	

The **Foreground latch load state** bits indicate which of the foreground latch registers (ECH through EFH) will be written to by the next write operation to Extended Register F0H. This value is reset to 0 when a read of F0H occurs. Sequential loading of all four foreground pattern registers (ECH through EFH) is accomplished by four sequential writes to this address.

The **Background latch load state** bits indicate which of the normal VGA processor latches will be written to by the next write operation to Extended Register F2H. This value is reset to 0 when a read of F2H occurs.

EXTENDED REGISTER F2H—FAST BACKGROUND PATTERN

Index Register Address: 3C4H   Index = F2H
Data Register Address: 3C5H

Bit 7	Bit 6	Bit 5	Bit 4	Bit 3	Bit 2	Bit 1	Bit 0
Input bytes for normal VGA processor latches.							

This is not an actual physical register. It permits sequential loading of all four normal VGA processor latches by four sequential writes to this address. Reading from this register will reset it so that the next write will be to the first VGA processor latch.

EXTENDED REGISTER F3H—MASKED WRITE CONTROL

Index Register Address: 3C4H   Index = F3H
Data Register Address: 3C5H

Bit 7	Bit 6	Bit 5	Bit 4	Bit 3	Bit 2	Bit 1	Bit 0
Not used.						Masked write source.	Masked write enable.

The **Masked write source** bit indicates the source of mask data if the Masked write enable bit is set to 1. When this bit is set to 1, the rotated CPU bit is used to provide a write mask for writing to each display memory plane. When this bit is set to 0, the mask is provided by Extended Register F4H—Masked Write Mask.

The **Masked write enable** bit, when set to 1, enables the masked write operation, which permits selected bits of a memory byte to be modified without first reading the byte, when V-RAM is used in the VGA card.

EXTENDED REGISTER F4H—MASKED WRITE MASK

Index Register Address: 3C4H   Index = F4H
Data Register Address: 3C5H

Bit 7	Bit 6	Bit 5	Bit 4	Bit 3	Bit 2	Bit 1	Bit 0
Masked write mask.							

The **Masked write mask** byte provides the mask for masked writes when Extended Register F3H bit 0 is set to 1 and bit 1 is set to 0.

EXTENDED REGISTER F5H—FOREGROUND/BACKGROUND PATTERN

Index Register Address: 3C4H   Index = F5H
Data Register Address: 3C5H

Bit 7	Bit 6	Bit 5	Bit 4	Bit 3	Bit 2	Bit 1	Bit 0
Foreground/background pattern.							

The **Foreground/background pattern** byte is one possible source of the pattern used in solid foreground/background mode, which is active when bits 3 and 2 of Extended Register FEH—Foreground/Background Control are 0 and 1, respectively.

EXTENDED REGISTER F6H—BANK SELECT

Index Register Address: 3C4H   Index = F6H
Data Register Address: 3C5H

Bit 7	Bit 6	Bit 5	Bit 4	Bit 3	Bit 2	Bit 1	Bit 0
Line compare bank reset.	Counter bank enable.	CRTC read bank select.		CPU read bank select.		CPU write bank select	

The **Line compare bank reset** bit, when set to 1, resets bits 17 and 16 of the memory address counter to 0 when the line compare condition becomes true. When set to 0, and the line compare condition becomes true, bits 17 and 16 of the memory address counter are loaded from bits 5 and 4 of this register.

The **Counter bank enable** bit, when set to 1, causes bits 17 and 16 of the memory address counter to address the 1 Mb DRAMs. When set to 0, this bit causes bits 5 and 4 from this register to provide the bit 17 and 16 addressing of the 1 Mb DRAMs.

The **CRTC read bank select** bits select one of four 256K banks of display memory from which the CRTC fetches video data for display.

The **CPU read bank select** bits select one of four 256K banks of display memory from which the CPU reads data when a display memory read occurs.

The **CPU write bank select** bits select one of four 256K banks of display memory to which the CPU writes data when a display memory write occurs.

EXTENDED REGISTER F7H—SWITCH READBACK

Index Register Address: 3C4H   Index = F7H
Data Register Address: 3C5H

Bit 7	Bit 6	Bit 5	Bit 4	Bit 3	Bit 2	Bit 1	Bit 0
Switch readback register.							

The **Switch readback register** byte determines the state of up to eight switches connected to CPU data lines 15 to 8. When an output to Extended Register EAH—Switch Strobe occurs, the buffer controlling these data lines is turned off, allowing the switches to set the line state through pull-down resistors. The value is then transferred to this register, from which it may be read at any time.

EXTENDED REGISTER F8H—CLOCK CONTROL

Index Register Address: 3C4H
Data Register Address: 3C5H

Index = F8H

Bit 7	Bit 6	Bit 5	Bit 4	Bit 3	Bit 2	Bit 1	Bit 0
Extended clock output.				External clock override.	Extended clock output source.	Extended clock direction .	Clock 0 only.

The **Extended clock output** bits perform the selection of the video clock when the Extended clock direction and Extended clock output source bits are set to 1.

The **Clock 3 on** bit, when set to 1, causes the clock selected to be grounded for IBM VGA compatibility (if Miscellaneous Output Register (3C2H) bits 3 and 2 are set to 1 (clock 3)) regardless of the mode of clock operation selected by Extended Register A4H—Extended Clock Select register and Extended register F8H—Clock Control.

The **External clock override** bit determines the external clock source when Miscellaneous Output Register (3C2H) bits 3 and 2 are set to 1 and 0, respectively (selecting the clock source from the feature connector). When this bit is 1, Extended Register A4H and this register select the clock. When this bit is 0, these two registers are ignored and the external clock is used.

The **Extended clock output source** bit, when set to 1, uses bits 7 to 5 of this register to select the clock source. When this bit is 0, then bit 4 of Extended Register A4 and bits 3 and 2 of the Miscellaneous Output Register (3C2) determine the clock source. When the **Extended clock direction** bit is 0, this bit has no effect.

The **Extended clock direction** bit, when set to 1, allows bits 7 to 5 of this register to be outputs to select the clock source. When this bit is set to 0, data can be written to bits 7 to 5 to select the desired clock.

The **Clock 0 only** bit, when set to 1, allows bit 4 of Extended Register A4H—Clock Select and bits 3 and 2 of the Miscellaneous

Output Register (3C2H) to select the current clock for the V7VGA. When this bit is 0, the clock source is determined by the clock select fields and bits 4, 3, and 1 of this register.

EXTENDED REGISTER F9H—PAGE SELECT

Index Register Address: 3C4H
Data Register Address: 3C5H

Index = F9H

Bit 7	Bit 6	Bit 5	Bit 4	Bit 3	Bit 2	Bit 1	Bit 0
							Extended page select.

The **Extended page select** bit is placed on memory address bit 0 when the Extended 256 color enable bit (Extended Register FCH, bit 2), the Chain 4 bit (Sequencer register 4, bit 3) and the Extended 256 color mode bit (Extended Register FCH, bit 1) are all set to 1. Otherwise, this bit is ignored.

EXTENDED REGISTER FAH—FOREGROUND COLOR

Index Register Address: 3C4H
Data Register Address: 3C5H

Index = FAH

Bit 7	Bit 6	Bit 5	Bit 4	Bit 3	Bit 2	Bit 1	Bit 0
				Foreground color.			

The **Foreground color** bits provide the foreground color used in solid foreground/background mode when bits 3 and 2 of Extended Register FEH—Foreground/background Control are 0 and 1, respectively.

EXTENDED REGISTER FBH—BACKGROUND COLOR

Index Register Address: 3C4H   Index = FBH
Data Register Address: 3C5H

Bit 7	Bit 6	Bit 5	Bit 4	Bit 3	Bit 2	Bit 1	Bit 0
				Background color.			

The **Background color** bits provide the background color used in
solid foreground/background mode when bits 3 and 2 of Extended
register FEH—Foreground/Background Control are 0 and 1,
respectively.

EXTENDED REGISTER FCH—COMPATIBILITY CONTROL

Index Register Address: 3C4H   Index = FCH
Data Register Address: 3C5H

Bit 7	Bit 6	Bit 5	Bit 4	Bit 3	Bit 2	Bit 1	Bit 0
Internal 3C3 enable.	Extended display enable skew.	Sequential chain 4.	Sequential chain.	Refresh skew control.	Extended 256 color enable.	Extended 256 color mode.	Extended attribute enable.

When the **Internal 3C3 enable** bit and the DISABLE pin, and bit 0
of the Video System Enable Register (3C3H) are all 1, the V7 VGA is
mapped into the host's input/output and memory space. Otherwise, all
addressing to the CPU is disabled.

When the **Extended display enable skew** bit is 1, the display
enable skew is greater than the skew selected by bits 6 and 5 of CRT
controller register 03H (the Horizontal blank end register). When this
bit is 0, the skew is as selected by CRT controller register 03H.

The **Sequential Chain 4** bit, when set to 1, causes sequential chain
4 bitmaps for 256 color modes to be stored at consecutive display
memory addresses. When this bit is set to 0, the 256 color data is
stored in the usual VGA manner.

The **Sequential Chain** bit, when set to 1, causes sequential chain 4 bitmaps for CGA color modes to be stored at consecutive display memory addresses. When this bit is set to 0, the CGA color data is stored in the usual CGA manner.

The **Refresh skew control** bit, when set to 1, causes the start of refresh to occur one character after the end of the skewed display enable signal (bits 6 and 5 of CRT controller register 03H). When this bit is set to 0, refresh begins one character after the end of the unskewed display enable signal.

The **Extended 256 color enable** bit, when set to 1, enables the enhanced 256 color mode selected by bit 1 of this register. When the bit is set to 0, the VGA operates in standard IBM mode.

The **Extended 256 color mode** bit selects the type of extended 256 color CPU addressing mode that is in effect when enhanced 256 color mode operation is taking place. When the bit is set to 1, the VGA is in the 128K extended 256 color mode. When the bit is 0, the VGA is in the 64K extended 256 color mode.

The **Extended attribute enable** bit, when set to 1, enables the extended text mode attribute obtained from memory plane 3 at the same time and from the same address as the character code and attribute byte. When this bit is 0, extended text attributes are disabled.

EXTENDED REGISTER FDH—TIMING SELECT

Index Register Address: 3C4H   Index = FDH
Data Register Address: 3C5H

Bit 7	Bit 6	Bit 5	Bit 4	Bit 3	Bit 2	Bit 1	Bit 0
Graphics 8-dot timing state select.				Text 8-dot timing state select.			

The **Graphics 8-dot timing state select** bits select the timing for 8 dot graphics modes.

The **Text 8-dot timing state select** bits select the timing state for 8 dot text modes.

The data entered in this register is usually fixed for the type of RAM and interleave modes used by the VGA and will not normally be changed by the programmer.

EXTENDED REGISTER FEH—FOREGROUND/BACKGROUND CONTROL

Index Register Address: 3C4H   Index = FEH
Data Register Address: 3C5H

Bit 7	Bit 6	Bit 5	Bit 4	Bit 3	Bit 2	Bit 1	Bit 0
Not used.				Foreground/ background mode.		Foreground/ background source.	Not used.

The **Foreground/background mode** bits select the source of the byte input to each of the four display memory planes as follows:

Bit 3	Bit 2	Mode of input operation
0	0	Set/reset output mode (IBM VGA).
0	1	Solid foreground/background mode.
1	0	Dithered foreground mode.
1	1	Not valid.

The **Foreground/background source** bit, when set to 1, selects the rotated CPU byte as the source for selecting between the solid foreground and background colors when in the solid foreground/background mode. When the bit is 0, the source is Extended register F5H—Foreground/Background Pattern.

EXTENDED REGISTER FFH—16 BIT INTERFACE CONTROL

Index Register Address: 3C4H   Index = FFH
Data Register Address: 3C5H

Bit 7	Bit 6	Bit 5	Bit 4	Bit 3	Bit 2	Bit 1	Bit 0
16 bit bus status.	Pointer bank select.		256K bank enable.	16 bit ROM interface enable.	Fast write enable.	16 bit I/O interface enable.	16 bit memory interface enable.

The **16 bit bus status** bit is a read only bit that reads back a 1 if the V7 VGA is installed in a 16 bit bus.

The **Pointer select** bits provide linear address bits 17 and 16 when addressing a pointer pattern.

The **256K bank enable** bit when set to 1, enables operation with four banks of 256K memory. When set to 0, it enables operation of four banks of 1Mb DRAMs.

The **16 bit ROM interface enable** bit, when set to 1, enables decoding of 16 bit ROMs. When set to 0, this bit enables the lower byte of the data bus for 8 bit ROM operation.

The **Fast write enable** bit, when set to 1, latches the VGA internally on CPU writes, releasing the CPU immediately. When this bit is set to 0, the CPU is held until the current memory display write is completed.

The **16 bit I/O interface enable** bit, when set to 1, provides a 16 bit input/output interface from the VGA. When set to 0, the bit provides an 8 bit input/output interface.

The **16 bit memory interface enable** bit determines the memory interface between the CPU and the VGA. When this bit is set to 1, the memory interface is 16 bits. When this bit is set to 0, the memory interface is 8 bits.

Additional Registers Used in the Logix VGA Display Adapter Card (Trident 8800CS Chip Set)

CRT CONTROLLER REGISTER 1FH—SCRATCH PAD

Index Register Address: Index = 1FH
    Monochrome Adapters: 3B4H
    Color Adapters: 3D4H
Data Register Address:
    Monochrome Adapters: 3B5H
    Color Adapters: 3D5H

Bit 7	Bit 6	Bit 5	Bit 4	Bit 3	Bit 2	Bit 1	Bit 0
Miscellaneous data.							

This register can be used to store data needed for a particular implementation of the VGA board using this chip set.

CRT CONTROLLER REGISTER 22H—LATCH READ BACK

Index Register Address: Index = 22H
    Monochrome Adapters: 3B4H
    Color Adapters: 3D4H
Data Read Only Register Address:
    Monochrome Adapters: 3B5H
    Color Adapters: 3D5H

Bit 7	Bit 6	Bit 5	Bit 4	Bit 3	Bit 2	Bit 1	Bit 0
Memory plane data.							

This register contains the processor latch data for the currently enabled display memory address and color plane.

CRT CONTROLLER REGISTER 24H—ATTRIBUTE CONTROLLER STATE

Index Register Address: Index = 24H
     Monochrome Adapters: 3B4H
     Color Adapters: 3D4H
Data Register Address:
     Monochrome Adapters: 3B5H
     Color Adapters: 3D5H

Bit 7	Bit 6	Bit 5	Bit 4	Bit 3	Bit 2	Bit 1	Bit 0
Attribute controller state.							

The **Attribute controller state** bit, when 0, indicates that the next write to the Attribute Register (3C0H) will be used to set the register index. When this bit is 1, the next write to the Attribute Register will write data to the Attribute Register whose index has already been selected.

CRT CONTROLLER REGISTER 26H—ATTRIBUTE CONTROLLER INDEX READ BACK

Index Register Address: Index = 26H
     Monochrome Adapters: 3B4H
     Color Adapters: 3D4H
Data Read Only Register Address:
     Monochrome Adapters: 3B5H
     Color Adapters: 3D5H

Bit 7	Bit 6	Bit 5	Bit 4	Bit 3	Bit 2	Bit 1	Bit 0
Attribute controller index value.							

This register contains the current value of the index for the attribute controller registers.

SEQUENCER REGISTER 0BH—HARDWARE VERSION

Index Register Address: 3C4H   Index = 0BH
Data Register Address: 3C5H

Bit 7	Bit 6	Bit 5	Bit 4	Bit 3	Bit 2	Bit 1	Bit 0
Reserved.				Hardware version number.			

Reading from this register causes the chip to enter the version 2 paging mode, which is normally used for extended mode programming. Writing to this register causes the chip to enter the version 1 paging mode.

SEQUENCER REGISTER 0EH—MODE CONTROL 1

Index Register Address: 3C4H   Index = 0EH
Data Register Address: 3C5H

Bit 7	Bit 6	Bit 5	Bit 4	Bit 3	Bit 2	Bit 1	Bit 0
Reserved.				64K page select.			

The **64K page select bits** indicate the display memory page number from which data is currently being displayed. This number must be written to the register with bit 1 inverted. When reading back, bit 1 will be read with the normal (not inverted) value.

Additional Registers Used in the Dell 310 Computer (Paradise VGA Card)

MODULE DISABLE REGISTER

Write Only Register Addresses: 46E8H, 56E8H, 66E8H, 76E8H

Bit 7	Bit 6	Bit 5	Bit 4	Bit 3	Bit 2	Bit 1	Bit 0
Not used.			Setup.	Enable I/O and memory accesses.	BIOS ROM page select.		

The **Setup** bit is set to 0 upon initialization, which results in the normal VGA mode of operation. When this bit is set to 1, all accesses to the VGA are disabled except for ports 46E8 and 102H.

The **Enable I/O and memory accesses** bit, when set to 1, permits CPU access to the VGA ports and memory. When the bit is set to 0, access to the I/O and memory is disabled.

The **BIOS ROM page select** bits select one of eight pages of VGA ROM BIOS memory. Upon initialization, page 6 is selected. Western Digital is planning to discontinue the ROM BIOS paging feature on future revisions of their VGA cards.

POS SLEEP BIT REGISTER

Write Only Register Addresses: 102H

Bit 7	Bit 6	Bit 5	Bit 4	Bit 3	Bit 2	Bit 1	Bit 0
Reserved.							VGA sleep.

The **VGA sleep** bit, when set to 1, enables the VGA for normal operation. When this bit is set to 0, the VGA is disabled.

GRAPHICS REGISTER 09H—ADDRESS OFFSET A

Index Register Address: 3CEH   Index = 09H
Data Register Address: 3CFH

Bit 7	Bit 6	Bit 5	Bit 4	Bit 3	Bit 2	Bit 1	Bit 0
Not used.	Page A page number minus 8.						

This register contains the number of a page number (minus 8) for a 32K memory block, which is page A. (For example, entering a 7 in this register will select page 15.)

GRAPHICS REGISTER 0AH—ADDRESS OFFSET B

Index Register Address: 3CEH   Index = 0AH
Data Register Address: 3CFH

Bit 7	Bit 6	Bit 5	Bit 4	Bit 3	Bit 2	Bit 1	Bit 0
Not used.	Page B page number minus 8.						

This register contains the number of a page number (minus 8) for a 32K memory block, which is page B. (For example, entering a 7 in this register will select page 15.)

GRAPHICS REGISTER 0BH—MEMORY SIZE

Index Register Address: 3CEH   Index = 0BH
Data Register Address: 3CFH

Bit 7	Bit 6	Bit 5	Bit 4	Bit 3	Bit 2	Bit 1	Bit 0
Memory size - Do not change these bits.				Enable alternate address offset.	1 = enable 16 bit inter-face to display RAM.	1 = enable 16 bit inter-face to BIOS ROM.	1 = disable BIOS ROM.

The **Memory size** bits are controlled internally and should not be modified.

The **Enable alternate address offset** bit, when set to 1, allows two pages of display memory to be accessed at the same time at two different memory addresses. The two base addresses are defined by Graphics controller registers 09H and 0AH (Address offset registers). This capability is useful in rapidly transferring data from one display page to another.

The **Enable 16 bit interface to display RAM** bit, when set to 1, sets up a 16 bit interface to the display RAM; when set to 0, an 8 bit interface is used.

The **Enable 16 bit interface to BIOS ROM** bit, when set to 1, sets up a 126 bit interface to the VGA card BIOS ROM extensions; when set to 0, a 98 bit interface is used.

The **Disable BIOS ROM** bit, when set to 1, disables the VGA BIOS ROM extensions; when set to 0, these ROM BIOS extensions are enabled.

GRAPHICS REGISTER 0CH—VIDEO SELECT

Index Register Address: 3CEH
Data Register Address: 3CFH

Index = 0CH

Bit 7	Bit 6	Bit 5	Bit 4	Bit 3	Bit 2	Bit 1	Bit 0
AT&T/M24 mode enable (400 line enable).	6845 compati- bility. 0=EGA/ VGA. 1= 6845.	Character map select.	Character clock period control.		Character map select (underline).	Third clock select line.	Force VCLK (overrides Sequencer Register 1 bit 3 .

The **AT&T/M24 mode enable** bit, when set to 1, sets up the 400 line display mode compatible with AT&T PCs.

The **6845 compatibility** bit, when set to 1, makes the CRT Controller Registers compatible with the 6845 display controller chip. When set to 0, this bit makes the CRT Controller Registers compatible with IBM EGA/VGA specifications.

The **Character map selector** bits (bits 5 and 2) select character maps from display memory planes 2 and 3 as follows:

D5	D2	Character Attribute	Display Memory Plane
0	0	Don't care.	2
0	1	Don't care.	2
1	0	Don't care.	3
1	1	0	2
1	1	1	3

The **Character clock control period** bits are used in text modes to determine the width of characters in dots as follows:

Bit 4	Bit 3	Character width
0	0	IBM VGA character clock (8 or 9 dots).
0	1	7 dots (used with 132 character modes).
1	0	9 dots.
1	1	10 dots.

The **Third clock select** bit provides a third clock select bit to work with bits 3 and 2 of the Miscellaneous output register to select additional clock frequencies.

The **Force VCLK** bit, when set to 1, overrides the setting of Sequencer register 1, bit 3, and forces the horizontal system timing clock of the CRT controller to run at the normal dot clock frequency.

GRAPHICS REGISTER 0DH—CRT LOCK CONTROL

Index Register Address: 3CEH   Index = 0DH
Data Register Address: 3CFH

Bit 7	Bit 6	Bit 5	Bit 4	Bit 3	Bit 2	Bit 1	Bit 0
Lock Vertical sync polarity.	Lock horizontal sync polarity.	Lock horizontal timing.	Bit 9 control.	Bit 8 control.	CRTC control.	Lock prevention.	Lock vertical timing.

The **Lock vertical sync polarity** bit locks the polarity of the vertical sync signal.

The **Lock horizontal sync polarity** bit locks the polarity of the horizontal sync signal.

The **Lock horizontal timing** bit, when set to 1, locks registers that control the horizontal timing signals.

The **Bit 9 control** bit, when set to 1, locks bit 9 of CRT Controller Register 0CH—Start Memory Address High and CRT Controller Register 0EH—Cursor Location High.

The **Bit 8 control** bit, when set to 1, locks bit 8 of CRT Controller Register 0CH—Start Memory Address High and CRT Controller Register 0EH—Cursor Location High.

The **CRTC control** bit, when set to 1, multiplies the cursor start, cursor stop, preset row scan, and maximum scan line register values by two.

The **Lock prevention** bit, when set to 1, inhibits locking of CRT Controller Registers 00H through 11H.

GRAPHICS REGISTER 0EH—VIDEO CONTROL

Index Register Address: 3CEH

Data Register Address: 3CFH

Index = 0EH

Bit 7	Bit 6	Bit 5	Bit 4	Bit 3	Bit 2	Bit 1	Bit 0
Blink/ Display enable.	PCLK = VCLK.	Tri-state video outputs.	Tri-state memory control outputs.	Override CGA enable input.	Lock internal palette and overscan registers.	EGA compatibility.	Extended 256 color shift register control .

The **Blink/display enable** bit, when set to 1, enables a mode using 8 colors, with the most significant color bit causing the pixel to blink. When set to 0, the 16 color mode is used with no blinking permitted.

The **PCLK=VCLK** bit, when set to 1, selects VCLK as the dot (pixel) clock frequency.

The **Tri-state video outputs** bit, when set to 1, disables all video outputs. When set to 0, this bit permits normal video outputs.

The **Tri-state memory control outputs** bit, when set to 1, disables all video memory control outputs. When set to 0, this bit permits normal video memory control outputs.

The **Override CGA enable** bit, when set to 1, overrides the CGA enable video bit 3 of the CGA Mode Register (3D8H) if it is in the CGA text mode.

The **Lock internal palette and overscan** bit, when set to 1, locks the palette and overscan registers.

The **EGA compatibility** bit, when set to 1, disables reads from all registers that are read only in the IBM EGA, and also disables reads from extended Graphics controller registers 09H to 0FH, thereby making the VGA fully EGA compatible.

The **Extended 256 color shift register control** bit, when set to 1, configures the video shift register to work with extended 256 color Super VGA modes.

GRAPHICS REGISTER 0FH—GENERAL PURPOSE STATUS

Index Register Address: 3CEH
Data Register Address: 3CFH

Index = 0FH

Bit 7	Bit 6	Bit 5	Bit 4	Bit 3	Bit 2	Bit 1	Bit 0
Read config-uration (7) status.	Read config-uration (6) status.	Read config-uration (5) status.	Read config-uration (4) status.	Read config-uration (8) status.	Unlock Graphics controller registers 09H to 0EH.		

The **Read configuration status** bits read back configuration register bits 4 through 8.

The **Unlock graphics controller register** bits, when set to 101, unlock the extended Graphics Controller Registers 09H through 0EH.

CRT CONTROLLER REGISTER 29H—UNLOCK SECOND BANK

Index Register Address: Index = 29H
      Monochrome Adapters: 3B4H
      Color Adapters: 3D4H
Data Register Address:
      Monochrome Adapters: 3B5H
      Color Adapters: 3D5H

Bit 7	Bit 6	Bit 5	Bit 4	Bit 3	Bit 2	Bit 1	Bit 0
Read enable bit.	Scratch pad.			Read enable bit.	Write enable.		

The **Read enable** bits (bits 7 and 3) must be set to 1 and 0, respectively, to read enable the register bank.

The **Write enable** bits (bits 2, 1 and 0) must be set to 101 binary to write enable the register bank.

CRT CONTROLLER REGISTER 2AH—EGA SWITCH

Index Register Address: Index = 2AH
      Monochrome Adapters: 3B4H
      Color Adapters: 3D4H
Data Register Address:
      Monochrome Adapters: 3B5H
      Color Adapters: 3D5H

Bit 7	Bit 6	Bit 5	Bit 4	Bit 3	Bit 2	Bit 1	Bit 0
EGA switch 4.	EGA switch 3.	EGA switch 2.	EGA switch 1.	EGA emulation on analog display.	Lock clock select.	Lock graphics and sequencer screen control.	Lock 8/9 dot character clock.

The **EGA configuration switch** bits (bits 7 through 4) are latched upon reset to the setting of the onboard switches. These bits can be used to change the EGA switch configuration by software control and can also be used to read the current switch configuration.

The **EGA emulation on analog display** bit, when set to 1, permits the display system to behave like an EGA digital display, even though the display monitor is actually an analog device.

The **Lock clock select** bit, when set to 1, prevents write access to the clock select bits.

The **Lock graphics controller/sequencer screen control** bit, when set to 1, prevents write access to Graphics Controller Register 05H, bits 5 and 6; Sequencer Register 01H, bits 2 through 5; and Sequencer Register 03H, bits 0 through 5.

The **Lock 8/9 dots** bit prevents write access to Sequencer Register 01H, bit 0.

CRT CONTROLLER REGISTER 2CH—INTERLACE H/2 START

Index Register Address: Index = 2CH
      Monochrome Adapters: 3B4H
      Color Adapters: 3D4H
Data Register Address:
      Monochrome Adapters: 3B5H
      Color Adapters: 3D5H

Bit 7	Bit 6	Bit 5	Bit 4	Bit 3	Bit 2	Bit 1	Bit 0
Interlaced H/2 start.							

This register contains the character count at which timing is modified so that odd horizontal lines are displayed in one vertical field, even horizontal lines are displayed in the next vertical fields and so forth in an alternating manner. The value for this register is determined as follows:

$$Interlaced\ \frac{H}{2}\ start = Horizontal\ sync\ start -$$
$$\frac{Horizontal\ total\ +\ 5}{2} + Horizontal\ sync\ skew$$

The Horizontal sync start value is found in CRT Controller Register 04H—Horizontal Sync Start. The Horizontal total is found in CRT Controller Register 00H—Horizontal Total. The Horizontal sync skew value is found in bits 6 and 5 of CRT Controller Register 05H—Horizontal Sync End.

CRT CONTROLLER REGISTER 2DH—INTERLACE H/2 END

Index Register Address: Index = 2DH
     Monochrome Adapters: 3B4H
     Color Adapters: 3D4H
Data Register Address:
     Monochrome Adapters: 3B5H
     Color Adapters: 3D5H

Bit 7	Bit 6	Bit 5	Bit 4	Bit 3	Bit 2	Bit 1	Bit 0
Enable IRQ.	Vertical double scan for EGA on PS/2 display.	Enable interlaced mode.	Interlaced H/2 end.				

The **Enable IRQ** bit, when set to 1, enables vertical interrupts. This bit can be used only on systems employing the AT bus; it doesn't work on the Micro Channel (PS/2) bus.

The **Vertical double scan** bit, when set to 1, causes the display adapter card to emulate EGA double scanning for certain display modes, when used with a PS/2 system.

The **Enable interlaced mode** bit, when set to 1, selects the interlaced mode of operation. Bit 7 and bits 4 through 0 of the CRT Controller Register 09H—Maximum Row Address must be set to 0. Line compare and double scan are not supported when operating in the interlaced mode.

The **Interlaced H/2 end** bits determine the horizontal sync width when using the interlaced mode.

CRT CONTROLLER REGISTER 2EH—MISCELLANEOUS CONTROL 1

Index Register Address:
     Monochrome Adapters: 3B4H
     Color Adapters: 3D4H
Data Register Address:
     Monochrome Adapters: 3B5H
     Color Adapters: 3D5H

Index = 2EH

Bit 7	Bit 6	Bit 5	Bit 4	Bit 3	Bit 2	Bit 1	Bit 0
Read 46E8H enable.	Low VCLK.	VCLK1, VCLK2 latched outputs.	VCLK= MCLK.	8514/A inter-laced com-patibility.	En-able page mode.	Select display enable timing	Disable border

The **Read 46E8H enable** bit, when set to 1, permits the 46E8H I/O port to be read by systems using the AT bus.

The **Low VCLK** bit, when set to 1, permits the system to use a video clock (VCLK) frequency that is much lower than the memory clock (MCLK) frequency. This bit should be set to 1 when the memory clock frequency is more than twice the video clock frequency.

The **VCLK1, VCLK2 latched outputs** bit, when set to 1, causes VCLK1 and VCLK2 outputs to be determined by bits 2 and 3 of the Miscellaneous output register. Other clock setting bits are ignored.

The **VCLK=MCLK** bit, when set to 1, causes the display adapter card to use the memory clock (MCLK) as the source of all video timing, ignoring other clock setting bits.

The **Enable page mode addressing** bit, when set to 1, causes screen memory refresh cycles to use page addressing in text modes. (The system automatically uses page mode addressing anyway in graphics modes.) This bit must be set before loading character sets into video RAM, since the addressing differs in the page and non-page modes.

The **Select display enable timing** bit determines the timing of the display enable command.

The **Disable border** bit, when set to 1, causes all video outputs to be 0 when the border (overscan) color would normally be displayed.

CRT CONTROLLER REGISTER 30H—MISCELLANEOUS CONTROL 3

Index Register Address: Index = 30H
    Monochrome Adapters: 3B4H
    Color Adapters: 3D4H
Data Register Address:
    Monochrome Adapters: 3B5H
    Color Adapters: 3D5H

Bit 7	Bit 6	Bit 5	Bit 4	Bit 3	Bit 2	Bit 1	Bit 0
Reserved.							Map out 2K in BIOS ROM.

The **Map out 2K in BIOS ROM** bit, when set to 1, disables ROM BIOS addresses C6000H to C67FFH on this VGA card so that it may coexist with adapters such as the IBM PGC that make use of this ROM BIOS space. This bit is normally set to 1 by the system reset.

Additional Registers Used in the ATI VGAWonder Display Adapter Card

The ATI VGAWonder Super VGA board has a lot of peculiarities in the way its registers are handled that make it uniquely different from the other boards described so far. First, although the I/O ports are usually 1CEH for index and 1CFH for data, ATI does not guarantee that these port addresses will be maintained. What they do guarantee, is that the I/O index port address will be found at memory address C0010H. Thus, if you're writing software for your ATI VGAWonder card and know the port addresses, you can use them, but if you want to write software for any VGAWonder card that ever may exist in the future, you need to make provision for reading the port address from memory and using that address, whatever it may be, from then on in your software. For convenience, the port addresses given previously are used in describing the VGAWonder registers, but don't expect this to mean that they will always work with any VGAWonder card.

The next peculiarity is in the way that reading and writing to the I/O registers takes place. Thus far, we have been accustomed to performing a write to set the index register and then either reading or writing to the data register thereby indexed. Although for safety we usually do this in two sequential steps, we would normally expect that, once an index was sent to the index register, it would remain there until changed. This is not true of the VGAWonder extended registers. After an index value is written to the index register, it is good for only one read or write from the data register. Then the index goes away and must be rewritten before the next data read or write. Finally, to read a VGAWonder extended register, you must first write the index with a byte instruction (*outportb* in C) and then read from the data register with another byte instruction (*inportb* in C). You can't do the job properly with a word I/O instruction. On the other hand, in writing to a VGAWonder extended register you must use the word I/O instruction (*outport* in C). Separate byte instructions for the index and data registers will not work when you want to write data to the extended registers.

ATI REGISTER B0H—DRAM TIMING

Index Register Address: 1CEH
Data Register Address: 1CFH

Index = B0H

Bit 7	Bit 6	Bit 5	Bit 4	Bit 3	Bit 2	Bit 1	Bit 0
Reserved.	Hercules 300 line emulation.	DRAM timing.	DRAM timing.	Enable 8 CRT accesses for each CPU access.	DRAM timing.	DRAM timing.	Reserved.

ATI REGISTER B1H—EGA COMPATIBILITY AND DOUBLE SCAN ENABLE

Index Register Address: 1CEH

Index = B1H

Data Register Address: 1CFH

Bit 7	Bit 6	Bit 5	Bit 4	Bit 3	Bit 2	Bit 1	Bit 0
Reserved.	1 = Divide vertical timing parameters by 2.	Double scanning/3 of 4 scanning enable. 001 = enable double scanning in graphics modes. 010 = enable 3 of 4 scanning in graphics modes. 101 = enable double scanning in text modes. 110 = enable 3 of 4 scanning in text modes.			General purpose read/ write.	1 = force all registers to be EGA compatible.	1 = force all I/O addresses to be EGA compatible.

ATI REGISTER B2H—MEMORY PAGE SELECT

Index Register Address: 1CEH

Index = B2H

Data Register Address: 1CFH

For Revision 1 chip:

Bit 7	Bit 6	Bit 5	Bit 4	Bit 3	Bit 2	Bit 1	Bit 0
Reserved.	External clock select.	Enable internal DIP switch settings (EGA mode).	Display memory page select.				1 = enable interlace mode.

For Revision 2 chip:

Bit 7	Bit 6	Bit 5	Bit 4	Bit 3	Bit 2	Bit 1	Bit 0
Read page select.			Reserved.	Page select.			Reserved.

The Revision 1 chip permits only one memory page to be selected at a time. The Revision 2 chip permits selection of two memory pages simultaneously, one for reading and one for writing. The dual page mode is enabled by setting bit 3 of ATI Register BEH to 1. The default setting upon power up yields the one page mode so that Revision 2 chips will be compatible with software written for Revision 1 chips.

ATI REGISTER B3H—ENABLE 1024 x 768 GRAPHICS

Index Register Address: 1CEH   Index = B3H
Data Register Address: 1CFH

Bit 7	Bit 6	Bit 5	Bit 4	Bit 3	Bit 2	Bit 1	Bit 0
Enable double scanning for 200 line modes.	Enable 1024 x 768 16 color mode.	Enable 16 bit opera- tion.	Disable memory beyond 256K.	EEPROM chip select.	Enable EEPROM interface.	EEPROM clock source.	EEPROM data input.

The information shown is for the Revision 2 chip only. For the Revision 1 chip, the data in this register is internally controlled and should not be modified by the programmer.

ATI REGISTER B4H—EMULATION CONTROL

Index Register Address: 1CEH   Index = B4H
Data Register Address: 1CFH

Bit 7	Bit 6	Bit 5	Bit 4	Bit 3	Bit 2	Bit 1	Bit 0
Override locking of CR117.	Lock CR0-CR7 rather than CR117.	Lock CR80- CR86 and CR140- CR144.	Lock cursor start and end.	Lock vertical timing reg- isters.	Lock CR90- CR94 and CR97.	Enable Hercules emulation.	Enable CGA emulation.

ATI REGISTER B5H—MISCELLANEOUS CONTROL

Index Register Address: 1CEH   Index = B5H
Data Register Address: 1CFH

Bit 7	Bit 6	Bit 5	Bit 4	Bit 3	Bit 2	Bit 1	Bit 0
Reserved.	Enable CGA cursor emulation.	Disable cursor blinking.	Enable 8 simultaneous fonts.	Select map 3 as programmable character generator.	Enable display signal skew.	Invert blanking signal polarity.	Select display enable as blanking signal.

The **Enable CGA cursor emulation** bit, when set to 1, adds five to CRT controller registers 0AH (Cursor start position register) and 0BH (Cursor end position register). This makes a cursor that is designed to be at the bottom of an 8 x 8 character cell or at the bottom of an 8 x 14 character cell, whichever has been selected.

The **Disable cursor blinking** bit, when set to 1, causes the cursor to be a steady, rather than a blinking, display.

ATI REGISTER B6H—HIGH RESOLUTION ENABLE

Index Register Address: 1CEH   Index = B6H
Data Register Address: 1CFH

Bit 7	Bit 6	Bit 5	Bit 4	Bit 3	Bit 2	Bit 1	Bit 0
Disable screen blanking in CGA and Hercules emulation modes.	Select composite sync for output.	Enable vertical interrupt.	Select 16 color high resolution modes.	Select 4 color high resolution modes.	Reserved.	Enable 640 x 400 Hercules emulation.	Reserved.

ATI REGISTER B8H—REGISTER WRITE PROTECT AND CLOCK SELECT

Index Register Address: 1CEH
Data Register Address: 1CFH

Index = B8H

Bit 7	Bit 6	Bit 5	Bit 4	Bit 3	Bit 2	Bit 1	Bit 0
Clock divider.		Lock vertical sync polarity.	Lock horizontal sync polarity.	Lock write to 3C2H.	Lock all VGA registers except CRTC start and end.	Lock overscan register in attribute controller.	Lock palette registers in attribute controller.

ATI REGISTER B9H—MISCELLANEOUS CONTROL 1

Index Register Address: 1CEH
Data Register Address: 1CFH

Index = B9H

Bit 7	Bit 6	Bit 5	Bit 4	Bit 3	Bit 2	Bit 1	Bit 0
Lock line compare register.	Set horizontal total.	Wait cycles for 16 bit access to ROM.		ROM address space.		Select input to clock chip.	Clock select.

ATI REGISTER BAH—MISCELLANEOUS CONTROL 2

Index Register Address: 1CEH   Index = BAH
Data Register Address: 1CFH

Bit 7	Bit 6	Bit 5	Bit 4	Bit 3	Bit 2	Bit 1	Bit 0
Delay chain resolution compensation.	Reserved.	Enable monochrome gray scale circuit.	Enable EGA color simulation for RGB monitors.	Disable secondary red output for RGB monitors.	Delay chain timing compensation.		

ATI REGISTER BBH—INPUT STATUS

Index Register Address: 1CEH   Index = BBH
Data Register Address: 1CFH

Bit 7	Bit 6	Bit 5	Bit 4	Bit 3	Bit 2	Bit 1	Bit 0
Reserved.		Memory size. 0 = 256K. 1 = 512K.	Reserved.	Display type. 0000 = EGA. 0001 = PS/2 analog monochrome. 0010 = TTL monochrome. 0011 = PS/2 color. 0100 = Analog RGB. 0101 = Multisync or similar. 0111 = IBM 8514. 1001 = NEC VGA monitor. 1101 = NEC Multisync XL.			

ATI REGISTER BDH—MISCELLANEOUS CONTROL 3

Index Register Address: 1CEH   Index = BDH
Data Register Address: 1CFH

Bit 7	Bit 6	Bit 5	Bit 4	Bit 3	Bit 2	Bit 1	Bit 0
EGA switch settings.				Reserved.			

ATI REGISTER BEH—MISCELLANEOUS

Index Register Address: 1CEH   Index = BEH
Data Register Address: 1CFH

Bit 7	Bit 6	Bit 5	Bit 4	Bit 3	Bit 2	Bit 1	Bit 0
Enable 1024x768 4 color mode.	Enable 1024x768 16 color mode.	Reserved.		Enable interlaced mode.	Select internal EGA DIP switch value.	Enable interlaced mode.	Unlock CRT Controller 12H– Vertical Display End.

Using Display Modes

When the IBM PC was first released, there were only two display adapter cards, the Monochrome Display Adapter (MDA), which produced only text characters on a black and white display, and the Color Graphics Adapter (CGA), which produced one of two sets of four colors on a color monitor. The display memory area was well defined with one address used for text displays and another address for graphics displays. Now, with a proliferation of display adapter cards, the situation has become very complicated. First, when EGA and VGA cards were developed, they were made compatible with the original display modes, but these modes were "improved" to take advantage of better resolution and more memory in the new cards. Therefore there are several versions of the original modes, which, while they run programs that were designed for the earlier display adapters flawlessly, still have different characteristics that you have to know about if you are developing new programs. Second, display adapter memory has increased, confusing the issue of how much memory is available and how many pages are supported for the older display modes, as well as new ones. Next, with the development of new display adapter cards, it has been found that there are additional display modes that can be used even though they aren't supported by IBM. Finally, the new Super VGA cards have lots of high resolution display modes, which unfortunately differ from one card to another in definition and the way they are used. In this chapter, we'll try to sort out all of this and give you as much definite information as possible about what modes exist and how they are used.

The function for setting your system to a particular display mode is very easy for the original display modes, but becomes considerably more complicated for undocumented display modes or for extended Super VGA modes. The situation is very complex for the Super VGA modes because there is little standardization, so that each manufacturer's technique for setting the extended modes is different from the others. Although you'll find the functions for setting display modes in many places throughout this book, we're going to include and explain all of them in this chapter, so that you'll be able to find all of the needed information in one place. If you don't quite understand how we use ROM BIOS calls, skip ahead to Chapter 11 to get this information.

MDA/CGA Display Modes

Table 5-1 lists the display modes that were supplied with the original IBM PC; modes 0–6 are the CGA display modes and mode 7 is the MGA display mode. You probably aren't very interested in these any more, but you will be interested in comparing them with the versions of the same modes that are used with the EGA and VGA.

TABLE 5-1. ORIGINAL IBM PC DISPLAY MODES

Mode	Type	Colors/ Shades	Char Format	Char Size	Display Size	Max Pgs	Memory Address
0	Text	2	40x25	8x8	320x200	8	B8000
1	Text	4/7	40x25	8x8	320x200	8	B8000
2	Text	2	80x25	8x8	640x200	8	B8000
3	Text	4/7	80x25	8x8	640x200	8	B8000
4	Graphics	4/7	40x25	8x8	320x200	8	B8000
5	Graphics	2	40x25	8x8	320x200	8	B8000
6	Graphics	2	80x25	8x8	640x200	1	B8000
7	Text	2	80x25	9x14	720x350	8	B0000

EGA Display Modes

Table 5-2 tabulates the display modes available for the EGA. Note two important things in perusing this table. First, in addition to the display modes common to the MGA and CGA, some new modes have been introduced that have better resolution and more colors. Second, some changes have been made to the original modes that provide more color capability and sometimes double line scanning, which makes the resolution of the display appear to be improved. These changes are all downward compatible so that any software originally written for the MGA or CGA will work with the EGA.

TABLE 5-2. ENHANCED GRAPHICS ADAPTER (EGA) DISPLAY MODES

Mode	Type	Colors/ Shades	Char Format	Char Size	Display Size	Max Pgs	Memory Address
0*	Text	16/64	40x25	8x14	320x350	8	B8000
1*	Text	16/64	40x25	8x14	320x350	8	B8000
2*	Text	16/64	40x25	8x14	640x350	8	B8000
3*	Text	16/64	40x25	8x14	640x350	8	B8000
4	Graphics	4/7	40x25	8x8	320x200	8	B8000
5	Graphics	4/7	40x25	8x8	320x200	8	B8000
6	Graphics	2	80x25	8x8	640x200	1	B8000
7	Text	2	80x25	9x14	720x350	8	B0000
D	Graphics	16/64	40x25	8x8	320x200	8	A0000
E	Graphics	16/64	80x25	8x8	640x200	4	A0000
F	Graphics	2	80x25	8x14	640x350	2	A0000
10	Graphics	16/64	80x25	8x14	640x350	1	A0000

VGA Display Modes

Table 5-3 tabulates the VGA display modes. As with the EGA, you will note that there are some new display modes, as well as some improvements to the previous modes that are downward compatible so that the VGA boards will work with software designed for the earlier display adapter cards. The VGA requires an analog monitor, while the display adapter cards previously described used digital monitors. However, this difference is all handled by the VGA card internally; except for a different connector being used to connect the monitor to the card and the existence of the newer display modes, you'll never notice any difference. It's now time to list the very simple function used to set the system video mode for all of the IBM supported video display modes (MGA, CGA, EGA, and VGA). The function is listed in Figure 5-1. The ROM BIOS service that supports this operation is service 0. Since this is normally entered in register AH and the mode in AL, we can set both these registers properly in one operation on AX. The video service interrupt is then called to perform the operations.

Figure 5-1. Listing of Function to Set Display Mode

```
/*

        setMode() = Function to set display mode

*/

void setMode(int mode)
{
     union REGS regs;

     regs.x.ax = mode;
     int86(&regs, &regs);
}
```

TABLE 5-3 VIDEO GRAPHICS ARRAY (VGA) DISPLAY MODES

Mode	Type	Colors/ Shades	Char Format	Char Size	Display Size	Max Pgs	Memory Address
0+	Text	16/ 256K	40x25	9x16	360x400	8	B8000
1+	Text	16/ 256K	40x25	9x16	360x400	8	B8000
2+	Text	16/ 256K	40x25	9x16	720x400	8	B8000
3+	Text	16/ 256K	40x25	9x16	720x400	8	B8000
4	Graphics	4/7	40x25	8x8	320x200	8	B8000
5	Graphics	4/7	40x25	8x8	320x200	8	B8000
6	Graphics	2	80x25	8x8	640x200	1	B8000
7+	Text	2	80x25	9x16	720x400	8	B0000
D	Graphics	16/ 256K	40x25	8x8	320x200	8	A0000
E	Graphics	16/ 256K	80x25	8x8	640x200	4	A0000
F	Graphics	2	80x25	8x14	640x350	2	A0000
10	Graphics	16/ 256K	80x25	8x14	640x350	1	A0000
11	Graphics	2	80x25	8x16	640x480	1	A0000
12	Graphics	16/ 256K	80x25	8x16	640x480	1	A0000
13	Graphics	256/ 256K	40x25	8x8	320x200	1	A0000

Display Modes for STB Powergraph VGA Board (Tseng Labs Chip Set)

Table 5-4 lists the extended modes available in addition to the regular VGA modes for the STB Powergraph VGA and other cards using the Tseng Labs chip set. These extended video modes are selected the same way as normal VGA modes using the function listed in Figure 5-1.

TABLE 5-4. TSENG LABS SUPER VGA EXTENDED DISPLAY MODES

Mode	Type	Colors/ Shades	Char Format	Char Size	Display Size	Max Pgs	Memory Address
18	Text	2	132x44	8x8	1056x352	2	B0000
19	Text	2	132x25	9x14	1188x350	4	B0000
1A	Text	2	132x28	9x13	1188x364	4	B0000
22	Text	16/256K	132x44	8x8	1056x352	2	B8000
23	Text	16/256K	132x25	8x14	1056x350	4	B8000
24	Text	16/256K	132x28	8x13	1056x364	4	B8000
25	Graphics	16/256K	80x60	8x8	640x480	1	A0000
26	Text	16/256K	80x60	8x8	640x480	2	B8000
29	Graphics	16/256K	100x40	8x16	800x600	1	A0000
2A	Text	16/256K	100x40	8x16	800x600	4	B8000
2D	Graphics	256/256K	80x25	8x14	640x350	1	A0000
2E	Graphics	256/256K	80x30	8x16	640x480	1	A0000
2F	Graphics	256/256K	80x25	8x16	640x480	1	A0000
30	Graphics	256/256K	100x37	8x16	800x600	1	A0000
37	Graphics	16/256K	128x48	8x16	1024x768	1	A0000
38	Graphics	256/256K	128x48	8x16	1024x768	1	A0000

Display Modes for the Headlands Technology Video Seven 1024i Display Adapter Card

Table 5-5 tabulates the extended modes that are available in addition to the regular VGA modes for the Headlands Technology Video Seven 1024i display adapter board. The regular VGA modes for the 1024i board are set in the normal manner, but the extended modes require quite a different procedure. First, an entirely new ROM BIOS video service (6FH) needs to be called with sub-service 05H in the AL register and the extended mode in the BL register. Then the extended functions have to be enabled by sending EAH to Sequencer Register 06H. Figure 5-2 shows a display mode setting function that can be used to set any mode on the 1024i board. You can simplify this quite a bit if you want the function to process only extended modes.

Figure 5-2. Listing of Function to Set Video Mode for Headlands Technology 1024i Display Adapter Card

```
/*

    setMode() Sets the video mode for Headlands Technology
                        1024i card

*/

void setMode(int mode)
{
        union REGS reg
        if (mode < 0x40)
        {
                reg.x.ax = mode;
                int86 (&reg, &reg);
        }
        else
        {
                reg.x.ax = 0x6F05;
                int86 (&reg, &reg)
                outpw(0x3C4, 0xEA06)
        }
}
```

TABLE 5-5. ADDITIONAL DISPLAY MODES FOR HEADLANDS TECHNOLOGY VIDEO SEVEN VGA 1024I

Mode	Type	Colors/ Shades	Char Format	Char Size	Display Size	Max Pgs	Memory Address
40	Text	16/256K	80x43	8x8	640x350	8	B8000
41	Text	16/256K	132x25	8x14	1056x350	4	B8000
42	Text	16/256K	132x43	8x8	1056x350	4	B8000
43	Text	16/256K	80x60	8x8	640x480	2	B8000
44	Text	16/256K	100x60	8x8	800x600	4	B8000
45	Text	16/256K	132x28	8x14	1056x392	4	B8000
60	Graphics	16/256K	94x51	8x8	752x410	1	A0000
61	Graphics	16/256K	90x67	8x8	720x540	2	A0000
62	Graphics	16/256K	100x75	8x8	800x600	1	A0000
63	Graphics	2/256K	128x96	8x8	1024x768	4	A0000
64	Graphics	4/256K	128x96	8x8	1024x768	1	A0000
65	Graphics	16/256K	128x96	8x8	1024x768	1	A0000
66	Graphics	256/ 256K	80x25	8x16	640x400	1	A0000
67	Graphics	256/ 256K	80x25	8x16	640x480	1	A0000

Display Modes for the Logix VGA Card (Trident Chip Set)

The additional display modes for the Logix Super VGA card (and others using this Trident chip set) are tabulated in Table 5-6. Like the Tseng Labs chip set, this chip set uses the standard ROM BIOS video service call for setting the display mode, so you can use the function in Figure 5-1 without any difficulty.

TABLE 5-6. ADDITIONAL DISPLAY MODES FOR TRIDENT VGA CARD

Mode	Type	Colors/ Shades	Char Format	Char Size	Display Size	Max Pgs	Memory Address
50	Text	16/256K	80x30	8x16	640x480	8	B8000
51	Text	16/256K	80x43	8x11	640x473	8	B8000
52	Text	16/256K	80x60	8x8	640x480	2	B8000
53	Text	16/256K	132x25	8x14	1056x350	2	B8000
54	Text	16/256K	132x30	8x16	1056x480	2	B8000
55	Text	16/256K	132x43	8x11	1056x473	1	B8000
56	Text	16/256K	132x60	8x8	1056x480	1	B8000
57	Text	16/256K	132x25	9x14	1188x350	1	B8000
58	Text	16/256K	132x30	9x16	1188x480	4	B8000
59	Text	16/256K	132x43	9x11	1188x473	1	B8000
5A	Text	16/256K	132x60	9x8	1188x480	1	B8000
5B	Graphics	16/256K	100x75	8x8	800x600	1	A0000
5C	Graphics	256/256K	80x25	8x16	640x400	1	A0000
5D	Graphics	256/256K	80x30	8x16	640x480	1	A0000
5F	Graphics	16/256K	128x48	8x16	1024x768	1	A0000
61	Graphics	16/256K	96x64	8x16	1024x768	1	A0000

Display Modes for the Paradise Chip Set (as Used in the Dell 310 Computer)

The extended display modes for the Paradise chip set (as used in the Dell 310 computer) are tabulated in Table 5-7. This is another Super VGA chip set in which the mode setting function is exactly the same as for the standard VGA, so that you can use the listing of Figure 5-1.

TABLE 5-7. ADDITIONAL DISPLAY MODES FOR DELL 310 (PARADISE VGA CARD)

Mode	Type	Colors/ Shades	Char Format	Char Size	Display Size	Max Pgs	Memory Address
54	Text	16/256K	132x43	8x8	1056x350	2	B8000
55	Text	16/256K	132x25	8x14	1056x350	2	B8000
56	Text	2/256K	132x43	8x11	1056x473	2	B8000
57	Text	2/256K	132x25	8x14	1056x350	2	B8000
58	Graphics	16/256K	100x37	8x16	800x600	2	A0000
59	Graphics	2/256K	100x37	8x16	800x600	2	A0000
5A	Graphics	2/256K	132x60	8x8	1024x768	1	A0000
5B	Graphics	4/256K	132x25	8x14	1024x768	1	A0000
5C	Graphics	16/256K	132x30	8x16	1024x768	1	A0000
5D	Graphics	256/256K	100x37	8x16	800x600	1	A0000
5E	Graphics	256/256K	80x25	8x16	640x400	1	A0000
5F	Graphics	256/256K	80x30	8x16	640x480	1	A0000

Display Modes for the ATI VGAWonder Display Adapter Card

Table 5-8 tabulates the extended display modes for the ATI VGAWonder display adapter card. This is another card where the setting the extended modes is fully compatible with the mode setting function for the original VGA card, so that the listing of Figure 5-1 can be used without alteration.

TABLE 5-8. ADDITIONAL DISPLAY MODES FOR ATI VGAWONDER VGA CARD

Mode	Type	Colors/ Shades	Char Format	Char Size	Display Size	Max Pgs	Memory Address
23	Text	16/256K	132x25	8x14	1056x350	1	B8000
27	Text	16/256K	132x25	8x14	1056x350	1	B8000
33	Text	16/256K	132x44	8x8	1056x352	1	B8000
37	Text	2/256K	132x44	8x8	1056x352	1	B8000
54	Graphics	16/256K	100x37	8x16	800x600	1	A0000
55	Graphics	16/256K	128x48	8x16	1024x768	1	A0000
61	Graphics	256/256K	80x25	8x16	640x400	1	A0000
62	Graphics	256/256K	80x30	8x16	640x480	1	A0000
63	Graphics	256/256K	100x37	8x16	800x600	1	A0000
65	Graphics	16/256K	128x48	8x16	1024x768	1	A0000
67	Graphics	4/256K	128x48	8x16	1024x768	1	A0000
6A	Graphics	16/256K	100x37	8x16	800x600	1	A0000

Display Modes for the VESA Standard

The first attempts at achieving some standardization of Super VGA modes have been achieved with the issuance of the VESA standard by:

Video Electronics Standards Association
1330 South Bascom Avenue
San Jose, CA 95128-4502

The VESA standard provides for extended modes in addition to those that may be included in any particular board. These modes used of through standardized extensions to the ROM BIOS. A number of manufacturers have already begun putting VESA modes in their boards and others will surely follow. The currently specified VESA modes are tabulated in Table 5-9. All of these modes are identified by 15 bit numbers; one of them (mode 102H) can also be called with a standard BIOS call to the 7 bit mode 6AH. The function for setting the VESA modes is listed in Figure 5-3. It makes use of the new ROM BIOS video service 4FH.

TABLE 5-9. VESA STANDARD ADDITIONAL DISPLAY MODES

Mode	Type	Colors/ Shades	Char Format	Char Size	Display Size	Max Pgs	Memory Address
100H	Graphics	256/256K	80x25	8x16	640x400	1	A0000
101H	Graphics	256/256K	80x30	8x16	640x480	1	A0000
102H	Graphics	16/256K	100x37	8x16	800x600	1	A0000
103H	Graphics	256/256K	100x37	8x16	800x600	1	A0000
104H	Graphics	16/256K	128x48	8x16	1024x768	1	A0000
105H	Graphics	256/256K	128x48	8x16	1024x768	1	A0000
106H	Graphics	16/256K	160x64	8x16	1280x1024	1	A0000
107H	Graphics	256/256K	160x64	8x16	1280x1024	1	A0000
108H	Text	16/256K	80x60	8x16	1280x1024	1	B8000
109H	Text	16/256K	132x25	8x16	1056x400	1	B8000
10AH	Text	16/256K	132x43	8x8	1056x350	1	B8000
10BH	Text	16/256K	132x50	8x8	1056x400	1	B8000
10CH	Text	16/256K	132x60	8x8	1056x480	1	B8000

Figure 5-3. Listing of Function to Set VESA Display Modes

```
/*

        setMode() = Function to set VESA display modes

*/

void setMode(int mode)
{
        union REGS reg;

        if (mode <= 0x6A)
        {
                reg.x.ax = mode;
        else
        {
                reg.x.ax = 0x4F02;
                reg.x.bx = mode;
        }
        int86(0x10, &reg, &reg);
}
```

Plotting a Point on the Graphics Screen

The starting point for plotting a point to the graphics screen is the ROM BIOS video service 0CH. This service supports all of the official IBM graphics modes for CGA, EGA and VGA color graphics adapter boards. Whether it supports the Hercules graphics card and its clones depends upon the BIOS extensions furnished with a particular card. Similarly, in using the extended or super VGA modes, this service may or may not be supported. Of course, if you decide to design your own graphics modes, the service will not be supported by the ROM BIOS extensions, and you will have to roll your own function. In any case, although the ROM BIOS video service for plotting a graphics point is a good place to start, it is usually much to slow to use for extensive graphics plotting operations.

The next approach might be to use the point plotting capabilities of the graphic package that comes with your compiler. For example the Borland family of C compilers (Turbo C, Turbo C++, Borland C++, etc.) has a function *putpixel* that does fast point plotting. However, Borland graphics is limited to normal IBM graphics modes, and not even all of them. Therefore many of the things that you would like to do with a point plotting function are not possible. Consequently, the rest of this chapter will be devoted to the design of point plotting functions that you can tailor to your exact applications.

Usually graphics information is plotted to the screen one pixel at a time. Each point may be plotted in any pixel location that is defined for the current graphics mode. The number of pixels on the screen differs widely for the different graphics modes. At the low end, the most used CGA color graphics mode is Mode 04H, which is 320 by 200 pixels by 4 colors. Thus for this mode, the screen has 64,000 pixels. The most common EGA color graphics mode is Mode 10H which is 640 by 350 pixels by 16 colors. This screen has 224,000 pixels. At the high end is the super VGA mode of 1024 by 768 pixels by 256 colors. This screen has 786,432 pixels. Fortunately, we don't have to call a point plotting function to plot every single one of these pixels; we can set up a background color and then call the point plotting function to plot only those pixels whose color must differ from the background. Nevertheless, you can see that we are going to be using the point plotting routine many many times in the course of creating a graphics display. Therefore it is important to plot each pixel as fast as possible so as to minimize the amount of time required to create a graphics display. We are going to begin by describing the slowest point plotting function, that using the ROM BIOS video service. Then, we'll go on to faster and more specialized point plotting functions until we've covered almost everything that you'll ever need to know.

Point Plotting with the ROM BIOS Video Services

Figure 6-1 is a listing of the function to plot a single point (pixel) using the ROM BIOS video services. This function should work for any of the video adapter cards that are compatible with the IBM CGA, EGA or VGA. (If you have a Hercules Graphics Adapter, you can try it and see what happens, but don't count on it working.) This function is very slow, partly because it uses of interrupts, which not only slow down operation, but also require that all register contents be saved to the stack and then recovered after the operation is complete; this requires a lot of extra time. Another thing that slows interrupt operations is that the interrupt must begin by reading the address of the routine that it is to use from a table in memory and must then jump to this address to find the routine to service the interrupt. As you can see, this function is pretty simple. You load the ROM BIOS Video Service number into register ah, the color into register al, set register bh to 0 (indicating page 0; if you want, you can add another parameter passed to this function to pass a different page number, which is sent to register bh), set registers cx and dx to the x and y coordinates of the desired pixel, and then call the ROM BIOS Video Service interrupt.

Figure 6-1. Plot Function Using ROM BIOS Video Services

```
/*

    plot() = Plots a point at location (x,y) in specified
             color using the ROM BIOS video services.

*/

void plot (int x, int y, int color)
{
    union REGS reg;

    reg.h.ah = 0x0C;
    reg.h.al = color;
    reg.h.bh = 0;
    reg.x.cx = x;
    reg.x.dx = y;
    int86 (0x10, &reg, &reg);
}
```

Plotting a Point on the CGA

The next function described will plot a point in color on the graphics screen when a CGA board is being used or when an EGA or VGA has its graphics mode set to emulate the CGA (mode 4, for example). Mode 4 consists of 320 by 200 pixels by four colors. In mode 4, the CGA has one page of graphics data located at address B8000H, so there is no need to worry about changing pages. (However, the page limitation is based upon the limited amount of memory that comes with a standard CGA; if you are using an EGA or VGA you may have enough memory to access more than one page in this mode and may wish to modify the plotting function to handle the additional pages.) Beginning at the top left-hand corner of the screen, each pixel is represented by two bits in video memory, which form a binary number from 0 to 3, representing the pixel color from 0 to 3, as defined by the selected palette. (For palette 0, color zero is the current background color and the other three colors in numerical order are green, red and brown. For palette 1, the colors are the current background color followed in numerical order by cyan, magenta and white.)

The arrangement of the bits in memory begins with pixel 0 (at the top left-hand corner of the screen), which is stored in the two most significant bits of memory address B8000H. The next pixel (pixel 1) in line is stored in the next two memory bits, and so forth until a complete line (320 pixels) has been stored (using up 80 bytes at 2 bits per pixel and 8 bits per byte). The first pixel in the next line is stored in the two most significant bits of memory address BA000H. The process continues, with pixels for even lines stored consecutively in the memory section beginning at address B8000H and pixels for odd lines stored consecutively in the memory section beginning at address BA000H. Using this information, we can create the point plotting function listed in Figure 6-2. Before we look at the actual function, we need to note how C compilers handle data of the type *char far **, which represents a far address. The compiler uses the four most significant hexadecimal digits to set the segment register and the lower four hexadecimal digits to set the memory address. Thus when we define an address as 0xA0000000L, the actual memory address is A0000H. This can be a little confusing if you don't fully understand that an address is defined by the contents of the segment register multiplied by 16 and added to the contents of the address byte. The function begins by computing the offset of the memory address from the base address of B8000H. Note that we use the number of lines modula 2 to add an offset of 2000H for odd lines, but not for even ones. Then we add in 80 bytes for each pair of lines plus the column value divided by four (since four pixels use up only one byte of memory). Next, we create a mask consisting of ones at the two bit positions for the selected pixel and zeroes elsewhere. We shift the color data to line up with the proper bit positions for the pixel. We then AND the contents of the selected memory address with the inverse of the mask and OR this with the combination of the shifted color data ANDed with the mask to create the new value of the contents of the selected memory address. The result is that the memory address contains new data for the two pixels at the selected address, and the display adapter card registers preserve the old data for the other three pixels in the byte. If you want to check the speed, write a program that goes to mode 4 and then writes several hundred points with the ROM BIOS services plot function and finally the same number of points with the function just described. The speed-up provided by this function will be obvious.

Figure 6-2. Plot Function for CGA (Mode 4) Using Direct Memory Access

```
/*

    plot() = Plots a point at (x,y) in selected color using
       CGA mode 4, sending data directly to display memory.

*/

void plot (int x, int y, int color)
{
        int offset, mask, temp;
        char far *address;

        offset = 0x2000*(y%2) + 80*(y>>1) + (x>>2);
        mask = 0xC0 >> ((x%4)<<1);
        address = 0xB8000000L + offset;
        temp = color<<(6-((x%4)<<1));
        *address = (*address & ~mask) | (temp & mask);
}
```

Point Plotting with the Hercules Graphics Adapter

The Hercules Graphics Adapter creates monochrome rather than color displays. There are thus only two choices for a pixel; it is either black or white. Hence a single memory bit can define each pixel's condition. The resolution of the Hercules display in its graphics mode is 720 columns by 348 rows. This means that each line of the display requires 90 bytes of memory. The memory storage technique used by Hercules is similar to that used for the CGA. However, where the CGA uses an odd/even interleaving scheme, the Hercules card uses four interleafs, with rows 0, 4, 8, 12, etc. being put into display memory beginning at memory address B0000H; rows 1, 5, 9, 13, etc. being put into display memory beginning at memory address B2000H; rows 2, 6, 10, 14, etc. being put into display memory beginning at memory address B4000H; and rows 3, 7, 11, 15, etc. being put into display memory beginning at memory address B6000H.

The Hercules card supports two graphics memory pages, whose memory addresses are separated by 8000H. Consequently we have created a Hercules point plotting function that checks to see which of the two pages is active and plots points to that page. If you are interested in using only one graphics page, you can remove the line that gets the page information and the part of the offset computation that inserts the page offset. Figure 6-3 is a listing of a plot function for the Hercules card.

Figure 6-3. Plot Function for Hercules Graphics Adapter

```
/*


    plot() = Plots a point at (x,y) in black or white for
                    Hercules Graphics Adapter.


*/

void plot (int x, int y, int color)
{
        unsigned int offset;
        int page;
        char mask;
        char far *address;

        page = getPage();
        offset = 0x2000*(y%4) + 0x8000*page + (90*(y>>2)) +
            x>>3;
        mask = 0x80 >> (x%8);
        if (color == 1)
                *address |= mask;
        else
                *address &= ~mask;
}
```

Point Plotting with 16 Color EGA/VGA Modes Using the Sequencer Registers

We already warned you in Chapter 2 that data on using the registers of the EGA and VGA boards was rather obscure. The memory portion of these cards consists of four memory planes. For the 16 color modes, each of these planes is located at the same starting address, namely A0000H. A single bit in the word at a memory address represents each pixel; the combination of the four memory planes in which this bit is activated determines which of the 16 colors is assigned to the pixel, with one plane representing red; one, green; one, blue; and the final one, intensity. Therefore, we can't simply send color information to the memory address; we also have to do some manipulation to assure that it gets distributed to the proper memory planes. There are at least three different ways of doing this. The first uses the sequencer registers. This function is listed in Figure 6-4. It requires an external parameter, *xres*, which is the number of bytes required for a full line of pixels in whichever 16 color mode was selected. The first thing that the function does is compute the offset from the base memory address by multiplying the number of lines by *xres* and then adding in the number of bytes required to reach the byte containing the desired pixel information. Next the address is determined by adding this offset to the base memory address. The function then sets up a mask that has a 1 only in the bit position representing the pixel being selected. Next, the function sends this mask out to Graphics Register 08H—Bit Mask. When a write to display memory occurs, the bits in the addressed word in each of the four bit planes that correspond in position to 0 in the bit mask register are immune to change. Where they correspond to 1 in the bit mask register, the bits in each of the bit planes may be changed by the write operation.

Next, OPERATOR is loaded into Graphics Register 03H—Data Rotate/Function Select. We're only concerned with bits 4 and 3 of this register that determine how the specified color of a pixel will interact with the color information previously present for that pixel. If bits 4 and 3 are 00B, the existing color data will be replaced by the newly specified color. If the bits are 01B, the new color will be ANDed with the existing color data. If the bits are 10B, the new color will be ORed with the existing color data. If the bits are 11B, the new color will be XORed with the existing color data. If you are concerned with only overwriting new color data, you can remove this line of the code and the default setting of 00B for these bits will do the job for you.

The function next does a read of the data at the selected display memory address. What is read by this operation is actually meaningless and is not used. When the computer attempts to read this memory, however, the contents of each of the four memory planes at this address is transferred to an individual register within the EGA/VGA board. We're going to be using Sequencer Register 02H—Map Mask to determine which planes are to have the color information written to them. The planes that are not enabled by Sequencer Register 02H—Map Mask will not be affected by a write operation. If any of these disabled planes already contains a 1 in the designated pixel position and we wish to replace it by a 0, we will be unable to do. Therefore, to assure that the proper color information is transferred, the function next sends 0 to clear all planes at the designated pixel location while Sequencer Register 02H—Map Mask is still in the default condition of all planes enabled. Next, the new color value is sent to Sequencer Register 02H—Map Mask, the map mask register. Ones in the color value permit the appropriate color planes to be written to when a memory write operation occurs; zeroes designate planes that are unaffected by the write operation. Finally another write to the selected memory location is performed, with an 0xFF sent, so that a 1 will be written for the pixel bit in every plane that is enabled. The registers of the EGA/VGA that were modified in this function are then reset to their default values and the function terminates.

Figure 6-4. Function to Plot a Point to the EGA/VGA Board in 16 Color Modes Using Sequencer Registers

```
/*

    plot() = Plots a point at (x,y) in selected color for
    EGA/VGA 16 color modes, using C port output functions
                  and sequencer register 2.

*/

void plot (int x, int y, int color)
{
        #define seq_out(index, val)   {outp(0x3C4,index);\
```
(continued)

```
                                       outp(0x3C5, val);}
    #define graph_out(index, val) {outp(0x3CE, index);\
                                       outp(0x3CF, val);}
    extern OPERATOR, xres;
    unsigned int offset;
    int dummy, mask;
    char far *address;

    offset = (long)y*xres + (x>>3);
    address = (char far *) 0xA0000000L + offset;
    mask = 0x80 >> (x%8);
    graph_out(8,mask);
    graph_out(3,OPERATOR);
    dummy = *address;
    *address = 0;
    seq_out(2,color);
    *address = 0xFF;
    seq_out(2,0x0F);
    graph_out(3,0);
    graph_out(8,0xFF);
}
```

Point Plotting with 16 Color EGA/VGA Modes Using the Graphics Registers

Another way of plotting a point to the EGA/VGA card in the 16 color mode is to use Graphics Register 01H—Enable Set/Reset, to control the color instead of using the Sequencer Register 02H_Map Mask. The function to do this is listed in Figure 6-5. Like the previous function, the first thing that the function does is compute the offset from the base memory address by multiplying the number of lines by 80 and then adding in the number of bytes required to reach the byte containing the desired pixel information. Next the address is determined by adding this offset to the base memory address. The function then sets up a mask that has a 1 only in the bit position representing the pixel being selected. Next, the function sends this mask out to Graphics Register 08H—Bit Mask. This is the bit map register; when a write to display memory occurs, the bits in the addressed word in each of the four bit planes that correspond in position to 0 in the bit map register are immune to change. Where there is a 1 in the bit map register, the bits in each of the bit planes may be changed by the write operation. This version of the plot function doesn't send the OPERATOR parameter to Graphics Register 03H—Data Rotate/Function Select to determine the interaction of the new and old colors, so that it only overwrites the existing data with the new data. (By referring to the previous function, you can easily add the feature if you need it.) Next, the function sends the inverse of the color data to graphics data register 1, the enable set/reset register. At each of the four least significant bits in this register where there is a 0, the associated color plane has data written to it by a memory write operation; where a bit is 1, the enabled color plane bits are reset to 0. Next, the function reads data at the selected display memory address. What is read by this operation is actually meaningless and is not used. When the computer attempts to read this memory, however, the contents of each of the four memory planes at this address is transferred to an individual register within the EGA/VGA board. Following this, we write 0FFH to the selected memory address, causing a 1 in the masked bits to be transferred to the selected memory planes and the selected bit in the remaining memory planes to be set to 0. The color planes are now set up for the proper color of the pixel, so the registers of the EGA/VGA that were modified in this function are then reset to their default values and the function terminates. This function uses a few less operations than the previous one and thus may be faster.

Figure 6-5. Function to Plot a Point to the EGA/VGA Board in 16 Color Modes Using Graphics Display Registers

```
/*

    plot() = Plots a point at (x,y) in selected color for
        EGA/VGA 16 color modes using C port output
            functions and graphics data register 1.

*/

void plot(int x, int y, int color)
{

        #define seq_out(index,val)      {outp(0x3C4,index);\
```
(continued)

```
                                           outp(0x3C5,val);}
      #define graph_out(index,val)   {outp(0x3CE,index);\
                                           outp(0x3CF,val);}


      unsigned int offset;
      int dummy,mask,page;
      char far * mem_address;


      offset = (long)y * xres + ((long)x / 8L);
      mem_address = (char far *) 0xA0000000L + offset;
      mask = 0x80 >> (x % 8);
      graph_out(8,mask);
      graph_out(1,~color);
      dummy = *mem_address;
      *mem_address = 0xFF;
      graph_out(1,0);
      graph_out(3,0);
      graph_out(8,0xFF);
}
```

Point Plotting with 16 Color EGA/VGA Modes Using Write Mode 2

A third way of plotting a point to the EGA/VGA card in the 16 color
mode is to use write mode 2, where color data transferred to memory
is sent directly to the color planes. The function to do this is listed in
Figure 6-6. Like the previous function, the first thing that the
function does is compute the offset from the base memory address by
multiplying the number of lines by *xres* and then adding in the
number of bytes required to reach the byte containing the desired
pixel information. Next the address is determined by adding this
offset to the base memory address. The function then sets up a mask
that has a 1 only in the bit position representing the pixel being
selected. Next, the function sends this mask out to Graphics Register
08H—Bit Mask. When a write to display memory occurs, the bits in
the addressed word in each of the four bit planes that correspond in
position to 0 in the bit mask register are immune to change. Where
there is a 1 in the bit mask register, the bits in each of the bit planes
may be changed by the write operation. This version of the plot
function doesn't send the OPERATOR parameter to Graphics Register
03H—Data Rotate/Function Select to determine the interaction of the
new and old colors, so that it only overwrites the existing data with

the new data. (By referring to the previous function, you can easily add the feature if you need it.) Next, Graphics Register 05H—Mode is set to write mode 2. IBM says that in this mode, when a write operation takes place, each bit in the character that is written is expanded to eight identical bits and transferred to one of the color planes. For example, if bit 1 is 1 and bit 0 is 0, then 11111111B would be sent to the selected address in the green memory plane and 00000000B would be sent to the address in the blue memory plane. However, we have set up the mask so that actually only one bit is sent to each color plane. Next, the function reads the data at the selected display memory address. Actually this read is used to cause the contents of each of the four memory planes at this address to be transferred to an individual register within the EGA/VGA board. The actual data read from memory is not used. Following this, we write the color information to the selected memory address, causing a 1 in the masked bits to be transferred to the selected memory planes. The color planes are now set up for the proper color of the pixel, so the registers of the EGA/VGA that were modified in this function are then reset to their default values and the function terminates. This function should be even faster than the previous one.

Figure 6-6. Function to Plot a Point to the EGA/VGA Board in 16 Color Modes Using Write Mode 2

```
/*

    plot() = Plots a point at (x,y) in selected color for
          EGA/VGA 16 color modes using C port output
                functions and write mode 2.

*/

void plot(int x, int y, int color)
{
        #define seq_out(index,val)   {outp(0x3C4,index);\
                                      outp(0x3C5,val);}
        #define graph_out(index,val)  {outp(0x3CE,index);\
                                      outp(0x3CF,val);}
        unsigned int offset;
```

(continued)

```
int dummy,mask,page;
char far * mem_address;

offset = (long)y * xres + ((long)x / 8L);
mem_address = (char far *) 0xA0000000L + offset;
mask = 0x80 >> (x % 8);
graph_out(8,mask);
graph_out(5,2);
dummy = *mem_address;
*mem_address = color;

graph_out(5,0);
graph_out(8,0xFF);
}
```

Point Plotting Using Assembly Language

It is possible to interface C code with assembly language to speed up the operation of a function. The amount of speed-up that is achieved depends primarily on the efficiency of your C compiler. A function similar to that of Figure 6-4, but using assembly language is listed in Figure 6-7. In order to compile it, you will need to have an assembler as well as a C compiler. Furthermore, some C compilers cannot handle assembly language instructions from within the integrated environment. If you are including the function in a program that is to be compiled with such a compiler, you will have to use the command line version of the compiler. I have used the regular C and assembly language versions of the plot function with a lot of different programs and have never really noticed any significant difference in speed. Therefore, I suggest that you stick with the regular C versions of the plot function unless you have a really compelling reason to do otherwise.

Figure 6-6. Function to Plot a Point to the EGA/VGA Board in 16 Color Mode 16 Using Sequencer Registers and Assembly Language

```
/*
```

```
    plot() = Plots a point at (x,y) in selected color for
    EGA/VGA 16 color modes using C port output functions,
        sequencer register 2, and assembly language.
```

```
*/

void plot (int x, int y, int color)
{
        extern xres;
        unsigned int offset;
        int dummy, mask;
        char far *address;
        offset = (long)y*xres + (x>>3);
        mask = 0x80 >> (x%8);
        _ES = 0xA000;
        _BX = offset;
        _CX = color;
        _AX = mask;
        asm MOV     AH,AL
        asm MOV     AL,08
        asm MOV     DX,03CEH
        asm OUT     DX,AX
        asm MOV     AX,0FF02H
        asm MOV     DL,0C4H
        asm OUT     DX,AX
        asm OR      ES:[BX],CH
        asm MOV     BYTE PTR ES:[BX],00
        asm MOV     AH,CL
        asm OUT     DX,AX
        asm MOV     BYTE PTR ES:[BX],0FFH
        asm MOV     AH,0FFH
        asm OUT     DX,AX
        asm MOV     DL,0CEH
        asm MOV     AX,0003
```

(continued)

```
        asm  OUT     DX,AX
        asm  MOV     AX,0FF08H
        asm  OUT     DX,AX
}
```

Point Plotting for 256 Color VGA Modes

The VGA mode 19 is 320 by 200 pixels by 256 colors. The four planes of display memory on the VGA board are used in a very different manner when in this display mode. As far as the user is concerned, all pixels are stored in display memory consecutively, with one byte allocated to describe the color of each pixel. The first byte (at the base memory address A0000H) represents the pixel at the top left-hand corner of the screen. As the memory address increases, pixels are stored for the first line until the right side is reached. The next address is that of the first pixel at the left of the next line, and so forth. Inside the VGA board, data is actually being rotated through the four memory planes, so that in any particular memory plane, only every fourth byte is actually used. However, this internal manipulation is completely transparent to the user, who may go ahead and treat the display memory as an ordinary block of memory. Figure 6-7 is the listing of a function to plot a point to the VGA in mode 19. The function first computes the offset from the base memory address of the desired pixel by taking 320 bytes per line plus the number of columns. This is then added to the base memory address to obtain the actual address of the pixel. The color number of the pixel is then sent to that address. The principle is the same for extended Super VGA 256 color modes.

Figure 6-7. Function to Plot a Point with VGA Mode 19 (320 × 200 Pixels × 256 Colors

```
/*

    plot() = Function to plot a point at (x,y) using VGA
        mode 19 with a specified color from 0 to 255.

*/
```

(continued)

```
void plot (int x, int y, int color)
{
     unsigned int offset
     char far *address;

     offset = 320*y + x;
     address = (char far *)(0xA0000000L + offset);
     *address = color;
}
```

Extended and Undocumented Display Modes

We've now given you complete information on plotting points with the usual graphics display modes for CGA, HGA, EGA and VGA. However, there are a number of additional plot functions that you need to be familiar with. First are those used for various undocumented display modes. These may turn out to be very useful for some graphics applications. They will be discussed in Chapter 8. Second are the plot functions associated with the extended Super VGA modes, which provide much higher resolution displays than the ordinary VGA is capable of. These will be discussed in Chapter 9.

Chapter 7

Lines and Rectangles

The next step after learning how to plot points on the graphics screen is to discover how to draw lines. If we are willing to get primitive enough, almost any geometric figure can be drawn out of a large number of tiny line segments. We're going to have somewhat more sophisticated techniques for creating many figures, but lines are still basic and essential. We'll start with a very simple function to draw a vertical line, and then progress to more complicated techniques. All of the line functions that are described in this chapter are listed as part of the file *Linetest.c*, the complete listing of which is in Figure 7-1. Each function will be described individually in the sections that follow and then at the chapter's end, the main function, which draws demonstrations of each line type, will be described. You can run this whole program to get an idea of how the various line functions can be used. You can also select those functions that you want to use in your own programs and either build them into a graphics library or make them a part of whatever program you wish to write. Note, however, that for each individual function you may need to include one or more of the standard C libraries with an *include* statement and also a particular function may make reference to external variables that you will have to define in your main program. Furthermore, many of the line and rectangle drawing functions make use of one of the two plot functions listed at the end of the program, which were already described in Chapter 6.

Figure 7-1. Listing of Linetest.c Program

```
/*


        LINETEST = Test of line drawing function

            By Roger T. Stevens   7-3-91


*/

#include <stdio.h>
#include <stdlib.h>
#include <dos.h>
#include <math.h>
void cls(int color);
void drawHorzLine1(int xstart, int xend, int y, int
    color);
void drawHorzLine2(int xstart, int xend, int y, int
    color);
void drawLine1(int xs, int ys, int xe, int ye, int color);
void drawLine2(int xs, int ys, int xe, int ye, int color);
void drawLine3(int xs, int ys, int xe, int ye, int color);
void drawLine4(int xs, int ys, int xe, int ye, int color);
void drawLine5(int xs, int ys, int xe, int ye, int color);
void drawLine6(int xs, int ys, int xe, int ye, int color);
void drawLine7(int xs, int ys, int length, int angle, int
    color);
void drawLine8(int xe, int ye, int color);
void drawVertLine2(int x, int ystart, int yend, int
    color);
void drawVertLine3(int x, int ystart, int yend, int
    color);
void drawVertLine4(int x, int ystart, int yend, int
    color);
void drawRect1(int x_one, int y_one, int x_two, int y_two,
    int color);
void drawRect2(int x_one, int y_one, int x_two, int y_two,
    int color);
void plot16(int x, int y, int color);
void plot256(int x, int y, int color);
```

(continued)

```
void setMode(int mode);
void setVGApalette(unsigned char *buffer);

typedef struct
{
    unsigned char red;
    unsigned char green;
    unsigned char blue;
} RGB;

RGB palette[256];
int angle, color, hue, i, j, k, length, LINEWIDTH, xs, ys;
char ch;
unsigned long int PATTERN = 0xFFFFFFFF;
int xres, yres, X, Y, x, y;
unsigned long int style[8] = {
    0xFFFFFFFF,0xC0C0C0C0,0xFF00FF00,0xFFF0FFF0,
    0xF000F000,0xFFFF0000,0xFFFFF0F0,0xFFF0F0F0};

void main()
{
    int i, xlength=130, ylength=90;

/*
```

```
                 320 x 200 Pixel x 256 Color Mode 19

                 Vertical Lines using drawVertLine1()
```

```
*/

    xres = 320;
    yres = 200;
    setMode(19);
    cls(0);
    color = 8;
    for (i=0; i<320; i+=45)
    drawVertLine1(i,0,199,color++);
    getch();
```

(continued)

```
/*
┌─────────────────────────────────────────────────────────────┐
│ ┌─────────────────────────────────────────────────────────┐ │
│ │                                                         │ │
│ │           640 x 350 Pixel x 16 Color Mode 16            │ │
│ │                                                         │ │
│ │           Vertical Lines using drawVertLine2()          │ │
│ │                                                         │ │
│ └─────────────────────────────────────────────────────────┘ │
└─────────────────────────────────────────────────────────────┘
*/

    xres = 640;
    yres = 350;
    setMode(16);
    cls(0);
    color = 8;
    for (i=0; i<640; i+=91)
        drawVertLine2(i,0,349,color++);
    getch();

/*
┌─────────────────────────────────────────────────────────────┐
│ ┌─────────────────────────────────────────────────────────┐ │
│ │                                                         │ │
│ │           320 x 200 Pixel x 256 Color Mode 19           │ │
│ │                                                         │ │
│ │         Wide Vertical Lines using drawVertLine3()       │ │
│ │                                                         │ │
│ └─────────────────────────────────────────────────────────┘ │
└─────────────────────────────────────────────────────────────┘
*/

    xres = 320;
    yres = 200;
    setMode(19);
    cls(0);
    color = 8;
    LINEWIDTH = 1;
    for (i=0; i<8; i++)
    {
        PATTERN = style[i];
        drawVertLine3(i*44,0,199,color++);
        LINEWIDTH++;
    }
    PATTERN = style[0];
    LINEWIDTH = 1;
```

(continued)

```
    getch();
```

```
/*
```

```
┌─────────────────────────────────────────────────────────────┐
│ ┌─────────────────────────────────────────────────────────┐ │
│ │                                                         │ │
│ │           640 x 350 Pixel x 16 Color Mode 16            │ │
│ │                                                         │ │
│ │        Wide Vertical Lines using drawVertLine4()        │ │
│ │                                                         │ │
│ └─────────────────────────────────────────────────────────┘ │
└─────────────────────────────────────────────────────────────┘
```

```
*/
```

```
    xres = 640;
    yres = 350;
    setMode(16);
    cls(0);
    color = 8;
    for (i=0; i<8; i++)
    {
        PATTERN = style[i];
        drawVertLine4(i*88,0,349,color++);
        LINEWIDTH++;
    }
    PATTERN = style[0];
    LINEWIDTH = 1;
    getch();
```

```
/*
```

```
┌─────────────────────────────────────────────────────────────┐
│ ┌─────────────────────────────────────────────────────────┐ │
│ │                                                         │ │
│ │           320 x 200 Pixel x 256 Color Mode 19           │ │
│ │                                                         │ │
│ │        Wide Horizontal Lines using drawHorzLine1()      │ │
│ │                                                         │ │
│ └─────────────────────────────────────────────────────────┘ │
└─────────────────────────────────────────────────────────────┘
```

```
*/
```

```
    xres = 320;
    yres = 200;
    setMode(19);
    cls(0);
    color = 8;
    LINEWIDTH = 1;
```

(continued)

```
for (i=0; i<8; i++)
{
    drawHorzLine1(10,310,i*24,color++);
    LINEWIDTH++;
}
PATTERN = style[0];
LINEWIDTH = 1;
getch();
```

```
/*
```

```
        640 x 350 Pixel x 16 Color Mode 16

    Wide Horizontal Lines using drawHorzLine2()
```

```
*/
```

```
xres = 640;
yres = 350;
setMode(16);
cls(0);
color = 8;
LINEWIDTH = 1;
for (i=0; i<8; i++)
{
    drawHorzLine2(10,630,i*48,color++);
    LINEWIDTH++;
}
PATTERN = style[0];
LINEWIDTH = 1;
getch();
```

(continued)

```
/*
```

```
        640 x 350 Pixel x 16 Color Mode 16

  Horizontal and Vertical Lines using drawHorzLine2()
                and drawVertLine4().
```

```
*/
```

```
    cls(7);
    color = 1;
    for (i=10; i<630; i += 30)
    {
        drawVertLine4(i,10,330,color++);
        color %= 16;
        if (color == 7)
            color++;
    }
    for (i=10; i<349; i+=20)
    {
        drawHorzLine2(10,630,i,color++);
        color %= 16;
        if (color == 7)
            color++;
    }
    getch();
```

```
/*
```

```
        320 x 200 Pixel x 256 Color Mode 19

        Wide Rectangle using drawRect2()
```

```
*/
```

```
    LINEWIDTH = 3;
    setMode(19);
    xres = 320;
    yres = 200;
```

(continued)

```
cls(1);
drawRect2(8,8,xres-6,yres-4,14);
getch();

/*
```

```
┌─────────────────────────────────────────────────────┐
│                                                       │
│        640 x 350 Pixel x 16 Color Mode 16            │
│                                                       │
│     Wide Horizontal Lines using drawHorzLine2()      │
│                                                       │
└─────────────────────────────────────────────────────┘
```

```
*/

LINEWIDTH = 5;
setMode(16);
xres = 640;
yres = 350;
cls(12);
drawRect1(8,8,xres-6,yres-4,1);
getch();

/*
```

```
┌─────────────────────────────────────────────────────┐
│                                                       │
│        640 x 350 Pixel x 16 Color Mode 16            │
│                                                       │
│        Line Pattern using drawLine1()                │
│                                                       │
└─────────────────────────────────────────────────────┘
```

```
*/

cls(1);
drawLine1(6,8,xres-6,8,11);
drawLine1(6,yres-4,xres-6,yres-4,11);
drawLine1(6,8,6,yres-4,11);
drawLine1(xres-6,8,xres-6,yres-4,11);
for (i=30; i< yres-10; i+=20)
    drawLine1(7,9,xres-7,i,13);
for (i=30; i< yres-10; i+=20)
    drawLine1(xres-7,yres-5,7,i,14);
for (i=30; i< yres-10; i+=20)
```

(continued)

```
        drawLine1(7,yres-5,xres-7,i,10);
    for (i=30; i< yres-10; i+=20)
        drawLine1(xres-7,9,7,i,12);
    getch();
```

/*

```
        320 x 200 Pixel x 256 Color Mode 19

        Line Pattern using drawLine2()
```

*/

```
    xres = 320;
    yres = 200;
    setMode(19);
    palette[0].red = 0;
    palette[0].green = 0;
    palette[0].blue = 0;
    for (i=0; i<6; i++)
        for(j=0; j<6; j++)
            for (k=1; k<8; k++)
            {
                palette[42*i+7*j+k].red = i*12+1;
                palette[42*i+7*j+k].green = j*12+1;
                palette[42*i+7*j+k].blue =
                    10*(k-1)+1;
            }

    setVGApalette(&palette[0].red);
    LINEWIDTH = 3;
    drawLine6(6,8,xres-5,8,42);
    drawLine6(6,yres-4,xres-5,yres-4,42);
    drawLine6(7,8,7,yres-4,42);
    drawLine6(xres-6,8,xres-6,yres-4,42);
    LINEWIDTH = 1;
    hue = 250;
    for (i=30; i< yres-10; i+=20)
    {
```

(continued)

```
            drawLine6(10,10,xres-8,i, hue--);
            drawLine6(xres-8,yres-6,10,i, hue--);
            drawLine6(10,yres-6,xres-8,i, hue--);
            drawLine6(xres-8,10,10,i, hue--);
        }
        getch();
```

/*

```
+-----------------------------------------------------------+
|                                                           |
|          640 x 350 Pixel x 16 Color Mode 16               |
|                                                           |
|      Line Pattern using drawRect1() and drawLine5()       |
|                                                           |
+-----------------------------------------------------------+
```

*/

```
        xres = 640;
        yres = 350;
        setMode(16);
        LINEWIDTH = 5;
        drawRect1(6,8,xres-6,yres-4,11);
        LINEWIDTH = 1;
        for (i=30; i< yres-10; i+=20)
            drawLine5(10,10,xres-6,i,13);
        for (i=30; i< yres-10; i+=20)
            drawLine5(634,yres-4,10,i,14);
        for (i=30; i< yres-10; i+=20)
            drawLine5(10,yres-4,xres-6,i,10);
        for (i=30; i< yres-10; i+=20)
            drawLine5(xres-6,10,10,i,12);
        getch();
```

/*

```
+-----------------------------------------------------------+
|                                                           |
|          640 x 350 Pixel x 16 color Mode 16               |
|                                                           |
|          Lines at an angle using drawLine(7)              |
|                                                           |
+-----------------------------------------------------------+
```

*/

(continued)

```
xres = 640;
yres = 350;
setMode(16);
while (ch != 0x0D)
{
    cls(1)
    for (i=0; i<80; i++)
    {
        length = random(80)+20;
        color = random(15) + 1;
        if (color == 1)
            color = 0;
        xs = random(640);
        ys = random(350);
        for (j=0; j<3600; j+=150,length/=1.02)
        {
            drawLine7(xs, ys, length, j, color);
        }
    }
    ch = getch();
}

/*
```

```
          640 x 350 Pixel x 16 Color Mode 16

  Wide Line Comparison between drawLine3() and drawLine5()
```

```
*/

    LINEWIDTH = 16;
    color = 13;
    cls(0);
    drawLine3(20,20,300,20,color);
    drawLine3(20,160,300,160,color);
    drawLine3(20,20,20,160,color);
    drawLine3(300,20,300,160,color);
    drawLine3(20,20,300,160,color);
    drawLine3(20,160,300,20,color);
    color = 14;
```

(continued)

165

```
    drawLine5(350,200,630,200,color);
    drawLine5(350,340,630,340,color);
    drawLine5(350,200,350,340,color);
    drawLine5(630,200,630,340,color);
    drawLine5(350,200,630,340,color);
    drawLine5(350,340,630,200,color);
    getch();
```

```
/*
```

┌───┐
│ ┌───┐ │
│ │   │ │
│ │   640 x 350 Pixel x 16 Color Mode 16   │ │
│ │   │ │
│ │   Wide Line End Test for drawLine4()   │ │
│ │   │ │
│ └───┘ │
└───┘

```
*/
```

```
    LINEWIDTH = 1;
    color = 1;
    cls(0);
    for(j=10; j<320; j+=120)
    {
        for(i=10; i<550   ; i+=160)
        {
            drawLine4(i,j,i+xlength,j+ylength,
                color);
            drawLine4(i,j+ylength,i+xlength,j,
                color);
            drawLine4(i,j,i+xlength,j,color);
            drawLine4(i,j+ylength,i+xlength, j+ylength,
                color);
            drawLine4(i,j,i,j+ylength,color);
            drawLine4(i+xlength,j,i+xlength, j+ylength,
                color);
            color++;
            if (color == 0)
                color++;
            LINEWIDTH++;
        }
    }
    getch();
```

(continued)

```
/*
```

```
                  640 x 480 Pixel x 16 Color Mode 18

                  Wide Line End Test for drawLine(5)
```

```
*/
    xres = 640;
    yres = 480;
    setMode(18);
    LINEWIDTH = 1;
    color = 1;
    cls(0);
    for(j=10; j<320; j+=120)
    {
        for(i=10; i<550   ; i+=160)
        {
            drawLine5(i,j,i+xlength,j+ylength,color);
            drawLine5(i,j+ylength,i+xlength,j,
                color);
            drawLine5(i,j,i+xlength,j,color);
            drawLine5(i,j+ylength,i+xlength, j+ylength,
                color);
            drawLine5(i,j,i,j+ylength,color);
            drawLine5(i+xlength,j,i+xlength, j+ylength,
                color);
            color++;
            if (color == 0)
                color++;
            LINEWIDTH++;
        }
    }
    getch();
}
```

(continued)

```
/*
┌─────────────────────────────────────────────────────────────┐
│ ┌─────────────────────────────────────────────────────────┐ │
│ │                                                         │ │
│ │         640 x 480 Pixel x 16 Color Mode 18              │ │
│ │                                                         │ │
│ │         Damped Sine Wave Using drawLine8()              │ │
│ │                                                         │ │
│ └─────────────────────────────────────────────────────────┘ │
└─────────────────────────────────────────────────────────────┘
*/

    setMode(18);
    xres = 640;
    yres = 480;
    LINEWIDTH = 3;
    X = 0;
    Y = 240;
    cls(2);
    for (i=0; i<=256; i++)
    {
        y = 240 - (220 * pow(2.718,-.01*i) *
            sin(6.283 * ((double)i)/64));
        x = 620 * (double)i/256;
        drawLine8 (x, y, 14);
        X = x;
        Y = y;
    }
    getch();

/*
┌─────────────────────────────────────────────────────────────┐
│ ┌─────────────────────────────────────────────────────────┐ │
│ │                                                         │ │
│ │         640 x 480 Pixel x 16 Color Mode 18              │ │
│ │                                                         │ │
│ │         Random Spirals Using drawLine8()                │ │
│ │                                                         │ │
│ └─────────────────────────────────────────────────────────┘ │
└─────────────────────────────────────────────────────────────┘
*/

    xres = 640;
    yres = 480;
    color = 1;
    LINEWIDTH = 1;
    setMode(18);
```

(continued)

```
    for (k=0; k<75; k++)
    {
        denom = random(40) + 8;
        xs = random(xres);
        X = xs;
        ys = random(yres);
        Y = ys;
        r = 2;
        iter = random(8) + 2;
        for (i=0; i<10; i++)
        {
            if (i>=iter)
                break;
            for (j=0; j<360; j+=2)
            {
                xb = xs + (r/denom) *
                    (cos(0.017453292 * j));
                yb = ys + (r/denom) *
                    (sin(0.017453292 * j));
                drawLine8(xb,yb,color);
                r++;
            }
        }
        color++;
        if (color == 16)
            color = 1;
    }
    getch();
}

/*
```

```
                 setMode() = Sets Video Mode
```

```
*/

void setMode(int mode)
{
    union REGS reg;
```

(continued)

```
    reg.h.ah = 0;
    reg.h.al = mode;
    int86 (0x10,&reg,&reg);
}
```

```
/*
```

```
         cls() = Clears the Screen to a Given Color
```

```
*/
```

```
void cls(int color)
{
    union REGS reg;

    reg.x.ax = 0x0600;
    reg.x.cx = 0;
    reg.x.dx = 0x3284;
    reg.h.bh = color;
    int86(0x10,&reg,&reg);
}
```

```
/*
```

```
    drawVertLine1 = Draws a vertical line on the screen
                    between two designated points using
                    a selected color for 256 color modes.
```

```
*/
```

```
void drawVertLine1(int x, int ystart, int yend, int color)
{
    int y;
    char far *address;

    for (y=ystart; y<=yend; y++)
    {
        address = (char far *) 0xA0000000L + (long)y * xres
```

(continued)

```
                + (long) x;
            *address = color;
        }
    }

/*
```

```
    drawVertLine2 = Draws a vertical line on the screen
                    between two designated points using
                    a selected color for 16 color modes.
```

```
*/

void drawVertLine2(int x, int ystart, int yend, int color)
{
    #define graph_out(index,val)  {outp(0x3CE,index);\
                                    outp(0x3CF,val);}

    int dummy, mask, y;
    char far * address;

    graph_out(5,2);
    mask = 0x80 >> (x % 8);
    graph_out(8,mask);
    for (y=ystart; y<=yend; y++)
    {
        address = (char far *) 0xA0000000L + (long)y *
            xres/8L + ((long)x / 8L);
        dummy = *address;
        *address = color;
    }
    graph_out(8,0xFF);
    graph_out(5,0);
}
```

(continued)

```
/*

       drawVertLine3 = Draws a vertical line of designated
                       width between two designated points
                       on screen using a selected color and
                       256 color video modes.

*/

void drawVertLine3(int x, int ystart, int yend, int color)
{
    struct SREGS segregs;

    int y, width, color_fill[640];
    unsigned long int style_mask;
    int srcseg, srcoff, destseg=0xA000, destoff;

    segread(&segregs);
    srcseg = segregs.ds;
    srcoff = (int) color_fill;
    width = LINEWIDTH/2;
    memset(color_fill,color,640);
    style_mask = 0x80000000L;
    for (y=ystart; y<=yend; y++)
    {
        style_mask = style_mask !=1 ? style_mask >> 1: \
            0x80000000;
        if (style_mask & PATTERN)
        {
            destoff = (long)y * xres + ((long)(x-width));
            movedata(srcseg,srcoff,destseg,destoff,
                LINEWIDTH);
        }
    }
}
```

(continued)

```
/*
```

```
    drawVertLine4 = Draws a vertical line of designated
                    width between two designated points
                    on screen using a selected color and
                    16 color video modes.
```

```
  */
```

```c
void drawVertLine4(int x, int ystart, int yend, int color)
{
    #define graph_out(index,val)  {outp(0x3CE,index);\
                            outp(0x3CF,val);}
    int dummy, i, mask=0, y, width;
    unsigned long int style_mask;
    char far * address;

    width = LINEWIDTH/2;
    graph_out(5,2);
    for (i=-width; i<=width; i++)
    {
        style_mask = 0x80000000L;
        mask |= (0x80 >> ((x+i) % 8));
        if ((((x+i) % 8) == 7) || (i==width))
        {
            graph_out(8,mask);
            for (y=ystart; y<=yend; y++)
            {
                style_mask = style_mask !=1 ? \
                    style_mask>>1 : 0x80000000;
                if (style_mask & PATTERN)
                {
                    address = (char far *) 0xA0000000L +
                        (long)y * xres /8L +
                        ((long)(x+i)/8L);
                    dummy = *address;
                    *address = color;
                }
            }
            mask = 0;
```

(continued)

```
            }
        }
        graph_out(8,0xFF);
        graph_out(5,0);
    }

/*
```

```
        drawHorzLine1 = Draws a horizontal line of designated
                        width between two designated points
                        on screen using a selected color and
                        256 color video modes.
```

```
*/

    void drawHorzLine1(int xstart, int xend, int y, int color)
    {
        char far * address;
        char line_store[1024];
        int x1, x2, length, width;
        int srcseg, srcoff, destseg, destoff;

        struct SREGS segregs;

        segread(&segregs);
        srcseg = segregs.ds;
        srcoff = (int) line_store;
        width = LINEWIDTH/2;
        x1 = min(xstart, xend) - width;
        x2 = max(xstart, xend) + width;
        length = (x2 - x1);
        memset(line_store,color,length);
        for (i=-width; i<=width; i++)
        {
            destseg = 0xA000;
            destoff = ((long) (y+i) * xres + ((long)x1)) + 1;
            movedata(srcseg, srcoff, destseg, destoff, length);
        }
    }
```

(continued)

```
/*
```

```
    drawHorzLine2 = Draws a horizontal line of designated
         width between two designated points on screen
              using a selected color and 16 color
                        video modes.
```

```
*/
```

```c
void drawHorzLine2(int xstart, int xend, int y, int color)
{
    #define graph_out(index,val)   {outp(0x3CE,index);\
                           outp(0x3CF,val);}
    char line_store[100];
    int dummy, i, x1, x2;
    int length, width, offset1, offset2;
    int srcseg, srcoff, destseg, destoff;
    long no_of_bytes;
    unsigned char mask;
    char far *start_address;
    char far *end_address;

    struct SREGS segregs;

    segread(&segregs);
    srcseg = segregs.ds;
    srcoff = (int) line_store;
    width = LINEWIDTH/2;
    x1 = min(xstart, xend) - width;
    x2 = max(xstart, xend) + width;
    offset1 = x1 % 8;
    offset2 = x2 % 8;
    length = ((x2 - x1) - ((8-offset1) + (offset2))) / 8L;
    for (i=-width; i<=width; i++)
    {
        start_address = (char far *)(0xA0000000L +
            ((long)(y+i) * xres/8L + ((long)x1 / 8L)));
        end_address = (char far *)(0xA0000000L +
            ((long)(y+i) * xres/8L + ((long)x2 / 8L)));
        no_of_bytes = end_address - start_address;
```

(continued)

```
                    mask = 0xFF << (7 - offset2);
                    if (!no_of_bytes)
                        mask &= 0xFF >> offset1;
                    dummy = *end_address;
                    graph_out(5,2);
                    graph_out(8,mask);
                    *end_address = color;
                    if (no_of_bytes)
                    {
                        mask = 0xFF >> offset1;
                        graph_out(8, mask);
                        *start_address = color;
                        graph_out(8, 0xFF);
                        memset(line_store,color,length);
                        destseg = 0xA000;
                        destoff = ((long) (y+i) * 80L + ((long)x1/8L))
                            + 1;
                        movedata(srcseg, srcoff, destseg, destoff,
                            length);
                    }
                }
            graph_out(8,0xFF);
            graph_out(5,0);
        }


    /*

    ┌─────────────────────────────────────────────────────────┐
    │                                                         │
    │  drawRect1() = Draws a rectangle in a selected color and │
    │       with a specified line width for 16 color modes.   │
    │                                                         │
    └─────────────────────────────────────────────────────────┘
    */

    void drawRect1(int x_one, int y_one, int x_two, int y_two,

        int color)
    {
        #define graph_out(index,val)  {outp(0x3CE,index);\
                            outp(0x3CF,val);}
        #define seq_out(index,val)  {outp(0x3C4,index);\
                            outp(0x3C5,val);}
```

(continued)

```
int j, page, x[2], y, offset, offset1, offset2;
char far * mem_address;
char line_store[100];
int dummy, i, x1, x2;
int length, width;
int srcseg, srcoff, destseg, destoff;
long no_of_bytes;
unsigned char mask;
char far *start_address1;
char far *start_address2;
char far *end_address1;
char far *end_address2;

struct SREGS segregs;

segread(&segregs);
srcseg = segregs.ds;
srcoff = (int) line_store;
width = LINEWIDTH/2;
x[0] = x_one;
x[1] = x_two;
for (i=-width; i<=width; i++)
{
    x1 = min(x_one, x_two) - width;
    x2 = max(x_one, x_two) + width;
    offset1 = x1 % 8;
    offset2 = x2 % 8;
    start_address1 = (char far *)(0xA0000000L +
        ((long)(y_one+i) * xres/8L + ((long)x1/8L)));
    end_address1 = (char far *)(0xA0000000L +
        ((long)(y_one+i) * xres/8L + ((long)x2/8L)));
    start_address2 = (char far *)(0xA0000000L +
        ((long)(y_two+i) * xres/8L + ((long)x1/8L)));
    end_address2 = (char far *)(0xA0000000L +
        ((long)(y_two+i) * xres/8L + ((long)x2/8L)));
    no_of_bytes = end_address1 - start_address1;
    length = ((x2 - x1) - ((8-offset1) +
        (offset2)))/8L;
    graph_out(5,2);
    mask = 0xFF << (7 - offset2);
    if (!no_of_bytes)
```

(continued)

```
                        mask &= 0xFF >> offset1;
                    graph_out(8,mask);
                    dummy = *end_address1;
                    *end_address1 = color;
                    dummy = *end_address2;
                    *end_address2 = color;
                    if (no_of_bytes)
                    {
                        mask = 0xFF >> offset1;
                        graph_out(8, mask);
                        *start_address1 = color;
                        *start_address2 = color;
                        graph_out(8, 0xFF);
                        memset(line_store,color,length);
                        destseg = 0xA000;
                        destoff = ((long)(y_one+i) * 80L +
                            ((long)x1/8L)) + 1;
                        movedata(srcseg, srcoff, destseg, destoff,
                            length);
                        destoff = ((long)(y_two+i) * 80L +
                            ((long)x1/8L)) + 1;
                        movedata(srcseg, srcoff, destseg, destoff,
                            length);
                    }
                }
                graph_out(8,0xFF);
                for (j=0; j<2; j++)
                {
                    for (i=-width; i<=width; i++)
                    {
                        mask|= (0x80 >> ((x[j]+i) % 8));
                        if ((((x[j]+i) % 8) == 7) || (i==width))
                        {
                            graph_out(8,mask);
                            for (y=y_one; y<=y_two; y++)
                            {
                                mem_address = (char far *) 0xA0000000L +
                                    (long)y * xres/8L +
                                    ((long)(x[j]+i)/8L);
                                dummy = *mem_address;
                                *mem_address = color;
```

(continued)

```
                    }
                  mask == 0;
              }
          }
      }
    graph_out(8,0xFF);
    graph_out(1,0x00);
    graph_out(5,0);
}


/*
```

```
  drawRect2() = Draws a rectangle in a selected color and
  with a specified line width in 256 color Mode 13.
```

```
*/

void drawRect2(int x_one, int y_one, int x_two, int y_two,
    int color)
{
    int j, page, x[2], y;
    char far * mem_address;
    char line_store[1024];
    int i, x1, x2;
    int length, width, offset, offset1, offset2;
    int srcseg, srcoff, destseg, destoff;

    struct SREGS segregs;

    segread(&segregs);
    srcseg = segregs.ds;
    srcoff = (int) line_store;
    width = LINEWIDTH/2;
    x[0] = x_one;
    x[1] = x_two;
    for (i=-width; i<=width; i++)
    {
        x1 = min(x_one, x_two) - width;
        x2 = max(x_one, x_two) + width;
        length = (x2 - x1);
```

(continued)

```
        memset(line_store,color,length);
        destseg = 0xA000;
        destoff = ((long) (y_one+i) * xres + ((long)x1)) +
            1;
        movedata(srcseg, srcoff, destseg, destoff, length);
        destoff = ((long) (y_two+i) * xres + ((long)x1)) +
            1;
        movedata(srcseg, srcoff, destseg, destoff, length);
    }
    for (j=0; j<2; j++)
    {
        memset(line_store,color,LINEWIDTH);
        for (y=y_one; y<=y_two; y++)
        {
            destoff = (long)y * xres + ((long)(x[j] -
                width));
            movedata(srcseg,srcoff,destseg,destoff,
                LINEWIDTH);
        }
    }
}


/*
```

```
    drawLine1() = Draws a single pixel wide line in a
       selected color using the plot function. Will
       work with any plot function. The one used in
       this example is for mode 16 (640 x 350 pixels
                    by 16 colors.
```

```
*/

void drawLine1(int xs, int ys, int xe, int ye, int color)
{

    int temp, dx, dy, i, x, y, x_sign, y_sing, decision;

    dx = abs(xe - xs);
    dy = abs(ye - ys);
    if (((dx > dy) && (xs > xe)) || ((dy > dx) && (ys >
```

(continued)

```
        ye)))
{
    temp = xs;
    xs = xe;
    xe = temp;
    temp = ys;
    ys = ye;
    ye = temp;
}
if ((ye - ys) < 0)
    y_sign = -1;
else
    y_sign = 1;
if ((xe - xs) < 0)
    x_sign = -1;
else
    x_sign = 1;
if (dx > dy)
{
    for (x=xs,y=ys,decision=0; x<=xe; x++,decision+=dy)
    {
        if (decision>=dx)
        {
            decision -= dx;
            y+= y_sign;
        }
        plot16(x,y,color);
    }
}
else
{
    for (x=xs,y=ys,decision=0; y<=ye;y++,decision+=dx)
    {
        if (decision>=dy)
        {
            decision -= dy;
            x += x_sign;
        }
        plot16(x,y,color);
    }
}
```

(continued)

```
}

/*
```

```
    drawLine2() = Draws a single pixel wide line from one
                  set of coordinates to another in
                  designated color using 256
                       color modes.
```

```
*/

void drawLine2(int xs, int ys, int xe, int ye, int color)
{
    int temp, dx, dy, i, x, y, x_sign, y_sign, decision;

    dx = abs(xe - xs);
    dy = abs(ye - ys);
    if (((dx > dy) && (xs > xe)) || ((dy > dx) && (ys >
        ye)))
    {
        temp = xs;
        xs = xe;
        xe = temp;
        temp = ys;
        ys = ye;
        ye = temp;
    }
    if ((ye - ys) < 0)
        y_sign = -1;
    else
        y_sign = 1;
    if ((xe - xs) < 0)
        x_sign = -1;
    else
        x_sign = 1;
    if (dx > dy)
    {
        for (x=xs,y=ys,decision=0; x<=xe; x++,decision+=dy)
        {
            if (decision>=dx)
```

(continued)

```
                {
                    decision -= dx;
                    y+= y_sign;
                }
                plot256(x,y,color);
            }
        }
        else
        {
            for (x=xs,y=ys,decision=0; y<=ye; y++,decision+=dx)
            {
                if (decision>=dy)
                {
                    decision -= dy;
                    x += x_sign;
                }
                plot256(x,y,color);
            }
        }
    }

/*
```

```
    drawLine3() = Draws a line of designated width from one
        set of coordinates to another in designated color
            plotting blocks of pixels to create width for
                        16 color modes.
```

```
*/

void drawLine3(int xs, int ys, int xe, int ye, int color)
{
    extern int LINEWIDTH;
    extern unsigned long int PATTERN;

    int temp, dx, dy, i, j, k, x, y, x_sign, y_sign,
        decision, width;
    unsigned long int mask;

    width = LINEWIDTH/2;
```

(continued)

```
dx = abs(xe - xs);
dy = abs(ye - ys);
if (((dx > dy) && (xs > xe)) || ((dy > dx) && (ys >
    ye)))
{
    temp = xs;
    xs = xe;
    xe = temp;
    temp = ys;
    ys = ye;
    ye = temp;
}
if ((ye - ys) < 0)
    y_sign = -1;
else
    y_sign = 1;
if ((xe - xs) < 0)
    x_sign = -1;
else
    x_sign = 1;
if (dx > dy)
{
    for (x=xs,y=ys,decision=0; x<=xe; x++,decision+=dy)
    {
        mask = mask !=1 ? mask >> 1 : 0x80000000;
        if (decision>=dx)
        {
            decision -= dx;
            y+= y_sign;
        }
        if (PATTERN & mask)
            for (j=-width; j<=width; j++)
            {
                for (k=-width; k<=width; k++)
                    plot16(x+k,y+j,color);
            }
    }
}
else
{
    for (x=xs,y=ys,decision=0; y<=ye; y++,decision+=dx)
```

(continued)

```
        {
            mask = mask !=1 ? mask >> 1 : 0x80000000;
            if (decision>=dy)
            {
                decision -= dy;
                x += x_sign;
            }
            if (PATTERN & mask)
                for (j=-width; j<=width; j++)
                {
                    for (k=-width; k<=width; k++)
                        plot16(x+k,y+j,color);
                }
        }
    }
}

/*
```

```
drawLine4() = Draws a line from one set of coordinates to
        another in designated color choosing proper
        direction for width but no compensating at
            end points. This function for 16
                    color modes.
```

```
*/

void drawLine4(int xs, int ys, int xe, int ye, int color)
{

    extern int LINEWIDTH;
    extern unsigned long int PATTERN;

    int temp, dx, dy, i, j, x, y, x_sign, y_sign,
        decision;
    unsigned long int mask;

    dx = abs(xe - xs);
    dy = abs(ye - ys);
    if (((dx > dy) && (xs > xe)) || ((dy > dx) && (ys >
```

(continued)

```
        ye)))
    {
        temp = xs;
        xs = xe;
        xe = temp;
        temp = ys;
        ys = ye;
        ye = temp;
    }
    if ((ye - ys) < 0)
        y_sign = -1;
    else
        y_sign = 1;
    if ((xe - xs) < 0)
        x_sign = -1;
    else
        x_sign = 1;
    if (dx > dy)
    {
        for (x=xs,y=ys,decision=0; x<=xe; x++,decision+=dy)
        {
            mask = mask !=1 ? mask >> 1 : 0x80000000;
            if (decision>=dx)
            {
                decision -= dx;
                y+= y_sign;
            }
            if (PATTERN & mask)
                for (j=-LINEWIDTH/2; j<=LINEWIDTH/2; j++)
                    plot16(x,y+j,color);
        }
    }
    else
    {
        for (x=xs,y=ys,decision=0; y<=ye; y++,decision+=dx)
        {
            mask = mask !=1 ? mask >> 1 : 0x80000000;
            if (decision>=dy)
            {
                decision -= dy;
                x += x_sign;
```

(continued)

```
            }
         if (PATTERN & mask)
            for (j=-LINEWIDTH/2; j<=LINEWIDTH/2; j++)
                plot16(x+j,y,color);
      }
   }
}
```

```
/*
```

```
drawLine5() = Draws a line from one set of coordinates to
another in designated color choosing proper direction for
 width and compensating at end points. This function for
                    16 color modes.
```

```
*/
```

```
void drawLine5(int xs, int ys, int xe, int ye, int color)
{
    extern int LINEWIDTH;
    extern unsigned long int PATTERN;

    int temp, dx, dy, i, j, k, x, y, x_sign, y_sign,
        decision, width;
    unsigned long int mask;

    width = LINEWIDTH >> 1;
    dx = abs(xe - xs);
    dy = abs(ye - ys);
    if (((dx > dy) && (xs > xe)) || ((dy > dx) && (ys >
        ye)))
    {
        temp = xs;
        xs = xe;
        xe = temp;
        temp = ys;
        ys = ye;
        ye = temp;
    }
    if ((ye - ys) < 0)
```

(continued)

```
        y_sign = -1;
    else
        y_sign = 1;
    if ((xe - xs) < 0)
        x_sign = -1;
    else
        x_sign = 1;
    if (dx > dy)
    {
        for (x=xs,y=ys,decision=0; x<=xe; x++,decision+=dy)
        {
            mask = mask !=1 ? mask >> 1 : 0x80000000;
            if (decision>=dx)
            {
                decision -= dx;
                y+= y_sign;
            }
            if (PATTERN & mask)
                for (j=-width; j<=width; j++)
                {
                    if ((x!=xs) && (x!=xe))
                        plot16(x,y+j,color);
                    else
                        for (k=-width; k<=width; k++)
                            plot16(x+k,y+j, color);
                }
        }
    }
    else
    {
        for (x=xs,y=ys,decision=0; y<=ye;
            y++,decision+=dx)
        {
            mask = mask !=1 ? mask >> 1 : 0x80000000;
            if (decision>=dy)
            {
                decision -= dy;
                x += x_sign;
            }
            if (PATTERN & mask)
                for (j=-width; j<=width; j++)
```

(continued)

```
                        {
                            if ((y!=ys) && (y!= ye))
                                plot16(x+j,y, color);
                            else
                                for (k=-width; k<=width; k++)
                                    plot16 (x+j, y+k, color);
                        }
                }
            }
    }

/*
```

```
┌─────────────────────────────────────────────────────────────┐
│ ┌───────────────────────────────────────────────────────── │
│ │                                                           │
│ │   drawLine6() = Draws a line from one set of coordinates to│
│ │ another in designated color choosing proper direction for │
│ │   width but no compensating at end points. This function  │
│ │                   for 256 color modes.                    │
│ │                                                           │
│ └───────────────────────────────────────────────────────── │
└─────────────────────────────────────────────────────────────┘
```

```
*/

void drawLine6(int xs, int ys, int xe, int ye, int color)
{
    extern int LINEWIDTH;
    extern unsigned long int PATTERN;

    int temp, dx, dy, i, j, x, y, x_sign, y_sign,
        decision;
    unsigned long int mask;

    dx = abs(xe - xs);
    dy = abs(ye - ys);
    if (((dx > dy) && (xs > xe)) || ((dy > dx) && (ys >
        ye)))
    {
        temp = xs;
        xs = xe;
        xe = temp;
        temp = ys;
        ys = ye;
        ye = temp;
```

(continued)

```
    }
    if ((ye - ys) < 0)
        y_sign = -1;
    else
        y_sign = 1;
    if ((xe - xs) < 0)
        x_sign = -1;
    else
        x_sign = 1;
    if (dx > dy)
    {
        for (x=xs,y=ys,decision=0; x<=xe; x++,decision+=dy)
        {
            mask = mask !=1 ? mask >> 1 : 0x80000000;
            if (decision>=dx)
            {
                decision -= dx;
                y+= y_sign;
            }
            if (PATTERN & mask)
                for (j=-LINEWIDTH/2; j<=LINEWIDTH/2; j++)
                plot256(x,y+j,color);
        }
    }
    else
    {
        for (x=xs,y=ys,decision=0; y<=ye; y++,decision+=dx)
        {
            mask = mask !=1 ? mask >> 1 : 0x80000000;
            if (decision>=dy)
            {
                decision -= dy;
                x += x_sign;
            }
            if (PATTERN & mask)
                for (j=-LINEWIDTH/2; j<=LINEWIDTH/2; j++)
                    plot256(x+j,y,color);
        }
    }
}
```

(continued)

```
/*

    drawLine7() = Draws a single pixel wide line in a
        selected color from the starting coordinates
          specified for a given length in a given
             direction using mode 16 (640 x 350
                    pixels x 16 colors).

*/

void drawLine7(int xs, int ys, int length, int angle,
    int color)
{
    int temp, dx, dy, xe, ye, i, x, y, x_sign, y_sign,
        decision;

    xe = xs + length * (cos(0.0017453292 * angle);
    ye = ys - length * (sin(0.0017453292 * angle);
    dx = abs(xe - xs);
    dy = abs(ye - ys);
    if (((dx > dy) && (xs > xe)) || ((dy > dx) && (ys >
        ye)))
    {
        temp = xs;
        xs = xe;
        xe = temp;
        temp = ys;
        ys = ye;
        ye = temp;
    }
    if ((ye - ys) < 0)
        y_sign = -1;
    else
        y_sign = 1;
    if ((xe - xs) < 0)
        x_sign = -1;
    else
        x_sign = 1;
    if (dx > dy)
    {
```

(continued)

```
              for (x=xs,y=ys,decision=0; x<=xe; x++,decision+=dy)
              {
                   if (decision>=dx)
                   {
                        decision -= dx;
                        y+= y_sign;
                   }
                   plot256(x,y,color);
              }
         }
         else
         {
              for (x=xs,y=ys,decision=0; y<=ye; y++,decision+=dx)
              {
                   if (decision>=dy)
                   {
                        decision -= dy;
                        x += x_sign;
                   }
                   plot256(x,y,color);
              }
         }
    }

/*
```

```
    drawLine8() = Draws a line from current position (in
         (X,Y) to a designated set of coordinates in a
            specified color using line width specified
                 by LINEWIDTH for 16 color modes.
```

```
*/

void drawLine8(int xe, int ye, int color)
{
    extern int LINEWIDTH;
    extern unsigned long int PATTERN;
    extern int X, Y;

    int dx, dy, i, j, temp, x, y, xs, ys, x_sign, y_sign,
        decision;
```

(continued)

```
unsigned long int mask;

xs = X;
ys = Y;
X = xe;
Y = ye;
dx = abs(xe - xs);
dy = abs(ye - ys);
if (((dx >= dy) && (xs > xe)) || ((dy > dx) && (ys >
    ye)))
{
    temp = xs;
    xs = xe;
    xe = temp;
    temp = ys;
    ys = ye;
    ye = temp;
}
if ((ye - ys) < 0)
    y_sign = -1;
else
    y_sign = 1;
if ((xe - xs) < 0)
    x_sign = -1;
else
    x_sign = 1;
if (dx >= dy)
{
    for (x=xs,y=ys,decision=0; x<=xe; x++,decision+=dy)
    {
        mask = mask !=1 ? mask >> 1 : 0x80000000;
        if (decision>=dx)
        {
            decision -= dx;
            y+= y_sign;
        }
        if (PATTERN & mask)
            for (j=-LINEWIDTH/2; j<=LINEWIDTH/2; j++)
                plot16(x,y+j,color);
    }
```

(continued)

```
}
```

```
        else
        {
            for (x=xs,y=ys,decision=0; y<=ye; y++,decision+=dx)
            {
                mask = mask !=1 ? mask >> 1 : 0x80000000;
                if (decision>=dy)
                {
                    decision -= dy;
                    x += x_sign;
                }
                if (PATTERN & mask)
                    for (j=-LINEWIDTH/2; j<=LINEWIDTH/2; j++)
                        plot16(x+j,y,color);
            }
        }
}

/*
```

```
  plot16() = Plots a point on the screen at the designated
  position using a selected color for the 16 color modes.
```

```
*/

void plot16(int x, int y, int color)
{
    #define graph_out(index,val)   {outp(0x3CE,index);\
                               outp(0x3CF,val);}
    int dummy,mask;
    char far * address;

    address = (char far *) 0xA0000000L + (long)y * xres/8L
        + ((long)x / 8L);
    mask = 0x80 >> (x % 8);
    graph_out(8,mask);
    graph_out(5,2);
    dummy = *address;
    *address = color;
    graph_out(5,0);
```

(continued)

```
    graph_out(8,0xFF);
```

```
}

/*
```

```
    plot256() = Plots a point on the screen at a designated
        position using a selected color for the 256 color
                            modes.
```

```
*/

void plot256(int x, int y, int color)
{
    char far * address;
    address = (char far *) 0xA0000000L + (long)y * xres +
        (long)x;
    *address = color;
}

/*
```

```
  setVGApalette() = Function to set all 256 color registers
```

```
*/

void setVGApalette(unsigned char *buffer)
{
    struct SREGS inreg;
    union REGS reg;

    reg.x.ax = 0x1012;
    segread(&inreg);
    inreg.es = inreg.ds;
    reg.x.bx = 0;
    reg.x.cx = 256;
    reg.x.dx = (int)&buffer[0];
    int86x(0x10,&reg,&reg,&inreg);
}
```

Drawing Vertical Lines in 256 Colors

One of the advantages of creating your own graphics functions is that you can simplify each function to do only the job that you need to have done, and nothing more. The first function that we are going to describe is extremely simple. It draws a vertical line one pixel wide, given an *x* coordinate and beginning and ending *y* coordinates using the 256 color mode (mode 19). This is the function *drawVertLine1* in the program listing. You will note a similarity between this and the function *plot256*, which plots a pixel to the screen in the 256 color modes. The *plot256* function simply determines the display memory address for the pixel by multiplying the row value by the number of pixels in a row (*xres*), adding the column position, and adding the base display memory address. The specified color (0 to 255) is then written to this memory address. (The internal logic of the VGA causes the color information to be stored at the proper point on the proper memory plane.) The *drawVertLine1* function differs only in that the pixel drawing actions are included within a *for* loop that iterates, starting with the initial row value and incrementing the row on each iteration, until the ending row value is operated upon.

Drawing Vertical Lines in 16 Colors

The function for drawing one pixel wide vertical lines in the 16 color modes, *drawVertLine2*, bears a similarity to the *plot16* function that plots pixels to the screen in the 16 color modes. Because each bit of a memory byte represents one pixel (which of the 16 colors is to appear is determined by the color planes that are written to) some VGA register manipulation and masking is required. All of this is explained in detail in the previous chapter. Fortunately, for a particular column, the register manipulation and masking is the same for every row, so the register operations need only be performed once. The pixels are then written within a *for* loop just as for the previous function. Since each byte now represents eight pixels, we have to divide by eight to get the right memory address and then use a mask to select the proper pixel within a byte. Unlike the 256 color mode, when using the 16 color mode, you must first do a dummy read at the selected memory address to set up the internal registers properly to accept the pixel information that is coming. When the loop is complete, the registers must be reset to their nominal values, whereupon the line drawing is complete.

Vertical Lines with Width and Style

If all you require in your program is a simple single pixel width line, you can select one of the two preceding vertical line functions, depending upon which display mode you are using. This is an advantage of tailoring your own graphic functions. The designer of a generalized graphics library has to decide just how many options to allow for a particular function. To make it compatible with all possible display modes, requires a number of tests which will slow down the function's operation. If extra features are needed, such as different widths or styles of lines, then the overhead for these operations slows down the function even when they aren't being used. Thus, by custom designing your own functions, you can include only the features you really need.

Now let's look look at how the vertical line drawing functions are modified to include drawing wide lines and lines having a repetitive pattern such as dashed lines, dotted lines, or center lines. The function to do this for 256 color modes is *drawVertLine3* and that for 16 color modes is *drawVertLine4*. First, let's just consider the generating of wide lines. If you observe carefully how this is done in the two functions, you can then introduce your own modifications to customize the functions to your requirements. The *drawVertLine3* function begins by finding the beginning address (in terms of segment and offset) for an array called *color_fill*. This array is 640 bytes long, which is adequate for all normal EGA and VGA graphics modes; if you are using a Super VGA mode, you may want to make it match the longest line length of your high resolution functions. The function uses the *memset* instruction to fill this array with the color to be drawn. Now, as with the single pixel function, we enter a *for* loop that iterates once for each value of *y*. Within that loop, we determine the offset part of the display memory address for the lefthand pixel of the wide line. We then use the *movedata* instruction to transfer a number of bytes corresponding to the line width from the *color_fill* array to display memory beginning at the selected address. Note that this technique, which is used in this and a number of the functions that follow, works only for the Tiny, Small, and Medium memory models of the Borland family of C compilers. For larger memory models, you will have to generate the address of the *color_fill* array differently.

Let's look at how we create line styles. Before beginning the line drawing loop, we set up a long integer called *style_mask* consisting of a single bit in the most significant position. Within the loop, we shift this bit one bit to the left at each loop iteration. When the bit reaches the least significant position, it is cycled around to the most significant position again. In the *Linetest.c* program is an array of eight long integers called *style* that contains line patterns. The first is 0xFFFFFFFF, which fills every bit with a 1 and thereby defines solid lines. Next is 0xC0C0C0C0, which is the binary pattern 11001100110011001100110011001100. The resulting line consists of two pixels followed by two blanks followed by two pixels. Before calling the line drawing function, you transfer one of these patterns (or any pattern of your own) to the global variable *PATTERN*. Within the loop for drawing the vertical line, instead of just drawing each pixel, the function compares *style_mask* with *PATTERN* and draws the pixel on the screen only if there is a one in the pattern at the current mask position. Thus as the loop is iterated to draw the line, the mask scans the selected pattern and reproduces it on the screen. A word of caution, however; the various line patterns are 32 bits long and therefore work well with lines that are 32 pixels long or longer. (Actually most of the patterns cycle more frequently than this and will therefore work reasonably well with smaller lines.) However, if you are using a number of very small line segments to reproduce a curve and you try to use one of the line styles, you may discover that you are using only a part of the pattern in which ones occur, thereby drawing a solid line instead of a patterned one. Worse yet, you may select a part of the pattern that is zeroes and draw nothing at all to the screen. Therefore use considerable care in using line styles with small line segments.

The function *drawVertLine4*, creates wide and stylized lines for the 16 color modes. The technique for creating stylized lines is just the same as for the previous function. The method for drawing wide lines is much different, however, because of the masking that is necessary. We start with a *for* loop that begins with minus half the line width and ends at plus half the line width. Within this loop, we OR together mask bits for each pixel position until we come to the end of a memory byte (identified by the fact that the *x* coordinate is divisible exactly by eight). At this point we run an inner *for* loop for each value of *y*, drawing the pixels represented by the mask on the screen. Thus if the line begins at some intermediate point on the screen, the first set of iterations of the inner loop draws the part of the line from the beginning of the line width to the end of each memory byte. Successive sets of inner loop iterations write a whole memory byte to the screen at once, until the line end is encountered. This last set of iterations of the inner loop draws the part of the line from the end of the last complete byte to the line width end. This method of drawing a wide vertical line is much faster than creating a wide line by drawing a number of one pixel wide vertical lines side by side.

Drawing Horizontal Lines

Because all of the pixels that compose a horizontal line are adjacent in display memory, we can use a very fast drawing technique that requires only three memory accesses, regardless of the line length. These functions are very important because we are going to use them repeatedly in later chapters to fill various geometric figures such as polygons and circles at very high speed. In fact, using the routines to be described here will speed up fill operations by at least an order of magnitude over techniques that plot pixels separately. One drawback, however, is that these functions can draw only solid lines, so that if you need a line of a different style, you will have to use the slower generalized line drawing functions.

The first function to be considered is *drawHorzLine1*. This is the function for drawing lines in the 256 color mode. The function begins by reading and storing the address of a data array called *line_store*. Then the beginning and end of the line (*x1* and *x2*) are set up with the line extended by half the specified line width at each end. This often makes a better fit when lines are joined together. If you don't like this feature drop the plus and minus *width* from the lines defining *x1* and *x2*. Observe that these expressions are set up so that the line is always drawn from left to right (minimum memory address to maximum memory address). The length of the line in memory bytes is then determined. The *line_store* array is then filled with this many bytes of the designated color. Next a *for* loop is entered that is iterated to draw a horizontal line for each pixel of the line width from the row coordinate minus half the line width to the row coordinate plus half the line width (so that the specified y coordinate is at the center of the line width). At each iteration of the loop, the offset for the beginning address in display memory is calculated and the *movedata* instruction is used to transfer the required number of bytes from the *line_store* array to display memory in a single operation which draws the entire horizontal line.

The function to draw a fast horizontal line in the 16 color modes is *drawHorzLine2*. This function is more complicated because these modes describe several pixels within a single byte of memory. The function begins the same way as the previous one. Once we have created the starting and ending points of the line in pixel terms, however, we now have to compute the quantities *offset1* and *offset2*, which are the bit number in a byte where the line starts and ends, respectively. Then the actual memory starting and ending addresses are computed. The number of bytes containing line information is then determined and the length for the byte transfer. We have three situations to consider: (1) the line begins and ends on a byte boundary; (2) the line begins or ends on a byte boundary, but not both; (3) the line neither begins nor ends on a byte boundary. In the first case, the length of the memory transfer is the number of bytes and we can do the transfer in one operation. In the second case, the length is one less than the number of bytes. We have to transfer one byte (at one end of the line) with a special mask; then *length* bytes are transferred in one operation. For the third case, the length is two less than the number of bytes. We have to transfer the beginning and ending bytes with special masks. Then *length* bytes in the middle are transferred in a single operation. Finally, there is a special case of (2) or (3) where the line is less than one byte (8 pixels) long.

The function begins by creating the mask for the ending byte. (If the line ends on a byte boundary, the mask is all ones; otherwise the part of the byte corresponding to the line is filled with ones and the rest of the byte with zeroes.) Now, if the line is less than a byte long, the mask is modified by replacing ones at the left hand side with zeroes so that only positions in the byte corresponding to actual line pixels are ones. The mask is then used to mask of the desired bits in the VGA through the mask register and the desired pixels are written to the display in the same way as for a single pixel in the *plot* function for 16 colors. This ends the function for lines less than a byte long. For longer lines, we next create the proper mask for the beginning of the line, send it to the mask register and write out the beginning byte to the display. Then the *line_store* array is filled with as many bytes of the desired color as are needed for the line memory bytes between the first and the last, the address for the first of these bytes is determined, and a *movedata* instruction is used to move the desired number of bytes from the array to display memory in one operation. This completes the drawing of the line. The display adapter registers are reset to their nominal values and the function terminates.

Drawing Rectangles

Using the vertical and horizontal line drawing functions, you can easily draw rectangles. However, since this type of figure is often used, it is convenient to have functions that are specially designed for rectangle drawing. Such a function for the 16 color modes is *drawRect1*. A corresponding function for 256 color modes is *drawRect2*. These functions just encapsulate the proper vertical and horizontal line drawing functions in a convenient package and make sure that the line lengths are correct. The input parameters are the coordinates of the top left corner of the rectangle, the coordinates of the bottom right corner, and the desired color of the rectangle. You will observe, however, that the vertical line drawing part of each rectangle function omits the feature of drawing stylized lines. The rectangles must be composed of solid lines, since this is all that the horizontal line drawing functions can draw.

Drawing Slanting Lines

Since the computer display screen is composed of discrete pixels, we can never draw a perfect slanting line on the screen. Given a starting point, the best we can do is step to the nearest pixel to the line's true position, and then continue this process until we reach the end of the line. A typical result of this process is shown in Figure 7-2. The result is that, especially for low resolution displays, the line has steps, the so-called jaggies that plague computer display line drawings. First let's take an overview of the situation. For the line shown in the figure, x increases more rapidly than y. Therefore, for each pixel step on the line we know that x is going to increase by one. The only question that remains is whether y will remain the same or increase. This will be determined through the use of a decision function. To obtain this decision function, we are going to use a method called Bresenham's algorithm. This method makes use of the derivative of the function, which is the change in y, given a small change in x. The equation of a line is

$$y = \frac{y_2 - y_1}{x_2 - x_1} x + b$$

(Equation 7-1)

Figure 7-2. Drawing a Line with Discrete Pixels

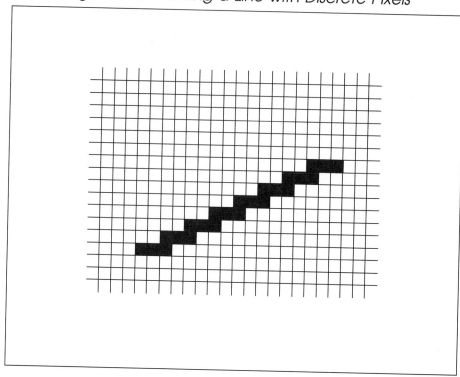

The derivative for a line is

$$dy = \frac{y_2 - y_1}{x_2 - x_1}\, dx$$

(Equation 7-2)

To use the derivative directly, we would let dx be equal to 1, since we are going to increase x by one pixel for each step. We would then increase y by the fractional part of the equation. However, we can actually only increase y in steps of 1, so we keep track of the actual value of y but do not actually increment y on the screen until the actual value of y has increased by 1. This is the first part of Bresenham's algorithm. It is not limited to straight lines, but can be applied to any curve for which we can take the derivative. The second part of Bresenham's algorithm modifies the decision function to speed up operation by eliminating any divisions. To do this, we multiply both sides of the derivative equation by x_2 - x_1. We then set up the decision function so that it starts at 0. Each time we increment x, we increase the decision function by $y_2 - y_1$. When the decision function exceeds $x_2 - x_1$, we increment y and decrease the decision function by $x_2 - x_1$. Mathematically, this is just the same as using the derivative, but it avoids all of the time consuming divisions. Finally, for Bresenham's algorithm to be complete, we need to consider a few other possibilities that have not yet been mentioned. First, the line in the figure is moving upward as it goes from right to left. If it were moving downward, although the derivative would then be negative, we can still use the same values in the decision function, but we have to decrement the y value instead of increment it each time a change in its value is called for. Next, suppose that we have a line with a slope of more than 45 degrees, so that at each step the y value increases, but the x value doesn't necessarily do so. If we use the algorithm as given previously, we will plot only the points where x increases, so although these points will be placed correctly, a lot of points will be left out. We can overcome this situation by interchanging x and y in the procedure.

A Single Pixel Wide Solid Slanting Line

Now we are ready to look at the function *drawLine1*, which draws a single pixel wide line for the 16 color modes. (Note that this function will draw horizontal and vertical lines as well as slanting ones, but the procedures that we have given for vertical and horizontal lines are better and faster. You might want to include all three cases in a single function with *if* statements or a *switch* statement to select the best routine for each line type.) The function begins by finding the distances between the x beginning and ending points and the y beginning and ending points of the line. Next is a complicated if statement which assures that for cases where the line is increasing faster in x than it is in y, the line is drawn from the smallest to the largest x and for cases where the line is increasing faster in y than it is in x, the line is drawn from the smallest to the largest y. Next *x_sign* and *y_sign* are determined. These determine the direction in which the second coordinate is to move for each of the loops that draw the line. Now, if the line is increasing faster in the x direction than in the y direction, we enter a *for* loop that begins at the starting line coordinates and with the decision function zero and continues until the ending x coordinate is reached. At each iteration, the x coordinate is incremented and the decision variable is increased by the y length. Within the loop, if the decision variable exceeds the x length, we reduce it by the x length and move y one unit in the appropriate direction. A point is then plotted to the screen at the current coordinates. For the case where the line is increasing faster in the y direction than in the x direction, the function goes instead to another *for* loop that is exactly the same in structure, except that the operations on x and y are interchanged.

The function *drawLine2* is exactly the same as *drawLine1* except that it calls a different function to plot the pixels to the screen so that it works for the 256 color modes rather than the 16 color modes. We have included it in its entirety in the listing so that if you are typing in the code, the listing will be complete and immediately workable without any jumps or repetitions.

Slanting Lines with Width and Style

As with vertical lines, we now want to progress from the simple line that is one pixel wide to wide lines that can not only be solid but also dotted, dashed, or another style. We didn't have much trouble widening vertical lines; we simply added pixels on both sides of the original one pixel line. With slanting lines, things get a little more complicated. When we draw a set of lines with a broad brush, we pretty much join them automatically, without thinking very much about how one line segment begins and another ends. When drawing lines with a computer, things get a little more complicated and if we aren't careful, the line junctions can be a little messy. We're going to start with a very simplistic approach in which we say that if a line is, say, six pixels wide, we will use the same line drawing algorithm but draw with rectangles that are six pixels on a side. In the test program, you'll find that the third screen from the last draws a magenta rectangle and two diagonals using this technique. The function that is used is *drawLine3*, which is very similar to *drawLine1*, except that each time *drawLine1* plots a point to the screen, *drawLine3* uses a pair of nested *for* loops to draw a square centered at the desired set of coordinates. As you watch the test program in action, you will note that the function is excruciatingly slow, mainly due to the large number of points that are redrawn a number of times during the function's operation. On the other hand, each end of a line segment is in the shape of a rectangle, which performs a pretty good job of joining line segments for the sample figure. You'll also observe that for display modes where the pixels are not square, the diagonal lines are wider that the vertical lines. It would be nice to have all lines that are supposed to be of the same width actually be the same width on the screen when using pixels that aren't square, but this doesn't happen without some complicated manipulation.

If we try to determine the fastest way to draw wide lines, the answers for two extreme cases are evident. For vertical lines, all we have to do is add pixels on either side of the line. For horizontal lines, all we have to do is add pixels at the top and bottom of the line. Now suppose that we take a horizontal line and begin tilting it. For a while, we can do a good job of making a wide line by simply adding pixels at the top and bottom of each pixel that is a point on the line. In fact, this method breaks down precisely at the point where y begins to increase faster than x. From then on, to make a good wide line, we have to add pixels at either side of each pixel that forms the line rather than at the top and bottom. Fortunately, our original line drawing function has separate loops for these two cases, so that we can provide an inner loop for each case that plots the added pixels with the appropriate coordinate modified. The function to do this is *drawLine4*. The next to last screen in the test program shows a number of figures of different widths drawn with this program. You'll observe that the ends of the line segments don't fit together very well, since the ends of the horizontal lines are vertical at the midpoint of the vertical lines and visa versa.

The function *drawLine5* is an attempt to improve the end point matching. This is accomplished by using the rectangle drawing method of *drawLine3* to draw the beginning and ending points of a line only and using the method of *drawLine4* to draw all of the rest of the points. This works very well for the test figure and is quite fast. It is used to draw a number of different width figures for the last screen display of the test program and also to draw the large yellow figure in the third from the last screen, which is compared with the magenta figure drawn by *drawLine3*. Watching this screen being drawn, you'll get a good idea of the speed difference between the two techniques. Although this approach works well for the test figure, you'll observe that, as the diagonals are being drawn, the ends have a very peculiar arrowish look. So this function would probably not be a good choice if you were drawing an isolated diagonal line that didn't have anything connected to its ends. Therefore, I wouldn't recommend using this function except in very special limited cases. The simplest solution is to use *drawLine4*, bearing in mind that you may have to lengthen some lines to get a perfect fit.

The technique that we used to permit stylized lines in the preceding functions is exactly the same that is used for vertical lines. There are no complications in transferring the technique from vertical to horizontal lines. Furthermore, since all these functions can also be used to draw horizontal lines, they are the ones to use for drawing horizontal lines when you want them stylized, even though they are much slower that the specialized functions to draw single pixel horizontal lines.

Thus far, all of the examples for drawing wide lines have been given for the 16 color modes. The function *drawLine6* is just the same as *drawLine4*, except that it plots using the proper function for the 256 color modes.

Drawing Lines with a Given Length and Angle

So far, we've considered only lines where the beginning and ending coordinates were specified. If you were constrained to the graphics package that came with a particular compiler, this might be the only option available to you. When you're creating your own functions, however, you have a lot of other options open. For example, suppose the parameters that are passed to the line drawing function are the starting coordinates, the line length, the line direction angle and the color. The function *drawLine7* does this. It requires addition of only a few lines at the beginning of the *drawLine4* function and the passing of different parameters. We've chosen to define the direction angle as being 0 degrees in the x direction and increasing counterclockwise. Plate 1 is a sample of a program used to test this line drawing function. It will be described in a later section.

Drawing Consecutive Lines

The function *drawLine8* is another example of how the line drawing function can be tailored to a special application with a few minor changes. In this case, we are going to drawing a lot of line segments consecutively. In other words, we draw one line segment between two coordinates, then draw the next line segment beginning where the first left off and continuing to a new set of coordinates, then draw the next from where the second left off to another new set of coordinates, and so forth. We could use one of our existing line drawing functions and simply specify both the beginning and ending coordinates each time, but this makes a lot of extra work and introduces the possibility of making errors each time a coordinate is repeated. This function solves that problem by drawing a line from the position specified in a set of global coordinates (X,Y) to a set of coordinates passed to the function. It then sets (X,Y) to the coordinate values that mark the end of the line just drawn. Thus for a set of consecutive lines, one needs only to set (X,Y) to the coordinates for the start of the first line segment, and then pass only end coordinates to the line drawing function for each line segment to be drawn after that.

The *Linetest.c* Program

This program is used to test the various line drawing functions described in the preceding section. By running it, you can verify the proper operation of each function before you transfer it to your own applications. Except for one case (to be described later), the program draws a screen and then waits while you view it. If you hit any key, the program will then draw the next screen. The first screen that is drawn makes use of *drawVertLine1* to draw a set of different colored vertical lines in the 256 color mode. The next screen uses *drawLine2* to draw a similar set of vertical lines using the 16 color modes. The next screen makes use of *drawVertLine3* to draw a set of vertical lines of different widths, styles, and colors in the 256 color mode. The next screen makes use of *drawVertLine3* to draw a set of vertical lines of different widths, styles, and colors in the 16 color modes. The next screen uses *drawHorzLine1* to draw a set of solid lines of varying widths and colors in the 256 color mode. The function itself draws only one pixel wide lines. We use a *for* loop to reiterate the function as many times as necessary for the specified line width, incrementing the *y* coordinate value each time.

The next screen uses *drawHorzLine2* to draw a set of solid lines of varying widths and colors in the 16 color modes. The function itself draws only one pixel wide lines. We use a *for* loop to reiterate the function as many times as necessary for the specified line width, incrementing the *y* coordinate value each time. The next screen uses *drawVertLine4* and *drawHorzLine2* to draw a rectangular grid of varicolored lines in mode 16 (640 by 350 pixel by 16 colors). The next screen draws a wide rectangle using *drawRect2* in mode 19 (320 by 200 pixels by 256 colors). The next screen draws a wide rectangle using *drawRect1* in mode 16 (640 by 350 pixels by 16 colors). The next screen draws a rectangular boundary and fills it with four different sets of slanting lines. Each set of lines is in a distinctive color, and each set begins at one of the corners of the bounding rectangle. The screen uses *drawLine1* and mode 16 (640 by 350 pixels by 16 colors). The next screen draws a rectangular boundary and fills it with four different sets of slanting lines. Each set of lines begins at one of the corners of the bounding rectangle. The screen uses *drawLine2* and mode 19 (320 by 200 pixels by 256 colors).

Before the line drawing begins, the VGA color registers are reset to a new set of colors that is more interesting for this display. Chapter 10 explains how this is done. Note that the earlier screen uses four separate *for* loops to draw the four sets of lines separately, whereas this screen uses a single *for* loop. The overall result is the same, but the way that the display is created is quite different. Watch both displays being generated and decide which technique you like best. Note also that this screen, instead of having a single color for each set of lines, uses a different color for each line. The color is incremented for each line that is drawn, so similar colors jump around the display. The next screen, shown in Plate 1, is the same as the first line pattern display (for 16 color modes) except that the boundary is drawn five pixels wide using the *drawRect1* function and the slanting lines are drawn with the *drawLine5* function.

The next set of screens is a very interesting one. It tests the *drawLine7* function by drawing sets of lines at 15 degree angle spacings from a common point. The line length is also reduced slightly for each line in the set that is drawn. Eighty of these sets are drawn to make up a screen. For each set, the origin, initial line length and color are selected randomly, so that each screen is unique and different. Since you may want to look at more that one of these screens, the program is set up so that the screen is drawn within a *while* loop, so that when the screen is complete, if you hit any key except the *Ent* key, a new version of this screen will be created. When you finally hit *Ent* the program will proceed to the next screen.

Because of the random selection of line parameters, each of the screens drawn is different and unique. Plate 2 shows a sample.

The next screen shows you the speed difference between drawing wide lines with the *drawLine3* function and the *drawLine5* function. The former is used to draw a yellow figure consisting of a rectangle and two diagonals. This function replaces each pixel with a rectangle to draw a wide line. As you can see, it is very slow. The latter function replaces each pixel of the line with either pixels on each side of the original pixel or pixels above and below the original pixel and automatically makes the decision as to which method is to be used for each particular case. It generates the same figure in magenta. You'll see when you generate this screen, that is much faster than the other method. The next screen draws a number of small figures of different widths and colors using *drawline4*. Since there is no compensation at the line ends, there is a gap that becomes more and more noticeable as the line width increases. By selectively changing the line lengths, however, you can correct this situation. The last screen shows the same figures as the previous screen, but they are drawn using *drawLine5*, which corrects for the line lengths to match the width changes. As you can see, this gives a good result for the test figure. However, if you observe the shape of the ends of the diagonal lines before the rectangles are drawn, you'll quickly get the idea that this function won't do at all well in drawing isolated slanting lines.

The next screen that is drawn is an example of using small straight line segments to approximate a complicated curve. The display shows four cycles of a damped sine wave, using 256 line segments drawn consecutively with *drawLine8*. This is illustrated in Plate 3. The next screen is another example of this technique. This screen draws spirals. There are 75 of them, each with a randomly selected center position, a random width between adjacent cycles, and a random number of cycles. Again the consecutive line drawing function *drawLine8* is used. Each display is unique, since the random processes are used. Plate 4 shows a typical spiral screen.

Chapter 8

Undocumented Display Modes: How to Create and Use Them

By a "documented display mode," we refer to a display mode that can be initialized through the ROM BIOS (usually by BIOS extensions that are included in the VGA card). Particularly, most documented display modes can be initialized through the use of ROM BIOS video service 00. All of these documented modes were described in Chapter 5. Due to the large number of registers internal to VGA cards, and the flexibility of these registers, it is possible to create a lot of different display modes that are not supported by the ROM BIOS video services. This is particularly true of the Super VGA cards, where the video modes that are supported by the manufacturer only begin to scratch the surface of what might be created. The undocumented display modes described in this chapter have the characteristic in common that they provide higher resolution 256 color modes than mode 19 (the 320 by 200 pixel by 256 color mode), without requiring any additional memory in the VGA card. They also have the unique characteristic that the data for four pixels is stored in two adjacent bytes of memory address space, with two adjacent bytes in memory plane 0 used to store the first of the four pixels, two adjacent bytes in memory plane 1 used to store the next pixel, etc. These modes were discovered by John Bridges and documented in several articles by Michael Abrash. Starting with the modes described here, with a good understanding of how the display adapter card registers work (as described in Chapter 4), you are ready to start creating your own display modes. There are two cautions to observe, however. First, make sure that you are not attempting to create a display mode that exceeds the memory capabilities of your VGA card. Furthermore, even if your card has adequate memory, you may need to institute a paging scheme if you exceed a 64K memory window. Second, you should be very careful if you attempt to create a display mode that changes the horizontal or vertical sweep rates from those used with one of the documented modes for your card. Many monitors are very limited in the sweep rates that they will accept, and some of them self-destruct if they are fed sweep rates outside the range they are capable of handling.

You'll note quite a little repetition in the undocumented mode descriptions if you read straight through the chapter. This is done deliberately, so that if you are interested in implementing only one of the undocumented modes you will have all of the necessary information together in one block and not have to look back through the chapter hunting for other necessary pieces of it.

The *xmodetst.c* Program

This program is listed in Figure 8-1. It is intended as a vehicle for testing the undocumented display modes on your VGA card and VGA monitor. The program makes use of a variant of the line pattern display that is part of the *Linetest.c* program described in Chapter 7. This program draws a wide rectangular border around the screen and then draws four sets of lines, each set radiating from one of the corners of the rectangle. Each line is a different color. (If there are more than 256 lines for the resolution specified, then the colors start repeating.) There are five different undocumented display modes. You will observe that the module for creating a pattern of lines for each display mode is the same as all the others except for the mode that is selected by the *setMode* function and for the values of *xres* and *yres* that are set to the horizontal and vertical resolutions respectively of the desired mode. The function for setting the VGA color registers (*setVGApalette*) is called at the beginning of each module, so that the module can be taken out and run as a self-contained program, if desired. If you don't care to do this, one statement at the beginning of the program to set the color registers is sufficient.

Figure 8-1. Listing of xmodetst.c Program to Demonstrate Undocumented 256 Color Modes

```
/*

    xmodetst.c = Program to do line test for all
        undocumented VGA graphics display modes.

        By Roger T. Stevens    7-12-91

*/

#include <dos.h>
#include <stdio.h>
#include <stdlib.h>
#include <mem.h>

void plot(int x, int y, int color);
void setMode(int mode);
void drawLine6(int xs, int ys, int xe, int ye, int color);
void setVGApalette(unsigned char *buffer);

typedef struct
{
    unsigned char red;
    unsigned char green;
    unsigned char blue;
} RGB;
RGB palette[256];

int color, hue, i, j, k, LINEWIDTH = 3;
int xres, yres;
unsigned long int PATTERN = 0xFFFFFFFF;

union REGS reg;

void main()
{
    palette[0].red = 0;
    palette[0].green = 0;
```

(continued)

```
        palette[0].blue = 0;
        for (i=0;  i<6;  i++)
            for(j=0;  j<6;  j++)
                for (k=1;  k<8;  k++)
                {
                    palette[42*i+7*j+k].red = i*12+1;
                    palette[42*i+7*j+k].green = j*12+1;
                    palette[42*i+7*j+k].blue = 10*(k-1)+1;
                }
```

```
/*
```

```
        Mode F0H = 320 x 400 pixels x 256 colors.
```

```
*/
```

```
        setMode(0xF0);
        setVGApalette(&palette[0].red);
        xres = 320; yres = 400;
        drawLine6(6,8,xres-5,8,42);
        drawLine6(6,yres-4,xres-5,yres-4,42);
        drawLine6(7,8,7,yres-4,42);
        drawLine6(xres-6,8,xres-6,yres-4,42);
        LINEWIDTH = 1;
        hue = 250;
        for (i=30; i< yres-10; i+=20)
        {
            drawLine6(10,10,xres-8,i, hue--);
            drawLine6(xres-8,yres-6,10,i, hue--);
            drawLine6(10,yres-6,xres-8,i, hue--);
            drawLine6(xres-8,10,10,i, hue--);
        }
        getch();
```

```
/*
```

```
        Mode F1H = 320 x 240 pixels x 256 colors.
```

```
*/
```

(continued)

```
setMode(0xF1);
setVGApalette(&palette[0].red);
LINEWIDTH = 3;
xres = 320; yres = 240;
drawLine6(6,8,xres-5,8,42);
drawLine6(6,yres-4,xres-5,yres-4,42);
drawLine6(7,8,7,yres-4,42);
drawLine6(xres-6,8,xres-6,yres-4,42);
LINEWIDTH = 1;
hue = 250;
for (i=30; i< yres-10; i+=20)
{
    drawLine6(10,10,xres-8,i, hue--);
    drawLine6(xres-8,yres-6,10,i, hue--);
    drawLine6(10,yres-6,xres-8,i, hue--);
    drawLine6(xres-8,10,10,i, hue--);
}
getch();

/*
```

```
          Mode F2H = 320 x 480 pixels x 256 colors.
```

```
*/

setMode(0xF2);
setVGApalette(&palette[0].red);
LINEWIDTH = 3;
xres = 320; yres = 480;
drawLine6(6,8,xres-5,8,42);
drawLine6(6,yres-4,xres-5,yres-4,42);
drawLine6(7,8,7,yres-4,42);
drawLine6(xres-6,8,xres-6,yres-4,42);
LINEWIDTH = 1;
hue = 250;
for (i=30; i< yres-10; i+=20)
{
    drawLine6(10,10,xres-8,i, hue--);
    drawLine6(xres-8,yres-6,10,i, hue--);
    drawLine6(10,yres-6,xres-8,i, hue--);
```

(continued)

215

```
            drawLine6(xres-8,10,10,i, hue--);
    }
    getch();
```

/*

```
┌─────────────────────────────────────────────────────────┐
│  ┌───────────────────────────────────────────────────┐  │
│  │                                                   │  │
│  │      Mode F3H = 360 x 400 pixels x 256 colors.    │  │
│  │                                                   │  │
│  └───────────────────────────────────────────────────┘  │
└─────────────────────────────────────────────────────────┘
```

*/

```
    setMode(0xF3);
    setVGApalette(&palette[0].red);
    LINEWIDTH = 3;
    xres = 360; yres = 400;
    drawLine6(6,8,xres-5,8,42);
    drawLine6(6,yres-4,xres-5,yres-4,42);
    drawLine6(7,8,7,yres-4,42);
    drawLine6(xres-6,8,xres-6,yres-4,42);
    LINEWIDTH = 1;
    hue = 250;
    for (i=30; i< yres-10; i+=20)
    {
        drawLine6(10,10,xres-8,i, hue--);
        drawLine6(xres-8,yres-6,10,i, hue--);
        drawLine6(10,yres-6,xres-8,i, hue--);
        drawLine6(xres-8,10,10,i, hue--);
    }
    getch();
```

/*

```
┌─────────────────────────────────────────────────────────┐
│  ┌───────────────────────────────────────────────────┐  │
│  │                                                   │  │
│  │      Mode F4H = 360 x 480 pixels x 256 colors.    │  │
│  │                                                   │  │
│  └───────────────────────────────────────────────────┘  │
└─────────────────────────────────────────────────────────┘
```

*/

```
    setMode(0xF4);
    setVGApalette(&palette[0].red);
    LINEWIDTH = 3;
    xres = 360; yres = 480;
```

(continued)

```
        drawLine6(6,8,xres-5,8,42);
        drawLine6(6,yres-4,xres-5,yres-4,42);
        drawLine6(7,8,7,yres-4,42);
        drawLine6(xres-6,8,xres-6,yres-4,42);
        LINEWIDTH = 1;
        hue = 250;
        for (i=30; i< yres-10; i+=20)
        {
            drawLine6(10,10,xres-8,i, hue--);
            drawLine6(xres-8,yres-6,10,i, hue--);
            drawLine6(10,yres-6,xres-8,i, hue--);
            drawLine6(xres-8,10,10,i, hue--);
        }
        getch();

        setMode(0x03);
}

/*

    ┌─────────────────────────────────────────────────────┐
    │                                                       │
    │  drawLine6() = Draws a line from one set of coordinates│
    │           to another in designated color.             │
    │                                                       │
    └─────────────────────────────────────────────────────┘

*/

void drawLine6(int xs, int ys, int xe, int ye, int color)
{
    extern int LINEWIDTH;
    extern unsigned long int PATTERN;

    int temp, dx, dy, i, j, x, y, x_sign, y_sign,
        decision;
    unsigned long int mask;

    dx = abs(xe - xs);
    dy = abs(ye - ys);
    if (((dx > dy) && (xs > xe)) || ((dy > dx) && (ys >
        ye)))
    {
```

(continued)

```
        temp = xs;
        xs = xe;
        xe = temp;
        temp = ys;
        ys = ye;
        ye = temp;
    }
    if ((ye - ys) < 0)
        y_sign = -1;
    else
        y_sign = 1;
    if ((xe - xs) < 0)
        x_sign = -1;
    else
        x_sign = 1;
    if (dx > dy)
    {
        for (x=xs,y=ys,decision=0; x<=xe; x++,decision+=dy)
        {
            mask = mask !=1 ? mask >> 1 : 0x80000000;
            if (decision>=dx)
            {
                decision -= dx;
                y+= y_sign;
            }
            if (PATTERN & mask)
                for (j=-LINEWIDTH/2; j<=LINEWIDTH/2; j++)
            plot(x,y+j,color);
        }
    }
    else
    {
        for (x=xs,y=ys,decision=0; y<=ye; y++,decision+=dx)
        {
            mask = mask !=1 ? mask >> 1 : 0x80000000;
            if (decision>=dy)
            {
                decision -= dy;
                x += x_sign;
            }
            if (PATTERN & mask)
```

(continued)

```
                    for (j=-LINEWIDTH/2; j<=LINEWIDTH/2; j++)
                        plot(x+j,y,color);
                }
            }
    }

    /*

    ┌──────────────────────────────────────────────────────────┐
    │                                                          │
    │  setMode() = Sets Video Mode (includes undocumented VGA  │
    │                       modes.)                            │
    │                                                          │
    └──────────────────────────────────────────────────────────┘

    */

    void setMode(int mode)
    {
        char result;
        unsigned int params[17] =
            {0x6b00,0x5901,0x5a02,0x8e03,0x5e04,0x8a05,
            0x4009,0x0014,0xe317,0x0d06,0x3e07,0xea10,0xac11,
            0xdf12,0xe715,0x0616,0x4109};
        char far * address;
        long int i;

        reg.h.ah = 0;

        switch(mode)
        {
            case 0xF0:  /* 320 x 400 pixel resolution */
                reg.h.al = 0x13;
                int86 (0x10,&reg,&reg);
                outport(0x3c4,0x0604);
                outportb(0x3d4,0x11);
                result = inportb(0x3d5);
                outportb(0x3d5,result & 0x7f);
                for (i=6; i<9; i++)
                    outport(0x3d4,params[i]);
                break;

            case 0xF1:  /* 320 x 240 pixels */
                reg.h.al = 0x13;
```

(continued)

```
            int86 (0x10,&reg,&reg);
            outport(0x3c4,0x0604);
            outport(0x3c4,0x0100);
            outportb(0x3c2,0xc3);
            outport(0x3c4,0x300);
            outportb(0x3d4,0x11);
            result = inportb(0x3d5);
            outportb(0x3d5,result & 0x7f);
            for (i=7; i<17; i++)
                outport(0x3d4,params[i]);
            break;

    case 0xF2:  /* 320 x 480 pixels */
            reg.h.al = 0x13;
            int86 (0x10,&reg,&reg);
            outport(0x3c4,0x0604);
            outport(0x3c4,0x0100);
            outportb(0x3c2,0xc3);
            outport(0x3c4,0x300);
            outportb(0x3d4,0x11);
            result = inportb(0x3d5);
            outportb(0x3d5,result & 0x7f);
            for (i=6; i<16; i++)
                outport(0x3d4,params[i]);
            outport(0x3d4,0x4009);
            break;

    case 0xF3:  /* 360 x 400 pixels */
            reg.h.al = 0x13;
            int86 (0x10,&reg,&reg);
            outport(0x3c4,0x0604);
            outport(0x3c4,0x0100);
            outportb(0x3c2,0x67);
            outport(0x3c4,0x300);
            outportb(0x3d4,0x11);
            result = inportb(0x3d5);
            outportb(0x3d5,result & 0x7f);
            for (i=0; i<9; i++)
                outport(0x3d4,params[i]);
            outport(0x3d4,0x2d13);
            break;
```

(continued)

```
            case 0xF4:  /* 360 x 480 pixels */
                reg.h.al = 0x13;
                int86 (0x10,&reg,&reg);
                outport(0x3c4,0x0604);
                outport(0x3c4,0x0100);
                outportb(0x3c2,0xe7);
                outport(0x3c4,0x300);
                outportb(0x3d4,0x11);
                result = inportb(0x3d5);
                outportb(0x3d5,result & 0x7f);
                for (i=0; i<16; i++)
                    outport(0x3d4,params[i]);
                outport(0x3d4,0x2d13);
                break;
            default:
                reg.h.al = mode;
                int86(0x10, &reg, &reg);
        }
        if (mode >= 0xF0)
        {
            outport(0x3c4,0x0f02);
            for(i=0; i<0xFFFF; i++)
            {
                address = (char far *) 0xA0000000L + i;
                *address = 0x00;
            }
        }
    }

    /*
```

```
    plot() = Function to plot point to VGA 256 color
             screen using undocumented modes.
```

```
    */

    void plot(int x, int y, int color)
    {
        #define seq_out(index,val) {outp(0x3c4, index);\
                                   outp(0x3c5, val);}
```

(continued)

```
    unsigned long int offset;
    char far *address;
    unsigned int plane;

    offset = (long)xres * y + x;
    plane = (0x01 << (offset % 4));
    seq_out(2,plane);
    offset >>= 2;
    address = (char far *)(0xA0000000L + offset);
    *address = color;
}
```

```
/*
```

```
        setVGApalette() = Function to set all 256 color
                            registers.
```

```
*/
```

```
void setVGApalette(unsigned char *buffer)
{
    struct SREGS inreg;
    union REGS reg;

    reg.x.ax = 0x1012;
    segread(&inreg);
    inreg.es = inreg.ds;
    reg.x.bx = 0;
    reg.x.cx = 256;
    reg.x.dx = (int)&buffer[0];
    int86x(0x10,&reg,&reg,&inreg);
}
```

Setting the Display Mode

Chapter 5 described in detail how to set the display modes for the documented modes and for the extended modes that are available on five representative Super VGA cards. In this chapter, we are going to describe a function that can set the display mode for any of the documented display modes or any one of the five undocumented display modes to be described in this chapter. This function, which is listed as part of Figure 8-1, is *setMode*. We have chosen to number the five undocumented modes F0H, F1H, F2H, F3H, and F4H. These are arbitrary numbers. Since there is no officially accepted standard, you may use any numbers that don't conflict with documented or extended mode numbers. The first thing that the program does is to set the *ah* register to 0, which selects the ROM BIOS video service for setting the display mode. Next, a switch statement is entered that determines what actions are to be taken for whatever mode was chosen. There is a case for each of the modes indicated and also a default case that is used for any other mode. The default case simply puts the selected mode into register *al* and then calls the ROM BIOS video services interrupt. This is the same thing we would have done with the plain vanilla function of Chapter 5. For each of the undocumented modes, we begin by setting register *al* to 13H and then calling the ROM BIOS video services interrupt. This sets everything up for the 320 by 200 pixel by 256 color mode, including clearing the display memory and setting the color registers to their default colors. We then modify some of the VGA registers to achieve the new VGA mode. After the registers are modified, if the mode that was selected was one of the undocumented ones, we send 0FH to Sequencer Register 2—Map Mask to enable all four color planes, and then enter a *for* loop that zeroes 64K of memory for all four display memory planes. The reason for this is that all of the undocumented modes have more resolution than the mode that was originally set, and therefore may use more display memory, so it is possible that clearing the original mode does not clear all of the memory displayed with the undocumented modes. To avoid strange things appearing on a supposedly cleared screen, we therefore zero all of the current window of display memory. This concludes the *setMode* function.

Setting the 320 × 400 Pixel × 256 Color Mode

The first thing that we do to modify mode 13H to this mode (mode F0H) is to send an 06H to Sequencer Register 04H—Memory Mode. This sets up the register so that the display planes are not chained (they were chained by mode 13H), sequential storage is used and memory greater than 64K is allowed. Mode 13 set things up to accept a byte (eight bits) of color information for each pixel. When the memory planes were chained together, the two least significant bits of the display memory offset from the base address were used to select which memory plane the color information was to be sent to and the remainder of the offset (shifted two bits to the right) became the actual offset from the base display memory address. As soon as we unchain the memory planes, the eight bits of color information are transferred to the four memory planes in sequence, the first going to the first plane, the second two to the next, and so forth, so that the fifth bit goes to the first memory plane again. Next, we select CRT Controller Register 11H. First we read the contents of this register and then OR it with 7FH and write it back again. This preserves all of the contents of the register except bit 7, which is changed to 0, thereby permitting us to write to CRT Controller Registers 00H to 07H. Next, we enter a *for* loop that outputs data to selected CRT Controller Registers from an array called *params*. For this mode, we do the following:

1. Set CRT Controller Register 09H–Maximum Row Address to 40H. The critical change here is to set bit 0 to 0, to allow one scan line per character row.
2. Set CRT Controller Register 14H—Underline Row Address to 00H. This changes from double word addressing to normal addressing, allowing scanning of all four memory planes.
3. Set CRT Controller Register 17H—Mode to E3H. The change here from mode 13H is in setting bit 6 to 1, so that we are in byte mode as for mode 12H, rather than in the word mode that was used in mode 13H.

Setting the 320 × 240 Pixel × 256 Color Mode

The first thing that we do to modify mode 13H to this mode (mode F1H) is to send an 06H to Sequencer Register 04H—Memory Mode. This sets up the register so that the display planes are not chained (they were chained by mode 13H), sequential storage is used and memory greater than 64K is allowed. Mode 13 set things up to accept a byte (eight bits) of color information for each pixel. When the memory planes were chained together, the two least significant bits of the display memory offset from the base address were used to select which memory plane the color information was to be sent to and the remainder of the offset (shifted two bits to the right) became the actual offset from the base display memory address. As soon as we unchain the memory planes, the eight bits of color information are transferred to the four memory planes in sequence, the first going to the first plane, the second two to the next, and so forth, so that the fifth bit goes to the first memory plane again. We then send 01H to Sequencer Register 00H—Reset to synchronously disable the timing signals while we change the clock frequency. Then we send C3H to miscellaneous output register to change the sync polarities to indicate to the display that there are 480 lines in a vertical frame. (Because the mode setting already provides for writing each scan line twice, we are actually in a 240 line mode, with each line being repeated to obtain the 480 lines.) We then send 03H to Sequencer Register 00H—Reset to restart the timing signals. Next, we select CRT Controller Register 11H. First we read the contents of this register and then OR it with 7FH and write it back again. This preserves all of the contents of the register except bit 7, which is changed to zero, thereby permitting us to write to CRT Controller Registers 00H to 07H. Next, we enter a *for* loop which outputs data to selected CRT Controller Registers from an array called *params*. For this mode, we do the following:

1. Set CRT Controller Register 14H—Underline Row Address to 00H. This changes from double word addressing to normal addressing, allowing scanning of all four memory planes.

2. Set CRT Controller Register 17H—Mode to E3H. The change here from mode 13H is in setting bit 6 to 1, so that we are in byte mode as for mode 12H, rather than in the word mode that was used in mode 13H.

3. Set CRT Controller Register 06H—Vertical Total to 0DH. This changes the vertical total to look for 240 scan lines rather than 200.

4. Set CRT Controller Register 07H—Vertical Sync Position to 3EH. A new value is required to properly set the vertical timing for 240 lines.

5. Set CRT Controller Register 10H—Vertical Sync Start to EAH. A new value is required to properly set the vertical timing for 240 lines.

6. Set CRT Controller Register 11H—Vertical Sync End to ACH. A new value is required to properly set the vertical timing for 240 lines.

7. Set CRT Controller Register 12H—Vertical Display End to DFH. A new value is required to properly set the vertical timing for 240 lines.

8. Set CRT Controller Register 15H—Start Vertical Blank to E7H. A new value is required to properly set the vertical timing

for 240 lines.

9. Set CRT Controller Register 16H—End Vertical Blank to 06H. A new value is required to properly set the vertical timing for 240 lines.

10. Set CRT Controller Register 09H—Max Row Address to 41H.

Setting the 320 × 480 Pixel × 256 Color Mode

The first thing that we do to modify mode 13H to this mode (mode F2H) is to send an 06H to sequencer register 4 (memory mode register). This sets up the register so that the display planes are not chained (they were chained by mode 13H), sequential storage is used and memory greater than 64K is allowed. Mode 13 set things up to accept a byte (eight bits) of color information for each pixel. When the memory planes were chained together, the two least significant bits of the display memory offset from the base address were used to select which memory plane the color information was to be sent to and the remainder of the offset (shifted two bits to the right) became the actual offset from the base display memory address. As soon as we unchain the memory planes, the eight bits of color information are transferred to the four memory planes in sequence, the first going to the first plane, the second two to the next, and so forth, so that the fifth bit goes to the first memory plane again. We then send 01H to sequencer register 0 (reset register) to synchronously disable the timing signals while we change the clock frequency. Then we send C3H to miscellaneous output register to change the sync polarities to indicate to the display that there are 480 lines in a vertical frame. We then send 03H to sequencer register 0 (reset register) to restart the timing signals. Next, we select CRT controller register 11H. First we read the contents of this register and then OR it with 7FH and write it back again. This preserves all of the contents of the register except bit 7, which is changed to 0, thereby permitting us to write to CRT controller registers 0 to 7. Next, we enter a *for* loop that outputs data to selected CRT controller registers from an array called *params*. For this mode, we do the following:

1. Set CRT Controller Register 09H—Maximum Row Address to 40H. The critical change here is to set bit 0 to 0, to allow one scan line per character row.

2. Set CRT Controller Register 14H—Underline Row Address to

00H. This changes from double word addressing to normal addressing, allowing scanning of all four memory planes.

3. Set CRT Controller Register 17H—Mode to E3H. The change here from mode 13H is in setting bit 6 to 1, so that we are in byte mode as for mode 12H, rather than in the word mode that was used in mode 13H.

4. Set CRT Controller Register 06H—Vertical Total to 0DH. This changes the vertical total to look for 480 scan lines rather than 400.

5. Set CRT Controller Register 07H—Vertical Sync Position to 3EH. A new value is required to properly set the vertical timing for 480 lines.

6. Set CRT Controller Register 10H—Vertical Sync Start to EAH. A new value is required to properly set the vertical timing for 480 lines.

7. Set CRT Controller Register 11H—Vertical Sync End to ACH. A new value is required to properly set the vertical timing for 480 lines.

8. Set CRT Controller Register 12H—Vertical Display End to DFH. A new value is required to properly set the vertical timing for 480 lines.

9. Set CRT Controller Register 15H—Start Vertical Blank to E7H. A new value is required to properly set the vertical timing for 480 lines.

10. Set CRT Controller Register 16H—End Vertical Blank to 06H. A new value is required to properly set the vertical timing for 480 lines.

11. Set CRT Controller Register 09H—Max Row Address to 41H.

Setting the 360 × 400 Pixel × 256 Color Mode

The first thing that we do to modify mode 13H to this mode (mode F3H) is to send an 06H to Sequencer Register 04H—Memory mode. This sets up the register so that the display planes are not chained (they were chained by mode 13H), sequential storage is used and memory greater than 64K is allowed. Mode 13 set things up to accept a byte (eight bits) of color information for each pixel. When the memory planes were chained together, the two least significant bits of the display memory offset from the base address were used to select which memory plane the color information was to be sent to and the remainder of the offset (shifted two bits to the right) became the actual offset from the base display memory address. As soon as we unchain the memory planes, the eight bits of color information are transferred to the four memory planes in sequence, the first going to the first plane, the second two to the next, and so forth, so that the fifth bit goes to the first memory plane again. We then send 01H to sequencer register 0 (reset register) to synchronously disable the timing signals while we change the clock frequency. Then we send 67H to miscellaneous output register to change the sync polarities to indicate to the display that there are 400 lines in a vertical frame and set the clock frequency for 90 characters (360 pixels) per scan line. We then send 03H to sequencer register 0 (reset register) to restart the timing signals. Next, we select CRT controller register 11H. First we read the contents of this register and then OR it with 7FH and write it back again. This preserves all of the contents of the register except bit 7, which is changed to 0, thereby permitting us to write to CRT controller registers 0 to 7. Next, we enter a *for* loop that outputs data to selected CRT controller registers from an array called *params*. For this mode, we do the following:

1. Set CRT Controller Register 00H—Total Horizontal Column to 6BH. This is required to adjust the horizontal timing signals for 360 pixels per line.
2. Set CRT Controller Register 01H—Horizontal Display End to 59H. This is required to adjust the horizontal timing signals for 360 pixels per line.
3. Set CRT Controller Register 02H—Start Horizontal Blank to 5AH. This is required to adjust the horizontal timing signals for 360 pixels per line.
4. Set CRT Controller Register 03H—End Horizontal Blank to 8EH. This is required to adjust the horizontal timing signals for 360 pixels per line.
5. Set CRT Controller Register 04H—Horizontal Sync Start to 5EH. This is required to adjust the horizontal timing signals for 360 pixels per line.
6. Set CRT Controller Register 05H—Horizontal Sync End to 8AH. This is required to adjust the horizontal timing signals for 360 pixels per line.
7. Set CRT Controller Register 09H—Maximum Row Address to 40H. The critical change here is to set bit 0 to 0, to allow one scan line per character row.
8. Set CRT Controller Register 14H—Underline Row Address to 00H. This changes from double word addressing to normal

addressing, allowing scanning of all four memory planes.

9. Set CRT Controller Register 17H—Modeto E3H. The change here from mode 13H is in setting bit 6 to 1, so that we are in byte mode as for mode 12H, rather than in the word mode that was used in mode 13H.

Setting the 360 × 480 Pixel × 256 Color Mode

The first thing that we do to modify mode 13H to this mode (mode F4H) is to send an 06H to Sequencer Register 04H—Memory Mode. This sets up the register so that the display planes are not chained (they were chained by mode 13H), sequential storage is used and memory greater than 64K is allowed. Mode 13 set things up to accept a byte (eight bits) of color information for each pixel. When the memory planes were chained together, the two least significant bits of the display memory offset from the base address were used to select which memory plane the color information was to be sent to and the remainder of the offset (shifted two bits to the right) became the actual offset from the base display memory address. As soon as we unchain the memory planes, the eight bits of color information are transferred to the four memory planes in sequence, the first going to the first plane, the second two to the next, and so forth, so that the fifth bit goes to the first memory plane again. We then send 01H to sequencer register 0 (reset register) to synchronously disable the timing signals while we change the clock frequency. Then we send E7H to miscellaneous output register to change the sync polarities to indicate to the display that there are 480 lines in a vertical frame and set the clock frequency for 90 characters (360 pixels) per scan line. We then send 03H to sequencer register 0 (reset register) to restart the timing signals. Next, we select CRT controller register 11H. First we read the contents of this register and then OR it with 7FH and write it back again. This preserves all of the contents of the register except bit 7, which is changed to 0, thereby permitting us to write to CRT controller registers 0 to 7. Next, we enter a *for* loop that outputs data to selected CRT controller registers from an array called *params*. For this mode, we do the following:

1. Set CRT Controller Register 00H—Total Horizontal Column to 6BH. This is required to adjust the horizontal timing signals for 360 pixels per line.
2. Set CRT Controller Register 01H—Horizontal Display End to

59H. This is required to adjust the horizontal timing signals for 360 pixels per line.

3. Set CRT Controller Register 02H—Start Horizontal Blank to 5AH. This is required to adjust the horizontal timing signals for 360 pixels per line.

4. Set CRT Controller Register 03H—End Horizontal Blank to 8EH. This is required to adjust the horizontal timing signals for 360 pixels per line.

5. Set CRT Controller Register 04H—Horizontal Sync Start to 5EH. This is required to adjust the horizontal timing signals for 360 pixels per line.

6. Set CRT Controller Register 05H—Horizontal Sync End to 8AH. This is required to adjust the horizontal timing signals for 360 pixels per line.

7. Set CRT Controller Register 09H—Maximum Row Address to 40H. The critical change here is to set bit 0 to 0, to allow one scan line per character row.

8. Set CRT Controller Register 14H—Underline Row Address to 00H. This changes from double word addressing to normal addressing, allowing scanning of all four memory planes.

9. Set CRT Controller Register 17H—Mode to E3H. This changes from the mode 13H setting of bit 6 as 1, to put us in byte mode as for mode 12H, rather than in the word mode that was used in mode 13H.

10. Set CRT Controller Register 06H—Vertical Total to 0DH. This changes the vertical total to look for 480 scan lines rather than 400.

11. Set CRT Controller Register 07H—Vertical Sync Position to 3EH. A new value is required to properly set the vertical timing for 480 lines.

12. Set CRT Controller Register 10H—Vertical Sync Start to EAH. A new value is required to properly set the vertical timing for 480 lines.

13. Set CRT Controller Register 11H—Vertical Sync End to ACH. A new value is required to properly set the vertical timing for 480 lines.

14. Set CRT Controller Register 12H—Vertical Display End to DFH. A new value is required to properly set the vertical timing for 480 lines.

15. Set CRT Controller Register 15H—Start Vertical Blank to E7H. A new value is required to properly set the vertical timing for 480 lines.

16. Set CRT Controller Register 16H—End Vertical Blank to 06H. A new value is required to properly set the vertical timing for 480 lines.

17. Set CRT Controller Register 09H—Max Row Address to 41H.

Plotting a Point to the Screen with Undocumented Modes

The function *plot* paints a point to the screen in the designated one of 256 colors at the selected coordinates. You'll observe some similarities but also so startling differences from the plot functions given in Chapter 6. Before we begin describing the function, we need to review how pixels are stored in display memory for the undocumented modes. Mode 13H chained all of the memory planes together and used the two least significant bits of the address sent to display memory to select which plane was to receive the eight bits of pixel color information. The color information was then set to the display memory address represented by the rest of the address word (shifted two bits to the right) and to the plane represented by the two least significant bits. Two things resulted from this. First, data rotated through the four planes, with the address increasing only after every fourth pixel. Second, because only 14 bits were left for the display memory address, only 16K of the 64K memory window could be used in this mode. When we disabled the memory plane chaining for the undocumented modes, the addressing again worked in straight-forward, normal fashion.

Now let's look at what the *plot* function does with this. We first set up the parameter *offset* to be the offset that would occur from the base memory display address if one byte were allowed for each pixel. We then take the quantity 01H and shift it to the left by *offset* modula 4 to find the number of the memory plane where this pixel's color data is to be stored. We output the result of this operation to Sequencer Register 02H—Map Mask to enable only the desired memory plane. Then *offset* is divided by four (because we're using four planes at the same memory address to store four pixels, the actual memory address offset is only one-fourth of that calculated previously). We then output the color value to display memory, and the VGA card takes care of putting it into the correct memory plane. The registers have already been set up so that the memory planes are scanned properly to transfer the color information to the monitor screen.

Chapter 9

Using Extended Super VGA Modes

Chapter 4 documented the extra registers and extra uses of existing VGA registers used by five of the representative Super VGA display adapter cards. Less than obvious was how these registers should be manipulated to actually use these cards in practical applications. In this chapter, we are going to make use of the same pattern of lines that was first used in the *Linetest.c* program and learn how to produce it in high resolution modes for each of the five Super VGAs. First, however, we must give a word of caution. VGAs are sold with different amounts of memory; your card must have enough memory to support the high resolution mode that you choose. In addition, VGA monitors do not always support all high resolution Super VGA modes. Thus the mode that we have chosen differs from one card to another, reflecting the capabilities of the VGA card and monitor combination that we were using for testing. For example, the Paradise card supplied with the Dell 310 computer will support higher resolution modes, but the monitor that came with our Dell would not. As another example, we were using a combination of the Logix VGA card (Trident chip set) and a standard IBM VGA monitor. You might think that, since the IBM monitor supports the 640 by 480 pixel by 16 color VGA mode, it would support a Trident 640 by 480 pixel by 256 color mode, because you would think that the horizontal and vertical frequencies supplied to the monitor would be the same. However, it turned out that we could never get the monitor to sync at this new mode. Substituting a Panasonic C1381 monitor made everything work all right. So if you're having trouble, try a lower resolution mode and see if this works out. If worst comes to worst and you really need a high resolution mode, you may need to replace your monitor with a multisync one.

We're going to begin by listing the entire program for the STB Powergraph VGA board that uses the Tseng Labs chip set. We were using this card with a Panasonic C1381 monitor. The listing for this program is given in Figure 9-1. After this has been described, we'll list the *setMode* and *plot* functions for the other four cards. You can insert the proper set to replace the functions given with the main program. The main program itself remains the same for each case. The program begins by setting the display mode, which differs depending upon the mode that you have chosen and the display card you are using. Next the program sets up the 256 color registers for a palette that provides pleasing colors for the display. After that, the border is drawn with a line width of five pixels. The line width is then set to one pixel and a *for* loop is used to draw the lines. Lines are drawn from each corner of the border rectangle to points along the opposite vertical border, beginning with close to a horizontal line and then moving the endpoint along the vertical border in steps of 20 pixels until the last line ends very close to the opposite corner of the display. Because the spacing is a fixed number of pixels and because the number of lines is varied to fill the particular display being drawn, the number of lines will vary with the resolution of the display, higher resolution displays having more lines, spaced closer together, than low resolution displays.

Basic Principle of Extended Resolution Displays

The basic principle used for extended resolution displays is the same for every Super VGA display adapter card. Unfortunately, the manner in which this is implemented is is a little bit different for just about every chip set, and sometimes is even different for different brand cards using the same chip set (since the card manufacturer designs the ROM BIOS extensions that are included with that card). The principle of operation is quite simple. For extended resolution, the amount of memory exceeds the 64K memory space available in the IBM memory addressing scheme for VGA display memory. (Some cards use 128K of memory, using up both the VGA and CGA memory address assignments.) The super VGA cards themselves contain a lot more than 64K of memory. The original IBM scheme was to have the VGA card contain 256K of memory in four memory planes. The four planes were all addressed at the same set of 64K of addresses, with internal registers and controls sorting out how data was to be transferred to the memory planes. Super VGA cards, however, usually contain 512K or 1M of memory. This is accessed through the 64K window of addressing space. In simplest form, a register contains a page address for one of however many 64K pages are needed to define the location of all the memory on the VGA card. The card is initialized with this register set for page 0, which makes everything compatible with the original VGA. When you use an extended resolution mode, you proceed to calculate a memory address at which you wish to write a pixel in just the same way as you would for ordinary VGA operation. If the address turns out to be outside the 64K window, you then need to reduce it to be within the window and then set the page register for the proper page for this address in VGA memory. How this is done will be described in detail later.

The sections that follow are going to show the way to write the *setMode* and *plot* functions for each of the five representative Super VGA boards. You can insert these functions into the test program to draw the line pattern in various high resolution modes. This is a good test of the capabilities of your particular board and monitor. When you have determined which high resolution modes your system is capable of handling, you can then use these two basic functions to incorporate high resolution graphics in your own applications. You should be aware that many of these Super VGA cards contain other advanced graphics capabilities that have not been described in detail in this chapter.

Using the STB Powergraph VGA Display Adapter (Tseng Labs Chip Set)

The STB Powergraph board is the easiest of all boards to program, since complicated register accesses are minimized. The original program, listed in Figure 9-1, contains the *setMode* and *plot* functions for this board. The *setMode* function is just like that used for the regular VGA modes. The board manufacturer takes care of all of the mode setting and initialization operations in the ROM BIOS extensions, so that you as the programmer do not need to do anything else. Now let's look at the *plot* function. This begins in the same way as other *plot* functions that we have encountered, by determining the offset from the base memory address where information on the desired pixel is to be stored. However, in this case, the offset must be a long integer, since for extended modes, the limits of an ordinary integer may be exceeded. Next the memory page is determined by dividing the offset into 64K (65536) pages. This is stored in *bank*. The offset in the 64K memory window is then determined by finding the remainder after dividing out the integral number of full pages through a modulus arithmetic operation. Next, we compare the *bank* variable with a global variable called *active_bank*. This contains the number of the page used in the previous call of the *plot* function. This is the page that is already set into the VGA registers; if it is the same as the page that we want to use this time, no action to change the page is necessary. If the page is different, we output the page value ORed with 40H to VGA register 3CDH, the Segment Select Register. The 40H sets bit 6, which selects a mode of two banks of eight 64K segments. The value of *bank* in the three least significant bits (bits 0 to 2) selects the page that the display information is written to. (Bits 3 to 5 could be used to select the page that display information is read from, but we don't need that capability for this operation.) The *active_bank* variable is then set to this new page number. The function then adds the offset to the base memory address and sends the color information for the desired pixel to that address, after which it will be displayed on the screen at the assigned location.

Figure 9-1. Listing of Function pwrgraph.c to Draw Line Pattern to STB The Powergraph Display Adapter in 800 × 600 Pixel × 256 Color Mode

```
/*

    pwrgraph.c = Program to do line test at 800 × 600
    pixel × 256 color mode for STB Powergraph Display
              Adapter (Tseng Labs chip set.)

          By Roger T. Stevens    8-27-91

*/

#include <dos.h>
#include <stdio.h>
#include <stdlib.h>
```

(continued)

```
void plot(int x, int y, int color);
void setMode(int mode);
void setVGApalette(unsigned char *buffer);
void drawLine(int x1, int y1, int x2, int y2, int color);

int xres=800, yres=600;
int active_bank = 0, color, hue,i, j, k, LINEWIDTH = 5;
unsigned long int PATTERN = 0xFFFFFFFF;

typedef struct
{
    unsigned char red;
    unsigned char green;
    unsigned char blue;
} RGB;

RGB palette[256];

union REGS reg;
struct SREGS inreg;

void main()
{
    setMode(0x30);
    palette[0].red = 0;
    palette[0].green = 0;
    palette[0].blue = 0;
    for (i=0; i<6; i++)
        for(j=0; j<6; j++)
            for (k=1; k<8; k++)
            {
                palette[42*i+7*j+k].red = i*12+1;
                palette[42*i+7*j+k].green = j*12+1;
                palette[42*i+7*j+k].blue = 10*(k-1)+1;
            }

    setVGApalette(&palette[0].red);

    drawLine(6,8,xres-5,8,42);
    drawLine(6,yres-4,xres-5,yres-4,42);
    drawLine(8,8,8,yres-4,42);
```

(continued)

```
        drawLine(xres-6,8,xres-6,yres-4,42);
        LINEWIDTH = 1;
        hue = 250;
        for (i=30; i< yres-10; i+=20)
        {
            drawLine(10,10,xres-8,i, hue--);
            drawLine(xres-8,yres-6,10,i, hue--);
            drawLine(10,yres-6,xres-8,i, hue--);
            drawLine(xres-8,10,10,i, hue--);
        }
        getch();
        setMode(0x03);
}

/*
```

```
      setVGApalette() = Function to set all 256 color
                            registers.
```

```
*/

void setVGApalette(unsigned char *buffer)
{
    reg.x.ax = 0x1012;
    segread(&inreg);
    inreg.es = inreg.ds;
    reg.x.bx = 0;
    reg.x.cx = 256;
    reg.x.dx = (int)&buffer[0];
    int86x(0x10,&reg,&reg,&inreg);
}

/*
```

```
    drawLine() = Draws a line from one set of coordinates
                to another in designated color.
```

```
*/
```

(continued)

```
void drawLine(int xs, int ys, int xe, int ye, int color)
{
    extern int LINEWIDTH;
    extern unsigned long int PATTERN;

    int temp, dx, dy, i, j, x, y, x_sign, y_sign,
        decision;
    unsigned long int mask;

    dx = abs(xe - xs);
    dy = abs(ye - ys);
    if (((dx > dy) && (xs > xe)) || ((dy > dx) && (ys >
        ye)))
    {
        temp = xs;
        xs = xe;
        xe = temp;
        temp = ys;
        ys = ye;
        ye = temp;
    }
    if ((ye - ys) < 0)
        y_sign = -1;
    else
        y_sign = 1;
    if ((xe - xs) < 0)
        x_sign = -1;
    else
        x_sign = 1;
    if (dx > dy)
    {
        for (x=xs,y=ys,decision=0; x<=xe; x++,decision+=dy)
        {
            mask = mask !=1 ? mask >> 1 : 0x80000000;
            if (decision>=dx)
            {
                decision -= dx;
                y+= y_sign;
            }
            if (PATTERN & mask)
                for (j=-LINEWIDTH/2; j<=LINEWIDTH/2; j++)
```

(continued)

```
                                 plot(x,y+j,color);
                }
        }
        else
        {
            for (x=xs,y=ys,decision=0; y<=ye; y++,decision+=dx)
            {
                mask = mask !=1 ? mask >> 1 : 0x80000000;
                if (decision>=dy)
                {
                    decision -= dy;
                    x += x_sign;
                }
                if (PATTERN & mask)
                    for (j=-LINEWIDTH/2; j<=LINEWIDTH/2; j++)
                        plot(x+j,y,color);
            }
        }
}

/*
```

```
            setMode() = Sets video mode.
```

```
*/

void setMode(int mode)
{
    reg.h.ah = 0;
    reg.h.al = mode;
    int86 (0x10,&reg,&reg);
}

/*
```

```
        plot() = Function to plot point to VGA 256 color
                           screen.
```

```
*/
```

(continued)

```
void plot(int x, int y, int color)
{
    long int offset;
    char far *address;
    int bank;

    offset = xres * (long)y + (long)x;
    bank = offset/65536L;
    offset = offset % 65536L;
    if (bank != active_bank)
    {
        active_bank = bank;
        outp(0x3CD,bank | 0x40);
    }
    address = (char far *)(0xA0000000L + offset);
    *address = color;
}
```

Using the Headlands Technology VGA 1024i Display Adapter

Figure 9-2 lists the *setMode* and *plot* functions for the Headlands Technology VGA 1024i display adapter card. This test, uses mode 67, which is the 640 by 480 pixel by 256 color mode. This mode was chosen to be compatible with the capabilities of the monitor being used with the 1024i board. Note that the mode numbers assigned to Super VGA modes by the different manufacturers are not alike and have different characteristics. These modes are described in Chapter 5, where you'll find all the information to determine which mode you want to use.

The *setMode* function differs from the one used for ordinary modes in that Headlands Technology uses an entirely new BIOS function to select the extended modes. This is BIOS function 6FH. Subfunction 5 is used to set the extended modes. (The *setMode* function as listed will work only for extended modes.) If you want a general purpose function, you should use the normal *setMode* function (described in Chapter 5) for modes less than or equal to 19 and the function listed here for modes higher than that. After the BIOS function is called, it is necessary to enable the extended registers of the 1024i card by writing EAH to Sequencer Register 06H.

The *plot* function begins in the same way as the *plot* function listed in the previous section. If a new page must be established, the bits representing the page number must be distributed among three registers. The least significant bit (bit 0) goes to bit 0 of register index F9H at port 3C4H. The next bit (bit 1) goes to bit 5 of the register at port 3C2. The remaining bits go to the least significant bits of register index F6H at port 3C4H. For the least significant bit, we only have to transfer this to the appropriate register. For the other bits, we have to first read the current contents of the register and then write both the page bits and the original contents of the other bits back out to the register. To further complicate the situation, the register that is output to port 3C2H must be read from port 3CCH. Looking at the listing, you can see the C operations used to perform all of this moving of page bits. When this is all through, we transfer the page number to *active_bank* and then send the color information to the memory address as before. (Note that for this board, the storage of the page information is totally different for 2, 4 and 16 color modes, so that a completely different technique is required.)

Figure 9-2. SetMode and Plot Files for Headlands Technology VGA 1024i Display Adapter Card

```
/*

    setMode and plot functions for Headlands Technology
          VGA 1024i board in 640 × 480 pixel × 256
                        color mode.



    Make the following changes in the main program

*/

    int xres=640, yres=480;
    setMode(0x67);
```

(continued)

```
/*
```

```
            setMode() = Sets the video mode.
```

```
*/
```

```c
void setMode(int mode)
{
    reg.x.ax = 0x6F05;
    reg.h.bl = mode;
    int86 (0x10,&reg,&reg);
    outpw(0x3C4,0xEA06);
}
```

```
/*
```

```
    plot() = Function to plot point to VGA 256 color
                         screen.
```

```
*/
```

```c
void plot(int x, int y, int color)
{
    long int offset;
    char far *address;
    int bank,temp,temp2;

    offset = xres * (long)y + (long)x;
    bank = offset/65536L;
    offset = offset % 65536L;
    if (bank != active_bank)
    {
        active_bank = bank;
        outport(0x3C4,0xF9 | ((bank & 0x01) << 8));
        temp = (inport(0x3CC)) & 0xDF;
        if ((bank & 0x02) != 0)
            temp = temp | 0x20;
        outport(0x3C2,temp);
        outportb(0x3C4,0xF6);
```

(continued)

243

```
                    temp = ((inport(0x3C5)) & 0xF0) | ((bank & 0x0C) >>
                        2) | (bank & 0x0C);
                    outportb(0x3C5,temp);
                }
                address = (char far *)(0xA0000000L + offset);
                *address = color;
            }
```

Using the Logix VGA Display Adapter (Trident Chip Set)

Figure 9-3 lists the *setMode* and *plot* functions for the Logix VGA adapter card using the Trident chip set. This card was also run in the 640 by 480 pixel by 256 color mode, so the resolutions are changed accordingly. The *setMode* function for the extended modes with this card is the same as the normal VGA *setMode* function. The mode number for the selected extended mode is 5DH.

The *plot* function begins in the same way as the *plot* function listed in the previous section. If a new page must be established, a paging mode must be set up that divides display memory into eight 64K pages. This is accomplished by first outputting the index 0BH to port 3C4H to select Sequencer Register 0BH—Hardware Version. Then a read of register 3C5 takes place (at index 0BH because the previous VGA host memory space must be set to 64K). To do this, the index 06H is output to register 3CE. The indexed register is then read into *temp* by an input from register port 3CF. The result is ANDed with F3H to zero bits 2 and 3 for the 64K memory space operation. Then this is output to register 3CF. We next output index 0EH to register 3C4. Then the register just indexed is read at port 3C5. The result is ANDED with F0H to clear the page definition bits and then ORed with the value in *bank* to store the current page. The result is stored with an output to port 3C5H. Note however, that something very weird occurs with this storage of the page data. The second least significant bit of this value (bit 1) must be inverted before being written to the register; yet when the value is read back from the register this bit is returned uninverted. To accomplish this writing properly, at the beginning of this section of the function, we first store the computed value of *bank* in *active_bank* and then invert bit 1 before sending the data to the VGA registers. It might appear that some of the register operations just described could be performed just once, under the *setMode* function, for example, and would then never have to be changed. This is not true; they must all be performed every time a page is changed. After storing the page data, the function continues by computing the display address and sending the color information there as with the other *plot* functions. Once these operations have been performed to store the page information, the function computes the display memory address and stores the color information for the pixel there as with the other *plot* functions.

Figure 9-3. SetMode and Plot Files for Logix VGA Display Adapter Card using Trident Chip Set

```
/*

    setMode and plot functions for Logix display adapter
    VGA board using Trident chip set in 640 × 480 pixel
                    × 256 color mode.


Make the following changes in the main program
*/

    int xres=640, yres=480;
    setMode(0x5D);

/*

            setMode() = Sets video mode

*/

void setMode(int mode)
{
    reg.h.ah = 0;
    reg.h.al = mode;
    int86 (0x10,&reg,&reg);
}
```

(continued)

```
/*

    ╔══════════════════════════════════════════════════════════════╗
    ║                                                                ║
    ║   plot() = Function to plot to VGA 256 color screen.           ║
    ║                                                                ║
    ╚══════════════════════════════════════════════════════════════╝

*/

void plot(int x, int y, int color)
{
    long int offset, base;
    char far *address;
    char bank,temp;
    offset = (long)xres * (long)y + (long)x;
    bank = offset/65536L;
    offset = offset % 65536L;
    if (bank != active_bank)
    {
        active_bank = bank;
        bank ^=  0x0002;
        outp(0x3C4,0x0B);
        temp = inp(0x3C5);
        outp(0x3CE,0x06);
        temp = inp(0x3CF);
        temp = (temp & 0xF3) | 0x04;
        outp(0x3CF,temp);
        outp(0x3C4,0x0E);
        temp = (inp(0x3C5) & 0xF0) | bank;
        outp(0x3C5,temp);
    }
    address = (char far *) (0xA0000000L + offset);
    *address = color;
}
```

Using the Paradise VGA Display Adapter

Figure 9-4 lists the *setMode* and *plot* functions for the Paradise VGA
adapter card as used in the Dell 310 computer. This card was run in
the 640 by 400 pixel by 256 color mode, so the resolutions are changed
accordingly. The *setMode* function for the extended modes with this
card is the same as the normal VGA *setMode* function. The mode
number for this extended mode is 5EH.

Figure 9-4. SetMode and Plot Files for Paradise VGA Display Adapter Card used in Dell 310 Computer

```
/*
```
```
        set and plot functions for Paradise display adapter
            VGA board used in Dell 310 Computer in 640 ×
                      400 pixel × 256 color mode.
```
```
Make the following changes in the main program
*/
```

```
        int xres=640, yres=480;
        setMode(0x5E);
```

```
/*
```
```
                    setMode() = Sets video mode
```
```
*/
```

```
void setMode(int mode)
{
    reg.h.ah = 0x00;
    reg.h.al = mode;
    int86 (0x10,&reg,&reg);
}
```

```
/*
```
```
        plot() = Function to plot point to VGA 256 color
                              screen.
```
```
*/
```

```
void plot(int x, int y, int color)
{
```

(continued)

```
#define graph_out(index,val)   {outp(0x3CE,index);\
                                 outp(0x3CF,val);}

long int offset;
char far *address;
int bank;

offset = (long)xres * (long)y + (long)x;
bank = offset/65536L;
offset = offset % 65536L;
if (bank != active_bank)
{
    active_bank = bank;
    graph_out(0x0F,0x05);
    graph_out(0x09,bank<<4);
    graph_out(0x0F,0x00);
}
address = (char far *)(0xA0000000L + offset);
*address = color;
}
```

Using the ATI VGAWonder VGA Display Adapter

Figure 9-5 lists the *setMode* and *plot* functions for the ATI VGAWonder VGA adapter card. This card was run in the 800 by 600 pixel by 256 color mode. The resolutions are the same as for the first program listed. The *setMode* function for the extended modes with this card is the same as the normal VGA *setMode* function. The mode number for this extended mode is 63H. Please note that the ATI VGAWonder card contains some non-volatile memory that must be set for extended modes by using a set-up program that is furnished with the card. If this is not done first, the card will not run in any of the extended modes.

*Figure 9-5. SetMode and Plot Files for ATI VGAWonder VGA
Display Adapter Card*

```
/*

    setMode and plot functions for ATI VGAWonder display
    adapter VGA board 800 × 600 pixel × 256 color mode.

Make the following changes in the main program
*/

int xres=800, yres=600;
int io_address;
setMode(0x63);

/*

                setMode() = Sets video mode

*/

void setMode(int mode)
{
    reg.h.ah = 0x00;
    reg.h.al = mode;
    int86 (0x10,&reg,&reg);
}

/*

    plot() = Function to plot point to VGA 256 color
 screen.

*/

void plot(int x, int y, int color)
```

(continued)

```
{
    long int offset;
    char far *address;
    int bank, temp;

    offset = (long)xres * (long)y + (long)x;
    bank = offset/65536L;
    offset = offset % 65536L;
    if (bank != active_bank)
    {
        active_bank = bank;
        outportb(0x1CE,0xB2);
        temp = inportb(0x1CF);
        temp = (((temp & 0xE1) | (bank << 1)) << 8) | 0xB2;
        outport(0x1CE,temp);
    }
    address = (char far *)(0xA0000000L + offset);
    *address = color;
}
```

EGA/VGA BIOS Functions

The EGA/VGA Basic Input Output System (BIOS) resides in Read Only Memory (ROM) on the EGA or VGA card. It is addressed at the computer memory space between C0000H and C4000H, and becomes a part of the overall computer BIOS automatically. (On boot up, the computer scans a designated memory space that includes the area just designated, looking for a header at 2K intervals, which indicates that a BIOS extension exists, and when such is found, it incorporates the necessary code to allow the BIOS extension to be accessed for all appropriate operations.) The BIOS extension consists of three sections. The first performs hardware checks when the computer is booted up, reporting EGA or VGA failures with various audible beep codes. (It is assumed that, if there are display hardware problems, it will be impossible to display any error code on the screen; therefore the audible error codes are used.) If all is well, the BIOS then initializes the display hardware and the monitor so that normal display operations can take place.

The next section of the BIOS extension contains a number of functions that are useful for manipulating the display. These are all accessed through an interrupt, 10H. The address of the interrupt handler code is stored in the interrupt vector table at memory address 40H. Because these functions must be addressed through the interrupt route, they tend to be relatively slow compared with direct access functions. When the interrupt is called, the computer must first store the contents of all its registers. It then loads some pertinent registers with new data. Next it gets the address of the interrupt handler from the interrupt vector table and jumps there. According to the register contents, it jumps to a selected function and performs the necessary actions. It saves some of the resulting register contents and then restores the original register contents. Finally it returns to the calling program. All of this additional overhead doesn't matter very much when you are performing an operation that occurs only occasionally, such as setting a display mode. However, if you are plotting pixels to the screen, where you would like to plot thousands of pixels that make up part of a display in a very short time, you'll find the EGA/VGA BIOS functions too slow, so that other measures are needed to achieve satisfactory speed.

The final section of the EGA/VGA BIOS contains character tables. For the EGA, 8 by 8 pixel, and 8 by 14 pixel color tables are supplied. For the VGA, both these and also an 8 by 16 pixel character table are available. Extensions are also available to make 9 pixel wide characters. Normally, selection of these character tables occurs automatically when a display mode is selected. You can access the tables however, and do interesting things like write different size characters to a display or write characters vertically to the screen. How to do all this will be described in Chapter 19.

In the remainder of this chapter, we are going to list all of the EGA/VGA BIOS functions and describe what they do. Along with most function descriptions, we're going to supply samples of functions written in C which make use of that BIOS function. The Borland family of C and C++ compilers has several ways of calling the interrupt driven functions. These include the function calls *int86, int86x, intr,* and *geninterrupt.* The first of these is useful when we have a function that uses only the normal registers *a* through *d.* This function also enables you to access the high and low bytes of each register separately, if that is desireable. The *int86x* function also makes use of the segment and pointer registers, when they are needed by the function. Both these functions are also supported by MicroSoft C. The *intr* function often provides a simpler way to communicate with a BIOS function that requires segment and pointer registers. We will use it to illustrate some applications in various functions, but if you are using MicroSoft C, you should be aware that it does not support this function and should modify your programs accordingly. We won't use the *geninterrupt* call at all, since it doesn't guarantee the condition of registers when it returns, which can sometimes cause some subtle complications that are hard to troubleshoot. The functions in this chapter have all been tested with Turbo C++ and Borland C++.

Since we have not usually used the C++ features, they should also work with older versions of Turbo C. Compiler manufactureres often make changes from one compiler version to another that require programming changes to get everything compatible again, so don't be surprised to see some problems if you are using a different compiler version.

Setting Display Modes (EGA/VGA Video Service 00H)

Register Inputs	Register Outputs
AX = Video mode	None

Chapter 5 describes the display modes in great detail, so we won't list or discuss them here. This BIOS video service supports all of the standard EGA modes (for an EGA card) and EGA and VGA modes (for a VGA card) and may also support extended modes. You can also use a mode call to clear the screen and return it to a clear black background. However, this method of clearing can be slow on some computers, and you'll find later that we have a better screen clearing technique that also lets you set the background color. Normally, the most significant bit of the lower register byte is 0. This causes the screen to be cleared when the mode is changed. If you OR the Video mode with 80H, to set the most significant bit of the lower register byte to 1, the mode change is made without clearing display memory. You might think that this would be a great way to switch from a graphics display to a text menu of some sort and then recover the graphics display, but it doesn't work out that way. First, although the test is addressed at a different place in memory that the graphics, only the addressing really changes; the actual memory locations overlap, so that whatever you do in the text mode will mess up the graphics display. Furthermore, even if you just reset the same graphics mode without clearing, it will do weird things to your display. Following are two functions for setting the display mode. You'll note that in most of these EGA/VGA BIOS video services, we put the service number into register *AH*, but for this special case where the value is zero, we can just put the mode into register *AX*, which automatically zeroes *AH*, and makes the program a little simpler.

```
/*

      ┌─────────────────────────────────────────────────┐
      │┌───────────────────────────────────────────────┐│
      ││                                               ││
      ││      setMode() = Function to set display mode ││
      ││                                               ││
      │└───────────────────────────────────────────────┘│
      └─────────────────────────────────────────────────┘
*/

void setMode(int mode)
{
      union REGS regs;

      regs.x.ax = mode;
      int86(&regs,&regs);
}
```

Alternate method of doing the same function.

```
/*

      ┌─────────────────────────────────────────────────┐
      │┌───────────────────────────────────────────────┐│
      ││                                               ││
      ││      setMode() = Function to set display mode ││
      ││                                               ││
      │└───────────────────────────────────────────────┘│
      └─────────────────────────────────────────────────┘
*/

void setMode(int mode)
{
      struct REGPACK regs;

      regs.r_ax = mode;
      intr(&regs);
}
```

Setting the Cursor Shape (EGA/VGA Video Service 01H)

Register Inputs	Register Outputs
AH = 01H CH = Scan line for start of cursor CL = Scan line for end of cursor	None

This video service sets the shape of the cursor by specifying the beginning and ending scan lines for which the cursor is to be displayed. The default cursor is a blinking single line, which is the last (bottom) line of the character box. The cursor is displayed only in the text modes; in the graphics modes it is not shown, but the BIOS does keep track of its position. If you enter a starting line (register CH) of 20H, the cursor will be turned off. Other than this, you should not enter values higher than the last line of the character box (which is 8, 14 or 16, depending upon the display mode selected). If you enter an ending line value that is less than the starting line value, for the EGA, this will result in the cursor beginning at the specified line and continuing to the bottom of the character box and then starting again at the top of the character box and continuing to the specified ending line. This results in a two part cursor with a space in the middle. If you try this same thing with the VGA, the cursor will simply not be displayed. In addition to controlling the shape of the cursor, this function stores the starting line value in memory location 461H and the ending line value in memory location 460H. The following is a C function to set the cursor shape:

```
/*

    setCursorShape() = Function to set the shape of the
                          cursor

*/

void setCursorShape (int start_line, int end_line)
{
      union REGS regs;
```

(continued)

```
        regs.h.ah = 0x01;
        regs.h.ch = start_line;
        regs.h.cl = end_line;
        int86(&regs,&regs);
}
```

Setting the Cursor Position (EGA/VGA Video Service 02H)

Register Inputs	Register Outputs
AH = 02H BH = Page number DH = Display row (y) DL = Display column (x)	None

This service establishes the cursor position at the specified column and row of the stated page. If you are in a text mode, the cursor will then appear at the specified position if you are viewing the stated page. The BIOS keeps track of the cursor position separately for each page and switches the cursor to the new position when you change pages. The number of pages for a particular display mode depends upon the amount of memory installed in your EGA/VGA card. If you are using a graphics mode, the cursor will not appear, but if you write out text, it will begin at the current cursor position. The first cursor position, at the top lefthand corner of the display is (0,0).

The last position at the bottom right depends upon the display mode. For display mode 10H, for example, the resolution is 640 by 350 pixels and the characters displayed are 80 by 25. Thus the last cursor position for this mode is (79,24). Note that the Borland C family has a *gotoxy* function which sets the cursor position, but it is referenced to the top lefthand corner of any window that has been specified. If the window is specified as the whole screen, the *gotoxy* function coordinates for the first position are (1,1) and for the example given earlier, the last position is (80,25). Therefore if you interchange it with functions that use the BIOS system of numbering, there will be a slight difference in position.The cursor location information is stored in memory in the memory locations beginning at 450H. The cursor column position for a given page is stored in location 450H + page number * 2 and the cursor row position for a given page is stored in location 451H + page number * 2. You have three choices when you write a function in C to set the cursor position. You can ignore the page number problem altogether and always set the cursor for page 0. In many cases, you'll be using only page 0 and this works just fine. Second, you can specifiy the desired page and write the cursor position to it. This gives the most flexibility, but requires passing an extra parameter. Third, you can have the function determine the current page and always write the cursor position to it. In this case, you are constrained to the page you are on. The function to do this first uses the video service 0FH to get the active page number. It returns in register BH, which is just where you want it for the cursor positioning service. The three functions follow:

```
/*

    gotoXY() = Function to set cursor position on page 0

*/

void gotoXY (int x, int y)
{
        union REGS regs;

        regs.h.ah = 0x03;
        regs.h.bh = 0;
        regs.h.dl = x;
        regs.h.dh = y;
        int86(0x10,&regs,&regs);
}

/*

    gotoXY() = Function to set cursor position on given
                          page

*/

void gotoXY (int x, int y, int page)
{
```

(continued)

```
union REGS regs;

    regs.h.ah = 0x03;
    regs.h.bh = page;
    regs.h.dl = x;
    regs.h.dh = y;
    int86(0x10,&regs,&regs);
}

/*
```

```
┌─────────────────────────────────────────────────────────┐
│                                                         │
│   gotoXY() = Function to set cursor position on current │
│                           page                          │
│                                                         │
└─────────────────────────────────────────────────────────┘
```

```
*/

void gotoXY (int x, int y)
{
    union REGS regs;

    regs.h.ah = 0x0F;
    int86 (0x10,&regs,&regs);
    regs.h.ah = 0x03;
    regs.h.dl = x;
    regs.h.dh = y;
    int86(0x10,&regs,&regs);
}
```

Reading the Cursor Position (EGA/VGA Video Service 03H)

Register Inputs	Register Outputs
AH = 03H BH = Page number	DL = Column DH = Row CH = Start line for cursor CL = End line for cursor

This is a double purpose video service which returns the cursor location and cursor shape location. The descriptions of the two previous services have pointed out where this information is stored in memory, and you can, if you desire, write a program to extract the information directly from memory. However, using this video service is usually easier. You'll probably never have a reason for reading information on the cursor shape. If it's visible (text mode) you can see what the shape is, and if it's invisible (graphics mode), the shape doesn't really matter. Similarly to the previous video service, you have the option of writing a function that will read the cursor position from page 0, from a specified page or from the current page. We won't list all varieties this time; you can see from the previous examples how to write the function you want. Function calls in C don't really handle returning two parameters very well. There are three basic ways to handle this situation. The first is to have two separate functions to get the cursor data. This works as follows:

```
/*

        getx = Function to get cursor x position

*/

int getx (void)
{
        union REGS regs;

        regs.h.ah = 0x03;
        int86(0x10,&regs,&regs);
        return (regs.h.dh);
}

/*

        gety = Function to get cursor y position

*/

int gety (void)
{
        union REGS regs;
```

(continued)

```
        regs.h.ah = 0x03;
        int86(0x10,&regs,&regs);
        return (regs.h.dl);
}
```

The next approach is to pass pointers to the function. This works as follows:

```
/*

        getxy = Function to get cursor position

*/
```

```
int getxy (int *x, int *y)
{
        union REGS regs;

        regs.h.ah = 0x03;
        int86(0x10,&regs,&regs);
        *x = regs.h.dh;
        *y = regs.h.dl;
}
```

Finally, we can make use of a *define* statement in connection with the first pair of functions that we listed above. This works as follows:

```
/*

        getxy() = Gets the position of the cursor

*/
```

```
#define getxy(x,y) {x=getx(); y=gety();}
```

This looks just like an ordinary function, but the values of x and y are replaced with the new cursor position just as if both functions could be returned by a function call.

Reading the Light Pen Position (EGA/VGA Video Service 04H)

Register Inputs	Register Outputs

AH = 04H	AH = 0: Light pen triggered
	    = 1: Light pen not triggered
	DL = Column
	DH = Row
	CH = Pixel line number (old
	    graphics modes)
	CX = Pixel line number (New
	    EGA and VGA graphics
	    modes
	BX = Pixel column number

When the IBM PC first came out, it seemed as if light pens were going to be a great way to communicate information to the computer. They never became very popular, however, and have been virtually replaced by the mouse or the trackball. Consequently, VGA cards do not support this video service, although it remains on the EGA as a relic from the past. If you ever come across a light pen, this is how it works. The light pen contains a light sensor. When you hold it up to the face of the monitor CRT, as the scanning electron beam passes the position where the light pen is being held, a pulse of light is emitted by the CRT's phosphorescent screen, which triggers the light pen circuits. This sets them to the light pen triggered mode and stores the coordinates of the position occupied by the beam when the trigger occurred. This video service reports back the fact that the system is in the triggered state and reports the position in terms of x and y graphics pixels as well as text column and row. Once the report is made, the circuits are cleared of position data and returned to the not triggered mode to wait for the next light pen trigger.

Selecting the Display Page (EGA/VGA Video Service 05H)

Register Inputs	Register Outputs
AH = 04H AL = Page to become active	None

Depending upon the display mode that has been selected, and the amount of video memory that is on the EGA or VGA card, there may be enough video memory to provide one to eight pages of text or full screen video graphics. However, only one page can be displayed at a time on the monitor. This video service determines which page will be displayed (the active page). The number of available pages for each mode and memory combination is listed in Chapter 5. The number of the active page is stored at memory location 462H and the address of the starting location of the active page in memory is stored in memory locations 44EH and 44FH. The active page can be changed by the following function:

```
/*

        setPage() = Function to set the active page

*/

void setPage (int page)
{
        union REGS regs;

        regs.h.ah = 0x05;
        regs.h.al = page;
        int86 (0x10,&regs, &regs);
}
```

Scrolling a Window up (EGA/VGA Video Service 06H)

Register Inputs	Register Outputs
AH = 06H AL = Number of character rows to scroll up BH = Attribute (color)to be used on new blank lines entering the window from the bottom CH = The number of the upper left character row of the window CL = The number of the upper left character column of the window DH = The number of the lower right character row of the window DL = The number of the lower right character column of the window	None

This video service defines a window on the screen and scrolls by moving all character rows within the window up (the top one(s) are removed from the screen) and inserting new blank rows having the specified attribute at the bottom. The term *attribute* is misleading, what is actually meant is the color of the lines that are inserted. This color is in terms of the colors from 0 to 16 that were defined in Chapter 5 (or whichever of the 64 available colors you have substituted for them) for the 16 EGA palettes when you are in a 16 color mode or the 256 colors of the 256 color modes. This is not really a background color, but a foreground color. consequently, if you do a *printf* command to one of these blank lines, whatever color you used for the blank lines in the window will be replaced with a background of black and a foreground of white for each printed character. If you enter a zero for the number of lines scanned, the entire window will be blanked to the specified color. This is about the fastest means of clearing the screen. There are several interesting things that you can do with this video service. Functions to perform these operations follow. The first function that we will consider is clearing the screen. We have already mentioned that this can be accomplished by telling a full screen window to scroll zero character rows. However, we need to observe that, while this will work for any of the EGA/VGA standard display modes, it probably won't be successful with the extended high resolution modes. The next question is: How big is a full screen window? For any display mode, we can find the number of character columns and rows in Chapter 5. However, the number of character rows is obtained by dividing the number of scan lines in that display mode by the number of scan lines that make up the character cell for the character font that is usually used with that mode. If we have gotten sophisticated and specified a different character set, we may also have changed the number of character rows without knowing it. However, let's assume that we are smart enough to determine the number of character columns and rows and thus determine the bottom right corner of a window that fills the whole screen. Do we then need a separate screen clearing function for every display mode? Actually this is the best way to work the function. It is fastest and avoids any peculiar problems. Of course, if we plan to use this function in only one or two graphics modes, we don't need to worry about any others. The two functions that follow are examples. The first is a special purpose function that clears a mode 10H screen. The second is a little more flexible. It clears the screen for several different display modes and can be expanded for others if you wish. It begins by using a video service that we haven't described yet to obtain the display mode and then uses a *switch* statement to select the right value for the bottom right hand corner of the window before performing the scrolling action.

```
/*

    cls() = Clears the screen to designated color for
                    display mode 10H

*/

void cls(int color)
{
        union REGS regs;

        regs.x.ax = 0x0600;
        regs.x.cx = 0;
```

(continued)

```
        regs.x.dx = 0x184F;
        regs.h.bh = color;
        int86(0x10,&regs,&regs);
}
```

```
/*
```

```
    cls() = Clears the screen to designated color for
                   various display modes
```

```
*/
```

```
void cls(int color)
{
        union REGS regs;
        int mode;

        regs.h.ah = 0x0F;
        int86 (0x10,&regs,&regs);
        switch(regs.h.al)
        {
                case 13:    /* 320 x 200 - 16 colors */
                case 14:    /* 640 x 200 - 16 colors */
                case 16:    /* 640 x 350 - 16 colors */
                case 19:    /* 320 x 200 - 256 colors */
                        regs.x.dx = 0x184F;
                        break;
                case 18:    /* 640 x 480 - 16 colors */
                        regs.x.dx = 0x1D4F;
                        break;
        }
        regs.x.ax = 0x0600;
        regs.x.cx = 0;
        regs.h.bh = color;
        int86(0x10,&regs,&regs);
}
```

With either of these functions, if you wish to end your clearing of the screen by positioning the cursor at the top lefthand corner, you can add the line

```
gotoXY(0,0);
```

just before the ending curly bracket. We said that this is the best way to clear the screen, but never really came to grips with what happens if we exceed the actual screen window size. Suppose, for example, that we assume 8 by 8 pixel characters and a 640 by 480 pixel screen and come up with a maximum of 80 character columns and 60 character rows. Why can't we use this for every display mode and have a very simple screen clearing function. The answer is that this will work in many cases. What is dangerous is that the BIOS code provides no protection against running beyond the end of the display memory window. If you get into a section of memory that is devoted to something else, your system can bomb in a hurry. So try to avoid this technique and play it safe.

Next, let's consider the situation where we want to create the background for a scene that has blue sky at the top and green grass at the bottom. We can use this same video service to clear the screen to two colors, one above a certain character row and the other below it. The function that does this follows. This version is tailored for mode 12H, but you can easily modify it to handle other display modes by following the examples shown previously. Note, however, that the line of demarcation between colors will not be at the same place on the screen for every display mode, since the total number of character rows may change for different modes, but character row number at which the color changes will remain the same, instead of changing proportionally to the display mode.

```
/*

    set_screen() = Sets the screen background colors for
                   display mode 12H

*/

void set_screen(int top_color, int bottom_color,
    int boundary)
{
    union REGS regs;
```

(continued)

```
        regs.h.ah = 0x06;
        regs.h.al = boundary;
        regs.x.cx = 0;
        regs.x.dx = 0x1D4F;
        regs.h.bh = top_color;
        int86(0x10,&regs,&regs);
        regs.h.ah = 0x06;
        regs.h.al = 30 - boundary;
        regs.h.bh = bottom_color;
        int86(0x10,&regs,&regs);
}
```

Next, let's look at a function that creates a window on a part of your screen. The top left and bottom right corners are defined in terms of character column and row coordinates. Because the *al* register (bottom byte of *ax*) is 0, the entire window is filled with blank lines of the designated color. As mentioned earlier, you can write characters to this window, but you need a function that will let you designate the character's background color; the *printf* function won't hack it since it draws white colors on a black background, no matter what color you have made the window. The window parameters are saved to a set of global variables so that if you are going to scroll the window no incompatibilities are introduced. You may put these parameters in a structure if you wish to do so.

```
/*

    window() = Makes a window on the display screen for
        display mode 12H at specified rectangle corners
                    in a specified color

*/

void window(int xl, int yt, int xr, int yb int color)
{
        union REGS regs;
        extern int window_xl, window_yt, window_xr,
                window_yb, window_color;

        regs.x.ax = 0x0600;
```

(continued)

```
        window_xl = regs.h.cl = xl;
        window_yt = regs.h.ch = yt;
        window_xr = regs.h.dl = xr;
        window_yb = regs.h.dh = yb;
        window_color = regs.h.bh = color;
        int86(0x10,&regs,&regs);
}
```

Once you have written to an empty window, you can use the scroll up video service to scroll everything up and add blank lines at the bottom. The following function is very similar to the preceeding one except that it puts the number of rows to be scrolled into the *al* register instead of a 0. Since very strange things happen if the scrolled window doesn't have the same dimensions and color as the window that you first created with the *window* function, the window parameters that were stored in global variables by the *window* function are used to define this window, instead of allowing you to pass any values that you want to the function. You can simplify this function a bit by limiting it to scrolling up a single line. Then you don't need to pass any parameters to it; instead you set the *al* register to one within the function.

```
/*
```

```
  scroll_up() = Scrolls a window on the display screen by
        a specified number of character rows for display
          mode 12H using coordinates and color specified
                        for window function
```

```
*/
```

```
void scroll_up(int rows)
{
        union REGS regs;

        extern int window_xl, window_yt, window_xr,
                window_yb, window_color;

        regs.h.ah = 0x06;
        regs.h.al = rows;
```

(continued)

```
        regs.h.cl = window_xl;
        regs.h.ch = window_yt;
        regs.h.dl = window_xr;
        regs.h.dh = window_yb;
        regs.h.bh = window_color;
        int86(0x10,&regs,&regs);
}
```

Scrolling a Window down (EGA/VGA Video Service 07H)

Register Inputs	Register Outputs

AH = 07H
AL = Number of character rows
    to scroll down
BH = Attribute (color) to be
    used on new blank lines
    entering the window
    from the top
CH = The number of the upper
    left character row of the
    window
CL = The number of the upper
    left character column of
    the window
DH = The number of the lower
    right character row of
    the window
DL = The number of the lower
    right character column
    of the window
	None

This video service is just the same as the one just described except that blank lines are added at the top instead of at the bottom and all lines within the window are moved downward, with the bottom lines dropping out of the window. All the functions described for scrolling up with work equally well when scrolling down.

Reading a Character and Its Attribute from the Screen (EGA/VGA Video Service 08H)

Register Inputs	Register Outputs
AH = 08H BH = Active page	AH = Attribute of text character AL = ASCII value of text character, if found

This video service attempts to read the character that is at the current cursor position. For text modes, the character code for each character on the screen is stored in display memory plane 0 and the character attribute is stored in display memory plane 1. These locations are simply read and returned by the video service. (A blank area of the screen contains space codes (20H).) In the graphics mode, things are much more complicated because we have control over every pixel on the display and can create patterns that are almost but not quite alphanumeric characters. In this case, the video service compares the contents of the character cell pointed to by the cursor and compares it with the character patterns stored in the BIOS for the lower 128 characters of the 256 character set. If a match is found, the character code is returned in register *AL*; otherwise this register is set 0. (You can't read a space in the graphics mode; a zero is returned to indicate no match was found.) The returned contents of register *AH* is meaningless for graphics modes. If you need to read characters from 128 to 255 in the graphics mode, you will need to run video service 11H, subservice 20H to set the pointer to the character table to the upper half of the table. This service and subservice will be described later.

When it comes to writing a C function to read a character from the screen, if we want to read text characters, we have the same old problem, C can return only one value from a function. We can handle this in two ways. The first is rather awkward; it returns the character directly and passes a pointer to the attribute to the function so that the variable pointed to will contain the attribute when we return. This function is as follows:

```
/*
```

```
/*

    getChar() = Reads a character and its attribute from
                         the screen

*/

char getChar (int page, char *attribute)
{
        union REGS regs;

        regs.h.ah = 0x08;
        regs.bh = page;
        int86 (0x10,&regs,&regs);
        *attribute = regs.h.ah;
        return (regs.h.al)
}
```

Here is a nicer way to do the same thing:

```
/*

    getChar() = Reads a character and its attribute from
                         the screen

*/

#define getChar(page,ch,attribute) {ch = get_ch(page);\
        attribute = get_attr(page);}

char get_ch (int page)
{
        union REGS regs;

        regs.h.ah = 0x08;
        regs.bh = page;
        int86 (0x10,&regs,&regs);
        return (regs.h.al)
}
```

(continued)

```
char get_attr (int page)
{
        union REGS regs;

        regs.h.ah = 0x08;
        regs.h.bh = page;
        int86 (0x10,&regs,&regs);
        return (regs.h.ah)
}
```

If you are going to use this function only when in the graphics modes, you don't need to worry about the attribute at all, so you can use this simple function:

```
/*

        getChar() = Reads a character from the screen

*/
```

```
char getChar (int page)
{
        union REGS regs;

        regs.h.ah = 0x08;
        regs.bh = page;
        int86 (0x10,&regs,&regs);
        return (regs.h.al)
}
```

Furthermore, if you want to work only with page 0, you don't need to pass the page parameter, but can set register *BH* to 0 instead.

Writing a Character and Its Attribute to the Screen (EGA/VGA Video Service 09H)

Register Inputs	Register Outputs
AH = 09H AL = ASCII character code of 　　　character to be written 　　　to the screen BL = Attribute of character to 　　　be written to screen BH = Active page CX = Number of times to write 　　　character and attribute 　　　to the screen	None

This service turns out to be quite different, depending upon whether you are writing a character in the text modes, the 16 color graphics modes, or the 256 color modes. For text modes, both foreground and background colors are written to the screen. However, the background can only be one of the eight non-intensified colors, since only palette numbers 0–7 are allowed. These can be the default colors or whichever of the 64 available colors you have set the palettes to. The foreground can be any of the 16 available palette colors (either default or as selected). The most significant bit determines whether the character will blink or not. The attribute byte for text modes is this:

Byte 7	Byte 6	Byte 5	Byte 4	Byte 3	Byte 2	Byte 1	Byte 0
Blink.	Background palette number (0–7).			Foreground palette number (0–15).			

In the 16 color graphics modes, only the foreground of the character is drawn; the background remains unchanged from the existing background color (whatever color is assigned to palette 0). This doesn't mean that you can write a character over a picture on the screen and have the background of the character remain unchanged, because the background of the character cell is rewritten to the current background color (which is usually black). The character itself is written in whichever of the 16 palette colors is selected. The most significant bit, when on, causes the character to be exclusive ORed with the current data. In this mode, nothing will appear different if you are writing to a background area of the screen. However, if you write the same character again in the same place, it will disappear. If you write on a varigated area of the screen, the color of various parts of the character may vary, depending upon the original character cell contents. Writing the same character a second time to the same place will cause the picture to return to its original contents. The attribute byte for 16 color graphics modes is this:

Byte 7	Byte 6	Byte 5	Byte 4	Byte 3	Byte 2	Byte 1	Byte 0
0 = overwrite character. 1 = XOR character with existing data.	Not used.			Foreground palette number (0–15).			

In the 256 color graphics mode, only the foreground of the character is drawn; the background remains unchanged from the existing background color (whatever color is assigned to palette 0). This doesn't mean that you can write a character over a picture on the screen and have the background of the character remain unchanged, because the background of the character cell is rewritten to the current background color (which is usually black). The character itself is written in the color specified by whichever of the 256 color registers is selected. The attribute byte for the 256 color graphics mode is this:

Byte 7	Byte 6	Byte 5	Byte 4	Byte 3	Byte 2	Byte 1	Byte 0
Foreground color register number.							

Note that whichever case you are using, you must be sure to set a value for register *CX* since this determines how many characters will be written to the screen. Normally this is set to 1, but it can be set to a different value if you want to fill an area with the same character. For text modes, this number should be no greater than the number of characters from the current cursor position to the end of the display screen. For graphics modes, this number should be no greater than the number of characters from the current cursor position to the end of the current line. If you use larger numbers than this, you won't like what happens. Strange spacings, overwrites, and blankings will occur.If you leave it at the default value of 0, you'll like what happens even less. Multiple partial characters will write and rewrite the screen.

A simple function to write a character to the screen using this video service is this

```
/*

        write_c() = Writes a character to the screen

*/
```

```
void write_c(character ch, int attribute, int page)
{
        union REGS regs;

        regs.h.ah = 0x09;
        regs.h.al = ch;
        regs.h.bl = attribute;
        regs.h.bh = page;
        regs.x.cx = 1;
        int86(0x10,&regs,&regs);
}
```

The only trouble with this function is that if you use it a number of times to write a bunch of characters, without any intervening steps, they will all be written on top of each other at the current cursor location. This is a real peculiarity of this BIOS video service, since if you set the *CX* register to write several characters, they will be written side by side rather than on top of each other, but the cursor position will not be changed, so the next time you write you'll start at the same location unless you change the cursor position. The following function increments the cursor position each time it writes a character and also moves it to the beginning of the next line when the end of the line is reached. When the last character on the page is written, it sets the cursor to the top lefthand corner of the page. The function requires two external variables, which contain the values of the number of characters in a line and the number of lines on the screen.

```
/*
```

```
        write_c() = Writes a character to the screen
```

```
*/
```

```
void write_c(char ch, int attribute, int page)
{
        union REGS regs;

        extern int no_of_rows;
        extern int no_of_cols;

        regs.h.ah = 0x09;
        regs.h.al = ch;
        regs.h.bl = attribute;
        regs.h.bh = page;
        regs.x.cx = 1;
        int86(0x10,&regs,&regs);
        regs.h.ah = 0x03;
        int86(0x10,&regs,&regs);
        regs.h.dl++;
        if (regs.h.dl >= no_of_cols)
        {
                regs.h.dl = 0;
                regs.h.dh = (regs.h.dh + 1) % no_of_rows;
        }
        regs.h.ah = 0x02;
        int86(0x10,&regs,&regs);
}
```

Now that you have a character writing function that takes care of the cursor position, you can create a string writing function that calls the character writing function, or you can build the character writing function right into the string writing function. The former is the simplest way; the latter is the fastest. Here are the two techniques:

```
/*
```

```
 write_s() = Writes a string to the screen using write_c
```

```
*/
```

```
void write_s(char *string, int attribute, int page)
{
      int i = 0;

      while (string[i])
            write_c(string[i], attribute, page);
}
```

```
/*
```

```
   write_c() = Writes a character to the screen (self-
                         contained)
```

```
*/
```

```
void write_s(char *string ch, int attribute, int page)
{
      union REGS regs;

      extern int no_of_rows;
      extern int no_of_cols;
      int i = 0;

      while (string[i])
      {
            regs.h.ah = 0x09;
            regs.h.al = string[i];
            regs.h.bl = attribute;
            regs.h.bh = page;
            regs.x.cx = 1;
            int86(0x10,&regs,&regs);
            regs.h.ah = 0x03;
            int86(0x10,&regs,&regs);
```

(continued)

```
                      regs.h.dl++;
                      if (regs.h.dl >= no_of_cols)
                      {
                              regs.h.dl = 0;
                              regs.h.dh = (regs.h.dh + 1) % no_of_rows;
                      }
                      regs.h.ah = 0x02;
                      int86(0x10,&regs,&regs);
              }
      }
```

Writing a Character to the Screen (EGA/VGA Video Service 0AH)

Register Inputs	Register Outputs
AH = 0AH AL = ASCII character code of character to be written to the screen BL = Attribute of character to be written to screen for graphics modes (not used for text modes) BH = Active page CX = Number of times to write character and attribute to the screen	None

This video service is just the same as the previous one for graphics modes. For text modes, the only difference from the previous service is that it uses the current attribute instead of the one that is in register *BL*.

Setting the CGA Color Palette (EGA/VGA Video Service 0BH)

Register Inputs	Register Outputs

AH = 0BH
BH = Palette color ID.
    0 = Set background color.
    1 = Set CGA Palette.
       Background color
BL = when BH = 0.
    Palette (0 or 1) when
    BH = 1.
	None

This video service should be used only for video modes 4 and 5, where the EGA/VGA is emulating a CGA. If used in EGA/VGA graphics modes, its effect on colors is unpredictable. When register *BH* is set to 0, the value set into register *BL* sets the background color to one of the 16 EGA palette colors. When register *BH* is set to 1, register *BL* may be set to 0 or 1 to select CGA palette 0 or 1, respectively. Each CGA palette consists of only four colors. These are as follows:

CGA Palette 0		CGA Palette 1	
Screen Color	**Equivalent EGA Palette Number**	**Screen Color**	**Equivalent EGA Palette Number**
0 = background color	—	0 = background color	—
1 = green	2	1 = cyan	11
2 = red	4	2 = magenta	13
3 = brown	6	3 = white	15

The following is a C function that may be used to set either the CGA background color or choose the palette. This function first checks the mode and inputs to assure that they are in the proper range of acceptable values. Consequently, the function is executed only if you are in display mode 4 or 5. Note that for register *BH* set to 0, register

BL is limited to a palette number from 0 to 15 and that for register BH set to 1, register BL is limited to the palette numbers 0 or 1.

```
/*

    setCGApalette() = Function to set CGA palette and
                      background color

*/

void setCGApalette(int id, int color)
{
    union REGS regs;
    char mode;

    regs.h.ah = 0x0F;
    if ((mode != 4) && (mode != 5)
        return;
    if (((id == 0) && (color >= 0) && (color < 16)) ||
        ((id != 1) && (color >= 0) && (color < 2)))
    {
        regs.h.ah = 0x0B;
        regs.h.bh = id;
        regs.h.bl = color;
        int86 (0x10,&regs,&regs);
    }
}
```

Writing a Pixel to the Screen (EGA/VGA Video Service 0CH)

Register Inputs	Register Outputs
AH = 0CH AL = Pixel color and write method for 16 color modes. Pixel color for 256 color mode. BH = Page CX = Pixel x position DX = Pixel y position	None

Note that you can write the pixel to any page, not just the active one. Therefore you can view one page while writing to another. In the 16 color graphics modes, the most significant bit, when on, causes the character to be exclusive ORed with the current data. The rest of the register contents determines which of the 16 EGA palette colors will be used to write the pixel. The register contents byte for 16 color graphics modes is this:

Byte 7	Byte 6	Byte 5	Byte 4	Byte 3	Byte 2	Byte 1	Byte 0
0 = overwrite character. 1 = XOR character with existing data.	Not used.			Foreground palette number (0–15).			

In the 256 color graphics mode, the color byte represents any one of the 256 color registers, and the pixel is written in that color. The byte content is

Byte 7	Byte 6	Byte 5	Byte 4	Byte 3	Byte 2	Byte 1	Byte 0
Foreground color register number.							

The following is a function to write a pixel to a display page. This function will work for any supported EGA/VGA mode, but, as pointed out in Chapter 6, it is very slow if you're going to plot very many pixels.

```
/*

        plot() = Plots a pixel to the specified page at
               coordinates (x,y) in designated color

*/

void plot(int x, int y, int page, int color)
{
        union REGS regs;
```

(continued)

```
      regs.h.ah = 0x0C;
      regs.h.al = color;
      regs.h.bh = page;
      regs.x.cx = x;
      regs.x.dx = y;
      int86 (0x10,&regs,&regs);
}
```

Reading a Pixel from the Screen (EGA/VGA Video Service 0DH)

Register Inputs	Register Outputs
AH = 0DH BH = Page CX = Pixel x position DX = Pixel y position	AL = Pixel color

Note that you don't have to read the pixel from the active page; it can be on any designated display page. For 16 color modes, this service returns a four bit number (0 to 15), representing the number of the EGA palette that was used to write the pixel to the page. For the 256 color mode, the service returns an eight bit number (0 to 255) representing the color register that was used to write the pixel to the page. The following is a C function to read a pixel using this service:

```
/*

      getPixel() = Function to read a pixel from the
                   designated page

*/

int getPixel (int x, int y, int page)
{
      union REGS regs;
      regs.h.ah = 0x0D;
      regs.h.bh = page;
```

(continued)

```
        regs.x.cx = x;
        regs.x.dx = y;
        int86 (0x10,&regs,&regs);
        return (regs.h.al);
}
```

Writing a TTY Character to the Active Page (EGA/VGA Video Service 0EH)

Register Inputs	Register Outputs
AH = 0EH AL = ASCII character to be written to the active page BH = Active page BL = Foreground color of character for the graphics modes	None

This video service is designed to permit your display to emulate a TTY type terminal. The page that is specified becomes the active page. The service writes a character to the screen (the active page) at the current cursor location. It then automatically advances the cursor position one character column and if the end of the line has been reached, moves it to the beginning of the next line. When the end of the screen is reached the entire display is scrolled upward one line. The new bottom line has the same color as the previous line. For text modes, the color parameter is ignored and the character is displayed in white. For 16 color modes, the character is displayed with the color designated by the EGA palette number (0 to 15) that is specified. For 256 color modes, the character is displayed in the color designated by the color register whose number is specified (0 to 255). The service intercepts the carriage return, line feed, backspace and bell characters and uses them to act on the display. These actions are as follows:

ASCII Number	Symbol	Name	Action
0DH	CR	Carriage return	Moves cursor to column zero of next character row
0AH	LF	Line feed	Moves cursor down one character row
08H	BS	Backspace	Moves cursor one character position to the left
07H	BELL	Bell	Generates a beep in the system speaker

The following is a C function to make use of this video service:

```
/*


  writeTTY() = Writes a character to the active page in
    TTY mode (using specified color for graphics modes)


*/

void writeTTY (char ch, int color, int page)
{
      union REGS regs;

      regs.h.ah = 0x0E;
      regs.h.al = ch;
      regs.h.bh = page;
      regs.h.bl = color;
      int86 (0x10,&regs,&regs);
}
```

Determining the Current Video Display Mode (EGA/VGA Video Service 0FH)

Register Inputs	Register Outputs
AH = 0FH	AL = Current video display mode AH = Number of characters per row BH = Number of active display page

This video service, which has been used before in some of the C functions previously described, reports back the current display mode. The most significant bit of this word is 0 if the display was cleared during the latest mode set and 1 if it was not cleared. The service also reports the current number of characters in a row and the number of the active display page. Probably you'll never need to determine the number of characters in a row. You can obtain the display mode and active page separately using the following C functions:

```
/*

    getMode() = Function to get current display mode

*/

int getMode (void)
{
    union REGS regs;

    regs.h.ah = 0x0F;
    int86 (0x10,&regs,&regs);
    return (regs.h.al & 0x7F);
}

/*

    getPage() = Function to get current active display page

*/
```

(continued)

```
int getPage (void)
{
     union REGS regs;

     regs.h.ah = 0x0F;
     int86 (0x10,&regs,&regs);
     return (regs.h.bh);
}
```

Setting an EGA Palette Register (EGA/VGA Video Service 10H, Subservice 00H)

Register Inputs	Register Outputs
AH = 10H AL = 00H BH = Color BL = Palette number	None

This service selects the color for an individual palette register. There are 64 available colors and 16 available palette registers. This service should be used with the 16 color display modes only; do not use it with the 256 color mode. A C function to use this service follows:

```
/*

   setEGApalette() = Sets the color of an EGA/VGA palette
                            register

*/
```

```
void setEGApalette(char palette, char color)
{
     union REGS regs;
     regs.x.ax = 0x1000;
     regs.h.bl = palette;
     regs.h.bh = color;
     int86 (0x10,&regs,&regs);
}
```

Setting the Border Color (EGA/VGA Video Service 10H, Subservice 01H)

Register Inputs	Register Outputs
AH = 10H AL = 01H BH = Border color	None

It's best to leave this service alone, as it can be a little erratic. The EGA doesn't work well in the 350 line graphics modes if the border is set to any color but black. The service works for the VGA only for 80 character per line modes; in these modes the border is restricted to one character wide.

Setting the Palette and Border Registers All at Once (EGA/VGA Video Service 10H, Subservice 02H)

Register Inputs	Register Outputs
AH = 10H AL = 02H ES:DX = Pointer to a 17 byte table of palette register and border register values	None

This video service permits setting all of the EGA palette registers and the border register in a single operation. A C function that uses this service follows. This function requires a global variable *char pal_color[17]* that is filled with the color values for the 16 palette registers and the overscan (border) register before the function is called.

```
/*

    setAllEGApals() = Sets all the EGA palette registers
                      and the border register

*/

void setAllEGApals(char *pal_colors)
{
    struct REGPACK regs;
    struct SREGS sregs;

    regs.r_ax = 0x1002;
    segread(&sregs);
    regs.r_es = sregs.ds;
    regs.r_dx = (int)pal_colors;
    intr (0x10,&regs);
}
```

Toggling the Blink/Intensity Bit (EGA/VGA Video Service 10H, Subservice 03H)

Register Inputs	Register Outputs
AH = 10H	None
AL = 03H	
BL = 0 Attribute bit 7 is intensity	
= 1 Attribute bit 7 is blink	

This video service applies to the text display modes only. In the default condition, the attribute byte, when writing characters to a page, can define only eight background colors. The most significant bit of the attribute byte, when set to 1, causes the character to blink. If this service is run with register *BL* set to 0, the most significant attribute bit becomes part of the background color definition, permitting display of 16 background colors. Running the service with register *BL* set to 1 returns to the default state. A C function to perform this operation follows:

```
/*

    setBlink() = Sets EGA/VGA for most significant
       attribute bit to represent blink or color

*/

void setBlink (char blink)
{
    union REGS regs;

    regs.h.ah = 0x10;
    regs.h.al = 0x03;
    regs.h.bl = blink;
    int86 (0x10, &regs, &regs);
}
```

Reading a Palette Color (EGA/VGA Video Service 10H, Subservice 07H)

Register Inputs	Register Outputs
AH = 10H AL = 07H BL = Number of palette register	BH = color value of designated palette register

This video service works with the VGA only. The EGA palette registers are write only, so the color information cannot be recovered from them. A C function to utilize this service follows:

```
/*

    getPalette() = Returns the palette register color

*/
```

(continued)

```
char getPalette (char palette)
{
      union REGS regs;

      regs.h.ah = 0x10;
      regs.h.al = 0x07;
      regs.h.bl = palette;
      int86 (0x10, &regs, &regs);
      return (regs.h.bh);
}
```

Reading the Overscan (Border) Register (EGA/VGA Video Service 10H, Subservice 08H)

Register Inputs	Register Outputs
AH = 10H AL = 08H	BH = Color value of overscan (border) register

This video service works with the VGA only. The EGA overscan register is write only so its value cannot be recovered. A C function to utilize this service follows:

```
/*

   getOverscan() = Returns color of the overscan register

*/
```

```
char getOverscan (void)
{
      union REGS regs;

      regs.h.ah = 0x10;
      regs.h.al = 0x08;
      int86 (0x10, &regs, &regs);
      return (regs.h.bh);
}
```

Getting the Palette and Border Registers All at Once (EGA/VGA Video Service 10H, Subservice 09H)

Register Inputs	Register Outputs
AH = 10H AL = 09H ES:DX = Pointer to a 17 byte table of palette register and border register values	Data is returned to a 17 byte table pointed to by ES:DX

This video service permits getting all of the palette registers and the border register in a single operation. It works only with the VGA, since the EGA registers are write only. The seventeen byte table to contain the values must be established in the calling program or as a global variable. A C function that uses this service follows:

```
/*


     getAllEGApals() = Gets all the palette register and the
                 border register color values


*/

void getAllEGApals(char *pal_colors)
{
      struct REGPACK regs;
      struct SREGS sregs;

      regs.r_ax = 0x1009;
      segread(&sregs);
      regs.r_es = sregs.ds;
      regs.r_dx = (int)pal_colors;
      intr (0x10,&regs);
}
```

Setting a VGA Color Register (EGA/VGA Video Service 10H, Subservice 10H)

Register Inputs	**Register Outputs**
AH = 10H AL = 10H BX = Number of color register DH = Red value CH = Green value CL = Blue value	None

This video service permits setting the value of a single VGA color register. It is not applicable to the EGA, which doesn't have color registers. The red, green and blue register values can be individually set to a value between 0 and 63. In the 256 color modes, all 256 colors can be displayed on the screen. In the 16 color modes, the 16 palette registers can be assigned to groups of 16 or 64 color registers, permitting rapid changes of the entire color palette without changing the color registers. A C function that uses this service to set the value of a single color register follows:

```
/*

       setColorReg() = Sets a VGA color register

*/

void setColorReg(char reg_no, char red, char green, char
       blue)
{
       union REGS regs;

       regs.x.ax = 0x1010;
       regs.h.bh = reg_no;
       regs.h.dh = red;
       regs.h.ch = green;
       regs.h.cl = blue;
       int86 (0x10,&regs,&regs);
}
```

Setting a Block of VGA Color Registers All at Once (EGA/VGA Video Service 10H, Subservice 12H)

Register Inputs	Register Outputs
AH = 10H AL = 12H BX = Number of first color register to be changed CX = Number of color registers to be changed ES:DX = Pointer to table of color values	None

This video service permits setting a block of VGA color registers in a single operation. The service requires a table of color values established either in the calling program or as a global array. The table should be of type *char* and should contain 768 members (3 for each of the maximum of 256 colors). The colors are entered in the table as triplets, in the order red, green, blue, red, green, blue, etc. A C function that uses this service follows:

```
/*

    setVGAcolors() = Sets the colors of a block of VGA
                     color registers

*/

void setVGAcolors(char first_reg, char number, char
    *pal_colors)
{
    struct REGPACK regs;
    struct SREGS sregs;

    regs.r_ax = 0x1012;
    segread(&sregs);
    regs.r_es = sregs.ds;
    regs.r_dx = (int)pal_colors;
```

(continued)

```
        regs.r_bx = first_reg;
        regs.r_cx = number;
        intr (0x10,&regs);
}
```

Normally you'll have an array *pal_colors* large enough to hold a triplet for each of the 256 color registers. Thus the triplet for register 0 will be in array members 0, 1 and 2, the triplet for register 1 will be in members 3, 4 and 5 and so forth. If you are going to change a block of color registers beginning somewhere beyond register 0, you need to make sure that the array address passed to its function is the address of the member of the array that corresponds to the first register to be changed. You can't just pass the address of the beginning of the array.

Selecting the Color Page (EGA/VGA Video Service 10H, Subservice 13H)

Register Inputs	Register Outputs

AH = 10H
AL = 13H
BL = 0 Select paging mode:
    BH = 0-4 pages of 64
    color registers
    BH = 1-16 pages of 16
    color registers
BL = 1 Select page
    BH = page number (0–3
    for paging mode 0) (0–15
    for paging mode 1)
	None

This video service works only with the VGA. It determines how the 16 EGA palette registers will interact with the 256 VGA color registers for the 16 color display modes. The default mode is paging mode 0 and page 0. This enables the EGA palette registers to be set to any of the first 64 color registers. By setting the page to 1, 2 or 3, the corresponding color registers in the second, third or fourth set of 64 color registers will be assigned to the palette registers. In paging mode 1, the palette registers should be set to 0 through 15, which correspond to the first 16 color registers. As the page number is increased, the color register table increases by 16 for each increase in page number, so as to assign the pallete registers to the next group of 16 color registers. A C function to set up the paging mode and page follows:

```
/*
```

```
        setVGApaging() = Sets the VGA page mode or page
```

```
*/
```

```
void setVGApaging(char mode, char page)
{
        union REGS regs;

        regs.x.ax = 0x1013;
        regs.h.bl = mode;
        regs.b.bh = page;
        int86(0x10,&regs,&regs);
}
```

Reading a VGA Color Register (EGA/VGA Video Service 10H, Subservice 15H)

Register Inputs	Register Outputs
AH = 10H AL = 15H BX = Number of color register	DH = Red value CH = Green value CL = Blue value

This video service permits reading the value of a single VGA color register. It is not applicable to the EGA, which doesn't have color registers. We want to return the three color components from the register. However, function calls in C don't really handle returning three parameters very well. There are three basic ways to handle this situation. The first is to have three separate functions to get the color data. This works as follows:

```
/*

        get_red = Function to get red register value

*/

char get_red (char color_reg)
{
        union REGS regs;

        regs.x.ax = 0x1015;
        regs.x.bx = color_reg;
        int86(0x10,&regs,&regs);
        return (regs.h.dh);
}

/*

        get_green = Function to get green register value

*/

char get_green (char color_reg)
{
        union REGS regs;

        regs.x.ax = 0x1015;
        regs.x.bx = color_reg;
        int86(0x10,&regs,&regs);
        return (regs.h.ch);
}

/*

        get_blue = Function to get blue register value

*/
```

(continued)

```
char get_blue (char color_reg)
{
      union REGS regs;
      regs.x.ax = 0x1015;
      regs.x.bx = color_reg;
      int86(0x10,&regs,&regs);
      return (regs.h.cl);
}
```

Another method is to pass pointers to the color variables to the function. This works as follows:

```
/*
```

```
       get_colors = Function to get colors from a color
                             register
```

```
*/
```

```
int get_colors (char reg_no, char *red, char *green, char
      *blue)
{
      union REGS regs;

      regs.x.ax = 0x1015;
      regs.x.bx = reg_no;
      int86(0x10,&regs,&regs);
      *red = regs.h.dh;
      *green = regs.h.ch;
      *blue = regs.h.cl;
}
```

Finally, we can make use of a *define* statement in connection with the first three functions just described. This works as follows:

```
/*

    ┌─────────────────────────────────────────────────────┐
    │                                                     │
    │    get_colors = Function to get colors from a color │
    │                        register                     │
    │                                                     │
    └─────────────────────────────────────────────────────┘

*/
```

```
#define get_colors(red,green,blue) {red=get_red();\
    green=get_green(); blue=get_blue();}
```

This looks just like an ordinary function, but the values of *red, green* and *blue* are replaced with the values from the color register just as if both functions could be returned by a function call.

Reading a Block of VGA Color Registers All At Once (EGA/VGA Video Service 10H, Subservice 17H)

Register Inputs	Register Outputs
AH = 10H AL = 17H BX = Number of first color register to be changed CX = Number of color registers to read ES:DX = Pointer to table of color values	Data returned in table pointed to by ES:DX

This video service permits reading a block of VGA color registers in a single operation. The service requires a table of color values established either in the calling program or as a global array. The table should be of type *char* and should contain 768 members (3 for each of the maximum of 256 colors). The colors are returned to the table as triplets, in the order red, green, blue, red, green, blue, etc. A C function that uses this service follows:

```
/*

    getVGAcolors() = Gets the colors of a block of VGA
                     color registers

*/

void getVGAcolors(char first_reg, char number, char
     *pal_colors)
{
     struct REGPACK regs;
     struct SREGS sregs;

     regs.r_ax = 0x1017;
     segread(&sregs);
     regs.r_es = sregs.ds;
     regs.r_dx = (int)pal_colors;
     regs.r_bx = first_reg;
     regs.r_cx = number;
     intr (0x10,&regs);
}
```

Getting the Current Color Page and Paging Mode (EGA/ VGA Video Service 10H, Subservice 1AH)

Register Inputs	Register Outputs
AH = 10H AL = 1AH	BH = Current page BL = Current paging mode

This video service works only with the VGA. It determines how the 16 EGA palette registers are currently set to interact with the 256 VGA color registers for the 16 color display modes. A C function to set up the paging mode and page follows:

```
/*
```

```
        getVGApage() = Gets the VGA page mode and page
```

```
*/

void getVGApage(char *mode, char *page)
{
        union REGS regs;

        regs.x.ax = 0x101A;
        *mode = regs.h.bl;
        *page = regs.b.bh;
        int86(0x10,&regs,&regs);
}
```

Summing Color Values to Gray Scale (EGA/VGA Video Service 10H, Subservice 1BH)

Register Inputs	Register Outputs

AH = 10H
AL = 1BH
BX = Number of first color
      register to be summed
CX = Number of registers to
      sum
	None

This video service works only with the VGA. It sums the color values of each color register that is operated upon to a gray value by the equation:

$$gray\ scale = (0.30 \times red) + (0.59 \times green) + (0.11 \times blue)$$

The resulting gray intensity value is placed in the red, green, and blue portions of the color register. If the original color register values resulted in a realistic color picture, the new gray scale values will produce a realistic black and white reproduction. A C function to use this video service follows:

```
/*

    setGrayScale() = Sets color registers to gray values

*/

void setGrayScale(char first_reg, char number)
{
        union REGS regs;

        regs.x.ax = 0x101B;
        regs.x.bx = first_reg;
        regs.x.cx = number;
        int86(0x10,&regs,&regs);
}
```

Loading a User Character Font (EGA/VGA Video Service 11H, Subservice 00H)

Register Inputs	Register Outputs
AH = 11H	None
AL = 00H	
BL = Number of character block in display memory to load	
BH = Number of bytes per character	
CX = Number of characters to load	
DX = Character offset into memory block	
ES:BP = Pointer to the user character table	

This video service works with text modes only. In the text modes, the EGA/VGA uses display memory plane 2 and/or 3 to store character fonts. The EGA has four memory blocks of 16K bytes each which are dedicated to holding character sets, but only the first 8K of each block may hold a font. The VGA has eight memory blocks of 8K each which can all be used to store character fonts. This service loads a user defined character font, stored in a memory array, to be transferred to the designated character block in display memory. An offset may be designated for the beginning of the load.

Loading the ROM Monochrome Character Set (EGA/VGA Video Service 11H, Subservice 01H)

Register Inputs	Register Outputs
AH = 11H AL = 01H BL = Number of character block in display memory to load	None

This video service works with text modes only. It loads a monochrome character set (8 x 14 character cell) from ROM into the designated character block in display memory.

Loading the ROM 8x8 Double Dot Character Set (EGA/VGA Video Service 11H, Subservice 02H)

Register Inputs	Register Outputs
AH = 11H AL = 02H BL = Number of character block in display memory to load	None

This video service works with text modes only. It loads the 8 x 8 character cell double dot character set from ROM into the designated character block in display memory. A C function to utilize this service follows:

```
/*

                    font_8x8 () = Load 8 x 8 font

*/

void font_8x8 (int block)
{
        union REGS regs;
        regs.x.ax = 0x1102;
        regs.x.bx = block;
        int86(0x10,&regs,&regs);
}
```

Setting the Block Specifier (EGA/VGA Video Service 11H, Subservice 03H)

Register Inputs	Register Outputs
AH = 11H AL = 03H BL = Character generator block specifier	None

This video service works with text modes only. When block A and block B are designated to be the same, then bit 3 of the attribute byte of each character is the most significant bit of the foreground color description, thereby permitting the foreground color to be any of the 16 colors available in the 16 color display modes. When block A is different from block B, bit 3 of the attribute byte of each character is the block selector, selecting the font from block A when 0 and the character font from block B when 1. The bits representing each block are as follows:

Bit 7	Bit 6	Bit 5	Bit 4	Bit 3	Bit 2	Bit 1	Bit 0
		Block B Bit 2	Block A Bit 2	Block B Bit 1	Block B Bit 0	Block A Bit 1	Block A Bit 0

If you want to use attribute bit 3 to switch font blocks, you need to prevent it from being considered a color bit; otherwise characters from the two different fonts will be displayed in two different colors. What needs to be done is to set Attribute Register 12H—Color Plane Enable, to allow only three color planes by sending it 07H. IBM suggests doing this with video service 10H, subservice 00H, which sets an individual palette register. However, this doesn't work with some EGA/VGA boards. The safest technique is to run the following function just before loading fonts to access the register directly:

```
/*

    colors_8() = Limits characters to 8 foreground colors

*/

void colors_8 (void)
{
      outportb(0x3C0,0x12);
      outportb(0x3C0,0x07);
}
```

The following is a C function that sets two blocks as the active fonts:

```
/*

    block_select() = Allows attribute 3 of character to
           select font block instead of color

*/

void block_select (char block_1, char block_2)
{
      union REGS regs;

      regs.x.ax = 0x1103;
      regs.h.bl = (block_1&0x03) | ((block_1&0x04)<<2) |
           ((block_2&0x03) << 2) | ((block_2&0x04)<<3);
      int86(0x10,&regs,&regs);
}
```

The following is a C program which will permit you to test using two fonts on a single display:

```
/*
```

```
    charsize = Program to test using two character fonts

              By Roger T. Stevens    10-12-91
```

```
*/

#include <stdio.h>
#include <dos.h>

void block_select (char block_1, char block_2);
void colors_8 (void);
void font_8x8 (int block);
void font_8x16 (int block);
void setMode(int mode);
void write_c(char ch, int attribute, int page, int replic);

int no_of_cols = 80, no_of_rows = 30;

void main(void)
{
     union REGS regs;
     int i,j,k;
     char st[128] = {"Now is the time for all good men to"\
          "come to the aid of their country or their "\
          "party or whatever...."};

     setMode(0x03);
     printf("This is a test....");
     getch();
     colors_8();
     font_8x8(1);
     font_8x16(2);
     block_select(1,2);
     regs.x.ax = 0x1103;
     regs.x.bx = 0x0009;
```

(continued)

```
int86(0x10,&regs,&regs);
for (i=0; i<40; i++)
{
      gotoxy(2+i,2);
      write_c(st[i],0x21,0,1);
}
for (i=0; i<40; i++)
{
      gotoxy(2+i,6);
      write_c(st[i],0x29,0,1);
}
for (i=41; i<79; i++)
{
      gotoxy(2+i,6);
      write_c(st[i],0x21,0,1);
}
gotoxy(2,8);
write_c('a',0x29,0,1);
gotoxy(3,8);
write_c('2',0x21,0,1);
gotoxy(4,8);
write_c(' ',0x29,0,1);
gotoxy(5,8);
write_c('+',0x29,0,1);
gotoxy(6,8);
write_c(' ',0x29,0,1);
gotoxy(7,8);
write_c('b',0x29,0,1);
gotoxy(8,8);
write_c('2',0x21,0,1);
gotoxy(9,8);
write_c(' ',0x29,0,1);
gotoxy(10,8);
write_c('=',0x29,0,1);
gotoxy(11,8);
write_c(' ',0x29,0,1);
gotoxy(12,8);
write_c('c',0x29,0,1);
gotoxy(13,8);
write_c('2',0x21,0,1);
getch();
```

(continued)

```
}

/*
```

```
              setMode() = Sets video mode
```

```
*/

void setMode(int mode)
{
      union REGS reg;

      reg.h.ah = 0;
      reg.h.al = mode;
      int86 (0x10,&reg,&reg);
}

/*
```

```
        write_c() Writes a character to the screen
```

```
*/

void write_c(char ch, int attribute, int page, int replic)
{
      union REGS reg;

      reg.h.ah = 0x09;
      reg.h.al = ch;
      reg.h.bl = attribute;
      reg.h.bh = page;
      reg.x.cx = replic;
      int86(0x10,&reg,&reg);
      reg.h.ah = 0x03;
      int86(0x10,&reg,&reg);
      reg.h.dl++;
      if (reg.h.dl >= no_of_cols)
      {
            reg.h.dl = 0;
```

(continued)

```
                    reg.h.dh = (reg.h.dh + 1) % no_of_rows;
          }
          reg.h.ah = 0x02;
          int86(0x10,&reg,&reg);
    }
```

Loading the ROM 8x16 Character Set (EGA/VGA Video Service 11H, Subservice 04H)

Register Inputs	Register Outputs
AH = 11H AL = 04H BL = Number of character block in display memory to load	None

This video service works with text modes only. In the text modes, the EGA/VGA uses display memory plane 2 and/or 3 to store character fonts. The EGA has four memory blocks (of 16K bytes each) which are dedicated to holding character sets, but only the first 8K of each block may hold a font. The VGA has eight memory blocks of 8K each which can all be used to store character fonts. This service loads the 8 x 16 character cell character set from ROM into the designated character block in display memory. A C function to utilize this service follows:

```
/*

          font_8x16() = Load 8 x 16 font

*/

void font_8x16 (int block)
{
      union REGS regs;

      regs.x.ax = 0x1104;
      regs.x.bx = block;
      int86(0x10,&regs,&regs);
}
```

Loading a User Character Font (EGA/VGA Video Service 11H, Subservice 10H)

Register Inputs	Register Outputs
AH = 11H	None
AL = 10H	
BL = Number of character block in display memory to load	
BH = Number of bytes per character	
CX = Number of characters to load	
DX = Character offset into memory block	
ES:BP = Pointer to the user character table	

This video service is identical to subservice 00H except that it changes the values of several of the CRT Controller Registers to match the selected character size and that it does not automatically execute a set mode before the character set is downloaded. Thus you should run a set mode BIOS call before running this service. In addition, this service can be invoked only if the active display page is page 0. This service transfer a user defined character font, stored in a memory array, to the designated character block in display memory. An offset may be designated for the beginning of the load. The following are the CRT controller registers affected by this service:

Register	New Contents
Maximum Row Register (09H)	Number of scan lines per character. (Bytes per character minus one).
Cursor Start Register (0AH)	EGA = Bytes per character minus one. VGA = Bytes per character minus two.
Cursor End Register (0BH)	EGA = 0 (cursor fills character cell). VGA = Bytes per character minus one (cursor fills bottom two lines of character cell).
Vertical Display End Register (12H)	350 or 480 line screen = (Number of rows plus one) multiplied by (number of bytes per character) minus one. 200 line screen = (Number of rows plus one) multiplied by (number of bytes per character) multiplied by two minus one.
Overflow Register (07H)	Bit 8 of the Vertical Display End value computed above is bit 1 of this register. VGA = Bit 9 of the Vertical Display End value computed previously is bit 6 of this register.

Loading the ROM Monochrome Character Set (EGA/VGA Video Service 11H, Subservice 11H)

Register Inputs	Register Outputs
AH = 11H AL = 11H BL = Number of character block in display memory to load	None

This video service is identical to subservice 01H except that it changes the values of several of the CRT Controller registers to match the selected character size and that it does not automatically execute a set mode before the character set is downloaded. Thus you should run a set mode BIOS call before running this service. In addition, this service can be invoked only if the active display page is page 0. This service loads a monochrome character set (8 x 14 character cell) from ROM into the designated character block in display memory.

Loading the ROM 8x8 Double Dot Character Set (EGA/VGA Video Service 11H, Subservice 12H)

Register Inputs	Register Outputs
AH = 11H AL = 12H BL = Number of character block in display memory to load	None

This video service is identical to subservice 02H except that it changes the values of several of the CRT Controller Registers to match the selected character size and that it does not automatically execute a set mode before the character set is downloaded. Thus you should run a set mode BIOS call before running this service. In addition, this service can be invoked only if the active display page is page 0. This service loads the 8 x 8 character cell double dot character set from ROM into the designated character block in display memory.

Loading the ROM 8x16 Character Set (EGA/VGA Video Service 11H, Subservice 14H)

Register Inputs	Register Outputs
AH = 11H AL = 14H BL = Number of character block in display memory to load	None

This video service is identical to subservice 04H except that it changes the values of several of the CRT Controller Registers to match the selected character size and that it does not automatically execute a set mode before the character set is downloaded. Thus you should run a set mode BIOS call before running this service. In addition, this service can only be invoked if the active display page is page 0. This service loads the 8 x 16 character cell character set from ROM into the designated character block in display memory.

Setting a Pointer for User Graphics Characters (EGA/VGA Video Service 11H, Subservice 20H)

Register Inputs	Register Outputs
AH = 11H AL = 20H ES:SP = Pointer to user table for characters having ASCII codes from 128 to 255	None

This video service only works with modes 4, 5 and 6. It loads a pointer to an 8 x 8 user defined character set for characters having ASCII codes from 128 to 255. For graphics modes, these characters have to be stored in regular computer memory, since all display memory is used by the graphics modes. The service requires an array of eight bytes for each of the 128 high order characters. A C function to perform this service follows:

```
/*

    setHighOrder() = Sets pointer to high order graphics
                            table

*/

void setHighOrder (int *high_order)
{
    struct REGPACK regs;
    struct SREGS sregs;

    regs.r_ax = 0x1120;
    segread(&sregs);
    regs.r_es = sregs.ds;
```

(continued)

```
    regs.r_bp = (int)high_order;
    intr (0x10,&regs);
}
```

Setting a Pointer for User Custom Character Set (EGA/VGA Video Service 11H, Subservice 21H)

Register Inputs	Register Outputs
AH = 11H AL = 21H BL = 0 (EGA Only) Number of 　　　character rows is in register 　　　DL 　= 1 = 14 character rows 　= 2 = 25 character rows 　= 3 = 43 character rows CX = Number of bytes per character ES:SP = Pointer to user custom 　　　character table	None

This video service loads a pointer to a variable size array of user defined characters. For graphics modes, these characters have to be stored in regular computer memory, since all display memory is used by the graphics modes. The service requires an array of eight bytes for each custom character.

Setting a Pointer for the 8x14 Character Set (EGA/VGA Video Service 11H, Subservice 22H)

Register Inputs	Register Outputs
AH = 11H AL = 22H BL = 0 (EGA Only) Number of 　　　character rows is in register DL 　= 1 = 14 character rows 　= 2 = 25 character rows 　= 3 = 43 character rows	None

This video service loads a pointer to the 8 x 14 character set located in the EGA/VGA BIOS ROM. For graphics modes, these characters have to remain stored in ROM, since all display memory is used by the graphics modes.

Setting A Pointer for the 8x8 Double Dot Character Set (EGA/VGA Video Service 11H, Subservice 23H)

Register Inputs	Register Outputs

AH = 11H
AL = 23H
BL = 0 (EGA Only) Number of
      character rows is in register DL
  = 1 = 14 character rows
  = 2 = 25 character rows
  = 3 = 43 character rows
	None

This video service loads a pointer to the 8 x 8 double dot character set located in the EGA/VGA BIOS ROM. For graphics modes, these characters have to remain stored in ROM, since all display memory is used by the graphics modes.

Setting a Pointer for the 8x16 Character Set (EGA/VGA Video Service 11H, Subservice 24H)

Register Inputs	Register Outputs

AH = 11H
AL = 24H
BL = 0 (EGA Only) Number of
      character rows is in
      register DL
  = 1 = 14 character rows
  = 2 = 25 character rows
  = 3 = 43 character rows
	None

This video service loads a pointer to the 8 x 16 character set located in the EGA/VGA BIOS ROM. For graphics modes, these characters have to remain stored in ROM, since all display memory is used by the graphics modes.

Getting Character Generation Information (EGA/VGA Video Service 11H, Subservice 30H)

Register Inputs	Register Outputs

AH = 11H
AL = 30H
BH = 0 = Get pointer to
        interrupt 1F (use 8 x 8 character
        set—upper 128 characters)
    = 1 = Get pointer to
        interrupt 43H (user 8 x 8 character
        set—lower 128 characters)
    = 2 = Get pointer to
        ROM 8 x 14 character set
    = 3 = Get pointer to
        ROM 8 x 8 character set
    = 4 = Get pointer to
        upper half of ROM 8 x 8 character set
    = 5 = Get pointer to
        ROM alternate 9 x 14 monochrome
        characters
    = 6 = Get pointer to
        ROM 8 x 16 character set
    = 7 = Get pointer to
        ROM alternate 9 x 16 characters
	CX = Bytes per
	        character
	DL = EGA—
	        Number of
	        character
	        rows on
	        screen
	        VGA—
	        Number of
	        character
	        rows on
	        screen
	        minus one
	ES:BP Pointer
	        requested
	        by BH
	        setting

There are a lot of interesting things that you can do with characters in the graphics modes if you have full control of your character writing functions. You could, of course, include in such functions complete tables of characters, but it is usually more efficient to make use of those that are already in ROM BIOS. The EGA ROM BIOS extensions have three character tables and the VGA ROM BIOS extensions have five character tables. This video service makes it possible to obtain the address of a desired character table, as well as the number of bytes per character and the number of lines that make up a display screen. The C function *findChar* permits you to get any character table address that you want by specifying the parameter *type*, which is the number that goes into the *BH* register in the preceding table to choose which table address you want. The function returns the table address. It also passes pointers to the parameters *lines* and *bytes_per_char*, which contain the number of lines in the display and the number of bytes per character, respectively, when the function returns. This function is included in the program that follows, which writes a string to the graphics screen with full control of the foreground and background colors. We won't describe the program in detail, since this is covered in Chapter 19. Meanwhile you can try it out, to get an idea of how to use video service.

```
/*
```

```
     charread = Program to test reading character table
                          address

              By Roger T. Stevens    10-13-91
```

```
*/
```

```
#include <stdio.h>
#include <dos.h>

void display(unsigned long int address, int color_plane,
     unsigned char ch);
unsigned char far *findChar (int type, int *lines,
     int *bytes_per_char);
void setMode(int mode);
void writeString(int col, int row,char *str, int color);

struct REGPACK reg;
char string[80] = {"This is the hour of destiny..."};
unsigned char far *char_table;
int lines, bytes_per_char;

void main (void)
{
     setMode(16);
     char_table = findChar (2, &lines, &bytes_per_char);
```

(continued)

```
    writeString(2,4,string,31);
    printf("\nlines: %d   bytes per character: %d   ",
       lines,bytes_per_char);
    getch();
}
```

```
/*
```

```
   findchar() = Returns the address of a character table
        and bytes per character and rows on screen
```

```
*/
```

```
unsigned char far *findChar (int type, int *lines,
    int bytes_per_char)
{
    unsigned char far *address;
    reg.r_bx = type << 8;
    reg.r_ax = 0x1130;
    intr(0x10, &reg);
    address = (unsigned char far *)(reg.r_es*0x10000 +
       reg.r_bp);
    *lines = reg.r_dx;
    *bytes_per_char = reg.r_cx;
    return (address);
}
```

```
/*
```

```
   writeString() = Writes a string of characters to the
                          screen
```

```
*/
```

```
void writeString(int col, int row,char *str, int color)
{
    int i = 0, j, k, mask1, mask2;
    unsigned int offset;
    char far * mem_address;
```

(continued)

317

```
int char_offset, foreground, background, width,
   point_color, dummy;
unsigned char char_test;

while (str[i])
{
   char_offset = str[i] * 14;
   for (k=0; k<14; k++)
   {
      offset = (long)(row*14+k) * 80L + col;
      mask1 = 0x10;
      mask2 = 0x01;
      for (j=0; j<4; j++)
      {
         if (((mask1 & color)!=0) && ((mask2 &
            color)!=0))
            display(offset,j,0xFF);
         else
         {
            if ((mask1 & color) != 0)
               display(offset,j,~char_table[char_offset
                  +k]);
            else
            {
               if ((mask2 & color) != 0)
                  display(offset,j,
                     char_table[char_offset + k]);
            }
         }
         mask1 <<= 1;
         mask2 <<= 1;
      }
   }
   i++;
   col++;
}
}
```

(continued)

```
/*
```

```
    display() = Writes a byte to one display memory plane
```

```
*/

void display(unsigned long int address, int color_plane,
    unsigned char ch)
{
    #define seq_out(index,val)  {outp(0x3C4,index);\
                        outp(0x3C5,val);}
    char far * mem_address;
    char dummy;

    mem_address = (char far *) 0xA0000000L + address;
    seq_out(2,(0x01 << color_plane));
    *mem_address = ch;
}
```

```
/*
```

```
                    setMode() = Sets video mode
```

```
*/

void setMode(int mode)
{
    union REGS reg;

    reg.h.ah = 0;
    reg.h.al = mode;
    int86 (0x10,&reg,&reg);
}
```

Getting EGA/VGA Video Information (EGA/VGA Video Service 12H, Subservice 10H)

Register Inputs	Register Outputs

AH = 12H
AL = 00H
BL = 10H
	BH = 0 = Current mode is color
	   = 1 = Current mode is monochrome
	BL = 00H = EGA/VGA memory size is 64K bytes
	   = 01H = EGA/VGA memory size is 128K bytes
	   = 02H = EGA/VGA memory size is 192K bytes
	   = 03H = EGA/VGA memory size is 256K bytes
	CH = Feature bits
	CL = Switch settings

This video service returns information on the configuration of the EGA/VGA and its current display mode. Most VGA and super VGA cards have paged memory greater than 256K, but since 256K is the maximum that can be read with this service, that is all that can be returned. The memory size report doesn't have much use any more. The feature bits are reported for the EGA only. Feature boards attached to the two EGA feature connectors never became popular, so this is another report that has little use. Typically the EGA has four sense switches located on its rear panel. These switches determine the EGA configuration. Their positions are reported by this video service in register *CL*. This also reports the configuration information for the VGA, although this is stored in software rather than by physical switches. The computer can have two types of display adapter card present, with one designated as primary and the other secondary. The configuration information indicates what combination is present. The following are the possible configurations:

Reg CL Hex	Switches				EGA/VGA	MGA	CGA
	1	2	3	4			
01	Off	Off	Off	On	Primary Color Display 80x25	Secondary	
02	Off	Off	On	Off	Primary Monochrome		Secondary
03	Off	Off	On	On	Secondary Enhanced Display Hi Res Mode	Primary	
05	Off	On	Off	Off	Secondary Monochrome		Primary 80 x 25
06	Off	On	On	Off	Primary Enhanced Display Hi Res Mode	Secondary	
07	Off	On	On	On	Secondary Color Display 80x25	Primary	
09	On	Off	Off	On	Primary Color Display 40x25	Secondary	
0A	On	Off	On	Off	Primary Monochrome		Secondary 40x25
0B	On	Off	On	On	Secondary Enhanced Display Hi Res Mode	Primary	
0D	On	On	Off	On	Secondary Monochrome		Primary 40x25
0E	On	On	On	Off	Primary Enhanced Display Emulation Mode	Secondary	
0F	On	On	On	On	Secondary Color Display 80x25	Primary	

Revector Print Screen (EGA/VGA Video Service 12H, Subservice 20H)

Register Inputs	Register Outputs
AH = 12H AL = 00H BL = 20H	None

Selecting Number of Scan Lines for Text Modes (EGA/VGA Video Service 12H, Subservice 30H)

Register Inputs	Register Outputs

AH = 12H
AL = 00H = 200 scan lines
    = 01H = 350 scan lines
    = 02H = 400 scan lines
BL = 30H
	AL = 12H indicates that this
	    video service is
	    supported

This video service works for the VGA in text modes only. It selects the number of scan lines and the default character set that are to be used in a text mode that is called for by the next mode set.

Specifying VGA Palette Loading (EGA/VGA Video Service 12H, Subservice 31H)

Register Inputs	Register Outputs

AH = 12H
AL = 00H = Enable palette
    loading
    = 01H = Disable palette
    loading
BL = 31H
	AL = 12H indicates that
	this video service is
	    supported

This video service works with the VGA only. It determines whether the default palette shall be loaded during a mode set. If this service is set for *Enable* the default values for the palette and color registers will be restored upon mode set. If set for *Disabled*, the current palette and color register settings will be kept when mode set takes place.

Video Enable or Disable (EGA/VGA Video Service 12H, Subservice 32H)

Register Inputs	Register Outputs
AH = 12H AL = 00H = Enable video = 01H = Disable video BL = 32H	AL = 12H indicates that this video service is supported

This video service works with the VGA only. When it is run to disable the VGA, all input and output to the VGA registers are disabled and all reads and writes to display memory of this VGA are disabled. This effectively takes the VGA out of the system and enables you to substitute some other device that uses the same memory and port addresses if you have the means for enabling it.

Summing Colors to a Gray Scale (EGA/VGA Video Service 12H, Subservice 33H)

Register Inputs	Register Outputs
AH = 12H AL = 00H = Enable summing = 01H = Disable summing BL = 33H	AL = 12H indicates that this video service is supported

This video service works only with the VGA. It sums the color values of each color register that is operated upon to a gray value by the equation:

$$gray\ scale = (0.30 \times red) + (0.59 \times green) + (0.11 \times blue)$$

Unlike video service 10H subservice 1BH, this service does not replace the color register contents with the gray intensity values that are obtained. Instead, it causes the gray value to be output to the screen instead of the color values when each register is designated in displaying a screen. This will result in a realistic black and white reproduction. A C function to use this video service follows:

```
/*

    displayGrayScale() = Displays a picture in monochrome

*/

void displayGrayScale(char enable)
{
    union REGS regs;

    regs.h.ah = 0x12;
    regs.h.al = enable;
    regs.h.bl = 0x33;
    int86(0x10,&regs,&regs);
}
```

Emulating the Cursor (EGA/VGA Video Service 12H, Subservice 34H)

Register Inputs	Register Outputs
AH = 12H AL = 00H = Enable emulation = 01H = Disable emulation BL = 34H	AL = 12H indicates that this video service is supported

This video service works with the VGA only. When disabled, the cursor is defined by the values passed in video service 01H. When this service is enabled, it assigns a different meaning to the cursor definition in video service 01H. The new definitions are as follows:

Video Service 01H Parameter Values	Cursor Type
Start line bit 5 = 1	No cursor
Start line < End line and <= 3	Overbar cursor
Start line + 2 >= End line	Underline cursor
Start line >= 2	Half-block cursor
Start line <= 2 or end line < start line	Full-block cursor

Switching the Display Adapter (EGA/VGA Video Service 12H, Subservice 35H)

Register Inputs	Register Outputs
AH = 12H AL = 00H = Initial switch off adapter video = 01H = Initial switch on planar video = 02H = Switch off active display = 03H = Switch on inactive display BL = 35H ES:DX = Pointer to 128 byte buffer for adapter or planar status	AL = 12H indicates that this video service is supported

This video service permits switching between a display adapter device on the motherboard (planar) and one on a plug-in card (adapter). If both types of display support are available, the system will try to initialize both upon power up. Should there be a conflict between port or memory addresses, only one device can be active at a time, so the system will (by default) disable the planar device and enable the adapter. To use this service, it should first be called with *AL* = 0, which switches off the adapter and stores its status in the designated buffer. The service should then be run with *AL* = 1 to turn on the planar video and store its status in the designated buffer. This reverses the default condition. After this, you can switch at will between the two devices by setting *AL* to 2 to turn off the active video and then to 3 to turn on the inactive video.

Turning off the Video Screen (EGA/VGA Video Service 12H, Subservice 36H)

Register Inputs	Register Outputs

AH = 12H
AL = 00H = Enable video
     output
   = 01H = Disable video
     output
BL = 36H
	AL = 12H indicates that this video service is supported

This output prevents all reads of the display memory by circuits that transfer memory information to the screen, thereby disabling output to the video screen, leaving the screen black. Normally, the computer can only refresh display memory when it is not being accessed by the display circuits. Therefore, when this service disables display circuit to display memory, more time is available for computer access, resulting in a substantial decrease in the time it takes to write a screen full of data to display memory. Whether you want to use this depends upon whether you would rather see a new display build up on the screen or gain speed by having the display black for a while and then have the full display pop up. A C function to utilize this video service follows:

```
/*

    ┌─────────────────────────────────────────────────────────┐
    │ ┌─────────────────────────────────────────────────────┐ │
    │ │                                                     │ │
    │ │   screen_enable() = Enables or disables the display │ │
    │ │                        screen                       │ │
    │ │                                                     │ │
    │ └─────────────────────────────────────────────────────┘ │
    └─────────────────────────────────────────────────────────┘

*/

void screen_enable (char enable)
{
    union REGS regs;

    regs.h.ah = 0x12;
    regs.h.bl = 0x36;
    regs.h.al = enable;
    int86 (0x10,&regs,&regs);
}
```

Writing a Character String on the Video Screen (EGA/VGA Video Service 13H)

Register Inputs	Register Outputs

AH = 13H
AL = 00H = Fixed attribute;
      cursor returns to starting
      position
      BL = Attribute
   = 01H = Fixed attribute;
      cursor stays at ending position
      BL = Attribute
   = 02H = String includes
      attributes; cursor returns to
      starting position
   = 03H = String includes
      attributes; cursor stays at
      ending position
BH = Page number
CX = Number of characters in string
DH = Character row
DL = Character column
	AL = 12H indicates
	that this video service
	is supported

This video service, which works with the VGA only, makes use of the TTY character writing service (video service 0EH) to write a string of characters. See the description of that service for a description of the way in which special characters are intercepted and used for display positioning, etc. This service gives you four options. The first two options (*AL* = 0 or 1) let you write the string with a fixed specified attribute and end with the cursor back at the beginning of the string or at the end, respectively. The second pair of options (*AL* = 2 or 3) give you the same choices for the cursor, but include an attribute for each character in the string, so that the string bytes are actually character, attribute, character, attribute, etc. The following is a C function that makes use of this video service. It uses only option 2, to write the string with a fixed attribute and leave the cursor at the end of the string. It doesn't allow you to set the string length; instead, it uses the C *strlen* function to determine the length of a standard C string. It uses a fixed value for page 0.

```
/*

    write_s() = Writes a string to the screen in TTY mode

*/

void write_s(int x, int y, char *string, char color)
{
    struct REGPACK regs;
    struct SREGS segregs;

    segread(&segregs);
    regs.r_es = segregs.ds;
    regs.r_bp = (int) string;
    regs.r_ax = 0x1301;
    regs.r_bx = color;
    regs.r_cx = strlen(string);
    regs.r_dx = (y<<8) | x;
    intr(0x10,&regs);
}
```

Reading or Writing the Display Combination Code (EGA/VGA Video Service 1AH)

Register Inputs	Register Outputs

AH = 1AH
AL = 00H = Read Display
    Combination Code
    = 01H = Write the Display
    Combination Code
BH = Inactive video system
    Display Combination Code
BL = Active video system
    Display Combination Code
	AL = 1AH indicates that
	    this video service is
	    supported
	BH = Inactive video
	    system Display
	    Combination Code
	BL = Active video system
	    Display
	    Combination Code

This service reads or writes the Display Combination Code into low memory. It is used when the computer is powered up. It is not normally used by the programmer. The Display Combination Codes are

Display Combination Code	Display
00H	No display
01H	Monochrome Display Adapter (MGA)
02H	Color Graphics Adapter (CGA)
04H	Enhanced Graphics Adapter (EGA) Monochrome monitor
05H	Enhanced graphics Adapter (EGA) Color monitor
06H	Professional Graphics Adapter (PGA)
07H	Video Graphics Array (VGA) Monochrome monitor
08H	Video Graphics Array (VGA) Color Monitor
0BH	Multi-Color Graphics Array (MCGA) Monochrome monitor
0CH	Multi-Color Graphics Array (MCGA) Color monitor

Reading VGA State Information (EGA/VGA Video Service 1BH)

Register Inputs	Register Outputs
AH = 1BH ES:DI Pointer to state information buffer	AL = 1BH indicates that this video service is supported ES:DI Pointer to state information buffer

This video service reads the EGA/VGA functionality/state information into a 40H byte buffer whose address must be specified by the programmer. After executing this video service, the buffer contents will be as follows:

Buffer Address	Size	Description
00H	word	Offset to static functionality information
02H	word	Segment to static functionality information
04H	byte	Video mode
05H	word	Number of columns on screen
07H	word	Length of regenerator buffer
09H	word	Start address of regenerator buffer
0BH	8*word	Cursor position (row,column) for 8 pages
1BH	word	Cursor type setting (start, end, value)
1DH	byte	Active display page
1EH	word	CRT controller address 3BX—monochrome 3DX—color
20H	byte	Current setting of 3x8 register (mode)
21H	byte	Current setting of 3x9 register
22H	byte	Rows on screen (character lines)
23H	word	Character height
25H	byte	Active display combination code
26H	byte	Alternate display combination code
27H	word	Colors supported by current video mode
29H	byte	Display pages supported in current video mode
2AH	byte	Scan lines in current video mode
2BH	byte	Primary character block
2CH	byte	Secondary character byte
2DH	byte	Miscellaneous state information

(continued)

Buffer Address	Size	Description
2EH	byte	Reserved
2FH	byte	Reserved
30H	byte	Reserved
31H	byte	Video memory available
32H	byte	Save pointer state information
33H–3FH	byte	Reserved

Saving or Restoring the Video State (EGA/VGA Video Service 1CH)

Register Inputs	Register Outputs
AH = 1CH AL = 00H = Return size of save/restore buffer = 01H = Save video state = 02H = Restore video state CX = 01H = Video hardware state = 02H = Video data areas = 04H = Video DAC state and color registers ES:BP = Pointer to save/restore buffer	AL = 1CH = indicates that this video service is supported BH = Inactive video system Display Combination Code BL = Active video system Display Combination Code

This service permits saving video state data to a host buffer and then restoring it to the video device. Three types of video data can be saved, depending upon the setting of the *CX* register. When utilizing this service, you should select the type of data that you want to save and then run the service with *AL* set to 0. This will return the size of the buffer needed to store the video data. Use this to set up the appropriate buffer and then run the service again to save the video data.

Chapter 11

System and Display Coordinates and How They Interact

In creating graphics displays, we need to have a coordinate system that we can use to define the location of every pixel that we want to draw on the screen. By default, if we don't do anything else, there is a screen coordinate system, but it is really designed for textual rather than graphics applications. The screen coordinate system always has the coordinate (0,0) at the top left-hand corner of the screen. The x coordinates increase as we move toward the right and the y coordinates increase as we move to the bottom of the screen. This is just like the page of a book, with the text flowing from left to right and the lines increasing from top to bottom. However, it is totally unlike most mathematical and geometrical coordinate systems. For a geometric system, you usually want to have the coordinate (0,0) at the center of the page, with increasingly positive values of x going toward the right, increasingly negative values of x going toward the left, increasingly positive values of y going upward and increasingly negative values of y going downward. In some cases, where you are going to be handling only negative numbers, you might want (0,0) to be at the bottom left corner of the page, with increasingly positive values of x going toward the right and increasingly positive values of y going upward. The fact that the screen coordinate system does not correspond with any coordinate system usually used in mathematical and geometric work is one good reason why you may not be satisfied with using the screen coordinate system and may want to create a coordinate system of your own.

The scale of the screen coordinate system depends upon the resolution of the display mode that you are using. For example, if you are using a display mode that has a resolution of 320 by 200 pixels, then you have 320 pixels across the screen in the x direction and 200 pixels down the screen in the y direction. Similarly a 640 by 350 pixel display mode has 640 pixels in the x direction and 350 in the y direction. It would be ideal if all display modes resulted in square pixels (pixels whose x and y dimensions were the same) but this is often not the case. Remembering that the aspect ratio of the display screen is 4:3 (in other words the height is 3/4 of the width), a display mode having square pixels would be 640 by 480 pixels. Thus the 640 by 350 pixel display mode would have pixels whose x dimension is only 0.7129166 of their y dimension. The unfortunate thing about this is that if you are drawing curves that are described by algebraic equations (circles, for example) their shape is only correct if you have square pixels. Thus, you can draw a circle without problems in the 640 by 480 pixel mode, but if you use the same technique in the 640 by 350 display mode, you will get an ellipse. This is another excellent reason for abandoning the screen coordinate system in favor of a coordinate system of your own.

Simple Coordinate Conversion

We'll begin with a very simple coordinate conversion problem. Suppose that we are using display mode 18 (640 pixels by 480 pixels by 16 colors). You'll note that the pixels are already square, so this is no problem, but we do want to move the center of the coordinate system to the center of the display. We are going to use a *#define* statement to set up a function that will perform this conversion at critical points. Since the use of this statement causes the defined code to be substituted for the function wherever it is called, we have the fastest mode of operation of which C is capable. The statement for this case is

```
#define convert(x,y) {x+=320; y = 240 - y;}
```

This makes a conversion from a system set of coordinates in which the x range is -320 (left) to +319 (right) and the y range is -240 (bottom) to +239 (top) to the standard screen coordinate system for the selected mode. Before going on, lets think about where we are going to use the *convert* function. Straight line drawing algorithms work just as well with screen coordinates as they do with system coordinates, so we can do our conversion at the beginning of the line drawing function for just the beginning and endpoints of the line. This is the fastest way to go. As long as the screen coordinate system has square pixels, the same reasoning applies for circle and ellipse drawing functions, but if the pixels are not square, we need to perform all of the circle and ellipse computations in the system coordinates. Then we will have to do a conversion on each set of points before we plot them to the screen.

More Complicated Conversions

Suppose we are using display mode 16 (640 pixels by 350 pixels by 16 colors). The pixels are not square, so we have a double reason for using system coordinates. The question is how we should define our coordinate system. First, the resolution with system coordinates must be as high or higher than that of screen coordinates. Suppose, for example, that we chose a set of system coordinates that had a resolution of 320 by 240. Then we would compute only one out of four points that were available on the screen, leaving blank areas and producing a display with only half the resolution of which it was capable. On the other hand, if we chose a resolution for the system coordinates of 1280 by 960, we would spend a lot of time computing points that we couldn't display, which isn't a very good idea either. So we're going to select a system coordinate resolution that matches the best resolution of the screen coordinate system, which says that the x resolution should be 640 pixels. Then, to be sure of square pixels, we need to have the y resolution 480 pixels. If we want our system coordinates to have the origin at the center of the display screen, we could then have a converting function of

```
#define convert(x,y) {x+=320; y = 175 - 0.7129166*y;}
```

This function will do the trick all right, but if it's speed you're after, the floating point multiplication will knock you dead. What we need is a way of converting without floating point operations. It also would be a good idea to avoid any integer divisions, since this is also a very slow process. Therefore we look for a fraction whose denominator is a power of two, so that the division operation can be converted to a shift. We find that 93/128 will do the job to within one pixel accuracy. Thus our conversion function becomes

```
#define convert(x,y) {x+=320; y = 175 - ((93*y) >> 7);}
```

You might suspect that a combination of shifts and additions could be substituted for the multiplication, and this is so, but experiments show that the multiplication is faster. If you're doing a more generalized version of this, you have to watch out for the limiting sizes of integer numbers. For example, another way to do this conversion is

```
#define convert(x,y) {x+=320; \
        y = ((240L - y) * 93) >> 7;}
```

Note that we have defined 240 to be a long integer, which causes all of the other integers involved in the subtraction, multiplication and shifting to be converted to long integers also. If we don't do this, some values of y will cause one of the intermediate products to exceed the bounds of regular integers, giving a wrong result. Surprisingly enough, the conversion to long integers doesn't seem to make the conversion appreciably slower.

When Two Different Conversions Are Required

Suppose that we have a program that begins with display mode 16 and then at some point switches to display mode 18. We can't really change the #*define* statement in the middle of the program, but we can make do by having the global variables $x\_off = 320$, $y\_mult = 93$, and $y\_shift = 7$. Now our conversion function for mode 16 becomes

```
#define convert(x,y) {x+=x_off; \
        y = ((240L - y) * y_mult) >> y_shift;}
```

You can check and see that this is the same as the previous conversion statement. Now, when we are ready to switch to mode 18, we simply set $y\_mult = 1$ and $y\_shift = 0$ and the conversion will be numerically equivalent to the one for mode 18. It's not quite as fast or elegant, however, since we are doing a couple of useless operations (multiplying by 1 and shifting zero places) but this is the price we have to pay for being able to use the same conversion function with two different modes.

Working with the 360 x 480 Pixel by 256 Color Mode

As just one more example of coordinate conversion, we're going to use the undocumented mode F4 described in Chapter 8. Our system coordinates are going to be the same 640 by 480 pixel set, with the origin at the center of the screen that we have used before. The program *undoccir.c* listed in Figure 11-1 uses the conversion technique in drawing a circle on a multicolored background. You've seen the undocumented mode in Chapter 8, but you'll have to take the circle function on faith until we explain circles in detail in Chapter 13. If you look at the beginning of the listing, you'll see how the *convert* function is defined for this case.

Figure 11-1. Listing of undoccir.c Program

```
/*

  undoccir.c = Drawing a circle in the 360 x 480 pixel x
               256 color mode (mode 74)

          By Roger T. Stevens    10-26-91

*/

#include <dos.h>
#include <stdio.h>
#include <stdlib.h>
#include <mem.h>

#define convert(x,y) {x = ((x + 320L) * 72) >> 7; \
                     y = 240 - y;}

void drawCircle(int x, int y, int r, int color);
void plot(int x, int y, int color);
void plots(int x, int y, int color);
void setMode(int mode);
void drawLine6(int xs, int ys, int xe, int ye, int color);
void setVGApalette(unsigned char *buffer);
```

(continued)

```
typedef struct
{
   unsigned char red;
   unsigned char green;
   unsigned char blue;
} RGB;

RGB palette[256];

int color, hue, i, j, k, LINEWIDTH = 3;
int xres, yres;
unsigned long int PATTERN = 0xFFFFFFFF;

union REGS reg;

void main()
{
   palette[0].red = 0;
   palette[0].green = 0;
   palette[0].blue = 0;
   for (i=0; i<6; i++)
      for(j=0; j<6; j++)
      for (k=1; k<8; k++)
      {
          palette[42*i+7*j+k].red = i*12+1;
          palette[42*i+7*j+k].green = j*12+1;
          palette[42*i+7*j+k].blue = 10*(k-1)+1;
      }

/*
```

```
          Mode F4H = 360 x 480 pixels x 256 colors
```

```
*/
   setMode(0xF4);
   setVGApalette(&palette[0].red);
   xres = 360; yres = 480;
   for (i=0; i<480; i++)
   {
       for (j=0; j<360; j++)
```

(continued)

```
            plot(j,i,random(253));
    }
    LINEWIDTH = 3;
    drawCircle(0,0,200,6);
    getch();
    setMode(0x03);
}
/*
```

```
   setMode() = Sets video mode (includes undocumented VGA
                              modes)
```

```
*/

void setMode(int mode)
{
    char result;
    unsigned int params[17] =
        {0x6b00,0x5901,0x5a02,0x8e03,0x5e04,0x8a05,
        0x4009,0x0014,0xe317,0x0d06,0x3e07,
        0xea10,0xac11,0xdf12,0xe715,0x0616,0x4109};
    char far * address;
    long int i;

    reg.h.ah = 0;

    switch(mode)
    {
        case 0xF0:  /* 320 x 400 pixel resolution */
            reg.h.al = 0x13;
            int86 (0x10,&reg,&reg);
            outport(0x3c4,0x0604);
            outportb(0x3d4,0x11);
            result = inportb(0x3d5);
            outportb(0x3d5,result & 0x7f);
            for (i=6; i<9; i++)
                outport(0x3d4,params[i]);
            break;

        case 0xF1:  /* 320 x 240 pixels */
```

(continued)

```
        reg.h.al = 0x13;
        int86 (0x10,&reg,&reg);
        outport(0x3c4,0x0604);
        outport(0x3c4,0x0100);
        outportb(0x3c2,0xc3);
        outport(0x3c4,0x300);
        outportb(0x3d4,0x11);
        result = inportb(0x3d5);
        outportb(0x3d5,result & 0x7f);
        for (i=7; i<17; i++)
            outport(0x3d4,params[i]);
        break;

    case 0xF2:   /* 320 x 480 pixels */
        reg.h.al = 0x13;
        int86 (0x10,&reg,&reg);
        outport(0x3c4,0x0604);
        outport(0x3c4,0x0100);
        outportb(0x3c2,0xc3);
        outport(0x3c4,0x300);
        outportb(0x3d4,0x11);
        result = inportb(0x3d5);
        outportb(0x3d5,result & 0x7f);
        for (i=6; i<16; i++)
            outport(0x3d4,params[i]);
        outport(0x3d4,0x4009);
        break;

    case 0xF3:   /* 360 x 400 pixels */
        reg.h.al = 0x13;
        int86 (0x10,&reg,&reg);
        outport(0x3c4,0x0604);
        outport(0x3c4,0x0100);
        outportb(0x3c2,0x67);
        outport(0x3c4,0x300);
        outportb(0x3d4,0x11);
        result = inportb(0x3d5);
        outportb(0x3d5,result & 0x7f);
        for (i=0; i<9; i++)
            outport(0x3d4,params[i]);
        outport(0x3d4,0x2d13);
```

(continued)

```
            break;

        case 0xF4:   /* 360 x 480 pixels */
            reg.h.al = 0x13;
            int86 (0x10,&reg,&reg);
            outport(0x3c4,0x0604);
            outport(0x3c4,0x0100);
            outportb(0x3c2,0xe7);
            outport(0x3c4,0x300);
            outportb(0x3d4,0x11);
            result = inportb(0x3d5);
            outportb(0x3d5,result & 0x7f);
            for (i=0;  i<16;  i++)
                outport(0x3d4,params[i]);
            outport(0x3d4,0x2d13);
            break;
        default:
            reg.h.al = mode;
            int86(0x10, &reg, &reg);
    }
    if (mode >= 0x70)
    {
        outport(0x3c4,0x0f02);  /* enable writes to all */
                            /* four planes */
        for(i=0;  i<0xFFFF;  i++)
        {
            address = (char far *) 0xA0000000L + i;
            *address = 0x00;
        }
    }
}


/*
```

```
 plot() = Function to plot point to VGA 256 color screen
          using mode 74 (360 x 480 pixels)
```

```
*/
```

(continued)

```
void plot(int x, int y, int color)
{
    #define seq_out(index,val) {outp(0x3c4, index);\
                        outp(0x3c5, val);}
    unsigned long int offset;
    char far *address;
    unsigned int plane;

    offset = (long)xres * y + x;
    plane = (0x01 << (offset % 4));
    seq_out(2,plane);
    offset >>= 2;
    address = (char far *)(0xA0000000L + offset);
    *address = color;
}
```

```
/*
```

```
    plots() = Function to plot a point to VGA 256 color
    screen using mode 74 (360 x 480 pixels) with system
                        coordinates.
```

```
*/
```

```
void plots(int x, int y, int color)
{
    #define seq_out(index,val) {outp(0x3c4, index);\
                        outp(0x3c5, val);}
    unsigned long int offset;
    char far *address;
    unsigned int plane;

    convert(x,y);
    offset = (long)xres * y + x;
    plane = (0x01 << (offset % 4));
    seq_out(2,plane);
    offset >>= 2;
    address = (char far *)(0xA0000000L + offset);
    *address = color;
}
```

(continued)

```
/*

    ┌──────────────────────────────────────────────────┐
    │                                                    │
    │   setVGApalette() = Function to set all 256 VGA color │
    │                         registers                  │
    │                                                    │
    └──────────────────────────────────────────────────┘

*/

void setVGApalette(unsigned char *buffer)
{
    struct SREGS inreg;
    union REGS reg;

    reg.x.ax = 0x1012;
    segread(&inreg);
    inreg.es = inreg.ds;
    reg.x.bx = 0;
    reg.x.cx = 256;
    reg.x.dx = (int)&buffer[0];
    int86x(0x10,&reg,&reg,&inreg);
}


/*

    ┌──────────────────────────────────────────────────┐
    │                                                    │
    │   drawCircle() = Draws a circle with specified center, │
    │      radius, and color, using line width in pixels │
    │                  specified by LINEWIDTH.           │
    │                                                    │
    └──────────────────────────────────────────────────┘

*/

void drawCircle(int x, int y, int r, int color)
{
    int i, row, col, px, py;
    long int sum;

    r += LINEWIDTH /2;
    py = r<<1;
    px = 0;
    sum = -(r<<1);
    while (px <= py)
```

(continued)

343

```
      {
    if ( !(px & 1))
    {
        col = x + (px>>1);
        row = y + (py>>1);
        for (i=0; i<LINEWIDTH; i++)
            plots(col,row-i,color);
        row = y - (py>>1);
        for (i=0; i<LINEWIDTH; i++)
            plots(col,row+i,color);
        col = x - (px>>1);
        for (i=0; i<LINEWIDTH; i++)
            plots(col,row+i,color);
        row = y + (py>>1);
        for (i=0; i<LINEWIDTH; i++)
            plots(col,row-i,color);
        col = x + (py>>1);
        row = y + (px>>1);
        for (i=0; i<LINEWIDTH; i++)
            plots(col-i,row,color);
        row = y - (px>>1);
        for (i=0; i<LINEWIDTH; i++)
            plots(col-i,row,color);
        col = x - (py>>1);
        for (i=0; i<LINEWIDTH; i++)
            plots(col+i,row,color);
        row = y + (px>>1);
        for (i=0; i<LINEWIDTH; i++)
            plots(col+i,row,color);
    }
    sum +=px++;
    if (sum >= 0)
        sum-=py--;
    }
}
```

Summary

You should now have a pretty good idea how to create fairly fast conversions from system coordinates to screen coordinates. The process can be systematized as follows:

1. Decide where you want the center of your coordinate system to be located.

2. Match your system coordinate resolution to the higher resolution of the two coordinates in the screen coordinate system.

3. Set the other coordinate resolution to a value that will create square pixels in the system coordinate system.

4. Use the *$define* expression to define your conversion function.

5. Don't use floating point operations in conversion. For a fractional multiplier, choose one whose denominator is a power of two, so that you can accomplish the division with a shift.

6. Make sure that you use long integers when necessary.

Just to reenforce the point about avoiding floating point operations, the function definition given previously that used a floating point operation took seven times as long to run as the integer function when a 386SX computer without a math coprocessor was used and 1.5 times as long to run when a 386 machine with a math coprocessor was used.

Chapter 12

Clipping Techniques

Many of the functions that have been described in this book involve plotting points to the display screen, but do not place any limits on the values that may be specified for the x and y coordinates of each point. It is up to the programmer to make sure that these values are such that the point will actually be at the proper point on the screen. It can sometimes be rather embarrassing if a point is specified to be outside the screen range. If you refer back to Chapter 6, you'll see that the plotting functions convert the x and y coordinates that you specify for a point location into an address in display screen memory. If you exceed the limit for the x coordinate, you usually end up with a point that moves to a memory location equivalent to the next line of the display and usually the left-hand side of the display instead of the right. If you exceed the limit for the y coordinate, you are likely to write to a different memory page, which you may never notice if you don't switch pages. If you do switch to another page, however, you may be unpleasantly surprised to discover that you have inadvertently already written something to a page that you thought was blank, or you may have overwritten something on the new page that you thought you were saving. One other unfortunate possibility is that you may send negative numbers to the coordinates, or numbers so big as to cause you to exceed the bounds of display memory. In either case, you may attempt to write sections of memory that are not reserved for the display, which can result in a number of strange effects.

A Simple Clipping Method

The simplest clipping method is to go directly to the plot function and enclose its whole body within an *if* statement similar to the following:

```
if (( x>= x_start) && (x < xend) && (y >= ystart) &&
    (y < yend))
{
    /*  body of plotting function */
}
```

This assures that a pixel will be plotted to the screen only if it is within the rectangle whose top left corner is *(x_start, y_start)* and whose bottom right corner is *(xend-1, yend-1)*. Usually these bounds will represent a rectangle corresponding to the whole screen area, but you can specify any other size rectangle within the screen area; and if you want to, you can pass the bounds to the plotting function, so that they can differ for different applications. Since this four way test must be made for each pixel, this is usually the slowest possible method of clipping. However, for such things as circles, ellipses and arcs, as described in the next three chapters, this primitive method is the only practical way that clipping can be achieved.

Clipping Straight Lines

If a line extends beyond the boundaries of a specified clipping rectangle, it may make sense to compute new beginning and/or ending points for the line that make it wholly within the clipping rectangle, and then plot this new line pixel by pixel, rather than performing the four way clipping test on each pixel. Whether this will reduce plotting time depends largely on how long a line you are going to draw. Determining the new line endpoints usually takes several times as long as would be required to use the primitive four way test on the beginning and ending pixels of the line, so if you are drawing lines that are just a few pixels long, you had better stick to the primitive method. On the other hand, if you are working with long lines, you can save a considerable amount of time by recomputing the endpoints. (The savings come about in two ways. First, the computer time to compute the new endpoints is much less than would be required to make the primitive four way test on each pixel in the line. Second, once the new endpoints are computed, you don't have to do anything for the parts of the original line that are outside the bounding rectangle.) Figure 12-1 lists a program called *cliptest.c* that tests the clipping of straight lines. For the moment, let's look only at the function called *clipline1*, which uses a straightforward mathematical approach to determining the new line endpoints. The generalized equation for a line is

$$y = mx + b$$

(Equation 12-1)

where m is the slope of the line and b represents an offset. The slope may also be written as

$$m = \frac{y_2 - y_1}{x_2 - x_1}$$

(Equation 12-2)

If we are looking for a new point on the line, we can put together the information in the two preceding equations to obtain the following equations:

$$y_3 = \frac{(x_3 - x_1)(y_2 - y_1)}{x_2 - x_1} + y_1$$

(Equation 12-3)

$$x_3 = \frac{(y_3 - y_1)(x_2 - x_1)}{y_2 - y_1} + x_1$$

Equation 12-4)

For a line that passes through any one of the four boundaries that make up the clipping rectangle, we can obtain the new line ending by setting the appropriate coordinate equal to the boundary value and then solving equation 12-3 if a new y value is required or equation 12-4 if a new x value is required. Ordinarily, we would have to make eight tests, one for the line beginning at each of the four boundaries and one for the line end at each of the four boundaries. We are going to begin the function, however, by swapping coordinates, if necessary, so that the starting coordinate set, *(xs,ys)*, is such that *xs* is always smaller (to the left of) *xe*. We then do a simple test that discards all lines that are totally to the left or right of the bounds of the clipping rectangle. This gets rid of all cases where *xe* is less that the left-hand boundary or where *xs* is greater than the right-hand boundary, so that we need to test only six more conditions. First, however, we have to treat separately the case of horizontal and vertical lines, since either of these would cause a divide by zero error in one of the six conditional boundary tests. For vertical lines, we don't know whether *ye* is greater than *ys* or vice versa, so we have to do four tests to assure that both ends of the line are limited to within the clipping rectangle boundaries. For the horizontal lines, we first need to discard any that are outside the clipping boundaries. Then we need only to make two tests since we already know that *xs* is smaller than *xe*. Next the function has a series of six *if* statements that check the six remaining boundary conditions and use the boundary conditions and the equations described earlier to compute a new line ending for each condition that applies. Note that a structure is used to define the line which makes it possible to return both sets of line coordinates when the function ends. (Once in a while, there is a pathological case in which truncation errors in computing new endpoints result in a point being plotted outside the clipping boundary.)

Figure 12-1. Listing of the cliptest.c Program

```
/*

    CLIPTEST = Test of functions for clipping lines

         By Roger T. Stevens   12-14-91

*/

#include <stdio.h>
#include <stdlib.h>
#include <dos.h>
```

(continued)

```c
#include <math.h>

typedef struct
{
      int xs;
      int ys;
      int xe;
      int ye;
} LINE;

LINE line, bounds;

void cls(int color);
LINE clipLine1(LINE line, LINE bounds);
LINE clipLine2(LINE line, LINE bounds);
void drawLine(LINE line, int color);
void drawRect(LINE bounds, int color);
void plot16(int x, int y, int color);
void setMode(int mode);

int i, j, lim, LINEWIDTH, test, xres, yres;

void main()
{
      randomize();

      LINEWIDTH = 3;
      setMode(16);
      xres = 640;
      yres = 350;
      cls(0);
      bounds.xs = 100;
      bounds.ys = 60;
      bounds.xe = 540;
      bounds.ye = 290;
      for (j=0; j<4; j++)
      {
            if (!(j % 2))
                  lim = 2500;
            else
                  lim = 250;
```

(continued)

```
                for (i=0; i<lim; i++)
                {
                    line.xs = random(640);
                    line.ys = random(350);
                    line.xe = random(640);
                    line.ye = random(350);
                    if ((j == 0) || (j == 2))
                        drawLine(line,(i %6) + 1);
                    if (j > 1)
                        line = clipLine2(line, bounds);
                    else
                        line = clipLine1(line, bounds);
                    if (line.xs != -999)
                        drawLine(line, (i % 6) + 9);
                }
                if (j%2)
                drawRect(bounds,15);
                getch();
                cls(0);
        }
}


/*
```

```
┌─────────────────────────────────────────────────┐
│                                                   │
│            setMode() = Sets video mode            │
│                                                   │
└─────────────────────────────────────────────────┘
```

```
*/

void setMode(int mode)
{
    union REGS reg;

    reg.h.ah = 0;
    reg.h.al = mode;
    int86 (0x10,&reg,&reg);
}
```

(continued)

```
/*

+----------------------------------------------------------+
| +------------------------------------------------------+ |
| |                                                      | |
| |     cls() = Clears the screen to a specified color   | |
| |                                                      | |
| +------------------------------------------------------+ |
+----------------------------------------------------------+

*/

void cls(int color)
{
        union REGS reg;

        reg.x.ax = 0x0600;
        reg.x.cx = 0;
        reg.x.dx = 0x3284;
        reg.h.bh = color;
        int86(0x10,&reg,&reg);
}

/*

+----------------------------------------------------------+
| +------------------------------------------------------+ |
| |                                                      | |
| |  drawRect() = Draws a rectangle in a specified color and | |
| |       a specified line width for 16 color modes.     | |
| |                                                      | |
| +------------------------------------------------------+ |
+----------------------------------------------------------+

*/

void drawRect(LINE bounds, int color)
{
     #define graph_out(index,val)   {outp(0x3CE,index);\
                                      outp(0x3CF,val);}
     #define seq_out(index,val)     {outp(0x3C4,index);\
                                      outp(0x3C5,val);}

        int j, page, x[2], y, offset, offset1, offset2;
        char far * mem_address;
        char line_store[100];
        int dummy, i, x1, x2;
        int length, width;
        int srcseg, srcoff, destseg, destoff;
        long no_of_bytes;
        unsigned char mask;
```

(continued)

```
char far *start_address1;
char far *start_address2;
char far *end_address1;
char far *end_address2;

struct SREGS segregs;

segread(&segregs);
srcseg = segregs.ds;
srcoff = (int) line_store;
width = LINEWIDTH/2;
x[0] = bounds.xs;
x[1] = bounds.xe;
for (i=-width; i<=width; i++)
{
    x1 = min(bounds.xs, bounds.xe) - width;
    x2 = max(bounds.xs, bounds.xe) + width;
    offset1 = x1 % 8;
    offset2 = x2 % 8;
    start_address1 = (char far *)(0xA0000000L +
        ((long)(bounds.ys+i) * xres/8L + ((long)x1
        / 8L)));
    end_address1 = (char far *)(0xA0000000L +
        ((long)(bounds.ys+i) * xres/8L + ((long)x2
        / 8L)));
    start_address2 = (char far *)(0xA0000000L +
        ((long)(bounds.ye+i) * xres/8L + ((long)x1
        / 8L)));
    end_address2 = (char far *)(0xA0000000L +
        ((long)(bounds.ye+i) * xres/8L + ((long)x2
        / 8L)));
    no_of_bytes = end_address1 - start_address1;
    length = ((x2 - x1) - ((8-offset1) +
        (offset2))) / 8L;
    graph_out(5,2);
    mask = 0xFF << (7 - offset2);
    if (!no_of_bytes)
        mask &= 0xFF >> offset1;
    graph_out(8,mask);
    dummy = *end_address1;
    *end_address1 = color;
```

(continued)

```
        dummy = *end_address2;
        *end_address2 = color;
        if (no_of_bytes)
        {
            mask = 0xFF >> offset1;
            graph_out(8, mask);
            *start_address1 = color;
            *start_address2 = color;
            graph_out(8, 0xFF);
            memset(line_store,color,length);
            destseg = 0xA000;
            destoff = ((long) (bounds.ys+i) * 80L +
            ((long)x1 /8L)) + 1;
            movedata(srcseg, srcoff, destseg, destoff,
                length);
            destoff = ((long) (bounds.ye+i) * 80L +
                ((long)x1 /8L)) + 1;
            movedata(srcseg, srcoff, destseg, destoff,
                length);
        }
    }
}
graph_out(8,0xFF);
for (j=0; j<2; j++)
{
    for (i=-width; i<=width; i++)
    {
        mask |= (0x80 >> ((x[j]+i) % 8));
        if ((((x[j]+i) % 8) == 7) || (i==width))
        {
            graph_out(8,mask);
            for (y=bounds.ys; y<=bounds.ye; y++)
            {
                mem_address = (char far *)
                    0xA0000000L + (long)y * xres
                    /8L + ((long)(x[j]+i) / 8L);
                dummy = *mem_address;
                *mem_address = color;
            }
            mask = 0;
        }
    }
```

(continued)

```
        }
    graph_out(8,0xFF);
    graph_out(1,0x00);
    graph_out(5,0);
}

/*
```

```
    drawLine() = Draws a single pixel wide line in a
selected color using the plot function. Will
        work with any plot function. The one used
            in this example is for mode 16 (640
                x 350 pixels by 16 colors.
```

```
*/

void drawLine(LINE line, int color)
{

    int temp, dx, dy, i, x, y, xs, xe, ys, ye, x_sign,
        y_sign, decision;

    xs = line.xs;
    ys = line.ys;
    xe = line.xe;
    ye = line.ye;
    dx = abs(xe - xs);
    dy = abs(ye - ys);
    if (((dx >= dy) && (xs > xe)) || ((dy > dx) && (ys >
        ye)))
    {
        temp = xs;
        xs = xe;
        xe = temp;
        temp = ys;
        ys = ye;
        ye = temp;
    }
    if ((ye - ys) < 0)
        y_sign = -1;
```

(continued)

```
     else
          y_sign = 1;
     if ((xe - xs) < 0)
          x_sign = -1;
     else
          x_sign = 1;
     if (dx >= dy)
     {
          for (x=xs,y=ys,decision=0; x<=xe;
              x++,decision+=dy)
          {
              if (decision>=dx)
              {
                   decision -= dx;
                   y+= y_sign;
              }
              plot16(x,y,color);
          }
     }
     else
     {
          for (x=xs,y=ys,decision=0; y<=ye;
              y++,decision+=dx)
          {
              if (decision>=dy)
              {
                   decision -= dy;
                   x+=x_sign;
              }
              plot16(x,y,color);
          }
     }
}

/*
```

```
     plot16() = Plots a point on the screen at a designated
       position using a selected color for 16 color modes.
```

```
*/
```

(continued)

```
void plot16(int x, int y, int color)
{

        #define graph_out(index,val)   {outp(0x3CE,index);\
                                        outp(0x3CF,val);}

        int dummy,mask;
        char far * address;

        if ((x>=0) && (x<xres) && (y>=0) && (y<yres))
        {
                address = (char far *) 0xA0000000L + (long)y *
                        xres/8L + ((long)x / 8L);
                mask = 0x80 >> (x % 8);
                graph_out(8,mask);
                graph_out(5,2);
                dummy = *address;
                *address = color;
                graph_out(5,0);
                graph_out(8,0xFF);
        }
}


/*

    ┌──────────────────────────────────────────────────────┐
    │                                                        │
    │   clipline1() = Changes line coordinates so that line  │
    │           will be within designated window.            │
    │                                                        │
    └──────────────────────────────────────────────────────┘
*/

LINE clipLine1(LINE line, LINE bounds)
{
        int dx, dy, temp;

        if (line.xs > line.xe)
        {
                temp = line.xe;
                line.xe = line.xs;
                line.xs = temp;
                temp = line.ye;
```

(continued)

```
            line.ye = line.ys;
            line.ys = temp;
    }
    if ((line.xs >= bounds.xe) || (line.xe <=
            bounds.xs))
    {
            line.xs = -999;
            return(line);
    }
    if (line.xs == line.xe)
    {
            line.ys = min(bounds.ye, line.ys);
            line.ys = max(bounds.ys, line.ys);
            line.ye = min(bounds.ye, line.ye);
            line.ye = max(bounds.ys, line.ye);
            return(line);
    }
    if (line.ys == line.ye)
    {
            if ((line.ys > bounds.ye) || (line.ys <
                    bounds.ys))
            {
                    line.xs = -999;
                    return(line);
            }
            line.xs = max(bounds.xs, line.xs);
            line.xe = min(bounds.xe, line.xe);
            return(line);
    }
    dy = line.ye - line.ys;
    dx = line.xe - line.xs;
    if (line.xs < bounds.xs)
    {
            line.ys = line.ys + (long)(bounds.xs -
                    line.xs)*dy/dx;
            line.xs = bounds.xs;
    }
    if (line.ys < bounds.ys)
    {
            line.xs = line.xs + (long)(bounds.ys -
                    line.ys)*dx/dy;
```

(continued)

```
                        line.ys = bounds.ys;
                }
                if (line.ys > bounds.ye)
                {
                        line.xs = line.xs + (long)(bounds.ye -
                                line.ys)*dx/dy;
                        line.ys = bounds.ye;
                }
                if (line.xe > bounds.xe)
                {
                        line.ye = line.ys + (long)(bounds.xe -
                                line.xs)*dy/dx;
                        line.xe = bounds.xe;
                }
                if (line.ye < bounds.ys)
                {
                        line.xe = line.xs + (long)(bounds.ys -
                                line.ys)*dx/dy;
                        line.ye = bounds.ys;
                }
                if (line.ye > bounds.ye)
                {
                        line.xe = line.xs + (long)(bounds.ye -
                                line.ys)*dx/dy;
                        line.ye = bounds.ye;
                }
                return(line);
        }


/*
```

```
    clipline2() = Changes line coordinates so that line
            will be within a designated window using
                Cohen-Sutherland algorithm.
```

```
*/

#define outcodes(x, y, bounds, outcode) { outcode = 0; \
        if (x < bounds.xs)          \
```

(continued)

```
                outcode |= 1;            \
        else                      \
            if (x > bounds.xe)      \
                outcode |= 2;        \
        if (y < bounds.ys)        \
            outcode |= 8;            \
        else                      \
            if (y > bounds.ye)      \
                outcode |= 4;}

        #define test {if (outcode1 & outcode2)  {        \
                                    line.xs = -999;   \
                                    return(line);}      \
                          if (! (outcode1 | outcode2))     \
                              return(line);  }

LINE clipLine2(LINE line, LINE bounds)
{
        int outcode1, outcode2, temp, dx, dy;

        if (line.xs > line.xe)
        {
            temp = line.xe;
            line.xe = line.xs;
            line.xs = temp;
            temp = line.ye;
            line.ye = line.ys;
            line.ys = temp;
        }
        outcodes(line.xs, line.ys, bounds, outcode1);
        outcodes(line.xe, line.ye, bounds, outcode2);
        test;
        dx = line.xe - line.xs;
        dy = line.ye - line.ys;
        while (1)
        {
            if (outcode1 & 1)
            {
                line.ys += (long)(bounds.xs - line.xs)
                    *dy/dx;
                line.xs = bounds.xs;
```

(continued)

```
                outcode1 = (line.ys > bounds.ye) ? 4 :
                    ((line.ys < bounds.ys) ? 8: 0);
        }
        test;
        if (outcode1 & 8)
        {
            line.xs += (long)(bounds.ys -
                line.ys)*dx/dy;
            line.ys = bounds.ys;
            outcode1 = (line.xs > bounds.xe) ? 2 :
                ((line.xs < bounds.xs) ? 1: 0);
        }
        test;
        if (outcode1 & 4)
        {
            line.xs += (long)(bounds.ye -
                line.ys)*dx/dy;
            line.ys = bounds.ye;
            outcode1 = (line.xs > bounds.xe) ? 2 :
                ((line.xs < bounds.xs) ? 1: 0);
        }
        test;
        if (outcode2 & 2)
        {
            line.ye = line.ys + (long)(bounds.xe -
                line.xs)*dy/dx;
            line.xe = bounds.xe;
            outcode2 = (line.ye > bounds.ye) ? 4 :
                ((line.ye < bounds.ys) ? 8: 0);
        }
        test;
        if (outcode2 & 8)
        {
            line.xe = line.xs + (long)(bounds.ys -
                line.ys)*dx/dy;
            line.ye = bounds.ys;
            outcode2 = (line.xe > bounds.xe) ? 2 :
                ((line.xe < bounds.xs) ? 1: 0);
        }
        test;
        if (outcode2 & 4)
```

(continued)

```
{
        line.xe = line.xs + (long)(bounds.ye -
            line.ys)*dx/dy;
        line.ye = bounds.ye;
        outcode2 = (line.xe > bounds.xe) ? 2 :
            ((line.xe < bounds.xs) ? 1: 0);
        test;
    }
}
}
```

Clipping with the Cohen-Sutherland Algorithm

Cohen and Sutherland developed a clipping algorithm based upon dividing the world into nine regions, one being within the clipping window and the others above, below, to the right and to the left of the window and combinations of these. Each region is then assigned a unique four bit identifying number. This scheme for dividing the world is shown in Figure 12-2. An identifying code is assigned to each endpoint of the line, depending upon which of the nine regions it lies in. The method of assigning codes has several nice features. First, it is very easy to generate the code that is assigned to each endpoint of the line. This is demonstrated in the macro at the beginning of the *clipline2* function. The code is first set to 0; then a check is made against the left boundary and the code ORed with 1 if the x coordinate is to the left. If this is the case, nothing further needs to be done with x. Otherwise, x is checked to see if it is to the right, and if so, the code is ORed with 2. In a similar manner, an 8 is ORed into the code if y is above the window and a 4 ORed in if y is below the window. That's all that needs to be done to generate the code for a coordinate pair. Another nice feature comes about in testing. If the both endpoints of the line are within the window, both codes are 0. If these codes are ORed together, the result is then 0, which indicates the function should return the line value, since it is in the window. If the codes for the endpoint have the same bit set to 1 in both, this indicates that the entire line is outside the window, which means that the line can be disregarded. This situation can be identified by the fact that ANDing the two codes yields a 1 if two corresponding bits are 1 and a 0 otherwise. For this situation, the function first changes the value of xs to -999. Since this value can never occur naturally, it is a signal to the calling function that the line is entirely outside the clipping boundaries and therefore should not be printed. Another way that you might want to handle this situation is to include a Boolean variable in the line structure which tells whether or not the line should be printed. This Boolean value would be set within the *clipline* function and would be automatically passed to the *drawLine* function to determine whether the line should be displayed or not.

Now lets look at the Cohen-Sutherland clipping function in a little more detail. As with the previous clipping function, it begins by swapping coordinate pairs, if necessary, so that *xs* is always less than *xe*. Then the *outcodes* macro is called to generate the *outcode* for each of the line endpoints. The macro *test* is then run to check whether we have a line totally outside the clipping rectangle or one totally inside it. In either of these two special cases, the function terminates, returning a set of line endpoint values. If neither of these trivial cases were true, the function would begin a *while* loop, which executes forever unless one of the subsequent calls to *test* causes the function to return to the calling program. In this *while* loop are the six boundary conditions that we described for the previous clipping function. Once a condition is found true and the new end point coordinates are computed, the *outcode* is modified appropriately. If you're not familiar with the *?* operator in C, this may seem a little obscure to you. A typical *outcode* modifying expression is

```
outcode1 = (line.ys > bounds.ye) ? 4: ((line.ys <
     bounds.ys) ? 8: 0);
```

This is equivalent to the following code:

```
if (line.ys > bounds.ye)
     outcode1 = 4;
else
     if (line.ys < bounds.ys)
         outcode = 8;
     else
         outcode = 0;
```

Then *test* is called to check whether the new line coordinates are both inside or outside of the clipping rectangle, thereby indicating that it is time to terminate. The loop continues to iterate until one of these conditions is met. We need to point out two things about this loop.

First, one pass through the loop should be sufficient to determine the new endpoints for any line. Unfortunately, however, there is an occasional pathological line where truncation errors during computation cause one pass through the loop to be insufficient. This occurs very rarely, but when it does, a second pass through the loop resolves the situation. Second, you might ask why after each coordinate change the whole *test* macro should be run, since it seems obvious that if a line is not totally outside the clipping rectangle to begin with, it will not become so after alteration. This is mathematically true, but when truncation errors creep in, a line right at the edge of the clipping rectangle can occasionally creep outside. Without some provision for this case, such a situation would cause the function to remain in the *while* loop forever, thereby locking up the computer.

The *cliptest.c* Program

The program *cliptest.c* is used to test the operation of the clipping functions. The program begins by running the *randomize* function, which results in every running of the program being different. Next, the program is put into the 640 pixel by 350 pixel by 16 color graphics mode and then the boundaries of a smaller clipping rectangle within the screen are defined. The program then begins a *for* loop which iterates four times. On the first pass, the program uses *clipline1* to perform the clipping. It randomly selects end points for 2500 lines, within the screen boundaries and draws each line in one of the six darker colors. Each line is then clipped and drawn in one of the six brighter colors. At the end of this loop, the boundaries of the clipping rectangle are very obvious on the screen. The resulting display is shown in Plate 5. On the next pass, the program generates 250 lines within the screen boundaries, clips them, and draws only the clipped lines. A rectangle representing the extent of the clipping box is then drawn around them. This shows very clearly that no part of any line extends beyond the clipping rectangle. The last two iterations of the loop repeat these two displays use *clipline2*, the Cohen-Sutherland algorithm clipping function. Although the Cohen-Sutherland algorithm is more elegant and does a better job of handling the pathological cases, it really doesn't show any remarkable increase in speed for actual operation. It appears that the clipping function is so much faster than the function for drawing a line that the latter determines the amount of computer time that will be used.

*Figure 12-2. Cohen-Sutherland Method of Dividing Space
Around a Clipping Rectangle (Window)*

Above Left (1001)	Above (1000)	Above Right (1010)
Left (0001)	Within (0000)	Right (0010)
Below Left (0101)	Below (0100)	Below Right (0110)

Clipping Filled Shapes

In the next four chapters, we are going to encounter functions for filling a wide variety of shapes such as circles, ellipses, irregular polygons and rounded rectangles. In most cases, such shapes are filled with horizontal lines. At some point in each function, the function has determined the top and bottom values of y for which the horizontal lines are to be drawn. You need to modify these values so that they are not beyond the top and bottom of the clipping rectangle. Then, for each horizontal line that is to be drawn, you need to modify the starting and ending values of x, if necessary, to be within the clipping rectangle. The one exception to this neat operation is the flood filling function. This function keeps changing the colors of points until it encounters the boundaries of a closed curve. If any part of a boundary is outside the screen limits, the function goes berserk and is likely to fill the whole screen. In using this function, then, you as the programmer must assure that the figure being operated upon never extends beyond the screen boundaries.

Chapter 13

Drawing and Filling Circles

Circles and ellipses are the most commonly used curves in graphics applications. In this chapter we are going to look at the theory involved in producing these figures and develop some functions that produce fast and accurate figures. These functions compare favorably in speed with commercial drawing packages, but offer the flexibility to design functions exactly the way you want them instead of being constrained by the preferences of the program designers.

The functions described and the test program to demonstrate them in operation are written for display mode 12H (640 by 480 pixels by 16 colors). The display screen is a rectangle having the aspect of 4 to 3. Thus, if the screen is divided into squares, they would contain 640/4 or 160 pixels in the horizontal direction and 480/3 or 160 pixels in the vertical direction. The pixels are therefore square and are thus ideally suited for displaying circles that actual appear circular on the screen. However, to give a little more flexibility, we are using a system coordinate system in which the coordinate (0,0) is at the center of the screen. The minimum horizontal value (at the left) is -319 and the maximum horizontal value (at the right) is +320 pixels. Similarly, the minimum vertical value (at the bottom) is -239 and the maximum vertical value (at the top) is +240 pixels. These are converted to actual screen coordinates in the *plots* function, just before the point is plotted to the screen. The program to test the circle drawing and filling functions is *circle.c*. This program is listed in Figure 13-1.

Figure 13-1. Listing of circle.c Function.

```
/*
```

```
              circle = Program to test circle drawing

                  By Roger T. Stevens    9-2-91
```

```
*/
```

```
#include <stdio.h>
#include <stdlib.h>
#include <math.h>
#include <dos.h>
#include <conio.h>

void cls(char colors);
void drawCircle(int x, int y, int r, int color);
void drawCircle1(int x, int y, int r, int color);
void drawCircle2(int x, int y, int r, int color);
void drawCircle3(int x, int y, int r, int color);
void fillCircle(int x, int y, int r, int color);
void fillLine(int x_one, int x_two, int y, int color);
void plots(int x, int y, int color);
void setMode(int mode);

#define convert(x,y)   {x += 320;  y = 240 - y;}

int xres=640, yres=480;
int color, angle;
int LINEWIDTH=1;
unsigned char OPERATOR = 0x00;
```

```
/*
```

```
                        MAIN PROGRAM
```

```
*/
```

(continued)

```
main()
{
    int i,j,x_cen, y_cen, radius,ran_param;

    randomize();
    setMode(0x12);
    cls(1);
    drawCircle1(-20,10,200,11);
    getch();
    cls(1);
    drawCircle2(-20,10,200,13);
    getch();
    cls(15);
    drawCircle1(-20,10,200,0);
    drawCircle2(-20,10,200,1);
    getch();
    cls(1);
    color = 9;
    for (i=2; i<200; i+=4)
       drawCircle1(-20,10,i,color++);
    getch();
    cls(1);
    color = 9;
    for (i=2; i<200; i+=4)
       drawCircle2(-20,10,i,color++);
    getch();
    cls(4);
    drawCircle2(-20,10,2,14);
    getch();
    randomize();
    color = random(16);
    cls(1);
    LINEWIDTH = 5;
    for (i=0; i<17; i++)
    {
       drawCircle3(0,0,14*i + 10,i);
    }
    getch();
    cls(1);
    for (i=0; i<100; i++)
    {
```

(continued)

```
        color = color%16;
        if (color == 1)
            color++;
        drawCircle2(random(640) - 320, random(480)-240,
            random(240), color++);
    }
    getch();
    cls(1);
    ran_param = 160;
    for (i=0; i<50; i++)
    {
        if (i == 15)
            ran_param = 0;
        color = 0;
        x_cen = random(640) - 320;
        y_cen = random(480) - 240;
        radius = random(80) + ran_param;
        for (j=0; j<17; j++)
        {
            drawCircle2(x_cen, y_cen, (radius * j)/16,
                color++);
            if (color == 1)
                color++;
        }
    }
    getch();
    cls(1);
    for (i=0; i<50; i++)
    {
        LINEWIDTH = random(20);
        color = (color + 1) % 16;
        if (color == 1)
            color++;
        drawCircle3(random(640) - 320, random(480) -
            240,  random(240), color);
    }
    getch();
    cls(1);
    fillCircle(-20,10,200,13);
    getch();
    cls(1);
```

(continued)

```
   for (i=0; i<70; i++)
   {
      color = (color + 1) % 16;
      if (color == 1)
          color++;
      fillCircle(random(840) - 420, random(680) - 340,
      random(150), color);
   }
   getch();
}

/*
```

```
      cls() = Clears the screen to a specified color
```

```
*/

void cls(char colors)
{
    union REGS reg;

    reg.x.dx = 0x2384F;
    reg.h.bh = colors;
    reg.x.ax = 0x0600;
    reg.x.cx = 0;
    int86(0x10,&reg,&reg);
    gotoxy(0,0);
}

/*
```

```
                  setMode() = Sets video mode
```

```
*/

void setMode(int mode)
{
    union REGS reg;
```

(continued)

```
    reg.h.ah = 0;
    reg.h.al = mode;
    int86 (0x10,&reg,&reg);
}

/*
```

```
    plots() = Plots a point on the screen at designated
            system coordinates using selected color.
```

```
*/

void plots(int x, int y, int color)
{
    unsigned int offset;
    int dummy,mask,page;
    char far * mem_address;

    convert(x,y);
    if ((x >= xres) || (x < 0) || (y >= yres) || (y < 0))
        return;
    offset = (long)y * xres/8L + ((long)x / 8L);
    mem_address = (char far *) 0xA0000000L + offset;
    mask = 0x8000 >> (x % 8);
    outport(0x3CE,mask | 0x08);
    outport(0x3CE,0x0205);
    dummy = *mem_address;
    *mem_address = color;
    outport(0x3CE,0xFF08);
    outport(0x3CE,0x0005);
}

/*
```

```
    drawCircle1() = Draws a circle with specified center,
            radius, and color, using a single pixel line
                            width.
```

```
*/
```

(continued)

```
void drawCircle1(int x, int y, int r, int color)
{

    int i, row, col, px, py;
    long int sum;

    py = r;
    px = 0;
    sum = -r;
    while (px <= py)
    {
        col = x + px;
        row = y + py;
        plots(col,row,color);
        row = y - py;
        plots(col,row,color);
        col = x - px;
        plots(col,row,color);
        row = y + py;
        plots(col,row,color);
        col = x + py;
        row = y + px;
        plots(col,row,color);
        row = y - px;
        plots(col,row,color);
        col = x - py;
        plots(col,row,color);
        row = y + px;
        plots(col,row,color);
        sum +=px++;
        if (sum >= 0)
        {
            sum-=py--;
        }
    }
}
```

(continued)

```
/*
```

```
    drawCircle2() = Draws a circle with specified center,
          radius, and color, using a single pixel line
                    width and increased accuracy.
```

```
*/
```

```
void drawCircle2(int x, int y, int r, int color)
{
    int i, row, col, px, py;
    long int sum;

    py = r<<1;
    px = 0;
    sum = -(r<<1);
    while (px <= py)
    {
        if ( !(px & 1))
        {
            col = x + (px>>1);
            row = y + (py>>1);
            plots(col,row,color);
            row = y - (py>>1);
            plots(col,row,color);
            col = x - (px>>1);
            plots(col,row,color);
            row = y + (py>>1);
            plots(col,row,color);
            col = x + (py>>1);
            row = y + (px>>1);
            plots(col,row,color);
            row = y - (px>>1);
            plots(col,row,color);
            col = x - (py>>1);
            plots(col,row,color);
            row = y + (px>>1);
            plots(col,row,color);
        }
        sum +=px++;
```

(continued)

```
        sum += px;
        if (sum >= 0)
        {
            sum-=py--;
            sum -=py;
        }
    }
}

/*
```

┌───┐
│   │
│ drawCircle3() = Draws a circle with specified center,   │
│   radius, and color, using line width in pixels   │
│   specified by LINEWIDTH.   │
│   │
└───┘

```
*/

void drawCircle3(int x, int y, int r, int color)
{
    extern int LINEWIDTH:

    int i, row, col, px, py;
    long int sum;

    r += LINEWIDTH /2;
    py = r<<1;
    px = 0;
    sum = -(r<<1);
    while (px <= py)
    {
        if ( !(px & 1))
        {
            col = x + (px>>1);
            row = y + (py>>1);
            for (i=0; i<LINEWIDTH; i++)
                plots(col,row-i,color);
            row = y - (py>>1);
            for (i=0; i<LINEWIDTH; i++)
                plots(col,row+i,color);
            col = x - (px>>1);
```

(continued)

```
                for (i=0; i<LINEWIDTH; i++)
                  plots(col,row+i,color);
                row = y + (py>>1);
                for (i=0; i<LINEWIDTH; i++)
                  plots(col,row-i,color);
                col = x + (py>>1);
                row = y + (px>>1);
                for (i=0; i<LINEWIDTH; i++)
                  plots(col-i,row,color);
                row = y - (px>>1);
                for (i=0; i<LINEWIDTH; i++)
                  plots(col-i,row,color);
                col = x - (py>>1);
                for (i=0; i<LINEWIDTH; i++)
                  plots(col+i,row,color);
                row = y + (px>>1);
                for (i=0; i<LINEWIDTH; i++)
                  plots(col+i,row,color);
                }
          sum +=px++;
          if (sum >= 0)
              sum-=py--;
        }
}


/*
```

```
     ┌──────────────────────────────────────────────────┐
     │ ┌──────────────────────────────────────────────┐ │
     │ │                                              │ │
     │ │    fillCircle() = Fills a circle with specified │ │
     │ │           center, radius, and color.         │ │
     │ │                                              │ │
     │ └──────────────────────────────────────────────┘ │
     └──────────────────────────────────────────────────┘
*/
```

```
void fillCircle(int x, int y, int r, int color)
{
    int i, row, col_start, col_end, t_row, t_col, px, py;
    long int sum;

    py = r<<1;
    px = 0;
    sum = -(r<<1);
```

(continued)

```
        while (px <= py)
        {
           if ( !(px & 1))
           {
               col_start = x - (px>>1);
               col_end = x + (px>>1);
               row = y + (py>>1);
               fillLine(col_start, col_end, row, color);
               col_start = x - (py>>1);
               col_end = x + (py>>1);
               row = y + (px>>1);
               fillLine(col_start, col_end, row, color);
               col_start = x - (px>>1);
               col_end = x + (px>>1);
               row = y - (py>>1);
               fillLine(col_start, col_end, row, color);
               col_start = x - (py>>1);
               col_end = x + (py>>1);
               row = y - (px>>1);
               fillLine(col_start, col_end, row, color);
           }
           sum +=px++;
           if (sum >= 0)
               sum-=py--;
        }
}

/*
```

```
  fillLine() = Fills a line with a specified color from
               x_one to x_two at row y.
```

```
*/

void fillLine(int x_one, int x_two, int y, int color)
{
    char color_buffer[100];
    int dummy, loop, i, x1, x2;
    int length, offset1, offset2;
    int srcseg, srcoff, destseg, destoff;
```

(continued)

```
long int no_of_bytes;
unsigned int mask;
char far *base1;
char far *base2;
struct SREGS segregs;

x_one += 320;
if (x_one < 0)
  x_one = 0;
if (x_one > xres)
  return;
x_two += 320;
if (x_two >= xres)
  x_two = xres - 1;
if (x_two < 0)
  return;
y = 240 - y;
segread(&segregs);
srcseg = segregs.ds;
srcoff = (int) color_buffer;
x1 = min(x_one, x_two);
x2 = max(x_one, x_two);
offset1 = x1 % 8;
offset2 = x2 % 8;
base1 = (char far *)(0xA0000000L + ((long)y * 80L +
  ((long)x1 / 8L)));
base2 = (char far *)(0xA0000000L + ((long)y * 80L +
  ((long)x2 / 8L)));
no_of_bytes = abs(base2 - base1);
length = ((x2 - x1) - ((8-offset1) + (offset2))) / 8L;
mask = 0xFF00 << (7 - offset2);
if (!no_of_bytes)
  mask &= (0xFF00 >> offset1) & 0xFF00;
dummy = *base2;
outport(0x3CE, mask | 0x08);
outport(0x3CE, 0x0205);
*base2 = color;
if (no_of_bytes)
{
  mask = (0xFF00 >> offset1) & 0xFF00;
  outport(0x3CE, mask | 0x08);
```

(continued)

```
            dummy = *base1;
            *base1 = color;
            mask = 0xFF00;
            outport(0x3CE, mask | 0x08);
            memset(color_buffer,color,length);
            destseg = 0xA000;
            destoff = ((long) y * 80L + ((long)x1 /8L)) + 1;
            movedata(srcseg, srcoff, destseg, destoff, length);
        }
        outport(0x3CE, 0xFF08);
        outport(0x3CE, 0x0005);
    }
```

Using Bresenham's Algorithm

To develop the circle drawing function, we are going to use Bresenham's algorithm, which was first described for drawing slanting lines in Chapter 7. The equation for a circle (assuming that the center is at the origin) is

$$x^2 + y^2 = r^2$$

(Equation 13-1)

where x and y indicate the coordinates and r is the radius of the circle. Bresenham's algorithm requires the derivative of this equation, which can be expressed as

$$dy = -\frac{x}{y}\,dx$$

(Equation 13-2)

We are going to begin Bresenham's algorithm with a point on the circumference of the circle at (0,r). At this point, we observe that if we increase x by one pixel, then y decreases by x/y pixels. We are working with discrete values, so we need to set up a decision function in which we store decreases in y until we have accumulated one whole pixel, at which point we actually change the y value. The second part of Bresenham's algorithm involves modifying the decision function so that we don't have to worry about floating point operations or divisions. We accomplish this by multiplying both sides of equation

379

13-2 by -*y*. We now have a decision function which we increase by *x* each time we increase *x* one pixel. When the decision function is greater than 0, we decrease *y* by one pixel and decrease the decision function by *y*. At this point you should look at the function *drawCircle1* in the program listing, which shows how the decision function is used. It also shows how we have completed Bresenham's algorithm for a circle. First, the decision function, *sum*, starts with a value of -*r*. This assures that we don't get an objectionable pip sticking out of the top of the circle due to the *y* coordinate being increased by one pixel on the very first iteration, even though it was too early for this to occur. Next, to cover all possibilities, we have to consider changes in the direction of *x* and *y* and of the decision function. Fortunately we can use the symmetry of a circle to plot eight octants of the circle while calculating the values of only one. Because this octant (from the radius making a 90 degree angle with the *x* axis to a 45 degree angle) is always increasing, *y* is always decreasing, and the decision function always changes in the same direction. You may find that the *drawCircle1* function is perfectly adequate for all of your circle drawing needs. However, there is a subtle problem with this implementation of the algorithm. When we decide to change the value of *y*, the decision function is almost always larger than 0, which means we are just a little late making the change. This means that our *y* values are always on or just inside the circle circumference, whereas, we would like then to be half on each side of the line to give a correct average value. For large circles, you'll never notice the difference, but for very small circles, you will observe a rather objectionable squarish shape to the circle.

Drawing Circles More Accurately

The function *drawCircle2* provides a way of drawing a more accurate circle. We begin by doubling the radius, and we then compute an octant of the circle that is twice the specified radius. Each time we change the decision function, we increase (or decrease) it once by the current coordinate value, then increment the coordinate and increase (or decrease) it again by the new coordinate value. Effectively, the result is that of using the derivative at an average of the values it assumes at the two points. When we plot all of the points of the circle, we use only half of the coordinate values, so that the resulting octant has the actual radius initially specified. The coordinate values are plotted only when the most rapidly changing coordinate value is even since these are the ones that represent the most accurate path for the circumference. When you run the test program, there are some examples, which will be described later, that show you the difference between circles drawn with the functions *drawCircle1* and *drawCircle2* so that you can decide for yourself which one you would prefer to use.

Drawing Wide Line Circles

The preceding functions are fine for drawing circles that are one pixel wide, but don't provide much help if you want to draw circles with wide lines. The function *drawCircle3* will enable you to draw circles with any line width that you desire. One way of doing this is to provide a *for* loop which begins with the smallest radius circle represented by the inside of the wide line and then draws a circle for each radius from this to the radius representing the outer edge of the wide line. Unfortunately, this does not result in a completely filled in line, since drawing concentric circles with a one pixel difference in their radii doesn't guarantee that all pixels within the inner and outer boundary will be included. If you want to use this technique, you need to remove the *if* statement that permits only the correct even valued coordinate sets from being plotted in *drawCircle2* so that there will be a lot of extra points plotted to fill in the gaps in the wide line. For best accuracy, however, this should not apply for the inner and outer boundary circles.

There is a better and faster way to accomplish the same result, however. You'll remember that we drew straight lines by drawing pixels on either side of the one pixel line for cases where *y* was increasing faster than *x* and by drawing pixels above and below the one pixel line for the opposite case. Fortunately, it is easy to identify which case is true for each octant of the circle and perform the proper operation. The only concern is whether the peculiar ends of each octant will meet properly or leave gaps. Fortunately, it turns out that in every case they overlap, so that the resulting circle is perfect. This technique doesn't leave any gaps inside the line either. The function to perform this operation is listed as *drawCircle3*.

Filling Circles

The function to produce filled in circles is *fillCircle*. You'll observe that this is very similar to *drawCircle2*, except that instead of plotting eight pixels at each iteration, (one for each of the eight octants that make up the circle) for four pairs of points, we determine the pair of points that are opposite each other on the same row of the circle and call *fillLine* to draw a fast horizontal line between them. This function is the same as *drawHorzLine2* described in Chapter 7, except that it only draws single pixel wide lines, since that is all that is necessary for the purpose of filling circles.

The *circle.c* Test Program

The *circle.c* program is used to test various aspects of the circle drawing and filling functions. The first screen produced by this program uses the *drawCircle1* function and shows the excellent quality of the circles produced by this program when large radii are involved. The second screen draws the same circle using the improved accuracy function *drawCircle2*. At this large a radius, it is hard to tell the difference between the two methods. The third screen superimposes circles drawn by the two methods, so that you can see how little difference there is between the two techniques. At this point, we might well be leaning toward drawing all our circles with the first function, which is much simpler. Screen 4 draws a series of concentric circles of different colors using the *drawCircle1* function. It is now evident that for small circles, there is an objectionable squareness to circles drawn with this technique. The next screen is the same display drawn with *drawCircle2*. Clearly the small circles are better with this technique. The next screen shows a very small circle (two pixel radius) drawn with the function *drawCircle2*. The next screen draws a set of 16 concentric circles having a line width of five pixels, using *drawCircle3*. The next screen shows 100 circles of one pixel line width drawn with *drawCircle2*. The center of each circle and its radius are selected randomly. Because of the random selection, each time this screen is drawn it appears differently. A typical display is shown in Plate 6. The next display draws 50 sets of 16 concentric circles using *drawCircle2*. The centers of these sets of circles are selected randomly throughout the display. The radii of the first 15 circles are selected randomly between 160 and 240 pixels. The radii of the remaining circles are selected randomly between 0 and 80 pixels. Again, each display is unique. A typical display is shown in Plate 7. The next display is of 50 circles whose widths, centers and radii are selected randomly. These are drawn using *drawCircle3*. Again, each display is unique. A typical one is shown in Plate 8. The next screen shows a large filled circle drawn with *fillCircle*. The next display is of 70 filled circles drawn with *fillCircle*. The center of each circle and its radius are selected randomly. A typical example of this display is shown in Plate 9.

Apollonian Packing of Circles

An interesting fractal, known as the Apollonian packing of circles, provides an excellent test of the circle filling function. In fact, using this program for testing, a major error in the first version of the circle filling function was discovered. This test program is listed in Figure 13-2. One must start out with defining three circles that are tangental to each other. The method I used was to set up a small program to draw and fill the three circles and experiment with their placing until they were somewhat of the size and in the proper locations that I desired. I then froze the values for the center coordinates of the first circle and the radii of the three circles and then calculated where the centers of the second and third circles had to be for all three circles to be tangental. You don't need to go through this, since the proper locations for the three initial circles have already been calculated and are in the program. The result after drawing the first three circles, is that a curvilinear triangle is found to be formed by the meeting of the three circles. The program then finds the largest circle that can be drawn within this triangle, making it tangental to each of the three original circles. The math for this is a little complex. It makes use of a relationship called Soddy's formula, which states

$$2\left(\frac{1}{a^2} + \frac{1}{b^2} + \frac{1}{c^2} + \frac{1}{r^2}\right) = \frac{1}{a} + \frac{1}{b} + \frac{1}{c} + \frac{1}{r}$$

(Equation 13-3)

You'll find all of the mathematical equations in the program listing if you are interested in pursuing the matter. At any rate, creating this new circle produces three more curvilinear triangles. We then fill each one with the largest possible circle, creating three new curvilinear triangles in each, and continue doing this for as long as we want to (in this program we do it eight times). Each circle is filled with a different color. The result is the interesting display shown in Plate 10.

Figure 13-2. Listing of apollon.c Program for Apollonian Packing of Circles

```
/*

     apollon = APOLLONIAN PACKING OF CIRCLES

          By Roger T. Stevens    8-28-91

*/

#include <dos.h>
#include <stdio.h>
#include <stdlib.h>
#include <math.h>

void drawHorzLine(int xstart, int xend, int y, int color);
void fillCircle(int x, int y, int r, int color);
void fillLine(int x_one, int x_two, int y, int color);
void rep_circle(float xa,float ya,float a,float xb,float
    yb, float b,float xc,float yc,float c, int level);
void node(float xa,float ya,float a,float xb,float yb,
    float b,float xc,float yc,float c, float xs,
    float ys, float s, int level);
void setMode(int mode);
void fillOval(float x_cen, float y_cen, float radius, int
    color, float aspect);

int color = 14;
int xres = 640, yres = 350;
int level = 8;

main()
{
    float a=625, b=375, c=945, xa=-725, xb=275, xc=180,
        ya=235, yb=268, yc=-1048,temp;
```

(continued)

```
    xa = -680;
    ya = 277;
    b = 500;
    xb = 445;
    yb = 276;
    c = 1045;
    xc = 60;
    yc = -1220;
    setMode(0x10);
    fillCircle(xa,ya,a,color--);
    fillCircle(xb,yb,b,color--);
    fillCircle(xc,yc,c,color--);
    rep_circle(xa,ya,a,xb,yb,b,xc,yc,c,level);
    getch();
}


/*
```

┌──┐
│   │
│   rep_circle() = Recursively replicates circles.   │
│   │
└──┘

```
*/

void rep_circle(float xa,float ya,float a,float xb,float
yb, float b,float xc,float yc,float c, int level)
{
    float s, xs, ys, mult;

    level--;
    s = 1/(1/a + 1/b + 1/c + 2*(sqrt(1/(b*c) + 1/(c*a) +
        1/(a*b)))));
    mult = (s+a)*(s+a) - (s+b)*(s+b) - xa*xa + xb*xb -
        ya*ya + yb*yb;
    ys = (mult*(xc-xa) - (xb - xa)*((s+a)*(s+a) -
        (s+c)*(s+c) - xa*xa + xc*xc - ya*ya +
        yc*yc))/(2*((yb-ya)*(xc-xa) - (yc-ya)* (xb - xa)));
    xs = (mult - 2*ys*(yb - ya))/(2*(xb - xa));
    color--;
    if (color == 0)
        color = 15;
    fillCircle(xs,ys,s,color);
```

(continued)

385

```
    color--;
       if (color == 0)
          color = 15;
       if (level > 0)
       {
          rep_circle(xa,ya,a,xb,yb,b,xs,ys,s,level);
          rep_circle(xb,yb,b,xc,yc,c,xs,ys,s,level);
          rep_circle(xa,ya,a,xc,yc,c,xs,ys,s,level);
       }
    }


/*
```

```
        fillCircle() = Fills a circle with specified
                    center, radius, and color.
```

```
*/

void fillCircle(int x, int y, int r, int color)
{
    int i, row, col_start, col_end, px, py;
    long int sum;

    py = r<<1;
    px = 0;
    sum = 0;
    while (px <= py)
    {
       col_start = max(x - (px>>1),-320);
       col_end = min(x + (px>>1),319);
       row = y + (py>>1);
       if ((col_start < 320) && (col_end > -320) && (row >
           -240) && (row < 240))
           fillLine(col_start, col_end, row, color);
       col_start = max(x - (py>>1),-320);
       col_end = min(x + (py>>1),319);
       row = y + (px>>1);
       if ((col_start < 320) && (col_end > -320) && (row >
           -240) && (row < 240))
           fillLine(col_start, col_end, row, color);
```

(continued)

```
            col_start = max(x - (px>>1),-320);
            col_end = min(x + (px>>1),319);
            row = y - (py>>1);
            if ((col_start < 320) && (col_end > -320) && (row >
                -240) && (row < 240))
                fillLine(col_start, col_end, row, color);
            col_start = max(x - (py>>1),-320);
            col_end = min(x + (py>>1),319);
            row = y - (px>>1);
            if ((col_start < 320) && (col_end > -320) && (row >
                -240) && (row < 240))
                fillLine(col_start, col_end, row, color);
        sum +=px++;
        sum += px;
        if (sum >= 0)
        {
            sum-=py--;
            sum -=py;
        }
    }
}


/*
```

```
     fillLine = Draws a horizontal line one pixel wide
       between two designated points on screen using
        a selected color and 16 color video modes.
```

```
*/

void fillLine(int x_one, int x_two, int y, int color)
{
    char color_buffer[100];
    int dummy, loop, i, x1, x2;
    int length, offset1, offset2;
    int srcseg, srcoff, destseg, destoff;
    long int no_of_bytes;
    unsigned int mask;
    char far *base1;
    char far *base2;
```

(continued)

387

```
    struct SREGS segregs;

       x_one += (xres>>1);
       x_two += (xres>>1);
       y = (yres>>1) - ((93*y) >> 7);
       segread(&segregs);
       srcseg = segregs.ds;
       srcoff = (int) color_buffer;
       x1 = min(x_one, x_two);
       x2 = max(x_one, x_two);
       offset1 = x1 % 8;
       offset2 = x2 % 8;
       base1 = (char far *)(0xA0000000L + ((long)y * xres/8L +
          ((long)x1 / 8L)));
       base2 = (char far *)(0xA0000000L + ((long)y * xres/8L +
          ((long)x2 / 8L)));
       no_of_bytes = abs(base2 - base1);
       length = ((x2 - x1) - ((8-offset1) + (offset2))) / 8L;
       mask = 0xFF00 << (7 - offset2);
       if (!no_of_bytes)
          mask &= (0xFF00 >> offset1) & 0xFF00;
       dummy = *base2;
       outport(0x3CE, mask | 0x08);
       outport(0x3CE, 0x0205);
       *base2 = color;
       if (no_of_bytes)
       {
          mask = (0xFF00 >> offset1) & 0xFF00;
          outport(0x3CE, mask | 0x08);
          dummy = *base1;
          *base1 = color;
          mask = 0xFF00;
          outport(0x3CE, mask | 0x08);
          memset(color_buffer,color,length);
          destseg = 0xA000;
          destoff = ((long) y * xres/8L + ((long)x1 /8L)) + 1;
          movedata(srcseg, srcoff, destseg, destoff, length);
       }
       outport(0x3CE, 0xFF08);
       outport(0x3CE, 0x0005);
    }
```

(continued)

```
/*

    setMode() = Sets video mode

*/

void setMode(int mode)
{
    union REGS reg;

    reg.h.ah = 0;
    reg.h.al = mode;
    int86 (0x10,&reg,&reg);
}
```

Serendipitous Errors

Back in Chapter 7, while discussing the *drawHorzLine2* function, we warned that this wouldn't work with the compact, large and huge memory models. The reason is that the fast horizontal line drawing function was set up to work with near addresses, and these memory modes use far addresses, which might result in the function going about anywhere in memory to get the color information that it is going to use to set the color of the line that is drawn. Plate 11 shows what happens when you use the wrong memory model to compile the program for the Apollonian packing of circles. The result is interesting and beautiful and probably not reproducible. Also, at least on my computer, it did funny things to memory that prevented me from saving the screen if the program was run from within the total integrated environment. Nonetheless, this shows that not every mistake turns out to produce disastrous results.

Chapter 14

Drawing and Filling Ellipses

Specifying the parameters for drawing a circle is easy. All you have to do is identify the coordinates for the circle's center and specify the radius. When we attempt to define an ellipse, things become much more complicated. Unlike the circle, which is symmetrical, the ellipse has a shape. It is long in one direction and short in the other. There are several ways in which we can specify this. One is to define an x axis value, which is the distance from the center of the ellipse to its circumference along the x axis, and a y axis value, which is the distance from the center of the ellipse to its circumference along the y axis. These values, along with the coordinates of the center of the ellipse are sufficient to completely define the ellipse. Another way to define the ellipse is to define the coordinates of the upper left corner and lower right corner of a rectangle, for which the ellipse is tangent to all four sides of the rectangle. These techniques define a well-behaved ellipse whose focii are on one of the two coordinate systems axes. Unlike the circle, however, the ellipse can be rotated, and appears different at each orientation. If we are going to allow rotation, the generation of the ellipse becomes much more complex, and we also have to specify the orientation angle. Finally, we may not want to use either of these methods for describing the ellipse, but may want to specify a point on the circumference of the ellipse at the end of one axis along with the two axis values. Don't despair at all these possibilities, however. Since you are creating your own functions for drawing and filling ellipses, you can tailor them to do exactly what you want and no more.

Using Bresenham's Algorithm

The version of Bresnham's algorithm that we used for drawing circles is almost the same as the one needed for drawing ellipses.The equation for an ellipse (assuming that the center is at the origin) is

$$\left(\frac{x}{a}\right)^2 + \left(\frac{y}{b}\right)^2 = 1$$

(Equation 14-1)

where x and y indicate the coordinates, a is the semi-major axis and b the semi-minor axis of the ellipse. Bresenham's algorithm requires the derivative of this equation, which can be expressed as

$$dy = -\frac{b^2 x}{a^2 y} dx$$

(Equation 14-2)

Comparing equation 14-2 with equation 13-2, we see that we can use the very same algorithm for drawing ellipses that we used for drawing circles, except that there is a different multiplication factor each time we increase the *sum* decision variable. The program *ovalchk.c* is used to demonstrate various examples of drawing and filling ellipses. It is listed in Figure 14-1. We are going to select three ellipse drawing techniques as examples from the many ones that are possible and one ellipse filling technique. Descriptions of these follow the program.

Figure 14-1. Listing of Ovalchk.c Function.

```
/*
```

```
    ovalchk.c = Program to check functions for drawing and
                       filling ovals.

                 By Roger T. Stevens   9-8-91
```

```
*/
```

```
#include <stdio.h>
#include <stdlib.h>
#include <math.h>
#include <dos.h>
#include <conio.h>

void cls(char colors);
void drawLine(int x1, int y1, int x2, int y2, int color);
void drawOval1(int xl, int yt, int xr, int yb, int color);
void drawOval2(int xl, int yt, int xr, int yb, int color);
void drawOval3(int xl, int yt, int xr, int yb, float
   angle, int color);
void drawOval2(int xl, int yt, int xr, int yb, int color);
void drawOval4(int x, int y, int x_axis, int y_axis, float
   angle, int color);
void fillOval(int x, int y, int x_axis, int y_axis, float
   angle, int color);
fillLine(int x_one, int x_two, int y, int color);
void plot(int x, int y, int color);
void plots(int x, int y, int color);
void setEGApalette(int palette, int color);
void setMode(int mode);

#define convert(x,y)  {x += 319; y = 175 - ((93*y) >> 7);}
#define compare(a,b,c)  {if (a<b) b = a; if (a>c) c = a;}

int color = 2, angle, xres=640, yres=350;
int LINEWIDTH=1, OPERATOR=0;
unsigned long int PATTERN=0xFFFFFFFF;
```

(continued)

```
/*
```

```
                              MAIN PROGRAM
```

```
*/
```

```
void main(void)
{
    int i, x, y, xc, yc, xa, ya, angle;

    randomize();
```

```
/*
```

```
         Draw three interlocked circles with 'drawOval1'
                640 x 350 pixel by 16 color mode.
```

```
*/
```

```
    setMode(0x10);
    cls (1);

    LINEWIDTH = 1;
    drawOval1(-270,190,-30,-50,14);
    drawOval1(-120,50,120,-190,14);
    drawOval1(30,190,270,-50,14);
    getch();
```

```
/*
```

```
    Draw three pairs of ovals; each pair with the same
              center, but axes lengths swapped.
               640 x 350 pixel x 16 color mode.
```

```
*/
```

```
    cls(1);
    drawOval2(-210,190,-90,-50,14);
```

(continued)

```
drawOval2(-60,50,60,-190,14);
drawOval2(90,190,210,-50,14);
drawOval2(-270,130,-30,10,14);
drawOval2(-120,-10,120,-130,14);
drawOval2(30,130,270,10,14);
getch();

/*
```

```
    Draw 80 ovals with random center, random axes and one
           pixel wide lines using 'drawOval2()'.
                640 x 350 pixel x 16 color mode.
```

```
*/
    cls(1);
    color = random(16);
    for (i=0; i<80; i++)
    {
        color = color%16;
        if (color == 1)
            color++;
        xc = random(640) - 320;
        yc = random(480) - 240;
        xa = xc + 10 + random(310 - xc);
        ya = yc - 10 - random(230 + yc);
        drawOval2(xc, yc, xa, ya,color++);
    }
    getch();

/*
```

```
    Draw 80 ovals with random centers, axes, and line widths
                      using 'drawOval2()'.
                640 x 350 pixel x 16 color mode.
```

```
*/

    cls(1);
    color = random(16);
```

(continued)

```
for (i=0; i<80; i++)
{
    LINEWIDTH = random(20) + 1;
    color = color%16;
    if (color == 1)
        color++;
    xc = random(640) - 320;
    yc = random(480) - 240;
    xa = xc + 10 + random(310) + 2*LINEWIDTH;
    ya = yc - 10 - random(230) - 2*LINEWIDTH;
    drawOval2(xc, yc, xa, ya,color++);
}
getch();
```

```
/*
```

```
        Draw long narrow ovals with 'drawOval1()' and
                'drawOval2()' for comparison.
            640 x 350 pixel x 16 color mode.
```

```
*/
```

```
cls(1);
LINEWIDTH = 20;
drawOval1(-200,90,200,50,13);
drawOval2(-200,-50,200,-90,12);
getch();
```

```
/*
```

```
        Draw two large ovals with axes swapped using
                    'drawOval3()'.
            640 x 350 pixel x 16 color mode.
```

```
*/
```

```
cls(1);
LINEWIDTH = 1;
color = 3;
```

(continued)

```
drawOval3(-200,100,200,-100,0,color++);
getch();
drawOval3(-200,100,200,-100,90,color++);
getch();
color = 9;
```

```
/*
```

```
        Draw very large and very small ovals using
                    'drawOval2()'.
              640 x 350 pixel x 16 color mode.
```

```
*/
```

```
cls(1);
drawOval2(-2,1,2,-1,color++);
drawOval2(-318,238,318,-238,color);
getch();
```

```
/*
```

```
   Draw two ovals with wide lines using 'drawOval2()'.
              640 x 350 pixel x 16 color mode.
```

```
*/
```

```
cls(1);
LINEWIDTH = 12;
drawOval2(-200,150,200,-150,12);
drawOval2(-308,228,308,-228,13);
getch();
```

```
/*
```

```
   Rotate ovals in 15 degree steps using 'drawOval3()'.
              640 x 350 pixel x 16 color mode.
```

```
*/
```

(continued)

```
LINEWIDTH = 1;
cls(1);
color = 3;
for (i=0; i<180; i+=15)
{
    drawOval3(-200,100,200,-100,i,color++);
}
getch();
```

```
/*

        Rotate smaller ovals in 15 degree steps using
                        'drawOval3()'.
            640 x 350 pixel x 16 color mode.

*/
    cls(1);
    color = 3;
    for (i=0; i<360; i+=15)
    {
        drawOval3(-120,50,120,-50,i,color++);
        if (color == 1)
            color++;
    }
    getch();
```

```
/*

        Rotate smaller ovals centered at upper right in 15
                degree steps using 'drawOval3()'.
            640 x 350 pixel x 16 color mode.

*/
    cls(1);
    color = 3;
    for (i=0; i<360; i+=15)
    {
        drawOval3(-220,150,20,50,i,color++);
```

(continued)

```
if (color == 1)
        color++;
   }
   getch();
```

/*

```
   Rotate ovals in 15 degree steps around one end using
                    'drawOval4()'.
           640 x 350 pixel x 16 color mode.
```

*/

```
   cls(1);
   color = 3;
   for (i=0; i<360; i+=15)
      drawOval4(0,0,200,100,i,color++);
   getch();
```

/*

```
   Compare rotated filled oval using 'fillOval()' with
          drawn rotated oval using 'drawOval4()'.
           640 x 350 pixel x 16 color mode.
```

*/

```
   cls(6);
   color = 13;
   fillOval(-227,-150,455,248,45,color);
   color = 15;
   drawOval4(-227,-150,455,248,45,color);
   getch();
```

(continued)

```
/*
```

```
┌─────────────────────────────────────────────────────────────┐
│ ┌─────────────────────────────────────────────────────────┐ │
│ │                                                         │ │
│ │           Make a Daisy with 'fillOval()'.               │ │
│ │           640 x 350 pixel x 16 color mode.              │ │
│ │                                                         │ │
│ └─────────────────────────────────────────────────────────┘ │
└─────────────────────────────────────────────────────────────┘
```

```
*/
```

```
    cls(1);
    setEGApalette(15,55);
    LINEWIDTH = 9;
    drawLine(0,80,-40,-239,2);
    for (angle=0; angle < 360; angle += 60)
    {
        x = 30 * cos(angle * 0.017453292);
        y = 80 + (30 * sin(angle * 0.017453292));
        fillOval(x,y,100,50,angle,14);
    }
    for (angle=30; angle < 360; angle += 60)
    {
        x = 30 * cos(angle * 0.017453292);
        y = 80 + (30 * sin(angle * 0.017453292));
        fillOval(x,y,100,50,angle,15);
    }
    fillOval(-30,80,64,64,0,6);
    getch();
```

```
/*
```

```
┌─────────────────────────────────────────────────────────────┐
│ ┌─────────────────────────────────────────────────────────┐ │
│ │                                                         │ │
│ │          Make three Daisies with 'fillOval()'.          │ │
│ │           640 x 350 pixel x 16 color mode.              │ │
│ │                                                         │ │
│ └─────────────────────────────────────────────────────────┘ │
└─────────────────────────────────────────────────────────────┘
```

```
*/
    cls(1);
    setEGApalette(15,55);
    LINEWIDTH = 9;
    drawLine(0,100,-40,-239,2);
    drawLine(-205,30,-38,-215,2);
    drawLine(195,-35,-40,-239,2);
    for (angle=0; angle < 360; angle += 60)
```

(continued)

```
    {
        x = 30 * cos(angle * 0.017453292);
        y = 100 + (30 * sin(angle * 0.017453292));
        fillOval(x,y,100,50,angle,14);
        x = 20 * cos(angle * 0.017453292);
        y = 100 + (20 * sin(angle * 0.017453292));
        fillOval(x-205,y-70,80,30,angle,14);
        fillOval(x+195,y-135,80,30,angle,14);
    }
    for (angle=30; angle < 360; angle += 60)
    {
        x = 30 * cos(angle * 0.017453292);
        y = 100 + (30 * sin(angle * 0.017453292));
        fillOval(x,y,100,50,angle,15);
        x = 20 * cos(angle * 0.017453292);
        y = 100 + (20 * sin(angle * 0.017453292));
        fillOval(x-205,y-70,80,30,angle,15);
        fillOval(x+195,y-135,80,30,angle,15);
    }
    fillOval(-30,100,64,64,0,6);
    fillOval(-235,30,55,55,0,6);
    fillOval(165,-35,55,55,0,6);
    getch();
}


/*

    drawOval1() = Draws an oval bounded by a box, with
            designated color using wide lines.

*/

void drawOval1(int xl, int yt, int xr, int yb, int color)
{
    int i, a, b, row, col, t_row, t_col, px, py, x, y;
    long int sum, asq, bsq;

    a = max((yt - yb + LINEWIDTH) >> 1,1);
    b = max((xr - xl + LINEWIDTH) >> 1,1);
    x = ((xl + xr)>>1) + 319;
```

(continued)

```
y = 175 - ((93*(yb + yt)) >> 8);
for (i=1; i<=LINEWIDTH; i++)
{
    asq = (long)a*a;
    bsq = (long)b*b;
    py = a << 1;
    px = 0;
    sum = 0;
    while (asq*px <= bsq*py)
    {
        if ((!(px & 1)) || ((i>1) && (i <
            LINEWIDTH)))
        {
            t_row = (93L*(py + 1)) >> 8;
            t_col = px >> 1;
            col = x + t_col;
            row = y + t_row;
            plot(col,row,color);
            row = y - t_row;
            plot(col,row,color);
            col = x - t_col;
            plot(col,row,color);
            row = y + t_row;
            plot(col,row,color);
        }
        sum += asq*px++;
        sum += asq*px;
        if (sum > 0)
        {
            sum -= bsq*py--;
            sum -= bsq*py;
        }
    }
    sum = 0;
    py = 0;
    px = b << 1;
    while (asq*px >= bsq*py)
    {
        if ((!(py & 1)) || ((i>1) && (i < LINEWIDTH)))
        {
            t_row = (93L*(py + 1)) >> 8;
```

(continued)

```
                    t_col = px >> 1;
                    col = x + t_col;
                    row = y + t_row;
                    plot(col,row,color);
                    row = y - t_row;
                    plot(col,row,color);
                    col = x - t_col;
                    plot(col,row,color);
                    row = y + t_row;
                    plot(col,row,color);
                }
            sum += bsq*py++;
            sum += bsq*py;
            if (sum > 0)
            {
                    sum -= asq*px--;
                    sum -= asq*px;
            }
        }
        a--;
        b--;
    }
}

/*
```

```
    drawOval2() = Draws an oval bounded by a box with
            designated color using wide lines.
```

```
*/

void drawOval2(int xl, int yt, int xr, int yb, int color)
{
    int i, a, b, row, col, t_row, t_col, px, py, x, y;
    long int sum, asq, bsq;

    a = max((yt - yb + (LINEWIDTH) >> 1),1);
    b = max((xr - xl + (LINEWIDTH) >> 1),1);
    x = (xl + xr) >> 1;
    y = (yb + yt) >> 1;
```

(continued)

```
asq = (long)a*a;
bsq = (long)b*b;
py = a << 1;
px = 0;
sum = -bsq*py;
while (asq*px <= bsq*py)
{
    if (!(px & 1))
    {
        col = x + (px>>1);
        row = y + (py>>1);
        for (i=0; i<LINEWIDTH; i++)
            plots(col,row-i,color);
        row = y - (py>>1);
        for (i=0; i<LINEWIDTH; i++)
            plots(col,row+i,color);
        col = x - (px>>1);
        for (i=0; i<LINEWIDTH; i++)
            plots(col,row+i,color);
        row = y + (py>>1);
        for (i=0; i<LINEWIDTH; i++)
            plots(col,row-i,color);
    }
    sum += asq*px++;
    sum += asq*px;
    if (sum > 0)
    {
        sum -= bsq*py--;
        sum -= bsq*py;
    }
}
py = 0;
px = b << 1;
sum = -asq*px;
while (asq*px >= bsq*py)
{
    if (!(py & 1))
    {
        col = x + (px>>1);
        row = y + (py>>1);
        for (i=0; i<LINEWIDTH; i++)
```

(continued)

```
                plots(col-i,row,color);
        row = y - (py>>1);
        for (i=0; i<LINEWIDTH; i++)
            plots(col-i,row,color);
        col = x - (px>>1);
        for (i=0; i<LINEWIDTH; i++)
            plots(col+i,row,color);
        row = y + (py>>1);
        for (i=0; i<LINEWIDTH; i++)
            plots(col+i,row,color);
    }
    sum += bsq*py++;
    sum += bsq*py;
    if (sum > 0)
    {
        sum -= asq*px--;
        sum -= asq*px;
    }
  }
}


/*
```

```
    drawOval3() = Draws an oval bounded by a box with
      designated angle and color using single pixel
                      wide lines.
```

```
*/

void drawOval3(int xl, int yt, int xr, int yb, float
    angle, int color)
{
    int i, a, b, row, col, t_row, t_col, px, py, x, y, ca,
        sa, tx, ty, tix, tiy;
    long int sum, asq, bsq;

    ca = cos(angle * 0.017453292) * 512;
    sa = sin(angle * 0.017453292) * 512;
    a = max((yt - yb) >> 1,1);
    b = max((xr - xl) >> 1,1);
```

(continued)

```
x = xl + b;
y = yb + a;
asq = (long)a*a;
bsq = (long)b*b;
py = a << 1;
px = 0;
sum = -bsq*py;
while (asq*px <= bsq*py)
{
    if (!(px & 1))
    {
        t_row = (py + 1) >> 1;
        t_col = px >> 1;
        tx =  (((long)t_col * ca) >> 9) -
            (((long)t_row * sa) >> 9);
        ty = (((long)t_col * sa) >> 9) +
            (((long)t_row * ca) >> 9);
        tix =  (((long)t_col * ca) >> 9) +
            (((long)t_row * sa) >> 9);
        tiy = (((long)t_col * sa) >> 9) -
            (((long)t_row * ca) >> 9);
        col = x + tx;
        row = y + ty;
        plots(col,row,color);
        col = x - tix;
        row = y - tiy;
        plots(col,row,color);
        col = x + tix;
        row = y + tiy;
        plots(col,row,color);
        col = x - tx;
        row = y - ty;
        plots(col,row,color);
    }
    sum += asq*px++;
    sum += asq*px;
    if (sum > 0)
    {
        sum -= bsq*py--;
        sum -= bsq*py;
    }
```

(continued)

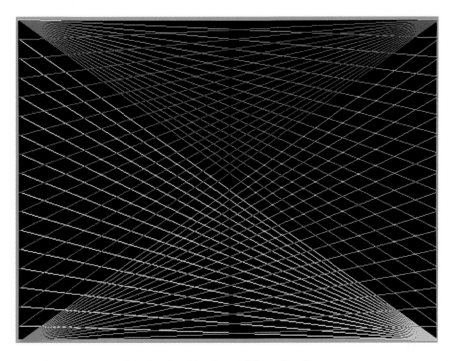

Plate 1. Straight Line Pattern

Plate 2. Random Starbursts of Straight Lines

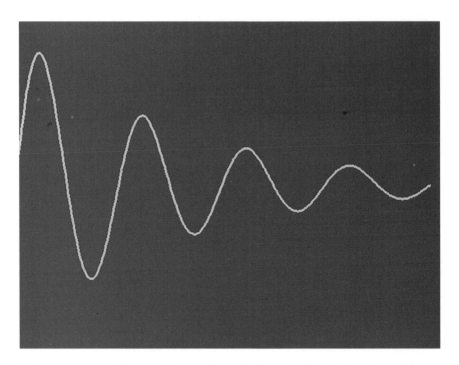

Plate 3. Damped Sine Wave Consisting of Straight Line Segments

Plate 4. Random Spirals Consisting of Straight Line Segments

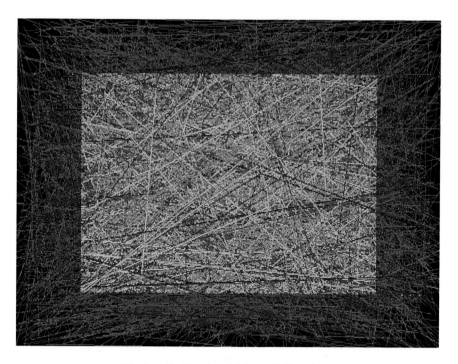

Plate 5. Test of Line Clipping

Plate 6. Random Circles

Plate 7. Random Sets of Concentric Circles

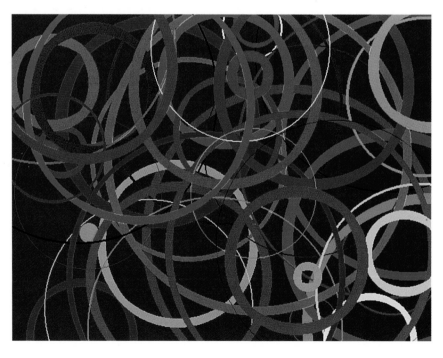

Plate 8. Randomly Located Circles of Random Width and Diameter

Plate 9. Random Filled Circles

Plate 10. Apollonian Packing of Circles

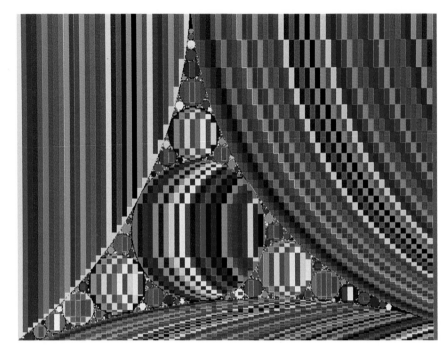

Plate 11. Apollonian Packing of Circles with Improper Color Selection

Plate 12. Daisies Made with Tilted Ellipses

Plate 13. Arcs of Random Diameter, Width, and Extent

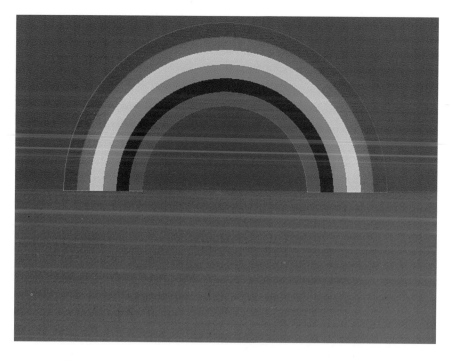

Plate 14. Rainbow Made with Arc Function

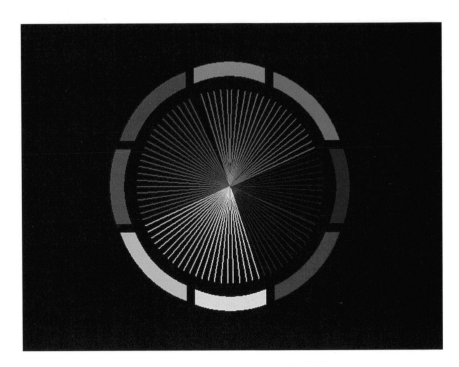

Plate 15. Arcs and Angled Lines

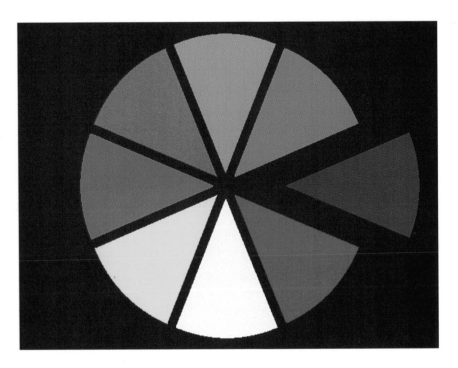

Plate 16. Pie Chart Made with Filled Arc Function

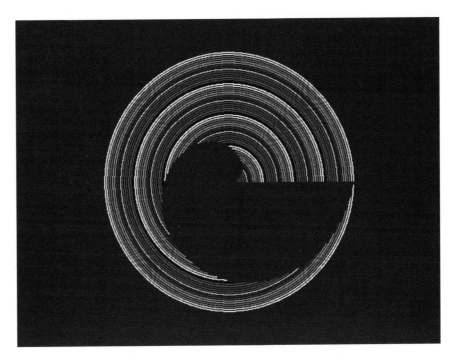

Plate 17. Testing of Arc Function

Plate 18. Filling Irregular Polygons

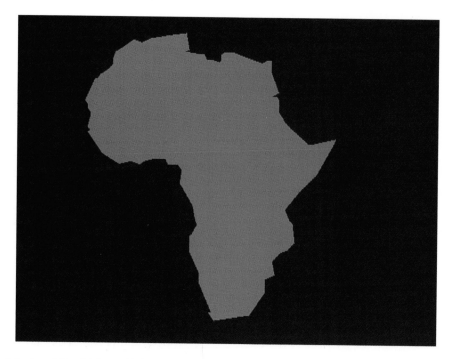

Plate 19. Africa Using Function for Filling Irregular Polygons

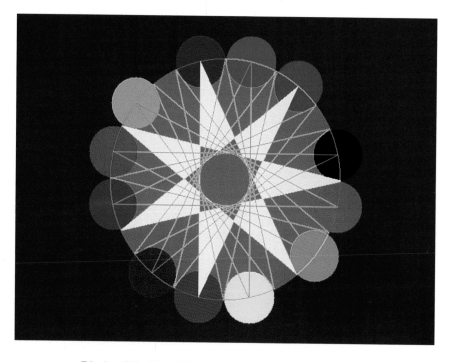

Plate 20. The New Jerusalem Diagram

Plate 21. Rounded Rectangles

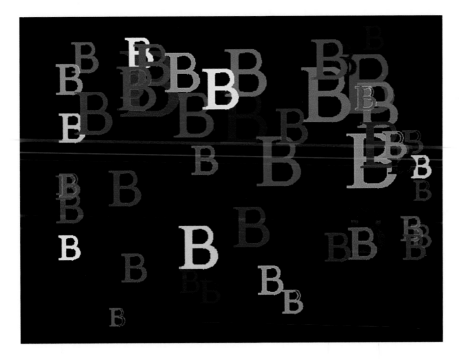

Plate 22. B's Generated by Filled Bezier Curves

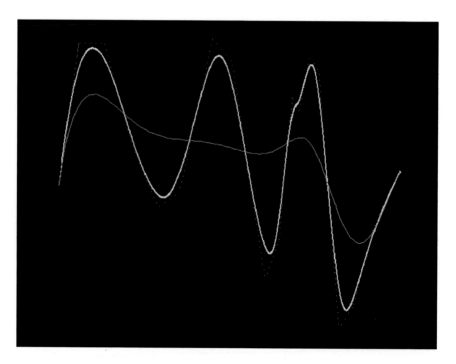

Plate 23. Bezier Curve and B-Spline Curve Approximations to Control Points

Plate 24. Functions for Generating Alphanumerics on a Graphic Display

Plate 25. Rotated Triangles

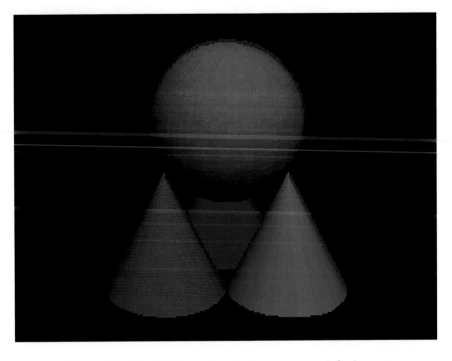

Plate 26. Solid Modeled Cones and Spheres

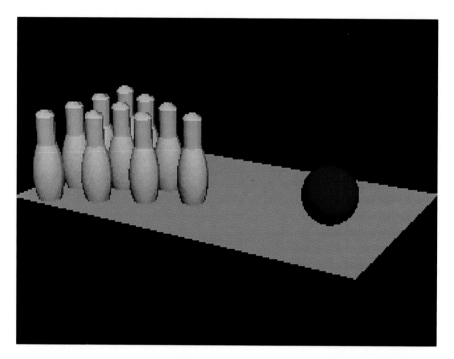

Plate 27. Bowling Using Solid Modeled Solids of Revolution and Sphere

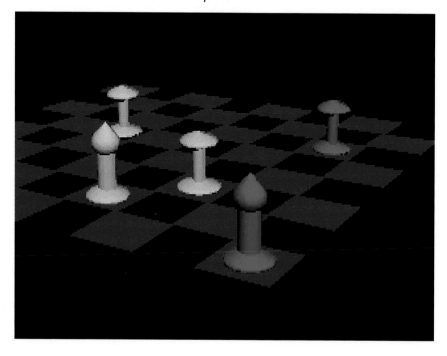

Plate 28. Chessboard Using Solid Modeled Solids of Revolution

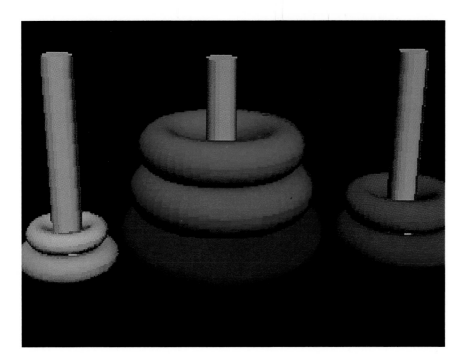

Plate 29. Towers of Hanoi Puzzle Using Solid Modeled Toroids

Plate 30. Teddy Bear Captured from Camcorder Image and
Saved to .PCX File

Plate 31. Peace Rose Captured from Camcorder Image and Saved to .PCX File

Plate 32. Chrysasnthemums Captured from Camcorder Image and Saved to .PCX File

```
    }
    py = 0;
    px = b << 1;
    sum = -asq*px;
    while (asq*px >= bsq*py)
    {
        if (!(py & 1))
        {
            t_row = (py + 1) >> 1;
            t_col = px >> 1;
            tx =  (((long)t_col * ca) >> 9) -
                (((long)t_row * sa) >> 9);
            ty = (((long)t_col * sa) >> 9) +
                (((long)t_row * ca) >> 9);
            tix =  (((long)t_col * ca) >> 9) +
                (((long)t_row * sa) >> 9);
            tiy = (((long)t_col * sa) >> 9) -
                (((long)t_row * ca) >> 9);
            col = x + tx;
            row = y + ty;
            plots(col,row,color);
            col = x - tix;
            row = y - tiy;
            plots(col,row,color);
            col = x + tix;
            row = y + tiy;
            plots(col,row,color);
            col = x - tx;
            row = y - ty;
            plots(col,row,color);
        }
        sum += bsq*py++;
        sum += bsq*py;
        if (sum > 0)
        {
            sum -= asq*px--;
            sum -= asq*px;
        }
    }
}
```

(continued)

```
/*

    drawOval4() = Draws an oval which has the following
            characteristics:
                (x,y)   = point on y axis at left end of x
                axis
                x_axis = length of x axis
                y_axis = length of y axis
                angle  = tilt angle of oval
                color  = color of oval

*/

void drawOval4(int x, int y, int x_axis, int y_axis, float
    angle, int color)
{
    int i, a, b, row, col, t_row, t_col, px, py, ca, sa;
    long int sum, asq, bsq;

    ca = cos(angle * 0.017453292) * 512;
    sa = sin(angle * 0.017453292) * 512;
    a = max((y_axis) >> 1,1);
    b = max((x_axis) >> 1,1);
    asq = 4L*a*a;
    bsq = 4L*b*b;
    py = a << 1;
    px = 0;
    sum = -bsq*py;
    while (asq*px <= bsq*py)
    {
        if (!(px & 1))
        {
            t_row = (py + 1) >> 1;
            t_col = px >> 1;
            col = x + (((long)(t_col + b)* ca) >> 9) -
                (((long)t_row * sa) >> 9);
            row = y + (((long)(t_col + b)* sa) >> 9) +
                (((long)t_row * ca) >> 9);
            plots(col,row,color);
            col = x - (((long)(t_col - b) * ca) >> 9) -
```

(continued)

```
                ((((long)t_row * sa) >> 9);
        row = y - (((long)(t_col - b)* sa) >> 9) +
            (((long)t_row * ca) >> 9);
        plots(col,row,color);
        col = x + (((long)(t_col + b) * ca) >> 9) +
            (((long)t_row * sa) >> 9);
        row = y + (((long)(t_col + b)* sa) >> 9) -
            (((long)t_row * ca) >> 9);
        plots(col,row,color);
        col = x - (((long)(t_col - b) * ca) >> 9) +
            (((long)t_row * sa) >> 9);
        row = y - (((long)(t_col - b) * sa) >> 9) -
            (((long)t_row * ca) >> 9);
        plots(col,row,color);
    }
    sum += asq*px++;
    sum += asq*px;
    if (sum > 0)
    {
        sum -= bsq*py--;
        sum -= bsq*py;
    }
}
py = 0;
px = b << 1;
sum = -asq*px;
while (asq*px >= bsq*py)
{
    if (!(py & 1))
    {
        t_row = (py + 1) >> 1;
        t_col = px >> 1;
        col = x + (((long)(t_col + b) * ca) >> 9) -
            (((long)t_row * sa) >> 9);
        row = y + (((long)(t_col + b) * sa) >> 9) +
            (((long)t_row * ca) >> 9);
        plots(col,row,color);
        col = x - (((long)(t_col - b) * ca) >> 9) -
            (((long)t_row * sa) >> 9);
        row = y - (((long)(t_col - b) * sa) >> 9) +
            (((long)t_row * ca) >> 9);
```

(continued)

```
                    plots(col,row,color);
                    col = x + (((long)(t_col + b) * ca) >> 9) +
                        (((long)t_row * sa) >> 9);
                    row = y + (((long)(t_col + b) * sa) >> 9) -
                        (((long)t_row * ca) >> 9);
                    plots(col,row,color);
                    col = x - (((long)(t_col - b) * ca) >> 9) +
                        (((long)t_row * sa) >> 9);
                    row = y - (((long)(t_col - b) * sa) >> 9) -
                        (((long)t_row * ca) >> 9);
                    plots(col,row,color);
                }
            sum += bsq*py++;
            sum += bsq*py;
            if (sum > 0)
            {
                sum -= asq*px--;
                sum -= asq*px;
            }
        }
    }

/*
```

```
    fillOval() = Fills an ellipse. The ellipse has the
            following characteristics:
                (x,y)  = point on y axis at left end of x
                axis
                x_axis = length of x axis
                angle  = tilt angle of ellipse
                color  = color of ellipse
```

```
*/

void fillOval(int x, int y, int x_axis, int y_axis,
    float angle, int color)
{
    int i, a, b, row, col, tx, ty, px, py, ca, sa,
        minrow=480, maxrow=0, coord[2][480];
    long int sum, asq, bsq;
```

(continued)

```
for (i=0; i<480; i++)
{
    coord[0][i] = 800;
    coord[1][i] = 0;
}
ca = cos(angle * 0.017453292) * 2048;
sa = sin(angle * 0.017453292) * 2048;
a = max (y_axis >> 1,1);
b = max (x_axis >> 1,1);
asq = (long)a*a;
bsq = (long)b*b;
py = a << 1;
px = 0;
sum = -bsq*py;
while (asq*px <= bsq*py)
{
    col = x + ((((long)(px + (b<<1)) * ca) -
        ((long)(py + 1) * sa)) >> 12);
    row = y + ((((long)(px + (b<<1)) * sa) +
        ((long)(py + 1) * ca)) >> 12);
    convert(col,row);
    compare(col,coord[0][row],coord[1][row]);
    compare(row,minrow,maxrow);
    col = x - ((((long)(px - (b<<1)) * ca) -
        ((long)(py + 1) * sa)) >> 12);
    row = y - ((((long)(px - (b<<1)) * sa) +
        ((long)(py + 1) * ca)) >> 12);
    convert(col,row);
    compare(col,coord[0][row],coord[1][row]);
    compare(row,minrow,maxrow);
    col = x + ((((long)(px + (b<<1)) * ca) +
        ((long)(py + 1) * sa)) >> 12);
    row = y + ((((long)(px + (b<<1)) * sa) -
        ((long)(py + 1) * ca)) >> 12);
    convert(col,row);
    compare(col,coord[0][row],coord[1][row]);
    compare(row,minrow,maxrow);
    col = x - ((((long)(px - (b<<1)) * ca) +
        ((long)(py + 1) * sa)) >> 12);
    row = y - ((((long)(px - (b<<1)) * sa) -
        ((long)(py + 1) * ca)) >> 12);
```

(continued)

```
        convert(col,row);
        compare(col,coord[0][row],coord[1][row]);
        compare(row,minrow,maxrow);
        sum += asq*px++;
        sum += asq*px;
        if (sum > 0)
        {
            sum -= bsq*py--;
            sum -= bsq*py;
        }
    }
    py = 0;
    px = b << 1;
    sum = -asq*px;
    while (asq*px >= bsq*py)
    {
        col = x + ((((long)(px + (b<<1)) * ca) -
            ((long)(py + 1) * sa)) >> 12);
        row = y + ((((long)(px + (b<<1)) * sa) +
            ((long)(py + 1) * ca)) >> 12);
        convert(col,row);
        compare(col,coord[0][row],coord[1][row]);
        compare(row,minrow,maxrow);
        col = x - ((((long)(px - (b<<1)) * ca) -
            ((long)(py + 1) * sa)) >> 12);
        row = y - ((((long)(px - (b<<1)) * sa) +
            ((long)(py + 1) * ca)) >> 12);
        convert(col,row);
        compare(col,coord[0][row],coord[1][row]);
        compare(row,minrow,maxrow);
        col = x + ((((long)(px + (b<<1)) * ca) +
            ((long)(py + 1) * sa)) >> 12);
        row = y + ((((long)(px + (b<<1)) * sa) -
            ((long)(py + 1) * ca)) >> 12);
        convert(col,row);
        compare(col,coord[0][row],coord[1][row]);
        compare(row,minrow,maxrow);
        col = x - ((((long)(px - (b<<1)) * ca) +
            ((long)(py + 1) * sa)) >> 12);
        row = y - ((((long)(px - (b<<1)) * sa) -
            ((long)(py + 1) * ca)) >> 12);
```

(continued)

```
            convert(col,row);
            compare(col,coord[0][row],coord[1][row]);
            compare(row,minrow,maxrow);
            sum += bsq*py++;
            sum += bsq*py;
            if (sum > 0)
            {
                sum -= asq*px--;
                sum -= asq*px;
            }
        }
        for (i=minrow; i<=maxrow; i++)
            fillLine(coord[0][i],coord[1][i], i, color);
    }


/*
+--------------------------------------------------------------+
|                                                              |
|    fillLine() = Draws a horizontal line in a selected        |
|                            color                             |
|                                                              |
+--------------------------------------------------------------+
*/

fillLine(int x_one, int x_two, int y, int color)
{
    char color_buffer[100];
    int dummy, loop, i, x1, x2;
    int length, offset1, offset2;
    int srcseg, srcoff, destseg, destoff;
    long int no_of_bytes;
    unsigned int mask;
    char far *base1;
    char far *base2;

    struct SREGS segregs;

    segread(&segregs);
    srcseg = segregs.ds;
    srcoff = (int) color_buffer;
    x1 = min(x_one, x_two);
    x2 = max(x_one, x_two);
```

(continued)

413

```
    offset1 = x1 % 8;
    offset2 = x2 % 8;
    base1 = (char far *)(0xA0000000L + ((long)y * 80L +
        ((long)x1 / 8L)));
    base2 = (char far *)(0xA0000000L + ((long)y * 80L +
        ((long)x2 / 8L)));
    no_of_bytes = abs(base2 - base1);
    length = ((x2 - x1) - ((8-offset1) + (offset2))) / 8L;
    mask = 0xFF00 << (7 - offset2);
    if (!no_of_bytes)
        mask &= (0xFF00 >> offset1) & 0xFF00;
    dummy = *base2;
    outport(0x3CE, mask | 0x08);
    outport(0x3CE, 0x0205);
    *base2 = color;
    if (no_of_bytes)
    {
        mask = (0xFF00 >> offset1) & 0xFF00;
        outport(0x3CE, mask | 0x08);
        dummy = *base1;
        *base1 = color;
        mask = 0xFF00;
        outport(0x3CE, mask | 0x08);
        memset(color_buffer,color,length);
        destseg = 0xA000;
        destoff = ((long) y * 80L + ((long)x1 /8L)) + 1;
        movedata(srcseg, srcoff, destseg, destoff, length);
    }
    outport(0x3CE, 0xFF08);
    outport(0x3CE, 0x0005);
}

/*

    setEGApalette() = sets the color for an EGA palette

*/

void setEGApalette(int palette, int color)
{
```

(continued)

```
    union REGS reg;

    reg.h.ah = 0x10;
    reg.h.al = 0;
    reg.h.bh = color;
    reg.h.bl = palette;
    int86(0x10,&reg,&reg);
}

/*
```

```
        cls() Clears the screen to a designated color
```

```
*/


void cls(char colors)
{
    union REGS reg;

    reg.x.dx = 0x184F;
    reg.h.bh = colors;
    reg.x.ax = 0x0600;
    reg.x.cx = 0;
    int86(0x10,&reg,&reg);
    gotoxy(0,0);
}

/*
```

```
                setMode() = Sets the video mode
```

```
*/

void setMode(int mode)
{
    union REGS reg;

    reg.h.ah = 0;
```

(continued)

```
      reg.h.al = mode;
      int86 (0x10,&reg,&reg);
}
```

```
/*
```

```
    plot() = Plots a point on the screen at designated
         screen coordinates using selected color.
```

```
*/
```

```
void plot(int x, int y, int color)
{
    unsigned int offset;
    int dummy,mask,page;
    char far * mem_address;
    offset = (long)y * 80L + ((long)x / 8L);
    mem_address = (char far *) 0xA0000000L + offset;
    mask = 0x8000 >> (x % 8);
    outport(0x3CE,mask | 0x08);
    outport(0x3CE,0x0205);
    dummy = *mem_address;
    *mem_address = color;
    outport(0x3CE,0xFF08);
    outport(0x3CE,0x0005);
}
```

```
/*
```

```
    plots() = Plots a point on the screen at designated
         system coordinates using selected color.
```

```
*/
```

```
void plots(int x, int y, int color)
{
    unsigned int offset;
    int dummy,mask,page;
    char far * mem_address;
```

(continued)

```
    convert(x,y);
    offset = (long)y * 80L + ((long)x / 8L);
    mem_address = (char far *) 0xA0000000L + offset;
    mask = 0x8000 >> (x % 8);
    outport(0x3CE,mask | 0x08);
    outport(0x3CE,0x0205);
    dummy = *mem_address;
    *mem_address = color;
    outport(0x3CE,0xFF08);
    outport(0x3CE,0x0005);
}


/*
    ┌─────────────────────────────────────────────────────┐
    │                                                     │
    │  drawLine() = Draws a line from one set of coordinates │
    │      to another in designated color choosing proper  │
    │                  direction for width.                │
    │                                                     │
    └─────────────────────────────────────────────────────┘
*/

void drawLine(int x1, int y1, int x2, int y2, int color)
{
    union REGS reg;
    extern int LINEWIDTH;
    extern unsigned long int PATTERN;
    #define sign(x) ((x) > 0 ? 1:  ((x) == 0 ? 0:  (-1)))
    int dx, dy,min, i, j, dmax, dmin, sdmax, sdmin, pl, ps,
        d;
    unsigned long int mask;

    convert(x1,y1);
    convert(x2,y2);
    dx = abs(x2-x1);
    dy = abs(y2-y1);
    if (dx >= dy)
    {
        sdmax = sign (x2 - x1);
        sdmin = sign(y2 - y1);
        pl = x1;
        ps = y1;
```

(continued)

```
    }
    else
    {
        sdmax = sign(y2 - y1);
        sdmin = sign(x2 - x1);
        pl = y1;
        ps = x1;
    }
    dmax = max(dx,dy);
    dmin = min(dx,dy);
    for (i=0,d=0; i<dmax; i++,d+=dmin)
    {
        mask = mask !=1 ? mask >> 1 : 0x80000000;
        if (d>=dmax)
        {
            d -= dmax;
            ps += sdmin;
        }
        pl += sdmax;
        if (PATTERN & mask)
        {
            for (j=-LINEWIDTH/2; j<=LINEWIDTH/2; j++)
            {
                if (dx >= dy)
                    plot(pl,ps+j,color);
                else
                    plot(ps+j,pl,color);
            }
        }
    }
}
```

Drawing a Wide Line Ellipse in a Box

First, we are going to look at *drawOval1*, which draws a wide line oval when the bounding rectangle is specified. The parameters that are sent to this function are the coordinates of the top left and bottom right corners of the bounding rectangle and the color. We first compute the semi-major and semi-minor axes of the ellipse, compensating for line width, so that the ellipse that will first be drawn is that of the inside of the line width. Then the coordinates of the center of the ellipse (x,y) are computed from the rectangle definition coordinates. We then find the squares of the semi-major and semi-minor axes, as these will be needed repeatedly in computing the decision function. Except for the use of these as multipliers, the rest of the function proceeds exactly like the function for drawing a wide line circle. This function, like the corresponding one for the circle, determines from the slope of the figure at any given point whether the wide line should be created by drawing additional pixels at either side of the current pixel on the screen or drawing additional pixels above and below the current pixel on the screen. You'll remember that in Chapter 7, when we discussed making wide straight lines, we commented on the difficulties of having wide line ends terminate properly. This didn't give us any problems in drawing circles, since the overlap between the line segments that are drawn to make up the circle does not usually extend beyond the boundaries of the next line segment. (You may note, however, that if we draw a very small circle with a very wide line width, the inside of the circle appears a little more squarish than it should be.) The problem gets much worse when we are drawing ellipses. When using a wide line to draw an ellipse that is long in one direction and very narrow at the other, the line ends of the wide line extend beyond where they should be, resulting in some funny tails on the ellipse. If you want to use this function, you'll need to experiment with the types of ellipses that you want to draw and the desired line widths to determine if the results are acceptable. Most normal ellipses will be all right, so you may well decide that this is the function for you. If this function will not do, you can use instead the function *drawOval2*. This function is a lot slower than the one just described, but it draws a more accurate ellipse. It begins by drawing the inner ellipse of a wide line ellipse and then increases the semi-minor and semi-major axes by one pixel and draws another ellipse and so forth until the dimensions of the outer ellipse are reached. One problem with this is that drawing this series of ellipses does not guarantee that all of the pixels inside the wide line boundaries will be selected, so that without further adjustment, there will be an objectionable pattern of holes within your wide line. Fortunately, the algorithm that we're using was originally designed to get the best approximation to the curve by calculating twice as many points as were necessary and then plotting only half of them to the screen. To get rid of the objectionable holes, we change this so that all of the points are plotted to the screen. This takes twice as long, and results in many points being plotted twice, but it does get rid of most of the objectionable holes.

Drawing an Ellipse at an Angle

The function *drawOval3* draws an ellipse at an desired angle orientation. This is very useful, but unfortunately it can be done only with single pixel wide ellipses, because for wide lines, the transformations used to perform the rotation produce many unfilled holes within the line width that there is no easy way of eliminating. The parameters passed to the function are the bounding rectangle coordinates, the rotation angle and the color. We are going to consider zero degrees of rotation as the position of the ellipse that occurs in the function just described and then rotate around the center of the ellipse in a counterclockwise direction. To do this, we have to transform every point that we plot using a standard coordinate rotation transformation that requires a sine and cosine. We need to do this in the most efficient manner possible to minimize the amount of time required to draw the ellipse. Essentially, this means that we need to use integer arithmetic and to avoid any divisions, since division is a lengthy process, even with integers. We also need to observe that we require only enough accuracy in the sine and cosine functions to obtain the right coordinate value to the nearest pixel. All of this is accomplished by first obtaining the sine and cosine of the angle and creating from each an integer that is 512 times the actual value. After we compute each point on the standard ellipse, we use the sine and cosine of the rotation angle to perform the proper transformation to obtain the new set of coordinates after the ellipse is rotated. We do this by multiplying by the integer functions that we computed earlier and then shifting the result to the right by nine bit positions, which is effectively a division by 512. This gives us the same result as if we had done a floating point operation using the sine or cosine. However, this technique is much faster and produces a complete tilted ellipse in a reasonable amount of time.

Ellipse Tilted from the End

The ellipse function just described rotates an ellipse around the center. Often, however, it is more convenient to specifiy an ellipse that is rotated around one end of the ellipse. The function *drawOval4* does this. If you will compare the listing of this function with that of *drawOval3*, you'll see that they are very similar in many ways. The main differences are that we pass to the new function the coordinates of a point at the left end of the x axis of the ellipse, instead of the center, and that we perform the rotation in such a way that the new coordinates for each point on the ellipse are computed in a coordinate system that has its origin at the position defined by this set of coordinates rather than having it at the center of the ellipse.

Filling a Tilted Ellipse

This function is very useful for creating such things as the petals of flowers. The function, like that just described, is passed the coordinates of a point at the left end of the x axis of the ellipse, the values of the x and y axes, a tilt angle and the desired color. At the very beginning of the function, we have a new array that consists of 2 by 480 elements. This is adequate for the highest resolution VGA display, which has a maximum of 480 lines; if you want to adapt this function for higher resolution Super VGAs, you'll need to increase the size of this array. The $(0,n)$ element of the array represents the value of x for the left-hand boundary of the ellipse at the y value of n. The $(1,n)$ element of the array represents the value of x for the right-hand boundary of the ellipse at the y value of n. The array is initialized with the left-hand boundaries all set to 800 and the right-hand boundaries all set to 0. The function then proceeds to compute the points on the circle boundary in the same way as the previous program, except that instead of plotting them to the screen, it performs a *compare* operation on each point. This operation, which is defined at the beginning of the program, compares the current point with *coord[0][y]* and *coord[1][y]*, where y indicates the vertical coordinate of the current point. If the x coordinate is smaller than the value for the left-hand boundary, it replaces that value; if it is larger than the value for the right- hand boundary, it replaces that value. Another *compare* is then performed, which replaces *minrow* or *maxrow* with the y coordinate of the current point if it is smaller than the first or larger than the second. At the end of this process, we have in *minrow* the smallest value of y for the ellipse and in *maxrow* the largest value of y. In all of the members of the *coord* array that are between these y values, we have the minimum value of x for the ellipse in *coord[0][y]* and the maximum value of x for the ellipse in *coord[1][y]*. We next enter a *for* loop that, for each row between *minrow* and *maxrow* draws a horizontal line between the minimum and maximum values of x as specified by the appropriate members of the *coord* array in the designated color. The result is a filled oval.

The *ovalchk.c* Test Program

The *ovalchk.c* test program displays a number of screens that demonstrate the proper operation of the ellipse drawing and filling functions. The first screen shows three interlocking circles drawn with *drawOval2*. The next screen shows three pairs of ellipses. One ellipse in each pair has the *x* axis the long axis and the *y* axis the short axis, while the other has the *x* axis the short axis and the *y* axis the long axis. These are all drawn with *drawOval2*. The next screen draws 80 single pixel line width ellipses with *drawOval2*, with the center coordinates and the two axes for each ellipse set randomly. The next screen draws 80 ellipses with *drawOval2*, with the center coordinates, the two axes for each ellipse, and the line width set randomly. The next screen draws two long narrow ellipses with wide lines, one with *drawOval1* and the other with *drawOval2* so that the two methods of obtaining wide lines can be compared for this extreme case. The next screen shows a large ellipse drawn with *drawOval3*. When any key is struck, the ellipse is drawn again in a different color with the axis values reversed. The next screen uses *drawOval2* to draw the largest and smallest ellipses that can appear fully on the screen. The next screen draws two wide line ellipses using *drawOval2*. The next screen uses *drawOval3* to draw a set of rotated ellipses at 15 degree intervals from 0 to 165 degrees, centered at the middle of the screen. The next screen uses *drawOval3* to draw a set of smaller rotated ellipses at 15 degree intervals from 0 to 345 degrees, centered at the middle of the screen. The next screen uses *drawOval3* to draw the same set of smaller rotated ellipses at 15 degree intervals from 0 to 345 degrees, centered at the upper left of the screen. The next screen uses *drawOval4* to draw a set of rotated ellipses at 15 degree intervals from 0 to 345 degrees. The left-hand end of the *x* axis is at the middle of the screen and the ellipses are rotated around this point. The next screen uses *fillOval* to fill a large tilted ellipse and then draws the boundary of the same ellipse with *drawOval4*. The program then changes a palette color so that two shades of yellow are available. The program then creates a daisy using *fillOval* and then makes its stem with *drawLine*. The last screen shows three daisies, created in the same way as the previous screen. These daisies are shown in Plate 12.

Chapter 15

Drawing and Filling Circular Arcs

Many functions for drawing and filling arcs make use of floating point operations using the sine and cosine to determine points on the arc as the angle moves in increments from the specified starting angle to the specified ending angle. This results in a function that is sluggish, to say the least. Furthermore, the angle increment needed to assure that every pixel on the arc is obtained varies with the radius of the circle, which introduces an additional complication. The technique that we shall use here uses exactly the same algorithm that we used to generate a circle in Chapter 13 to actually compute the points on an octant of the arc and extend this to obtain points for all eight octants. However, instead of actually plotting all of these points, we test each one to determine whether it is in the specified arc or not and plot only those points that are within the proper range. It is a bit complicated to sort out all of the tests that are needed, but once this is done, the function produces fast arcs. Even in the case of a very small arc (one or two degrees), where the function is at a disadvantage because it still has to compute all of the points in an octant, it is still much faster than functions that use floating point operations. Figure 15-1 lists a program called *arctest.c* which includes the arc drawing and filling functions and produces a number of screens which test these functions.

Figure 15-1. Listing of arctest.c Program to Test Drawing and Filling of Arcs

```
/*

    arctest.c = Program to test arc drawing and filling
                            functions

                 By Roger T. Stevens   9-19-91

*/

#include <conio.h>
#include <stdio.h>
#include <math.h>
#include <dos.h>
#include <stdlib.h>

void arc_data (int x, int y, int test_var, int type, int
    color, int start_test, int end_test);
void arc_plot (int x, int y, int test_var, int type, int
    color, int x_start_test, int x_end_test);
void cls(char colors);
void drawArc (int xc, int yc, int radius, float
    start_angle, float end_angle, int color);
void drawLine(int xs, int ys, int length, float angle, int
    color);
void fillArc(int xc, int yc, int radius, float
    start_angle, float end_angle, int color);
void fillLine(int x_one, int x_two, int y, int color);
void Line(int xs, int ys, int xe, int ye, int color);
void plots(int x, int y, int color);
void setEGApalette(int palette, int color);
void setMode(int mode);
void set_screen(int top_color, int bottom_color, int
    boundary);

#define convert(x,y)    {x += 319;    y = 240 - y;}
#define compare(a,b,c)  {if (a<b) b = a; if (a>c) c = a;}
```

(continued)

```
int LINEWIDTH = 1, color, coord[2][800], minrow, maxrow;
int xres=640, yres=480;

void main(void)
{
    int i, start, end, xc, yc, radius;
```

```
/*
```

```
    Draw very small and very large 350 degree arcs with
         'drawArc() and single pixel width lines.
             640 x 350 pixel x 16 color mode
```

```
*/
```

```
    setMode(0x12);
    cls(1);
    randomize();
    drawArc(0,0,2,1,359,10);
    drawArc(0,0,238,1,359,14);
    getch();
```

```
/*
```

```
    Draw 100 arcs with random angles and centers and single
            pixel wide lines using 'drawArc()'.
             640 x 350 pixel x 16 color mode
```

```
*/
```

```
    cls(1);
    color = random(16);
    for (i=0; i<100; i++)
    {
        color = color%16;
        if (color == 1)
            color++;
        start = random(360);
        end = random(360) + start;
```

(continued)

425

```
        xc = random(640) - 320;
        yc = random(480) - 240;
        radius = 10 + random(225);
        drawArc(xc, yc, radius, start, end,color++);
    }
    getch();
```

```
/*
```

```
    Draw 80 arcs with random angles, centers, and line
                widths using 'drawArc()'.
             640 x 350 pixel x 16 color mode
```

```
*/
```

```
    cls(1);
    color = random(16);
    for (i=0; i<80; i++)
    {
        LINEWIDTH = random(20);
        color = color%16;
        if (color == 1)
            color++;
        start = random(360);
        end = random(360) + start;
        end = (start + end) % 360;
        xc = random(640) - 320;
        yc = random(480) - 240;
        radius = random(235);
        drawArc(xc, yc, radius, start, end,color++);
    }
    getch();
```

(continued)

```
/*
```

```
Draw single pixel wide arcs from 0 to 179 degrees, from 91
       to 270 degrees, and from 1 to 359 degrees, using
                         'drawArc()'.
                640 x 350 pixel x 16 color mode
```

```
*/
```

```
        LINEWIDTH = 1;
        cls(1);
        drawArc(0,0,238,0,179,11);
        getch();
        drawArc(0,0,75,91,270,10);
        getch();
        drawArc(0,0,150,1,359,10);
        getch();
```

```
/*
```

```
                    Draw rainbow using 'drawArc()'.

                640 x 350 pixel x 16 color mode
```

```
*/
```

```
        set_screen(13,2,16);
        LINEWIDTH=20;
        setEGApalette(9,44);
        setEGApalette(10,52);
        setEGApalette(11,62);
        setEGApalette(12,58);
        setEGApalette(13,57);
        setEGApalette(14,45);
        drawArc(0,-16,235,0,180,9);
        drawArc(0,-16,215,0,180,10);
        drawArc(0,-16,195,0,180,11);
        drawArc(0,-16,175,0,180,12);
        drawArc(0,-16,155,0,180,1);
```

(continued)

```
drawArc(0,-16,135,0,180,14);
getch();
```

```
/*
```

```
        Draw spaced octant arcs using 'drawArc()'.
              640 x 350 pixel x 16 color mode
```

```
*/
```

```
setMode(0x12);
cls(1);
LINEWIDTH = 20;
drawArc(20,0,150,337.5,22.5,9);
for (i=337; i<382; i+=4)
    drawLine (0,0,140,i,9);
drawArc(14,14,150,22.5,67.5,10);
for (i=24; i<67; i+=4)
    drawLine (0,0,140,i,10);
drawArc(0,20,150,67.5,112.5,11);
for (i=68; i<112; i+=4)
    drawLine (0,0,140,i,11);
drawArc(-14,14,150,112.5,157.5,12);
for (i=116; i<157; i+=4)
    drawLine (0,0,140,i,12);
drawArc(-20,0,150,157.5,202.5,13);
for (i=160; i<202; i+=4)
    drawLine (0,0,140,i,13);
drawArc(-14,-14,150,202.5,247.5,14);
for (i=204; i<247; i+=4)
    drawLine (0,0,140,i,14);
drawArc(0,-20,150,247.5,292.5,15);
for (i=248; i<292; i+=4)
    drawLine (0,0,140,i,15);
drawArc(14,-14,150,292.5,337.5,2);
for (i=292; i<337; i+=4)
    drawLine (0,0,140,i,2);
getch();
```

(continued)

```
/*
```

```
                    Pie chart using 'fillArc()'.
                 640 x 350 pixel x 16 color mode
```

```
*/
```

```
    cls(1);
    fillArc(90,0,200,337.5,22.5,9);
    fillArc(14,14,200,22.5,67.5,10);
    fillArc(0,20,200,67.5,112.5,11);
    fillArc(-14,14,200,112.5,157.5,12);
    fillArc(-20,0,200,157.5,202.5,13);
    fillArc(-14,-14,200,202.5,247.5,14);
    fillArc(0,-20,200,247.5,292.5,15);
    fillArc(14,-14,200,292.5,337.5,2);
    getch();
```

```
/*
```

```
Filled arc from 45 degrees around to 22.5 degrees using
                        'fillArc()'.

              640 x 350 pixel x 16 color mode
```

```
*/
```

```
    cls(1);
    fillArc(0,0,150,45.0,22.5,10);
    getch();
```

```
/*
```

```
    Test of arcs with 6 degree starting increments and 4
          degree lengths. Hit any key to terminate.
                640 x 350 pixle x 16 color mode
```

```
*/
```

(continued)

```
        setMode(0x12);
        cls(1);
        LINEWIDTH = 1;
        for (start=0; start<360; start+=4)
        {
            color = 0;
            for (end=0; end<360; end+=6)
            {
                drawArc(0,0,10+end/2,start,end+start+4,
                    color);
                if ((color = (color + 1) % 16) == 1)
                    color = 2;
            }
            delay(2500);
            if (bioskey(1) != 0)
                break;
            cls(1);
        }
    }

/*
```

```
    drawArc() = Draws an arc centered at (xc, yc), with x
        axis 'b' and y axis 'a' from starting angle
        'start_angle'to ending angle 'end_angle' in
                degrees in color 'color'.
            640 x 350 pixel x 16 color mode
```

```
*/

void drawArc (int xc, int yc, int radius, float
    start_angle, float end_angle, int color)
{
    int arc[8], i, j, n, row, col, px, py, x, y
        ,start_sector, end_sector, temp, x_start_test,
        x_end_test, y_start_test, y_end_test;
    long int sum, asq, bsq;

    void arc_plot (int x, int y, int test_var, int type,
        int color, int x_start_test, int x_end_test);
```

(continued)

```
while (start_angle >= 360)
    start_angle -= 360;
while (end_angle >= 360)
    end_angle -= 360;
radius = max(radius - (LINEWIDTH>>1),1);
for (j=0; j<8; j++)
    arc[j] = 0;
start_sector = (int)(start_angle/45) % 8;
end_sector = (int)(end_angle/45) % 8;
x_start_test = xc+radius*cos(start_angle*.017453);
x_end_test = xc+radius*cos(end_angle*.017453);
y_start_test = yc+radius*sin(start_angle*.017453);
y_end_test = yc+radius*sin(end_angle*.017453);
if (start_sector == end_sector)
{
    if (end_angle < start_angle)
    {
        arc[start_sector] = 5;
        for (i=0; i<8; i++)
        {
            if (i != start_sector)
                arc[i] = 2;
        }
    }
    else
        arc[start_sector] = 4;
}
else
{
    arc[start_sector] = 1;
    arc[end_sector] = 3;
    for (i=(start_sector+1)%8; i!=end_sector; i=
        (i+1)%8)
        arc[i] = 2;
}
for (j=0; j<LINEWIDTH; j++)
{
    py = radius << 1;
    px = 0;
    sum = -py;
    while (px <= py)
```

(continued)

```
                {
                    arc_plot (xc+(px>>1), yc+(py>>1),
                        -xc-(px>>1), arc[1], color,
                        -x_start_test, -x_end_test);
                    arc_plot (xc+(px>>1), yc-(py>>1),
                        xc+(px>>1), arc[6], color, x_start_test,
                        x_end_test);
                    arc_plot (xc-(px>>1), yc+(py>>1),
                        -xc+(px>>1), arc[2], color,
                        -x_start_test, -x_end_test);
                    arc_plot (xc-(px>>1), yc-(py>>1),
                        xc-(px>>1), arc[5], color, x_start_test,
                        x_end_test);
                    arc_plot (xc+(py>>1), yc+(px>>1),
                        yc+(px>>1), arc[0], color, y_start_test,
                        y_end_test);
                    arc_plot (xc+(py>>1), yc-(px>>1),
                        yc-(px>>1), arc[7], color, y_start_test,
                        y_end_test);
                    arc_plot (xc-(py>>1), yc+(px>>1),
                        -yc-(px>>1), arc[3], color,
                        -y_start_test, -y_end_test);
                    arc_plot (xc-(py>>1), yc-(px>>1),
                        -yc+(px>>1), arc[4], color,
                        -y_start_test, -y_end_test);
                    sum += px++;
                    sum += px;
                    if (sum > 0)
                    {
                        sum -= py--;
                        sum -= py;
                    }
                }
                radius++;
            }
        }
```

(continued)

```
/*
```

┌───┐
│ ┌───┐ │
│ │   │ │
│ │ arc_plot() = Determines which points should be plotted │ │
│ │   on the screen.   │ │
│ │   │ │
│ └───┘ │
└───┘

```
*/

void arc_plot (int x, int y, int test_var, int type, int
    color, int start_test, int end_test)
{
    switch(type)
    {
        case 1:
            if (test_var>=start_test)
                plots(x,y,color);
            break;
        case 2:
            plots(x,y,color);
            break;
        case 3:
            if (test_var<=end_test)
                plots(x,y,color);
            break;
        case 4:
            if ((test_var>=start_test) &&
                (test_var<=end_test))
                plots(x,y,color);
            break;
        case 5:
            if ((test_var<=end_test) ||
                (test_var>=start_test))
                plots(x,y,color);
            break;
    }
}
```

(continued)

```
/*
```

```
    plots() = Plots a point on the screen at designated
            system coordinates using selected color.
```

```
*/
```

```
void plots(int x, int y, int color)
{
    #define seq_out(index,val)   {outp(0x3C4,index);\
                                    outp(0x3C5,val);}
    #define graph_out(index,val)  {outp(0x3CE,index);\
                                    outp(0x3CF,val);}

    unsigned int offset;
    int dummy,mask,page;
    char far * address;

    convert(x,y);

    if ((x>=0) && (x<xres) && (y>=0) && (y<yres))
    {
        address = (char far *) 0xA0000000L + (long)y *
            xres/8L + ((long)x / 8L);
        mask = 0x80 >> (x % 8);
        graph_out(8,mask);
        graph_out(5,2);
        dummy = *address;
        *address = color;
        graph_out(5,0);
        graph_out(8,0xFF);
    }
}
```

```
/*
```

```
            setMode() = Sets the video mode.
```

```
*/
```

(continued)

```
void setMode(int mode)
{
    struct REGPACK reg;

    reg.r_ax = mode;
    intr (0x10,&reg);
}

/*
```

```
        cls() = Clears the screen to selected color.
```

```
*/

void cls(char colors)
{
    union REGS reg;
    char ch;
    int columns,mode;

    reg.x.dx = 0x1D4F;
    reg.h.bh = colors;
    reg.x.ax = 0x0600;
    reg.x.cx = 0;
    int86(0x10,&reg,&reg);
}

/*
```

```
    setEGApalette() = Sets the color for an EGA palette
                            number
```

```
*/

void setEGApalette(int palette, int color)
{
    union REGS reg;

    reg.h.ah = 0x10;
```

(continued)

435

```
        reg.h.al = 0;
        reg.h.bh = color;
        reg.h.bl = palette;
        int86(0x10,&reg,&reg);
}


/*
```

```
        set_screen() = Sets the screen background colors.
```

```
*/


void set_screen(int top_color, int bottom_color, int
        boundary)
{
        union REGS reg;
        reg.h.ah = 0x06;
        reg.h.al = boundary;
        reg.x.cx = 0;
        reg.x.dx = 0x1D4F;
        reg.h.bh = top_color;
        int86(0x10,&reg,&reg);
        reg.h.ah = 0x06;
        reg.h.al = 30 - boundary;
        reg.x.cx = 0;
        reg.x.dx = 0x1D4F;
        reg.h.bh = bottom_color;
        int86(0x10,&reg,&reg);
}


/*
```

```
    fillArc() = Fills an arc centered at (x,y) with radius
          'radius' from starting angle 'start_angle' in
                tenths of a degree to ending angle
              'end_angle' in tenths of a degree
                    in color 'color'.
```

```
*/
```

(continued)

```
void fillArc(int xc, int yc, int radius, float
    start_angle, float end_angle, int color)
{
    #define sign(x) ((x) > 0 ? 1:  ((x) == 0 ? 0:  (-1)))

    long int sum, asq, bsq;
    int arc[8], i, j, row, col, px, py, x, y
        ,start_sector, end_sector, temp, x_start_test,
        x_end_test, y_start_test, y_end_test, dx, dy,
        sdmax, sdmin,pl,ps,dmax,dmin,d, flag=1;
    float temp_angle;

    void arc_data (int x, int y, int test_var, int type,
        int color, int x_start_test, int x_end_test);

    while (start_angle >= 360)
        start_angle -= 360;
    while (end_angle >= 360)
        end_angle -= 360;
    temp_angle = end_angle - start_angle;
    if (temp_angle < 0)
        temp_angle+= 360;
    if (temp_angle > 180)
    {
        flag++;
        temp_angle = end_angle;
        end_angle = (start_angle + 180);
        if (end_angle >= 360)
            end_angle -= 360;
    }
    radius = max(radius,1);
    while (flag > 0)
    {
        minrow = 800;
        maxrow = 0;
        for (i=0; i<480; i++)
        {
            coord[0][i] = 800;
            coord[1][i] = 0;
        }
        for (j=0; j<8; j++)
```

(continued)

```
            arc[j] = 0;
start_sector = (int)(start_angle/45) % 8;
end_sector = (int)(end_angle/45) % 8;
x_start_test = xc+radius *
    cos(start_angle*.017453);
x_end_test = xc+radius*cos(end_angle*.017453);
y_start_test = yc+radius *
    sin(start_angle*.017453);
y_end_test = yc+radius*sin(end_angle*.017453);
if (start_sector == end_sector)
{
    if (end_angle < start_angle)
    {
        arc[start_sector] = 5;
        for (i=0; i<8; i++)
        {
            if (i != start_sector)
                arc[i] = 2;
        }
    }
    else
        arc[start_sector] = 4;
}
else
{
    arc[start_sector] = 1;
    arc[end_sector] = 3;
    for (i=(start_sector+1)%8; i!=end_sector; i=
        (i+1)%8)
        arc[i] = 2;
}
py = radius << 1;
px = 0;
sum = -py;
while (px <= py)
{
    if (!(px & 1))
    {
        arc_data (xc+(px>>1), yc+(py>>1),
            -xc-(px>>1), arc[1], color,
            -x_start_test, -x_end_test);
```

(continued)

```
                arc_data (xc+(px>>1), yc-(py>>1),
                    xc+(px>>1), arc[6], color,
                    x_start_test, x_end_test);
                arc_data (xc-(px>>1), yc+(py>>1),
                    -xc+(px>>1), arc[2], color,
                    -x_start_test, -x_end_test);
                arc_data (xc-(px>>1), yc-(py>>1),
                    xc-(px>>1), arc[5], color,
                    x_start_test, x_end_test);
                arc_data (xc+(py>>1), yc+(px>>1),
                    yc+(px>>1), arc[0], color,
                    y_start_test, y_end_test);
                arc_data (xc+(py>>1), yc-(px>>1),
                    yc-(px>>1), arc[7], color,
                    y_start_test, y_end_test);
                arc_data (xc-(py>>1), yc+(px>>1),
                    -yc-(px>>1), arc[3], color,
                    -y_start_test, -y_end_test);
                arc_data (xc-(py>>1), yc-(px>>1),
                    -yc+(px>>1), arc[4], color,
                    -y_start_test, -y_end_test);
            }
        sum += px++;
        sum += px;
        if (sum > 0)
        {
            sum -= py--;
            sum -= py;
        }
    }
Line(xc, yc, x_end_test, y_end_test, color);
Line(xc, yc, x_start_test,y_start_test, color);
for (i=minrow; i<=maxrow; i++)
{
    if (coord[0][i] == coord[1][i])
        if ((i != minrow) && (i != maxrow))
        {
            coord[0][i] = (coord[0][i-1] +
                coord[0][i+1])/2;
            coord[1][i] = (coord[1][i-1] +
                coord[1][i+1])/2;
```

(continued)

439

```
                    }
                    fillLine(coord[0][i],coord[1][i], i,
                        color);
              }
         for (i=0; i<8; i++)
              arc[i] = 0;
         flag--;
         start_angle = end_angle;
         end_angle = temp_angle;
    }
}


/*
```

```
      fillLine() = Draws a horizontal line in a selected
                           color.
```

```
*/

void fillLine(int x_one, int x_two, int y, int color)
{
    char color_buffer[100];
    int dummy, loop, i, x1, x2;
    int length, offset1, offset2;
    int srcseg, srcoff, destseg, destoff;
    long int no_of_bytes;
    unsigned int mask;
    char far *base1;
    char far *base2;
    struct SREGS segregs;

    segread(&segregs);
    srcseg = segregs.ds;
    srcoff = (int) color_buffer;
    x1 = min(x_one, x_two);
    x2 = max(x_one, x_two);
    offset1 = x1 % 8;
    offset2 = x2 % 8;
    base1 = (char far *)(0xA0000000L + ((long)y * 80L +
        ((long)x1 / 8L)));
```

(continued)

```
    base2 = (char far *)(0xA0000000L + ((long)y * 80L +
        ((long)x2 / 8L)));
    no_of_bytes = abs(base2 - base1);
    length = ((x2 - x1) - ((8-offset1) + (offset2))) / 8L;
    mask = 0xFF00 << (7 - offset2);
    if (!no_of_bytes)
        mask &= (0xFF00 >> offset1) & 0xFF00;
    dummy = *base2;
    outport(0x3CE, mask | 0x08);
    outport(0x3CE, 0x0205);
    *base2 = color;
    if (no_of_bytes)
    {
        mask = (0xFF00 >> offset1) & 0xFF00;
        outport(0x3CE, mask | 0x08);
        dummy = *base1;
        *base1 = color;
        mask = 0xFF00;
        outport(0x3CE, mask | 0x08);
        memset(color_buffer,color,length);
        destseg = 0xA000;
        destoff = ((long) y * 80L + ((long)x1 /8L)) + 1;
        movedata(srcseg, srcoff, destseg, destoff,
            length);
    }
    outport(0x3CE, 0xFF08);
    outport(0x3CE, 0x0005);
}


/*

+----------------------------------------------------------+
|                                                          |
|                                                          |
| arcData() = Determines whether point on a circle should  |
|                        be saved.                         |
|                                                          |
+----------------------------------------------------------+

*/


void arc_data (int x, int y, int test_var, int type, int
    color, int start_test, int end_test)
{
    convert(x,y);
```

(continued)

```
switch(type)
{
    case 1:
        if (test_var>=start_test)
        {
            compare(x,coord[0][y],coord[1][y]);
            compare(y,minrow,maxrow);
        }
        break;
    case 2:
        {
            compare(x,coord[0][y],coord[1][y]);
            compare(y,minrow,maxrow);
        }
        break;
    case 3:
        if (test_var<=end_test)
        {
            compare(x,coord[0][y],coord[1][y]);
            compare(y,minrow,maxrow);
        }
        break;
    case 4:
        if ((test_var>=start_test) &&
            (test_var<=end_test))
        {
            compare(x,coord[0][y],coord[1][y]);
            compare(y,minrow,maxrow);
        }
        break;
    case 5:
        if ((test_var<=end_test) ||
            (test_var>=start_test))
        {
            compare(x,coord[0][y],coord[1][y]);
            compare(y,minrow,maxrow);
        }
        break;
}
}
```

(continued)

```
/*
```

```
Line() = Draws a single pixel wide line from one set of
   coordinates to another in designated color using 16
                    color mode.
```

```
*/

void Line(int xs, int ys, int xe, int ye, int color)
{
    int temp, dx, dy, y_sign, i, x, y, decision;

    convert(xs,ys);
    convert(xe,ye);
    if (xs > xe)
    {
        temp = xs;
        xs = xe;
        xe = temp;
        temp = ys;
        ys = ye;
        ye = temp;
    }
    dx = abs(xe - xs);
    dy = abs(ye - ys);
    if ((ye - ys) < 0)
        y_sign = -1;
    else
        y_sign = 1;
    if (dx > dy)
    {
        for (x=xs,y=ys,decision=0; x<=xe;
            x++,decision+=dy)
        {
            if (decision>=dx)
            {
                decision -= dx;
                y+= y_sign;
            }
            compare(x,coord[0][y], coord[1][y]);
```

(continued)

443

```
                    compare(y,minrow,maxrow);
            }
        }
        else
        {
            for (x=xs,y=ys,decision=0; y!=ye;
                y+=y_sign,decision+=dx)
            {
                if (decision>=dy)
                {
                    decision -= dy;
                    x++;
                }
                compare(x,coord[0][y], coord[1][y]);
                compare(y,minrow,maxrow);
            }
        }
}

/*
```

```
    drawLine() = Draws a single pixel wide line in a
         selected color from specified starting
              coordinates in a given angular
                  direction in degrees.
```

```
*/

void drawLine(int xs, int ys, int length, float angle, int
    color)
{
    int temp, dx, dy, xe, ye, i, x, y, x_sign, y_sign,
        decision;

    xe = xs + length * (cos(0.017453292 * angle));
    ye = ys + length * (sin(0.017453292 * angle));
    dx = abs(xe - xs);
    dy = abs(ye - ys);
    if (((dx >= dy) && (xs>xe)) || ((dy>dx) && (ys>ye)))
    {
```

(continued)

```
            temp = xs;
            xs = xe;
            xe = temp;
            temp = ys;
            ys = ye;
            ye = temp;
     }
     if ((ye - ys) < 0)
            y_sign = -1;
     else
            y_sign = 1;
     if ((xe - xs) < 0)
            x_sign = -1;
     else
            x_sign = 1;
     if (dx >= dy)
     {
            for (x=xs,y=ys,decision=0; x<=xe;
                x++,decision+=dy)
            {
                if (decision>=dx)
                {
                    decision -= dx;
                    y+= y_sign;
                }
                plots(x,y,color);
            }
     }
     else
     {
            for (x=xs,y=ys,decision=0; y<=ye;
                y++,decision+=dx)
            {
                if (decision>=dy)
                {
                    decision -= dy;
                    x += x_sign;
                }
                plots(x,y,color);
            }
     }
}
```

Drawing an Arc

The function for drawing an arc is *drawArc*. First, just glance through the listing of this function and observe that the method for computing the points of the wide line circle is just the same as that used for the circle in the function *drawCircle3*, which was described in the Chapter 13. However, instead of plotting each point directly to the screen, the function *arc_plot* is called. Before we describe this function, we need to look at some additional things that are done at the beginning of the *drawArc* function. First, two *while* loops are used to assure that the start and end angles are between 0 and 360 degrees. They do this by repeatedly subtracting 360 degrees until the resulting angle falls within the desired range. This works just fine as long as you don't specify any negative angles. If you use this function and are worried about that possibility, you need to add a couple more loops to handle the negative cases. The program then clears the values in the array *arc* to 0. This array contains the status of each octant that makes up the circle. Next, the number of the octant in which the arc starts is found by dividing the starting angle by 45 degrees and taking the result modula 8. This gives us a starting octant from 0 to 7. The same procedure is then performed to find the ending octant. At this point, the function uses some simple geometry to find the *x* and *y* coordinates of the starting and ending points on the arc. It then proceeds to fill *arc* array. There are six possible values to represent the contents of each octant. They are:

0 = this octant does not contain any part of the arc.

1 = the arc starts in this octant but ends in another octant.

2 = this octant is entirely filled by a portion of the arc, which starts and ends in other octants.

3 = the arc starts in another octant and ends in this octant.

4 = the arc begins and ends in this octant and does not extend into any other octant.

5 = the arc starts and ends in this octant, but makes nearly a full revolution, filling all other octants.

The function first checks whether the starting and ending octants are the same. If so, it next checks whether the end angle is less than the start angle. If this is the case, we have an arc that fills all of the circle except the space between the end angle and the start angle in this octant. Hence we set this octant's value to 5 and set all of the other octants to a value of 2. If the end angle was larger than or equal to the start angle, we have an arc that extends from the start angle to the end angle in this octant and doesn't appear in any other octant. Consequently, we set this octant to 4 and do nothing to the other octants. If the starting and ending octants are not the same, first set the value for the starting octant to 1 and then set the value of the ending octant to 3. We then enter a *for* loop that fills all of the octants from the one next to the starting octant around to the one next to the ending octant with a value of 2. We use modulus arithmetic to assure that no problems are encountered if we pass from octant 7 to octant 0 during this loop. Now we are ready to compute the points on the circle. We make use of a *for* loop to do this repeatedly for wide lines, beginning with a radius that is at the inside of the circle line and incrementing the radius for each iteration until the last circle is drawn at the outside boundary of the wide line. The circle drawing algorithm is just the same as that given for *drawCircle4* in Chapter 13, except that instead of plotting each point, we send it to *arc_plot*, which decides whether the point should be plotted or not.

Now take a look at the listing for *arc_plot*. The parameters that are passed to this are the x and y coordinates of the point to be plotted, a variable to be tested to determine what plotting action to take, the type of octant (0 to 5 as listed previously), and the starting and ending test values. The function consists of a *switch* statement that causes the function to perform a different action for each type of octant. Let's look at these actions first and later go into more detail about how the tests work. The simplest case is an octant of type 0 (no plotting within this octant). It isn't covered by the *switch* statement, so the function does nothing. The next simplest is an octant of type 2; for this case the entire octant is included in the arc, so the function just plots every point. For an octant of type 1, where the arc begins in the octant, but ends elsewhere, the program begins plotting points when the test variable achieves the value of the *start_test* parameter and continues to the end of the octant. Similarly, for type 3, where the arc begins elsewhere, but ends in this octant, the function plots points from the beginning of the octant until the value of the test variable reaches the value of the *end_test* parameter; after this it doesn't plot any more points. For type 4, where the arc is included only in this octant, the function starts plotting points when the test variable achieves the value of the *start_test* parameter and stops plotting points when the value of the test variable reaches the value of the *end_test* parameter. For type 5, where the arc begins and ends in this octant and extends through all the other octants (almost, but not quite a complete circle) the program plots points from the beginning of the octant until the test variable reaches the value of the *end_test* parameter and then stops plotting points until the test variable reaches the value of the *start_test* parameter. It then begins plotting points again and continues to do so until the end of the octant is reached. (This description seems to imply that we are plotting points in some particular direction around the circle, but actually, the appropriate test is made for every point, to determine whether it should be plotted, and it doesn't really matter in what order the points are computed.)

This describes what the *arc_plot* function does, but sorting out what variable is to be tested against what is a little more complicated. The first thing to observe is that, in any octant, it is sufficient to test against either the *x* or the *y* coordinate of the starting or ending point, and for angles around multiples of 45 degrees, it doesn't really matter which test is made. However at angles that are multiples of 90 degrees, the situation is different. At 0 and 180 degrees, the *y* value is changing very rapidly, while the *x* value is changing very slowly. Therefore, octants that include these values should be tested for the *y* coordinate, since this gives the most precise test and stops or starts the arc at the closest point to the specified angle. For the case of 90 or 270 degrees, the reverse situation is true, so the most precise test is performed with the *x* variable. Once we have determined which octants are associated with *x* tests and which with *y* tests, we pass the parameters *x, x_start_test,* and *x_end_test* to *arc_plot* for the former cases and *y, y_start_test,* and *y_end_test* to *arc_plot* for the latter cases. Finally, we have to note that all of the tests, as just described, assume that the coordinate being tested is increasing toward the test parameter. However, in some octants, the coordinate being tested starts at a higher value than the test parameter and decreases toward it. In these cases, the direction of the test inequality should be reversed (less than instead of greater than or vice-versa). Since the inequalities are a part of the *arc_test* function, they cannot easily be switched, but we can accomplish the same result by passing the negative of the coordinate being tested and the start and end test parameters to the function. To sum up, we now have an arc drawing function that computes all of the points on a circle and then determines for each point whether it is within the bounds of a specified arc. If it is, the point is plotted to the screen.

Filling an Arc

We need to begin this section by defining what we mean by filling an arc. What we refer to is filling the area bounded by an arc that forms part of the circumference of a circle and by two straight lines which begin at the center of the circle and extend to the beginning and end of the arc, respectively. You'll find this function much like that for drawing the arc in many ways, but there are some significant differences. You'll recall that we filled a circle by drawing horizontal lines between the beginning and ending x values for each vertical row that made up the circle, and that in the more complicated situation of the tilted ellipse we first let each x value be compared to the proper row values of two arrays, one of which contained minimum values of x for each row and the other maximum values of x for each row. The minimums and maximums were saved and after the ellipse was completely calculated, a horizontal line was drawn from the minimum x to the maximum x for each row of the ellipse. For the filled arc, we need to use this latter procedure to process all points in the arc and in each of the straight lines, and then we draw the appropriate filled lines. Unfortunately, if we have an arc that extends for an angle greater than 180 degrees, we may have a situation where a particular row contains two filled portions separated by a blank space. Our procedure for filling the ellipse would, in this case, result in a single horizontal line being drawn from the minimum x value to the maximum x value, which would include filling in that portion of each line that we really wanted to be empty. To avoid this problem, we first determine the difference between the starting and ending angle. If it is greater than 180 degrees, we increment a flag that was initialized to 1 and then save the original ending angle and create a new ending angle 180 degrees greater than the starting angle. We then enter a *while* loop that executes the entire arc filling process and then decrements the flag for as long as the flag is not 0. At the end of this loop, the starting angle is changed to the ending angle (starting angle + 180 degrees) and the ending angle is changed to the original ending angle. Thus, if the original difference in arc starting and ending angles was 180 degrees or less, the original angles are preserved and the loop is executed once. However, if the angle difference was more than 180 degrees, a first pass is made through the loop to cover the section of the arc from the beginning angle to 180 degrees plus that angle and a second pass is made through the loop to fill the rest of the arc. Since each pass through the loop fills an arc of 180 degrees or less, there are no ambiguities and the arc is filled perfectly.

The only other differences between this function and the function for drawing an arc are that we initialize two coordinate arrays at the beginning of the program, and then instead of calling *arc_plot* to test whether a point should be plotted and plot it if it should, we call *arc_data*, which performs the same test, but if the point is part of the arc, instead of plotting it, checks whether it should replace the appropriate member of one of the coordinate arrays, and if it should, performs the replacement. After the circle has been computed completely, we call the function *Line* twice for the two straight lines that are needed to form the remaining boundaries of the figure to be filled. This function is similar to the line drawing functions that we looked at in Chapter 7, except that instead of plotting each point of the line to the screen, it checks whether it should be used to replace the appropriate member of each of the two coordinate arrays and, if it should, performs the replacement. At the same time, both for these lines and the arc, we keep track of the maximum and minimum row values that occur. When we are through, the arrays contain the values for the beginning and end of a straight line to be drawn at each of the rows that make up the figure. We then use a *for* loop to draw all of these lines, resulting in a final filled arc.

Elliptical Arcs

If you need to draw and/or fill elliptical arcs, you can often achieve the desired result by using the functions just described, but inserting the ellipse drawing or filling algorithms given in Chapter 14 instead of the circle drawing or filling algorithms of Chapter 13. These work well for most starting and ending angles, but there are a few angles for which the function breaks down. The problem is that we begin by defining eight octants as portions of the ellipse that cover a 45 degree angle. When we actually compute the points that make up the ellipse, we compute from 0, 90, 180 or 270 degrees until the point at which the x and y coordinates are equal. This point is exactly a multiple of

45 degrees for a circle, so that each octant is consistent from one definition to the other and we have no problems. For the ellipse, however, this point is not a multiple of 45 degrees; the actual angle differs, depending upon the shape of the ellipse. We have an ambiguous region at one boundary of each pair of octants, where the angular definition says that the start and end test coordinates are in one octant, but the algorithm for actually computing the points says they are in another. If your starting or ending angle is in this region, strange results occur. If you can live with these regions of uncertainty, you'll have no problem with elliptical arcs. I've created such a function and used it for making a lot of arcs without any difficulties. If you really need a perfect function, you'll have to create a lot more complex method of determining the octant boundaries at the beginning of the program. You should be able to calculate the angles at which the two coordinates are equal for each quadrant and from these determine what the actual angular boundaries of each octant are. Once you determine the proper type for each octant, based upon its actual boundaries, the algorithm should work perfectly for every case.

The *arctest.c* Program for Testing Arcs

The *arctest.c* program generates a lot of test screens which you can use to assure that your arc functions are working properly. The first screen shows a very small arc and one that is as large as can be shown without going off the screen. Each of these arcs goes from 1 degree to 359 degrees. (For the very small arc, you just can't see the opening, so the result appears to be a complete circle.) The next screen draws 100 arcs with random centers and random starting and ending angles. All of these arcs are drawn with single pixel wide lines. If your *drawArc* function is doing anything peculiar, it ought to turn up in one of these arcs. The next screen draws 80 arcs with random centers, random starting and ending angles and random line widths. This screen should show up any problems with creating wide line arcs. The screen is illustrated in Plate 13. The next screen draws three arcs on one screen, one at a time. You have to hit a key after each one is drawn before you get the next one. The first arc is drawn from 0 to 179 degrees, the second from 91 to 270 degrees, and the third from 1 to 359 degrees. If your arc function is giving problems near the angles 0, 90, 180 or 270 degrees, they should show up in this screen. The next screen draws a rainbow using wide line arcs. First, we reset the EGA palette colors to give a prettier rainbow picture.

This screen is shown in Plate 14. The next screen shows segmented arcs around a circle combined with the use of a version of the *drawLine* function to produce matching radials. This screen is shown in Plate 15. The next screen is a segmented pie chart with one section partially removed. It shows the capabilities of the *fillArc* function. It is illustrated in Plate 16. The next screen shows a filled arc that extends from 45 degrees around to 22.5 degrees. This screen reveals any problems with the *fillArc* function filling in regions that are supposed to be unfilled. (If your function has a problem in this area, this screen will appear as a fully filled circle instead of as a pie with a slice removed.) The next set of screens performs a full check of the *drawArc* function. It begins by drawing arcs that start at zero degrees and end in 4 degree increments from 4 degrees to 356 degrees. It then pauses 2.5 seconds and then erases the screen and draws the set of arcs beginning at 6 degrees. It continues this process with the starting angle increasing in 6 degree steps until it reaches 354 degrees. This gives you a chance to see whether almost any arc that can be drawn is drawn correctly. Since this is a lengthy process, you can terminate it at any time. A typical screen is shown in Plate 17.

Chapter 16

Drawing and Fast Filling Polygons

There are many cases in which you will want to create some enclosed figure with a number of straight line segments. Of course, you could repeatedly call a *drawLine* function until every line segment was drawn, but this is a rather tedious process. It makes a lot more sense to have a function that will take a lot of sets of coordinates defining points and draw lines from one to the next, to the next, and so forth. The main decision that needs to be made is whether to pass all of the coordinates to the function in the calling statement or to have them stored in an array that the function references. We shall show functions that use each of these techniques. You may also want to fill one of these enclosed figures with solid color. We'll show some very fast ways of doing this and also a very slow one that, however, turns out to be very effective if you know that you have a closed area but don't really know the locations of the boundary lines that make up the figure. Figure 16-1 lists a program called *polytest* which includes all of the polygon drawing and filling functions and provides some examples of how they are used. All of the displays in the demonstration use mode 16 (640 x 350 pixels x 16 colors), which will run on either the EGA or VGA. The New Jerusalem display uses mode 18 (640 x 480 pixels x 16 colors) and will run only on a VGA. The demonstration program includes a number of functions that have already been described in previous chapters. We won't describe them again here, but we have repeated them in the program listing so that you'll have a complete self-contained program to work with, rather than having to search through the book for missing functions. In particular, the New Jerusalem curve, which is the last screen displayed, is a good example of how several different drawing and filling functions can be combined to produce interesting displays.

Figure 16-1. Listing of polytest.c Program

```
/*


    polytest = Program to demonstrate polygon and flood
                        fill functions

            By Roger T. Stevens   10-15-91

*/

#include <stdio.h>
#include <stdlib.h>
#include <stdarg.h>
#include <math.h>
#include <dos.h>
#include <conio.h>

void cls(char colors);
void drawCircle(int x, int y, int r, int color);
void drawLine(int xs, int ys, int xe, int ye, int color);
void drawPoly(int color, ...);
void draw2Poly(int color,int *point);
void fill (int x, int y, int color);
void fillCircle(int x, int y, int r, int color);
void fillLine(int x_one, int x_two, int y, int color);
void fillPoly(int color,...);
void fill2Poly(int color,int *point);
void fillTriangle (int x1, int y_one, int x2, int y2, int
    x3, int y3, int color);
void fillQuad (int xa, int ya, int xb, int yb, int xc, int
    yc, int xd, int yd, int color);
char readPixel(int x, int y);
void setMode(int mode);
```

(continued)

```
void set_screen(int top_color, int bottom_color, int
    boundary);
void display(unsigned long int address, int color_plane,
    unsigned char ch);
void plot(int x, int y, int color);
void plot_char(int x, int y, int char_offset,int color,
    int type);
void plots(int x, int y, int color);
int sort_function (const long int *a, const long int *b);

#define convert(x,y)  {x += 320; \
                   y = yoff - ((ymult*y)>>yshift);}

int yoff = 175, ymult = 93, yshift = 7;
int color = 2;
int color, angle, xc[28], yc[28];
int xres = 640, yres = 480;
int i, radius=175;
long int coord[2000];
int poly1[128] = {-300,-36,-260,-108,-204,-108,-164,-84,
    -148,-108,-124,-108,-68,-68,-68,-12,-76,28,-100,-36,
    -108,-28,-92,36,-44,44,-44,52,-20,52,-28,84,-76,68,-76,
    100, 4,92,-12,108,4,124,-20,164,-92,172,-108,148,
    -108,100,-156,68,-196,36,-220,-12,-236,-76,
    -260,-92,-268,-88,-284,-44,-999};

int poly2[128] = {50,50,58,66,82,90,114,102,178,106,202,
    110,226,110,242,106,262,82,270,66,298,42,270,58,274,18,
    266,-6,250,-22,242,-22,234,-14,230,-6,234,-2,238,-10,
    242,-10,254,-2,258,18,258,34,242,50,214,50,202,38,194,
    26,206,-38,182,-38,174,18,170,-38,166,-38,150,18,114,
    18,114,-38,98,-38,94,18,70,50,58,34,58,18,62,2,50,18,
    50,50,-999};

int poly3[128] = {-100,-172,-82,-142,-58,-142,-40,-148,
    -28,-136,-40,-124,-46,-112,-22,-112,-28,-88,2,-94,14,
    -70,32,-82,56,-58,68,-88,92,-82,98,-106,116,-106,110,
    -124,122,-124,116,-148,134,-142,134,-154,152,-142,158,
    -154,170,-154,164,-166,152,-184,116,-190,56,-184,56,
    -208,26,-208,14,-190,-4,-190,-10,-208,-46,-208,-34,
    -184,-70,-190,-82,-184,-94,-196,-100,-196,-999};
```

(continued)

```
int africa[256] = {-217,115,-202,146,-198,146,-194,153,
    -183,161,-175,168,-175,176,-171,187,-164,191,-145,203,
    -133,199,-118,206,-95,210,-65,214,-61,191,-69,187,-50,
    184,-38,184,-34,176,-27,176,-15,172,-12,176,-12,184,-8,
    187,3,187,48,172,56,176,63,176,63,161,75,130,63,123,
    71,123,75,119,75,100,82,92,86,85,94,77,120,54,124,54,
    162,62,158,54,132,9,109,-13,86,-40,94,-59,98,-62,101,
    -89,90,-100,79,-104,67,-116,71,-135,56,-142,56,-161,33,
    -195,-19,-203,-27,-192,-23,-192,-42,-150,-42,-135,-57,
    -104,-57,-81,-53,-78,-46,-66,-50,-51,-53,-36,-72,-5,
    -69,16,-76,24,-88,24,-91,24,-95,32,-110,32,-126,28,
    -133,24,-145,28,-164,24,-190,39,-213,70,-209,73,-213,
    77,-209,92,-209,100,-213,104,-213,111,-999};

void main(void)
{
    setMode(16);

    /*
```

```
        Draw irregular polygons with passed parameters
```

```
    */

    set_screen(9,10,14);
    drawPoly(2,-300,-36,-260,-108,-204,-108,-164,-84,-148,
        -108,-124,-108,-68,-68,-68,-12,-76,28,-100,-36,
        -108,-28,-92,36,-44,44,-44,52,-20,52,-28,84,-76,68,
        -76,100,4,92,-12,108,4,124,-20,164,-92,172,-108,
        148,-108,100,-156,68,-196,36,-220,-12,-236,-76,
        -260,-92,-268,-88,-284,-44,-999);
    drawPoly(7,50,50,58,66,82,90,114,102,178,106,202,110,
        226,110,242,106,262,82,270,66,298,42,270,58,274,18,
        266,-6,250,-22,242,-22,234,-14,230,-6,234,-2,238,
        -10,242,-10,254,-2,258,18,258,34,242,50,214,50,
        202,38,194,26,206,-38,182,-38,174,18,170,-38,
        166,-38,150,18,114,18,114,-38,98,-38,94,18,70,50,
        58,34,58,18,62,2,50,18,50,50,-999);
    drawPoly(12,-100,-172,-82,-142,-58,-142,-40,-148,-28,
        -136,-40,-124,-46,-112,-22,-112,-28,-88,2,-94,14,
```

(continued)

```
    -70,32,-82,56,-58,68,-88,92,-82,98,-106,116,-106,
    110,-124,122,-124,116,-148,134,-142,134,-154,152,
    -142,158,-154,170,-154,164,-166,152,-184,116,-190,
    56,-184,56,-208,26,-208,14,-190,-4,-190,-10,-208,
    -46,-208,-34,-184,-70,-190,-82,-184,-94,-196,-100,
    -196,-999);
getch();
```

```
/*
```

```
        Flood fill the irregular polygons
```

```
*/
```

```
    fill (-120,0,2);
    fill (140,30,7);
    fill (0,-100,12);
    getch();
```

```
/*
```

```
        Generate triangles and bars
```

```
*/
    cls(1);
    for (i=25; i<284; i++)
        fillLine(321,327,i,14);
    for (i=20; i<284; i++)
        fillLine(617,623,i,14);
    for (i=20; i<284; i++)
        fillLine(17,23,i,14);
    fillTriangle(-250,-150,4,220,250,-150,13);
    fillTriangle(-123,35,125,35,0,-150,10);
    getch();
```

(continued)

```
/*
```
```
                    Generate quadrilaterals
```
```
*/
    cls(10);
    fillQuad(-250,-150,-190,220,270,200,-180,-180,9);
    fillQuad(-220,35,40,210,45,10,-215,-165,14);
    getch();
```

```
/*
```
```
        Fill irregular polygons with parameter array
```
```
*/
    cls(1);
    fill2Poly(11,poly1);
    fill2Poly(12,poly2);
    fill2Poly(14,poly3);
    getch();
```

```
/*
```
```
        Draw irregular polygons with parameter array
```
```
*/
    cls(1);
    draw2Poly(11,poly1);
    draw2Poly(12,poly2);
    draw2Poly(14,poly3);
    getch();
```

```
/*
```
```
        Fill irregular polygons with passed parameters
```
```
*/
```

(continued)

```
cls(1);
fillPoly(10,-300,-36,-260,-108,-204,-108,-164,-84,-148,
-108,-124,-108,-68,-68,-68,-12,-76,28,-100,-36,-108,
-28,-92,36,-44,44,-44,52,-20,52,-28,84,-76,68,-76, 100,
4,92,-12,108,4,124,-20,164,-92,172,-108,148,-108,100,
-156,68,-196,36,-220,-12,-236,-76,-260,-92,-268,-88,
-284,-44,-999);
fillPoly(11,50,50,58,66,82,90,114,102,178,106,202,110,
    226,110,242,106,262,82,270,66,298,42,270,58,274,
    18,266,-6,250,-22,242,-22,234,-14,230,-6,234,-2,
    238,-10,242,-10,254,-2,258,18,258,34,242,50,214,
    50,202,38,194,26,206,-38,182,-38,174,18,170,-38,
    166,-38,150,18,114,18,114,-38,98,-38,94,18,70,50,
    58,34,58,18,62,2,50,18,50,50,-999);
fillPoly(13,-100,-172,-82,-142,-58,-142,-40,-148,-28,
    -136,-40,-124,-46,-112,-22,-112,-28,-88,2,-94,14,
    -70,32,-82,56,-58,68,-88,92,-82,98,-106,116,-106,
    110,-124,122,-124,116,-148,134,-142,134,-154,152,
    -142,158,-154,170,-154,164,-166,152,-184,116,-190,
    56,-184,56,-208,6,-208,14,-190,-4,-190,-10,-208,
    -46,-208,-34,-184,-70,-190,-82,-184,-94,-196,-100,
    -196,-999);
getch();
```

```
/*
```

```
                    Generate map of Africa
```

```
*/
```

```
cls(1);
fill2Poly(10,africa);
getch();
```

```
/*
```

```
                Generate New Jerusalem figure
```

```
*/
```

(continued)

```
setMode(0x12);
yoff = 240;
ymult = 1;
yshift = 0;
cls(1);
fillCircle(0,0,radius,13);
for (i=0; i<28; i++)
{
    xc[i] = radius * cos(.22439947 * i);
    yc[i] = radius * sin(.22439947 * i);
}
fillCircle(xc[1],yc[1],37,0);
fillCircle(xc[4],yc[4],37,2);
fillCircle(xc[6],yc[6],37,3);
fillCircle(xc[8],yc[8],37,4);
fillCircle(xc[11],yc[11],37,7);
fillCircle(xc[13],yc[13],37,6);
fillCircle(xc[15],yc[15],37,9);
fillCircle(xc[18],yc[18],37,8);
fillCircle(xc[20],yc[20],37,5);
fillCircle(xc[22],yc[22],37,14);
fillCircle(xc[25],yc[25],37,11);
fillCircle(xc[27],yc[27],37,12);
drawCircle(0,0,radius,13);
for (i=0; i<28; i+=4)
{
    drawLine(xc[i],yc[i],xc[(i+12)%28],yc[(i+12)%28],
        15);
}
fill(0,50,15);
fill(50,0,15);
fill(50,50,15);
fill(-50,50,15);
fill(-30,-50,15);
fill(-50,-50,15);
fill(50,-50,15);
for (i=0; i<28; i++)
{
    if ((i%4) != 0)
        drawLine(xc[i],yc[i],xc[(i+12)%28],
            yc[(i+12)%28],10);
```

(continued)

```
    }
    getch();
}

/*
```

```
          readPixel() = Read a pixel from the screen
```

```
*/

char readPixel(int x, int y)
{
    union REGS reg;

    gotoxy(2,22);
    reg.h.ah = 0x0D;
    reg.x.cx = x;
    reg.x.dx = y;
    reg.h.bh = 0;
    int86 (0x10,&reg,&reg);
    return (reg.h.al);
}

/*
```

```
              setMode() = Sets the video mode
```

```
*/

void setMode(int mode)
{
    union REGS reg;

    reg.h.ah = 0;
    reg.h.al = mode;
    int86 (0x10,&reg,&reg);
}
```

(continued)

```
/*

    drawPoly() = Draws a polygon in a designated color by
       drawing lines between sets of coordinates specified
          and then drawing a line from last coordinates
                            to first.

*/

void drawPoly(int color,...)
{
    va_list coord;
    int temp, dx, dy, y_sign, i=0, j, x, y, xs, ys, xe, ye,
        decision, xpoint[150],ypoint[150];

    va_start(coord,color);
    while (((xpoint[i]=va_arg(coord,int)) >= -500) &&
        ((ypoint[i]=va_arg(coord,int)) >= -500) &&
        ((i++)<150));
    va_end(coord);
    if (i<3) return;
    xpoint[i] = xpoint[0];
    ypoint[i++] = ypoint[0];
    for (j=0; j<i-1; j++)
    {
        xs = xpoint[j];
        ys = ypoint[j];
        xe = xpoint[j+1];
        ye = ypoint[j+1];
        drawLine(xs,ys,xe,ye,color);
    }
}
```

(continued)

```
/*
```

```
    draw2Poly() = Draws a polygon in a designated color by
       drawing lines between sets of coordinates specified
           and then drawing a line from last coordinates
                to first. Coordinates are in an array.
```

```
*/
```

```
void draw2Poly(int color,int *point)
{
    int i=0, j;

    while (point[i++] > -500);
    if (i<6) return;
    for (j=0; j<i-3; j+=2)
        drawLine(point[j], point[j+1], point[j+2],
            point[j+3],color);
    drawLine(point[j], point[j+1], point[0],
        point[1],color);
}
```

```
/*
```

```
    plot() = Plots a point on the screen at a designated
           position using a selected color for the 16
                          color modes.
```

```
*/
```

```
void plot(int x, int y, int color)
{
    #define graph_out(index,val)  {outp(0x3CE,index);\
                              outp(0x3CF,val);}

    int dummy,mask;
    char far * address;

    address = (char far *) 0xA0000000L + (long)y * xres/8L
```

(continued)

```
           + ((long)x / 8L);
        mask = 0x80 >> (x % 8);
        graph_out(8,mask);
        graph_out(5,2);
        dummy = *address;
        *address = color;
        graph_out(5,0);
        graph_out(8,0xFF);
    }


    /*
```

```
    fill() = Fills an area bounded by a designated color
            when a point within the area is specified.
```

```
    */

    void fill (int x, int y, int color)
    {
        int dy, sp=0, start, x1, x2;
        struct
        {
            int y, xl, xr, dy;
        } buffer[5000];

        convert(x,y);
        buffer[sp].y = y;
        buffer[sp].xl = x;
        buffer[sp].xr = x;
        buffer[sp++].dy = 1;
        buffer[sp].y = y + 1;
        buffer[sp].xl = x;
        buffer[sp].xr = x;
        buffer[sp++].dy = -1;
        while (sp > 0)
        {
            dy = buffer[--sp].dy;
            y = buffer[sp].y + dy;
            x1 = buffer[sp].xl;
            x2 = buffer[sp].xr;
```

(continued)

```
        x = x1;
        while ((x>=0) && (readPixel(x,y) != color))
            plot(x--,y,color);
        if (x >= x1)
            goto enter;
        start = x + 1;
        if (start < x1)
        {
            buffer[sp].y = y;
            buffer[sp].xl = start;
            buffer[sp].xr = x1 - 1;
            buffer[sp++].dy = -dy;
        }
        x = x1 + 1;
        do
        {
            while ((x < xres) && (readPixel(x,y) != color))
                plot(x++,y,color);
            buffer[sp].y = y;
            buffer[sp].xl = start;
            buffer[sp].xr = x - 1;
            buffer[sp++].dy = dy;
            if (x > (x2 + 1))
            {
                buffer[sp].y = y;
                buffer[sp].xl = x2 + 1;
                buffer[sp].xr = x - 1;
                buffer[sp++].dy = -dy;
            }
enter:      x++;
            while ((x <= x2) && (readPixel(x,y) == color))
                x++;
            start = x;
        }
        while (x <= x2);
    }
}
```

(continued)

```
/*

┌─────────────────────────────────────────────────────────────┐
│ ┌─────────────────────────────────────────────────────────┐ │
│ │                                                         │ │
│ │     set_screen() = Sets the screen background colors     │ │
│ │                                                         │ │
│ └─────────────────────────────────────────────────────────┘ │
└─────────────────────────────────────────────────────────────┘

*/

void set_screen(int top_color, int bottom_color, int
    boundary)
{
    union REGS reg;

    reg.h.ah = 0x06;
    reg.h.al = boundary;
    reg.x.cx = 0;
    reg.x.dx = 0x184F;
    reg.h.bh = top_color;
    int86(0x10,&reg,&reg);
    reg.h.al = 25 - boundary;
    reg.x.cx = 0;
    reg.x.dx = 0x184F;
    reg.h.bh = bottom_color;
    int86(0x10,&reg,&reg);
}


/*

┌─────────────────────────────────────────────────────────────┐
│ ┌─────────────────────────────────────────────────────────┐ │
│ │                                                         │ │
│ │     cls() = Clears the screen to a specified color       │ │
│ │                                                         │ │
│ └─────────────────────────────────────────────────────────┘ │
└─────────────────────────────────────────────────────────────┘

*/

void cls(char colors)
{
    union REGS reg;

    reg.x.dx = 0x284F;
    reg.h.bh = colors;
    reg.x.ax = 0x0600;
    reg.x.cx = 0;
    int86(0x10,&reg,&reg);
```

(continued)

```
    gotoxy(0,0);
}

/*
```

```
    plots() = Plots a point on the screen at designated
        system coordinates using a selected color.
```

```
*/

void plots(int x, int y, int color)
{

    unsigned int offset;
    int dummy,mask,page;
    char far * mem_address;

    convert(x,y);
    offset = (long)y * (xres/8L) + ((long)x / 8L);
    mem_address = (char far *) 0xA0000000L + offset;
    mask = 0x8000 >> (x % 8);
    outport(0x3CE,mask | 0x08);
    outport(0x3CE,0x0205);
    dummy = *mem_address;
    *mem_address = color;
    outport(0x3CE,0xFF08);
    outport(0x3CE,0x0005);
}

/*
```

```
    drawCircle() = Draws a circle with specified center,
        radius, and color, using single pixel wide line.
```

```
*/

void drawCircle(int x, int y, int r, int color)
{
    int i, row, col, px, py;
```

(continued)

```
long int sum;
py = r<<1;
px = 0;
sum = 0;
while (px <= py)
{
    if (!(px & 1))
    {
        col = x + (px>>1);
        row = y + (py>>1);
        plots(col,row,color);
        row = y - (py>>1);
        plots(col,row,color);
        col = x - (px>>1);
        plots(col,row,color);
        row = y + (py>>1);
        plots(col,row,color);
        col = x + (py>>1);
        row = y + px>>1;
        plots(col,row,color);
        row = y - (px>>1);
        plots(col,row,color);
        col = x - (py>>1);
        plots(col,row,color);
        row = y + (px>>1);
        plots(col,row,color);
    }
    sum+=px++;
    sum += px;
    if (sum >= 0)
    {
        sum-=py--;
        sum-=py;
    }
}
}
```

(continued)

```
/*

┌─────────────────────────────────────────────────────────┐
│                                                           │
│    fillCircle() = Fills a circle with specified center,   │
│                    radius, and color.                     │
│                                                           │
└─────────────────────────────────────────────────────────┘

*/

void fillCircle(int x, int y, int r, int color)
{
    int i, row, col_start, col_end, t_row, t_col, px, py;
    long int sum;

    py = r<<1;
    px = 0;
    sum = 0;
    while (px <= py)
    {
        col_start = max(x - (px>>1),-320) + 320;
        col_end = min(x + (px>>1),319) + 320;
        row = 240 - (y + (py>>1));
        fillLine(col_start, col_end, row, color);
        col_start = max(x - (py>>1),-320) + 320;
        col_end = min(x + (py>>1),319) + 320;
        row = 240 - (y + (px>>1));
        fillLine(col_start, col_end, row, color);
        col_start = max(x - (px>>1),-320) + 320;
        col_end = min(x + (px>>1),319) + 320;
        row = 240 - (y - (py>>1));
        fillLine(col_start, col_end, row, color);
        col_start = max(x - (py>>1),-320) + 320;
        col_end = min(x + (py>>1),319) + 320;
        row = 240 - (y - (px>>1));
        fillLine(col_start, col_end, row, color);
        sum +=px++;
        sum += px;
        if (sum >= 0)
        {
            sum-=py--;
            sum -=py;
        }
```

(continued)

```
      }
}

/*
```

```
      fillLine() = Fast draws a horizontal line
```

```
*/

void fillLine(int x_one, int x_two, int y, int color)
{
    char color_buffer[100];
    int dummy, loop, i, x1, x2;
    int length, offset1, offset2;
    int srcseg, srcoff, destseg, destoff;
    long int no_of_bytes;
    unsigned int mask;
    char far *base1;
    char far *base2;

    struct SREGS segregs;

    segread(&segregs);
    srcseg = segregs.ds;
    srcoff = (int) color_buffer;
    x1 = min(x_one, x_two);
    x2 = max(x_one, x_two);
    offset1 = x1 % 8;
    offset2 = x2 % 8;
    base1 = (char far *)(0xA0000000L + ((long)y * 80L +
        ((long)x1 / 8L)));
    base2 = (char far *)(0xA0000000L + ((long)y * 80L +
        ((long)x2 / 8L)));
    no_of_bytes = abs(base2 - base1);
    length = ((x2 - x1) - ((8-offset1) + (offset2))) / 8L;
    mask = 0xFF00 << (7 - offset2);
    if (!no_of_bytes)
        mask &= (0xFF00 >> offset1) & 0xFF00;
    dummy = *base2;
    outport(0x3CE, mask | 0x08);
```

(continued)

```
    outport(0x3CE, 0x0205);
    *base2 = color;
    if (no_of_bytes)
    {
        mask = (0xFF00 >> offset1) & 0xFF00;
        outport(0x3CE, mask | 0x08);
        dummy = *base1;
        *base1 = color;
        mask = 0xFF00;
        outport(0x3CE, mask | 0x08);
        memset(color_buffer,color,length);
        destseg = 0xA000;
        destoff = ((long) y * 80L + ((long)x1 /8L)) + 1;
        movedata(srcseg, srcoff, destseg, destoff, length);
    }
    outport(0x3CE, 0xFF08);
    outport(0x3CE, 0x0005);
}


/*
```

```
    drawLine() = Draws a single pixel wide line in a
      selected color using the plot function. Will
              work with any plot function.
```

```
*/

void drawLine(int xs, int ys, int xe, int ye, int color)
{
    int temp, dx, dy, y_sign, i, x, y, decision;

    convert(xs,ys);
    convert(xe,ye);

    if (xs > xe)
    {
        temp = xs;
        xs = xe;
        xe = temp;
        temp = ys;
```

(continued)

471

```
            ys = ye;
            ye = temp;
        }
    dx = abs(xe - xs);
    dy = abs(ye - ys);
    if ((ye - ys) < 0)
        y_sign = -1;
    else
        y_sign = 1;
    if (dx > dy)
    {
        for (x=xs,y=ys,decision=0; x<=xe; x++,decision+=dy)
        {
            if (decision>=dx)
            {
                decision -= dx;
                y+= y_sign;
            }
            plot(x,y,color);
        }
    }
    else
    {
        for (x=xs,y=ys,decision=0; y!=ye;
            y+=y_sign,decision+=dx)
        {
            if (decision>=dy)
            {
                decision -= dy;
                x++;
            }
            plot(x,y,color);
        }
    }
}
```

(continued)

```
/*

    fillTriangle() = Fills a triangle with a specified
                         color

*/

void fillTriangle (int xa, int ya, int xb, int yb, int xc,
    int yc, int color)
{
    #define compare(a,b,c)  {if (a<b) b=a; if (a>c) c=a;}
    #define sign(x) ((x) > 0 ? 1:  ((x) == 0 ? 0:  (-1)))

    int coord[2][800], dx, dxabs, dy, dyabs, i, k, old_sdy,
        minrow, maxrow, sdx, sdy, sy0, x, xe, xpoint[4],
        xs, y, ypoint[4];
    int temp, y_sign, decision, ye, ys;

    minrow = 800;
    maxrow = 0;
    for (i=0; i<480; i++)
    {
        coord[0][i] = 800;
        coord[1][i] = 0;
    }
    convert(xa,ya);
    convert(xb,yb);
    convert(xc,yc);
    xpoint[0] = xa;
    ypoint[0] = ya;
    xpoint[1] = xb;
    ypoint[1] = yb;
    xpoint[2] = xc;
    ypoint[2] = yc;
    xpoint[3] = xa;
    ypoint[3] = ya;

    for (i=0; i<3; i++)
    {
        xs = xpoint[i];
```

(continued)

```
            ys = ypoint[i];
            xe = xpoint[i+1];
            ye = ypoint[i+1];
            if (xs > xe)
            {
                temp = xs;
                xs = xe;
                xe = temp;
                temp = ys;
                ys = ye;
                ye = temp;
            }
            compare(xs,coord[0][ys],coord[1][ys]);
            compare(ys,minrow,maxrow);
            dx = abs(xe - xs);
            dy = abs(ye - ys);
            if ((ye - ys) < 0)
                y_sign = -1;
            else
                y_sign = 1;
            if (dx > dy)
            {
                for (x=xs,y=ys,decision=0; x<=xe;
                    x++,decision+=dy)
                {
                    if (decision>=dx)
                    {
                        decision -= dx;
                        y+= y_sign;
                    }
                    compare(x,coord[0][y],coord[1][y]);
                    compare(y,minrow,maxrow);
                }
            }
            else
            {
                for (x=xs,y=ys,decision=0; y!=ye;
                    y+=y_sign,decision+=dx)
                {
                    if (decision>=dy)
                    {
```

(continued)

```
                    decision -= dy;
                    x++;
                }
                compare(x,coord[0][y],coord[1][y]);
                compare(y,minrow,maxrow);
            }
        }
    }
    for (i=minrow; i<=maxrow; i++)
    {
        xs = coord[0][i];
        xe = coord[1][i];
        fillLine(xs, xe, i, color);
    }
}
```

```
/*
```

```
┌──────────────────────────────────────────────────────────┐
│                                                            │
│  fillQuad() = Fills a quadrilateral in a specified color   │
│                                                            │
└──────────────────────────────────────────────────────────┘
```

```
*/
```

```
void fillQuad (int xa, int ya, int xb, int yb, int xc, int
yc, int xd,       int yd, int color)
{
    fillTriangle (xa,ya,xb,yb,xc,yc, color);
    fillTriangle (xc,yc,xd,yd,xa,ya,color);
}
```

```
/*
```

```
┌──────────────────────────────────────────────────────────┐
│                                                            │
│  sort_function() = Sorting function for Turbo C++ qsort    │
│                                                            │
└──────────────────────────────────────────────────────────┘
```

```
*/
```

```
int sort_function (const long int *a, const long int *b)
{
    if (*a < *b)
    return(-1);
```

(continued)

```
            if (*a == *b)
            return(0);
            if (*a > *b)
            return(1);
        }

    /*
```

```
         fillPoly() = fills a polygon in specified color by
            filling in boundaries resulting from connecting
              specified points in the order given and then
                connecting last point to first. Calling
                  program passes coordinates to function.
```

```
    */

    void fillPoly(int color,...)
    {
        #define sign(x) ((x) > 0 ? 1:  ((x) == 0 ? 0:  (-1)))

        va_list coords;
        int dx, dy, dxabs, dyabs, i=0, index=0, j, k, px, py,
            sdx, sdy, x, y, xs, xe, ys, ye, toggle=0, old_sdy,
            sy0, point[600];
        long int coord[4000];

        va_start(coords,color);
        while ((((point[i]=va_arg(coords,int)) >= -500) &&
            ((point[i+1]=va_arg(coords,int)) >= -500) &&
            (i<559))
            i+=2;
        va_end(coords);
        if (i<6) return;
        point[i] = point[0];
        point[i+1] = point[1];
        for (j=0; j<=i; j+=2)
            convert(point[j],point[j+1]);
        px = point[0];
        py = point[1];
        if (point[1] == point[3])
```

(continued)

```
{
    coord[index++] = px | (long)py << 16;
}
for (j=0; j<i; j+=2)
{
    dx = point[j+2] - point[j];
    dy = point[j+3] - point[j+1];
    sdx = sign(dx);
    sdy = sign(dy);
    if (j==0)
    {
        old_sdy = sdy;
        sy0 = sdy;
    }
    dxabs = abs(dx);
    dyabs = abs(dy);
    x = 0;
    y = 0;
    if (dxabs >= dyabs)
    {
        for (k=0; k<dxabs; k++)
        {
            y += dyabs;
            if (y>=dxabs)
            {
                y -= dxabs;
                py += sdy;
                if (old_sdy != sdy)
                {
                    old_sdy = sdy;
                            index--;
                }
                coord[index++] = (px + sdx) | (long)py <<
                    16;
            }
            px += sdx;
            plot(px,py,color);
        }
    }
    else
    {
```

(continued)

```
                for (k=0; k<dyabs; k++)
                {
                    x += dxabs;
                    if (x>=dyabs)
                    {
                        x -= dyabs;
                        px += sdx;
                    }
                    py += sdy;
                    if (old_sdy != sdy)
                    {
                        old_sdy = sdy;
                        if (sdy != 0)
                            index--;
                    }
                        plot(px,py,color);
                        coord[index] = px | (long)py << 16;
                        index++;
                }
            }
        }
    if (sy0 + sdy == 0)
        index--;
    qsort(coord,index,sizeof(coord[0]),(int(*)
        (const void *, const void *))sort_function);
    for (i=0; i<index; i++)
    {
        xs = min(639,(max(0,(int)coord[i])));
        xe = min(639,(max(0,(int)coord[i + 1])));
        ys = min(639,(max(0,(int)(coord[i] >> 16))));
        ye = min(639,(max(0,(int)(coord[i + 1] >> 16))));
        if ((ys == ye) && (toggle == 0))
        {
            fillLine(xs, xe, ys, color);
            toggle = 1;
        }
        else
            toggle = 0;
    }
}
```

(continued)

```
/*
```

```
    fil2Poly() = fills a polygon in specified color by
       filling in boundaries resulting from connecting
        specified points in the order given and then
         connecting last point to first. Uses an
                array to store coordinates.
```

```
*/
```

```c
void fill2Poly(int color,int *point)
{
    #define sign(x) ((x) > 0 ? 1:  ((x) == 0 ? 0:  (-1)))

    int dx, dy, dxabs, dyabs, i=0, index=0, j, k, px, py,
        sdx, sdy, x, y, xs, xe, ys, ye, toggle=0, old_sdy,
        sy0;
    long int coord[4000];

    while (point[i++] > -500);
    if (i<6) return;
    px = point[0];
    py = point[1];
    convert(px,py);
    if (point[1] == point[3])
    {
        coord[index++] = px | (long)py << 16;
    }
    for (j=0; j<=i-3; j+=2)
    {
        xs = point[j];
        ys = point[j+1];
        if ((j == (i-3)) || (j == (i-4)))
        {
            xe = point[0];
            ye = point[1];
        }
        else
        {
            xe = point[j+2];
```

(continued)

```
        ye = point[j+3];
    }
    convert (xs,ys);
    convert (xe,ye);
    dx = xe - xs;
    dy = ye - ys;
    sdx = sign(dx);
    sdy = sign(dy);
    if (j==0)
    {
        old_sdy = sdy;
        sy0 = sdy;
    }
    dxabs = abs(dx);
    dyabs = abs(dy);
    x = 0;
    y = 0;
    if (dxabs >= dyabs)
    {
        for (k=0; k<dxabs; k++)
        {
            y += dyabs;
            if (y>=dxabs)
            {
                y -= dxabs;
                py += sdy;
                if (old_sdy != sdy)
                {
                    old_sdy = sdy;
                    index--;
                }
                coord[index++] = (px + sdx) |
                    (long)py<<16;
            }
            px += sdx;
            plot(px,py,color);
        }
    }
    else
    {
        for (k=0; k<dyabs; k++)
```

(continued)

```
        {
            x += dxabs;
            if (x>=dyabs)
            {
                x -= dyabs;
                px += sdx;
            }
            py += sdy;
            if (old_sdy != sdy)
            {
                old_sdy = sdy;
                if (sdy != 0)
                    index--;
            }
            plot(px,py,color);
            coord[index] = px | (long)py << 16;
            index++;
        }
    }
}
if (sy0 + sdy == 0)
    index--;
qsort(coord,index,sizeof(coord[0]),(int(*)
    (const void *, const void *))sort_function);
for (i=0; i<index; i++)
{
    xs = min(639,(max(0,(int)coord[i])));
    xe = min(639,(max(0,(int)coord[i + 1])));
    ys = min(639,(max(0,(int)(coord[i] >> 16))));
    ye = min(639,(max(0,(int)(coord[i + 1] >> 16))));
    if ((ys == ye) && (toggle == 0))
    {
        fillLine(xs, xe, ys, color);
        toggle = 1;
    }
    else
        toggle = 0;
}
}
```

Drawing a Polygon with Passed Parameters

The first function that we are going to look at is *drawPoly*. This function passes all the pairs of coordinate values in the call to the function. Since there are a variable number of these, we have to make use of some C functions that are specifically designed for cases where the number of variables passed is not known in advance. The fixed parameters are passed to the function at the beginning of the parameter list. In this case, there is just one, the color. This is followed by a comma and then three dots, which indicate that there may follow any number of parameters. At the beginning of the function, we define a parameter array called *coord* to be of type *va_list*. This type is mandatory for receiving the variable length parameter list. Next, to prepare for reading the list, we run *va_start*. This function has two parameters, first the parameter list that we just defined and second the name of the last fixed parameter that is passed to the function *drawPoly* before the variable length parameter list begins. In order to get each member of the variable length list transferred to the *drawPoly* function, we have to successively run the function *va_arg* for each parameter in the list. Its two parameters are the name of the list (*coord*) and the type of the parameter passed (for this function always an integer). You'll note that the procedure just described has no way of knowing when to stop getting parameter values. It's up to you to tell it when to stop; if it keeps on going, the results will be disastrous. For this function, we have set up a *while* loop that keeps reading coordinate pairs and storing them in the *xpoint* and *ypoint* arrays until either 150 pairs of coordinates have been stored (which is all we have room for) or until one of the coordinates has a value less than -500. Since we are operating in the system coordinate space, which can have x values of -320 to +320 and y values of -240 to +240, there can never be a coordinate that has an actual value of less than -500. Thus when we deliberately insert such a value into the list of parameters being passed, it is a sign to stop. The function then runs *va_end* to end the variable parameter list process. If this function isn't run, weird results can occur in the rest of your program. We now have a couple arrays with the coordinate values in them. To complete these arrays, we set the next member of the array to be the same as the first member, so that the final line that is drawn will close the figure. Now we are ready to begin a *for* loop that calls *drawLine* to draw a line between each successive pair of coordinates in the selected color. When this loop is complete, we have drawn our enclosed regular polygon.

Drawing a Polygon with a Parameter Array

While the polygon drawing procedure that was just described works very well with a reasonably small number of points, if we have a polygon made up of a large number of line segments, passing all of their coordinates within the function call gets to be a rather cumbersome process. Hence, we have another variation of the polygon drawing function called *draw2Poly*, which passes only the address of a coordinate array and then works on the array members within the function. This function is very simple and elegant. It first scans the array of coordinate points to find one that is less than -500, indicating the end of the array. Then it enters a *for* loop that draws each line segment, with the proper two points from the coordinate array being passed to the line drawing function at each iteration of the loop. For the last iteration, the loop uses the last pair of points in the array as the beginning of the line segment and the first set of points in the array as the end of the line segment, thereby closing the bounded surface.

Flood Filling a Bounded Area

Next we are going to look at a program that starts at any point within an area on the screen which is bounded with a given color and fills the entire area with that color. It can not only be used for filling regular polygons, but also for filling circles and many other types of closed curves. This function is rather slow, so that often you will be able to use a much faster function with better results. However, there are many times when nothing but this function will do. In particular, we may have several crossing lines that define a bounded area we want to fill. However, we don't know the exact coordinates of the crossing points, so we can't define an irregular polygon to which we can apply the fast filling functions. However, the flood filling technique will fill such an area just fine. Flood filling is difficult, because an irregular polygon may have some strange areas that are off the beaten track, which may easily get lost as the flood fill takes place and never get filled at all. The algorithm used here is based on one in Andrew Glassner's book *Graphics Gems*. It works just fine as long as you choose a starting point that is actually within the bounded area and as long as you make sure there are no gaps in the bounding line. It begins by putting the beginning point and one on the next line onto a stack. It then begins processing the stack, reading pixels from the screen to the right of the selected point and redrawing them in the designated color until a pixel of that color is read, indicating that the boundary has been reached. It then repeats this process to the right of the selected starting point. While it is doing this, it is storing the coordinates of appropriate points above and below the current line on the stack, to assure that no part of the figure is overlooked. When one line is finished, the function then processes the next stack entry and repeats this process until the stack is empty.

Filling Triangles and Quadrilaterals

We now turn our attention to fast methods of filling polygons. We need to consider two special cases first. These are filling triangles and filling quadrilaterals. These are used fairly frequently in building up representations of three-dimensional figures from a number of facets. Since with a maximum of four sides, a figure can have no funny dips or spurs that have to be considered, we can come up with some very fast and straightforward filling methods. The function *fillTriangle* is used for fast filling triangles. It is passed three pairs of coordinates, one pair for each vertex of the triangle, and also the desired fill color. The heart of this function is an array called *coord* that consists of two members for each y coordinate (line) position. The first member is the minimum x value for that line and the second is the maximum x value. With a triangle, there can be no more than two edges passing through this line. The minimum (left-hand values are all initialized to 800 and the maximum (right) values are all initialized to 0. We also have the parameters *minrow* and *maxrow,* which identify the minimum and maximum rows, respectively, that the triangle occupies. The function next converts the three vertices from system coordinates to screen coordinates and then puts the converted values into a pair of arrays. The function then begins a *for* loop that iterates once for each of the three lines which make up the boundary of the triangle. For each iteration of the loop, the function performs the same procedure that was described in Chapter 7 to draw a line. However when each new point on the line is calculated, it is not plotted to the screen. Instead, it is compared with the minimum and maximum values of x that are in the y members of the *coord* array. If the point's x value is smaller than the minimum, it is used to replace the minimum; if it is larger than the maximum, it is used to replace the maximum. The y value is compared with *minrow* and *maxrow* and if it is smaller than the minimum, it is used to replace *minrow* or if it is larger than the maximum it is used to replace *maxrow*. At the end of the three iterations of the *for* loop, *minrow* contains the minimum row that is intersected by the triangle and *maxrow* contains the maximum row that is intersected by the triangle. The values of the *coord* array for the range of row values between minimum and maximum contain the minimum and maximum *x* values for each row. The function now goes through another *for* loop. This loop iterates once for each *y* value from minimum to maximum. At each iteration it uses the fast horizontal line drawing function *fillLine* to draw a line from the left-hand to right-hand values of *x* for that particular value of *y*. The result is a very fast fill of the designated triangle.

The function *fillQuad* is used to draw a fast quadrilateral. The function is passed the coordinates of four pairs of points that make up the quadralateral and the designated color. You could use the same procedure that is used for the triangle to compute the four line segments of the triangle and store the minimum and maximum values in an array, but it is nearly as fast to simply divide the quadralateral into two triangles and call *fillTriangle* to fill each one of them, so that is what we have done here.

Filling an Irregular Polygon with Passed Parameters

We're now going to consider a much more general function for filling polygons. This function is called *fillPoly*. It is passed a color and a variable number of coordinate pairs. It begins just like the corresponding function for drawing a polygon with an undetermined number of coordinate pairs, which was described earlier. After setting up the array of points to define a closed curve, we enter a *for* loop to calculate all of the necessary line segments just as with the analogous drawing function. Instead of plotting each point that is determined, we're going to put the data into an array. We can't do like we did for the triangle and put beginning and ending *x* values into an array member whose other index is the *y* coordinate, however, because we may have a number of *x* values for each *y* coordinate. We don't know how many values of *x* there are for each *y* or which are the beginnings and which the ends of line segments. Therefore, at this point, we are going to have one member of an array for each coordinate pair that is computed. It is going to consist of a single number so that we can sort with each coordinate as an entity. We do this by using a long integer, which has the *y* value as its 16 most significant bits and the *x* value as its 16 least significant bits. When the loop has finished computing all of these array values for every line segment that makes up a polygon, we use Turbo C++'s *qsort* function (or its equivalent) to put all these array members in order. Because of the way that each array member was created, the list is sorted on y first and then on x. Observe that the sorting function requires that you create your own function to actually make the comparison between two members of the array and pass back a result that indicates which is larger. After the array is sorted, we start with the first (left-hand) x value for the lowest line and draw a fast line to the next x value for that line. We then start with the next x value for the same line (if there is one) and draw to the next x value. We then repeat the process for the next line up, and so forth, until we have used every coordinate pair that was inserted into the array. Note that, for each coordinate pair, we first assure that neither coordinate exceeds the bounds of the display.

Filling an Irregular Polygon using a Coordinate Array

As with the case of the polygon drawing functions, the preceding method of filling a polygon gets cumbersome if there is a large number of coordinate pairs. Therefore, as with the polygon drawing functions, we have another version that passes only the address of an array of coordinate pairs. As with the previous function, this function enters a *for* loop that computes the points along each line segment and stores these values in an array if the proper comparison dictates that this should be done. At the beginning of each iteration of the loop, the beginning and ending points of the line segment are extracted from the proper members of the coordinate array whose address was passed to the function. At the final iteration of the loop, the last pair of coordinates is the beginning of the line segment and the very first pair of coordinates is used for the end of the line segment, thereby closing the boundary of the polygon. As with the previous function, when this loop is complete, the stored coordinate values are sorted and then fast horizontal lines drawn between them as appropriate to fill the polygon.

For either of these functions for filling irregular polygons, you should note that they work correctly only if the bounding line segments form a continuous boundary that does not cross itself. The responsibility for assuring that the lines do not cross is up to you, the programmer; the function provides no tests or safeguards to prevent this. If you want to experiment with crossing lines, you can do so. What usually happens is that some area of the polygon does not get filled. No one can say for sure what will happen for any particular case, however, so you're on your own when lines start crossing.

The *polytest.c* Program

The *polytest.c* program provides a number of examples of how the polygon drawing and filling programs are used. The program begins by using *set_screen* to make a background of sky and grass. It then draws the outlines of three irregular polygons reminiscent of dinosaurs, using the passed parameter function *drawPoly*. It then uses the flood fill function *fill* to fill each of these polygons. The result is shown in Plate 18. Next the program draws three bars with the fast horizontal drawing function *fillLine* and superimposes two triangles on them with *fillTriangle*. The program next fills two quadrilaterals using the *fillQuad* function. Next, the program fills the dinosaur figures using coordinates from an array and the function *fill2Poly*. The program then uses the same coordinate arrays to draw the outlines of the figures using *draw2Poly*. The same figures are then drawn and filled with passed parameters using *fillPoly*. The program then draws and fills a map of Africa using coordinates from an array and the function *fill2Poly*. This map is shown in Plate 19. Finally, the program uses a variety of functions that have previously been described to create the New Jerusalem figure. This figure, which is illustrated in Plate 20, is supposed to be associated with the New Jerusalem as described in the bible in the book of Revelations, because it combines the mystical numbers 7 and 12 that are used in the Revelations descriptions.

Drawing and Filling Rounded Rectangles

The rectangle with rounded corners makes a pleasing background on which to display menus or similar alphanumeric messages while in a graphics mode. By judicious combination of the functions that have already been developed in previous chapters, we can produce functions that will draw or fill rounded rectangles. The functions, together with a program to use them, are in the file *rndrect.c*, which is listed in Figure 17-1. The program uses display mode 12H (640 x 480 pixels x 16 colors), which works only on the VGA. The parameters that describe the bounds and radius of the rounded rectangles are in system coordinates, where x can vary from -320 to +319 and y from -240 to -239. If you are changing to another display mode, you'll have to modify various places in the functions where conversion from the system coordinates to display screen coordinates takes place.

Figure 17.1. Listing of the rndrect.c Program

```
/*
```

```
        rndrect = Program to test drawing and filling of
                        rounded rectangles

               By Roger T. Stevens   10-20-91
```

```
*/
```

```c
#include <stdio.h>
#include <stdlib.h>
#include <math.h>
#include <dos.h>
#include <conio.h>

void cls(char colors);
void drawRndRect(int xl, int yt, int xr, int yb, int r, int
    color);
void drawVertLine(int x, int ystart, int yend, int color);
void fillRndRect(int xl, int yt, int xr, int yb, int r, int
    color);
void fillLine(int x_one, int x_two, int y, int color);
void plots(int x, int y, int color);
void setMode(int mode);

#define convert(x,y)    {x += 320;  y = 240 - y;}

int xres=640, yres=480;
int color, angle;
int LINEWIDTH=1;
unsigned char OPERATOR = 0x00;
```

```
/*
```

```
                        MAIN PROGRAM
```

```
*/
```

(continued)

```
main()
{
    int i,j,x_cen, y_cen, radius,ran_param;

    setMode(0x12);
    fillRndRect (-320,240,319,-239,30,13);
    getch();
    LINEWIDTH = 3;
    drawRndRect (-310,230,310,-230,30,15);
    getch();
    fillRndRect (-300,210,-120,-210,30,9);
    fillRndRect (-90,210,90,-210,30,10);
    fillRndRect (120,210,300,-210,30,14);
    getch();
}

/*
```

```
            setMode() = Sets the video mode
```

```
*/

void setMode(int mode)
{
    union REGS reg;

    reg.h.ah = 0;
    reg.h.al = mode;
    int86 (0x10,&reg,&reg);
}

/*
```

```
    plots() = Plots a point on the screen at designated
          system coordinates using selected color
```

```
*/
```

(continued)

```
void plots(int x, int y, int color)
{
    unsigned int offset;
    int dummy,mask,page;
    char far * mem_address;

    convert(x,y);
    if ((x >= xres) || (x < 0) || (y >= yres) || (y < 0))
        return;
    offset = (long)y * xres/8L + ((long)x / 8L);
    mem_address = (char far *) 0xA0000000L + offset;
    mask = 0x8000 >> (x % 8);
    outport(0x3CE,mask | 0x08);
    outport(0x3CE,0x0205);
    dummy = *mem_address;
    *mem_address = color;
    outport(0x3CE,0xFF08);
    outport(0x3CE,0x0005);
}

/*
```

```
drawRndRect() = Draws a rounded rectangle with top left
and bottom right corners specified, using line width in
                pixels specified by LINEWIDTH.
```

```
*/

void drawRndRect(int xl, int yt, int xr, int yb, int r, int
    color)
{
    int i, row, col, px, py;
    long int sum;

    r += LINEWIDTH /2;
    for (i=yb; i<=yb+LINEWIDTH; i++)
        fillLine(xl + r,xr - r,i,color);
    for (i=yt-LINEWIDTH; i<=yt; i++)
        fillLine(xl + r,xr - r,i,color);
    drawVertLine(xl+320,240 - (yt - r),240 - (yb + r),color);
```

(continued)

```
drawVertLine(xr+320,240 - (yt - r),240 - (yb + r),color);
xl += r;
xr -= r;
yt -= r;
yb += r;
py = r<<1;
px = 0;
sum = -(r<<1);
while (px <= py)
{
    if ( !(px & 1))
    {
        col = xl - (px>>1);
        row = yt + (py>>1);
        for (i=0; i<LINEWIDTH; i++)
            plots(col,row-i,color);
        row = yb  - (py>>1);
        for (i=0; i<LINEWIDTH; i++)
            plots(col,row+i,color);
        col = xr + (px>>1);
        for (i=0; i<LINEWIDTH; i++)
            plots(col,row+i,color);
        row = yt + (py>>1);
        for (i=0; i<LINEWIDTH; i++)
            plots(col,row-i,color);
        col = xr + (py>>1);
        row = yb - (px>>1);
        for (i=0; i<LINEWIDTH; i++)
            plots(col-i,row,color);
        row = yt + (px>>1);
        for (i=0; i<LINEWIDTH; i++)
            plots(col-i,row,color);
        col = xl - (py>>1);
        for (i=0; i<LINEWIDTH; i++)
            plots(col+i,row,color);
        row = yb - (px>>1);
        for (i=0; i<LINEWIDTH; i++)
            plots(col+i,row,color);
    }
    sum +=px++;
    if (sum >= 0)
```

(continued)

```
sum-=py--;

        }
    }

    /*
```

```
  fillRndRect() = Fills a rounded rectangle when top left
       and bottom right corners, radius and color are
                        specified
```

```
    */

    void fillRndRect(int xl, int yt, int xr, int yb, int r, int
        color)
    {
        int i, row, col_start, col_end, t_row, t_col, px, py;
        long int sum;

        yt -= r;
        yb += r;
        for (i=yb; i<=yt; i++)
            fillLine(xl,xr,i,color);
        xl += r;
        xr -= r;
        py = r<<1;
        px = 0;
        sum = -(r<<1);
        while (px <= py)
        {
            if ( !(px & 1))
            {
                col_start = xl - (px>>1);
                col_end = xr + (px>>1);
                row = yt + (py>>1);
                fillLine(col_start, col_end, row, color);
                col_start = xl - (py>>1);
                col_end = xr + (py>>1);
                row = yt + (px>>1);
                fillLine(col_start, col_end, row, color);
```

(continued)

```
            col_start = xl - (px>>1);
            col_end = xr + (px>>1);
            row = yb - (py>>1);
            fillLine(col_start, col_end, row, color);
            col_start = xl - (py>>1);
            col_end = xr + (py>>1);
            row = yb - (px>>1);
            fillLine(col_start, col_end, row, color);
        }
        sum +=px++;
        if (sum >= 0)
            sum-=py--;
    }
}


/*
```

```
            fillLine() = Fast fills a horizontal line
```

```
*/

void fillLine(int x_one, int x_two, int y, int color)
{
    char color_buffer[100];
    int dummy, loop, i, x1, x2;
    int length, offset1, offset2;
    int srcseg, srcoff, destseg, destoff;
    long int no_of_bytes;
    unsigned int mask;
    char far *base1;
    char far *base2;

    struct SREGS segregs;

    x_one += 320;
    if (x_one < 0)
        x_one = 0;
    if (x_one > xres)
        return;
    x_two += 320;
```

(continued)

```
if (x_two >= xres)
    x_two = xres - 1;
if (x_two < 0)
    return;
y = 240 - y;
segread(&segregs);
srcseg = segregs.ds;
srcoff = (int) color_buffer;
x1 = min(x_one, x_two);
x2 = max(x_one, x_two);
offset1 = x1 % 8;
offset2 = x2 % 8;
base1 = (char far *)(0xA0000000L + ((long)y * 80L +
    ((long)x1 / 8L)));
base2 = (char far *)(0xA0000000L + ((long)y * 80L +
    ((long)x2 / 8L)));
no_of_bytes = abs(base2 - base1);
length = ((x2 - x1) - ((8-offset1) + (offset2))) / 8L;
mask = 0xFF00 << (7 - offset2);
if (!no_of_bytes)
    mask &= (0xFF00 >> offset1) & 0xFF00;
dummy = *base2;
outport(0x3CE, mask | 0x08);
outport(0x3CE, 0x0205);
*base2 = color;
if (no_of_bytes)
{
    mask = (0xFF00 >> offset1) & 0xFF00;
    outport(0x3CE, mask | 0x08);
    dummy = *base1;
    *base1 = color;
    mask = 0xFF00;
    outport(0x3CE, mask | 0x08);
    memset(color_buffer,color,length);
    destseg = 0xA000;
    destoff = ((long) y * 80L + ((long)x1 /8L)) + 1;
    movedata(srcseg, srcoff, destseg, destoff, length);
}
outport(0x3CE, 0xFF08);
outport(0x3CE, 0x0005);
}
```

(continued)

```
/*

    drawVertLine = Draws a vertical line on the
        screen between two designated points
            using a selected color and of
            width LINEWIDTH using 16 color
                  display modes.

*/

void drawVertLine(int x, int ystart, int yend, int color)
{
    #define graph_out(index,val)  {outp(0x3CE,index);\
                        outp(0x3CF,val);}

    int dummy, i, mask, y;
    char far * address;

    graph_out(5,2);
    for (i=x-LINEWIDTH/2; i<=x+LINEWIDTH/2; i++)
    {
        mask = 0x80 >> (i % 8);
        graph_out(8,mask);

        for (y=ystart; y<=yend; y++)
        {
            address = (char far *) 0xA0000000L + (long)y *
                xres/8L + ((long)i / 8L);
            dummy = *address;
            *address = color;
        }
    }
    graph_out(8,0xFF);
    graph_out(5,0);
}
```

Drawing a Rounded Rectangle

The function *drawRndRect* draws a rounded rectangle whose lines
have the line width that is placed in the parameter *LINEWIDTH*. The

parameters passed to this function are the coordinates of the top left-hand corner of the unrounded rectangle, the coordinates of the bottom right-hand corner, the color and the radius of the rounding circle. The function first uses the *fillLine* function to draw the straight horizontal portions of the rounded rectangle. Two *for* loops are used to draw enough adjacent straight lines to make the lines as wide as specified by *LINEWIDTH*. Next the function *drawVertLine* is used to draw the vertical straight line portions. This function includes the capability to draw the lines of the proper width, but it does not include conversion to display screen coordinates, so this has to be done before the coordinates are passed to the function. After the straight line portions have been drawn, we enter a part of the function that is just like the function for drawing wide line circles described in Chapter 13. However, instead of drawing eight 45 degree arcs around the center coordinates of a circle, we draw eight arcs that are offset to fit with the straight line portions of the rectangle to supply the rounded corners. Before entering this section of the function, the coordinates of the two corners of the unrounded rectangle are modified, using the rounding circle radius, to locate them properly to provide the correct arc offsets. When this circle portion of the function is complete, we have a completed rounded rectangle drawn on the screen.

Filling a Rounded Rectangle

The function *fillRndRect* is used to create a filled rounded rectangle. It turns out to be a little simpler than the function for drawing a rounded rectangle. It begins by modifying the values of y for the top and bottom corners so that they mark the top and bottom of the straight vertical portions of the rounded rectangle. Then a *for* loop is used to fill all lines between these two limits using *fillLine*, the fast horizontal line drawing function. Next we use a circle drawing procedure similar to that used for the previous function for drawing rounded rectangles. However, instead of simply plotting the points of the eight arcs, after properly displacing them, we pair up the arcs at the left and right sides of the rounded rectangle and use *fillLine* to draw a fast horizontal line between each matching pair of x values which have a common y coordinate. The result, when this procedure finishes, is a completely filled rounded rectangle.

The *rndrect.c* Program

This program gives a short demonstration of rounded rectangles. The program first fills a rounded rectangle that occupies the full screen. When you enter a character, the program continues by drawing a three pixel wide rounded rectangle inside and just a little smaller than the previous filled rectangle. Next, the program fills three small rounded rectangles withing the bounds of the rectangle just drawn. The resulting display is shown in Plate 21.

Chapter 18

Smooth Curves with Bezier and B-Spline Functions

When you want to draw a smooth curve of some unusual shape that can't be represented by a circle or ellipse or a standard conic section, you may find yourself resorting to representing the curve by a large number of short straight line segments. This is not a very good solution, however, because it requires specifying a large number of points for line beginnings and endings and because it is often difficult to get the curve to look as smooth as you would like to have it. Fortunately, there are some methods for specifying a smooth curve of a desired shape through the use of a limited number of control points. The resulting curves are called *Bezier* and *B-spline* curves. The Bezier curve was developed in the early 1970's by Pierre Bezier, who was attempting to use computers to design automobiles. The B-spline curve is similar, but uses a different weighting of the control points, so that the shape of the curve is different. In this chapter we're only going to look at Bezier and B-spline curves in two dimensions, but the same techniques can easily be extended to three dimensions to generate pleasingly curved three-dimensional shapes such as automobile hoods and fenders.

One of the primary uses of Bezier curves is in the design of type fonts for reproducing text on a computer printer. Adobe and other companies that sell a variety of type font software, rely heavily on Bezier curves to define the shape of each character in each different type face. One of our examples in this chapter will be a typical letter from a type face. You shouldn't expect this simple example to be quite as polished as the type faces from Adobe, but it will give you some idea of how the technique is used. A number of different functions for generating Bezier and B-spline curves are going to be discussed. They are all included in a demonstration program called *Bezier.c*, which provides a lot of examples of how they are used. Plate 22 shows variations of the letter *B*, produced with Bezier curves, and Plate 23 shows an example of a number of control points connected by straight lines and then used as control points to draw Bezier and B-spline curves. This latter plate gives you a good idea of the differences between the Bezier curve and a B-spline curve using the same controls.

Figure 18-1. Listing of the Bezier.c Program.

```
/*

    bezier = Program to draw Bezier and B-Spline curves

              By Roger T. Stevens   11-13-91

*/

#include <dos.h>
#include <graphics.h>
#include <conio.h>
#include <string.h>
#include <stdio.h>
#include <stdlib.h>
#include <math.h>
#include <stdarg.h>
#include <time.h>

int B_level = 0;

typedef struct
{
    float x,y;
} XY;
```

(continued)

```
typedef struct
{
    XY a, b, c, d;
} box;

void cls(int color);
void draw_alpha(int x,int y, int last, box letter[], float
    size, int color);
void draw_bezier1(box *bcurve,int color);
int draw_bezier2(box *bcurve, int color);
void draw_bezier3(box *bcurve, int color);
void drawBezier(int color,...);
void draw_bspline(box *bcurve, int color);
void drawBspline(int color,...);
void drawLine8(int xe, int ye, int color);
void fill (int x, int y, int color);
void plot16(int x, int y, int color);
void print_usage(void);
char readPixel(int x, int y);
void setMode(int mode);

int xres=640, yres = 480;
int LINEWIDTH;
int dummy1,dummy2,X, Y, x, y, size, color;
char type = NULL;
unsigned long int PATTERN=0xFFFFFFFF;
unsigned long int style[8] = { 0xFFFFFFFF, 0xC0C0C0C0,
    0xFF00FF00, 0xFFF0FFF0, 0xF000F000, 0xFFFF0000,
    0xFFFFF0F0, 0xFFF0F0F0};

void main(void)
{
    box upper_b[24] = { 0,0,450,0,450,0,0,0,
        0,0,0,20,0,20,0,0,
        0,20,80,20,100,30,100,80,
        100,70,100,600,100,600,100,70,
        100,600,100,640,70,650,0,650,
        0,650,0,670,0,670,0,650,
        0,670,450,670,450,670,0,670,
        400,670,600,670,600,360,450,360,
        450,360,700,360,700,0,400,0,
```

(continued)

```
                210,320,400,320,400,320,210,320,
                210,320,210,120,210,120,210,320,
                210,380,350,380,350,380,210,380,
                210,380,210,550,210,550,210,380,
                400,320,570,320,570,50,380,50,
                340,630,540,630,540,380,350,380,
                400,50,255,50,255,50,400,50,
                350,630,250,630,250,630,350,630,
                210,120,210,60,220,50,310,50,
                210,550,210,620,220,630,280,630,
                0,0,150,30,0,0,0,0
        };
    box bline;
    int i;

    randomize();
    for (;;)
    {
        setMode(3);
        printf("\nSelect one rendering method:");
        printf("\n    Literal (L)\n    Bernstein blend");
        printf(" (B)");
        printf("\n    deCasteljau (D)\n    B spline (S)");
        printf("\n    Quit (Q)    ");
        while(type != 'D' && type != 'L' && type != 'B' &&
            type != 'S' && type != 'Q')
        {
            scanf("%c",&type);
            type = toupper(type);
        }
        setMode(0x12);
        if (type == 'Q')
            break;
        draw_alpha(0,170,19,upper_b,200.0,13);
        draw_alpha(230,190,19,upper_b,175.0,14);
        draw_alpha(425,210,19,upper_b,140.0,9);
        draw_alpha(520,290,19,upper_b,95.0,15);
        draw_alpha(410,330,19,upper_b,65.0,11);
        draw_alpha(320,370,19,upper_b,48.0,12);
        getch();
        cls(0);
```

(continued)

```
        color = 1;
        for (i=0; i<50; i++)
        {
            x = random(560) + 48;
            y = random(400) + 48;
            size = min(640 - x,x);
            size = min(480-y,size);
            size = min(size,y);
            size = random(size-48) + 48;
            draw_alpha(x,y,19,upper_b,size,color++);
            if (color == 16)
                color = 1;
        }
        getch();
        type = 0;
    }
    cls(0);
    LINEWIDTH = 1;
    PATTERN = style[1];
    X = 270;
    Y = 260;
    drawLine8(270,240,3);
    drawLine8(320,240,3);
    drawLine8(320,360,3);
    drawLine8(160,360,3);
    drawLine8(120,40,3);
    drawLine8(410,90,3);
    drawLine8(380,200,3);
    drawLine8(520,300,3);
    drawLine8(580,210,3);
    PATTERN = style[0];
    drawBezier(14,270,260,270,240,320,240,320,360,160,
        360,120,40,410,90,380,200,520,300,580,210,-999);
    getch();
    cls(0);
    PATTERN = style[1];
    X = 40;
    Y = 265;
    drawLine8(20,20,3);
    drawLine8(240,30,3);
    drawLine8(280,265,3);
```

(continued)

505

```
drawLine8(480,265,3);
drawLine8(620,265,5);
drawLine8(620,50,5);
drawLine8(360,30,5);
drawLine8(150,460,5);
PATTERN = style[0];
drawBezier(10,40,265,20,20,240,30,280,265,480,265,
    -999);
drawBezier(12,480,265,620,265,620,50,360,30,150,460,
    -999);
getch();
cls(0);
PATTERN = style[1];
X = 70;
Y = 240;
drawLine8(100,40,3);
drawLine8(140,40,3);
drawLine8(180,180,3);
drawLine8(220,270,3);
drawLine8(250,250,3);
drawLine8(300,32,3);
drawLine8(330,65,3);
drawLine8(380,370,3);
drawLine8(400,320,3);
drawLine8(420,115,3);
drawLine8(430,135,3);
drawLine8(445,55,3);
drawLine8(460,80,3);
drawLine8(490,440,3);
drawLine8(510,410,3);
drawLine8(540,300,3);
drawLine8(580,220,3);
PATTERN = style[0];
drawBspline(14,70,240,100,40,140,40,180,180,220,270,
    250,250,300,32,330,65,380,370,400,320,420,115,
    430,135,445,55,460,80,490,440,510,410,540,300,
    580,220,-999);
drawBezier(10,70,240,100,40,140,40,180,180,220,270,
    250,250,300,32,330,65,380,370,400,320,420,115,
    430,135,445,55,460,80,490,440,510,410,540,300,
    580,220,-999);
```

(continued)

```
        getch();
        cls(0);
        PATTERN = style[1];
        X = 100;
        Y = 140;
        drawLine8(100,340,15);
        drawLine8(540,340,15);
        drawLine8(540,140,15);
        drawLine8(100,140,15);
        PATTERN = style[0];
        drawBspline(14,100,140,100,340,540,340,540,140,-999);
        drawBezier(13,100,140,100,340,540,340,540,140,-999);
        getch();
        setMode(3);
}

/*

    cls() = Clears the screen to a designated color

*/

void cls(int color)
{
        union REGS reg;

        reg.x.ax = 0x0600;
        reg.x.cx = 0;
        reg.x.dx = 0x3284;
        reg.h.bh = color;
        int86(0x10,&reg,&reg);
}

/*

    drawAlpha() = Draws an alphanumeric character using
                  Bezier or B-Spline curves

*/
```

(continued)

507

```
void draw_alpha(int x, int y, int last, box letter[],
    float size, int color)
{
    int i;
    box bline;
    float scale;

    scale = size / 1000.0;
    for (i=0; i<last; i++)
    {
        bline.a.x = x + (letter[i].a.x * scale);
        bline.a.y = y - (letter[i].a.y * scale);
        bline.b.x = x + (letter[i].b.x * scale);
        bline.b.y = y - (letter[i].b.y * scale);
        bline.c.x = x + (letter[i].c.x * scale);
        bline.c.y = y - (letter[i].c.y * scale);
        bline.d.x = x + (letter[i].d.x * scale);
        bline.d.y = y - (letter[i].d.y * scale);
        if ((bline.a.x == bline.d.x) && (bline.a.y ==
            bline.d.y) && (bline.b.x == bline.c.x) &&
            (bline.b.y == bline.c.y))
        {
            X = bline.d.x;
            Y = bline.d.y;
            drawLine8(bline.b.x,bline.b.y,color);
        }
        else
        {
            switch(type)
            {
                case 'L':
                    draw_bezier1(&bline, color);
                    break;
                case 'D':
                    draw_bezier2(&bline, color);
                    break;
                case 'B':
                    draw_bezier3(&bline, color);
                    break;
                case 'S':
                    draw_bspline(&bline, color);
```

(continued)

```
                }
            }
        }
        fill((int) (x + letter[i].b.x * scale),
            (int) (y - letter[i].b.y * scale), color);
}

/*
```

```
  draw_bezier1 = Draws Bezier curve using literal method
```

```
*/

void draw_bezier1(box *bcurve, int color)
{
    float x,y;
    float tm;
    float t;

    X = (int)bcurve->a.x;
    Y = (int)bcurve->a.y;
    for (t=0.0; t<=1.0; t+= 0.01)
    {
        x=(1-t) * (1-t) * (1-t) * bcurve->a.x + 3 * t *
            (t-1) * (t-1) * bcurve->b.x + 3 *t *t * (1-t)
            * bcurve->c.x + t * t * t * bcurve->d.x;
        y=(1-t) * (1-t) * (1-t) * bcurve->a.y + 3 * t *
            (t-1) * (t-1) * bcurve->b.y + 3 *t *t * (1-t)
            * bcurve->c.y + t * t * t * bcurve->d.y;
        drawLine8(x,y,color);
    }
}

/*
```

```
  draw_bezier2() = Draws Bezier curve using deCasteljau
  method
```

```
*/
```

(continued)

```
int draw_bezier2(box *bcurve, int color)
{
    extern int B_level;
    box box1, box2;
    XY a0, a1, a2, a3, b1, b2, c1, d0;

    if (B_level >= 3)
    {
        X = bcurve->a.x;
        Y = bcurve->a.y;
        drawLine8(bcurve->b.x,bcurve->b.y, color);
        drawLine8(bcurve->c.x,bcurve->c.y, color);
        drawLine8(bcurve->d.x,bcurve->d.y, color);
        return(0);
    }
    B_level++;
    box1.a.x = bcurve->a.x;
    box1.a.y = bcurve->a.y;
    box2.d.x = bcurve->d.x;
    box2.d.y = bcurve->d.y;
    box1.b.x = (box1.a.x + bcurve->b.x) /2;
    box1.b.y = (box1.a.y + bcurve->b.y) /2;
    b1.x = (bcurve->b.x + bcurve->c.x) /2;
    b1.y = (bcurve->b.y + bcurve->c.y) /2;
    box2.c.x = (bcurve->c.x + bcurve->d.x) /2;
    box2.c.y = (bcurve->c.y + bcurve->d.y) /2;
    box1.c.x = (box1.b.x + b1.x) /2;
    box1.c.y = (box1.b.y + b1.y) /2;
    box2.b.x = (b1.x + box2.c.x) /2;
    box2.b.y = (b1.y + box2.c.y) /2;
    box1.d.x = (box1.c.x + box2.b.x) /2;
    box1.d.y = (box1.c.y + box2.b.y) /2;
    box1.d.x = box1.d.x;
    box1.d.y = box1.d.y;
    box2.a.x = box1.d.x;
    box2.a.y = box1.d.y;
    draw_bezier2(&box1,color);
    draw_bezier2(&box2,color);
    B_level--;
    return(0);
}
```

(continued)

```
/*
┌─────────────────────────────────────────────────────────────┐
│ ┌─────────────────────────────────────────────────────────┐ │
│ │                                                         │ │
│ │   draw_bezier3() = Draws Bezier curve using Bernstein   │ │
│ │                       polynomials                       │ │
│ │                                                         │ │
│ └─────────────────────────────────────────────────────────┘ │
└─────────────────────────────────────────────────────────────┘
*/

void draw_bezier3(box *bcurve, int color)
{
    int i,j,k;
    float x,y,b,t,xpoint[4],ypoint[4];

    xpoint[0] = bcurve->a.x;
    ypoint[0] = bcurve->a.y;
    xpoint[1] = bcurve->b.x;
    ypoint[1] = bcurve->b.y;
    xpoint[2] = bcurve->c.x;
    ypoint[2] = bcurve->c.y;
    xpoint[3] = bcurve->d.x;
    ypoint[3] = bcurve->d.y;
    X = xpoint[0];
    Y = ypoint[0];
    for (t=0.0; t<=1.0; t+= 0.01)
    {
        x = 0;
        y = 0;
        for (j=0; j<=3; j++)
        {
            b = 1.0;
            for (k=3; k>j; k--)
                b *= k;
            for (k=3-j; k>1; k--)
                b /= k;
            for (i=1; i<=j; i++)
                b *= t;
            for (i=1; i<=3-j; i++)
                b *= (1-t);
            x += xpoint[j]*b;
            y += ypoint[j]*b;
        }
```

(continued)

```
                    drawLine8(x,y,color);
            }
    }

    /*
```

```
      drawBezier() = Draws Bezier curve using Bernstein
                polynomials with multipoint input
```

```
    */

    void drawBezier(int color,...)
    {
            va_list coord;
            int xpoint[20],ypoint[20],i=0,j,k,end;
        float b,t,x,y;

        va_start(coord,color);
        while (((xpoint[i]=va_arg(coord,int)) >= -320) &&
            ((ypoint[i]=va_arg(coord,int)) >= -320) &&
            (i++<=20));
        va_end(coord);
        end = --i;
        X = xpoint[0];
        Y = ypoint[0];
        for (t=0.0; t<=1.0; t+=0.01)
        {
            x = 0;
            y = 0;
            for (j=0; j<=end; j++)
            {
                b = 1.0;
                for (k=end; k>j; k--)
                    b *= k;
                for (k=end-j; k>1; k--)
                    b /= k;
                for (i=1; i<=j; i++)
                    b *= t;
                for (i=1; i<=end-j; i++)
                    b *= (1-t);
```

(continued)

```
              x += xpoint[j]*b;
              y += ypoint[j]*b;
         }
         if (t>0.0)
             drawLine8(x,y,color);
      }
}


/*
```

```
                draw_bspline() = Draws B-Spline curve
```

```
*/

void draw_bspline(box *bcurve, int color)
{
    float x,y;
    float nc1, nc2, nc3, nc4, t;
    int xpoint[7], ypoint[8], i, last;
    xpoint[0] = bcurve->a.x;
    ypoint[0] = bcurve->a.y;
    xpoint[1] = bcurve->a.x;
    ypoint[1] = bcurve->a.y;
    xpoint[2] = bcurve->b.x;
    ypoint[2] = bcurve->b.y;
    xpoint[3] = bcurve->c.x;
    ypoint[3] = bcurve->c.y;
    xpoint[4] = bcurve->d.x;
    ypoint[4] = bcurve->d.y;
    xpoint[5] = xpoint[4];
    ypoint[5] = ypoint[4];
    xpoint[6] = xpoint[4];
    ypoint[6] = ypoint[4];
    X = bcurve->a.x;
    Y = bcurve->a.y;
    last = 4;
    for(i=0; i<last; i++)
    {
        for (t=0.0; t<=1.0; t+=0.01)
        {
```

(continued)

```
              nc1=-(t*t*t/6)+t*t/2-t/2+1.0/6;
              nc2=t*t*t/2-t*t+2.0/3;
              nc3=(-t*t*t+t*t+t)/2 + 1.0/6;
              nc4=t*t*t/6;
              x = (nc1*xpoint[i] + nc2*xpoint[i+1] +
                  nc3*xpoint[i+2] + nc4*xpoint[i+3]);
              y = (nc1*ypoint[i] + nc2*ypoint[i+1] +
                  nc3*ypoint[i+2] + nc4*ypoint[i+3]);
              if ((x!=X) || (y != Y))
                  drawLine8(x,y,color);
          }
      }
}

/*
```

```
+--------------------------------------------------------+
|                                                        |
|  drawBspline() = Draws a B-Spline curve with multipoint|
|                          inputs                        |
|                                                        |
+--------------------------------------------------------+
```

```
*/

void drawBspline(int color,...)
{
    union REGS reg;

    va_list coord;
        int xpoint[24],ypoint[24],j=1,i,x,y;
    float t,nc1,nc2,nc3,nc4;

    va_start(coord,color);
    while (((xpoint[j]=va_arg(coord,int)) >= -320) &&
        ((ypoint[j]=va_arg(coord,int)) >= -320) &&
        (j++<=20));
    va_end(coord);
    xpoint[0]=xpoint[1];
    ypoint[0]=ypoint[1];
    X = xpoint[0];
    Y = ypoint[0];
    xpoint[j]=xpoint[j-1];
    ypoint[j]=ypoint[j-1];
```

(continued)

```
                xpoint[j+1]=xpoint[j];
                ypoint[j+1]=ypoint[j];
                xpoint[j+2]=xpoint[j];
                ypoint[j+2]=ypoint[j];
                for(i=0; i<j; i++)
                {
                    for (t=0.0; t<=1.0; t+=0.01)
                    {
                        nc1=-(t*t*t/6)+t*t/2-t/2+1.0/6;
                        nc2=t*t*t/2-t*t+2.0/3;
                        nc3=(-t*t*t+t*t+t)/2 + 1.0/6;
                        nc4=t*t*t/6;
                        x = (nc1*xpoint[i] + nc2*xpoint[i+1] +
                            nc3*xpoint[i+2] + nc4*xpoint[i+3]);
                        y = (nc1*ypoint[i] + nc2*ypoint[i+1] +
                        nc3*ypoint[i+2] + nc4*ypoint[i+3]);
                        if ((x!=X) || (y != Y))
                            drawLine8(x,y,color);
                    }
                }
        }

        /*
```

```
    drawLine8() = Draws a line of designated width from the
        current position to a designated set of coordinates
            in a specified color in a width specified by
                    LINEWIDTH for 16 color modes.
```

```
        */

        void drawLine8(int xe, int ye, int color)
        {
            extern int LINEWIDTH;
            extern unsigned long int PATTERN;
            extern int X, Y;

            int dx, dy, i, j, temp, x, y, xs, ys, x_sign, y_sign,
                decision;
            unsigned long int mask=0x8000000;;
```

(continued)

```
xs = X;
ys = Y;
X = xe;
Y = ye;
dx = abs(xe - xs);
dy = abs(ye - ys);
if (((dx >= dy) && (xs > xe)) || ((dy > dx) && (ys >
    ye)))
{
    temp = xs;
    xs = xe;
    xe = temp;
    temp = ys;
    ys = ye;
    ye = temp;
}
if ((ye - ys) < 0)
    y_sign = -1;
else
    y_sign = 1;
if ((xe - xs) < 0)
    x_sign = -1;
else
    x_sign = 1;
if (dx >= dy)
{
    for (x=xs,y=ys,decision=0; x<=xe;
        x++,decision+=dy)
    {
        mask = mask !=1 ? mask >> 1 : 0x80000000;
        if (decision>=dx)
        {
            decision -= dx;
            y+= y_sign;
        }
        if (PATTERN & mask)
            for (j=-LINEWIDTH/2; j<=LINEWIDTH/2; j++)
                plot16(x,y+j,color);
    }
}
else
```

(continued)

```
    {
        for (x=xs,y=ys,decision=0; y<=ye;
            y++,decision+=dx)
        {
            mask = mask !=1 ? mask >> 1 : 0x80000000;
            if (decision>=dy)
            {
                decision -= dy;
                x += x_sign;
            }
            if (PATTERN & mask)
                for (j=-LINEWIDTH/2; j<=LINEWIDTH/2; j++)
                    plot16(x+j,y,color);
        }
    }
}

/*
```

```
    fill() = Fills an area bounded by a designated color
         when a point within the area is specified
```

```
*/

void fill (int x, int y, int color)
{
    int dy, sp=0, start, x1, x2;
    struct
    {
        int y, xl, xr, dy;
    } buffer[5000];

    buffer[sp].y = y;
    buffer[sp].xl = x;
    buffer[sp].xr = x;
    buffer[sp++].dy = 1;
    buffer[sp].y = y + 1;
    buffer[sp].xl = x;
    buffer[sp].xr = x;
    buffer[sp++].dy = -1;
```

(continued)

```
        while (sp > 0)
        {
            dy = buffer[--sp].dy;
            y = buffer[sp].y + dy;
            x1 = buffer[sp].xl;
            x2 = buffer[sp].xr;
            x = x1;
            while ((x>=0) && (readPixel(x,y) != color))
                plot16(x--,y,color);
            if (x >= x1)
                goto enter;
            start = x + 1;
            if (start < x1)
            {
                buffer[sp].y = y;
                buffer[sp].xl = start;
                buffer[sp].xr = x1 - 1;
                buffer[sp++].dy = -dy;
            }
            x = x1 + 1;
            do
            {
                while ((x < xres) && (readPixel(x,y) !=
                    color))
                    plot16(x++,y,color);
                buffer[sp].y = y;
                buffer[sp].xl = start;
                buffer[sp].xr = x - 1;
                buffer[sp++].dy = dy;
                if (x > (x2 + 1))
                {
                    buffer[sp].y = y;
                    buffer[sp].xl = x2 + 1;
                    buffer[sp].xr = x - 1;
                    buffer[sp++].dy = -dy;
                }
enter:          x++;
                while ((x <= x2) && (readPixel(x,y) == color))
                    x++;
                start = x;
            }
```

(continued)

```
            while (x <= x2);
        }
    }


    /*
    ┌────────────────────────────────────────────────────┐
    │ ┌──────────────────────────────────────────────────┐ │
    │ │                                                  │ │
    │ │  plot16() = Plots a point on the screen at a designated │ │
    │ │    position using a selected color for 16 color modes  │ │
    │ │                                                  │ │
    │ └──────────────────────────────────────────────────┘ │
    └────────────────────────────────────────────────────┘
    */

    void plot16(int x, int y, int color)
    {
        #define graph_out(index,val)  {outp(0x3CE,index);\
                            outp(0x3CF,val);}

        int dummy,mask;
        char far * address;

        if ((x>=0) && (x<xres) && (y>=0) && (y<yres))
        {
            address = (char far *) 0xA0000000L + (long)y *
                xres/8L + ((long)x / 8L);
            mask = 0x80 >> (x % 8);
            graph_out(8,mask);
            graph_out(5,2);
            dummy = *address;
            *address = color;
            graph_out(5,0);
            graph_out(8,0xFF);
        }
    }


    /*
    ┌────────────────────────────────────────────────────┐
    │ ┌──────────────────────────────────────────────────┐ │
    │ │                                                  │ │
    │ │      readPixel() = Read a pixel from the screen   │ │
    │ │                                                  │ │
    │ └──────────────────────────────────────────────────┘ │
    └────────────────────────────────────────────────────┘
    */
```

(continued)

```
char readPixel(int x, int y)
{
    union REGS reg;

    gotoxy(2,22);
    reg.h.ah = 0x0D;
    reg.x.cx = x;
    reg.x.dx = y;
    reg.h.bh = 0;
    int86 (0x10,&reg,&reg);
    return (reg.h.al);
}

/*
```

```
         setMode() = Sets video mode
```

```
*/

void setMode(int mode)
{
    union REGS reg;

    reg.x.ax = mode;
    int86 (0x10,&reg,&reg);
}
```

Mathematics of the Bezier Curve

The Bezier curve is represented by the general equation

$$p(u) = \sum_{i=0}^{n} a_i \, C_{(n,i)} \, t^{\,i} \, (1 - t)^{n-t}$$

(Equation 18-1)

The coefficient $C_{(n,i)}$ is the binomial coefficient, so equation 18-1 can also be written in the form

$$p(t) = \sum_{i=0}^{n} \frac{n!}{i!(n-i)!} a_i t^i (1 - t)^{n-t}$$

(Equation 18-2)

These two equations give the Bezier curve for any desired value of n, where n is the number of control points that directly influence the shape of the Bezier curve. Once we have selected a value for n, it is possible to write the Bezier curve equation in a third form using matrix notation. For $n = 4$ the matrix form is

$$p(t) = \begin{bmatrix} t^3 & t^2 & t & 1 \end{bmatrix} \begin{bmatrix} -1 & 3 & -3 & 1 \\ 3 & -6 & 3 & 0 \\ -3 & 3 & 0 & 0 \\ 1 & 0 & 0 & 0 \end{bmatrix} \begin{bmatrix} q_1 \\ q_2 \\ q_3 \\ q_4 \end{bmatrix}$$

(Equation 18-3)

The most commonly used form of the Bezier curve is with four control points. Figure 18-2 shows a box along with the resulting Bezier and B-spline curves. The Bezier curve is the one nearest the top of the figure; the B-spline curve is closer to the bottom. The control points are the corners of the box in the order: top left, bottom left, bottom right and top right. Observe how the Bezier curve with four control points has its beginning at the first control points; is tangental with the line between the first and second control points; has its ending at the fourth control point and is tangental to the line between the third and fourth control points. This gives you some idea of how each curve segment will be shaped if you are designing a curved figure out of Bezier curve segments. It's not quite so easy to determine where the center of the curve is located; a little trial and error is necessary.

Figure 18-2. Bezier and B-spline Curves with Four Control Points.

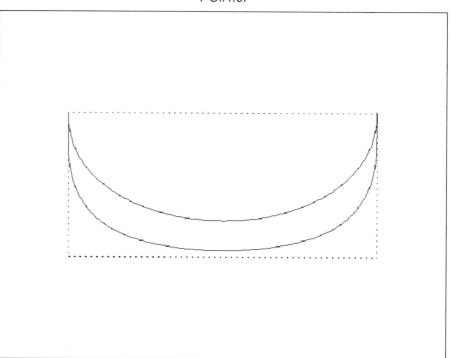

Mathematics of the B-Spline Curve

Like the Bezier curve, the B-spline curve can be controlled by a specified number, n, of points. For a given number of points, the curve can be defined in the same way as the matrix representation of the Bezier curve, except that the weightings of the control points are different. Since these weightings can be varied as desired, there can be a whole family of B-spline curves. Just one of these, for four control points, is represented by the following equation

$$p(t) = \begin{bmatrix} t^3 & t^2 & t & 1 \end{bmatrix} \begin{bmatrix} -1 & 3 & -3 & 1 \\ 3 & -6 & 3 & 0 \\ -3 & 0 & 3 & 0 \\ 1 & 4 & 1 & 0 \end{bmatrix} \begin{bmatrix} q_1 \\ q_2 \\ q_3 \\ q_4 \end{bmatrix}$$

(Equation 18-4)

You will note from Figure 18-2 that the B-spline curve tends to be closer to the control points than the Bezier curve. The first point of the B-spline curve has to be designated twice if the curve is to progress smoothly from the starting point. Furthermore, the B-spline curve does not normally end at the fou/rth control point; to make this behavior occur, you have to designate the fourth control point at least three times.

The Literal Bezier Curve

The function *draw_bezier1*, in the program listing uses a literal rendering of equation 18-1 to generate a Bezier curve in the box defined by four control points. The function uses this equation to compute the x and y coordinates separately for increments of t of 0.01 over the range from 0 to 1. After each increment is calculated, a line is drawn from the previous position to the new one. Because of the very small steps, the line lengths are very short in most cases, so there is no point in trying to draw a line having a pattern (such as a dashed or dotted line), since even though the line drawing function has this capability, each line segment is so short that the pattern just becomes a filled in line. This is true of all of the Bezier and B-spline drawing functions that follow. It is also possible that a line segment may be so short that it begins and ends on the same pixel. If this is true, you don't really have to draw it, so you may want to insert a test to throw out such line segments. This is done in the function *drawBezier* whose description follows.

Bezier Curves with the deCasteljau Method

The deCasteljau method is a geometric technique that gives the same results as the literal method, but is much faster. It is by far the fastest of the three Bezier curve drawing methods described in this chapter. Figure 18-3 illustrates the technique that is used. The process is a recursive one; the figure shows the result after two iterations. One begins by finding the mid-points (a_1, b_1 and c_1) of the first three sides of the box defined by the four control points (a_0, b_0, c_0 and d_0). Next, a line is constructed from the first to the second mid-points and from the second to the third mid-points and the mid-points (a_2 and b_2) of these two lines are found. Then a line is constructed between these two mid-points and its mid-point (a_3) is found. This yields two new boxes, one defined by the points a_0, a_1, a_2 and a_3, and the other by the points a_3, b_2, c_1 and d_0.

We now perform exactly the same procedure for these two new boxes. We can repeat this procedure as many times as we want to achieve the resolution of the curve that we desire. At the last step, instead of further subdividing, we draw the curve along the set of line segments that define the newest set of boxes, as shown by the heavy line in the figure. The function to do all this is *draw_bezier2* in the listing. The function begins by testing whether the recursion level has reached the point at which the figure is to be drawn. If so, three line segments are drawn to connect the corners of the current box. If the final level has not been reached, the level is incremented, the four corners of each of two new boxes are computed and *draw_bezier2* is called recursively to perform the same procedure for each of the two boxes. The level is then decremented to make it correct for the previous level of the function before returning.

Figure 18-3. DeCasteljau Method for Generating Bezier Curve

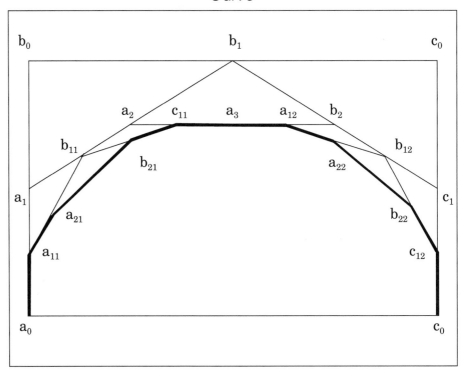

Drawing Bezier Curves with Bernstein Polynomials

The third technique for drawing Bezier curves makes use of what are called *Bernstein polynomials*. It a little faster than the literal method but much slower than the deCasteljau method. It is included in the listing as *draw_bezier3*. Basically the mathematics is the same as the literal method, but the function makes use of a series of *for* loops to perform the mathematical operations in sections. The beauty of this method is that not only does it work for the four control point version, by setting the upper limit of *j* to 3 in the second *for* loop, but it can be extended to any number of control points by simply increasing the upper limit of the second *for* loop without any other changes in the code.

Bezier Curves with Many Control Points

Thus far, we have restricted ourselves to the case where the Bezier curve is solely defined by four control points. There are two ways that we can extend the Bezier curve capability. The first is to create a more complex curve by combining individual Bezier curves that were generated using four control points. Since we know the direction that individual curves are taking at each end point and we also know exactly where each end point is, we can make sure that the ends of individual Bezier curves fit together well. The other option is to generate a complex Bezier curve by having many control points. The function *drawBezier* in the listing uses this option. We make use of the C functions *va_start, va_end* and *va_arg* together with a variable of the type *va_list* to extract parameters from a variable size list passed to the function. Any number of parameters may be passed by this technique, but we have limited ourselves to 20 pairs of coordinates by the size that we define in the function for the variables *xpoint* and *ypoint*. If you need more control points, simply increase the dimensions of these arrays. We've set things up in such a way that when the function encounters a parameter that is less than -320, it stops reading in parameters. Thus the last value passed to the function must be less than -320. Once the parameters have all been loaded into the arrays, the function uses the same method of Bernstein polynomials that was used for *drawBezier3* above, except that in the second *for* loop we let the upper limit be the same as the number of control points that were passed to the function. The function is set up in such a way that the individual line segments that are drawn are very small. In fact, it is possible that a line segment may turn out to be so small that it begins and ends on the same pixel. If this is the case, we don't want to bother to draw the line, so before each line segment is drawn, the function tests to make sure that it is longer than a single pixel, and if not, the line segment is not drawn.

Drawing B-Spline Curves

The function *draw_bspline* uses a literal rendering of equation 18-4 to generate a B-spline curve using four control points. The function first loads the parameters from the structure of four points that is passed to it into two point arrays. The point arrays consist of eight points. The first two points are duplicates of the starting point and the last four points are duplicates of the fourth point. The B-spline mathematics is repeated four times, for the first four points (points 0 through 3), then for points 1 through 4, for points 2 through 5, and finally for points 3 through 6.

Drawing a B-Spline Curve with Many Points

When dealing with many points, it might be better to use the same technique used with the Bezier curve and let all of the points influence the shape of the curve. To do so, however, would require a very large blending matrix. Since we don't have a good repetitive means of programming the process, the mathematics would get very cumbersome. So instead, we have produced a function that will use the B-spline function already developed to draw a piece of the curve, using the four nearest control points, then draw the next piece with the four control points nearest it and so forth. The function begins by assigning a variable number of passed parameters to point arrays, just like the many-point Bezier function. It then enters a *for* loop that is iterated for each set of four control points. Within this loop, the mathematics is just the same as those for the B-spline function described earlier.

Creating Type Characters with Bezier Curves

In the demonstration program whose description follows, we are going to create some variations of the letter *B* as an example of how typographical characters can be created with Bezier curves. They won't be quite as polished as those produced by a type font program, but they show clearly the nature of the process involved. The vehicle for doing this is the function *drawAlpha* that is given in the program listing. This function is passed the *x* and *y* location of the character starting point, the number of sets of control points that define the alphanumeric, a pointer to the beginning of an array of control point boxes, the character size and the character color. The program begins by defining the scale multiplier that sets the character size. To get this, we first scale the control point parameters to a range of 0 to 1 and then multiply the result by the specified character size. A loop is then entered which is iterated for each set of control points in the control point array. It begins by determining the values of the control points for the box currently being processed. These are the character control points offset by the specified location parameters and multiplied by the scale factor. Next the control point information is used to generate a curve segment. Any alphanumeric is made up of straight line segments and curves. We could use a control point box that is actually a straight line to draw a Bezier curve that would also be a straight line and thus have the same operation performed for every line segment of the character whether it is a straight line or a curve. This is not a very good idea, however. First, the Bezier curve functions often don't react quite right to a straight line control box, sometimes resulting in a need to fudge the control points, since the resulting straight line stops short of the specified end. Second, a lot of extra work is required to just draw a simple straight line, greatly lengthening the curve drawing process. To avoid these difficulties, the first thing that is done after the control box parameters have been defined is to test whether the control box is actually a straight line. If it is, the function just draws the line. If the box is a quadrilateral, the function enters a *switch* statement which selects one of the three types of Bezier curve rendering or the B-spline curve rendering, as selected by the user. The proper function is then used to draw the curve segment. Finally the flood fill function (*fill*) is used to fill the resulting character outline.

The control points for making a *B* are in the array *upper_b* at the beginning of the program. They were obtained by tracing a large *B* on graph paper, breaking it up into curve segments, determining the control points that would be the ends of each curve segment and then placing the other two control points experimentally so that the curve would have the proper direction (tangental to the lines between control points 0 and 1 and between control points 3 and 4) and the curve would have the proper shape.

Demonstrating the Use of Bezier and B-Spline Curves

The program *Bezier.c*, which is listed in Figure 18-1, provides a number of display screen that illustrate the use of Bezier and B-spline functions. The program begins with a *for* loop that iterates forever. The first thing the loop does is provide a screen display that enables the user to select from the three renderings of the Bezier curve (literal, deCasteljau or Bernstein polynomials) or to quit. If this last is selected, the program breaks out of the loop and continues to run the rest of the program. As long as one of the rendering methods is selected, the program then creates a screen that shows six variations of the letter *B* in different sizes and colors and in different positions. These characters are rendered by the selected rendering technique. When any character on the keyboard is hit, this display ends and another display is created. This one generates 50 variations of the letter *B*, sequencing through the available colors and selecting the character size and starting coordinates randomly. This display will be different each time you run it. A sample of the display is shown in Plate 22. An attempt has been made to assure that the character is never too small and that it does not fall outside the screen boundaries. Either of these conditions confuses the flood fill function and will result in part of the character not being filled or, worse yet, in the function attempting to fill the entire screen with a solid color. One eccentricity of the flood fill function that you'll also observe is that if it attempts to fill a character outline that is partially superimposed on another character of the same color, the fill will be incomplete.

After you are tired of looking at different renditions of *B*, and select the quit option, the program will next draw a curved line using the many point Bezier technique. The control points for this curve are connected with dashed lines so that you can see the shape of the hull which determines the curve. Next two connected many point Bezier curves are drawn in different colors, with their hulls also shown in different colors by dashed lines. The next display is a quite complex curve whose hull is shown in dashed lines and then the B-spline and Bezier curves generated by these control points are drawn in different curves. This screen shows clearly how the B-spline follows the points quite closely (while smoothing) whereas the Bezier curve is much smoother and looses a lot of detail in the original graph. Finally, a rectangular hull is shown, together with the resulting Bezier and B-spline curves. This shows how, for a simple curve, the B-spline curve approaches closer to the intermediate control points and has a more boxy shape than the Bezier curve. The resulting display is shown in Plate 23.

Chapter 19

Displaying Text in the Graphics Modes

C programmers are all familiar with the C text output function *printf* and know how to use it to produce all sorts of informative displays in the text display modes. You can also use *printf* in the regularly supported graphics modes, but regardless of what colors you have on the screen, the data displayed by *printf* will be in white on a black background. I have seen some peculiar cases where *printf* produced a totally garbage output on a graphics display, but I've never been able to isolate the exact conditions that cause this, and usually *printf* is pretty well behaved, even with graphics modes. There are, however, a lot of graphics situations in which you want to go beyond the capabilities of *printf*. We're going to look at a lot of these situations in this chapter and discover some very interesting ways to make use of alphanumerics in graphics displays. All of the functions that we are going to describe, together with a demonstration program that shows them in operation, are included in a file called *chartest.c*. This program is listed in Figure 19-1.

Figure 19-1. Listing of chartest.c Program

```
/*

    chartest = Program to demonstrate display of characters
                        in graphics modes

                By Roger T. Stevens   11-2-91

*/

#include <stdio.h>
#include <stdarg.h>
#include <math.h>
#include <dos.h>
#include <conio.h>

void cls(int color);
void color_printf (char *fmt,int color,...);
void display(unsigned long int address, int color_plane,
    unsigned char ch);
unsigned char far *findChar (int type, int *lines, int
    *bytes_per_char);
void setMode(int mode);
void writeVchar(int x, int y, int ch, int color);
void writeHchar(int x, int y, char ch, int color);
void writeHstring(int x, int y, char *string, int color);
void writeString(int x, int y, char *string, int color);
void writeVstring(int x, int y, char *string, int color);
void writeBigChar(int x, int y, int ch, int color);
void writeBigString(int x, int y, char *string, int
    color);
void writeVideoChar(int x, int y, int ch, int color);
void writeVideoString(int x, int y, char *string, int
    color);

union REGS reg;

unsigned char far *char_table;
int color;
```

(continued)

```
int xres = 640, yres = 350;
int lines,type;

void main(void)
{
    struct REGPACK reg;
    int k, x, y, bytes_per_char;
    directvideo = 0;
    type = 2;
    char_table = findChar (type, &lines, &bytes_per_char);
    setMode(0x10);
    cls(1);
    textbackground(3);
    textcolor(13);
    writeBigString(20,10,"Big Letters",158);
    writeVideoString(20,70,"Video Letters",243);
    writeBigChar(560,10,'O',63);
    writeBigChar(590,10,'K',63);
    writeVideoChar(400,220,'O',62);
    writeVideoChar(430,220,'K',62);
    x= 45;
    y= 115;
    for (k=0; k<93; k++)
    {
        if (!(k%25))
        {
            y+=20;
            x = 45;
        }
        writeHchar(x, y, k+33, 31);
        x += 16;
    }
    x= 520;
    y= 291;
    for (k=0; k<93; k++)
    {
        if (!(k%17))
        {
            x += 16;
            y = 291;
        }
```

(continued)

```
        writeVchar(x, y, k+33, 47);
        y -= 10;
    }
    writeHstring(30,300,"Sorry to have to be this way, "
        "but we need to have a string that is long enough"
        " to extend over more than one row so as to make "
        "sure that the program works properly for "
        "automatically moving to the next line...",95);
    writeVstring(480,258, "This is a vertical string...",
        159);
    gotoxy(6,17);
    printf("This string uses 'printf'...");
    gotoxy(6,19);
    cprintf("This string uses 'cprintf'...");
    gotoxy(6,21);
    color_printf("This string uses 'color_printf'...",
        241);
    getch();
```

```
/*
```

```
┌────────────────────────────────────────────────────────┐
│                                                          │
│        Mode 70H = 320 x 400 pixels x 256 colors          │
│                                                          │
└────────────────────────────────────────────────────────┘
```

```
*/
```

```
    setMode(0x70);
    xres = 320; yres = 400;
    type = 2;
    char_table = findChar (type, &lines, &bytes_per_char);
    writeString(10,80,"These are the times that "
        "try men's souls. The summer soldier and "
        "the sunshine patriot...",31);
    getch();
```

```
/*
```

```
┌────────────────────────────────────────────────────────┐
│                                                          │
│        Mode 71H = 320 x 240 pixels x 256 colors          │
│                                                          │
└────────────────────────────────────────────────────────┘
```

```
*/
```

(continued)

```
setMode(0x71);
xres = 320; yres = 240;
writeString(10,80,"These are the times that try "
    men's souls. The summer soldier and the "
    sunshine patriot...",31);
getch();
```

```
/*
```

```
Mode 72H = 320 x 480 pixels x 256 colors
```

```
*/
```

```
setMode(0x72);
xres = 320; yres = 480;
writeString(10,80,"These are the times that try \
    men's souls. The summer soldier and the \
    sunshine patriot...",31);
getch();
```

```
/*
```

```
Mode 73H = 360 x 400 pixels x 256 colors
```

```
*/
```

```
setMode(0x73);
xres = 360; yres = 400;
writeString(10,80,"These are the times that try "
    "men's souls. The summer soldier and the "
    "sunshine patriot...",31);
getch();
```

```
/*
```

```
Mode 74H = 360 x 480 pixels x 256 colors
```

```
*/
```

(continued)

```
        setMode(0x74);
        xres = 360; yres = 480;
        writeString(10,80,"These are the times that try "
            "men's souls. The summer soldier and the "
            "sunshine patriot...",31);
        getch();

        setMode(0x03);
}

/*
```

```
  +-------------------------------------------------------+
  |                                                       |
  |   setMode() = Sets video modes (includes undocumented VGA |
  |                          modes)                       |
  |                                                       |
  +-------------------------------------------------------+
```

```
*/

void setMode(int mode)
{
    char result;
    unsigned int params[17] = {0x6b00,0x5901,0x5a02,
        0x8e03,0x5e04,0x8a05,0x4009,0x0014,0xe317,
        0x0d06,0x3e07,0xea10,0xac11,0xdf12,0xe715,
        0x0616,0x4109};
    char far * address;
    long int i;

    reg.h.ah = 0;

    switch(mode)
    {
        case 0x70:  /* 320 x 400 pixel resolution */
            reg.h.al = 0x13;
            int86 (0x10,&reg,&reg);
            outport(0x3c4,0x0604);
            outportb(0x3d4,0x11);
            result = inportb(0x3d5);
            outportb(0x3d5,result & 0x7f);
            for (i=6; i<9; i++)
                outport(0x3d4,params[i]);
```

(continued)

```
        break;

case 0x71:  /* 320 x 240 pixels */
    reg.h.al = 0x13;
    int86 (0x10,&reg,&reg);
    outport(0x3c4,0x0604);
    outport(0x3c4,0x0100);
    outportb(0x3c2,0xc3);
    outport(0x3c4,0x300);
    outportb(0x3d4,0x11);
    result = inportb(0x3d5);
    outportb(0x3d5,result & 0x7f);
    for (i=7; i<17; i++)
        outport(0x3d4,params[i]);
    break;

case 0x72:  /* 320 x 480 pixels */
    reg.h.al = 0x13;
    int86 (0x10,&reg,&reg);
    outport(0x3c4,0x0604);
    outport(0x3c4,0x0100);
    outportb(0x3c2,0xc3);
    outport(0x3c4,0x300);
    outportb(0x3d4,0x11);
    result = inportb(0x3d5);
    outportb(0x3d5,result & 0x7f);
    for (i=6; i<16; i++)
        outport(0x3d4,params[i]);
    outport(0x3d4,0x4009);
    break;

case 0x73:  /* 360 x 400 pixels */
    reg.h.al = 0x13;
    int86 (0x10,&reg,&reg);
    outport(0x3c4,0x0604);
    outport(0x3c4,0x0100);
    outportb(0x3c2,0x67);
    outport(0x3c4,0x300);
    outportb(0x3d4,0x11);
    result = inportb(0x3d5);
    outportb(0x3d5,result & 0x7f);
```

(continued)

```
                    for (i=0;  i<9;  i++)
                        outport(0x3d4,params[i]);
                    outport(0x3d4,0x2d13);
                    break;

                case 0x74:   /* 360 x 480 pixels */
                    reg.h.al = 0x13;
                    int86 (0x10,&reg,&reg);
                    outport(0x3c4,0x0604);
                    outport(0x3c4,0x0100);
                    outportb(0x3c2,0xe7);
                    outport(0x3c4,0x300);
                    outportb(0x3d4,0x11);
                    result = inportb(0x3d5);
                    outportb(0x3d5,result & 0x7f);
                    for (i=0;  i<16;  i++)
                        outport(0x3d4,params[i]);
                    outport(0x3d4,0x2d13);
                    break;
                default:
                    reg.h.al = mode;
                    int86(0x10, &reg, &reg);
        }
        if (mode >= 0x70)
        {
            outport(0x3c4,0x0f02);
            for(i=0; i<0xFFFF; i++)
            {
                address = (char far *) 0xA0000000L + i;
                *address = 0x00;
            }
        }
}


/*
```

```
        writeString() = writes a string horizontally using
                        undocumented display modes
```

```
*/
```

(continued)

```
void writeString(int x, int y, char *string, int color)
{
    #define seq_out(index,val)   {outp(0x3C4,index);\
                    outp(0x3C5,val);}
    #define graph_out(index,val)   {outp(0x3CE,index);\
                    outp(0x3CF,val);}
    unsigned char char_test, exist_color;
    int i, j, k, foreground,background, point_color;
    unsigned long int offset;
    char far *address;
    unsigned int plane;
    int char_offset,p=0,lines;

    switch(type)
    {
        case 0:
        case 1:
        case 3:
        case 4:
            lines = 8;
            break;
        case 2:
        case 5:
            lines = 14;
            break;
        case 6:
        case 7:
            lines = 16;
    }
    foreground = color & 0x0F;
    background = (color & 0xF0) >> 4;
    while (string[p])
    {
        char_offset = (string[p]) * lines;
        for (i=0; i<lines; i++)
        {
            for (j=0; j<8; j++)
            {
                char_test = 0x80 >> j;
                if ((char_table[char_offset+i] &
                    char_test) != 0)
```

(continued)

```
                                point_color = foreground;
                          else
                                point_color = background;
                          offset = (long)xres * (y+i) + x + j;
                          plane = (0x01 << (offset % 4));
                          seq_out(2,plane);
                          offset >>= 2;
                          address = (char far *)(0xA0000000L +
                              offset);
                          *address = point_color;
                     }
                }
                x += 8;
                if (x>xres-8)
                {
                     x=0;
                     y += lines;
                }
                p++;
          }
     }

/*
```

```
    findChar() = Returns the address of a character table
        as well as finding the bytes per character and
                    rows on the screen.
```

```
*/

unsigned char far *findChar (int type, int *lines, int
     *bytes_per_char)
{
     struct REGPACK reg;
     unsigned char far *address;

     reg.r_bx = type << 8;
     reg.r_ax = 0x1130;
     intr(0x10,&reg);
     address = (unsigned char far*)(reg.r_es*0x10000 +
```

(continued)

```
              reg.r_bp);
        *lines = reg.r_dx & 0xFF;
        *bytes_per_char = reg.r_cx;
        return(address);
}

/*
```

```
        cls() = Clears the screen to a designated color
```

```
*/

void cls(int color)
{
        union REGS reg;

        reg.x.ax = 0x0600;
        reg.x.cx = 0;
        reg.x.dx = 0x184F;
        reg.h.bh = color;
        int86(0x10,&reg,&reg);
}

/*
```

```
        writeHchar() = writes a character horizontally
```

```
*/

void writeHchar(int x, int y, char ch, int color)
{
    #define seq_out(index,val)  {outp(0x3C4,index);\
                    outp(0x3C5,val);}
    #define graph_out(index,val)  {outp(0x3CE,index);\
                    outp(0x3CF,val);}

    unsigned int offset;
    char far * mem_address;
    unsigned char char_test, exist_color;
```

(continued)

```
int i, j, k, foreground,background, height, width,
    point_color,dummy,mask;
int char_offset,lines;

switch(type)
{
    case 0:
    case 1:
    case 3:
    case 4:
        lines = 8;
        break;
    case 2:
    case 5:
        lines = 14;
        break;
    case 6:
    case 7:
        lines = 16;
}
char_offset = ch * lines;
foreground = color & 0x0F;
background = (color & 0xF0) >> 4;
for (i=0; i<lines; i++)
{
    for (j=0; j<8; j++)
    {
        height = y+i;
        width = x+j;
        char_test = 0x80 >> j;
        if ((char_table[char_offset+i] &char_test) !=
            0)
            point_color = foreground;
        else
            point_color = background;
        offset = (long)(height) * 80L
            + ((long) (width) / 8L);
        mem_address = (char far *)0xA0000000L +
            offset;
        mask = 0x80 >> ((width) % 8);
        graph_out(8,mask);
```

(continued)

```
                seq_out(2,0x0F);
                dummy = *mem_address;
                *mem_address = 0;
                seq_out(2,point_color);
                *mem_address = 0xFF;
            }
        }
        seq_out(2,0x0F);
        graph_out(3,0);
        graph_out(8,0xFF);
    }


    /*
    ┌─────────────────────────────────────────────────┐
    │ ┌─────────────────────────────────────────────┐ │
    │ │                                             │ │
    │ │    writeVchar() = writes a character vertically │ │
    │ │                                             │ │
    │ └─────────────────────────────────────────────┘ │
    └─────────────────────────────────────────────────┘
    */

    void writeVchar(int x, int y, int ch, int color)
    {
        #define seq_out(index,val)  {outp(0x3C4,index);\
                            outp(0x3C5,val);}
        #define graph_out(index,val)  {outp(0x3CE,index);\
                            outp(0x3CF,val);}

        unsigned int offset;
        char far * mem_address;
        unsigned char char_test, exist_color;
        int i, j, k, foreground,background, height, width,
            point_color,dummy,mask;

        int char_offset,lines;

        switch(type)
        {
            case 0:
            case 1:
            case 3:
            case 4:
                lines = 8;
```

(continued)

```
                    break;
            case 2:
            case 5:
                lines = 14;
                break;
            case 6:
            case 7:
                lines = 16;
        }
        char_offset = ch * lines;
        foreground = color & 0x0F;
        background = (color & 0xF0) >> 4;
        for (i=0; i<lines; i++)
        {
            for (j=0; j<8; j++)
            {
                height = y-j;
                width = x+i;
                char_test = 0x80 >> j;
                if ((char_table[char_offset+i] & char_test) !=
                    0)
                    point_color = foreground;
                else
                    point_color = background;
                offset = (long)(height) * 80L
                    + ((long)(width) / 8L);
                mem_address = (char far *)0xA0000000L +
                    offset;
                mask = 0x80 >> ((width) % 8);
                graph_out(8,mask);
                seq_out(2,0x0F);
                dummy = *mem_address;
                *mem_address = 0;
                seq_out(2,point_color);
                *mem_address = 0xFF;
            }
        }
        seq_out(2,0x0F);
        graph_out(3,0);
        graph_out(8,0xFF);
    }
```

(continued)

```
/*
┌─────────────────────────────────────────────────────────────┐
│                                                               │
│        writeHstring() = Writes a string horizontally          │
│                                                               │
└─────────────────────────────────────────────────────────────┘
*/

void writeHstring(int x, int y, char *string, int color)
{
    #define seq_out(index,val)   {outp(0x3C4,index);\
                        outp(0x3C5,val);}
    #define graph_out(index,val)  {outp(0x3CE,index);\
                        outp(0x3CF,val);}

    unsigned int offset;
    char far * mem_address;
    unsigned char char_test, exist_color;
    int i, j, k, foreground,background, height, width,
        point_color,dummy,mask;

    int char_offset,p=0,lines;

    switch(type)
    {
        case 0:
        case 1:
        case 3:
        case 4:
            lines = 8;
            break;
        case 2:
        case 5:
            lines = 14;
            break;
        case 6:
        case 7:
            lines = 16;
    }
    while (string[p])
    {
        char_offset = (string[p]) * lines;
```

(continued)

```
        foreground = color & 0x0F;
        background = (color & 0xF0) >> 4;
        for (i=0; i<lines; i++)
        {
            for (j=0; j<8; j++)
            {
                height = y+i;
                width = x+j;
                char_test = 0x80 >> j;
                if ((char_table[char_offset+i] &
                    char_test) != 0)
                    point_color = foreground;
                else
                    point_color = background;
                offset = (long)(height) * 80L +
                    ((long)(width) / 8L);
                mem_address = (char far *)0xA0000000L +
                    offset;
                mask = 0x80 >> ((width) % 8);
                graph_out(8,mask);
                seq_out(2,0x0F);
                dummy = *mem_address;
                *mem_address = 0;
                seq_out(2,point_color);
                *mem_address = 0xFF;
            }
        }
        seq_out(2,0x0F);
        graph_out(3,0);
        graph_out(8,0xFF);
        x += 8;
        if (x>xres-8)
        {
            x=0;
            y += lines;
        }
        p++;
    }
}
```

(continued)

```
/*

        writeVstring() = Writes a string vertically

*/
void writeVstring(int x, int y, char *string, int color)
{
    #define seq_out(index,val)  {outp(0x3C4,index);\
                        outp(0x3C5,val);}
    #define graph_out(index,val)  {outp(0x3CE,index);\
                        outp(0x3CF,val);}

    unsigned int offset;
    char far * mem_address;
    unsigned char char_test, exist_color;
    int i, j, k, foreground,background, height, width,
        point_color,dummy,mask;

    int char_offset,p=0,lines;

    switch(type)
    {
        case 0:
        case 1:
        case 3:
        case 4:
            lines = 8;
            break;
        case 2:
        case 5:
            lines = 14;
            break;
        case 6:
        case 7:
            lines = 16;
    }
    while (string[p])
    {
        char_offset = (string[p]) * lines;
```

(continued)

```
            foreground = color & 0x0F;
            background = (color & 0xF0) >> 4;
            for (i=0; i<lines; i++)
            {
                for (j=0; j<8; j++)
                {
                    height = y-j;
                    width = x+i;
                    char_test = 0x80 >> j;
                    if ((char_table[char_offset+i] &
                        char_test) != 0)
                        point_color = foreground;
                    else
                        point_color = background;
                    offset = (long)(height) * 80L +
                        ((long)(width) / 8L);
                    mem_address = (char far *)0xA0000000L +
                        offset;
                    mask = 0x80 >> ((width) % 8);
                    graph_out(8,mask);
                    seq_out(2,0x0F);
                    dummy = *mem_address;
                    *mem_address = 0;
                    seq_out(2,point_color);
                    *mem_address = 0xFF;
                }
            }
            seq_out(2,0x0F);
            graph_out(3,0);
            graph_out(8,0xFF);
            y -= 8;
            if (y<8)
            {
                y = yres - 8;
                x += lines;
            }
            p++;
        }
    }
```

(continued)

```
/*
```

```
          writeBigChar() = Writes a big character
```

```
*/
```

```
void writeBigChar(int x, int y, int ch, int color)
{
    #define seq_out(index,val)  {outp(0x3C4,index);\
                     outp(0x3C5,val);}
    #define graph_out(index,val)  {outp(0x3CE,index);\
                     outp(0x3CF,val);}

    unsigned int offset;
    char far * mem_address;
    unsigned char char_test, exist_color;
    int i, j, k, m, foreground,background, height, width,
        point_color,dummy,mask;

    int char_offset,lines;

    switch(type)
    {
        case 0:
        case 1:
        case 3:
        case 4:
            lines = 8;
            break;
        case 2:
        case 5:
            lines = 14;
            break;
        case 6:
        case 7:
            lines = 16;
    }
    char_offset = ch * lines;
    foreground = color & 0x0F;
    background = (color & 0xF0) >> 4;
```

(continued)

```
    for (i=0; i<lines; i++)
    {
        for (j=0; j<8; j++)
        {
            for (m=0; m<4; m++)
            {
                for (k=0; k<4; k++)
                {
                    height = y+4*i+k;
                    width = x+4*j+m;
                    char_test = 0x80 >> j;
                    if  ((char_table[char_offset + i] &
                        char_test) != 0)
                        point_color = foreground;
                    else
                        point_color = background;
                    offset = (long)(height) * 80L +
                        ((long)(width) / 8L);
                    mem_address = (char far*)0xA0000000L +
                        offset;
                    mask = 0x80 >> ((width) % 8);
                    graph_out(8,mask);
                    seq_out(2,0x0F);
                    dummy = *mem_address;
                    *mem_address = 0;
                    seq_out(2,point_color);
                    *mem_address = 0xFF;
                }
            }
        }
    }
    seq_out(2,0x0F);
    graph_out(3,0);
    graph_out(8,0xFF);
}
```

(continued)

```
/*

    writeVideoChar() = Writes a big video-type character

*/

void writeVideoChar(int x, int y, int ch, int color)
{
    #define seq_out(index,val)   {outp(0x3C4,index);\
                            outp(0x3C5,val);}
    #define graph_out(index,val)   {outp(0x3CE,index);\
                            outp(0x3CF,val);}

    unsigned int offset;
    char far * mem_address;
    unsigned char char_test, exist_color;
    int i, j, k, m, foreground,background, height, width,
        point_color,dummy,mask;

    int char_offset,lines;

    switch(type)
    {
        case 0:
        case 1:
        case 3:
        case 4:
            lines = 8;
            break;
        case 2:
        case 5:
            lines = 14;
            break;
        case 6:
        case 7:
            lines = 16;
    }
    char_offset = ch * lines;
    foreground = color & 0x0F;
    background = (color & 0xF0) >> 4;
```

(continued)

```
for (i=0; i<lines; i++)
{
    for (j=0; j<8; j++)
    {
        for (m=1; m<4; m++)
        {
            for (k=1; k<4; k++)
            {
                height = y+4*i+k;
                width = x+4*j+m;
                char_test = 0x80 >> j;
                if ((char_table[char_offset+i] &
                    char_test) != 0)
                    point_color = foreground;
                else
                    point_color = background;
                offset = (long)(height) * 80L +
                    ((long)(width) / 8L);
                mem_address = (char far *)
                    0xA0000000L + offset;
                mask = 0x80 >> ((width) % 8);
                graph_out(8,mask);
                seq_out(2,0x0F);
                dummy = *mem_address;
                *mem_address = 0;
                seq_out(2,point_color);
                *mem_address = 0xFF;
            }
        }
    }
}
seq_out(2,0x0F);
graph_out(3,0);
graph_out(8,0xFF);
}
```

(continued)

```
/*
```

```
    writeBigString() = Writes a string of big characters
```

```
*/
```

```
void writeBigString(int x, int y, char *string, int color)
{
    #define seq_out(index,val)   {outp(0x3C4,index);\
                        outp(0x3C5,val);}
    #define graph_out(index,val)   {outp(0x3CE,index);\
                        outp(0x3CF,val);}

    unsigned int offset;
    char far * mem_address;
    unsigned char char_test, exist_color;
    int i, j, k, m, foreground,background, height, width,
        point_color,dummy,mask;

    int char_offset,p=0,lines,start,end;

    switch(type)
    {
        case 0:
        case 1:
        case 3:
        case 4:
            lines = 8;
            break;
        case 2:
        case 5:
            lines = 14;
            break;
        case 6:
        case 7:
            lines = 16;
    }
    start = 0;
    end = 4;
    while (string[p])
```

(continued)

```
{
    char_offset = string[p] * lines;
    foreground = color & 0x0F;
    background = (color & 0xF0) >> 4;
    for (i=0; i<lines; i++)
    {
        for (j=0; j<8; j++)
        {
            for (m=start; m<end; m++)
            {
                for (k=start; k<end; k++)
                {
                    height = y+4*i+k;
                    width = x+4*j+m;
                    char_test = 0x80 >> j;
                    if ((char_table[char_offset+i] &
                        char_test) != 0)
                        point_color = foreground;
                    else
                        point_color = background;
                    offset = (long)(height) * 80L +
                        ((long)(width) / 8L);
                    mem_address = (char far *)
                        0xA0000000L + offset;
                    mask = 0x80 >> ((width) % 8);
                    graph_out(8,mask);
                    seq_out(2,0x0F);
                    dummy = *mem_address;
                    *mem_address = 0;
                    seq_out (2, point_color);
                    *mem_address = 0xFF;
                }
            }
        }
    }
    seq_out(2,0x0F);
    graph_out(3,0);
    graph_out(8,0xFF);
    x += 32;
    if (x>607)
    {
```

(continued)

```
            x=0;
            y += 56;
        }
        p++;
    }
}


/*
```

┌───┐
│ ┌───┐ │
│ │   │ │
│ │ writeVideoString() = Writes a string of big video-type │ │
│ │   characters   │ │
│ │   │ │
│ └───┘ │
└───┘

```
*/

void writeVideoString(int x, int y, char *string, int
    color)
{
    #define seq_out(index,val)   {outp(0x3C4,index);\
                        outp(0x3C5,val);}
    #define graph_out(index,val)   {outp(0x3CE,index);\
                        outp(0x3CF,val);}

    unsigned int offset;
    char far * mem_address;
    unsigned char char_test, exist_color;
    int i, j, k, m, foreground,background, height, width,
        point_color,dummy,mask;
    int char_offset,p=0,lines,start,end;

    switch(type)
    {
        case 0:
        case 1:
        case 3:
        case 4:
            lines = 8;
            break;
        case 2:
        case 5:
            lines = 14;
```

(continued)

```
            break;
        case 6:
        case 7:
            lines = 16;
    }
    start = 1;
    end = 4;
    while (string[p])
    {
        char_offset = string[p] * lines;
        foreground = color & 0x0F;
        background = (color & 0xF0) >> 4;
        for (i=0; i<lines; i++)
        {
            for (j=0; j<8; j++)
            {
                for (m=start; m<end; m++)
                {
                    for (k=start; k<end; k++)
                    {
                        height = y+4*i+k;
                        width = x+4*j+m;
                        char_test = 0x80 >> j;
                        if ((char_table[char_offset+i] &
                            char_test) != 0)
                            point_color = foreground;
                        else
                            point_color = background;
                        offset = (long)(height) * 80L +
                            ((long)(width) / 8L);
                        mem_address = (char far *)
                            0xA0000000L + offset;
                        mask = 0x80 >> ((width) % 8);
                        graph_out(8,mask);
                        seq_out(2,0x0F);
                        dummy = *mem_address;
                        *mem_address = 0;
                        seq_out (2, point_color);
                        *mem_address = 0xFF;
                    }
                }
```

(continued)

```
            }
        }
        seq_out(2,0x0F);
        graph_out(3,0);
        graph_out(8,0xFF);
        x += 32;
        if (x>607)
        {
            x=0;
            y += 56;
        }
        p++;
    }
}


/*
```

```
    color_printf() = Version of printf with control of
            foreground and background colors
```

```
*/

void color_printf (char *fmt,int color,...)
{
    #define seq_out(index,val)  {outp(0x3C4,index);\
                        outp(0x3C5,val);}
    union REGS reg;
    char ch, string[200];
    int i = 0 ,j, k, mask1, mask2;
    char far *address;
    int char_offset, foreground, background, width,
        point_color, dummy;
    unsigned char char_test;
    va_list ap;

    va_start (ap,color);
    vsprintf(string,fmt,ap);
    va_end(ap);
    while ((ch=string[i++]) != '\0')
    {
```

(continued)

```
            if (ch == 0x0A)
            {
                reg.h.ah = 3;
                int86(0x10,&reg,&reg);
                reg.h.dl = 0;
                reg.h.dh++;
                reg.h.ah = 2;
                int86(0x10,&reg,&reg);
            }
            else
            {
                reg.h.ah = 3;
                reg.h.bh = 0;
                int86(0x10,&reg,&reg);
                char_offset = ch * 14;
                for (k=0; k<14; k++)
                {
                    seq_out(2,(0x01 << j));
                    address = (char far *) 0xA0000000L +
                        (long)(reg.h.dh*14+k)*80L + reg.h.dl;
                    mask1 = 0x10;
                    mask2 = 0x01;
                    for (j=0; j<4; j++)
                    {
                        if (((mask1 & color) != 0) && ((mask2
                            & color) != 0))
                            *address = 0xFF;
                        else
                        {
                            if ((mask1 & color) != 0)
                                *address = ~char_table
                                    [char_offset + k];
                            if ((mask2 & color) != 0)
                                *address = char_table
                                    [char_offset + k];
                        }
                        mask1 <<= 1;
                        mask2 <<= 1;
                    }
                }
                reg.h.bh = 0;
```

(continued)

```
                reg.x.dx++;
                reg.h.ah = 2;
                int86(0x10,&reg,&reg);
          }
     }
     seq_out(2,0x0F);
}
```

The *cprintf* Function

Borland C++ and Turbo C++ have a function called *cprintf*. This function is designed to be used with a global variable called *directvideo*. When this variable is set to 0, the console output uses the ROM BIOS video services to access the screen; when it is set to 1, direct video RAM drivers are used to create the console output. The *cprintf* function only works with *directvideo* set to 0. When used in this way, *cprintf* is much like *printf* except that the foreground and background colors with which it prints characters can be specified by two functions called *textcolor* and *textbackground*, respectively. Setting of the foreground and background colors using these functions does not affect any characters already written on the screen; they affect only characters written after they are called. We could often use this flexibility in our programs, but unfortunately, *cprintf* has two drawbacks. The first, and most serious, is that the background setting function does not work for graphics modes, so that regardless of how hard you try, the background when using *cprintf* is always black. Second, even if you're in a text mode, the *textbackground* function can set only the eight low intensity colors, so you cannot have high intensity background colors using *cprintf*.

Using the Built-in Fonts

The functions described in the rest of this chapter make it possible for you to display characters on the screen that have various capabilities not available with the two functions just described. In order for any of these functions to work, however, you need a table that defines the characteristics of each character in the font. For each character, we're going to be using an 8 pixel wide character, but the lengths (number of character lines) may be 8, 14 or 16 lines. Therefore an array of 8, 14 or 16 bytes for each character is needed. If you want to, you can design each character on a sheet of grid paper and then convert the characters into array definitions, but it's a lot easier to make use of one of the character fonts that is already built into the ROM BIOS extensions that are part of your EGA or VGA card. To access one of these fonts, all you need to know is the address where the font array begins. To find this, we set up a pointer called *char_table* of type *unsigned char far ** and then call the function *findChar* to load this pointer with the font array address by means of the ROM BIOS video services. The parameter *type* that is passed to this function determines which font's address will be returned; for cases 0, 1, 3 and 4 an 8 bit high font is pointed to, for cases 2 and 5 a 14 bit high font is pointed to and for cases 6 and 7 a 16 bit high font is pointed to.

The *color_printf* Function

The *color_printf* function is designed to do everything that *printf* does but also to give you both foreground and background control of each individual character. This version of *color_printf* works only with 16 color graphics modes and the 8×14 pixel character set but once you understand how it operates, you can easily make a comparable function that will work with 256 color graphics modes, with undocumented or extended modes, or with text modes. The function begins by using the C functions and variables *va_start, va_end, va_list* and *vsprintf* to produce the exact ASCII string that *printf* would normally output to the screen, but instead of sending it to the screen, place it in an array *string*. We've set *string* to be 200 bytes in size, which gives you about two and a half lines of text. If you think you're going to need more than this for a single *color_printf* call, you can increase the size of the array. The function then enters a *while* loop that gets the first character from *string* and then on each iteration gets the next character until a NULL is encountered, indicating that the string is exhausted. At each iteration, the function first checks to see if the character is a line feed. If it is, a ROM BIOS video service is called to get the current cursor position, the row value of this position is incremented and another ROM BIOS video service is used to store the new cursor position. If the character was not a line feed, the function continues by getting the cursor position. It then computes the offset into the character table for the character just read from the string. The function then enters a *for* loop that is iterated once for each of the 14 lines of the character. Within this loop, the function first computes the memory location of the first line of the character.

It then initializes two masks for use with the background and foreground color determination. Then another *for* loop is entered, which iterates once for each of the four color planes. Sequencer register 2 is first set to activate only the color plane indicated by the loop index. At each iteration of the loop, the function then checks whether the background and foreground colors for this color plane are both unequal to 0. If this is the case, both foreground and background colors require each memory bit to be set to 1, so the display memory location is sent an 0xFF to set all these bits to 1. If both colors weren't to be set for this character line, the function next checks whether the background color is to be set for this color plane. If so, it sends the inverse of the contents of the character table for this character line to display memory, causing all background bits to be set to 1. The function next checks whether the foreground color is to be set for this color plane. If so, it sends the contents of the character table for this character line to display memory, causing all foreground bits to be set to 1. You'll notice that, if both these *if* statements were found to be true, the second addressing of display memory would override the first, causing an incorrect memory setting. However, this can never occur, since the case of both foreground and background colors being set in this plane was already handled by the previous conditional test, so that this section occurs only if one of the two colors was 0 for this color plane. After sending data to memory, the function shifts the location of the mask bits and performs another iteration of the loop. Once all four color planes have been processed, the function loops to the next character line, until all 14 character lines have been written to display memory. The function then increments the column position of the cursor position data and stores this through the ROM BIOS video service.

Writing a Horizontal Character

The *color_printf* function given previously is fast and efficient and gives you complete color control. So why not use it for every application? There are two situations when it just isn't satisfactory. The first situation is when you are going to move the beginning of the screen to some line partway down the screen. This situation will be described in detail in Chapter 25. The point we want to make here is that the cursor positions used by *color_printf* cover only rows and columns on the normal display screen. If you want to write characters on a screen that has been shifted upward, you just can't do it with that function. Second, *color_printf* can select character positions using only text character coordinates. Thus, for example, a mode 16 graphics screen has 80×25 character positions, but it also has 640×350 pixel positions. If you are willing to satisfy yourself with locating a character at one of the 80×25 character positions, *color_printf* will do just fine. However, if you want the higher resolution, if you want to start a character one-fourth of the distance between two columns and one-half of the distance between two rows (for example), *color_printf* just won't do the job. For such unusual situations, we have created the function *writeHchar*. This function writes a single character horizontally, beginning at the position specified in pixel coordinates by the parameters x and y passed to the function. The function works only with the 16 color graphics modes. The function begins by using the global parameter *type* to determine whether the character is to have 8, 14 or 16 lines. (Thus this function can handle any eight pixel wide type font.) The function then computes the offset into the character table for each character. It determines the foreground and background colors from the color parameter that was passed to it. The function then enters a pair of *for* loops. The outer loop iterates once for each line of the character. The inner loop iterates once for each pixel of character width (eight in all). Each loop iteration begins by determining the position of the current pixel of the character being drawn. The *char_test* mask is then set to mask the bit corresponding to the current pixel of character width that is being processed. The appropriate bit in the character table is masked out and, if it is a 0, the variable *point_color* is set to the background color, whereas if it is a 1, the variable is set to the foreground color. Next the display memory address for the current pixel is determined. A mask is set and output to graphics control register 8 to assure that only the currently selected pixel will be modified. Sequencer register 2 is then set for all color planes, and a dummy read of the appropriate memory address is performed to get the data from the color planes into the proper EGA/VGA registers. Then a 0 is sent to the memory address to zero out the selected bit in all color planes. Sequencer register 2 is set to activate only those color planes corresponding to the desired pixel color. An *FFH* is sent to the memory address to turn on the pixel bit in the proper color planes. When the two loops are complete, this process has been performed for eight pixels in a row for each line that makes up the desired character. Finally, the registers are reset to their nominal values and the function is complete.

Writing a Vertical Character to the Screen

None of the C compilers, either in their normal or graphics modes of operation, is capable of writing characters to the screen vertically. Yet this is often a desired option in creating graphics displays. The function *writeVchar* will write a character to the screen vertically, in any specified foreground and background colors, at a designated pixel position. The function works for any 16 color graphics mode. If you look at the listing for this function, you'll see that it is nearly identical to the *writeHchar* function, the only difference being that the addressing of the x and y coordinates is interchanged. If you use a mode having square pixels (such as mode 18 that is 640×480 pixels) the vertical characters will look exactly the same as horizontal characters, except that they are rotated 90 degrees. If you use a mode that doesn't have square pixels, then the characters appear a little distorted as compared with the horizontal characters, but they are still readable. This function cause characters to be written from top to bottom of the screen. Once you understand how this one works, it should be a simple matter for you to write a similar function that writes characters from top to bottom.

Writing a Horizontal String to the Screen

Suppose that we want to write a whole string of characters horizontally to the screen. Of course, we could use the *writeHchar* string once for each character, being careful to supply the correct position coordinates each time the function was called. However, we have chosen to create a function called *writeHstring* that will do the whole job in one simple operation. The heart of this function is a *while* loop that keeps reading characters from the string and processing them until a NULL is encountered to indicate that the string is complete. Within this loop, the function operates pretty much like *writeHchar*. There are a few extra things that we have to take care of, however. After each character has been written to the screen, we have to increase the x position coordinate by 8 (the character width) to position it properly to write the next character. Next, we have to check whether we have reached the end of the row. If so, we set the x position coordinate to 0 and increase the y position coordinate by the character height in pixels to properly position for the next character. Finally, we have to increment the pointer that is pointing at the current string character.

Writing a Vertical String to the Screen

The function *writeVstring* uses same techniques that were used to write a horizontal string to the screen but interchanges the x and y values to cause the string to be written vertically up the screen.

Writing Big Horizontal Characters

If you want some really nice big horizontal characters, you need to design each character on a large grid and convert the resulting information into a character table. Then you can use a version of *writeHchar* or *writeHstring* to display these large characters. If you don't want to go to all of this trouble, the function *writeBigChar* will use one of the existing character fonts and enlarge each pixel to a 4×4 pixel block. The result is a little chunky, but not at all bad. If you look at the listing for this function, you'll see that it is very much like the function for writing an ordinary horizontal character, except that the information for each pixel of the character is written in a 4×4 block of pixels instead of a single pixel. You can use this same technique to write a function for displaying vertical characters now that you understand how to do it.

Writing a String of Big Characters

The function *writeBigString* is very similar to those already described. It is used to write a string of big characters to the screen horizontally.

Writing Video Characters

If we take the function for writing big characters and write only a 3×3 pixel square for each character pixel, within a 4×4 pixel space, we have a very interesting effect, similar to lighted signs on a theater marque. The function *writeVideoChar* does this job.

Writing a String of Video Characters

The function *writeVideoString* is very similar to those already described. It is used to write a string of video characters to the screen horizontally.

Writing a String in the Undocumented Modes

The undocumented 256 color display modes described in Chapter 8 are another place where the normal methods of displaying text will not work. You need to create your own function for displaying text in these modes. The function *writeString* will do this for you. As with the other similar functions, you have to get the address of the desired font table before you use it. You can then use the function with either 8, 14 or 16 pixel long characters, whichever font you have selected. The function is just the same as the *writeHstring* function except for the part that writes the pixels out to display memory. That section is the same as the technique described for writing a pixel in Chapter 8. The mode numbers used in this part of the program are different from those used in Chapter 8, demonstrating the fact that for undocumented modes, the mode number selection is arbitrary as long as it doesn't overlap those modes assigned by IBM.

The *chartest.c* Program

The program *chartest.c* provides a demonstration of the various character drawing techniques described in this chapter. The program begins by setting the display mode to mode 16 (640×350 pixels × 16 colors). It next finds the address of the 8×14 pixel font. It then displays "Big Letters", using the *writeBigString* function, "Video Letters", using the *writeVideoString* function, and "OK", using the *writeBigChar* and *writeVideoChar* functions. Next the program uses the *writeHchar* function to write the font of ASCII characters from 33 to 125. The program then uses the function *writeVchar* to write these same characters. The program uses the function *writeHstring* to write a very long horizontal string, to demonstrate that carrying over from the end of one row to the beginning of the next works properly. The program writes a vertical string using the function *writeVstring*. The program then writes strings using *printf, cprintf* and *color_printf*. The resulting display is shown in Plate 24. After this display screen is completed, each time a key is pressed, the program sets up one of the undocumented modes described in Chapter 8 and uses the function *writeString* to display a string on the screen, until all undocumented modes have been displayed.

Chapter 20

Rotating Geometric Figures

In Chapter 14 we had a brief introduction to figure rotation with one of the ellipse drawing functions, which permitted the orientation of the ellipse to be specified. However, at that point, there wasn't much discussion of the principle involved. In this chapter, we'll look at the mathematics of coordinate rotation and come up with some techniques that can be used to rotate triangles and rectangles and that can easily be extended to just about any other type of geometric figure. The functions and a test program are all included in the file *testrot.c*, which is listed in Figure 20-2.

Rotation Geometry

Figure 20-1 shows the geometry that is involved in a rotation. The coordinate system is rotated through an angle θ. One pair of rectangles shows what happens when a rectangle at the origin is rotated and another pair shows what happens when rotation occurs for a rectangle that is not centered at the origin. The dotted triangle is similar to the one formed by the original and rotated x coordinates, from which the distance expressions given in the diagram can be computed. From these, it can be seen that the new coordinates of a point *(x1,y1)* are related to the original coordinates *(x,y)* as follows:

Figure 20-1. Coordinate Rotation Geometry

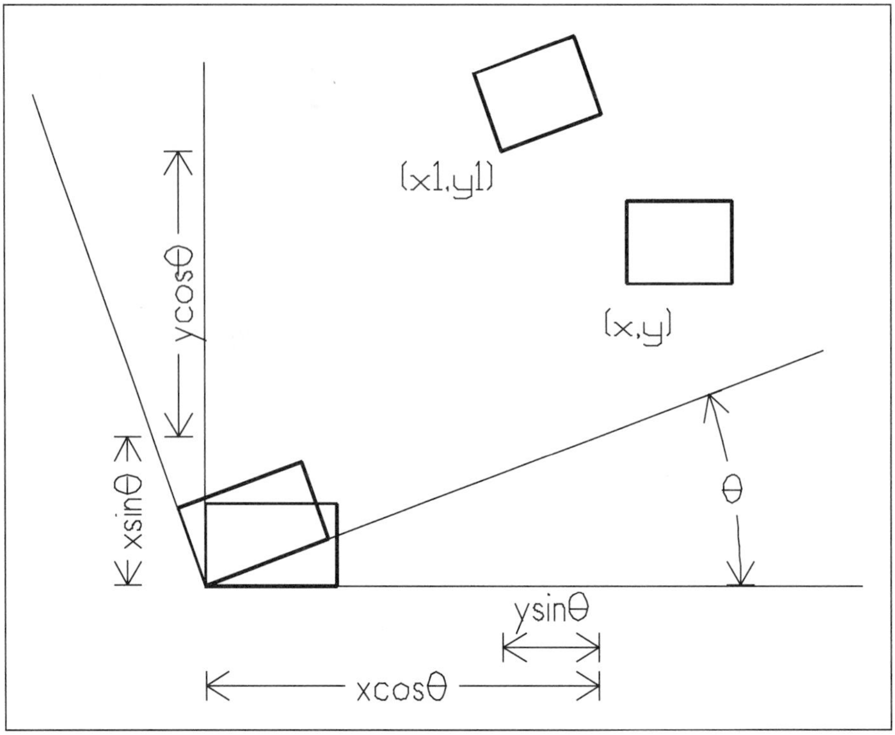

$$x1 = x\cos\theta - y\sin\theta$$

(Equation 20-1)

$$y1 = x\sin\theta + y\cos\theta$$

(Equation 20-2)

Before actually using these expressions in a function, we need to decide the location of the origin about which we want to rotate our geometric figures. Often, we won't want to rotate our whole display. Instead we will want to rotate each geometric shape individually. This requires that we temporarily shift the coordinate system so that its origin is at the point about which we wish to rotate the shape, perform the mathematics of rotation and then shift the coordinate system back to where it was originally. In our rotation program, we have two geometric shapes, a rectangle and a triangle. The function for the rectangle is set up to rotate it about the top left-hand corner of the rectangle. The function for the triangle is set up to rotate it about the first of the three vertices that are passed to the function to specify the triangle. Once you get the feel for how this is done, you should be able to extend the process to any other geometric shape and to change the point about which you are rotating each shape to meet your particular requirements. Some of the functions you will need are listed in Figure 20-2.

Figure 20-2. Listing of testrot.c Program for Testing Object Rotation

```
/*

    testrot = Program to test rotating of rectangles and
                         triangle.

              By Roger T. Stevens   12-18-91

*/

#include <stdio.h>
#include <stdlib.h>
#include <math.h>
#include <dos.h>
#include <conio.h>

typedef struct
{
    long int xs;
    long int ys;
    long int xe;
    long int ye;
} LINE;

typedef struct
```

(continued)

```
    {
        long int xa;
        long int ya;
        long int xb;
        long int yb;
        long int xc;
        long int yc;
    } TRIANGLE;

LINE line, bounds;
TRIANGLE triangle;

LINE clipLine(LINE line, LINE bounds);
void cls(char colors);
void drawLine(LINE line, LINE bounds, int color);
void drawRect(LINE line, LINE bounds, float angle, int
    color);
void drawTriangle(TRIANGLE triangle, LINE bounds, float
    angle, int color);
void plot(int x, int y, int color);
void setMode(int mode);

#define convert(x,y)  {x += 319; \
                  y = 175 - ((93*y) >> 7);}

int color = 2, angle, xres=640, yres=350;

/*
```

```
+-------------------------------------------------------+
|                                                       |
|                   MAIN PROGRAM                        |
|                                                       |
+-------------------------------------------------------+
```

```
*/

void main(void)
{
    int i, j, angle;

    randomize();
    setMode(0x10);
    cls (1);
```

(continued)

```
color = 3;
bounds.xs = 0;
bounds.ys = 0;
bounds.xe = xres-1;
bounds.ye = yres-1;
line.xs = 0;
line.ys = 0;
line.xe = 200;
line.ye = 100;
for (i=0; i<360; i+=15)
    drawRect(line,bounds,i,color++);
getch();
cls (1);
color = 2;
triangle.xa = 0;
triangle.ya = 0;
triangle.xb = 150;
triangle.yb = 50;
triangle.xc = 100;
triangle.yc = -35;
for (i=0; i<360; i+=15)
{
    drawTriangle(triangle,bounds,i,color);
    color = (color + 1) % 16;
    if (color==1)
        color++;
}
getch();
cls(4);
color = 0;
for (i=0; i<20; i++)
{
    color = (++color)%16;
    if (color == 4)
        color++;
    if (random(2) == 0)
    {
        line.xs = random(640) - 329;
        line.ys = random(480) - 240;
        line.xe = line.xs + random(100);
        line.ye = line.ys + random(75);
```

(continued)

```
                for (j=0; j<360; j+=15)
                    drawRect(line,bounds,j,color);
            }
            else
            {
                triangle.xa =  random(640) - 320;
                triangle.ya =  random(480) - 240;
                triangle.xb = triangle.xa + random(100);
                triangle.yb = triangle.xa + random(75);
                triangle.xc = triangle.xa + random(100);
                triangle.yc = triangle.xa + random(75);
                for (j=0; j<360; j+=15)
                    drawTriangle(triangle, bounds, j,color);
            }
        }
        getch();
    }

    /*
```

```
        drawRect() = Draws a rectangle within a clipping
          boundary having the following characteristics:
                        line = top left hand corner and bottom
                            right-hand corner of rectangle
                        angle = tilt angle of rectangle (around
                                        top left corner)
                        color = color of oval
```

```
    */

    void drawRect(LINE line, LINE bounds, float angle, int
        color)
    {
        LINE t1, t2, t3, t4;
        int ca, sa;

        ca = cos(angle * 0.017453292) * 512;
        sa = sin(angle * 0.017453292) * 512;

        t4.xe = t1.xs = line.xs;
```

(continued)

```
        t4.ye = t1.ys = line.ys;
        t2.xs = t1.xe = t1.xs + (((long)(line.xe - t1.xs) *
            ca) >> 9) - (((long)(line.ys - t1.ys) * sa) >> 9);
        t2.ys = t1.ye = t1.ys + (((long)(line.xe - t1.xs) *
            sa) >> 9) + (((long)(line.ys - t1.ys) *) >> 9);
        t3.xs = t2.xe = t1.xs + (((long)(line.xe - t1.xs) *
            ca) >> 9) - (((long)(line.ye - t1.ys) * sa) >> 9);
        t3.ys = t2.ye = t1.ys + (((long)(line.xe - t1.xs) *
            sa) >> 9) + (((long)(line.ye - t1.ys) * ca) >> 9);
        t4.xs = t3.xe = t1.xs + (((long)(line.xs - t1.xs) *
            ca) >> 9) - (((long)(line.ye - t1.ys) * sa) >> 9);
        t4.ys = t3.ye = t1.ys + (((long)(line.xs - t1.xs) *
            sa) >> 9) + (((long)(line.ye - t1.ys) * ca) >> 9);
        drawLine(t1, bounds, color);
        drawLine(t2, bounds, color);
        drawLine(t3, bounds, color);
        drawLine(t4, bounds, color);
}


/*
```

```
     drawTriangle() Draws a triangle within a clipping
  rectangle which has the following characteristics:
            (xa,ya), (xb,yb), (xc,yc) = vertices of
                        triangle
            angle = tilt angle of triangle
            color = color of oval
```

```
*/

void drawTriangle(TRIANGLE triangle, LINE bounds, float
    angle, int color)
{
    LINE t1, t2, t3;
    int ca, sa;

    ca = cos(angle * 0.017453292) * 512;
    sa = sin(angle * 0.017453292) * 512;

    t3.xe = t1.xs = triangle.xa;
```

(continued)

573

```
        t3.ye = t1.ys = triangle.ya;
        t2.xs = t1.xe = t1.xs + (((long)(triangle.xb - t1.xs)
            * ca) >> 9) - (((long)(triangle.yb - t1.ys)*sa) >>
            9);
        t2.ys = t1.ye = t1.ys + (((long)(triangle.xb - t1.xs)
            * sa) >> 9) + (((long)(triangle.yb - t1.ys)*ca) >>
            9);
        t3.xs = t2.xe = t1.xs + (((long)(triangle.xc - t1.xs)
            * ca) >> 9) - (((long)(triangle.yc - t1.ys)*sa) >>
            9);
        t3.ys = t2.ye = t1.ys + (((long)(triangle.xc - t1.xs)
            * sa) >> 9) + (((long)(triangle.yc - t1.ys)*ca) >>
            9);
        drawLine(t1, bounds, color);
        drawLine(t2, bounds, color);
        drawLine(t3, bounds, color);
    }


    /*
    ┌─────────────────────────────────────────────────────┐
    │                                                     │
    │                cls() = Clears the screen            │
    │                                                     │
    └─────────────────────────────────────────────────────┘
    */

    void cls(char colors)
    {

        union REGS reg;

        reg.x.dx = 0x184F;
        reg.h.bh = colors;
        reg.x.ax = 0x0600;
        reg.x.cx = 0;
        int86(0x10,&reg,&reg);
        gotoxy(0,0);
    }
```

(continued)

```
/*
```

```
              setMode() = Sets video mode
```

```
*/
```

```
void setMode(int mode)
{
    union REGS reg;

    reg.h.ah = 0;
    reg.h.al = mode;
    int86 (0x10,&reg,&reg);
}
```

```
/*
```

```
    plot() = Plots a point on the screen at designated
            screen coordinates using selected color
```

```
*/
```

```
void plot(int x, int y, int color)
{
    unsigned int offset;
    int dummy,mask,page;
    char far * mem_address;

    offset = (long)y * 80L + ((long)x / 8L);
    mem_address = (char far *) 0xA0000000L + offset;
    mask = 0x8000 >> (x % 8);
    outport(0x3CE,mask | 0x08);
    outport(0x3CE,0x0205);
    dummy = *mem_address;
    *mem_address = color;
    outport(0x3CE,0xFF08);
    outport(0x3CE,0x0005);
}
```

(continued)

```
/*
```

```
    drawLine() = Draws a single pixel wide line within a
        clipping rectangle in a selected color using the
        plot function. Will work with any plot function.
            The one used in this example is for mode 16
                    (640×350 pixels × 16 colors
```

```
*/

void drawLine(LINE line, LINE bounds, int color)
{

    int temp, dx, dy, i, x, y, xs, xe, ys, ye, x_sign,
        y_sign, decision;

    convert(line.xs,line.ys);
    convert(line.xe,line.ye);
    if (line.xs > line.xe)
    {
        temp = line.xe;
        line.xe = line.xs;
        line.xs = temp;
        temp = line.ye;
        line.ye = line.ys;
        line.ys = temp;
    }
    if ((line.xs > bounds.xe) || (line.xe <= bounds.xs) ||
        ((line.ye > bounds.ye) && (line.ys > bounds.ye))
        || ((line.ys < bounds.ys) && (line.ye <
        bounds.ys)))
        return;
    if (line.xs == line.xe)
    {
        line.ys = min(bounds.ye, line.ys);
        line.ys = max(bounds.ys, line.ys);
        line.ye = min(bounds.ye, line.ye);
        line.ye = max(bounds.ys, line.ye);
    }
    else
```

(continued)

```
{
    if (line.ys == line.ye)
    {
        if ((line.ys > bounds.ye) || (line.ys <
            bounds.ys))
        {
            return;
        }
        line.xs = max(bounds.xs, line.xs);
        line.xe = min(bounds.xe, line.xe);
    }
    else
    {
        dy = line.ye - line.ys;
        dx = line.xe - line.xs;
        if (line.xs < bounds.xs)
        {
            line.ys = line.ys + (long)(bounds.xs -
                line.xs)*dy/dx;
            line.xs = bounds.xs;
        }
        if (line.ys < bounds.ys)
        {
            line.xs = line.xs + (long)(bounds.ys -
                line.ys)*dx/dy;
            line.ys = bounds.ys;
        }
        if (line.ys > bounds.ye)
        {
            line.xs = line.xs + (long)(bounds.ye -
                line.ys)*dx/dy;
            line.ys = bounds.ye;
        }
        if (line.xe > bounds.xe)
        {
            line.ye = line.ys + (long)(bounds.xe -
                line.xs)*dy/dx;
            line.xe = bounds.xe;
        }
        if (line.ye < bounds.ys)
        {
```

(continued)

```
                line.xe = line.xs + (long)(bounds.ys -
                    line.ys)*dx/dy;
                line.ye = bounds.ys;
        }
        if (line.ye > bounds.ye)
        {
                line.xe = line.xs + (long)(bounds.ye -
                    line.ys)*dx/dy;
                line.ye = bounds.ye;
        }
    }
}
xs = line.xs;
ys = line.ys;
xe = line.xe;
ye = line.ye;
dx = abs(xe - xs);
dy = abs(ye - ys);
if ((dy > dx) && (ys > ye))
{
    temp = xs;
    xs = xe;
    xe = temp;
    temp = ys;
    ys = ye;
    ye = temp;
}
if ((ye - ys) < 0)
    y_sign = -1;
else
    y_sign = 1;
if ((xe - xs) < 0)
    x_sign = -1;
else
    x_sign = 1;
if (dx >= dy)
{
    for (x=xs,y=ys,decision=0; x<=xe;
        x++,decision+=dy)
    {
        if (decision>=dx)
```

(continued)

```
            {
                decision -= dx;
                y+= y_sign;
            }
            plot(x,y,color);
        }
    }
    else
    {
        for (x=xs,y=ys,decision=0; y<=ye;
            y++,decision+=dx)
        {
            if (decision>=dy)
            {
                decision -= dy;
                x+=x_sign;
            }
            plot(x,y,color);
        }
    }
}
```

Drawing Lines for Rotated Figures

The two representative functions that are used in illustrating rotation simply draw a series of straight lines to represent the desired figure. Without some constraints, you can get into a lot of trouble trying to rotate and then draw lines. The first constraint that we impose is to make use of the set of system coordinates, in which the origin is at the center of the display screen. (The left-hand side of the screen has an x value of -320 and the right side a value of +319. The bottom of the screen has a y value of -240 and the top a value of +239.) Therefore if we rotate a figure whose center of rotation is at the origin *(0,0)*, it will rotate right around the center of the screen. The second constraint is that we are going to clip each line before we draw it, so that it fits within the bounds of the screen. Even if we have a figure that is totally on the screen before we begin rotating, it may be partly off the screen after a rotation occurs. This can cause all kinds of complicated and unusual displays if clipping is not employed. Now take a look at the special version of the function *drawLine* that we have employed in the program listing. This function incorporates the two constraints just given so that the figures can be drawn with the origin at the screen center and can be drawn when they are partially off the edge of the screen without any undue complications. Looking at the function listing, you will note at the very beginning that we use the macro *convert* to make the conversion to screen coordinates from system coordinates. This macro is set up to make the conversion for the mode 16 display (640×350 pixels × 16 colors) but can easily be changed to accomodate any other display mode. Next, the function runs through a procedure that is just like that used by the function *clipLine1* described in Chapter 12. The only difference is that at various places, *clipLine1* sets *xs* to -999 and then returns the new line values. This indicates that the routine to draw the line should not be entered since the line is outside of the clipping boundary. In this function, the line drawing is incorporated within the same function with the clipping, so these special cases require only that the function immediately return to the calling program, since this results in the line not being drawn. After coordinate conversion and clipping have taken place, the function proceeds in the same manner as the *drawLine* functions described in Chapter 7 to draw the line either between the original endpoints if they were within the clipping boundary, or between the new (clipped) endpoints.

Rotated Rectangles and Triangles

Next, lets look at the *drawRect* function. Note that this function makes use of a structure that contains two sets of coordinates. Normally, the first is used to designate the beginning point of a line and the second the endpoint of the line. In this case, however, a structure of this type is passed to indicate the top left and bottom right corners of the rectangle to be drawn and a second structure is passed to show the corresponding corners of the clipping rectangle. The function first generates integers that are the sine and cosine of the rotation angle multiplied by 512. This is enough precision to determine the rotated position of a set of coordinates to within one pixel. Next, the function generates the coordinates for the starting and endpoints of the four rotated lines of the rectangle. After each enlarged sine or cosine is used to multiply a coordinate position, the product is shifted nine places (the same as dividing by 512) to make the mathematics correct. Using integers and enlarging the sine and cosine and then reducing them back by shifting after the product is obtained is a much faster way of performing the operations than if floating point numbers were used. The very first pair of coordinates are the same as the top left corner of the rectangle, since this is the point around which the rectangle is to be rotated and therefore remains constant. The remaining points are computed using the mathematics of equations 20-1 and 20-2, with the endpoint of each line segment corresponding to the starting point of the next, and the endpoint of the fourth and final end segment corresponding to the starting point of the first line segment. The *drawLine* function is then used four times to draw each of the line segments that make up the rectangle.

The function *drawTriangle* is passed a structure of three pairs of coordinates, each of which represents one vertex of the desired triangle. The function works much like *drawRect*, calculating the rotated values for the endpoints of the three line segments that make up the triangle. Observe that the first vertex specified for the triangle is the point around which the triangle is rotated. For this function, *drawLine* needs to be called only three times to draw the three lines that make up the triangle.

The *testrot.c* Program

The *testrot.c* program begins by setting the bounds of the clipping rectangle. It sets up the coordinates of a rectangle whose top left-hand corner is at the origin (the center of the display screen). It then enters a *for* loop that draws the rectangle on the screen rotated by multiples of 15 degrees from 15 to 345 degrees, each in a different color. Next the program sets the three vertices of a triangle and then enters another *for* loop that draws the triangle at rotations that increase in 15 degree steps from 0 to 345 degrees. The resulting screen is shown in Plate 25. The program then enters another *for* loop. This loop iterates 20 times. At each iteration, the program decides randomly whether rectangles or triangles are to be drawn. It then sets the points of the selected figure randomly and then draws the figure rotated by 15 degree increments from 0 to 345 degrees.

The Mathematics of Modeling Solids

In the following chapter, we are going to describe a program for modeling solid objects on the display screen. We're going to use two- and three-dimensional vectors to represent many of the quantities needed to perform the modeling tasks. To move, scale and reorient these vectors, we'll use 4×4 matrices. We need a lot of mathematical tools to handle these operations. Some of them are the simple tools of vector and matrix manipulation that you learned in school, but since they aren't a part of the mathematical repertory of the C libraries, we will have to create them for ourselves. Other functions are oriented more to the solid modeling task, but still need to be generalized for use in many operations. Before we get into the modeling itself, we will use this chapter to describe all of these mathematical techniques and how they are used. All of the vector, matrix and mathematical functions are part of the solid modeling program *solid.c*, which is listed in Figure 22-1 in the following chapter. Refer to the listing as you read the descriptions of the functions here.

Adding, Subtracting and Multiplying Vectors

The thing that determines how we are going to define vectors in the first place is that we would like to have the basic mathematical operations on vectors be as much like the same operations with numbers as possible. As we shall see in the Chapter 23, if we were using C++ we could have a vector operation exactly the same as a number operation, for example

$$c = a + b$$

(Equation 21-1)

We can't do this in C; the closest we can come is to use a function. A C function can return only one entity, but that entity can be a structure consisting of several variables. Therefore, we define a vector as

```
typedef struct
{
        float x,y,z;
} vector;
```

We can then define vector addition, for example, so that we can add two vectors in the following manner:

```
c = addvec(a,b);
```

Vector addition and subtraction are pretty simple; we simply add or subtract each pair of corresponding elements to obtain a new vector. You'll note in the listing that we have functions to do these operations for two types of vectors, floating point vectors and integer vectors. Vector multiplication becomes a little more complicated. We have a pretty simple multiplication function called *multelemvec*, which is passed a floating point number and two vectors. The function multiplies together each pair of corresponding elements of the two vectors and then multiplies the product by the floating point number. The result is a new vector. Another form of vector multiplication is the dot product of two vectors. This is a number obtained by multiplying together each pair of corresponding vector elements and then adding together the results. The dot product can also be expressed as

$$a \cdot b = AB \cos\theta$$

(Equation 21-2)

where a and b are the two vectors, A and B are the vector lengths respectively, and θ is the angle between the two vectors. We have two vector dot product functions, *dotvec* for floating point vectors and *dotvecint* for integer vectors.

The vector cross product is a combination of vector element products. You can plainly see the math involved in the function *cross*. The result is a vector that is at right angles to the two input vectors and which has a length:

$$|a \times b| = AB \sin\theta$$

(Equation 21-3)

The *cross* function gives the vector cross product for floating point vectors; for integer vectors the vector cross product is obtained from the function *crossint*.

The function *scalemult* multiplies a vector by a scalar for floating point vectors. This simply multiplies each element of the vector by the scalar. A similar function, *scalemultint* performs the same operation for an integer and an integer vector.

Length of a Vector

The function *lengthvec* obtains the length of a vector. The math is simple: the length is the square root of the sum of the squares of each of the vector elements.

Normalizing a Vector

When a vector is normalized, a new vector is created that has the same direction as the original vector but whose length is 1. This is easily obtained by dividing each of the original vector elements by the length of the original vector. The function *normvec* performs this operation.

Multiplying a Vector by a Matrix

We're now going to look at some functions that involve 4×4 element matrices. When a vector is multiplied by such a matrix, the result is a new vector that can represent a translation, rotation, or scaling of the old vector or a combination of all three, depending upon the values of the matrix elements. The actual multiplication process is quite similar to that used in obtaining the cross product of two vectors. You can see how the math is done by examining the function *mat_cross_vec*.

Translating a Vector

The matrix for translating a vector by t_x in the x direction, t_y in the y direction and t_z in the z direction is as follows:

$$
T = \begin{bmatrix} 1 & 0 & 0 & 0 \\ -t_x & 1 & 0 & 0 \\ -t_y & 0 & 1 & 0 \\ -t_z & 0 & 0 & 1 \end{bmatrix}
$$

(Equation 21-4)

Creating this matrix is accomplished by the function *translate*. This function is passed a vector that consists of the three translation parameters. It then generates the appropriate translation matrix. When the matrix operates upon a vector, the length and direction of the vector are unchanged but its position is changed as specified by the three parameters.

Scaling a Vector

The matrix for scaling a vector by s_x in the x direction, s_y in the y direction and s_z in the z direction is as follows:

$$S = \begin{bmatrix} s_x & 0 & 0 & 0 \\ 0 & s_y & 0 & 0 \\ 0 & 0 & s_z & 0 \\ 0 & 0 & 0 & 1 \end{bmatrix}$$

(Equation 21-5)

Creating this matrix is accomplished by the function *scale*. This function is passed a vector that consists of the three scaling parameters. It then generates the appropriate scaling matrix. When the matrix operates upon a vector, the position of the vector is unchanged but its length in each of the three axis directions is modified by the corresponding scaling parameter. Note that the scaling can differ for each axis direction, so that a cube could be scaled to become a rectangular parallelepiped or a sphere could be scaled to become an ellipsoid.

Rotating a Vector

A simple rotation matrix can be applied to a vector to rotate it about one of the three coordinate axes. One function, called *rotate*, is used for these operations; the first parameter passed to it represents the axis about which rotation is to take place; the second parameter is the angle of rotation in degrees. The matrix for scaling a vector around the x axis is:

$$R_x = \begin{bmatrix} 1 & 0 & 0 & 0 \\ 0 & \cos\theta & \sin\theta & 0 \\ 0 & -\sin\theta & \cos\theta & 0 \\ 0 & 0 & 0 & 1 \end{bmatrix}$$

(Equation 21-6)

The matrix for scaling a vector around the y axis is:

$$R_y = \begin{bmatrix} \cos\theta & 0 & -\sin\theta & 0 \\ 0 & 1 & 0 & 0 \\ -\sin\theta & 0 & \cos\theta & 0 \\ 0 & 0 & 0 & 1 \end{bmatrix}$$

(Equation 21-7)

The matrix for scaling a vector around the z axis is:

$$R_z = \begin{bmatrix} \cos\theta & \sin\theta & 0 & 0 \\ -\sin\theta & \cos\theta & 0 & 0 \\ 0 & 0 & 1 & 0 \\ 0 & 0 & 0 & 1 \end{bmatrix}$$

(Equation 21-8)

The function begins by zeroing all elements of the new matrix. It next sets all of the matrix elements that are to be 1. It then computes the sine and cosine of the rotation angle and places them in the proper elements (with the proper sign) for the rotation axis selected. The effect of this matrix on a vector is that the vector retains the same length and the same orientation on the plane defined by the two axes not selected, but is rotated by the specified angle around the selected axis.

Multiplying Two Matrices

The function *mult_mat* multiplies two 4×4 matrices together by taking the products of various element pairs and combining them together with the proper sign in a manner similar to that used for obtaining a vector cross product. You should be able to follow the math from the function listing; if you really want to get into the nitty gritty of it, refer to any textbook on matrices.

Putting It All Together

The function *transform* makes use of the function *mult_mat* to combine the scaling, translation and rotations about each of the three coordinate axes into a single matrix that performs all of the operations you want to do on a vector. You will see in the next chapter that we will have a transformation matrix that defines these operations for a particular object in a scene and that we will then apply it to the coordinates of every facet that makes up the object.

Projection from Three to Two Dimensions

To understand how the conversion is made from a three-dimensional scene to a two-dimensional picture, we need to examine how the positions of object in the scene are defined. Each object is specified by its position in a three-dimensional space in which *x* is to the left, *y* is forward, and *z* is up. At some point in this space is the location of the viewer, who is looking at the picture. The viewer position is initially specified in spherical coordinates, where *view_theta* is the angle from the *x* axis counterclockwise in the *x-y* plane, *view_phi* is the angle between the *z* axis and a line from the origin to the viewer, and *view_rho* is the length of the line from the origin to the viewer. Interposed between the viewer and the scene is a transparent screen upon which the projected image of the scene appears. The position and orientation of the screen are specified by the vector *screen*. The geometry of this situation is shown in Figure 21-1. Now it's time to turn to the listing of the function *map* to see what's involved in going from three to two dimensions. The equations listed are the result of a lot of vector manipulation to convert from the scene coordinates to a set of coordinates oriented in the plane of the screen and then to identify what a point in the scene will appear like on the screen to the viewer at his position. A vector specifying the three-dimensional coordinates of a point in the scene is passed to the map function, and it returns the column and row positions for the point in pixels on the display screen.

Figure 21-1. Geometry of Three-Dimensional to Two-Dimensional Conversion

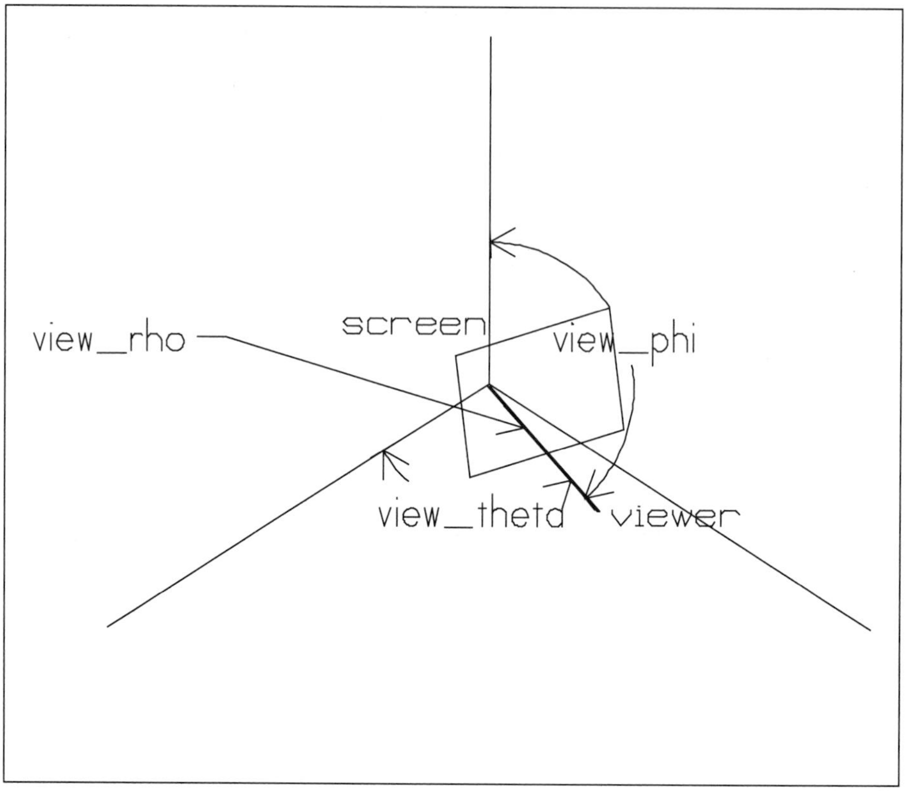

Chapter 22

Solid Modeling Techniques

Now that we've examined the mathematical operations that are needed for creating solid objects and then projecting their images onto a two-dimensional display, we're going to get into the actual mechanics of creating a program to perform the solid modeling process. Although this program is somewhat large and cumbersome, it really consists of just a few basic steps. First, we have to define each solid that we want to model as a collection of facets, each of which is a small quadrilateral. Together, these quadrilaterals approximate the surface of the solid. We are going to define each generic solid as a collection of quadrilaterals that are centered at the origin and fit within a box that is + or - 1 unit in each direction. Next we need the mathematics that translates, scales and rotates each generic object to make it into an object of the size we desire and in the position we desire it to be in the scene that we are creating. We then operate upon each facet of the object. Using information that has been stored for the position of the light source illuminating the scene, we determine the surface normal to the light projected upon the facet and from this compute the intensity of the light reflected from this facet back to the viewer. Finally, we determine the projection of the facet upon the two-dimensional screen and paint it on the screen in the appropriate color and brightness. Two things need to be noted here. First, as a rule, we have tried to define each object in such a way that the back of the object is painted on the screen first, followed by the front of the object. This assures that the front parts of the object will overdraw the back parts, which gives the effect that you would normally see in a scene. A test is also included that prevents painting a facet at all if the surface normal is pointed away from the viewer, indicating that it is a facet that cannot be seen. However, if you radically change the viewing angle, you may have to modify the order in which the facets of an object are painted to the screen to assure that the front parts of the object are drawn last. Also, there are some cases where all of this is just not enough. For example, in the Tower of Hanoi scene, we want to have a cylinder go down through the middle of several tori. The only way that this can be done is to paint the back half of each torus to the screen, then paint each cylinder, and finally paint the front half of each torus. To make this possible, we've set up the torus drawing function so that it can be called to draw each half of a torus separately. The second thing to note is that no provision has been made for properly ordering the painting of solids in the scene. For the scene to appear natural, you must paint the object that is farthest from the viewer first, followed by the next farthest, and so forth until the nearest object is painted last. It is up to you to determine the placement of the objects and place them in the proper order in your program. If you paint some of the nearest objects before the farther ones, you will get a very strange looking scene. By just looking, it is sometimes hard to determine just what's wrong, but you'll surely know that something is wrong. The entire program for modeling solids, including some typical scenes, is listed in Figure 22-1.

Figure 22-1. Listing of solid.c Program to Generate Scenes Made up of Solid Objects

```
/*


        SOLID = Program to model 3D Objects


        By Roger T. Stevens   11-8-91


*/

#include <stdio.h>
#include <dos.h>
#include <conio.h>
#include <math.h>
#include <string.h>
```

(continued)

```
#include <alloc.h>
#include <stdlib.h>

typedef struct
{
    float x,y,z;
} vector;

typedef struct
{
    int x,y,z;
} vecint;

typedef struct
{
    float elem[4][4];
} matrix;

typedef struct
{
    int col, row;
} plane;

typedef struct
{
    unsigned char red;
    unsigned char green;
    unsigned char blue;
} RGB;

RGB palette[256];

/*
```

```
                          Function Prototypes
```

```
*/

vector addvec(vector a,vector b);
void cls(int color);
```

(continued)

```
void cone(int no_facets, int color);
vector copy(vector a);
vector cross(vector a, vector b);
void cylinder(int no_facets, int color);
void cube(int color);
float dotvec(vector a, vector b);
void display_facet(vector facet3D[],int Color);
void draw(int xs, int ys, int xe, int ye, int color);
void draw_quad(plane v[], int color);
void fill_quad (plane quad[], int color);
float lengthvec(vector a);
plane map(vector a);
vector mat_cross_vec(vector a, matrix m);
vector multelemvec(float r, vector a, vector b);
matrix mult_mat(matrix a, matrix b);
vector normvec(vector a);
void plot256(int x, int y, int color);
matrix rotate(int axis, float angle);
matrix scale(vector a);
vector scalemult(float r, vector a);
vecint scalemultint(int r, vecint a);
void setMode(int s_mode);
vector setvec(float x, float y, float z);
vecint setvecint(int x, int y, int z);
void setVGAcolors(RGB palette[]);
void setVGApalette(unsigned char *buffer);
void solid_rev(int type, int color);
vector subvec(vector a,vector b);
void surface(int color);
vector surface_normal(vector facet3D[]);
void sphere(int color);
void toroid(int type, int no_facets, float r1, float r2,
    int    color);
matrix transform(vector tr, vector sc, vector ro);
matrix translate(vector a);

#define light_phi 45
#define light_theta 45
#define light_max 35
#define compare(a,b,c)  {if (a<b) b = a; if (a>c) c = a;}
```

(continued)

```
int view_theta = 240, view_phi = 18, view_rho = 500;
vector view, screen;
matrix trans1;
const xres = 320;
const yres = 200;
int mode=2;
matrix mat,zero={0,0,0,0,0,0,0,0,0,0,0,0,0,0,0,0};
vector surf_norm, light, tr,sc,ro;
float CP,SP,CT,ST;
int x_center, y_center;

/*
```

```
                          Main Program
```

```
*/

void main(void)
{
    float r, s;
    int i,j;
    vector trans[12], toroid_vecs[7], facet3D[4];
    float phi, theta;
    float x, y, z;

    setMode(3);
    textcolor(YELLOW);
    textbackground(BLUE);
    clrscr();
    printf("Three-dimensional modeling of solids\n\n");
    perspective = setvec(0,-25,450);
    x_center=(xres-1) >> 1;
    y_center=(yres-1) >> 1;
    CT=cos(0.017453292*angle);
    ST=sin(0.017453292*angle);
    CP=cos(0.017453292*tilt);
    SP=sin(0.017453292*tilt);
    view = setvec(-CP*ST,-CP*CT,SP);
    screen = setvec(0, -25, 450);
    printf("View Direction is %d around the z-Axis\n",
```

(continued)

```
                    view_theta);
        printf("                    %d off the z-Axis\n",
            view_phi);
        printf("Light Direction is %d around the z-Axis"
            " and\n", light_phi);
        printf("                    %d off the z-Axis\n",
            light_theta);
        phi=0.017453292*light_phi;
        theta=0.017453292*light_theta;
        light = setvec(sin(theta)*cos(phi),
            sin(theta)*sin(phi), cos(theta));
        printf("\nHit any key to continue...");
        getch();
```

```
/*
```

```
                            Cube
```

```
*/
```

```
        setMode(19);
        setVGAcolors(palette);
        setVGApalette(palette);
        r= 32.0;
        s= -48.0;
        sc = setvec(r,r,r);
        ro = setvec(0,0,0);
        tr = setvec(0,0,0);
        trans[6];
        cube(5);
        getch();
```

```
/*
```

```
                          Cylinders
```

```
*/
```

```
        setMode(19);
```

(continued)

```
setVGAcolors(palette);
setVGApalette(palette);
r= 24.0;
s= -80.0;
trans[6] = setvec(r, 0.293*r, -s-4.6*r);
trans[7] = setvec(-2*r, 0.293*r, -s-3.5*r);
trans[8] = setvec(0.0, -1.8*r, -s-4.1*r);
sc = setvec(r,r,1.5*r);
ro = setvec(0,0,0);
tr = trans[6];
cylinder(90,1);
sc = setvec(r,r,1.5*r);
ro = setvec(0,0,0);
tr = trans[7];
cylinder(90,4);
sc = setvec(r,r,1.5*r);
ro = setvec(0,0,0);
tr = trans[8];
cylinder(90,3);
getch();

/*
```

```
                    Sphere and three cones
```

```
*/

r= 32.0;
s= 80.0;
setMode(19);
setVGApalette(palette);
trans[6] = setvec(r, 0.293*r, s-2.6*r);
trans[7] = setvec(-r, 0.293*r, s-2.6*r);
trans[8] = setvec(0.0, -1.5*r, s-2.6*r);
trans[9] = setvec(0.0, -0.34*r, s-4.3*r);
sc = setvec(r,r,r);
ro = setvec(0,0,0);
tr = trans[6];
cone(60,1);
sc = setvec(r,r,r);
```

(continued)

```
ro = setvec(0,0,0);
tr = trans[7];
cone(60,4);
sc = setvec(r,r,r);
ro = setvec(0,0,0);
tr = trans[8];
cone(60,3);
sc = setvec(1.3*r,1.3*r,1.3*r);
ro = setvec(0,0,0);
tr = trans[9];;
sphere(2);
getch();

/*
```

Stacked cones

```
*/

r=16.0;
s=16.0;
trans[0] = setvec(2.0*r, r, -s-r);
trans[1] = setvec(0.0, r, -s-r);
trans[2] = setvec(-2.0*r, r, -s-r);
trans[3] = setvec(r, -0.866*r, -s-r);
trans[4] = setvec(-r, -0.866*r, -s-r);
trans[5] = setvec(0.0, -2.732*r, -s-r);
trans[6] = setvec(r, 0.293*r, -s-2.6*r);
trans[7] = setvec(-r, 0.293*r, -s-2.6*r);
trans[8] = setvec(0.0, -1.5*r, -s-2.6*r);
trans[9] = setvec(0.0, -0.5*r, -s-4.4*r);
setMode(19);
setVGApalette(palette);
sc = setvec(r,r,r);
ro = setvec(0,0,0);
for(i=0; i<10; i++)
{
    tr = trans[i];
    cone(60,(i%7) + 1);
}
```

(continued)

```
getch();
```

```
/*
```

```
                        Stacked spheres
```

```
*/
```

```
    setMode(19);
    setVGApalette(palette);
    sc = setvec(r,r,r);
    ro = setvec(0,0,0);
    for(i=0; i<10; i++)
    {
        tr = trans[i];
        sphere((i%7) + 1);
    }
    getch();
```

```
/*
```

```
                        Stacked pyramids
```

```
*/
```

```
    setMode(19);
    setVGApalette(palette);
    for(i=0; i<10; i++)
    {
        sc = setvec(r,r,r);
        ro = setvec(0,0,0);
        tr = trans[i];
        cone(4,(i%7) + 1);
    }
    getch();
```

(continued)

```
/*
```

```
                              .Bowling
```

```
*/
```

```
    setMode(19);
    setVGApalette(palette);
    sc = setvec(70,112,1);
    ro = setvec(0,0,0);
    tr = setvec(45,25,0);
    trans1 = transform(tr, sc, ro);
    facet3D[0] = setvec(1,1,0),
    facet3D[0] = mat_cross_vec(facet3D[0],trans1);
    facet3D[1] = setvec(-1,1,0);
    facet3D[1] = mat_cross_vec(facet3D[1],trans1);
    facet3D[2] = setvec(-1,-1,0);
    facet3D[2] = mat_cross_vec(facet3D[2],trans1);
    facet3D[3] = setvec(1,-1,0);
    facet3D[3] = mat_cross_vec(facet3D[3],trans1);
    display_facet(facet3D,6);
    sc = setvec(2*r,2*r,2*r);
    ro = setvec(0,0,0);
    trans[0] = setvec(152,184,0);
    trans[1] = setvec(120,184,0);
    trans[2] = setvec(88,184,0);
    trans[3] = setvec(56,184,0);
    trans[4] = setvec(136,152,0);
    trans[5] = setvec(104,152,0);
    trans[6] = setvec(72,152,0);
    trans[7] = setvec(120,120,0);
    trans[8] = setvec(88,120,0);
    trans[9] = setvec(104,88,0);
    for (i=0; i<10; i++)
    {
        tr = trans[i];
        solid_rev(2,7);
    }
    r=18.0;
    sc = setvec(r,r,r);
```

(continued)

```
tr = setvec(80,-30,0);
sphere(1);
getch();
```

/*

```
+--------------------------------------------------+
|                                                  |
|                   Chessboard                     |
|                                                  |
+--------------------------------------------------+
```

*/

```
setMode(19);
setVGAcolors(palette);
setVGApalette(palette);
ro = setvec(0,0,0);
sc = setvec(20,20,0);
for (j=-40; j<250; j+=80)
    for (i=-40; i<250; i+=80)
    {
        tr = setvec(j,i,0);
        surface(4);
    }
for (j=0; j<250; j+=80)
    for (i=0; i<250; i+=80)
    {
        tr = setvec(j,i,0);
        surface(4);
    }
sc = setvec(22,22,20);
tr = setvec(90,70,0);
solid_rev(0,7);
tr = setvec(178,202,0);
solid_rev(0,7);
tr = setvec(225,25,0);
solid_rev(0,3);
sc = setvec(22,22,26);
tr = setvec(55,125,0);
solid_rev(1,7);
tr = setvec(12,-12,0);
solid_rev(1,3);
getch();
```

(continued)

601

```
/*

┌─────────────────────────────────────────────────────────────┐
│ ┌───────────────────────────────────────────────────────────┐ │
│ │                                                           │ │
│ │                      Towers of Hanoi                      │ │
│ │                                                           │ │
│ └───────────────────────────────────────────────────────────┘ │
└─────────────────────────────────────────────────────────────┘

*/

    setMode(19);
    setVGAcolors(palette);
    setVGApalette(palette);
    ro = setvec(0,0,0);
    toroid_vecs[0] = setvec(-45,-20,-17);
    toroid_vecs[1] = setvec(-45,-20,-38);
    toroid_vecs[2] = setvec(-45,-20,-59);
    toroid_vecs[3] = setvec(20,-90,-7);
    toroid_vecs[4] = setvec(20,-90,-24);
    toroid_vecs[5] = setvec(-80,50,-1);
    toroid_vecs[6] = setvec(-80,50,-13);
    for (i=0; i<7;i++)
    {
        sc = setvec(50-5*i,50-5*i,50-5*i);
        tr = toroid_vecs[i];
        toroid(1,60,.75,.25,i+1);
    }
    sc = setvec(7,7,55);
    tr = setvec(20,-90,-45);
    cylinder(90,7);
    tr = setvec(-45,-20,-45);
    cylinder(90,7);
    tr = setvec(-80,50,-45);
    cylinder(90,7);
    for (i=0; i<7;i++)
    {
        sc = setvec(50-5*i,50-5*i,50-5*i);
        tr = toroid_vecs[i];
        toroid(0,60,.75,.25,i+1);
    }
    getch();
    setMode(3);
}
```

(continued)

```
/*

     display_facet() = Displays and shades a facet on screen

*/

void display_facet(vector facet3D[],int Color)
{
    float ambient=0.30;
    float diffuse=0.50;
    float specular=0.20;
    float glossiness=5.0;
    float cos_theta, cos_alpha, cos_beta;
    vector temp;
    int intensity;
    int i;
    plane facet2D[4], temp2;
    surf_norm = surface_normal(facet3D);
    temp = multelemvec(1.0, view, surf_norm);
    cos_beta=temp.x + temp.y + temp.z;
    if (cos_beta > 0.0)
    {
        cos_theta = dotvec(surf_norm, light);
        if(cos_theta<=0.0)
            intensity = light_max * ambient;
        else
        {
            temp = scalemult(cos_theta, surf_norm);
            temp = normvec(temp);
            temp = subvec(temp, light);
            temp = normvec(temp);
            cos_alpha = dotvec(view, temp);
            intensity = light_max * (ambient +
                diffuse * cos_theta + specular *
                pow(cos_alpha, glossiness));
        }
        if(intensity>=1)
        {
            for(i=0; i<4; i++)
                facet2D[i] = map(facet3D[i]);
```

(continued)

603

```
                      facet2D[4] = facet2D[0];
                      if(mode == 0)
                      {
                          plot256(facet2D[0].col, facet2D[0].row,
                              light_max*Color);
                          plot256(facet2D[1].col, facet2D[1].row,
                              light_max*Color);
                          plot256(facet2D[2].col, facet2D[2].row,
                              light_max*Color);
                          plot256(facet2D[3].col, facet2D[3].row,
                              light_max*Color);
                      }
                      if(mode == 1)
                          draw_quad(facet2D,light_max*Color);
                      if(mode == 2)
                          fill_quad (facet2D,((light_max+1) *
                              (Color-1)+intensity) & 255);
                  }
              }
      }


/*
```

```
  surface_normal() = Computes surface normal to a facet
```

```
*/

vector surface_normal(vector facet3D[])
{
    float length1, length2;
    vector dir1, dir2, srf_normal1, srf_normal2;

    dir1 = subvec(facet3D[1], facet3D[0]);
    dir2 = subvec(facet3D[3],facet3D[0]);
    srf_normal1 = cross(dir1, dir2);
    length1 = lengthvec(srf_normal1);
    dir1 = subvec(facet3D[3],facet3D[2]);
    dir2 = subvec(facet3D[1],facet3D[2]);
    srf_normal2 = cross(dir1, dir2);
    length2 = lengthvec(srf_normal2);
```

(continued)

```
        if(length1 == 0.0)
            srf_normal1 = normvec(srf_normal2);
        else
        {
            srf_normal1 = normvec(srf_normal1);
            if(length2 != 0.0)
            {
                srf_normal2 = normvec(srf_normal2);
                srf_normal1 = addvec(srf_normal1,srf_normal2);
                srf_normal1 = scalemult(0.5, srf_normal1);
            }
        }
        return(srf_normal1);
}

/*
┌─────────────────────────────────────────────────────────┐
│                                                         │
│                   GRAPHICS FUNCTIONS                    │
│                                                         │
└─────────────────────────────────────────────────────────┘
*/

/*
┌─────────────────────────────────────────────────────────┐
│                                                         │
│                cls() = Clears the screen                │
│                                                         │
└─────────────────────────────────────────────────────────┘
*/

void cls(int color)
{
    union REGS reg;

    reg.x.ax = 0x0600;
    reg.x.cx = 0;
    reg.x.dx = 0x3284;
    reg.h.bh = color;
    int86(0x10,&reg,&reg);
}
```

(continued)

```
/*
```

```
    draw() = Draws a line between two sets of coordinates
            in designated color using 256color mode.
```

```
*/
```

```c
void draw(int xs, int ys, int xe, int ye, int color)
{
    int temp, dx, dy, y_sign, i, x, y, decision;

    if (xs > xe)
    {
        temp = xs;
        xs = xe;
        xe = temp;
        temp = ys;
        ys = ye;
        ye = temp;
    }
    dx = abs(xe - xs);
    dy = abs(ye - ys);
    if ((ye - ys) < 0)
        y_sign = -1;
    else
        y_sign = 1;
    if (dx > dy)
    {
        for (x=xs,y=ys,decision=0; x<=xe;
            x++,decision+=dy)
        {
            if (decision>=dx)
            {
                decision -= dx;
                y+= y_sign;
            }
            plot256(x,y,color);
        }
    }
    else
```

(continued)

```
    {
        for (x=xs,y=ys,decision=0; y!=ye; y+=y_sign,
            decision+=dx)
        {
            if (decision>=dy)
            {
                decision -= dy;
                x++;
            }
            plot256(x,y,color);
        }
    }
}

/*

    ┌─────────────────────────────────────────────────┐
    │                                                 │
    │       draw_quad() = Draws a quadrilateral       │
    │                                                 │
    └─────────────────────────────────────────────────┘
*/

void draw_quad(plane v[], int color)
{
    draw(v[0].col, v[0].row, v[1].col, v[1].row, color);
    draw(v[1].col, v[1].row, v[2].col, v[2].row, color);
    draw(v[2].col, v[2].row, v[3].col, v[3].row, color);
    draw(v[3].col, v[3].row, v[0].col, v[0].row, color);
}

/*

    ┌─────────────────────────────────────────────────┐
    │                                                 │
    │   fill_quad() = Fills a quadrilateral in a specified │
    │                        color                    │
    │                                                 │
    └─────────────────────────────────────────────────┘
*/

void fill_quad (plane quad[], int color)
{
    #define sign(x) ((x) > 0 ? 1:  ((x) == 0 ? 0:  (-1)))
    int dx, dy, dxabs, dyabs, i, j, px, py, sdx, sdy, x,
```

(continued)

```
        y, xpoint[5], ypoint[5], minrow=480, maxrow=0,
        coord[2][1024];

    for (i=0; i<4; i++)
    {
        xpoint[i] = quad[i].col;
        ypoint[i] = quad[i].row;
    }
    xpoint[4] = xpoint[0];
    ypoint[4] = ypoint[0];
    for (i=0; i<yres; i++)
    {
        coord[0][i] = 2048;
        coord[1][i] = 0;
    }
    for (j=0; j<4; j++)
    {
        px = xpoint[j];
        py = ypoint[j];
        dx = xpoint[j+1] - xpoint[j];
        dy = ypoint[j+1] - ypoint[j];
        sdx = sign(dx);
        sdy = sign(dy);
        dxabs = abs(dx);
        dyabs = abs(dy);
        x = 0;
        y = 0;
        if (dxabs >= dyabs)
        {
            for (i=0; i<dxabs; i++)
            {
                y += dyabs;
                if (y>=dxabs)
                {
                    y -= dxabs;
                    py += sdy;
                }
                px += sdx;
                compare(px,coord[0][py],coord[1][py]);
                compare(py,minrow,maxrow);
            }
```

(continued)

```
        }
        else
        {
            for (i=0; i<dyabs; i++)
            {
                x += dxabs;
                if (x>=dyabs)
                {
                    x -= dyabs;
                    px += sdx;
                }
                py += sdy;
                compare(px,coord[0][py],coord[1][py]);
                compare(py,minrow,maxrow);
            }
        }
    }
    for (i=minrow; i<=maxrow; i++)
        for (j=coord[0][i]; j<=coord[1][i]; j++)
            plot256(j,i,color);
}

/*
```

```
  plot256() = Plots a point on the screen at a designated
    position using a selected color for 256 color modes.
```

```
*/

void plot256(int x, int y, int color)
{
    char far * address;

    if ((x>0) && (x<320) && (y>0) && (y<200))
    {
        address = (char far *) 0xA0000000L + (long)y *
            xres + (long)x;
        *address = color;
    }
}
```

(continued)

```
/*
```

```
                    setMode() = Sets video mode
```

```
*/
```

```
void setMode(int s_mode)
{
    union REGS reg;

    reg.x.ax = s_mode;
    int86 (0x10,&reg,&reg);
}
```

```
/*
```

```
  setVGAcolors() = Function to generate 256 color array
```

```
*/
```

```
void setVGAcolors(RGB palette[])
{
    int i;

    for(i=0; i<252; i++)
    {
        if (i>107)
            palette[i].red = 1.8*(i%36);
        else
            palette[i].red = 0.;
        if ((i>35 && i<108) || (i>179))
            palette[i].green = 1.8*(i%36);
        else
            palette[i].green = 0.;
        if((i<36) || (i>71 && i<108) || (i>143 && i<180)
            || (i>215))
            palette[i].blue = 1.8*(i%36);
        else
            palette[i].blue = 0.;
```

(continued)

```
        }

    }

    /*
```

```
        setVGApalette() = Function to set all 256 color
                          registers
```

```
    */

    void setVGApalette(unsigned char *buffer)
    {
        struct SREGS inreg;
        union REGS reg;

        reg.x.ax = 0x1012;
        segread(&inreg);
        inreg.es = inreg.ds;
        reg.x.bx = 0;
        reg.x.cx = 256;
        reg.x.dx = (int)&buffer[0];
        int86x(0x10,&reg,&reg,&inreg);
    }

    /*
```

```
                    VECTOR AND MATHEMATICAL FUNCTIONS
```

```
                        setvec() = Set vector values
```

```
    */

    vector setvec(float x, float y, float z)
    {
        vector a;
```

(continued)

```
        a.x = x;
        a.y = y;
        a.z = z;
        return(a);
    }

/*
```

```
            setvecint() = Set integer vector values
```

```
*/

vecint setvecint(int x, int y, int z)
{
    vecint a;

    a.x = x;
    a.y = y;
    a.z = z;
    return(a);
}

/*
```

```
                addvec() = Adds two vectors
```

```
*/

vector addvec(vector a,vector b)
{
    vector c;

    c.x = a.x + b.x;
    c.y = a.y + b.y;
    c.z = a.z + b.z;
    return(c);
}
```

(continued)

```
/*
```

```
        subvec() = Subtracts one vector from another
```

```
*/

vector subvec(vector a,vector b)
{
    vector c;

    c.x = a.x - b.x;
    c.y = a.y - b.y;
    c.z = a.z - b.z;
    return(c);
}

/*
```

```
            addvecint() Add two integer vectors
```

```
*/

vecint addvecint(vecint a,vecint b)
{
    vecint c;

    c.x = a.x + b.x;
    c.y = a.y + b.y;
    c.z = a.z + b.z;
    return(c);
}

/*
```

```
  subvecint() = Subtracts one integer vector from another
```

```
*/
```

(continued)

```
vecint subvecint(vecint a,vecint b)
{
    vecint c;

    c.x = a.x + b.x;
    c.y = a.y + b.y;
    c.z = a.z + b.z;
    return(c);
}

/*
```

```
    dotvec() = Computes the dot product of two vectors
```

```
*/

float dotvec(vector a, vector b)
{
    return (a.x*b.x + a.y*b.y + a.z*b.z);
}

/*
```

```
   dotvecint() = Computes the dot product of two integer
                            vectors
```

```
*/

int dotvecint(vecint a, vecint b)
{
    return (a.x*b.x + a.y*b.y + a.z*b.z);
}

/*
```

```
    cross() = Computes the cross product of two vectors
```

```
*/
```

(continued)

```
vector cross(vector a, vector b)
{
    vector c;

    c.x = a.y*b.z - a.z*b.y;
    c.y = a.z*b.x - a.x*b.z;
    c.z = a.x*b.y - a.y*b.x;
    return(c);
}

/*
```

```
crossint() = Computes the cross product of two integer
                        vectors
```

```
*/

vecint crossint(vecint a, vecint b)
{
    vecint c;

    c.x = a.y*b.z - a.z*b.y;
    c.y = a.z*b.x - a.x*b.z;
    c.z = a.x*b.y - a.y*b.x;
    return(c);
}

/*
```

```
multelemvec() = Multiplies each element of a vector by
                the same element of another vector
```

```
*/

vector multelemvec(float r, vector a, vector b)
{
    vector c;

    c.x = r*a.x*b.x;
```

(continued)

```
            c.y = r*a.y*b.y;
            c.z = r*a.z*b.z;
            return(c);
        }
```

```
/*
```

┌───┐
│   │
│   lengthvec() = Finds the length of a vector   │
│   │
└───┘
```
*/
```

```
float lengthvec(vector a)
{
        return(sqrt(a.x*a.x + a.y*a.y + a.z*a.z));
}
```

```
/*
```

┌───┐
│   │
│   normvec() = Finds a normalized vector   │
│   │
└───┘
```
*/
```

```
vector normvec(vector a)
{
        float length;

        length = lengthvec(a);
        a.x /= length;
        a.y /= length;
        a.z /= length;
        return(a);
}
```

```
/*
```

┌───┐
│   │
│   translate() = Creates a matrix to translate vectors   │
│   │
└───┘
```
*/
```

(continued)

```
matrix translate(vector a)
{
    matrix b;
    int i;

    b = zero;
    for (i=0; i<4; i++)
        b.elem[i][i] = 1.0;
    b.elem[0][3] = -a.x;
    b.elem[1][3] = -a.y;
    b.elem[2][3] = -a.z;
    return(b);
}

/*
┌────────────────────────────────────────────────────┐
│ ┌────────────────────────────────────────────────┐ │
│ │                                                │ │
│ │    scale() = Creates a matrix to scale vectors │ │
│ │                                                │ │
│ └────────────────────────────────────────────────┘ │
└────────────────────────────────────────────────────┘
*/

matrix scale(vector a)
{
    matrix b;

    b = zero;
    b.elem[0][0] = a.x;
    b.elem[1][1] = a.y;
    b.elem[2][2] = a.z;
    b.elem[3][3] = 1.0;
    return(b);
}

/*
┌────────────────────────────────────────────────────┐
│ ┌────────────────────────────────────────────────┐ │
│ │                                                │ │
│ │   rotate() = Creates a matrix to rotate vectors│ │
│ │                                                │ │
│ └────────────────────────────────────────────────┘ │
└────────────────────────────────────────────────────┘
*/

matrix rotate(int axis, float angle)
```

(continued)

617

```
    {
        int  i,j;
        matrix a;
        float c,s;

        a = zero;
        a.elem[axis-1][axis-1] = 1.0;
        a.elem[3][3] = 1.0;
        i = (axis % 3) + 1;
        j = i %3;
        i -= 1;
        c = cos(angle * 0.017453292);
        s = sin(angle * 0.017453292);
        a.elem[i][i] = c;
        a.elem[i][j] = s;
        a.elem[j][j] = c;
        a.elem[j][i] = -s;
        return(a);
    }

    /*
```

```
┌──────────────────────────────────────────────────────────┐
│  ┌────────────────────────────────────────────────────┐  │
│  │                                                    │  │
│  │        mult_mat() = Multiplies two matrices        │  │
│  │                                                    │  │
│  └────────────────────────────────────────────────────┘  │
└──────────────────────────────────────────────────────────┘
```

```
    */

    matrix mult_mat(matrix a, matrix b)
    {
        int  i,j,k;
        matrix c;

        c = zero;
        for (i=0; i<4; i++)
        {
            for (j=0; j<4; j++)
            {
                for (k=0; k<4; k++)
                    c.elem[i][j] += a.elem[i][k]*b.elem[k][j];
            }
        }
```

(continued)

```
        return(c);
}

/*
```

```
┌─────────────────────────────────────────────────────────────┐
│ ┌─────────────────────────────────────────────────────────┐ │
│ │                                                         │ │
│ │   transform() = Creates a vector transformation matrix  │ │
│ │                                                         │ │
│ └─────────────────────────────────────────────────────────┘ │
└─────────────────────────────────────────────────────────────┘
```

```
*/

matrix transform(vector tr, vector sc, vector ro)
{
    matrix a1,a2,a3,a4,a5,temp;

    a1 = scale(sc);
    a2 = rotate(1,ro.x);
    a3 = rotate(2,ro.y);
    a4 = rotate(3,ro.z);
    a5 = translate(tr);
    temp = mult_mat(a2,a1);
    temp = mult_mat(a3,temp);
    temp = mult_mat(a4,temp);
    temp = mult_mat(a5,temp);
    return(temp);
}

/*
```

```
┌─────────────────────────────────────────────────────────────┐
│ ┌─────────────────────────────────────────────────────────┐ │
│ │                                                         │ │
│ │      scalemult() = Multiplies a vector by a scalar      │ │
│ │                                                         │ │
│ └─────────────────────────────────────────────────────────┘ │
└─────────────────────────────────────────────────────────────┘
```

```
*/

vector scalemult(float r, vector a)
{
    vector b;

    b.x = r*a.x;
    b.y = r*a.y;
    b.z = r*a.z;
    return(b);
```

(continued)

```
}

/*
┌─────────────────────────────────────────────────────────────┐
│                                                             │
│    scalemultint() = Multiplies an integer vector by an      │
│                          integer                            │
│                                                             │
└─────────────────────────────────────────────────────────────┘
*/

vecint scalemultint(int r, vecint a)
{
    vecint b;

    b.x = r*a.x;
    b.y = r*a.y;
    b.z = r*a.z;
    return(b);
}

/*
┌─────────────────────────────────────────────────────────────┐
│                                                             │
│    mat_cross_vec() = Multiplies a vector by a matrix        │
│                                                             │
└─────────────────────────────────────────────────────────────┘
*/

vector mat_cross_vec(vector a, matrix m)
{
    vector b;

    b.x = m.elem[0][0]*a.x + m.elem[0][1]*a.y +
        m.elem[0][2]*a.z + m.elem[0][3];
    b.y = m.elem[1][0]*a.x + m.elem[1][1]*a.y +
        m.elem[1][2]*a.z + m.elem[1][3];
    b.z = m.elem[2][0]*a.x + m.elem[2][1]*a.y +
        m.elem[2][2]*a.z + m.elem[2][3];
    return(b);
}
```

(continued)

```
/*

  ┌─────────────────────────────────────────────────────┐
  │                                                       │
  │    map() = Maps a three-dimensional vector to a two   │
  │                 dimensional surface                   │
  │                                                       │
  └─────────────────────────────────────────────────────┘

*/


plane map(vector a)
{
    float x, y, temp;
    plane b;

    x = screen.x + a.x*CT - a.y*ST;
    y = screen.y + a.x*ST*SP + a.y*CT*SP + a.z*CP;
    temp = view_rho/(screen.z + a.x*ST*CP + a.y*CT*CP -
        a.z*SP);
    b.col = x_center + 1.2*temp*x);
    b.row = y_center - temp*y;
    return(b);
}


/*

  ┌─────────────────────────────────────────────────────┐
  │                                                       │
  │        cone() = Displays a cone on the screen         │
  │                                                       │
  └─────────────────────────────────────────────────────┘

*/


void cone(int no_facets, int color)
{
    int theta, d_theta, phi, d_phi, i;
    vector facet3D[4];
    vector temp1,temp2;
    matrix trans;

    d_theta = 180/no_facets;
    theta = d_theta;
    trans = transform(tr, sc, ro);
    for (i=0; i<no_facets; i++)
    {
```

(continued)

```
              facet3D[0] = setvec((cos((theta-d_theta) *
                  0.017453292)), (sin((theta-d_theta) *
                  0.017453292)), -1.0);
              facet3D[0] = mat_cross_vec(facet3D[0],trans);
              facet3D[1] = setvec((cos((theta+d_theta) *
                  0.017453292)), (sin((theta+d_theta) *
                  0.017453292)), -1.0);
              facet3D[1] = mat_cross_vec(facet3D[1],trans);
              facet3D[2] = setvec(0.0,0.0,1.0);
              facet3D[2] = mat_cross_vec(facet3D[2],trans);
              facet3D[3] = setvec(0.0, 0.0, 1.0);
              facet3D[3] = mat_cross_vec(facet3D[3],trans);
              display_facet(facet3D,color);
              theta += 2*d_theta;
          }
      }


  /*
```

```
          sphere() = Displays a sphere on the screen
```

```
  */


  void sphere(int color)
  {
      int horizontal=60, vertical=45, theta, d_theta, phi,
          d_phi, i, j;
      float sp, cp;
      vector facet3D[4];
      vector temp1,temp2;
      matrix trans;

      d_theta=180/horizontal;
      theta=d_theta;
      d_phi=90/vertical;
      phi=d_phi;
      trans = transform(tr, sc, ro);
      for (i=0; i<vertical; i++)
      {
          for (j=0; j<horizontal; j++)
```

(continued)

```
        {
            sp=sin((phi+d_phi)*0.017453292);
            cp=cos((phi+d_phi)*0.017453292);
            facet3D[0] = setvec((sp*cos((theta-d_theta) *
                0.017453292)), (sp*sin((theta-d_theta) *
                0.017453292)), cp);
            facet3D[0] = mat_cross_vec(facet3D[0],trans);
            facet3D[1] = setvec((sp*cos((theta+d_theta) *
                0.017453292)), (sp*sin((theta+d_theta) *
                0.017453292)), cp);
            facet3D[1] = mat_cross_vec(facet3D[1],trans);
            sp=sin((phi-d_phi)*0.017453292);
            cp=cos((phi-d_phi)*0.017453292);
            facet3D[2] = setvec((sp*cos((theta+d_theta) *
                0.017453292)), (sp*sin((theta+d_theta) *
                0.017453292)), cp);
            facet3D[2] = mat_cross_vec(facet3D[2],trans);
            facet3D[3] = setvec((sp*cos((theta-d_theta) *
                0.017453292)), (sp*sin((theta-d_theta) *
                0.017453292)), cp);
            facet3D[3] = mat_cross_vec(facet3D[3],trans);
            display_facet(facet3D,color);
            theta += 2*d_theta;
        }
        theta=d_theta;
        phi += 2*d_phi;
    }
}

/*
```

```
        toroid() = Displays a toroid on the screen
```

```
*/

void toroid(int type, int no_facets, float r1, float r2,
    int color)
{
    int theta, d_theta, phi, d_phi, i, start, stop;
    float ctm, stm, ctp, stp, rcpm, rspm, rcpp, rspp;
```

(continued)

```
vector facet3D[4];
vector temp1,temp2;
matrix trans;

d_theta = 180/no_facets;
d_phi = d_theta;
if (type == 1)
{
    start = d_theta + 90;
    stop = d_theta + 270;
}
else
{
    start = d_theta + 270;
    stop =  d_theta + 450;
}
trans = transform(tr, sc, ro);
for (theta=start; theta < stop; theta+=(2*d_theta))
{
    ctm = cos((theta-d_theta)*0.017453292);
    stm = sin((theta-d_theta)*0.017453292);
    ctp = cos((theta+d_theta)*0.017453292);
    stp = sin((theta+d_theta)*0.017453292);
    for (phi=d_phi; phi<d_phi+360; phi+=(2*d_phi))
    {
        rcpm = r2*cos((phi-d_phi)*0.017453292);
        rspm = r2*sin((phi-d_phi)*0.017453292);
        rcpp = r2*cos((phi+d_phi)*0.017453292);
        rspp = r2*sin((phi+d_phi)*0.017453292);
        facet3D[0] = setvec((r1 + rcpm)*ctm,(r1 +
            rcpm)*stm,rspm);
        facet3D[0] = mat_cross_vec(facet3D[0],trans);
        facet3D[1] = setvec((r1 + rcpm)*ctp,(r1 +
            rcpm)*stp,rspm);
        facet3D[1] = mat_cross_vec(facet3D[1],trans);
        facet3D[2] = setvec((r1 + rcpp)*ctp,(r1 +
            rcpp)*stp,rspp);
        facet3D[2] = mat_cross_vec(facet3D[2],trans);
        facet3D[3] = setvec((r1 + rcpp)*ctm,(r1 +
            rcpp)*stm,rspp);
        facet3D[3] = mat_cross_vec(facet3D[3],trans);
```

(continued)

```
                    display_facet(facet3D,color);
            }
       }
}


/*
```

```
  ┌─────────────────────────────────────────────────────┐
  │ ┌─────────────────────────────────────────────────┐ │
  │ │                                                 │ │
  │ │   cylinder() = Displays a cylinder on the screen │ │
  │ │                                                 │ │
  │ └─────────────────────────────────────────────────┘ │
  └─────────────────────────────────────────────────────┘
*/
```

```
void cylinder(int no_facets, int color)
{
    int theta, d_theta, phi, d_phi, i, no_cap_facets;
    vector facet3D[4];
    vector temp1,temp2;
    matrix trans;

    no_cap_facets = no_facets/2 - 1;
    d_theta = 180/no_cap_facets;
    if ((no_cap_facets & 1) == 1)
        theta = 90 + d_theta;
    else
        theta = 90 + 2*d_theta;
    trans = transform(tr, sc, ro);
    for (i=0; i<no_cap_facets; i++)
    {
        facet3D[0] = setvec((cos((theta-d_theta) *
            0.017453292)), (sin((theta-d_theta) *
            0.017453292)), 1.0);
        facet3D[0] = mat_cross_vec(facet3D[0],trans);
        facet3D[1] = setvec((cos((theta+d_theta) *
            0.017453292)), (sin((theta+d_theta) *
            0.017453292)), 1.0);
        facet3D[1] = mat_cross_vec(facet3D[1],trans);
        facet3D[2] = setvec((cos((180-theta-d_theta) *
            0.017453292)), (sin((180-theta-d_theta) *
            0.017453292)), 1.0);
        facet3D[2] = mat_cross_vec(facet3D[2],trans);
        facet3D[3] = setvec((cos((180-theta+d_theta) *
```

(continued)

625

```
                0.017453292)), (sin((180-theta+d_theta) *
                0.017453292)), 1.0);
        facet3D[3] = mat_cross_vec(facet3D[3],trans);
        display_facet(facet3D,color);
        theta += 2*d_theta;
    }
    d_theta = 180/no_facets;
    theta = d_theta;
    for (i=0; i<no_facets; i++)
    {
        facet3D[0] = setvec((cos((theta-d_theta) *
                0.017453292)), (sin((theta-d_theta) *
                0.017453292)), -1.0);
        facet3D[0] = mat_cross_vec(facet3D[0],trans);
        facet3D[1] = setvec((cos((theta+d_theta) *
                0.017453292)), (sin((theta+d_theta) *
                0.017453292)), -1.0);
        facet3D[1] = mat_cross_vec(facet3D[1],trans);
        facet3D[2] = setvec((cos((theta+d_theta) *
                0.017453292)), (sin((theta+d_theta) *
                0.017453292)), 1.0);
        facet3D[2] = mat_cross_vec(facet3D[2],trans);
        facet3D[3] = setvec((cos((theta-d_theta) *
                0.017453292)), (sin((theta-d_theta) *
                0.017453292)), 1.0);
        facet3D[3] = mat_cross_vec(facet3D[3],trans);
        display_facet(facet3D,color);
        theta += 2*d_theta;
    }
}


/*
```

```
    solid_rev() = Displays a solid of revolution on the
                           screen
```

```
*/

void solid_rev(int type, int color)
{
```

(continued)

```
int i, j, theta, d_theta;
float z_step, dz;
vector facet3D[4];
vector temp1,temp2;
matrix trans;
float surface[60];

if (type == 0)    /* pawn */
{
    for (i=0; i<10; i++)
        surface[i] = 0.2 + sin(0.017453292 * (9 - i) *
            12.0) * 0.5;
    for (i=10; i<43; i++)
        surface[i] = 0.2;
    for (i=43; i<60; i++)
        surface[i] = sin(0.017453292 * (59 - i) * 9.0)
            * 0.6;
}
if (type == 1)    /* bishop */
{
    for (i=0; i<10; i++)
        surface[i] = 0.2 + sin(0.017453292 * (9 - i) *
            12.0) * 0.5;
    for (i=9; i<38; i++)
        surface[i] = 0.3;
    for (i=38; i<60; i++)
        surface[i] = sin(0.017453292 * (59 - i) * 6) *
            0.45;
}
if (type == 2)   /* bowling pin */
{
    for (i=0; i<38; i++)
        surface[i] = -0.65 + cos(0.017453292 * (i -
            16)*1.5);
    for (i=38; i<56; i++)
        surface[i] = 0.2;
    for (i=56; i<60; i++)
        surface[i] =  sin(0.017453292 * (59 - i) *
            30.0) * 0.2;
}
trans = transform(tr, sc, ro);
```

(continued)

```
d_theta = 3;
theta = 93;
dz = 1/60.0;
for (i=0; i<60; i++)
{
    z_step = dz - 1.0;
    for (j=0; j<60; j++)
    {
        facet3D[0] = setvec((cos((theta-d_theta) *
            0.017453292)) * surface[j],
            (sin((theta-d_theta) * 0.017453292)) *
            surface[j], z_step - dz);
        facet3D[0] = mat_cross_vec(facet3D[0],trans);
        facet3D[1] = setvec((cos((theta+d_theta) *
            0.017453292)) * surface[j],
            (sin((theta+d_theta) * 0.017453292))*
            surface[j], z_step - dz);
        facet3D[1] = mat_cross_vec(facet3D[1],trans);
        facet3D[2] = setvec((cos((theta+d_theta) *
            0.017453292))* surface[j+1],
            (sin((theta+d_theta) * 0.017453292))*
            surface[j+1], z_step + dz);
        facet3D[2] = mat_cross_vec(facet3D[2],trans);
        facet3D[3] = setvec((cos((theta-d_theta) *
            0.017453292)) * surface[j+1],
            (sin((theta-d_theta)*0.017453292))*
            surface[j+1], z_step + dz);
        facet3D[3] = mat_cross_vec(facet3D[3],trans);
        display_facet(facet3D,color);
        z_step += 2*dz;
    }
    theta += 2*d_theta;
}
}

/*
```

```
            cube() = Displays a cube on the screen
```

```
*/
```

(continued)

```
void cube(int color)
{
    int i;
    vector facet3D[4];
    vector temp1,temp2;
    matrix trans;
    float side[6][4][3] = {1,1,1,-1,1,1,-1,-1,1,1,-1,1,
        1,1,-1,1,-1,-1,-1,-1,-1,-1,1,-1,
        1,1,1,1,-1,1,1,-1,-1,1,1,-1,
        -1,1,1,-1,1,-1,-1,-1,-1,-1,-1,1,
        1,1,1,1,1,-1,-1,1,-1,-1,1,1,
        1,-1,1,-1,-1,1,-1,-1,-1,1,-1,-1};

    trans = transform(tr, sc, ro);
    for (i=0; i<6; i++)
    {
        facet3D[0] = setvec(side[i][0][0],
            side[i][0][1],side[i][0][2]);
        facet3D[0] = mat_cross_vec(facet3D[0],trans);
        facet3D[1] = setvec(side[i][1][0],
            side[i][1][1],side[i][1][2]);
        facet3D[1] = mat_cross_vec(facet3D[1],trans);
        facet3D[2] = setvec(side[i][2][0],
            side[i][2][1],side[i][2][2]);
        facet3D[2] = mat_cross_vec(facet3D[2],trans);
        facet3D[3] = setvec(side[i][3][0],
            side[i][3][1],side[i][3][2]);
        facet3D[3] = mat_cross_vec(facet3D[3],trans);
        display_facet(facet3D,color);
    }
}

/*

        surface() = Displays a surface on the screen

*/

void surface(int color)
{
```

(continued)

```
vector facet3D[4];
vector temp1,temp2;
matrix trans;

trans = transform(tr, sc, ro);
facet3D[0] = setvec(1,1,0);
facet3D[0] = mat_cross_vec(facet3D[0],trans);
facet3D[1] = setvec(-1,1,0);
facet3D[1] = mat_cross_vec(facet3D[1],trans);
facet3D[2] = setvec(-1,-1,0);
facet3D[2] = mat_cross_vec(facet3D[2],trans);
facet3D[3] = setvec(1,-1,0);
facet3D[3] = mat_cross_vec(facet3D[3],trans);
display_facet(facet3D,color);
}
```

Modeling Solids

The raw material that we're going to operate upon consists of a number of functions that create primitive solids. These include a cone, a pyramid (a cone with only four facets), a sphere, a torus, a cylinder, a cube, a surface (a single facet) and a solid of revolution. This last allows you to specify a profile of 60 points, which is then rotated around the z axis. It comes with three types of profile, a chess pawn, a chess bishop and a bowling pin. The functions to produce these objects are listed at the end of the program, they differ in some details, but have the same principles, so only the function for the cone will be described. This particular function, *cone*, allows you to pass to it the number of facets to be used to make up the object, and the object color. The first thing that the function does is to divide 180 degrees by the number of facets to obtain the angle increment that will be used to define each facet. Since integers are used at this point, you need to enter a number of facets that will divide evenly into 180. The function next finds a starting value for the angle and then invokes the function *transform* that creates a transformation matrix, *trans*, from the global vectors *tr*, for translation of the object, *sc*, for scaling of the object, and *ro*, for rotation of the object. These vectors are set to the proper values before the function is called. Next the function begins a *for* loop that is repeated once for each facet that is to make up the cone. The four vertices of a facet are computed and placed in each of four vectors that make up *facet3D*. For the cone, two of the vertices are spaced along the circumference of the circle that forms the base of the cone and the other two are at the apex of the cone for every facet. (Therefore, in this case, the facets are actually triangles rather than quadrilaterals.) Note that the solid is designed to be centered at the origin and to fit into a box defined by the limits of -1 and +1 for each dimension. After each vertex is computed, it is transformed by the transformation matrix *trans* to the desired size, position and rotation for its proper place in the scene being generated. You should also note that numbers given for the *z* dimension are reversed, which makes the picture come out properly in the screen coordinate system, where *y* is the reverse of what is normally accepted. After all four vertices of each facet are computed, it is painted onto the screen. The angle is then increased and the loop is iterated again for another facet. Although the mathematics is different for each primitive object, the principles used to generate and display each facet are the same.

Displaying a Facet on the Screen

The first step that takes place in the function *display_facet*, which displays a facet on the screen, is to calculate a surface normal to the facet surface. This is accomplished by the function *surf_norm*. This function first finds a vector between the first two vertices of the facet and then finds another vector between the first and last vertices of the facet. Next, the cross product of these two vectors is taken to give a vector normal (at right angles) to the plane determined by the two vectors (the facet surface). The length of the normal vector is then computed. In a similar manner, the normal to the vectors from the last vertex of the facet to the second and third vertices of the facet is determined and its length obtained. Now, if the length of the first normal vector is 0, the second normal vector is normalized and the result becomes the surface normal vector for the facet. If the first length isn't 0, it is normalized and if the second normal has length 0, then the first normalized vector becomes the surface normal. If neither normal vector has zero length, they are averaged to find the surface normal vector. The function doesn't make any provision for what happens if both normal vectors have zero length.

Getting back to *display_facet*, the function now computes the angle between the viewer position vector and the facet surface normal vector (beta). If the cosine of this angle is less than or equal to 0, the facet cannot be seen by the viewer, so the function returns without drawing it to the screen, or doing anything else, for that matter. Otherwise, the function computes the angle between the light source position vector and the surface normal vector of the facet (theta). If the cosine of this angle is less than or equal to 0, none of the light from the light source illuminates the facet, so its light intensity is set to that of ambient light. Otherwise, the surface normal vector is multiplied by the cosine of theta, the resulting vector is normalized and then the light vector subtracted from it and the resulting vector normalized again. The angle between this vector and the viewer vector (alpha) is then determined. The intensity of the facet is the sum of the ambient light, the diffuse lighting from the surface multiplied by the cosine of theta and the specular light from the surface multiplied by the cosine of alpha raised to the *glossiness* power. This last term is the Phong shading, which creates the highlights that are seen in illuminating curved objects.

Now, if the intensity is greater than or equal to 1 (otherwise the facet is not illuminated so it need not be drawn), the *map* function described in the previous chapter is used to project the facet onto the two-dimensional display screen. Three possible display modes are incorporated in the program. In mode 0, a point is plotted to the screen for each vertex. This gives a series of dots that depict the shape of the solid. In mode 1, the function *drawQuad* is called, which draws straight lines between adjacent vertices to outline each facet of the object. In mode 2, the function *fill_quad* is called, which fills the quadrilateral with the proper shade of the designated color.

The *solid.c* Program

The main program paints a series of scenes on the screen that give some idea of the capabilities of the solid modeling technique. With these as examples, you can define other pictures that you would like to create. You may have to experiment a little to get the proper size and position for each object. The first screen that is created is simply a large magenta colored cube. The next screen consists of three cylinders. The *cylinder* function paints only the top cap of the cylinder; if you change the viewing orientation such that the bottom cap of the cylinder is visible, you'll need to add a bottom cap to the function. The next scene shows a large sphere balanced upon three cones. This is shown in Plate 26. The next scene shows 10 stacked cones. The positioning of each cone is the same used for the display of 10 stacked spheres. (This is the next display to be shown by the program.) The spacing was adjusted to be correct for the spheres; it isn't quite correct for the cones. You can change the values around, if you like, to get them perfect for the cones. Following the 10 stacked spheres, the next display is of stacked pyramids. This display is exactly like the one for stacked cones except that each cone is specified to have 4 facets rather than 60. The next display is of 10 bowling pins and a bowling ball. The very first thing that is generated in this display is a single facet that represents the bowling alley. This scene is shown in Plate 27. The next scene is of a chessboard with two bishops and three pawns. The bishops and pawns, as well as the bowling pins of the previous scene, were created with the *solid_of_rev* function. By passing a type number to the function the proper profile for one of these three objects is selected. You can add more profiles if you desire to be able to make other symmetrical objects. At the beginning of this scene, two nested *for* loops are used to draw the alternate rows of red squares on the chessboard. Another pair of *for* loops are then used to fill in the red squares in the rows between. The resulting chessboard display is shown in Figure 28. The next scene is reminiscent of the Towers of Hanoi puzzle. The puzzle begins with seven rings stacked on a rod, each ring being smaller than the one below it. The goal is to move rings to the other two rods and back, until all seven rings are stacked on another of the rods. However, you can never put a bigger ring on top of a smaller one. To create this picture, we have to draw the back half of all of the tori and then draw the cylindrical rods. Finally the front half of each torus is drawn. The function *toroid* handles the tori, generating the back half of a torus when it is passed the type 1 and the front half when it is passed the type 0. The resulting display is shown in Plate 29.

Chapter 23

Solid Modeling with C++

There is an old Greek fable about Procrustes, the robber innkeeper who placed his unwary lodgers in a bed and then stretched or cut off their legs until they fit the size of the bed exactly. This is hard on people, and you can accomplish similar undesirable effects by attempting to force your computer problems to fit a language that they are not suited for. You've probably heard a lot of hype about how object oriented programming should be used for everything, since it is the natural way that people think. The truth is that certain types of problems are naturally better suited to an object oriented language, but other problems can be solved much easier by straightforward mathematical techniques, and if you try to fit either one into the other's environment, the result is a much degraded program. The beauty of C++ as a computer language is that it permits you to use all of the power and elegance of C to handle problems that beg for a mathematical treatment and yet can easily be used in an object-oriented mode for problems best solved using that technique. Don't however, try to force everything into one mold or the other; the result can be only disaster.

Where Objects Shine

Back in Chapter 20, we discussed the rotation of objects. As examples, we had functions that could be used to draw rotated rectangles and rotated triangles. Suppose we have a long list of objects that we want to rotate. Some of them are rectangles and some are triangles, but we don't know in advance just in what order these types of objects are going to appear. We could set up a program that would somehow test each object and would then decide which function to run to rotate it. But using C++, there is a much better way. We set up a class of objects called *triangle* and another class called *rectangle*, both of which are subclasses of the class *object*. Within each of these subclasses we have a function *drawObject*. The version of this function that is part of the *triangle* class is exactly the same as the function we used in Chapter 20 to draw triangles and the version that is part of the *rectangle* class is the same as the one used to draw rectangles. Now, we can simply call *drawObject* for every object that we want to rotate, and C++ automatically takes care of determining which class of object is encountered at each function call and using the right one of the two functions to draw the rotated object on the screen.

Using C++ with the Solid Modeling Program

Using the solid modeling program described in the previous chapter, we're going to make use of C++ in a slightly different way that is equally powerful. You'll note in the previous chapter that we used structures to define vectors and matrices. This is as close to C++ as you can get using ordinary C, since a C structure and a C++ class are virtually identical if all of the internal variables of the class are made public. What we are going to do is make use of the powerful capability of C++ to overload mathematical operators. As an example, C++ makes it possible for you to use the + sign to add two vectors or matrices or whatever with exactly the same form that you would use to add two numbers, but using your own functions to perform the addition in the appropriate way for the classes you have defined. In other words, as programmer, you simply create the proper addition function, and then each time you want to add two vectors (for example) you simply write

$$c = a + b$$

(Equation 23-1)

We've set up the *vector* class so that the normal rules apply for most vector operations and so that the operator % is used for taking the dot product of two vectors, the operator ^ is used for taking the cross product of two vectors, and the operator ~ is used to normalize a vector. In the remainder of the chapter, in Figure 23-1, we're going to give a listing of the *solid.cpp* program, which is parallel to the *solid.c* program of the previous chapter. You can compare the two to observe how the overloading of mathematical operators makes the program easier to understand and simpler to write.

Figure 23-1. Listing of solid.c Program using C++

```
/*

        SOLID = Program to model 3D Objects

        By Roger T. Stevens   12-23-91

*/

#include <stdio.h>
#include <dos.h>
#include <conio.h>
#include <math.h>
#include <string.h>
#include <alloc.h>
#include <stdlib.h>
#include <stream.h>


typedef struct
{
    int col, row;
} plane;

typedef struct
{
    unsigned char red;
    unsigned char green;
    unsigned char blue;
} RGB;

RGB palette[256];
```

(continued)

```
#define light_phi 45
#define light_theta 45
#define light_max 35
#define compare(a,b,c)  {if (a<b) b = a; if (a>c) c = a;}

/*
```

```
VECTOR AND MATHEMATICAL FUNCTIONS
```

```
*/

class vector {
    public:
    float x, y, z;

    vector();
    vector(float x1, float y1, float z1);
    vector (vector &);
    vector operator+(vector &);
    vector operator-(vector &);
    vector operator-();
    vector operator=(vector &);
    vector operator*(vector &);
    vector operator*(float);
    vector operator/(float);
    float operator%(vector &);      // dot product
    vector operator^(vector &);     // cross product;
    vector operator~();             // normalize vector;
    float length();
};

class matrix {
    public:
    float elem[4][4];

    matrix();
    vector operator*(vector &);
    matrix operator*(matrix &);
};
```

(continued)

```
/*
```

┌──┐
│   │
│   FUNCTION PROTOTYPES   │
│   │
└──┘

```
*/

void cls(int color);
void cone(int no_facets, int color);
void cylinder(int no_facets, int color);
void cube(int color);
void display_facet(vector facet3D[],int Color);
void draw(int xs, int ys, int xe, int ye, int color);
void draw_quad(plane v[], int color);
void fill_quad (plane quad[], int color);
plane map(vector a);
void plot256(int x, int y, int color);
void setMode(int s_mode);
void setVGAcolors(RGB palette[]);
void setVGApalette(RGB palette[]);
void solid_rev(int type, int color);
void surface(int color);
vector surface_normal(vector facet3D[]);
void sphere(int color);
void toroid(int type, int no_facets, float r1, float r2,
    int color);
matrix transform(vector tr, vector sc, vector ro);
matrix scale(vector &);
matrix rotate(int axis, float angle);
matrix translate(vector &);

int view_theta = 240, view_phi = 18, view_rho = 500;
vector view, screen;
const xres = 320;
const yres = 200;
int mode=2;
float CP,SP,CT,ST;
int   x_center, y_center;
matrix trans1;
vector surf_norm, light, tr,sc,ro;
```

(continued)

```
/*
```

```
                              Vector constructors
```

```
*/
```

```
vector::vector()
{
    x = 0;
    y = 0;
    z = 0;
}
```

```
vector::vector(float x1, float y1, float z1)
{
    x = x1;
    y = y1;
    z = z1;
}
```

```
vector::vector(vector & othervector)
{
    x = othervector.x;
    y = othervector.y;
    z = othervector.z;
}
```

```
/*
```

```
                         Vector overload of + operator
```

```
*/
```

```
vector vector::operator+(vector & b)
{
    vector c;

    c.x = x + b.x;
    c.y = y + b.y;
```

(continued)

```
    c.z = z + b.z;
    return(c);
}
```

```
/*
```

```
┌─────────────────────────────────────────────────────────────┐
│                                                               │
│         Vector overload of - operator (a - b)                 │
│                                                               │
└─────────────────────────────────────────────────────────────┘
```

```
*/
```

```
vector vector::operator-(vector & b)
{
    vector c;

    c.x = x - b.x;
    c.y = y - b.y;
    c.z = z - b.z;
    return(c);
}
```

```
/*
```

```
┌─────────────────────────────────────────────────────────────┐
│                                                               │
│         Vector overload of - operator (-a)                    │
│                                                               │
└─────────────────────────────────────────────────────────────┘
```

```
*/
```

```
vector vector::operator-()
{
    vector c;

    c.x = -x;
    c.y = -y;
    c.z = -z;
    return(c);
}
```

(continued)

```
/*
```

┌───┐
│   │
│   Vector overload of * operator (corresponding elements   │
│   multiplied together)   │
│   │
└───┘

```
*/

vector vector::operator*(vector & b)
{
    vector c;

    c.x = x*b.x;
    c.y = y*b.y;
    c.z = z*b.z;
    return(c);
}

/*
```

┌───┐
│   │
│   Vector overload of * operator (vector x float)   │
│   │
└───┘

```
*/

vector vector::operator*(float b)
{
    vector c;

    c.x = x*b;
    c.y = y*b;
    c.z = z*b;
    return(c);
}

/*
```

┌───┐
│   │
│   Vector overload of / operator (vector / float)   │
│   │
└───┘

```
*/
```

(continued)

```
vector vector::operator/(float b)
{
    vector c;

    c.x = x/b;
    c.y = y/b;
    c.z = z/b;
    return(c);
}

/*
```

```
                    Vector overload of = operator
```

```
*/

vector vector::operator=(vector &b)
{
    x = b.x;
    y = b.y;
    z = b.z;
    return *this;
}

/*
```

```
            Vector overload of % operator (dot product)
```

```
*/

float vector::operator%(vector &b)
{
    float c;

    c = x*b.x + y*b.y + z*b.z;
    return c;
}
```

(continued)

```
/*

    +--------------------------------------------------------------+
    |                                                              |
    |     Vector overload of ^ operator (cross product)            |
    |                                                              |
    +--------------------------------------------------------------+
*/

vector vector::operator^(vector &b)
{
    vector c;

    c.x = y*b.z - z*b.y;
    c.y = z*b.x - x*b.z;
    c.z = x*b.y - y*b.x;
    return c;
}

/*

    +--------------------------------------------------------------+
    |                                                              |
    |       Vector overload of ~ operator (normalize)              |
    |                                                              |
    +--------------------------------------------------------------+
*/

vector vector::operator~()
{
    vector c;
    float length;

    length = *this % *this;
    length = sqrt(length);
    c.x = x/length;
    c.y = y/length;
    c.z = z/length;
    return c;
}
```

(continued)

```
/*

┌─────────────────────────────────────────────────────────┐
│ ┌─────────────────────────────────────────────────────┐ │
│ │                                                     │ │
│ │        length() = Finds the length of a vector      │ │
│ │                                                     │ │
│ └─────────────────────────────────────────────────────┘ │
└─────────────────────────────────────────────────────────┘
*/

float vector::length()
{
    return(sqrt(x*x + y*y + z*z));
}


/*

┌─────────────────────────────────────────────────────────┐
│ ┌─────────────────────────────────────────────────────┐ │
│ │                                                     │ │
│ │                 Matrix constructors                 │ │
│ │                                                     │ │
│ └─────────────────────────────────────────────────────┘ │
└─────────────────────────────────────────────────────────┘
*/

matrix::matrix()
{
    int i,j;

    for (i=0; i<4; i++)
        for (j=0; j<4; j++)
            elem[i][j] = 0;
}


/*

┌─────────────────────────────────────────────────────────┐
│ ┌─────────────────────────────────────────────────────┐ │
│ │                                                     │ │
│ │    Matrix overload of * operator (matrix x matrix)  │ │
│ │                                                     │ │
│ └─────────────────────────────────────────────────────┘ │
└─────────────────────────────────────────────────────────┘
*/

matrix matrix::operator*(matrix &b)
{
    int i,j,k;
    matrix c;

    c = matrix();
```

(continued)

```
    for (i=0; i<4; i++)
    {
        for (j=0; j<4; j++)
        {
            for (k=0; k<4; k++)
                c.elem[i][j] += elem[i][k]*b.elem[k][j];
        }
    }
    return(c);
}

/*
```

```
    Matrix overload of * operator (matrix x vector)
```

```
*/

vector matrix::operator*(vector &a)
{
    vector b;
    b.x = elem[0][0]*a.x + elem[0][1]*a.y + elem[0][2]*a.z
        + elem[0][3];
    b.y = elem[1][0]*a.x + elem[1][1]*a.y + elem[1][2]*a.z
        + elem[1][3];
    b.z = elem[2][0]*a.x + elem[2][1]*a.y + elem[2][2]*a.z
        + elem[2][3];
    return(b);
}

/*
```

```
    map() = Maps a three-dimensional vector to a
              two-dimensional surface
```

```
*/

plane map(vector a)
{
    float x, y, temp;
```

(continued)

```
    plane b;

    x = screen.x + a.x*CT - a.y*ST;
    y = screen.y + a.x*ST*SP + a.y*CT*SP + a.z*CP;
    temp = view_rho/(screen.z + a.x*ST*CP + a.y*CT*CP -
        a.z*SP);
    b.col = x_center + 1.2*temp*x;
    b.row = y_center - temp*y;
    return(b);
}


/*
```

```
    translate() = Creates a matrix to translate vectors
```

```
*/

matrix translate(vector &a)
{
    matrix b;
    int i;

    b = matrix();
    for (i=0; i<4; i++)
        b.elem[i][i] = 1.0;
    b.elem[0][3] = -a.x;
    b.elem[1][3] = -a.y;
    b.elem[2][3] = -a.z;
    return(b);
}


/*
```

```
        scale() = Creates a matrix to scale vectors
```

```
*/

matrix scale(vector &a)
{
```

(continued)

```
        matrix b;

        b = matrix();
        b.elem[0][0] = a.x;
        b.elem[1][1] = a.y;
        b.elem[2][2] = a.z;
        b.elem[3][3] = 1.0;
        return(b);
}
```

```
/*
```

```
      rotate() = Creates a matrix to rotate vectors
```

```
*/
```

```
matrix rotate(int axis, float angle)
{
    int i,j;
    matrix a;
    float c,s;

    a = matrix();
    a.elem[axis-1][axis-1] = 1.0;
    a.elem[3][3] = 1.0;
    i = (axis % 3) + 1;
    j = i %3;
    i -= 1;
    c = cos(angle * 0.017453292);
    s = sin(angle * 0.017453292);
    a.elem[i][i] = c;
    a.elem[i][j] = s;
    a.elem[j][j] = c;
    a.elem[j][i] = -s;
    return(a);
}
```

(continued)

```
/*

    transform() = Creates a vector transformation matrix

*/

matrix transform(vector tr, vector sc, vector ro)
{
    matrix a1,a2,a3,a4,a5,temp;

    a1 = scale(sc);
    a2 = rotate(1,ro.x);
    a3 = rotate(2,ro.y);
    a4 = rotate(3,ro.z);
    a5 = translate(tr);
    temp = a2*a1;
    temp = a3*temp;
    temp = a4*temp;
    temp = a5*temp;
    return(temp);
}


/*

                        MAIN PROGRAM

*/

void main(void)
{
    vector toroid_vecs[8];
    float r, s;
    int i,j;
    vector trans[10], facet3D[4];
    float phi, theta;
    float x, y, z;

    setMode(3);
    textcolor(YELLOW);
```

(continued)

```
textbackground(BLUE);
clrscr();
printf("Three-dimensional modeling of solids\n\n");
x_center=(xres-1) >> 1;
y_center=(yres-1) >> 1;
CT=cos(0.017453292*view_theta);
ST=sin(0.017453292*view_theta);
CP=cos(0.017453292*view_phi);
SP=sin(0.017453292*view_phi);
view = vector(-CP*ST,-CP*CT,SP);
screen = vector(0,-25,450);
printf("View Direction is %d around the z-Axis\n",
    view_theta);
printf("                    %d off the z-Axis\n",
    view_phi);
printf("Light Direction is %d around the z-Axis"
    " and\n", light_phi);
printf("                    %d off the z-Axis\n",
    light_theta);
phi=0.017453292*light_phi;
theta=0.017453292*light_theta;
light = vector(sin(theta)*cos(phi),
    sin(theta)*sin(phi), cos(theta));
delay(5000);

/*
```

```
┌────────────────────────────────────────────────┐
│                                                  │
│                      Cube                        │
│                                                  │
└────────────────────────────────────────────────┘
```

```
*/

setMode(19);
setVGAcolors(palette);
setVGApalette(palette);
r= 32.0;
s= -48.0;
sc = vector(r,r,r);
ro = vector(0,0,0);
tr = vector(0,0,0);
cube(5);
```

(continued)

```
        getch();
```

```
/*
```

```
┌─────────────────────────────────────────────┐
│ ┌─────────────────────────────────────────┐ │
│ │                                         │ │
│ │             Three cylinders             │ │
│ │                                         │ │
│ └─────────────────────────────────────────┘ │
└─────────────────────────────────────────────┘
```

```
*/
```

```
        setMode(19);
        setVGAcolors(palette);
        setVGApalette(palette);
        r= 32.0;
        s= -80.0;
        trans[6] = vector(r, 0.293*r, -s-4.6*r);
        trans[7] = vector(-2*r, 0.293*r, -s-3.5*r);
        trans[8] = vector(0.0, -1.5*r, -s-2.6*r);
        sc = vector(r,r,r);
        ro = vector(0,0,0);
        tr = trans[6];
        cylinder(60,1);
        sc = vector(r,r,r);
        ro = vector(0,0,0);
        tr = trans[7];
        cylinder(60,7);
        sc = vector(r,r,r);
        ro = vector(0,0,0);
        tr = trans[8];
        cylinder(60,3);
        getch();
```

```
/*
```

```
┌─────────────────────────────────────────────┐
│ ┌─────────────────────────────────────────┐ │
│ │                                         │ │
│ │           Sphere and three cones        │ │
│ │                                         │ │
│ └─────────────────────────────────────────┘ │
└─────────────────────────────────────────────┘
```

```
*/
```

```
        r= 32.0;
        s= -80.0;
        setMode(19);
```

(continued)

```
setVGApalette(palette);
trans[6] = vector(r, 0.293*r, -s-2.6*r);
trans[7] = vector(-r, 0.293*r, -s-2.6*r);
trans[8] = vector(0.0, -1.5*r, -s-2.6*r);
trans[9] = vector(0.0, -0.34*r, -s-4.3*r);
sc = vector(r,r,r);
ro = vector(0,0,0);
tr = trans[6];
cone(60,1);
sc = vector(r,r,r);
ro = vector(0,0,0);
tr = trans[7];
cone(60,4);
sc = vector(r,r,r);
ro = vector(0,0,0);
tr = trans[8];
cone(60,3);
sc = vector(1.3*r,1.3*r,1.3*r);
ro = vector(0,0,0);
tr = trans[9];;
sphere(2);
getch();

/*
```

```
                            Stacked cones
```

```
*/

r=16.0;
s=16.0;
trans[0] = vector(2.0*r, r, -s-r);
trans[1] = vector(0.0, r, -s-r);
trans[2] = vector(-2.0*r, r, -s-r);
trans[3] = vector(r, -0.866*r, -s-r);
trans[4] = vector(-r, -0.866*r, -s-r);
trans[5] = vector(0.0, -2.732*r, -s-r);
trans[6] = vector(r, 0.293*r, -s-2.6*r);
trans[7] = vector(-r, 0.293*r, -s-2.6*r);
trans[8] = vector(0.0, -1.5*r, -s-2.6*r);
```

(continued)

```
    trans[9] = vector(0.0, -0.5*r, -s-4.4*r);
    setMode(19);
    setVGApalette(palette);
    sc = vector(r,r,r);
    ro = vector(0,0,0);
    for(i=0; i<10; i++)
    {
        tr = trans[i];
        cone(60,(i%7) + 1);
    }
    getch();
```

```
/*
```

```
                       Stacked spheres
```

```
*/
```

```
    setMode(19);
    setVGApalette(palette);
    sc = vector(r,r,r);
    ro = vector(0,0,0);
    for(i=0; i<10; i++)
    {
        tr = trans[i];
        sphere((i%7) + 1);
    }
    getch();
```

```
/*
```

```
                       Stacked pyramids
```

```
*/
```

```
    setMode(19);
    setVGApalette(palette);
    for(i=0; i<10; i++)
    {
```

(continued)

```
        sc = vector(r,r,r);
        ro = vector(0,0,0);
        tr = trans[i];
        cone(4,(i%7) + 1);
    }
```

```
/*
```

```
                              Bowling
```

```
*/
```

```
    setMode(19);
    setVGApalette(palette);
    sc = vector(70,112,1);
    ro = vector(0,0,0);
    tr = vector(45,25,0);
    trans1 = transform(tr, sc, ro);
    facet3D[0] = vector(1,1,0),
    facet3D[0] = trans1 *facet3D[0];
    facet3D[1] = vector(-1,1,0);
    facet3D[1] = trans1 * facet3D[1];
    facet3D[2] = vector(-1,-1,0);
    facet3D[2] = trans1 * facet3D[2];
    facet3D[3] = vector(1,-1,0);
    facet3D[3] = trans1 * facet3D[3];
    display_facet(facet3D,6);
    sc = vector(2*r,2*r,2*r);
    ro = vector(0,0,0);
    trans[0] = vector(152,184,0);
    trans[1] = vector(120,184,0);
    trans[2] = vector(88,184,0);
    trans[3] = vector(56,184,0);
    trans[4] = vector(136,152,0);
    trans[5] = vector(104,152,0);
    trans[6] = vector(72,152,0);
    trans[7] = vector(120,120,0);
    trans[8] = vector(88,120,0);
    trans[9] = vector(104,88,0);
    for (i=0; i<10; i++)
```

(continued)

```
{
    tr = trans[i];
    solid_rev(2,7);
}
r=18.0;
sc = vector(r,r,r);
tr = vector(80,-30,0);
sphere(1);
getch();
```

```
/*
```

```
┌─────────────────────────────────────────────────────┐
│                                                       │
│                                                       │
│                     Chessboard                        │
│                                                       │
│                                                       │
└─────────────────────────────────────────────────────┘
```

```
*/
```

```
setMode(19);
setVGAcolors(palette);
setVGApalette(palette);
ro = vector(0,0,0);
sc = vector(20,20,0);
for (j=-40; j<250; j+=80)
    for (i=-40; i<250; i+=80)
    {
        tr = vector(j,i,0);
        surface(4);
    }
for (j=0; j<250; j+=80)
    for (i=0; i<250; i+=80)
    {
        tr = vector(j,i,0);
        surface(4);
    }
sc = vector(22,22,20);
tr = vector(90,70,0);
solid_rev(0,7);
tr = vector(178,202,0);
solid_rev(0,7);
tr = vector(225,25,0);
solid_rev(0,3);
```

(continued)

```
        sc = vector(22,22,26);
        tr = vector(55,125,0);
        solid_rev(1,7);
        tr = vector(12,-12,0);
        solid_rev(1,3);
        getch();
```

```
/*
```

┌───┐
│   │
│   Towers of Hanoi   │
│   │
└───┘

```
*/
```

```
        setMode(19);
        setVGAcolors(palette);
        setVGApalette(palette);
        ro = vector(0,0,0);
        toroid_vecs[0] = vector(-45,-20,-17);
        toroid_vecs[1] = vector(-45,-20,-38);
        toroid_vecs[2] = vector(-45,-20,-59);
        toroid_vecs[3] = vector(20,-90,-7);
        toroid_vecs[4] = vector(20,-90,-24);
        toroid_vecs[5] = vector(-80,50,-1);
        toroid_vecs[6] = vector(-80,50,-13);
        for (i=0; i<7;i++)
        {
            sc = vector(50-5*i,50-5*i,50-5*i);
            tr = toroid_vecs[i];
            toroid(1,60,.75,.25,i+1);
        }
        sc = vector(7,7,55);
        tr = vector(20,-90,-45);
        cylinder(90,7);
        tr = vector(-45,-20,-45);
        cylinder(90,7);
        tr = vector(-80,50,-45);
        cylinder(90,7);
        for (i=0; i<7;i++)
        {
            sc = vector(50-5*i,50-5*i,50-5*i);
```

(continued)

```
            tr = toroid_vecs[i];
            toroid(0,60,.75,.25,i+1);
        }
        getch();
        setMode(3);
    }

    /*
```

```
    display_facet() = Displays and shades a facet on the
                              screen
```

```
    */

    void display_facet(vector facet3D[],int Color)
    {
        float ambient=0.30;
        float diffuse=0.50;
        float specular=0.20;
        float glossiness=5.0;
        float cos_theta, cos_alpha, cos_beta;
        vector temp;
        int intensity;
        int i;
        plane facet2D[4], temp2;

        surf_norm = surface_normal(facet3D);
        temp = view * surf_norm;
        cos_beta=temp.x + temp.y + temp.z;
        if (cos_beta > 0.0)
        {
            cos_theta = surf_norm % light;
            if(cos_theta<=0.0)
                intensity = light_max * ambient;
            else
            {
                temp = surf_norm * cos_theta;
                temp = ~temp;
                temp = temp - light;
```

(continued)

```
                    temp = ~ temp;
                    cos_alpha = view % temp;
                    intensity = light_max * (ambient + diffuse *
                        cos_theta + specular * pow(cos_alpha,
                        glossiness));
            }
            if(intensity>0)
            {
                for(i=0; i<4; i++)
                    facet2D[i] = map(facet3D[i]);
                facet2D[4] = facet2D[0];
                if (intensity > light_max)
                    intensity = light_max;
                if(intensity>=1)
                {
                    if(mode == 0)
                    {
                        plot256(facet2D[0].col,
                            facet2D[0].row, light_max*Color);
                        plot256(facet2D[1].col,
                            facet2D[1].row, light_max*Color);
                        plot256(facet2D[2].col,
                            facet2D[2].row, light_max*Color);
                        plot256(facet2D[3].col,
                            facet2D[3].row, light_max*Color);
                    }
                    if(mode == 1)
                        draw_quad(facet2D,light_max*Color);
                    if(mode == 2)
                        fill_quad (facet2D, ((light_max+1) *
                            (Color-1) + intensity));
                }
            }
        }
    }

/*
```

```
    surface_normal() = Computes the surface normal vector
                   to a facet surface
```

```
*/

vector surface_normal(vector facet3D[])
{
    float length1, length2;
    vector dir1, dir2, srf_normal1, srf_normal2;

    dir1 = facet3D[1] - facet3D[0];
    dir2 = facet3D[3] - facet3D[0];
    srf_normal1 = dir1 ^ dir2;
    length1 = srf_normal1.length();
    dir1 = facet3D[3] - facet3D[2];
    dir2 = facet3D[1] - facet3D[2];
    srf_normal2 = dir1 ^ dir2;
    length2 = srf_normal2.length();
    if(length1 == 0.0)
        srf_normal1 =  ~srf_normal2;
    else
    {
        srf_normal1 =  ~srf_normal1;
        if(length2 != 0.0)
        {
            srf_normal2 =  ~srf_normal2;
            srf_normal1 = srf_normal1 + srf_normal2;
            srf_normal1 = srf_normal1 * 0.5;
        }
    }
    return(srf_normal1);
}

/*
```

```
                        GRAPHICS FUNCTIONS
```

```
*/
```

(continued)

```
/*
```

```
                            cls() Clears the screen
```
```
*/

void cls(int color)
{
    union REGS reg;

    reg.x.ax = 0x0600;
    reg.x.cx = 0;
    reg.x.dx = 0x3284;
    reg.h.bh = color;
    int86(0x10,&reg,&reg);
}


/*

    draw() = Draws a single pixel wide line from one set of
        coordinates to another in 256 color modes.

*/

void draw(int xs, int ys, int xe, int ye, int color)
{

    int temp, dx, dy, y_sign, i, x, y, decision;

    if (xs > xe)
    {
        temp = xs;
        xs = xe;
        xe = temp;
        temp = ys;
        ys = ye;
        ye = temp;
    }
    dx = abs(xe - xs);

    dy = abs(ye - ys);
```

(continued)

```
        if ((ye - ys) < 0)
            y_sign = -1;
        else
            y_sign = 1;
        if (dx > dy)
        {
            for (x=xs,y=ys,decision=0; x<=xe;
                x++,decision+=dy)
            {
                if (decision>=dx)
                {
                    decision -= dx;
                    y+= y_sign;
                }
                plot256(x,y,color);
            }
        }
        else
        {
            for (x=xs,y=ys,decision=0; y!=ye; y+=y_sign,
                decision+=dx)
            {
                if (decision>=dy)
                {
                    decision -= dy;
                    x++;
                }
                plot256(x,y,color);
            }
        }
}

/*
```

```
            draw_quad() = Draws a quadrilateral
```

```
*/

void draw_quad(plane v[], int color)
```

(continued)

```
{
```

```
        draw(v[0].col, v[0].row, v[1].col, v[1].row, color);
        draw(v[1].col, v[1].row, v[2].col, v[2].row, color);
        draw(v[2].col, v[2].row, v[3].col, v[3].row, color);
        draw(v[3].col, v[3].row, v[0].col, v[0].row, color);
}


/*
```

```
    fill_quad() = Fills a quadrilateral in specified color
```

```
*/

void fill_quad (plane quad[], int color)
{

    #define sign(x) ((x) > 0 ? 1:  ((x) == 0 ? 0:  (-1)))

    int dx, dy, dxabs, dyabs, i, j, px, py, sdx, sdy, x,
        y, xpoint[5], ypoint[5], minrow=480, maxrow=0,
        coord[2][1024];

    for (i=0; i<4; i++)
    {
        xpoint[i] = quad[i].col;
        ypoint[i] = quad[i].row;
    }
    xpoint[4] = xpoint[0];
    ypoint[4] = ypoint[0];
    for (i=0; i<yres; i++)
    {
        coord[0][i] = 2048;
        coord[1][i] = 0;
    }
    for (j=0; j<4; j++)
    {
        px = xpoint[j];
        py = ypoint[j];
        dx = xpoint[j+1] - xpoint[j];
        dy = ypoint[j+1] - ypoint[j];
        sdx = sign(dx);
```

(continued)

```
        sdy = sign(dy);
        dxabs = abs(dx);
        dyabs = abs(dy);
        x = 0;
        y = 0;
        if (dxabs >= dyabs)
        {
            for (i=0; i<dxabs; i++)
            {
                y += dyabs;
                if (y>=dxabs)
                {
                    y -= dxabs;
                    py += sdy;
                }
                px += sdx;
                compare(px,coord[0][py],coord[1][py]);
                compare(py,minrow,maxrow);
            }
        }
        else
        {
            for (i=0; i<dyabs; i++)
            {
                x += dxabs;
                if (x>=dyabs)
                {
                    x -= dyabs;
                    px += sdx;
                }
                py += sdy;
                compare(px,coord[0][py],coord[1][py]);
                compare(py,minrow,maxrow);
            }
        }
    }
    for (i=minrow; i<=maxrow; i++)
        for (j=coord[0][i]; j<=coord[1][i]; j++)
            plot256(j,i,color);
}
```

(continued)

```
/*
```

```
  plot256() = Plots a point on the screen at a designated
  position using a selected color for 256 color modes.
```

```
*/
```

```c
void plot256(int x, int y, int color)
{
    char far * address;
    address = (char far *) 0xA0000000L + (long)y * xres +
        (long)x;
    *address = color;
}
```

```
/*
```

```
                    setMode() = Sets video mode
```

```
*/
```

```c
void setMode(int s_mode)
{

    union REGS reg;

    reg.x.ax = s_mode;
    int86 (0x10,&reg,&reg);
}
```

```
/*
```

```
  setVGAcolors() = Function to generate 256 color array
```

```
*/
```

```c
void setVGAcolors(RGB palette[])
{
```

(continued)

```
        int i;

        for(i=0; i<252; i++)
        {
            if (i>107)
                palette[i].red = 1.8*(i%36);
            else
            palette[i].red = 0.;
        if ((i>35 && i<108) || (i>179))
            palette[i].green = 1.8*(i%36);
        else
            palette[i].green = 0.;
        if((i<36) || (i>71 && i<108) || (i>143 && i<180) ||
            (i>215))
            palette[i].blue = 1.8*(i%36);
        else
            palette[i].blue = 0.;
    }
}


/*
```

```
        setVGApalette() = Function to set all 256 color
                            registers
```

```
*/

void setVGApalette(RGB palette[])
{
    struct SREGS inreg;
    union REGS reg;

    reg.x.ax = 0x1012;
    segread(&inreg);
    inreg.es = inreg.ds;
    reg.x.bx = 0;
    reg.x.cx = 256;
    reg.x.dx = (int)&palette[0].red;
    int86x(0x10,&reg,&reg,&inreg);
}
```

(continued)

```
/*
┌─────────────────────────────────────────────────────────┐
│ ┌───────────────────────────────────────────────────┐   │
│ │                                                   │   │
│ │      sphere() = Displays a sphere on the screen   │   │
│ │                                                   │   │
│ └───────────────────────────────────────────────────┘   │
└─────────────────────────────────────────────────────────┘
*/

void sphere(int color)
{
    int horizontal=60, vertical=45, theta, d_theta, phi,
        d_phi, i, j;
    float sp, cp;
    matrix trans;
    vector facet3D[4];

    trans = transform(tr, sc, ro);
    d_theta=180/horizontal;
    theta=d_theta;
    d_phi=90/vertical;
    phi=d_phi;
    for (i=0; i<vertical; i++)
    {
        for (j=0; j<horizontal; j++)
        {
            sp=sin((phi+d_phi)*0.017453292);
            cp=cos((phi+d_phi)*0.017453292);
            facet3D[0] = vector((sp*cos((theta-d_theta) *
                0.017453292)), (sp*sin((theta-d_theta) *
                0.017453292)), cp);
            facet3D[0] = trans * facet3D[0];
            facet3D[1] = vector((sp*cos((theta+d_theta) *
                0.017453292)), (sp*sin((theta+d_theta) *
                0.017453292)), cp);
            facet3D[1] = trans * facet3D[1];
            sp=sin((phi-d_phi)*0.017453292);
            cp=cos((phi-d_phi)*0.017453292);
            facet3D[2] = vector((sp*cos((theta+d_theta) *
                0.017453292)), (sp*sin((theta+d_theta) *
                0.017453292)), cp);
            facet3D[2] = trans * facet3D[2];
            facet3D[3] = vector((sp*cos((theta-d_theta) *
```

(continued)

666

```
                0.017453292)), (sp*sin((theta-d_theta) *
                0.017453292)), cp);
            facet3D[3] = trans * facet3D[3];
            display_facet(facet3D,color);
            theta += 2*d_theta;
        }
        theta=d_theta;
        phi += 2*d_phi;
    }
}


/*
```

```
           cone() = Displays a cone on the screen
```

```
*/

void cone(int no_facets, int color)
{
    int theta, d_theta, phi, d_phi, i;
    vector facet3D[4];
    matrix trans;

    d_theta = 180/no_facets;
    theta = d_theta;
    trans = transform(tr,sc,ro);
    for (i=0; i<no_facets; i++)
    {
        facet3D[0] = vector((cos((theta-d_theta) *
            0.017453292)), (sin((theta-d_theta) *
            0.017453292)), -1.0);
        facet3D[0] = trans * facet3D[0];
        facet3D[1] = vector((cos((theta+d_theta) *
            0.017453292)), (sin((theta+d_theta) *
            0.017453292)), -1.0);
        facet3D[1] = trans * facet3D[1];
        facet3D[2] = vector(0.0,0.0,1.0);
        facet3D[2] = trans * facet3D[2];
        facet3D[3] = vector(0.0, 0.0, 1.0);
        facet3D[3] = trans * facet3D[3];
```

(continued)

```
            display_facet(facet3D,color);
            theta += 2*d_theta;
        }
    }


/*
```

┌───┐
│   │
│   cylinder() = Displays a cylinder on the screen   │
│   │
└───┘

```
*/

void cylinder(int no_facets, int color)
{
    int theta, d_theta, phi, d_phi, i, no_cap_facets;
    vector facet3D[4];
    matrix trans;

    no_cap_facets = no_facets/2 - 1;
    d_theta = 180/no_cap_facets;
    if ((no_cap_facets & 1) == 1)
        theta = 90 + d_theta;
    else
        theta = 90 + 2*d_theta;
    trans = transform(tr,sc,ro);
    for (i=0; i<no_cap_facets; i++)
    {
        facet3D[0] = vector((cos((theta-d_theta) *
            0.017453292)), (sin((theta-d_theta) *
            0.017453292)), 1.0);
        facet3D[0] = trans * facet3D[0];
        facet3D[1] = vector((cos((theta+d_theta) *
            0.017453292)), (sin((theta+d_theta) *
            0.017453292)), 1.0);
        facet3D[1] = trans * facet3D[1];
        facet3D[2] = vector((cos((180-theta-d_theta) *
            0.017453292)), (sin((180-theta-d_theta) *
            0.017453292)), 1.0);
        facet3D[2] = trans * facet3D[2];
        facet3D[3] = vector((cos((180-theta+d_theta) *
            0.017453292)), (sin((180-theta+d_theta) *
```

(continued)

```
                0.017453292)), 1.0);
            facet3D[3] = trans * facet3D[3];
            display_facet(facet3D,color);
            theta += 2*d_theta;
        }
        d_theta = 180/no_facets;
        theta = d_theta;
        for (i=0; i<no_facets; i++)
        {
            facet3D[0] = vector((cos((theta-d_theta) *
                0.017453292)), (sin((theta-d_theta) *
                0.017453292)), -1.0);
            facet3D[0] = trans * facet3D[0];
            facet3D[1] = vector((cos((theta+d_theta) *
                0.017453292)), (sin((theta+d_theta) *
                0.017453292)), -1.0);
            facet3D[1] = trans * facet3D[1];
            facet3D[2] = vector((cos((theta+d_theta) *
                0.017453292)), (sin((theta+d_theta) *
                0.017453292)), 1.0);
            facet3D[2] = trans * facet3D[2];
            facet3D[3] = vector((cos((theta-d_theta) *
                0.017453292)), (sin((theta-d_theta) *
                0.017453292)), 1.0);
            facet3D[3] = trans * facet3D[3];
            display_facet(facet3D,color);
            theta += 2*d_theta;
        }
    }


    /*

    ┌─────────────────────────────────────────────────────────┐
    │                                                         │
    │        toroid() = Displays a toroid on the screen       │
    │                                                         │
    └─────────────────────────────────────────────────────────┘

    */

    void toroid(int type, int no_facets, float r1, float r2,
        int color)
    {
        int theta, d_theta, phi, d_phi, i, start, stop;
```

(continued)

```
float ctm, stm, ctp, stp, rcpm, rspm, rcpp, rspp;
vector facet3D[4];
vector temp1,temp2;
matrix trans;

d_theta = 180/no_facets;
d_phi = d_theta;
if (type == 1)
{
    start = d_theta + 90;
    stop = d_theta + 270;
}
else
{
    start = d_theta + 270;
    stop =  d_theta + 450;
}
trans = transform(tr, sc, ro);
for (theta=start; theta < stop; theta+=(2*d_theta))
{
    ctm = cos((theta-d_theta)*0.017453292);
    stm = sin((theta-d_theta)*0.017453292);
    ctp = cos((theta+d_theta)*0.017453292);
    stp = sin((theta+d_theta)*0.017453292);
    for (phi=d_phi; phi<d_phi+360; phi+=(2*d_phi))
    {
        rcpm = r2*cos((phi-d_phi)*0.017453292);
        rspm = r2*sin((phi-d_phi)*0.017453292);
        rcpp = r2*cos((phi+d_phi)*0.017453292);
        rspp = r2*sin((phi+d_phi)*0.017453292);
        facet3D[0] = vector((r1 + rcpm)*ctm,(r1 +
            rcpm)*stm,rspm);
        facet3D[0] = trans * facet3D[0];
        facet3D[1] = vector((r1 + rcpm)*ctp,(r1 +
            rcpm)*stp,rspm);
        facet3D[1] = trans * facet3D[1];
        facet3D[2] = vector((r1 + rcpp)*ctp,(r1 +
            rcpp)*stp,rspp);
        facet3D[2] = trans  * facet3D[2];
        facet3D[3] = vector((r1 + rcpp)*ctm,(r1 +
            rcpp)*stm,rspp);
```

(continued)

```
            facet3D[3] = trans * facet3D[3];
            display_facet(facet3D,color);
        }
    }
}

/*
┌─────────────────────────────────────────────────────────┐
│ ┌───────────────────────────────────────────────────────┐ │
│ │                                                       │ │
│ │   solid_rev() = Displays a solid of revolution on the │ │
│ │                           screen                      │ │
│ │                                                       │ │
│ └───────────────────────────────────────────────────────┘ │
└─────────────────────────────────────────────────────────┘
*/

void solid_rev(int type, int color)
{
    int i, j, theta, d_theta;
    float z_step, dz;
    vector facet3D[4];
    vector temp1,temp2;
    matrix trans;
    float surface[60];

    if (type == 0)    /* pawn */
    {
        for (i=0; i<10; i++)
            surface[i] = 0.2 + sin(0.017453292 * (9 - i) *
                12.0) * 0.5;
        for (i=10; i<43; i++)
            surface[i] = 0.2;
        for (i=43; i<60; i++)
            surface[i] = sin(0.017453292 * (59 - i) * 9.0)
                * 0.6;
    }

    if (type == 1)    /* bishop */
    {
        for (i=0; i<10; i++)
            surface[i] = 0.2 + sin(0.017453292 * (9 - i) *
                12.0) * 0.5;
        for (i=9; i<38; i++)
```

(continued)

671

```
            surface[i] = 0.3;
            for (i=38; i<60; i++)
                surface[i] = sin(0.017453292 * (59 - i) *
                    6) * 0.45;
    }

    if (type == 2)   /* bowling pin */
    {
        for (i=0; i<38; i++)
            surface[i] = -0.65 + cos(0.017453292 * (i -
                16)*1.5);
        for (i=38; i<56; i++)
            surface[i] = 0.2;
        for (i=56; i<60; i++)
            surface[i] =  sin(0.017453292 * (59 - i) *
                30.0) * 0.2;
    }
    trans = transform(tr, sc, ro);
    d_theta = 3;
    theta = 93;
    dz = 1/60.0;

    for (i=0; i<60; i++)
    {
        z_step = dz - 1.0;
        for (j=0; j<60; j++)
        {
            facet3D[0] = vector((cos((theta-d_theta) *
                0.017453292))*surface[j],
                (sin((theta-d_theta) * 0.017453292))*
                surface[j], z_step - dz);
            facet3D[0] = trans * facet3D[0];
            facet3D[1] = vector((cos((theta+d_theta) *
                0.017453292))*surface[j],
                (sin((theta+d_theta) * 0.017453292))*
                surface[j], z_step - dz);
            facet3D[1] = trans * facet3D[1];
            facet3D[2] = vector((cos((theta+d_theta) *
                0.017453292))*surface[j+1],
                (sin((theta+d_theta) * 0.017453292))*
                surface[j+1], z_step + dz);
```

(continued)

```
                    facet3D[2] = trans * facet3D[2];
                    facet3D[3] = vector((cos((theta-d_theta) *
                        0.017453292))*surface[j+1],
                        (sin((theta-d_theta)*0.017453292))*
                        surface[j+1], z_step + dz);
                    facet3D[3] = trans * facet3D[3];
                    display_facet(facet3D,color);
                    z_step += 2*dz;
                }
            theta += 2*d_theta;
        }
}


/*
+------------------------------------------------------------------+
|                                                                  |
|          cube() = Displays a cube on the screen                  |
|                                                                  |
+------------------------------------------------------------------+
*/

void cube(int color)
{
    int i;
    vector facet3D[4];
    vector temp1,temp2;
    matrix trans;
    float side[6][4][3] = {1,1,1,-1,1,1,-1,-1,1,1,-1,1,
        1,1,-1,1,-1,-1,-1,-1,-1,-1,1,-1,
        1,1,1,1,-1,1,1,-1,-1,1,1,-1,
        -1,1,1,-1,1,-1,-1,-1,-1,-1,-1,1,
        1,1,1,1,1,-1,-1,1,-1,-1,1,1,
        1,-1,1,-1,-1,1,-1,-1,-1,1,-1,-1};

    trans = transform(tr, sc, ro);
    for (i=0; i<6; i++)
    {
        facet3D[0] = vector(side[i][0][0],
            side[i][0][1],side[i][0][2]);
        facet3D[0] = trans * facet3D[0];
        facet3D[1] = vector(side[i][1][0],
            side[i][1][1],side[i][1][2]);
```

(continued)

```
            facet3D[1] = trans * facet3D[1];
            facet3D[2] = vector(side[i][2][0],
                side[i][2][1],side[i][2][2]);
            facet3D[2] = trans * facet3D[2];
            facet3D[3] = vector(side[i][3][0],
                side[i][3][1],side[i][3][2]);
            facet3D[3] = trans * facet3D[3];
            display_facet(facet3D,color);
        }
    }

    /*
```

```
        surface() = Displays a surface on the screen
```

```
    */

    void surface(int color)
    {
        vector facet3D[4];
        vector temp1,temp2;
        matrix trans;

        trans = transform(tr, sc, ro);
        facet3D[0] = vector(1,1,0);
        facet3D[0] = trans * facet3D[0];
        facet3D[1] = vector(-1,1,0);
        facet3D[1] = trans * facet3D[1];
        facet3D[2] = vector(-1,-1,0);
        facet3D[2] = trans * facet3D[2];
        facet3D[3] = vector(1,-1,0);
        facet3D[3] = trans * facet3D[3];
        display_facet(facet3D,color);
    }
```

Chapter 24

Saving and Restoring Displays with the *.PCX* Format

The next three chapters cover the general subject of saving the contents of a display screen to a disk file and then restoring that file to the screen. Many graphics displays require a good deal of computation, sometimes resulting in hours of computer usage to produce a single display. To avoid such a lengthly process every time we want to reproduce a display, it becomes important to have a technique for saving such pictures on disk and recalling them quickly. Straightforward saving of screen information requires huge files, so that some form of data compression is a necessity if we are to save pictures in reasonable file sizes. Another problem is that there are a wide variety of screen resolutions and formats, and our programs must be capable of determining how to handle each that is encountered. This is further complicated when we want to display a file that is in one of the existing "standard" formats, since some of these are interested mostly in storing picture data and are really quite incompatible with the display screen characteristics. In general, the file formats consist of a header that gives information about the file contents followed by the picture content in some compressed form.

The *.PCX* file format was developed by

ZSoft Corporation
450 Franklin Road, Suite 100
Marietta, GA 30067   Phone: (404) 428-0008

Shannon in their technical support group was most helpful to me in furnishing detailed specifications of this format. The format, which was first developed with the PC Paintbrush painting program, is one of the oldest and most widely used methods for storing and recovering graphics display information. To create a *.PCX* file, the screen is scanned on a pixel by pixel basis. For multicolor displays, one line of each of the four color planes is scanned, then the next line for four color planes, etc. The program is capable of handling a 64K×64K image size, but such large sizes are rarely used (they wouldn't fit on most disks, for one thing), so we will confine ourselves to sizes corresponding to EGA and VGA display resolutions. The format can handle monochrome displays, 16 color EGA/VGA displays and 256 color VGA displays. You may encounter any one of three *.PCX* versions. Version 2.5 is the earliest version. It supports 16 color EGA/VGA displays using the standard color palette only; no palette modifications are allowed. Version 2.8 supports 16 color EGA/VGA displays and contains palette information that allows each of the 16 colors to be selected from any of 64 available colors. Version 3.0 supports 256 color EGA/VGA images, permitting definition of each of the 256 colors from 262,144 possible colors. The palette data is appended at the end of the *.PCX* file.

The *.PCX* Header Format

The *.PCX* header consists of 128 bytes at the beginning of the file. The contents of this header are described in Table 24-1. Most of the information is self-explanatory. A little further detail is required for the palette information, however. If you are writing a program to save a display screen as a *.PCX* file, you will have two bits available to specify one of four levels for each of R, G and B for every one of the 16 palettes. You can process this any way you want that will come up with a number within the proper range for the particular level for each palette triple. If you are writing for a VGA card, you can read the palette setting from the VGA registers. The corresponding registers in the EGA, however, are write-only. Therefore, when you are generating the color display initially, you need to be very careful to store somewhere the changes that you make in palette color settings, so that you have this information available for the *.PCX* file header. Otherwise you will never be able to recover your original color settings. In the reverse direction, when you are writing a program to convert the disk file to a display screen, you have to carefully perform

TABLE 24-1. *PCX* FILE HEADER CONTENTS

Byte #	Name	Description
0	Manufacturer ID	Always set to 0AH
1	Version number	0 = Version 2.5 1 = Version 2.8 2 = Version 2.8 with palette 3 = Version 3.0
2	Encoding technique	1 = Simple RLE. This is the normal setting for all *.PCX* files. Other values are reserved for future encoding techniques that have not yet been implemented.
3	Bits per plane per pixel	Number of bits required in each plane to store 1 pixel. (Bit 65 gives the number of planes.) 1 = EGA/VGA 16 color modes 2 = CGA 4 color modes 8 = VGA 256 color modes
4-11	Window dimensions	4 integers (2 bytes each) defining top left and bottom right corners of the display box in the order xl, yt, xr, yb.
12-13	Horizontal resolution	Horizontal resolution of display device. Common values are 640 for EGA/VGA (16 color) 320 for CGA or VGA 256 color 720 for Hercules

(continued)

TABLE 24-1. *PCX* FILE HEADER CONTENTS (CONT.)

Byte #	Name	Description
14-15	Vertical resolution	Vertical resolution of display device (rows). Common values are 480 for VGA 350 for EGA 200 for CGA or VGA 256 color 348 for Hercules
16-63	Color map	Sets EGA/VGA palette registers. Colors are specified as 16 RGB triplets. Each color number ranges from 0 to 255, but actually only four color levels are available. The numbers are therefore interpreted as follows: 0-63 = Level 0 64-127 = Level 1 128-192 = Level 2 193-254 = Level 3
64	Reserved	Always set to 0
65	Number of bit planes	Bit planes used for representing a pixel. Normally 4 for EGA/VGA 16 color modes and 1 otherwise.
66-67	Bytes per scan line per plane	Number of bytes per scan line per color plane. Must be an even number compatible with the window size definition (bytes 4-5 and 8-9).
68-69	Palette Information	How to interpret palette 1 = color or B&W 2 = Gray scale (Usually ignored)
70-127	Filler	Blanks to fill out 128 byte header.

the conversion from the header triplets to the EGA/VGA palette numbers in such a way that the proper one of the four levels is obtained for every value within the range of numbers that represent that color level.

Information on 256 Colors

The VGA has the capability to display 256 out of 262,144 colors. To define the triplet for each of the 256 color registers requires more space than is available in the .*PCX* header, so this information is appended at the end of the .*PCX* file. First you should ascertain that the version number data in the header (byte 1) is 5 (version 3.0), since this is the only version that supports 256 color information. If the version is correct, you should go to the end of the file and then count back 769 bytes. If the value in this byte position is *0CH* (12 decimal), the information that follows is 256 color register data.

Run-Length Encoding

When storing data, it is read from the screen, horizontally from left to right, starting at the pixel position for the upper left corner. For 16 color EGA/VGA modes, pixel information must be read from four color memory planes. In these modes, a line is read from the red plane from the beginning to the end of the window boundary. Then the green information for the same line is read, then the blue, and finally the intensity information. The functions that we will develop below work only if the horizontal pixel boundaries are at a byte interface (the column number must be divisible by eight.) Data is run-length encoded in the following way. A single byte that is unlike the ones on either side of it is written directly to the file if its two most significant bits are not 1. The two most significant bits being 1 represents a flag to indicated that repeated byte data is to follow. If the display contains a repeated series of the same byte, a count is made of the number of like bytes (up to 63) and this count is ANDed with *C0H* and the result written to the file, followed by the value of the byte. (Thus the byte that gives the count has its two most significant bits set to 1 by the *C0H*.) If there are more than 63 successive like bytes, the count for 63 and *C0H* (resulting in *FFH*) is written followed by the byte value. The count then begins all over again. (Note that a singular byte having the two most significant bits 1 is handled by writing a count byte with a count of 1 followed by the byte value. This is the only case where there is actually an expansion in size, one byte of the original being replaced by two bytes in the "compressed" code. Fortunately the situation doesn't come up often so that the "compressed" file is almost always considerably smaller than the uncompressed data.)

Restoring .PCX Files to the Screen

Figure 24-1 is a listing of a general purpose program for restoring .PCX files to the display screen. The principal problem encountered in developing a program like this is determining how to go from the specification of window dimensions to a real-life display format. In this program, a check is first made as to whether 256 color information is available. If it is, the 320×200 pixel × 256 color mode is chosen. Otherwise, the window size is checked against those resolutions that correspond to EGA/VGA modes and, if a match is found, that display mode is selected. This gives us a lot of flexibility. For a moment, however, let's look at what the program will not do. Then you can begin to think about what modifications you might make to the code to add to the current capabilities. First, if you have a picture that doesn't correspond to a standard size, the program simply rejects it. You might want to add the capability to show a part of such a picture, if it is larger than a standard format, or show the picture as a small section of the screen if it is smaller than a standard format. In Chapter 25 we'll show how to do these things with the .IMG file. Second, as far as I know, no one has ever designed program that will store and display 256 colors in the undocumented VGA modes. This isn't a very difficult problem, however. Using the framework of the programs listed in Figures 24-1 and 24-2, you should be able to use the information from Chapter 8 to create such programs.

The program listing begins by defining the values for the arrow keys, the outputs used in accessing the display adapter card and an expression for obtaining the next character from the buffer. The buffer is initially filled with 32,768 characters from the designated disk file. Each time a character is read from the buffer, the index is incremented, and when the buffer is exhausted it is automatically refilled. You can reduce the buffer size if it is too large to coexist with the rest of the data in your program, but this may slow up generating the display. The prototypes for the functions used in the program are given next, followed by the global variable list. Note that these include a structure *pcx_header,* which is set up to contain all of the file header information.

The actual program begins by initiating an infinite *for* loop. At each iteration of this loop, the display mode is first set to text, and the display foreground and background colors defined. A window is then created. The next group of instructions draws a double line boundary around this window. At the top of the window is displayed the legend "Select file name with cursor arrows: ". The program next makes use of some Turbo C/Borland C++ functions to extract the names of all files in the default directory that end in the extension *.PCX*. If you're using another C compiler that doesn't have these functions, you'll have to roll your own. Also note that only the default directory is read, so that you need to be in the directory where your *.PCX* files reside before calling the program. The program can handle 64 *.PCX* files in one directory; if you have more than this, you'll need to modify the code to prevent running past the end of the file name buffer with disastrous results. When all the file names have been read, the C *qsort* function is used to sort them into alphabetical order. This function requires a user designed function to make the actual comparisons. That function is *sort_function,* which simply calls the string compare function and returns the result. Next the file names are displayed. After each 18 names, the file name is location is shifted so that the next group is moved over one column. The file name corresponding to the index *dir_index* is displayed in reverse colors; all other file names are displayed in the normal color selection.

The program next calls the function *dir_menu.* This function begins with a *while* loop that iterates until either a carriage return or an escape key is entered on the keyboard. The loop begins by getting a character from the keyboard. If the character is a NULL (00) this indicates a key that has a two character designation. In that case, the second character is read and 256 is added to it to distinguish it from ordinary alphanumeric key codes. Next the foreground and background colors are set for the normal display and the cursor is positioned at the file name designated by *dir_index* and the name rewritten. (This was the name that was shown in reverse colors; it is now rewritten in normal colors.) The function then enters a *switch* statement that changes the value of *dir_index* according to which arrow key is selected. For an up or down arrow, the index is moved one line up or down. If it is already at the first line of the entire display and is moved up, it moves to the last line. If it is already at the bottom line of the entire display and moves down, it moves to the first line of the display. For right and left arrows, the index moves one column to the right or left if there is a file name in that location; otherwise it doesn't change. After leaving the *switch* operation, the colors are changed for reverse video and the line at the index position is rewritten. The function remains in the *for* loop, changing index position for arrow key executions (or ignoring other keys) until a carriage return or an escape key is hit. The loop then terminates. The file name designated by the index is copied to the global variable *filename*, and the function terminates, returning the designation of the last key entered (which must be a carriage return or an escape key). The net result of all this is that the user may use the arrow keys to move a reverse color line around on the display of file names until the desired name is selected and then may terminate the function by entering a carriage return or escape key.

We've now returned to the main program. If the last key struck was an escape key, we break out of the infinite loop and the program terminates. Otherwise, the program calls the function *restore_screen* to display the file selected by the above preceding, whose name is now in *filename*. The file is displayed and remains on the screen until a keystroke is entered. The legend "Hit 'E' to erase this file...or any other key to continue..." is then displayed and the program waits for a keystroke. If it is an *E* or an *e* the file is erased. Next the infinite *for* loop repeats, calling up the directory menu again to allow the selection of another file for display. This makes it possible for you to view each of a list of files and erase those that aren't worth saving.

Figure 24-1. Listing of PCX Program to Display a .PCX File

```
/*

    PCX = Program to read and display .PCX files

         By Roger T. Stevens   9-9-91

*/
```

(continued)

```
#include <stdio.h>
#include <stdlib.h>
#include <string.h>
#include <math.h>
#include <dos.h>
#include <conio.h>
#include <ctype.h>
#include <dir.h>

#define UP_ARROW        328
#define DOWN_ARROW      336
#define LEFT_ARROW      331
#define RIGHT_ARROW     333
#define BACKSPACE         8
#define seq_out(register,val)  {outp(0x3C4,register);\
                        outp(0x3C5,val);}
#define graph_out(register,val)  {outp(0x3CE,register);\
                        outp(0x3CF,val);}
#define next_char(ch, index) {ch = file_buf[index];\
                if ((index = (++index) % 32768) == 0)\
                fread(file_buf,32768,1,fsave);}
#define next_comp(ch, index) {ch =~ file_buf[index];\
                if ((index = (++index) % 32768) == 0)\
                fread(file_buf,32768,1,fsave);}

void cls(int color);
int dir_menu(int last_entry);
void plot256(int x, int y, int color);
int restore_screen(char file_name[]);
void save_pcx(char filename[13]);
void setEGApalette(int palette, int color);
void setVGApalette(unsigned char *buffer);
void setMode(int mode);
int sort_function(const void *a, const void *b);

union REGS reg;

struct SREGS segregs;

struct {
    char password;
```

(continued)

```
    char version;
    char encoding;
    char bits_per_pixel;
    int xmin, ymin, xmax, ymax;
    int xres, yres;
    unsigned char palette[48];
    char reserved;
    char no_of_planes;
    int bytes_per_line;
    int palette_type;
    char filler[58];
    } pcx_header;

unsigned char palette_data[256][3];
int srcseg, srcoff, destseg, destoff;
int xres, yres, active_bank, bank;
int attr, i, j, k, dir_index= 0, type, length[7];
char Host_Array[100];
unsigned char PALETTE[16] = {0,1,2,3,4,5,20,7,56,57,58,
    59,60,61,62,63};
int column, end, done, level,key, cursor_pos[16] = {16,
    25,30,25,26,30,30,30,28,28,21,14,21,20,12,18},
    start_x, start_y, start_angle, cursor_x, cursor_y,
    mode;
char filename[32], buffer[64],div_buf[64],ch,
    dirbuf[64][13];
struct ffblk ffblk;
long int col,row;

main()
{
    for(;;)
    {
        setMode(3);
        textbackground(1);
        textcolor(15);
        window(2,2,78,23);
        clrscr();
        gotoxy(1,1);
        printf("╔");
        for (i=0; i<74; i++)
```

(continued)

```
        printf("=");
printf("╗");
for (i=2; i<22; i++)
{
    gotoxy(1,i);
    printf("║");
    gotoxy(76,i);
    printf("║");
}
gotoxy(1,22);
printf("╚");
for (i=0; i<74; i++)
    printf("=");
printf("╝");
gotoxy(19,2);
filename[0] = NULL;
cprintf("Select file name with cursor arrows: ");
textcolor(14);
end = 0;
done = findfirst("*.pcx",&ffblk,0);
while(!done)
{
    strcpy(dirbuf[end++],ffblk.ff_name);
    done = findnext(&ffblk);
}
qsort((void *)dirbuf,end,sizeof(dirbuf[0]),
    sort_function);
textbackground(1);
textcolor(14);
for (i=0; i<end; i++)
{
    column = i/19;
    if (i == dir_index)
    {
        textbackground(7);
        textcolor(1);
    }
    gotoxy(2+19*column,(i%19)+3);
    cprintf("%s",dirbuf[i]);
    textbackground(1);
    textcolor(14);
```

(continued)

```
            }
        key = dir_menu(end);
        if (key == 0x1B)
            break;
        restore_screen(filename);
        getch();
        printf("     Hit 'E' to erase this file..."
            "or any other key to continue...");
        ch = getch();
        if (toupper(ch) == 'E')
            remove(filename);
    }
}

/*
```

```
     setEGApalette() = Sets the color for an EGA palette
                          register
```

```
*/

void setEGApalette(int palette, int color)
{
    union REGS reg;

    PALETTE[palette] = color;
    reg.h.ah = 0x10;
    reg.h.al = 0;
    reg.h.bh = color;
    reg.h.bl = palette;
    int86(0x10,&reg,&reg);
}


/*
```

```
                  setMode() = Sets video mode
```

```
*/
```

(continued)

```
void setMode(int imode)
{
    reg.x.ax = imode;
    int86 (0x10,&reg,&reg);
}


/*
```

```
        restore_screen() = Reads and displays a file
```

```
*/

int restore_screen(char file_name[])
{
    FILE *fsave;
    unsigned char ch,color,buffer[650],file_buf[32768];
    int i,j,k,m,pass,col,row,plane,index=0;

    segread(&segregs);
    srcseg = segregs.ds;
    srcoff = (int) buffer;
    destseg = 0xA000;
    if ((fsave = fopen(file_name,"rb")) == NULL)
    {
        printf("\nCan't find %s.\n",file_name);
        return(0);
    }
    else
    {
        fread(&pcx_header,1,128,fsave);
        if (pcx_header.password != 0x0A)
        {
            printf("\n%s is not a valid ZSoft file.\n",
                file_name);
            fclose(fsave);
            return(0);
        }
    }
    fseek(fsave,-769L,SEEK_END);
    ch = fgetc(fsave);
```

(continued)

```
if (ch == 0x0C)
{
    fread(file_buf,768,1,fsave);
    for (i=0,k=0; i<256; i++)
        for (j=0; j<3; j++)
        {
            palette_data[i][j] = file_buf[k++] >> 2;
        }
    if ((pcx_header.xres == 320) && (pcx_header.yres
        == 200))
    setMode(0x13);
    else
    {
        if ((pcx_header.xres == 640) &&
            (pcx_header.yres == 480))
            setMode(0x67);
        else
        {
            printf ("\n%s is not a Mode 13H or "
                "Mode 67H file.\n", file_name);
            fclose(fsave);
            return(1);
        }
    }
    setVGApalette(&palette_data[0][0]);
    fseek(fsave,128L,SEEK_SET);
    if (index == 0)
        fread(file_buf,32768,1,fsave);
    for (row=pcx_header.ymin; row<=pcx_header.ymax;
        row++)
    {
        for (col=pcx_header.xmin;
            col<=pcx_header.xmax; col++)
        {
            next_char(ch,index);
            if ((ch & 0xC0) != 0xC0)
                pass = 1;
            else
            {
                pass = ch & 0x3F;
                next_char(ch,index);
```

(continued)

```
                }
                for (m=0; m<pass; m++)
                    buffer[col++] = ch;
                col--;
            }
            destoff = row *
                (long)pcx_header.bytes_per_line +
                (long) pcx_header.xmin;
            movedata(srcseg,srcoff,destseg,destoff,
                pcx_header.bytes_per_line);
        }
        fclose(fsave);
        return(0);
    }
    else
    {
        fseek(fsave,128L,SEEK_SET);
        if ((pcx_header.xres == 640) && (pcx_header.yres
            == 480))
            setMode(18);
        if ((pcx_header.xres == 640) && (pcx_header.yres
            == 350))
            setMode(16);
        if ((pcx_header.xres == 640) && (pcx_header.yres
            == 200))
            setMode(14);
        for (i=0; i<48; i+=3)
        {
            k = i/3;
            color = ((pcx_header.palette[i] & 0x40) >> 1)
                | ((pcx_header.palette[i] & 0x80) >> 5) |
                ((pcx_header.palette[i+1] & 0x40) >> 2) |
                (pcx_header.palette[i+1] & 0x80) >> 6 |
                ((pcx_header.palette[i+2] & 0x40) >> 3) |
                ((pcx_header.palette[i+2] & 0x80) >> 7);
            PALETTE[k] = color;
            setEGApalette(k,PALETTE[k]);
        }
        graph_out(8,0xFF);
        graph_out(3,0x00);
        for (row=pcx_header.ymin; row<=pcx_header.ymax;
```

(continued)

```
                            row++)
                {
                    col = pcx_header.xmin/8;
                    plane = 0;
                    if (index == 0)
                        fread(file_buf,32768,1,fsave);
                    while (plane<4)
                    {
                        next_char(ch,index);
                        if ((ch & 0xC0) != 0xC0)
                            pass = 1;
                        else
                        {
                            ch &= 0x3F;
                            pass = ch;
                            next_char(ch,index);
                        }
                        for (m=0; m<pass; m++)
                        {
                            buffer[col++] = ch;
                            if (col > pcx_header.xmax/8)
                            {
                                col = pcx_header.xmin/8;
                                seq_out(2,(0x01 << plane++));
                                destoff = row * 80L + (long) col;
                                movedata(srcseg,srcoff, destseg,
                                    destoff,
                                    pcx_header.bytes_per_line);
                            }
                        }
                    }
                }
            }
        graph_out(3,0);
        graph_out(8,0xFF);
        graph_out(5,0);
        fclose(fsave);
        return(pcx_header.xmax);
    }
}
```

(continued)

```
/*
```

```
        sort_function() = Directory sorting function
```

```
*/
```

```c
int sort_function(const void *a, const void *b)
{
    return( strcmp(a,b));
}
```

```
/*
```

```
        setVGApalette() = Function to set all 256 color
                          registers
```

```
*/
```

```c
void setVGApalette(unsigned char *buffer)
{
    union REGS reg;
    struct SREGS inreg;

    reg.x.ax = 0x1012;
    segread(&inreg);
    inreg.es = inreg.ds;
    reg.x.bx = 0;
    reg.x.cx = 256;
    reg.x.dx = (int)&buffer[0];
    int86x(0x10,&reg,&reg,&inreg);
}
```

```
/*
```

```
      plot256() = Function to plot point to VGA 256 color
                          screen
```

```
*/
```

(continued)

```
void plot256(int x, int y, int color)
{
    long int offset;
    char far *address;
    int temp,temp2;

    offset = (long)pcx_header.xres * (long)y + (long)x;
    bank = offset/65536L;
    offset = offset % 65536L;
    if (bank != active_bank)
    {
        active_bank = bank;
        reg.h.ah = bank & 0x01;
        reg.h.al = 0xF9;
        outport(0x3C4,reg.x.ax);
        temp = inport(0x3CC);
        temp = temp & 0xDF;
        if ((bank & 0x02) != 0)
            temp = temp | 0x20;
        outport(0x3C2,temp);
        outportb(0x3C4,0xF6);
        temp = inport(0x3C5);
        temp = temp & 0xF0;
        temp2 = ((bank & 0x0C) >> 2) | (bank & 0x0C);
        temp = temp | temp2;
        outportb(0x3C5,temp);
    }
    address = (char far *)(0xA0000000L + offset);
    *address = color;
}


/*
```

```
            dir_menu() = Menu function for directory
```

```
*/

int dir_menu(int last_entry)
{
    int ch1 = NULL;
```

(continued)

```c
    while ((ch1 != 0x0D) && (ch1 != 0x1B))
    {
        ch1 = getch();
        if (ch1 == 0x00)
        {
            ch1 = getch() + 256;
            textbackground(1);
            textcolor(14);
            column = dir_index/19;
            gotoxy(2+19*column,(dir_index%19)+3);
            cprintf("%s",dirbuf[dir_index]);
            switch(ch1)
            {
                case DOWN_ARROW:
                    ++dir_index;
                    dir_index = dir_index % last_entry;
                    break;
                case UP_ARROW:
                    --dir_index;
                    if (dir_index<0)
                        dir_index = last_entry - 1;
                    break;
                case RIGHT_ARROW:
                    if ((dir_index + 19) < last_entry)
                        dir_index += 19;
                    break;
                case LEFT_ARROW:
                    if (dir_index > 19)
                        dir_index -= 19;
                    break;
            }
            textbackground(7);
            textcolor(1);
            column = dir_index/19;
            gotoxy(2+19*column,(dir_index%19)+3);
            cprintf("%s",dirbuf[dir_index]);
        }
    }
    strcpy(filename,dirbuf[dir_index]);
    return(ch1);
}
```

Displaying the Screen

The function *restore_screen* performs the operations necessary to convert the disk file to an actual screen display. It begins by finding the base address and offsets for the buffer that is to be used to contain file data and defines the base address of the display area. Next the function attempts to open the selected file. If it cannot do this, it displays a diagnostic message and returns. (This should never occur, since the specified file name has to be that of a good file as obtained from the directory.) If the file is opened successfully, the function reads the header into the header storage area. It then checks whether the first character is *0AH* If not, the file is not a legitimate *.PCX* file. The function closes the file, displays a message reporting this result, and returns.

If the file is a *.PCX* file, the function next looks at the character that is 769 bytes before the end of the file. If this is *0CH* the file contains 256 color information. If this is the case, the function reads the color data into a buffer called *palette_data*. The function then has to decide which display mode to select. For this program, we have provided two options. If the resolution data in the header shows that the file is 320×200 pixels, the function sets the display mode to mode 13H. If the resolution is 640×480 pixels, the function assumes that a Headlands Technology 1024i VGA board is present and sets the display mode to the extended mode 67H. (The reading and displaying functions are compatible with this extended mode.) If neither of these resolutions is present, the function displays a diagnostic message and returns. If one of the modes was selected, the function sets the color registers from the data that was read, repositions the file pointer to the first byte after the file header and reads 32,768 bytes into the buffer. Next a *for* loop begins that iterates once for each row from the top to the bottom of the window specified in the header. Nested within is another *for* loop that begins at the column designated for the left side of the window and continues until it reaches the column at the right side of the window. Within this inner loop, the function first uses *next_char* to get a character from the buffer. The expression is defined at the beginning of the program. It transfers a character from the buffer at the index specified by the second passed parameter to the variable specified by the first passed parameter. It then increments the index, and takes the remainder after dividing by 32,768. If this is 0, it indicates that the last character in the buffer has been used. If this is the case, it reloads the buffer with another 32,768 characters.

Next, the function checks whether the two most significant bits of the character are each 1. If not, it puts the value of 1 into the variable *pass*. If each of the two most significant bits was 1, it strips off these bits, puts the remaining number into *pass*, and then gets the next character from the buffer. In either case, we now have the character to be sent to the display in *ch* and the number of times it is to be repeated in *pass*. The function then begins another *for* loop, which puts the character into the next *pass* bytes of a line buffer. When the line buffer is full (with one line of display) the inner of the two nested *for* loops is complete. The offset address for the display memory is computed and the entire line is transferred from the line buffer to display memory. This process is repeated by the outer *for* loop until all of the lines of the display have been sent to display memory, after which the function closes the disk file and returns to the main program.

The next section of the function code is used when the 256 color information was not found at the end of the file. This indicates that a 16 color mode is being used. (This program doesn't handle the case where a black and white picture has been saved.) The function first checks the resolution information in the header. If the picture is 640×480 pixels, mode 18 is set up, if 640×350 pixels, mode 16 is set up, and if 640×200, mode 14 is set up. Other modes are not handled by this program. The program next takes the information from each color triplet in the header palette information and converts it into color information to be passed to the palette register. The function *setEGApalette* is then called to set up the 16 palette registers to the proper colors. The EGA/VGA registers are then initialized, and the program then enters a pair of nested *for* loops as described in the previous paragraph. The procedure is just the same as that described earlier, except that when a line of data is collected in the line buffer, it is passed to the display memory plane 0 (by properly setting sequencer register 2). The line is not incremented yet; instead another line of data is collected for the same line number and passed to display memory plane 1, and so forth until a line of data has been sent to each of the four display memory planes. Then the line is incremented, and the process is repeated for the four memory planes for the next display line. When the display is complete, the EGA/VGA registers are reset, the file is closed and the function returns to the main program.

Real Pictures in *.PCX* format

The VGA limitation of 256 colors, together with the limited resolution that is available, might make it seem that any attempt to display real color pictures on a PC screen would be doomed to failure. Actually, it is pretty surprising what good quality can be achieved within the limitations of the VAG 256 color mode. The last three color plates show examples of what can be done. Plate 30 is a picture of a teddy bear. Plate 31 is a close-up of a Peace rose. Plate 32 is a close-up of some chrysanthemums. These pictures were all taken with a Sony camcorder using a tripod to keep the picture as steady as possible. They were then transferred to the computer with a board called ComputerEyes Professional, manufactured by

> Digital Vision, Inc.
> 270 Bridge Street
> Dedham, MA 02026-9912

This board requires about 16 seconds to capture an image, so your camcorder taped picture must be stationary for at least that long. Software is available to change picture colors and to save it in any desired form. These pictures were saved as *.PCX* files and can thus be viewed using the software described in this book. You will find that transferring real-life pictures to the computer in this way is an extremely interesting activity. Furthermore, once you have the picture in the form of a *.PCX* file, you can add data or alpha-numerics using PC Paintbrush or any other drawing program that can accept *.PCX* files.

Saving a Display Screen in the *.PCX* Format

The function *save_pcx* is designed to be inserted into your program at a point just after you have generated a graphics display. It will then save the display to a disk file. The function is listed in Figure 24-2 as part of a program that first generates a simple display of colored bars and then saves the resulting display to a *.PCX* file using *save_pcx*. As you look at this program, please note that the *for* loop and the horizontal line drawing function within it are the only parts of the program involved in creating the display. Everything else is used in saving the display. This includes the header structure, variable definitions, etc. You'll need to include this information in your program along with the actual screen saving function. You also need to make a couple decisions about how the function is to be used. The first is what you are going to name the file of display information that is to be saved. This program just calls it *example.pcx*, so any file by that name will always be overwritten when this program runs. You may want to make some provision for allowing the user to enter a file name and for modifying the name that is entered or taking some other action if a file by that name already exists. The second consideration is when to save a graphics screen to disk. This program saves the screen to disk every time it is run. You may want to give the user an option as to whether or not the screen should be saved. If you need to print out some information offering this option, you can't just print it on top of the graphics display or it will be saved also. One way is to set the EGA/VGA registers so that alphanumeric data is XORed with the graphics picture. Then a second XOR of the same data returns the screen to its original condition.

The main program sets the graphics mode, draws 16 different colored horizontal bars, reads the 256 color VGA color registers into an array, and then saves the display screen to a *.PCX* file. (The reading of the color registers is shown for completeness, since it is needed for 256 color displays, but it isn't really used for anything in this case.) The function *save_pcx* begins by reading the display mode from the EGA/VGA card. It then sets up the header data to define the display mode that is currently in use. Some modes are not handled by this function. For these the function displays, "Cannot save this display mode..." and then exits back to DOS. The function next checks to see whether the display adapter card is a VGA. If so, the function gets the current palette information and stores it in the array *PALETTE*. This array is initially set to the default palette colors. If you have an EGA and are changing palette colors, it is your responsibility to update this array properly. Otherwise, your screen display will be saved with the default colors. (If you have a VGA, the palette information is automatically updated as described previously.) The program next takes each palette color assignment and converts it into a *.PCX* type color triplet, which is stored in the appropriate place in the header structure. The function then opens the disk file and stores the header at its beginning. The program determines some parameters needed to process the current display mode. Then, it enters a *for* loop which iterates from the top of the display window to the bottom of the display window. At each iteration, the loop first gets the starting character for the line. (This is at an address that increases by *xres* bytes per line for 256 color modes and by *xres/8* bytes per line for 16 color modes.) Next a pair of nested *for* loops are entered. The first iterates once for each memory plane used in the display mode, and the second iterates once for each byte making up the display line from the left to the right of the designated window. For all except the very first character, the following procedure takes place. If the character is the last one, it is set to an arbitrary value of 1 less than the preceeding character, forcing the buffer to be cleared out to the disk file at the end of each line. Otherwise, if the next character is the same as the current character, a parameter called *number* is incremented and we go on to the next loop. If the next character is different from the current character, then *number* is modified to make its two most significant bits ones and the result sent to the disk file. The current character is then sent to the disk file and the new character replaces the current character ready for the next loop. There is one exception to this. When the current value of *number* is 1 and the two most significant bits of the current character are not naturally 1, the numerical byte is not saved to the file; only the character byte is saved. All of this accomplishes the run-length compression that was described earlier. When all of the screen display data has been saved, if the 256 color mode was being used, a *C0H* is sent to the disk file, followed by the 768 bytes of color data for the 256 color registers.

Figure 24-2. Test Program for Storing .PCX File

```
/*

    SAVETEST = Program to store .PCX graphics files

            By Roger T. Stevens    11-22-91

*/

#include <stdio.h>
#include <stdlib.h>
#include <math.h>
#include <dos.h>
#include <conio.h>

#define graph_out(register,val)    {outp(0x3CE,register);\
```

(continued)

```
                              outp(0x3CF,val);}

void drawHorzLine2(int xstart, int xend, int y, int
    color);
int getMode(void);
char getPalette(int palette);
int getVGA(void);
unsigned char getByte(unsigned long int address, int
    color_plane, unsigned char mode);
void save_pcx(char filename[13]);
void setMode(int mode);
void getVGApalette(unsigned char *buffer);

union REGS reg;
struct REGPACK regs;
struct SREGS segregs;

struct {
    char password;
    char version;
    char encoding;
    char bits_per_pixel;
    int xmin, ymin, xmax, ymax;
    int xres, yres;
    unsigned char palette[48];
    char reserved;
    char no_of_planes;
    int bytes_per_line;
    int palette_type;
    char filler[58];
} pcx_header;

char VGA_data[64];
int srcseg, srcoff, destseg, destoff, xres, yres, i,
    start_x, start_y, start_angle, mode;
int LINEWIDTH;
unsigned char
PALETTE[16]={0,1,2,3,4,5,20,7,56,57,58,59,60,61,62,63};
char filename[13] = {"example.pcx"};
long int col,row;
unsigned char far *address;
```

(continued)

```
unsigned char palette_data[768];

void main(void)
{
    int i;

    xres = 640;
    yres = 350;
    setMode(16);
    LINEWIDTH = 18;
    for (i=0; i<16; i++)
        drawHorzLine2(10,630,i*22,i);
    getVGApalette(palette_data);
    save_pcx(filename);
    getch();
    setMode(3);
}

/*

    save_pcx() = Save display screen to .PCS disk file

*/

void save_pcx(char filename[13])

{
    int index = 0, i,j,k,add1,add2,number,num_out, end,
        start_line, end_line, planes;
    unsigned char ch,ch1,old_ch, file_buf[800];
    FILE *fsave;
    char far *video_address;

    mode = getMode();
    pcx_header.password = 0x0A;
    pcx_header.version = 0x05;
    pcx_header.encoding = 0x01;
    pcx_header.xmin = 0;
    pcx_header.ymin = 0;
    pcx_header.reserved = 0;
```

(continued)

```
pcx_header.palette_type = 0;
switch(mode)
{
    case 4:          /* 320 x 200 - 4 colors */
    case 5:
    case 6:      /* 640 x 200 - 2 colors */
    case 15:     /* 640 x 350 - 4 colors */
    case 17:     /* 640 x 480 - 2 colors */
        printf("\nCannot save this display "
            "mode...\n");
        exit(0);
    case 13:         /* 320 x 200 - 16 colors */
        pcx_header.bits_per_pixel = 0x01;
        pcx_header.xmax = 319;
        pcx_header.ymax = 199;
        pcx_header.xres = 320;
        pcx_header.yres = 200;
        pcx_header.no_of_planes = 4;
        pcx_header.bytes_per_line = 0x50;
        break;
    case 14:     /* 640 x 200 - 16 colors */
        pcx_header.bits_per_pixel = 0x01;
        pcx_header.xmax = 639;
        pcx_header.ymax = 199;
        pcx_header.xres = 640;
        pcx_header.yres = 200;
        pcx_header.no_of_planes = 4;
        pcx_header.bytes_per_line = 0x50;
        break;
    case 16:     /* 640 x 350 - 16 colors */
        pcx_header.bits_per_pixel = 0x01;
        pcx_header.xmax = 639;
        pcx_header.ymax = 349;
        pcx_header.xres = 640;
        pcx_header.yres = 350;
        pcx_header.no_of_planes = 4;
        pcx_header.bytes_per_line = 0x50;
        break;
    case 18:     /* 640 x 480 - 16 colors */
        pcx_header.bits_per_pixel = 0x01;
        pcx_header.xmax = 639;
```

(continued)

```
            pcx_header.ymax = 479;
            pcx_header.xres = 640;
            pcx_header.yres = 480;
            pcx_header.no_of_planes = 4;
            pcx_header.bytes_per_line = 0x50;
            break;
        case 19:    /* 320 x 200 - 256 colors */
            pcx_header.bits_per_pixel = 0x08;
            pcx_header.no_of_planes = 1;
            pcx_header.bytes_per_line = 320;
            pcx_header.xmax = 319;
            pcx_header.ymax = 199;
            pcx_header.xres = 320;
            pcx_header.yres = 200;
            break;
    }
    if (getVGA() == 0x1B)
    {
        for (i=0; i<16; i++)
            PALETTE[i] = getPalette(i);
    }
    for (i=0; i<16; i++)
    {
        pcx_header.palette[3*i] = ((PALETTE[i] & 0x20)
            << 1) | ((PALETTE[i] & 0x04) << 5);
        pcx_header.palette[3*i + 1] = ((PALETTE[i] & 0x10)
            << 2) | ((PALETTE[i] & 0x02) << 6);
        pcx_header.palette[3*i + 2] = ((PALETTE[i] & 0x08)
            << 3) | ((PALETTE[i] & 0x01) << 7);
    }
    fsave = fopen(filename,"wb");
    fwrite(&pcx_header,1,128,fsave);
    if (mode == 19)
    {
        start_line = pcx_header.xmin;
        end_line = pcx_header.xmax + 1;
        planes = 1;
    }
    else
    {
        start_line = pcx_header.xmin>>3;
```

(continued)

```
        end_line = (pcx_header.xmax>>3) + 1;
        planes = 4;
    }
    for (k=pcx_header.ymin; k<=pcx_header.ymax; k++)
    {
        number = 1;
        if (mode==19)
            old_ch = getByte(320*k + start_line,0,mode);
        else
            old_ch = getByte((pcx_header.xres>>3)*k +
                start_line,0,mode);
        for (j=0; j<planes; j++)
        {
            for (i=start_line; i<=end_line; i++)
            {
                if ((i==start_line) && (j == 0))
                    continue;
                if (i==end_line)
                    if (j == planes-1)
                        ch = old_ch - 1;
                    else
                        continue;
                else
                {
                    if (mode==19)
                        ch = getByte(320*k + i,j, mode);
                    else
                        ch = getByte((pcx_header.xres >>
                            3)*k + i,j,mode);
                }
                if ((ch == old_ch) && number < 63)
                    number++;
                else
                {
                    num_out = ((unsigned char) number |
                        0xC0);
                    if ((number != 1) || ((old_ch & 0xC0)
                        == 0xC0))
                        file_buf[index++] = num_out;
                    file_buf[index++] = old_ch;
                    old_ch = ch;
```

(continued)

```
                        number = 1;
                    }
                }
            }
        fwrite(file_buf,index,1,fsave);
        index = 0;
    }
    if (mode == 19)
    {
        fputc(0xC0,fsave);
        for (i=0; i<768; i++)
            fputc((palette_data[i] << 2),fsave);
    }
    fclose(fsave);
}
```

```
/*
┌─────────────────────────────────────────────────────┐
│                                                       │
│              setMode() = Sets video mode              │
│                                                       │
└─────────────────────────────────────────────────────┘
*/
```

```
void setMode(int mode)
{
    reg.x.ax = mode;
    int86 (0x10,&reg,&reg);
}
```

```
/*
┌─────────────────────────────────────────────────────┐
│                                                       │
│           getMode() = Returns the video mode          │
│                                                       │
└─────────────────────────────────────────────────────┘
*/
```

```
int getMode(void)
{
    reg.h.ah = 0x0F;
    int86 (0x10,&reg,&reg);
    return (reg.h.al);
```

(continued)

```
}

/*

        getVGA() = Returns VGA information

*/

int getVGA(void)
{
    segread(&segregs);
    regs.r_es = segregs.ds;
    regs.r_di = (int) VGA_data;
    regs.r_ax = 0x1B00;
    intr (0x10,&regs);
    return (regs.r_ax & 0xFF);
}

/*

    getPalette() = Returns the contents of a palette
                   register (for VGA only)

*/

char getPalette(int palette)
{
    union REGS reg;
    struct SREGS inreg;

    reg.x.ax = 0x1007;
    reg.h.bl = palette;
    int86x(0x10,&reg,&reg,&inreg);
    return(reg.h.bh);
}
```

(continued)

```
/*
    ┌─────────────────────────────────────────────────────┐
    │┌───────────────────────────────────────────────────┐│
    ││                                                   ││
    ││        getByte() = Reads a byte from the screen   ││
    ││                                                   ││
    │└───────────────────────────────────────────────────┘│
    └─────────────────────────────────────────────────────┘
*/

unsigned char getByte(unsigned long int address, int
    color_plane, unsigned char mode)
{

    #define graph_out(index,val)  {outp(0x3CE,index);\
                        outp(0x3CF,val);}
    char far * video_address;

    video_address = (char far *) 0xA0000000L + address;
    if (mode != 19)
    {
        graph_out(4,color_plane);
        graph_out(5,0);
    }
    return (*video_address);
}


/*
    ┌─────────────────────────────────────────────────────┐
    │┌───────────────────────────────────────────────────┐│
    ││                                                   ││
    ││  getVGApalette() = Function to read all 256 VGA color ││
    ││                          registers                ││
    ││                                                   ││
    │└───────────────────────────────────────────────────┘│
    └─────────────────────────────────────────────────────┘
*/

void getVGApalette(unsigned char *buffer)
{
    struct REGPACK regs;
    struct SREGS sregs;

    regs.r_ax = 0x1017;
    segread(&sregs);
    regs.r_es = sregs.ds;
    regs.r_bx = 0;
```

(continued)

```
        regs.r_cx = 256;
        regs.r_dx = (int)buffer;
        intr(0x10,&regs);
}


/*
    ┌─────────────────────────────────────────────────────────┐
    │ ┌─────────────────────────────────────────────────────┐ │
    │ │                                                     │ │
    │ │ drawHorzLine2() = Draws a horizontal line of designated │ │
    │ │  width between two designated points on screen using a  │ │
    │ │       selected color and 16 color video modes.         │ │
    │ │                                                     │ │
    │ └─────────────────────────────────────────────────────┘ │
    └─────────────────────────────────────────────────────────┘
*/


void drawHorzLine2(int xstart, int xend, int y, int color)
{
    #define graph_out(index,val)   {outp(0x3CE,index);\
                         outp(0x3CF,val);}
    char line_store[100];
    int dummy, i, x1, x2;
    int length, width, offset1, offset2;
    int srcseg, srcoff, destseg, destoff;
    long no_of_bytes;
    unsigned char mask;
    char far *start_address;
    char far *end_address;

    struct SREGS segregs;

    segread(&segregs);
    srcseg = segregs.ds;
    srcoff = (int) line_store;
    width = LINEWIDTH/2;
    for (i=-width; i<=width; i++)
    {
        x1 = min(xstart, xend) - width;
        x2 = max(xstart, xend) + width;
        offset1 = x1 % 8;
        offset2 = x2 % 8;
        start_address = (char far *)(0xA0000000L +
            ((long)(y+i) * xres/8L + ((long)x1 / 8L)));
```

(continued)

```
                    end_address = (char far *)(0xA0000000L +
                        ((long)(y+i) * xres/8L + ((long)x2 / 8L)));
                    no_of_bytes = end_address - start_address;
                    length = ((x2 - x1) - ((8-offset1) + (offset2))) /
                        8L;
                    mask = 0xFF << (7 - offset2);
                    if (!no_of_bytes)
                        mask &= 0xFF >> offset1;
                    dummy = *end_address;
                    graph_out(5,2);
                    graph_out(8,mask);
                    *end_address = color;
                    if (no_of_bytes)
                    {
                        mask = 0xFF >> offset1;
                        graph_out(8, mask);
                        *start_address = color;
                        graph_out(8, 0xFF);
                        memset(line_store,color,length);
                        destseg = 0xA000;
                        destoff = ((long)(y+i)*80L + ((long)x1/8L))
                            +1;
                        movedata(srcseg, srcoff, destseg, destoff,
                            length);
                    }
                }
            graph_out(8,0xFF);
            graph_out(5,0);
        }
```

Chapter **25**

Displaying *.IMG* Format Files

The *.IMG* file format can be used for saving and restoring monochrome or 16 color displays. In the 16 color mode, it is a plane oriented format like the *.PCX* format, and therefore quite efficient with the EGA/VGA four plane memory structure. The format has been around quite awhile, so you'll probably often encounter pictures in this format that you would like to display. However, because of some strange discrepancies in the handling of the color palette, you'll be much better off to save your 16 color files in one of the other two formats described in this book. Therefore, we are going to supply only a program for displaying the *.IMG* files. The *.IMG* format was developed by

Digital Research, Inc.
P. O. Box DRI
Monterey, CA 93942   Phone: (408) 649-3896

The format is used in storing files for the GEM drawing and painting products. Digital Research is not noted for their customer service, as you will discover if you try to get information on this file format. Several times, I was promised a specification on the file format, and actually received a couple of packages, but each time, the enclosures were something totally irrelevant to what I had asked for.

The *.IMG* Header Format

Table 25-1 describes the contents of the *.IMG* file header. As can be seen, the information in the header is minimal. You should note that no color information is given. The *.IMG* file, in the 16 color mode, uses only the 16 default EGA colors, so that if you have changed the palette, these changes will be lost. Furthermore, the colors are treated in a rather strange way, as will be described later.

Data Compression in the *.IMG* File

Like the *.PCX* file, the *.IMG* file uses a form of run-length compression. There are two bytes that have special meanings in the *.IMG* format. They are *00H* and *80H*. The *00H* byte has two possible meanings. If it occurs at the beginning of a scan line and is followed by the bytes *00H* and *FFH*, the next byte is a replication count, which indicates how many times the decoded scan line that follows is to be replicated on the screen. If the special byte *00H* is followed by anything other than another *00H*, the second byte is a run-length byte, which indicates the number of times that a particular pattern of bytes is to be replicated on the screen. The pattern length is given in the header; the actual bytes that make up the pattern follow directly after the run-length byte. The special byte *80H* is followed by a run-length byte, which indicates the number of bytes that follow that are to be written directly to the screen. Finally, for all bytes having values other than 00H and 80H, the high order byte is masked off and the remaining number indicates the number of bytes that are to be written to the screen. If the high order byte was 0, these bytes are all to be *00H*; if the high order byte was 1, these bytes are all to be filled pixels (*FFH*).

Problems with 16 Color *.IMG* Files

You might suppose that the *.IMG* file for 16 colors would be like the *.PCX* file in reading a line from each of the four color planes of the EGA in turn, compressing it and storing it. Unfortunately this turns out not to be true. Although *.IMG* file generating programs cannot recognize the EGA palettes and assume a default palette, what they do to the colors is totally unlike what you might expect. The colors reported by the *.IMG* generating programs for the standard 16 color

TABLE 25-1. *.IMG* FILE HEADER

Byte #	Name	Description
0-1	Version number	This word must always be set to 1.
2-3	Header length in words	An eight word header is normal. (Ventura Publisher creates *.IMG* files that may be incompatible with the method of display described in this book. They have a nine bit header.)
4-5	Number of planes	1 = monochrome 2 = 16 colors (see the discussion of the handling of 16 color files).
6-7	Pattern length (for data compression)	Default is 2 bytes. Allowable range is 1 to 8 bytes.
8-9	Pixel width	Microns. (Normally not used. Graphics displays specify resolution in dots and printers specify resolution in dots per inch.)
10-11	Pixel height	Microns. (Normally not used. Graphics displays specify resolution in dots and printers specify resolution in dots per inch.)
12-13	Image width	Pixels (maximum is 65535)
14-15	Image height	Pixels (maximum is 65535)

palette are shown in Table 25-2 for two alternate methods of reading the color data. Method 1 is the most straight-forward way of reading the color information, but it turns out to be right only for black and intense white. All other colors are different from the normal palette setting so that you have to reset the palette registers for your picture to have the proper coloring. Unfortunately, your display is then incompatible with everything else in the world. The second method of reading color data gets all of the colors right except for palette registers 0, 7, 8 and 15. Therefore you still have to change these four registers to make the picture come out right. Unfortunately, if you are using C and attempt to use *printf* to write something to the screen, you'll find that it expects to use palette register 0 as the background color and palette register 7 as the foreground color, so after you've modified these palette registers, your *printf* function will produce something other than a white character on a black background.

Handling a Large *.IMG* File

You'll remember that for *.PCX* files, we simply checked to see if the x and y resolutions of the file matched any of the standard EGA/VGA display modes. If they did, we selected that display mode; if none matched, we simply aborted without displaying anything. A lot of *.IMG* files around that are much larger than any of our display formats. In fact it is possible to have a file with a display resolution of 65536×65536 pixels, although this is unlikely and would result in a pretty big file, even if compressed. In decoding and displaying the *.IMG* files, we're going to take a different approach. If the designated display resolution is the same as one of the standard EGA/VGA formats, we'll use that display mode. If the file display resolution is larger, we'll select the highest display resolution available for 16 colors on the VGA (640×480 pixels) and then indicate the resolution of the file on the screen and allow the user to enter the starting pixel values for x and y. Thus, although you cannot view all of a large picture at once, you can view it piece by piece.

The *img.c* Program

The *img.c* program, which selects and displays *.IMG* files, is listed in Figure 25-1. The program begins by reading and displaying a directory of all *.IMG* files in the default directory and permitting the

TABLE 25-2. PALETTE DATA FOR *.IMG* FILES

Palette No.	IMG Data Method #1	IMG Data Method #2
0 (0000)	0000	0111
1 (0001)	0011	0001
2 (0010)	0101	0010
3 (0011)	0001	0011
4 (0100)	0110	0100
5 (0101)	0010	0101
6 (0110)	0100	0110
7 (0111)	1000	1111
8 (1000)	0111	0000
9 (1001)	1011	1001
10 (1010)	1101	1101
11 (1011)	1001	1011
12 (1100)	1110	1100
13 (1101)	1010	1101
14 (1110)	1100	1110
15 (1111)	1111	1000

user to select one of these for display. This is done in the same manner that was described for *.PCX* files in the previous chapter. Once a file has been selected, the function *restore_screen* is called to display the selected file. The display remains until a key is struck on the keyboard. The program then gives the user the option of erasing this file. Whether or not the file is erased, the program returns to the directory display of *.IMG* files and continues to iterate in this manner until the *Esc* key is hit to terminate the program.

The *restore_screen* function begins by opening the designated file. It then reads the header, checks the first five bytes of the header and if they do not match those for a *.IMG* file, displays a diagnostic message and returns to the directory. The x and y resolutions are then checked. The program is set up to handle files with a maximum resolution of 8192. If the x resolution is greater than this, the program prints a diagnostic message and then returns to the directory. Next, if the y resolution is greater than or equal to 480, mode 18 (640×480 pixels) is selected. If the y resolution is less than this, mode 16 (640×350 pixels) is selected. Next, if either file resolution is greater than the resolution of the selected display mode, the program prints out the screen width (the display mode x resolution and the file x resolution and then lets the user enter the value that he or she wants to use for the starting x point. This can be any integer; no protection is provided against the user entering an incorrect value. The same process is then repeated to allow the user to enter a y starting value. The program then reads the next 16,384 bytes from the file (or until end of file is reached), sets the display mode, sets the EGA palette registers to show the proper colors and finally determines the end values for x and y. The function then enters a *while* loop that iterates once for each row in the file. (Note that whether we want to display beginning at the first row or have selected a row further down to begin the display, we have to process all of the file data and decode it; only what is actually displayed changes.) The function then looks for the code indicating duplicated rows and, if it is found, sets up to duplicate rows. Then the function checks for a repeated pattern and, if one is found, sends it out to the line buffer the indicated number of times. Next the function looks for the code indicating a string of characters and, if found, stores the characters in the string in the line buffer. Finally, the function checks for strings of a continuous fill color and stores them in the line buffer if found. This process continues until the line buffer is filled with a full line for for each color plane (one for monochrome or four for 16 color). Then, the function sets the sequencer registers for the proper color plane and transfers a line of data to the display memory for each color plane. Data is transferred only for lines that are to be displayed and only for that part of the file line that is to be displayed. In this function we are doing a perfectly straightforward transfer of the color planes in order, resulting in the palette color selection of mode 1.

A *restore_screen* Function for Mode 2

Figure 25-2 lists a version of the *restore_screen* function that will produce the colors listed for mode 2. The first thing to note is that we are reading all information in inverted form. Consequently for a black and white picture to be reproduced properly, we don't tamper with the palette, but we reinvert all of the data before display. For the 16 color display, we reinvert the data for the fourth memory plane only. Second, we don't transfer the data to display memory in the normal color plane order. Instead we transfer in the order 3, 2, 1 and 4. This gives the color selection shown for mode 2, and we then do some manipulation of the palette registers so that the colors will be correct.

Figure 25-1. Listing of Program to Display .IMG Files

```
/*



        IMG = Program to read .IMG graphics files


              By Roger T. Stevens   9-23-91



*/

'#include <stdio.h>
#include <stdlib.h>
#include <string.h>
#include <math.h>
#include <dos.h>
#include <conio.h>
#include <ctype.h>
#include <dir.h>

#define UP_ARROW      328
#define DOWN_ARROW    336
#define LEFT_ARROW    331
#define RIGHT_ARROW   333
#define BACKSPACE       8
#define seq_out(register,val)  {outp(0x3C4,register);\
                  outp(0x3C5,val);}
```

(continued)

```
#define graph_out(register,val)  {outp(0x3CE,register);\
                        outp(0x3CF,val);}
#define next_char(ch, index) {ch = file_buf[index];\
                if ((index = (++index) % 16384) == 0)\
                fread(file_buf,16384,1,fsave);}
#define next_comp(ch, index) {ch =~ file_buf[index];\
                if ((index = (++index) % 16384) == 0)\
                fread(file_buf,16384,1,fsave);}

void cls(int color);
char menu(int last_entry);
int dir_menu(int last_entry);
void plot16(int x, int y, int color);
char read_char_from_screen(int x, int y);
int restore_screen(char file_name[]);
void setMode(int mode);
void setAllEGApals(char *pal_colors);
int sort_function(const void *a, const void *b);

union REGS reg;

struct SREGS segregs;

long int srcseg, srcoff, destseg, destoff;
int pattern_size, xres, yres;
int attr, i, j, k, dir_index= 0, type, length[7];
char Host_Array[100];
int column, end, done, level,key, cursor_pos[16] =
    {16,25,30,25,26,30,30,30,28,28,21,14, 21,20,12,18},
    start_x, start_y, start_angle, cursor_x, cursor_y,
    mode, end_x, end_y, mode;
char filename[32],
buffer[64],div_buf[64],ch,dirbuf[64][13];
unsigned char header[16];
struct ffblk ffblk;
long int col,row;
char palette[17] = {0,3,5,1,20,2,4,7,56,59,61,57,62,
    58,60,63};

main()
{
```

(continued)

```
for(;;)
{
    setMode(3);
    textbackground(1);
    textcolor(15);
    window(2,2,78,23);
    clrscr();
    gotoxy(1,1);
    printf("\xC9");
    for (i=0; i<74; i++)
        printf("\xCD");
    printf("\xBB");
    for (i=2; i<22; i++)
    {
        gotoxy(1,i);
        printf("\xBA");
        gotoxy(76,i);
        printf("\xBA");
    }
    gotoxy(1,22);
    printf("\xC8");
    for (i=0; i<74; i++)
        printf("\xCD");
    printf("\xBC");
    gotoxy(19,2);
    filename[0] = NULL;
    cprintf
        ("Select file name with cursor arrows: ");
    textcolor(14);
    end = 0;
    done = findfirst("*.img",&ffblk,0);
    while(!done)
    {
        strcpy(dirbuf[end++],ffblk.ff_name);
        done = findnext(&ffblk);
    }
    qsort((void *)dirbuf,end,sizeof(dirbuf[0]),
        sort_function);
    textbackground(1);
    textcolor(14);
    for (i=0; i<end; i++)
```

(continued)

717

```
                {
                    column = i/19;
                    if (i == dir_index)
                    {
                        textbackground(7);
                        textcolor(1);
                    }
                    gotoxy(2+19*column,(i%19)+3);
                    cprintf("%s",dirbuf[i]);
                    textbackground(1);
                    textcolor(14);
                }
                key = dir_menu(end);
                if (key == 0x1B)
                    break;
                restore_screen(filename);
                getch();
                printf("     Hit 'E' to erase this file...or any"
                    " other key to continue...");
                ch = getch();
                if (toupper(ch) == 'E')
                    remove(filename);
            }
    }


/*
┌─────────────────────────────────────────────────────────┐
│                                                           │
│              setMode() = Sets video mode                  │
│                                                           │
└─────────────────────────────────────────────────────────┘
*/

void setMode(int imode)
{
    mode = imode;
    reg.h.ah = 0;
    reg.h.al = mode;
    int86 (0x10,&reg,&reg);
}
```

(continued)

```
/*
┌─────────────────────────────────────────────────────┐
│                                                     │
│    restore_screen() = Reads and displays a .IMG file │
│                                                     │
└─────────────────────────────────────────────────────┘
*/

int restore_screen(char file_name[])
{
    FILE *fsave;
    unsigned char ch,color,buffer[4][8192],
        file_buf[16384];
    int i,j,k,m,pass,col,row,dup_rows=1,no_planes,plane,
        max_col, max_row, start_col=0, start_row=0,type;
    unsigned char plane_sel[4] = {1,2,4,8};
    long int index=0;
    int ch1=0x0D;

    segread(&segregs);
    srcseg = segregs.ds;
    srcoff = (int) buffer;
    destseg = 0xA000;
    if ((fsave = fopen(file_name,"rb")) == NULL)
    {
        printf("\nCan't find %s.\n",file_name);
        return;
    }
    fread(header,1,16,fsave);
    if (memcmp("\x00\x01\x00\x08\x00",header,5))
    {
        printf("\nImproper format in file %s...\n",
            file_name);
        return;
    }
    pattern_size = header[7] + (header[6] << 8);
    no_planes = header[5];
    max_col = header[13] + (header[12] << 8);
    max_row = header[15] + (header[14] << 8);
    xres = 640;
    if (max_row >= 480)
    {
```

(continued)

```
        mode = 18;
        yres = 480;
    }
    else
    {
        mode = 16;
        yres = 350;
    }
    if (max_col > 8192)
    {
        printf("\nResolution not supported...\n");
        return;
    }
    if ((max_col<xres) || (max_row > yres))
    {
        textbackground(1);
        textcolor(15);
        window(0,0,79,24);
        clrscr();
        printf("\n   Screen width: %d",xres);
        printf("\n   Picture width: %d",max_col);
        printf("\n   Enter starting column: ");
        scanf("%d",&start_col);
        printf("\n   Screen height: %d",yres);
        printf("\n   Picture height: %d",max_row);
        printf("\n   Enter starting line: ");
        scanf("%d",&start_row);
    }
    fread(file_buf,16384,1,fsave);
    setMode(mode);
    setAllEGApals(palette);
    graph_out(8,0xFF);
    index = 0;
    row = 0;
    end_x = min(xres/8,(max_col - start_col)/8);
    end_y = min(start_row + yres,max_row);
    while (row < end_y)
    {
        col = 0;
        plane = 0;
        dup_rows = 1;
```

(continued)

```
while (plane<no_planes)
{
    next_char(ch, index);
    if (ch == 0x00)
    {
        j = pattern_size;
        next_char(ch,index);
        if (ch == 0x00)
        {
            next_char(ch,index);
            next_char(dup_rows,index);
        }
        else
        {
            while (j--)
                next_comp(buffer[plane][col++],
                    index);
            k = ch-1;
            while(k--)
            {
                memcpy(&buffer[plane][col],
                    &buffer[plane][col -
                    pattern_size],
                    pattern_size);
                col += pattern_size;
            }
        }
    }
    else
    {
        if (ch == 0x80)
        {
            next_char(i,index);
            while (i--)
                next_comp (buffer[plane]
                    [col++],index);
        }
        else
        {
            if (ch > 0x80)
            {
```

(continued)

```
                        i = ch & 0x7F;
                        while (i--)
                            buffer[plane][col++] = 0x00;
                }
                else
                {
                        i = ch & 0x7F;
                        while (i--)
                            buffer[plane][col++] = 0xFF;
                }
            }
        }
        if (col >= max_col/8)
        {
            col = 0;
            plane++;
        }
    }
    while (dup_rows-- > 0)
    {
        if (no_planes == 1)
        {
            seq_out(2,0xFF);
            if (row >= start_row)
            {
                destoff = (row - start_row) * 80L;
                movedata(srcseg,
                    srcoff+(start_col/8), destseg,
                    destoff, end_x);
            }
        }
        else
        {
            for (i=0; i<no_planes; i++)
            {
                seq_out(2,plane_sel[i]);
                if (row >= start_row)
                {
                    destoff = (row - start_row) * 80L;
                    movedata(srcseg,
                        srcoff+(start_col/8)+8192*i,
```

(continued)

```
                                    destseg, destoff, end_x);
                        }
                    }
                }
            }
            row++;
        }
        graph_out(8,0xFF);
        graph_out(5,0);
        fclose(fsave);
}

/*
```

```
        sort_function() = Directory sorting function
```

```
*/

int sort_function(const void *a, const void *b)
{
    return( strcmp(a,b));
}

/*
```

```
        dir_menu() = Menu function for directory
```

```
*/

int dir_menu(int last_entry)
{
    int ch1 = NULL;

    while ((ch1 != 0x0D) && (ch1 != 0x1B))
    {
        ch1 = getch();
        if (ch1 == 0x00)
        {
            ch1 = getch() + 256;
```

(continued)

```
            textbackground(1);
            textcolor(14);
            column = dir_index/19;
            gotoxy(2+19*column,(dir_index%19)+3);
            cprintf("%s",dirbuf[dir_index]);
            switch(ch1)
            {
                case DOWN_ARROW:
                    ++dir_index;
                    dir_index = dir_index % last_entry;
                    break;
                case UP_ARROW:
                    --dir_index;
                    if (dir_index<0)
                        dir_index = last_entry - 1;
                    break;
                case RIGHT_ARROW:
                    if ((dir_index + 19) < last_entry)
                        dir_index += 19;
                    break;
                case LEFT_ARROW:
                    if (dir_index > 19)
                        dir_index -= 19;
                    break;
            }
            textbackground(7);
            textcolor(1);
            column = dir_index/19;
            gotoxy(2+19*column,(dir_index%19)+3);
            cprintf("%s",dirbuf[dir_index]);
        }
    }
    strcpy(filename,dirbuf[dir_index]);
    return(ch1);
}
```

(continued)

```
/*
```

```
    setAllEGApals() = Sets all the EGA palette registers
                  and the border register
```

```
*/
```

```c
void setAllEGApals(char *pal_colors)
{

    struct REGPACK regs;
    struct SREGS sregs;

    regs.r_ax = 0x1002;
    segread(&sregs);
    regs.r_es = sregs.ds;
    regs.r_dx = (int)pal_colors;
    intr(0x10,&regs);
}
```

```
/*
```

```
  plot16() = Plots a point on the screen at a designated
   position using a selected color for 16 color modes.
```

```
*/
```

```c
void plot16(int x, int y, int color)
{
    #define graph_out(index,val)  {outp(0x3CE,index);\
                        outp(0x3CF,val);}

    int dummy,mask;
    char far * address;

    if ((x>=0) && (x<xres) && (y>=0) && (y<yres))
    {
        address = (char far *) 0xA0000000L + (long)y *
            xres/8L + ((long)x / 8L);
```

(continued)

```
        mask = 0x80 >> (x % 8);
        graph_out(8,mask);
        graph_out(5,2);
        dummy = *address;
        *address = color;
        graph_out(5,0);
        graph_out(8,0xFF);
    }
}
```

Figure 25-2. Listing of restore_screen Function for Mode 2

```
/*
```

```
restore_screen = Reads and displays a file using mode 2
```

```
*/
```

```
int restore_screen(char file_name[])
{
    FILE *fsave;
    unsigned char ch,color,buffer[8192],file_buf[16384];
    int i,j,k,m,pass,col,row,dup_rows=1,no_planes,plane,
        max_col, max_row, start_col=0, start_row=0,type;
    unsigned char plane_sel[4] = {4,2,1,8};
    long int index=0;
    int ch1=0x0D;
    segread(&segregs);
    srcseg = segregs.ds;
    srcoff = (int) buffer;
    destseg = 0xA000;
    if ((fsave = fopen(file_name,"rb")) == NULL)
    {
        printf("\nCan't find %s.\n",file_name);
        return;
    }
    fread(header,1,16,fsave);
    if (memcmp("\x00\x01\x00\x08\x00",header,5))
    {
```

(continued)

```
        printf("\nImproper format in file %s...\n",
            file_name);
        return;
    }
    pattern_size = header[7] + (header[6] << 8);
    no_planes = header[5];
    max_col = header[13] + (header[12] << 8);
    max_row = header[15] + (header[14] << 8);
    xres = 640;
    if (max_row >= 480)
    {
        mode = 18;
        yres = 480;
    }
    else
    {
        mode = 16;
        yres = 350;
    }
    if (max_col > 8192)
    {
        printf("\nResolution not supported...\n");
        return;
    }
    if ((max_col<xres) || (max_row > yres))
    {
        textbackground(1);
        textcolor(15);
        window(0,0,79,24);
        clrscr();
        printf("\n   Screen width: %d",xres);
        printf("\n   Picture width: %d",max_col);
        printf("\n   Enter starting column: ");
        scanf("%d",&start_col);
        printf("\n   Screen height: %d",yres);
        printf("\n   Picture height: %d",max_row);
        printf("\n   Enter starting line: ");
        scanf("%d",&start_row);
    }
    fread(file_buf,16384,1,fsave);
    setMode(mode);
```

(continued)

727

```
if (no_planes == 4)
    setAllEGApals(palette);
graph_out(8,0xFF);
index = 0;
row = 0;
end_x = min(xres/8,(max_col - start_col)/8);
end_y = min(start_row + yres,max_row);
while (row < end_y)
{
    col = 0;
    plane = 0;
    while (plane<no_planes)
    {
        next_char(ch, index);
        if (ch == 0x00)
        {
            j = pattern_size;
            next_char(ch,index);
            if (ch == 0x00)
            {
                next_char(ch,index);
                next_char(dup_rows,index);
            }
            else
            {
                while (j--)
                    next_char(buffer[col++], index);
                k = ch-1;
                while(k--)
                {
                    memcpy(&buffer[col],
                        &buffer[col-pattern_size],
                        pattern_size);
                    col += pattern_size;
                }
            }
        }
        else
        {
            if (ch == 0x80)
            {
```

(continued)

```
            next_char(i,index);
            while (i--)
                next_char (buffer[col++],index);
    }
    else
    {
        if (ch > 0x80)
        {
            i = ch & 0x7F;
            while (i--)
                buffer[col++] = 0xFF;
        }
        else
        {
            i = ch & 0x7F;
            while (i--)
                buffer[col++] = 0x00;
        }
    }
}
if (col >= max_col/8)
{
    col = 0;
    if (no_planes == 1)
    {
        seq_out(2,0xFF);
    }
    else
    {
        seq_out(2,plane_sel[plane]);
    }
    if ((plane == 3) || (no_planes == 1))
    {
        for (i=0; i<end_x; i++)
            buffer[i] = ~buffer[i];
    }
    plane++;
    if (row >= start_row)
    {
        destoff = (row - start_row) * 80L;
        movedata(srcseg,
```

(continued)

```
                                   srcoff+start_col/8,
                                   destseg,destoff,
                                   end_x);
                    }
              }
         }
         row++;
    }
    graph_out(8,0xFF);
    graph_out(5,0);
    fclose(fsave);
}
```

Saving and Restoring Displays with the *.GIF* Format

The Graphics Interchange Format (GIF) was developed by:

CompuServe Incorporated
P. O. Box 20212
Columbus, OH 43220   Phone: (614) 457-8650

Graphics Interchange Format and *GIF* are trademarks of Compu-Serve, Incorporated, an H&R Block Company. You can download the latest specification for the *.GIF* format from CompuServe if you are interesting in studying the details of this format. It is stored in a file called *GIF89A.ARC*. The *.GIF* uses Lempel-Ziv–Welch (LZW) compression, a highly effective method for compressing files. If you have a display with variegated colors, this compression technique will usually produce a file that is smaller than obtained by any of the run-length encoding techniques described in the two previous chapters. On the other hand, for pictures having large areas of a solid color, the run-length methods may be more efficient. The *.GIF* technique reads the screen pixel by pixel rather than on a memory plane oriented basis, so that it is most effective with 256 color modes, whereas the *.IMG* and *.PCX* formats are more effective with 16 color modes. Finally, *.GIF* encoders tend to be a little slow. However, decoding is on a par with the other methods. In this case, speed of encoding was sacrificed to small file size, which is most important when the files are to be transmitted over the telephone lines.

Lempel-Ziv–Welch Compression

The LZW compression technique makes use of a table of strings of characters, each of which is assigned a code. Rather than save the character string, only the code is saved. The beauty of the technique is that the table is generated as the data is scanned, with entries assigned to strings only as they occur, and the code can be regenerated easily from the saved data. Figure 26-1 shows a sample length of character data to illustrate how the technique works. In the example, there only four characters. The table is initialized with only four entries, *0* being *a*, *1* being *b*, *2* being *c*, and *3* being *d*. The process begins by taking as many characters from the data stream as match an existing string in the table. At the beginning this amounts to only one character. The next character is then read and a new string, consisting of the previous string that was found (only one character in this case), with the new character appended. The string from the table is then saved to the data file. With the new character as the beginning of a data string, a search of the table is made for a matching string (there has to be some match, even if for only a single character). When the match is found, the next character is read, appended to the string that was found, and the new string assigned to the next entry in the table. Again the string that was found in the table is sent to the file and the final character that was just read from the data stream becomes the beginning of the next string of data for which a match is sought. The figure shows how the process works for the sample data stream. The original and compressed data streams are shown in Figure 26-2, and the table generated during compression is in Figure 26-3. It turns out that reading this encoded data is very simple. At least the first two codes that we read from the file are characters that have already been assigned values in the table. We work in the same way as for encoding, generating codes for new strings. If you note how the compressed data stream was created, it is obvious that for just about every case, a table entry has already been created when reading before a reference to that string number occurs.

The *GIF* Program for Viewing *.GIF* Files

The *GIF* program is very similar to the *PCX* program described in Chapter 24, except for the use of the different compression technique. It is listed in Figure 26-4. The program begins by entering an infinite

Figure 26-1. Lempel-Ziv–Welch Data Compression

a	b	b	c	d	a	b	b	d	a	a	b	b	b	c	b	b	b
ab=5																	
	bb=6																
		bc=7															
			cd=8														
				da=9													
					abb=5b=10												
						bd=11											
							daa=9a=12										
								abbb=10b=13									
									bcb=7b=14								
										bbb=6b= 15							

Figure 26-2. Original and Compressed Data Streams

Original Data	a b b c d a b b d a a b b b c b b b
Compressed Data	1 2 2 3 4 5 2 9 10 7 6 2

for loop, which at each iteration starts by displaying a box containing a sorted directory of all of the files ending with a *.GIF* extension in the default directory. The user is given an opportunity to move around in this directory and select a program for display. All of this is done in just the same way as for the *PCX* program. Once a file is selected, the *restore_screen* function is run to display the file on the screen. This is where everything is different. After a file is displayed, hitting any key presents the user with an opportunity to erase the file. If an *E* or *e* is entered, the file will be erased. Then the program loops to give

Figure 26-3. Table Entries Generated in LZW Compression Process

Code	String	Alternate	Code	String	Alternate
1	a	0	9	da	4a
2	b	1	10	abb	5b
3	c	2	11	bd	2d
4	d	3	12	daa	9a
5	ab	1b	13	abab	10b
6	bb	2b	14	bcd	7b
7	bc	2c	15	bb	6b
8	cd	3d			

the user another chance to select a file for display. This continues until the user hits the *Esc* key to exit from the program.

Now let's look at the *restore_screen* function. This begins by opening the selected file. If the file cannot be opened, a diagnostic message is printed and the function returns to the main program. This shouldn't ever occur, however, because the file name selected must match one in the directory. Next the function reads the header information and checks to see if the first three characters were *GIF*. If not, a message is displayed indicating that the file is not really a *.GIF* file and the function returns to the main program. Figure 26-5 shows the header information for the *.GIF* file. If a genuine *.GIF* file was encountered, the function breaks up the packed header byte into various parameters. It then reads a color table of the proper size if one was specified. If 16 colors were specified, the EGA palette values are calculated from the color information; if 256 colors were specified, the color table is modified to be compatible with the VGA. The *.GIF* file format can specify many more than the 256 colors that the VGA can handle. If this program encounters a lot more color information, it won't know what to do and will attempt to read it all into an array that will only hold 256 colors, resulting in disaster. You might want to put a limit on the color information in some way to avoid this problem. The function then enters a *switch* statement which takes action depending upon the next character to be read from the file. If it is a semicolon, the data is complete and the program terminates. If the character is an exclamation point, the next block of data is an extension block, which has no direct relation to an ordinary *.GIF* picture. In this case, the data in the block is read, but not used. Then the next character is read. If it is not a comma, the function terminates. If the first read character or the character read after an extension block is a comma, the function reads the image description, unpacks its packed byte and reads any local color data that is required. The image descriptor block is shown in Figure 26-6.

We now have to cope with how to handle the various display resolutions that may be specified for a picture. You will remember that for the *.PCX* files, as described in Chapter 24, we checked the specified file resolutions in x and y against the sizes allowed for the various VGA modes, and if we didn't find a match, we rejected the file completely. In Chapter 25, we took a different approach to the *.IMG* files and selected the next higher resolution mode, if there was one. Otherwise, we used the highest resolution VGA mode and let the user select the starting points for x and y and then, from that beginning point, displayed as much of the picture as we could. In this chapter, we take another approach altogether. For 16 color pictures, we select the lowest resolution VGA mode that will include the entire picture; if the picture is too high for the highest resolution mode, we use it and display as much as we can. For 256 color pictures, we use the normal VGA 320 pixel × 200 pixel × 256 color mode if the picture will fit in it. If the picture is too big, we use the 640 pixel × 480 pixel × 256 color VESA mode. If your Super VGA board doesn't include the VESA extensions, you can get a program from the board manufacturer that will load and remain in memory and allow the VESA extensions to the BIOS to be used by any program. Unfortunately, to be compatible with these BIOS extensions, we had to use the BIOS function for plotting pixels to the screen, which makes the program very slow in this mode. The program, as written, doesn't check to assure that a VESA compatible board is present, so that if the board (and/or software) is not there, the display doesn't do much. You might want to add a test and revert to the normal VGA 256 color mode if the system is not VESA compatible. Once the display mode has been determined, the *setMode* function is used to set the proper display mode. Note that this function is the version that is modified to run VESA modes. We then set up heights and widths for the display, which are either the dimensions of the file or of the display, whichever is smaller. For 256 color modes, the color registers are set to the locally specified colors if they are available; otherwise to the globally specified colors. For 16 color modes, the EGA palette is set to the 16 local EGA palette colors if they are available; otherwise to the globally specified palette colors. The function then calls the function *decoder* to decode the LZW data for an image.

Figure 26-4. Listing of GIF Program to View .GIF Files

```
/*


          GIF = Program to read .GIF graphics files

    GIF and 'Graphics Interchange Format' are trademarks
    (TM) of Compuserve, Incorporated, an H&R Block Company

                By Roger T. Stevens   12-9-91


*/

#include <stdio.h>
#include <stdlib.h>
#include <string.h>
#include <math.h>
#include <dos.h>
#include <conio.h>
#include <ctype.h>
#include <dir.h>

#define  UP_ARROW           328
#define  DOWN_ARROW         336
#define  LEFT_ARROW         331
#define  RIGHT_ARROW        333
#define  BACKSPACE            8
#define  seq_out(register,val)   {outp(0x3C4,register);\
                 outp(0x3C5,val);}
#define  graph_out(register,val)   {outp(0x3CE,register);\
```

(continued)

```
                    outp(0x3CF,val);}

void decoder(int linewidth);
void cls(int color);
char menu(int last_entry);
int dir_menu(int last_entry);
int next_code(void);
void restore_screen(char file_name[]);
void setEGApalette(unsigned char *buffer);
void setVGApalette(unsigned char *buffer);
void setMode(int mode);
int sort_function(const void *a, const void *b);
int next_code(void);
void line_out(char *pixels, int linelen);

union REGS reg;

struct
{
    char name[3];
    char version[3];
    int xres, yres;
    unsigned int packed;
    char back_col_index;
    char aspect_ratio;
} gif_header;

struct
{
    char red;
    char green;
    char blue;
} color_table[256],loc_color_table[256];

struct
{
    int start_col;
    int start_row;
    int width;
    int height;
    char packed;
```

(continued)

```
    } image_descriptor;

char buffer[64], ch, color_flag, color_res,
    col_tab_flag, dirbuf[64][13], filename[32],
    interlace_flag, loc_sort_flag, sort_flag;
unsigned char bytes = 0, b1, display_line[2049],
    file_buf[512], last[4096], stack[4096];
unsigned char PALETTE[17] = {0,1,2,3,4,5,20,7,56,57,58,
    59,60,61,62,63,0},
LOC_PALETTE = {0,1,2,3,4,5,20,7,56,57,58,59,60,61,62,63,
    0};
int active_page = 0, bits_left = 0, code_size, clear,
    col_tab_size, column, dir_index= 0, disp_height, done,
    end, finished, i, index = 0, j, k, key, linewidth,
    loc_col_tab_size, mode, newcodes, rows, slot, top,
    xres;
unsigned int height, link[4096], width;
long int col,row;
FILE *fin;
struct ffblk ffblk;

void main(void)
{
    for(;;)
    {
        setMode(3);
        textbackground(1);
        textcolor(15);
        window(2,2,78,23);
        clrscr();
        gotoxy(1,1);
        printf("\xC9");
        for (i=0; i<74; i++)
            printf("\xCD");
        printf("\xBB");
        for (i=2; i<22; i++)
        {
            gotoxy(1,i);
            printf("\xBA");
            gotoxy(76,i);
            printf("\xBA");
```

(continued)

```
    }
    gotoxy(1,22);
    printf("\xC8");
    for (i=0; i<74; i++)
        printf("\xCD");
    printf("\xBC");
    gotoxy(19,2);
    filename[0] = NULL;
    cprintf("Select file name with cursor arrows: ");
    textcolor(14);
    end = 0;
    done = findfirst("*.gif",&ffblk,0);
    while(!done)
    {
        strcpy(dirbuf[end++],ffblk.ff_name);
        done = findnext(&ffblk);
    }
    qsort((void *)dirbuf,end,sizeof(dirbuf[0]),
        sort_function);
    textbackground(1);
    textcolor(14);
    for (i=0; i<end; i++)
    {
        column = i/19;
        if (i == dir_index)
        {
            textbackground(7);
            textcolor(1);
        }
        gotoxy(2+19*column,(i%19)+3);
        cprintf("%s",dirbuf[i]);
        textbackground(1);
        textcolor(14);
    }
    key = dir_menu(end);
    if (key == 0x1B)
        break;
    restore_screen(filename);
    getch();
    printf("    Hit 'E' to erase this file...or any"
        " other key to continue...");
```

(continued)

```
            ch = getch();
            if (toupper(ch) == 'E')
                remove(filename);
    }
}

/*
```

```
    setVGApalette() = Function to set all 256 color
                            registers
```

```
*/

void setVGApalette(unsigned char *buffer)
{
    union REGS reg;
    struct SREGS inreg;

    reg.x.ax = 0x1012;
    segread(&inreg);
    inreg.es = inreg.ds;
    reg.x.bx = 0;
    reg.x.cx = 256;
    reg.x.dx = (int)&buffer[0];
    int86x(0x10,&reg,&reg,&inreg);
}

/*
```

```
    setEGApalette() = Sets the color for all EGA palettes
```

```
*/

void setEGApalette(unsigned char *buffer)
{
    union REGS reg;
    struct SREGS inreg;

    reg.x.ax = 0x1002;
```

(continued)

```
    segread(&inreg);
    inreg.es = inreg.ds;
    reg.x.dx = (int)&buffer[0];
    int86x(0x10,&reg,&reg,&inreg);
}


/*
```

```
        restore_screen() = Reads and displays a file
```

```
*/

void restore_screen(char file_name[])
{
    char color;

    if ((fin = fopen(file_name,"rb")) == NULL)
    {
        printf("\nCan't find %s.\n",file_name);
        return;
    }
    else
    {
        fread(&gif_header,1,13,fin);
        if ((gif_header.name[0] != 'G') ||
            (gif_header.name[1] != 'I')
            || (gif_header.name[2] != 'F'))
        {
            printf("\n%s is not a valid GIF file.\n",
            file_name);
            fclose(fin);
            return;
        }
    }
    setMode(3);
    color_flag = (gif_header.packed & 0x80) >> 7;
    color_res = (gif_header.packed & 0x70) >> 4;
    sort_flag = (gif_header.packed & 0x08) >> 3;
    col_tab_size = (int)pow(2,(gif_header.packed &
        0x07)+1.0);
```

(continued)

741

```
    if (col_tab_size > 0)
        fread(color_table,1,col_tab_size *3,fin);
    for (i=0; i<16; i++)
    {
        PALETTE[i] = ((color_table[i].red & 0x40) >> 1) |
            ((color_table[i].red & 0x80)    >> 5) |
            ((color_table[i].green & 0x40) >> 2) |
            (color_table[i].green & 0x80) >> 6 |
            ((color_table[i].blue & 0x40) >> 3) |
            ((color_table[i].blue & 0x80) >> 7);
    }
    for (i=0; i<256; i++)
    {
        color_table[i].red >>=  2;
        color_table[i].green >>=  2;
        color_table[i].blue >>=  2;
    }
    rows = 0;
    finished = 0;
    while (!finished)
    {
        ch = fgetc(fin);

        switch (ch)
        {
            case ';':      /*End of .GIF data */
                finished = 1;
                break;

            case '!':   /* .GIF extension block - read */
                        /* and discard */
                fgetc(fin);
                i = fgetc(fin);
                fread(file_buf,i,1,fin);
                if (fgetc(fin) != ',')
                    break;
            case ',':   /* read image description */
                fread(&image_descriptor,1,9,fin);
                width = image_descriptor.width;
                linewidth = min(640,width);
                height = image_descriptor.height;
```

(continued)

```c
col_tab_flag = (image_descriptor.packed &
    0x80) >> 7;
interlace_flag = (image_descriptor.packed
    & 0x40) >> 6;
loc_sort_flag = (image_descriptor.packed &
    0x20) >> 5;
loc_col_tab_size = (int)pow(2,
    (image_descriptor.packed
    & 0x07) + 1.0);
if (col_tab_flag == 1)
fread(loc_color_table,1,loc_col_tab_size
    *3,fin);
for (i=0; i<16; i++)
{
    LOC_PALETTE[i] = ((color_table[i].red
        & 0x40) >> 1) |
        ((color_table[i].red & 0x80) >> 5)
        | ((color_table[i].green & 0x40)
        >> 2) | (color_table[i].green &
        0x80) >> 6 | ((color_table[i].blue
        & 0x40) >> 3) |
        ((color_table[i].blue & 0x80) >>
        7);
}
for (i=0; i<256; i++)
{
    loc_color_table[i].red >>=  2;
    loc_color_table[i].green >>=  2;
    loc_color_table[i].blue >>=  2;
}
if (col_tab_size == 256)
{
    if ((height > 200) || (width > 320))
    {
        disp_height = min(400,height);
        linewidth = min(640,width);
        mode = 0x101;
        xres = 640;
    }
    else
    {
```

(continued)

```
                disp_height = min(200,height);
                linewidth = min(320,linewidth);
                mode = 19;
                xres = 320;
            }
            setMode(mode);
            if ((mode == 19) || (mode == 0x101))
            {
                if (col_tab_flag == 1)
                    setVGApalette
                    (loc_color_table);
                else
                    setVGApalette(color_table);
            }
        }
        else
        {
            if (image_descriptor.height <= 200)
            {
                mode = 14;
                disp_height = min (height,200);
            }
            else
            {
                if (image_descriptor.height <=
                    350)
                {
                    disp_height = min
                        (height,350);
                    mode = 16;
                }
                else
                {
                    disp_height = min (height,
                        480);
                    mode = 18;
                }
            }
            setMode(mode);
            linewidth = min(640,width);
            if (col_tab_flag == 1)
```

(continued)

```
                    setEGApalette(LOC_PALETTE);
               else
                    setEGApalette(PALETTE);
               decoder(width);
          }
          break;
     default:
          finished = 1;
          break;
     }
}
fclose(fin);
}

/*
```

```
     sort_function() = Directory sorting function
```

```
*/

int sort_function(const void *a, const void *b)
{
    return( strcmp(a,b));
}

/*
```

```
          dir_menu() = Menu function for directory
```

```
*/

int dir_menu(int last_entry)
{
    int ch1 = NULL;

    while ((ch1 != 0x0D) && (ch1 != 0x1B))
    {
        ch1 = getch();
        if (ch1 == 0x00)
```

(continued)

745

```
                    {
                  ch1 = getch() + 256;
                  textbackground(1);
                  textcolor(14);
                  column = dir_index/19;
                  gotoxy(2+19*column,(dir_index%19)+3);
                  cprintf("%s",dirbuf[dir_index]);
                  switch(ch1)
                  {
                      case DOWN_ARROW:
                          ++dir_index;
                          dir_index = dir_index % last_entry;
                          break;
                      case UP_ARROW:
                          --dir_index;
                          if (dir_index<0)
                              dir_index = last_entry - 1;
                          break;
                      case RIGHT_ARROW:
                          if ((dir_index + 19) < last_entry)
                              dir_index += 19;
                          break;
                      case LEFT_ARROW:
                          if (dir_index > 19)
                              dir_index -= 19;
                          break;
                  }
                  textbackground(7);
                  textcolor(1);
                  column = dir_index/19;
                  gotoxy(2+19*column,(dir_index%19)+3);
                  cprintf("%s",dirbuf[dir_index]);
              }
          }
      strcpy(filename,dirbuf[dir_index]);
      return(ch1);
  }
```

(continued)

```
/*

        line_out() = Displays a line on the screen

*/

void line_out(char *pixels, int linelen)
{
    unsigned long int offset;
    char far *address;
    char mask, dummy;
    int page;

    if (mode==19)
    {
        for (i=0; i<linelen; i++)
        {
            offset = (long)xres * (long)rows + (long)i;
            address = (char far *)(0xA0000000L + offset);
            *address = pixels[i];
        }
    }
    else
    {
        if (mode == 0x101)
        {
            for (i=0; i<linelen; i++)
            {
                reg.h.ah = 0x0C;
                reg.h.al = pixels[i];
                reg.h.bh = 0;
                reg.x.cx = i;
                reg.x.dx = rows;
                int86(0x10,&reg,&reg);
            }
        }
        else
        {
            offset = (long)rows * 640/8L;
            for (i=0; i<linelen; i++)
```

(continued)

```
                    {
                        graph_out(5,2);
                        if (i%8 == 0)
                            address = (char far *) 0xA0000000L +
                                offset + ((long)i / 8L);
                        mask = 0x80 >> (i % 8);
                        graph_out(8,mask);
                        dummy = *address;
                        *address = pixels[i];
                    }
                    graph_out(5,0);
                    graph_out(8,0xFF);
            }
        }
        rows++;
}


/*
```

```
                        decoder() = .GIF File decode
```

```
*/

void decoder(int width)
{
    int code, fc=0, old_code=0, counter;
    int ch, size, ret;
    int s_index=0;
    int l_index=0;

    size = fgetc(fin);
    code_size = size + 1;
    top = 1 << code_size;
    clear = 1 << size;
    end = clear + 1;
    slot = newcodes = end + 1;
    counter = width;
    bits_left = 0;
    b1 = 0;
    bytes = 0;
```

(continued)

```
while ((ch = next_code()) != end)
{
    if (ch == clear)
    {
        code_size = size + 1;
        slot = newcodes;
        top = 1 << code_size;
        ch = next_code();
        old_code = fc = ch;
        display_line[l_index++] = ch;
        counter--;
    }
    else
    {
        code = ch;
        if (code >= slot)
        {
            code = old_code;
            stack[s_index++] = fc;
        }
        while (code >= newcodes)
        {
            stack[s_index++] = last[code];
            code = link[code];
        }
        stack[s_index++] = code;
        if (slot < top)
        {
            fc = code;
            last[slot] = code;
            link[slot++] = old_code;
            old_code = ch;
        }
        if (slot >= top)
            if (code_size < 12)
            {
                top <<= 1;
                ++code_size;
            }
        while (s_index > 0)
        {
```

(continued)

```
                    display_line[l_index++] =
                        stack[--s_index];
                    if (--counter == 0)
                    {
                        line_out(display_line, linewidth);
                        if (rows >= disp_height)
                            return;
                        l_index = 0;
                        counter = width;
                    }
                }
            }
        }
    }
    if (counter != linewidth)
        line_out(display_line, linewidth-counter);
}


/*
```

```
        next_code() = Reads next code from file
```

```
*/

int next_code()
{
    int flag=0;
    unsigned long int code;

    if (bits_left == 0)
        flag == 1;
    code = b1 >> (8 - bits_left);
    while (code_size > bits_left)
    {
        if (bytes <= 0)
        {
            index = 0;
            bytes = fgetc(fin);
            fread(file_buf,bytes,1,fin);
        }
        b1 = file_buf[index++];
```

(continued)

```
    if (flag == 1)
    {
        code = b1 >> (8 - bits_left);
        flag == 0;
    }
    else
        code |= b1 << bits_left;
    bits_left += 8;
    --bytes;
    }
    bits_left -= code_size;
    code &= 0xFFF >> (12 - code_size);
    return((int)(code));
}

/*
```

```
                setMode() = Sets video mode
```

```
*/

void setMode(int mode)
{
    if (mode <= 0x6A)
        reg.x.ax = mode;
    else
    {
        reg.x.ax = 0x4F02;
        reg.x.bx = mode;
    }
    int86(0x10, &reg, &reg);
}
```

Decoding an LZW Image

The function *decoder* converts the LZW encoded data to a decompressed data string for display. The function begins by reading the LZW minimum code size. This is the minimum initial number of bits used for LZW codes in the image data. From this, the functions sets up the values for the top (which is 1 shifted to the left by 1 more

Figure 26-5. .GIF File Header Contents

Byte	Description	Bit							
		0	**1**	**2**	**3**	**4**	**5**	**6**	**7**
0	Signature	G							
1		I							
2		F							
3	Version	8							
4		7 or 9							
5		a							
6	Logical Screen Width	Width in pixels							
7	Logical Screen Height	Height in pixels							
8									
9	Packed Fields	Global Color Table Flag 0 = No tables 1 = Table follows	Color Resolution			Sort Flag 0=No order 1=Reverse importance	Global Color Table		
10									
11	Background Color	Color number 0–256							
12	Pixel Aspect Ratio	0 = No aspect ratio given 1–255 = (Pixel aspect ratio + 15) / 64							

Figure 26-6. .GIF File Image Descriptor Contents

Byte	Description	Bit							
		0	1	2	3	4	5	6	7
0	Image Seperator	2CH (,)							
1 2	Image Left Position	Left edge column number in pixels							
3 4	Image Top Position	Top edge row number in pixels							
5 6	Image Width	Image width in pixels							
7 8	Image Height	Image height in pixels							
9	Packed Fields	Local Color Table Flag 0 = No tables 1 = Table follows	Interlace flag 0=Not inter- laced 1=In- terlaced	Sort Flag =No order 1=Re- verse impor- tance	Re- served		Size of Local Color Table		

than the number of bits), for the clear code (which is 1 shifted to the left by the number of bits) and for the end code (which is 1 more than the clear code value). The current slot in the table and the point at which new codes may begin are set to 1 beyond the end code value. The function is then ready to begin a *while* loop that continues until the end code is read, indicating the end of the data. At each iteration of this loop, the function *next_code* is called. This function has two jobs. First, if *file_buf* is empty, it reads the next character (the block size) from the file. It then reads a block of this size from the file into *file_buf*. Second, it uses whatever bits are available from a previous character plus whatever bits are needed from the next character to assemble the next code from the packed data in the buffer. Back in the *decoder* function, if the code is a clear code, the various parameters are reset, the next code value is obtained and saved in the display line buffer. If a clear code was not encountered, the function first checks for a pathological case where a code is larger than any code currently in the table. It then takes the last character value given for the code and puts it onto a stack. It then sets the *code* variable to the *link* value given for the current code and puts the last character value onto the stack and changes the *code* value until a *code* value is obtained that is less than the *newcodes* value, indicating that we are at a code value for a single character. This is the first character of the string. We next have to put the entries for *last* and *link* for this new string into the table, increment the value of *slot* and, if it is greater than *top*, increment the number of bits for a code and change *top* accordingly. The function then enters a *while* loop that takes all of the accumulated characters of the string off the stack, beginning with the first character in the string (the last character to be sent to the stack), and places them in the display line buffer. When a counter shows that this buffer has accumulated a full line, the line is sent to the display by the function *line_out*, which is similar to the plot functions that we have encountered earlier in the book, except that it sends a whole line of data to the display rather than a single pixel. The counter is then reset for the next line. The loop continues until all display data has been processed.

Saving Screens to *.GIF* Files

The program *savegif.c* creates two representative color screens and saves them in *.GIF* file format. The first is a 16 color display showing wide lines of each of the 16 EGA default colors. The second is a 256 color display showing single pixel wide lines of each of the 200 first colors. The program generates these using a simplified, but slow, horizontal line drawing function. After each screen is displayed, the program calls the function *save_screen* to convert the screen to a *.GIF* file and save it to the screen. This program is an example of how you can use the function *save_screen* to save a *.GIF* file within your own graphics program. However, as you will see, some of the tables and variables have to be defined within the main program. The entire program is listed in Figure 26-7.

Figure 26-7. Listing of Program to Save Screens to .GIF Files

```
/*


    savegif = Program to save a screen in a .GIF graphics
        file GIF and "Graphics Interchange Format" are
    trademarks (TM) of Compuserve,  Incorporated, an H&R
                  Block Company

           By Roger T. Stevens   12-31-91


*/

#include <stdlib.h>
#include <stdio.h>
#include <dos.h>

union REGS reg;
struct REGPACK regs;
struct SREGS segregs;
struct
{
    char red;
    char green;
    char blue;
} color_table[256],loc_color_table[256];

struct
{
    char name[3];
    char version[3];
    int xres, yres;
    unsigned int packed;
    char back_col_index;
```

(continued)

```
        char aspect_ratio;
} gif_header;
struct
{
    int start_col;
    int start_row;
    int width;
    int height;
    char packed;
} image_descriptor;

void drawHorzLine(int xstart, int xend, int y, int color);
int getMode(void);
char getPalette(int palette);
int getPixel(int x, int y);
void getVGApalette(unsigned char *buffer);
void initialize(void);
void plot16(int x, int y, int color);
void plot256(int x, int y, int color);
void setMode(int mode);
void write_code(unsigned int code);

FILE *fsave;
char VGA_data[64];
int clear, codebits, colors, destoff, destseg, end, i,
    length, lastentry, LINEWIDTH, mode, nbits, nbytes,
    entries, actual, srcoff, scrseg, startbits, xres,
    yres;
unsigned char buffer[16384], block[266], test[100];
unsigned char PALETTE[16]={0,1,2,3,4,5,20,7,56,57,58,59,
    60,61,62,63};
unsigned int hashcode, next, str_index[5003];

void main(void)
{
    mode = 16;
    xres = 640;
    yres = 350;
    setMode(16);
    LINEWIDTH = 18;
    for (i=0; i<16; i++)
```

(continued)

```
            drawHorzLine(10,630,i*22,i);
        getch();
        save_screen("gtest.gif");
        getch();
        xres = 320;
        yres = 200;
        mode = 19;
        setMode(19);
        LINEWIDTH = 1;
        for (i=0; i<200; i++)
            drawHorzLine(10,310,i,i);
        getch();
        save_screen("g256test.gif");
        getch();
}


/*
```

```
  drawHorzLine = Draws a horizontal line of designated
  width between two designated points on screen using a
  selected color and 16 color or 256 color video modes.
```

```
*/

void drawHorzLine(int xstart, int xend, int y, int color)
{
    int i, j;

    for (i=y-(LINEWIDTH/2); i<=y+(LINEWIDTH/2); i++)
        for (j=xstart; j<=xend; j++)
            if (mode == 19)
                plot256(j,i,color);
            else
                plot16(j,i,color);
}
```

(continued)

```
/*

      ┌─────────────────────────────────────────────────────┐
      │                                                     │
      │         setMode() = Sets the video mode             │
      │                                                     │
      └─────────────────────────────────────────────────────┘
*/

void setMode(int mode)
{
    reg.x.ax = mode;
    int86 (0x10,&reg,&reg);
}


/*

      ┌─────────────────────────────────────────────────────┐
      │                                                     │
      │            save_screen() = GIF encoder              │
      │                                                     │
      └─────────────────────────────────────────────────────┘
*/

save_screen(char *filename)
{
    int i, j, row, col, color, barcolor=2, temp;
    unsigned int hashentry;
    unsigned char bits, x;

    if ((fsave=fopen(filename,"wb")) == NULL)
    {
        printf("\nCan't create file %s \n",filename);
        return(0);
    }
    mode = getMode();
    strcpy(gif_header.name,"GIF");
    strcpy(gif_header.version, "87a");
    switch(mode)
    {
        case 4:     /* 320 x 200 - 4 colors */
        case 5:
        case 6:     /* 640 x 200 - 2 colors */
        case 15:    /* 640 x 350 - 4 colors */
        case 17:    /* 640 x 480 - 2 colors */
```

(continued)

```
                printf("\nCannot save this display"
                    " mode...\n");
                exit(0);
            case 13:    /* 320 x 200 - 16 colors */
                gif_header.xres = 320;
                gif_header.yres = 200;
                gif_header.packed = 0xD3;
                bits = 4;
                colors = 16;
                break;
            case 14:    /* 640 x 200 - 16 colors */
                gif_header.xres = 640;
                gif_header.yres = 200;
                gif_header.packed = 0xD3;
                bits = 4;
                colors = 16;
                break;
            case 16:    /* 640 x 350 - 16 colors */
                gif_header.xres = 640;
                gif_header.yres = 350;
                gif_header.packed = 0xD3;
                bits = 4;
                colors = 16;
                break;
            case 18:    /* 640 x 480 - 16 colors */
                gif_header.xres = 640;
                gif_header.yres = 480;
                gif_header.packed = 0xD3;
                bits = 4;
                colors = 16;
                break;
            case 19:    /* 320 x 200 - 256 colors */
                gif_header.xres = 320;
                gif_header.yres = 200;
                gif_header.packed = 0xF7;
                bits = 8;
                colors = 256;
                break;
    }
    gif_header.back_col_index = 0;
    gif_header.aspect_ratio = 0;
```

(continued)

```
fwrite(&gif_header,1,13,fsave);
if (getVGA() == 0x1B)
{
    for (i=0;  i<16;  i++)
        PALETTE[i] = getPalette(i);
}
if (gif_header.packed == 0xD3)
{
    for (i=0;  i<16;  i++)
    {
        color_table[i].red = ((PALETTE[i] & 0x20) <<
            1) | ((PALETTE[i] & 0x04) << 5);
        color_table[i].green = ((PALETTE[i] & 0x10) <<
            2) | ((PALETTE[i] & 0x02) << 6);
        color_table[i].blue = ((PALETTE[i] & 0x08) <<
            3) | ((PALETTE[i] & 0x01) << 7);
    }
    fwrite(&color_table,1,48,fsave);
}
if (gif_header.packed == 0xF7)
{
    getVGApalette(color_table);
    for (i=0;  i<256;  i++)
    {
        color_table[i].red <<=  2;
        color_table[i].green <<=  2;
        color_table[i].blue <<=  2;
    }
    fwrite(&color_table,1,768,fsave);
}
fputc(',',fsave);
fputc(0,fsave);
fputc(0,fsave);
fputc(0,fsave);
fputc(0,fsave);
fwrite(&xres,1,2,fsave);
fwrite(&yres,1,2,fsave);
fputc(0,fsave);
startbits = bits+1;
clear = 1 << (startbits - 1);
end = clear+1;
```

(continued)

```
fputc(bits,fsave);
codebits = startbits;
nbytes = 0;
nbits = 0;
for (i = 0; i < 266; i++)
    block[i] = 0;
initialize();
for (row = 0; row < yres; row++)
{
    for (col = 0; col < xres; col++)
    {
        color = getPixel(col,row);
        test[0] = ++length;
        test[length] = color;
        switch(length)
        {
            case 1:
                lastentry = color;
                break;
            case 2:
                hashcode = 301 * (test[1]+1);
            default:
                hashcode *= (color + length);
                hashentry = ++hashcode % 5003;
                for( i = 0; i < 5003; i++)
                {
                    hashentry = (hashentry + 1) %
                        5003;
                    if (memcmp(&buffer[str_index
                        [hashentry]+2], test,
                        length+1) == 0)
                        break;
                    if (str_index[hashentry] == 0)
                        i = 5003;
                }
                if (str_index[hashentry] != 0 &&
                    length < 97)
                {
                    memcpy(&lastentry,
                        &buffer[str_index
                        [hashentry]],2);
```

(continued)

```
                                break;
                        }
                        write_code(lastentry);
                        entries++;
                        if (str_index[hashentry] == 0)
                        {
                            temp = entries+end;
                            str_index[hashentry] = next;
                            memcpy(&buffer[next],&temp,2);
                            memcpy(&buffer[next+2],
                                test,length+1);
                            next += length+3;
                            actual++;
                        }
                        test[0] = 1;
                        test[1] = color;
                        length = 1;
                        lastentry = color;
                        if ((entries+end) == (1<<codebits))
                            codebits++;
                        if ( entries + end > 4093 || actual >
                            3335 || next > 15379)
                        {
                            write_code(lastentry);
                            initialize();
                        }
                }
        }
        if (!(row % 4))
        if (++barcolor >= colors)
            barcolor = 0;
        for (i = 0; 300*i < xres; i++)
        {
            if (mode == 19)
            {
                plot256(i,row,barcolor);
                plot256(xres-1-i,row,barcolor);
            }
            else
            {
                plot16(i,row,barcolor);
```

(continued)

```
                plot16(xres-1-i,row,barcolor);
            }
        }
    }
    write_code(lastentry);
    write_code(end);
    fputc(0,fsave);
    fputc(';',fsave);
    fclose(fsave);
    printf(" Screen saved as %s \n",filename);
}

/*
```

```
              initialize() = Initializes tables
```

```
*/

void initialize(void)
{
    write_code(clear);
    entries = 0;
    actual = 0;
    next = 1;
    length = 0;
    codebits = startbits;
    buffer[0] = NULL;
    memset(str_index,0x00,10006);
}

/*
```

```
            write_code() = Writes codes to disk file
```

```
*/

void write_code(unsigned int code)
{
    block[nbytes  ] |= ((code << nbits) & 0xFF);
```

(continued)

```
            block[nbytes+1] |= ((code >> (8 - nbits)) & 0xFF);
            block[nbytes+2] |= (((code>>(8 - nbits)) >> 8) &
                0xFF);
        nbits += codebits;
        while (nbits >= 8)
        {
            nbits -= 8;
            nbytes++;
        }
        if (nbytes < 251 && code != end)
            return;
            if (code == end)
                while (nbits > 0)
                {
                    nbits -= 8;
                    nbytes++;
                }
            fputc(nbytes,fsave);
            fwrite(block,nbytes,1,fsave);
            memcpy(block,&block[nbytes],5);
            memset(&block[5],0x00,260);
            nbytes = 0;
}


/*
```

```
         getMode() = Returns the video mode
```

```
*/

int getMode(void)
{
    reg.h.ah = 0x0F;
    int86 (0x10,&reg,&reg);
    return (reg.h.al);
}
```

(continued)

```
/*
```

```
                  getVGA() = Returns VGA information
```

```
*/
```

```
int getVGA(void)
{
    segread(&segregs);
    regs.r_es = segregs.ds;
    regs.r_di = (int) VGA_data;
    regs.r_ax = 0x1B00;
    intr (0x10,&regs);
    return (regs.r_ax & 0xFF);
}
```

```
/*
```

```
     getPalette() = Returns the contents of a palette
                             register
```

```
*/
```

```
char getPalette(int palette)
{
    union REGS reg;
    struct SREGS inreg;

    reg.x.ax = 0x1007;
    reg.h.bl = palette;
    int86x(0x10,&reg,&reg,&inreg);
    return(reg.h.bh);
}
```

(continued)

```
/*
```

```
        getVGApalette() = Function to read all 256 color
                            registers
```

```
*/
```

```c
void getVGApalette(unsigned char *buffer)
{

    struct REGPACK regs;
    struct SREGS sregs;

    regs.r_ax = 0x1017;
    segread(&sregs);
    regs.r_es = sregs.ds;
    regs.r_bx = 0;
    regs.r_cx = 256;
    regs.r_dx = (int)buffer;
    intr(0x10,&regs);
}
```

```
/*
```

```
        getPixel() = Reads a pixel from the screen
```

```
*/
```

```c
int getPixel(int x, int y)
{
    reg.h.ah = 0x0D;
    reg.h.bh = 0x00;
    reg.x.cx = x;
    reg.x.dx = y;
    int86(0x10,&reg,&reg);
    return(reg.h.al);
}
```

(continued)

```
/*
```

```
   plot16() = Plots a point on the screen at a designated
     position using a selected color for 16 color modes.
```

```
*/
```

```c
void plot16(int x, int y, int color)
{
    #define graph_out(index,val)   {outp(0x3CE,index);\
                        outp(0x3CF,val);}
    int dummy,mask;
    char far * address;

    address = (char far *) 0xA0000000L + (long)y * xres/8L
        + ((long)x / 8L);
    mask = 0x80 >> (x % 8);
    graph_out(8,mask);
    graph_out(5,2);
    dummy = *address;
    *address = color;
    graph_out(5,0);
    graph_out(8,0xFF);
}
```

```
/*
```

```
   plot256() = Plots a point on the screen at a designated
     position using a selected color for 256 color modes.
```

```
*/
```

```c
void plot256(int x, int y, int color)
{
    char far * address;
    address = (char far *) 0xA0000000L + (long)y * xres +
        (long)x;
    *address = color;
}
```

The *save_screen* Function

The *save_screen* function begins by attempting to open the specified file for writing. If this can't be done for any reason, the function displays a diagnostic message and terminates. Otherwise, the program gets the current video mode. It loads the header and version number into the *GIF* header. It then enters a *switch* statement which sets up the rest of the header information as appropriate for the current display mode and then writes the *GIF* header to the disk file. Next, it checks whether a VGA is present. If so, it gets the current EGA palette information; otherwise it uses the default EGA palette. If a 16 color display mode is being used, the first 16 members of the *color_table* array are filled with the EGA palette data, and this is written out to the file. If a 256 color mode is being used, the values in *color_table* are changed from VGA to *GIF* values and the entire color table is written out to the file. The function then writes the character to indicate that an image follows, followed by the image descriptor data, for a case where no local color information is provided. The function initializes the various tables and parameters used in the compression process. Next the function enters a pair of nested *for* loops. The outer loop iterates once for each row of the display; the inner loop iterates once for each pixel of the display. The first thing that is done within the inner loop is to get the designated pixel character. This character is put into the *test* array at the position designated by *length*. The function then enters a *switch* statement which simply sets up the character as *lastentry* if *length* is 1. If *length* is 2, the *hashcode* variable is initialized. For hash codes other than 1, the hash code technique is used to search the buffer for a string that matches the stream of pixels being read from the display. When a match is found (even if it is only a single character), its code ends up in *lastentry*. It is then packed and ultimately written to the file by the function *write_code*. In addition, a new string is created for the buffer consisting of the matching string with the current character appended. This is just the procedure that was described under the section that explained LZW compression. After every line is displayed the function changes the edges of the display to a color that is incremented every four rows, to give an indication of the progress of the function in compressing and saving the display. When all lines of the screen have been saved, a semicolon is output to the file to indicate that the image is complete. The file is then closed and the message "Screen saved as " is displayed on the screen followed by the file name under which the display was saved.

Bibliography

Abrash, Michael, "Higher 256-Color Resolution on the VGA," *Programmer's Journal*, Vol. 7.1, January–February 1989, pp. 18–30.

Abrash, Michael, "Mode X: 256-Color VGA Magic," *Dr. Dobb's Journal*, Vol. 16, No. 7, July 1991, pp. 133–138.

Abrash, Michael, "Still Higher 256-Color VGA Resolutions," *Programmer's Journal*, Vol. 7.5, September-October 1989, pp. 24–36.

Adams, Lee, *High Performance Interactive Graphics*, Blue Ridge Summit, PA TAB Books, 1987.

Barkakati, Nabajyoti, "Graphics: Simple Plots with the Enhanced Graphics Adapter," *Dr. Dobb's Journal*, Vol. 11, No. 5, May 1986, pp. 42, 72–77.

Batty, Michael, *Microcomputer Graphics*, London, Chapman and Hall, 1987.

Blinn, James F., "How Many Ways Can You Draw a Circle?" *Dr. Dobb's Journal*, Vol. 12, No. 9, September 1987, pp. 18–26.

Duvanenko, Victor, Robbins, W. E., and Gyurcsik, Ronald S., "Improved Line Segment Clipping," *Dr. Dobb's Journal*, Vol. 15, No. 7, July 1990, pp.36–45.

Ferraro, Richard F., *Guide to the EGA and VGA Cards*, Reading, MA, Addison-Wesley Publishing Co., 1989.

Glassner Andrew S., *Graphics Gems*, San Diego, CA, Academic Press, 1990.

Harbison, Samuel P. and Steele, Guy L. Jr., *C: A Reference Manual*, Englewood Cliffs, NJ, Prentice-Hall, 1987.

Johnson, Nelson, *Advanced Graphics in C*, Berkeley, CA, Osborne McGraw-Hill, 1987.

King, Todd, "Drawing Character Shapes with Bezier Curves," *Dr. Dobb's Journal*, Vol. 15, No. 7, July 1990, pp.46–52.

Patterson, Tim, "Circles and the Digital differential Analyzer," *Dr. Dobb's Journal*, Vol. 15, No. 7, July 1990, pp.30–35.

Porter, Kent, "A Graphics Toolbox for Turbo C (Part 1)," *Dr. Dobb's Journal*, Vol. 12, No. 11, November 1987, pp. 30–36, 82–86.

Porter, Kent, "A Graphics Toolbox for Turbo C (Part 2)," *Dr. Dobb's Journal*, Vol. 12, No. 12, December 1987, pp. 54–61, 106–108.

Porter, Kent, "Curves, Bezier-Style," *Turbo Technix*, March-April 1988, pp. 34–39.

Rimmer, Steve, *Bit-Mapped Graphics*, Blue Ridge Summit, PA, Windcrest Books, 1990.

Stevens, Roger T., and Watkins, Christopher D., *Advanced Graphics Programming in C and C++*, Redwood City, CA, M&T Publishing, 1991.

Stevens, Roger T., *Fractal Programming in C*, Redwood City, CA, M&T Publishing, 1989.

Stevens, Roger T., *Graphics Programming in C*, Redwood City, CA, M&T Publishing, 1988.

Sutty, George and Blair, Steve, *Advanced Programmer's Guide to SuperVGAs*, New York, Brady, 1990.

Wegner, Timothy and Peterson, Mark, *Fractal Creations*, Mill Valley, CA, 94941, Waite Group Press, 1991.

Welch, Terry A., "A Technique for High-Performance Data Compression," *Computer*, June 1984.

Index